DATE			

Representations of
Commonsense
Knowledge

Ernest Davis
Courant Institute for Mathematical Sciences

Morgan Kaufmann Publishers, Inc.
San Mateo, California

Sponsoring Editor   *Michael B. Morgan*
Production Editor   *Sharon E. Montooth*
Cover Designer   *Joy Dickenson*
Copyeditor   *Linda Medoff*
Composition   *Technically Speaking Publications*
Artist   *Technically Speaking Publications*

Credits:

Figure 6.17: Dana H. Ballard/Christopher M. Brown, *Computer Vision,* copyright 1982, p. 250. Reprinted by permission of Prentice-Hall, Inc., Englewood Cliffs, NJ.

Figure 6.20: This figure first appeared in the journal, *Artificial Intelligence* published by North-Holland Publishing Co., Amsterdam. © 1981 by **North-Holland** Publishing Co. It is reprinted here by permission of the publisher.

Figure 7.8: This figure first appeared in *Artificial Intelligence In Engineering Journal*, **Computational Mechanics Publications**. The article in which it appeared is "A Logical Framework for Commonsense Predictions of Solid Object Behavior," by Ernest Davis, pp. 125–140.

Library of Congress Cataloging-in-Publication Data

Davis, Ernest.
    Representations of commonsense knowledge / Ernest Davis.
        p.   cm. -- (Morgan Kaufmann series in representation and reasoning. ISSN 1046-9567)
    Includes bibliographical references and index.
    ISBN 1-55860-033-7
    1. Artificial intelligence. 2. Common sense. 3. Reasoning.
I. Title. II. Series.
Q335.D37   1990
006.3--dc20   90-41289
                                                                                    CIP

ISBN 1-55860-033-7
MORGAN KAUFMANN PUBLISHERS, INC.
Editorial Office:
    2929 Campus Drive
    San Mateo, California 94403
Order from:
    P.O. Box 50490
    Palo Alto, CA 94303-9953

©1990 by Morgan Kaufmann Publishers, Inc.
All rights reserved.
Printed in the United States.

Dedication

To my parents
Philip and Hadassah Davis

Preface

A major problem in artificial intelligence is to endow computers with commonsense knowledge of the world and with the ability to use that knowledge sensibly. A large body of research has studied this problem through careful analysis of typical examples of reasoning in a variety of commonsense domains. The immediate aim of this research is to develop a rich language for expressing commonsense knowledge, and inference techniques for carrying out commonsense reasoning. This book provides an introduction and a survey of this body of research. It is, to the best of my knowledge, the first book to attempt this.

The book is designed to be used as a textbook for a one-semester graduate course on knowledge representation. (Drafts of chapters have been used for courses at New York University, Brown, and Yale.) The one absolute prerequisite is that the student be familiar with the notation and the meaning of the predicate calculus (first-order logic). A review of the predicate calculus is given in Section 2.3, but too briefly to be useful to the student who is not already familiar with it. It is not necessary that the student be familiar with either metalogic (topics such as soundness and completeness) or with computational logic (topics such as Skolemization and resolution). It will be very helpful if the student has had a general course in AI, though more for general motivation than for specific content. Mathematical sophistication is also an asset, particularly in reading Chapters 3, 4, and 6.

The following diagram shows the interdependence of chapters:

$$(2.5, 2.6) \quad (2.7, 2.8) \quad (8) \quad (9) \quad (10)$$

$$(1) \quad (2.1 - 2.4) \quad (3) \quad (5)$$

$$(4) \quad (6) \quad (7)$$

Additional dependencies of individual sections are indicated in the text. These dependencies should not be taken too seriously; in particular, the reader who finds Chapter 2 heavy going should not, on that account, be discouraged from reading the rest of the book.

Exercises are provided at the end of each chapter. Difficult exercises are marked with an asterisk. Instructors assigning starred exercises should keep in mind that they vary quite widely in difficulty, length, and the degree of prior knowledge, particularly mathematical knowledge that they require. Some of the exercises contain results of moderate interest that are not mentioned elsewhere in the text; the reader, therefore, may find it worth his while to glance through them even if he has no intention of working them out.

When I began work on this book in early 1985, the subject of domain-specific representations was somewhat obscure. The existing textbooks barely treated the issue, and almost no significant collections of papers had been published. The student or teacher was therefore obliged to search through journals, conference proceedings, technical reports, and unpublished papers to collect the important work in the area; and he had to form his own synthesis of the many different outlooks and techniques. The field was also small. When I planned this book, I thought I could survey virtually the entire relevant AI literature.

All this has changed spectacularly in the last five years. New textbooks, particularly [Charniak and McDermott 1985] and [Genesereth and Nilsson 1987] treat domain-specific representations at considerable length. Numerous collections of research papers, both on knowledge representation generally and on various subareas, have been published in book form, greatly simplifying the student's literature search.

At the same time, research in the area has expanded explosively. More than half the AI papers cited in the bibliography of this book were first published in 1985 or later. Today, a comprehensive bibliography would be a very substantial undertaking and a comprehensive survey would be nearly impossible.

Nonetheless, I feel that this book serves important functions. The student who has completed this book will be able to read any but the most narrowly technical paper published in the area. The researcher studying commonsense representations can find here a rich vocabulary of primitives presented within an integrated framework, and a collection of domain axioms and techniques that supports a variety of nontrivial commonsense inferences. The integration achieved here of theories of various commonsense domains makes it possible to get an overall view of how much commonsense reasoning can currently be expressed in computational terms. Compared to the powers of human commonsense reasoning, of course, we are just scratching the surface, but I think that we have made enough progress to be optimistic.

Three important omissions should be noted:

1. Domain-independent architectures for knowledge representations: semantic nets, production systems, logic programming, and so on.

2. Representations of knowledge based on linguistic considerations.

3. "Scruffy" representation of human interactions, particularly those developed by Roger Schank and his students.

The first two categories are omitted for the usual reasons: lack of time, energy, and knowledge, and a personal judgment that these issues were not central to the purposes of this book. In the case of the first category, I also felt that the subject was well covered in other texts. This is certainly not the case (as far as I know) for linguistically derived representations; a systematic survey of these would be of great value, but it is outside my personal competence.

The omission of Schankian representations is more serious. It is, in fact, a substantial disappointment to me; one of my original purposes in this book was to show how "scruffy" representation could be incorporated into a "neat" theory. In the event, however, I found this integration very hard to achieve. The problem is not so much technical; it is not difficult, using Procrustean methods, to squeeze Schankian primitives into neat categories. Rather, it is a problem of conflicting criteria in choosing primitives and inference rules. I still feel that this integration is one of the major problems in knowledge representation, but I have not found any satisfactory solution. (Section 9.5 gives a short account of Schank's categorization of goals; Appendix 10.A gives a summary of conceptual dependency.)

My friends and colleagues have been extraordinarily generous in helping me with suggestions, criticisms, and encouragement. Above all, I thank Drew McDermott, who taught me most of what I know about AI; and Leora Morgenstern, who read every draft of every chapter, and whose suggestions and comments pervade the text. Thanks also to

Sanjaya Addanki	S. Bhasker	Ron Brachman
Pasquale Caianiello	Eugene Charniak	Joey Davis
Philip Davis	Tom Dean	Sam Fleischacker
Hector Geffner	Benjamin Grosof	Pat Hayes
Jerry Hobbs	Leo Joskowicz	Ken Klein
Tomas Ksiezyk	Larry Manevitz	Chris Riesbeck
Yoav Shoham	John Sterling	Arthur Walker
Dan Weld		

The writing of this book has been supported in part by NSF grants numbers DCR-8402309, DCR-8603758, and IRI-8801529.

Finally, I thank my family for their support and encouragement. Most of all, thanks to Bianca, for her patience and love.

Contents

List of Tables

List of Figures

List of Named Axioms

PROP.1 – 9: Propositional calculus
FOL.1 – 13: First-order logic
EQL.1 – 2: Equality
SET.1 – 7: Set theory
MODAL.1 – 13: Modal logic
ORD.1 – 3: Ordering
DIFF.1 – 6: Differential space
MULT.1 – 6: Multiplication
MON.1 – 5: Monotonic dependence
DRV.1 – 5: Derivatives
MODE.1 – 5: Mode transitions
QDE.1 – 2: Qualitative differential equations
NEG.1 – 6: Infinitesimal (negligible) quantities
BW.1 – 18: Blocks world
FRA.1 – 9: Frame axioms: Framing by events and fluents
FRB.1 – 7: Frame axioms: Framing primitive fluents by events
FRC.1 – 7: Frame axioms: Framing primitive events
BR.1 – 3: Chronicles in branching time
BW.3 – 9: Blocks-world state-coherence axioms using set notation
CE.1 – 7: Compound events
EP.1 – 6: Compound events from primitive components
MTIME.1 – 10: Modal temporal logic
BW.3 – 5, 15–18: Blocks-world axioms in modal notation
HF.1 – 11: Heat flow
SO.1 – 5: Solid objects: Kinematics
PO.1 – 19: Point object: Kinematics and dynamics
LI.1 – 14: Liquids
BEL.1 – 14: Belief (modal Formulation)
BEL.1 – 8: Belief (possible-worlds formulation)
BEL.1 – 14: Belief (syntactic formulation)
DBEL.1 – 7: Degree of belief
KNOW.1 – 6: Knowledge
KB.1 – 5: Knowledge and belief
KW.1 – 2: Knowing what and whether
BT.1 – 3: Knowledge and belief over time
PL.1 – 3: Plans and goals
KPG.1 – 7: Knowledge of plans and goals
KPS.1 – 8: Knowledge preconditions
RAP.1 – 6: Reactive plan

CK.1 – 5: Common knowledge
IL.1 – 8: Illocutionary acts
ETH.1 – 5: Ethics
POS.1 – 4: Possession

Chapter 1

Automating Common Sense

Most of their remarks were the sort it would not be easy to disagree with: "What I always say is, when a chap's hungry, he likes some victuals," or "Getting dark now; always does at night," or even, "Ah, you've come over the water. Powerful wet stuff, ain't it?"

C. S. Lewis, *The Voyage of the Dawn Treader*

In order for an intelligent creature to act sensibly in the real world, it must know about that world and be able to use its knowledge effectively. The common knowledge about the world that is possessed by every schoolchild and the methods for making obvious inferences from this knowledge are called common sense. Commonsense knowledge and commonsense reasoning are involved in most types of intelligent activities, such as using natural language, planning, learning, high-level vision, and expert-level reasoning. How to endow a computer program with common sense has been recognized as one of the central problems of artificial intelligence since the inception of the field [McCarthy 1959].

It is a very difficult problem. Common sense involves many subtle modes of reasoning and a vast body of knowledge with complex interactions. Consider the following quotation from *The Tale of Benjamin Bunny*, by Beatrix Potter:

Peter did not eat anything; he said he would like to go home.
Presently, he dropped half the onions.

Except that Peter is a rabbit, there is nothing subtle or strange here, and the passage is easily understood by five-year-old children. Yet the three clauses involve, implicitly or explicitly, concepts of quantity,

1

space, time, physics, goals, plans, needs, and communication. To understand the passage, an intelligent system needs relevant knowledge from each of these domains, and the ability to connect this knowledge to the story. To design such a system, we must create theories of all the commonsense domains involved, determine what kind of knowledge in each domain is likely to be useful, determine how it can be effectively used, and find a way of implementing all this in a working computer program.

Since common sense consists (by definition) of knowledge and reasoning methods that are utterly obvious to us, we often overlook its astonishing scope and power. The variety of domains involved in a commonsense understanding of the world is not much less than the variety involved in all of human knowledge about the world; that is, most domains of human knowledge have some basis in a commonsense understanding. Likewise, the kinds of reasoning involved in common sense include, in simple form, most if not all of the kinds of reasoning that are consciously usable by human intelligence. In short, most of what we know and most of the conscious thinking we do has its roots in common sense. Thus, a complete theory of common sense would contain the fundamental kernel of a complete theory of human knowledge and intelligence.

The purpose of this introductory chapter is to give a general feeling for the field of AI commonsense reasoning and introduce some basic ideas and terminology. We will discuss the kinds of issues that a theory of commonsense reasoning must address, or avoid; the general structure of these kinds of theories; the most important methodological debates in the field; and the relationship between theories of commonsense reasoning and other fields of study. Chapters 2 and 3 will lay a more detailed groundwork by describing the various logical theories we will use in this book.

The remaining chapters will each deal with one particular commonsense domain: quantities, time, space, physics, cognition, purposive actions, and interpersonal relations. Human common sense, of course, encompasses many other areas as well; there are commonsense theories of biology, terrestrial and astronomical phenomena, aesthetics, and so on. We have omitted these areas here simply because they have not been extensively studied in AI. This neglect is rather a pity; the restricted commonsense domains studied in AI sometimes give the feeling that the world consists of four blocks, five electronic devices, three people, an elephant, and a penguin.

This book entirely omits any discussion of the development of common sense: which aspects of common sense are innate and which aspects are learned, how they are learned, and to what extent they depend on the culture and the individual. Though these issues are ultimately of the highest importance in AI and cognitive psychology, at present we know very little about them. This theory will require a combination of major advances in AI, developmental psychology, and comparative anthropology. Therefore, this book makes no attempt to arrive at theories that are innate or culture independent. The theories presented here are almost entirely the products of people born in the twentieth century and educated in Western culture generally and in science and math in particular, and they reflect this origin. Some aspects of these theories would certainly have appeared quite unnatural in many times and places; for example, the sharp division made between physical and psychological phenomena and the omission of the divine or spiritual as a central category.

1.1 Knowledge Bases

Commonsense reasoning in AI programs can be viewed as largely the performance of *inference* on a body of *object-level* information. Object-level information is information that describes the subject matter of the reasoning, as opposed to *control-level* information, which describes the internal state of the reasoning process itself.[1] Inference is the process of deriving new information from old information. Programs that do this kind of reasoning are generally designed as *knowledge-based systems*. A knowledge-based system is a program consisting of two parts:

- The *knowledge base* — a data structure that encodes a body of object-level information.

- The *knowledge base manager* — a collection of procedures that perform inferences on the information in the knowledge base, possibly modifying the knowledge base in the process.

In general, any object-level information that cannot be foreseen by the programmer, particularly problem-specific information, must be represented in the knowledge base. Information that can be foreseen by the programmer, such as fixed rules governing the subject domain, may be represented in the knowledge base, called a *declarative* representation, or it may be incorporated into the inference procedures, called a *procedural* representation. Typically, declarative representations have the advantage that the information may be more easily

---

[1]This distinction breaks down in a program that can introspect on its own reasoning process.

changed, that the information may be used in more different ways, and that the program may reason directly about its use of the information. Procedural representations typically have the advantage of efficiency.

All other modules of the program use the knowledge-base manager to access or change the information in the knowledge base. A knowledge-base manager generally includes procedures for *assimilation,* adding some new information to the knowledge base and drawing appropriate conclusions; and *query answering,* providing requested information on the basis of the information in the knowledge base. Some knowledge bases also provide facilities for *deletion,* the removing of information from the knowledge base and the withdrawal of all conclusions drawn from it.

Various different modes of inference are used in common sense. An inference is *deductive* if it is logically sound; the inferred information is necessarily true if the starting information is true. An inference is *abductive* if it offers a plausible explanation of some particular fact. For instance, if you see that there is no mail in your mailbox, you may infer that your spouse has come home; this is an abduction, but not a deduction, since other explanations are possible. An inference is *inductive* if it infers a general rule as an explanation or characterization of some number of particular instances. For example, if you come to a new town, and three or four times you see a white fire truck, you may infer the rule, "In this town, fire trucks are white."

There are substantial advantages to using deductive inferences, when possible. First, no other type of inference is fully understood. Second, the fact that deductive inference preserves truth greatly simplifies the design of knowledge bases. If a knowledge base uses only deductive inference, and all the information that is assimilated is true, then all the conclusions it draws will be true. If a knowledge base uses nondeductive inference, then it runs the risk of making false conclusions even if all the given information is true. We must therefore consider the problem of what to do when the inference is discovered to be false. Unfortunately, much of commonsense reasoning is inescapably nondeductive by nature.

1.2 Methodology

The focus of this book is on the development of declarative representations for the knowledge used in commonsense inferences. The basic approach used here, as in much of the research in automating commonsense reasoning, is to take a number of examples of commonsense inference in a commonsense domain, generally deductive inference; identify the general domain knowledge and the particular problem specification used in the inference; develop a formal language in which this knowledge can be expressed; and define the primitives of the language as carefully and precisely as possible. Only occasionally is there any discussion here of the algorithms, the control structures, or the organization of data that would be used in an actual reasoning system.[2] The reader may therefore wonder how any of this contributes to the building of actual AI programs. In this section, we answer this question by discussing the relation between this kind of analysis and the process of designing an AI program.

Our approach rests on three general methodological assumptions:

1. In designing a reasoning system, it is generally worthwhile to characterize the object-level information that the system will use and the inferences that it will perform, independently of determining how the system should perform these inferences.

2. A number of fundamental commonsense domains arise so frequently in designing reasoning systems that it is worthwhile for the research community to study the basic structure of commonsense inference in these domains independently of any particular application. Results from this study will be useful across a large range of applications. The more domain information can be represented declaratively, the easier it will be to design systems that can handle this information flexibly.

3. Certain characteristics of the knowledge used in commonsense inference make it particularly important that the language used to express this knowledge be very carefully and tightly defined. In particular: (a) Commonsense inferences tend to use a great variety of partial and incomplete knowledge. Representations for partial knowledge whose meaning is left at all open to the intuitive understanding of the programmer are very liable to be ambiguous or unclear in important respects. (b) The very familiarity of commonsense concepts and their close connection to basic natural language forms renders them liable to ambiguity. Unless particular care is taken, it is very easy for a symbol or formula to be interpreted in one way in one part of a program, and in a way that is subtly but importantly different in a different part.

---

[2]There is almost no discussion of domain-independent techniques; some references are given at the end of the chapter. A number of domain-specific algorithms are described.

We may clarify these points by contrasting commonsense reasoning with other areas of computer science. In standard algorithmic or numerical analysis, the domains of discourse, such as graph theory or differential analysis, are very restricted and mathematical. The domains have generally been given precise definitions and characterized; the researcher can focus on finding effective algorithms. In database system design, the details of finding effective primitives for a particular application are generally considered to be the problem of the user, and the theory gives him little guidance. The design of the database system is concerned with providing an architecture for the manipulation of information, not with giving a language for its expression. Moreover, database systems typically deal with only limited forms of partial information, such as missing tuples, or null values. (Some recent work in database theory has been drawing close to AI issues.)

Based on these assumptions, we suggest that a commonsense reasoning system be designed as a knowledge base, recording information and performing inference on object-level information about some *microworld*. A microworld is a restricted, idealized model of the world containing only those relations and entities of interest in the particular reasoning system being designed. The analysis of the microworld takes place on three levels:

1. The definition of the microworld: its entities, its relations, and the rules that govern them. This definition is called the *ontology* of the domain.

2. The analysis of the type of information that the system must record and the types of inferences it must perform. The result of this analysis is generally a *formal language*, in which facts of the microworld can be expressed, and *axioms* or *rules of inference,* which characterize inferences that are reasonable within the microworld.

3. An *implementation* of the information in mutable data structures and of the inferences in procedures and predefined data structures.

The analysis also specifies connections between these levels. The formal language is connected to the ontology by a *semantics*, which specifies how sentences in the language are interpreted as facts about the microworld. The implementation is connected to the language by formal definitions given for the data structures, and by arguments establishing that the inference procedures carry out legitimate inferences. (Figure 1.1.)

For a simple example, suppose that we are constructing a knowledge base recording family relationships between individual people.

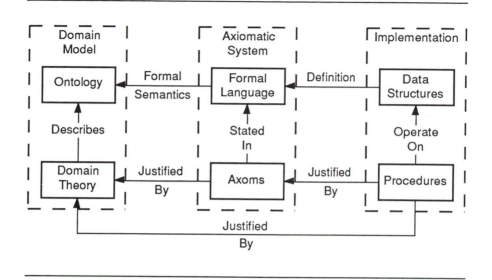

Figure 1.1 Theory structure

That is, we want to be able to input a collection of facts about individuals, like "Fleur is Soames's daughter," "Winifred is Soames's sister," "James is Winifred's father," and then make queries like, "Who is Fleur's aunt?" or "How is Fleur related to James?"

Our ontology for the domain can be very simple: the only entities we need consider are people, which are *atomic* (not decomposable). People have various relations defined on them. In particular, people have a sex, male or female; there is a binary parent-child relation; and there is a binary husband-wife relationship.

We can construct a simple first-order language[3] for this domain using four predicate symbols: "male(X)", "female(X)", "parent(X, Y)", and "married(X, Y)", together with constant symbols for individual people. The semantics for this language is established by relating the symbols to the corresponding relations of the microworld.

We can now study the power of this language by studying the kinds of facts that can be expressed in it. Any fact asserting a specific relation between two people can be expressed. For instance "Winifred is Soames's sister" can be expressed in the form

$$\text{female(winifred)} \land \exists_X \text{ parent}(X,\text{winifred}) \land \text{parent}(X,\text{soames})$$

---

[3] We assume that the reader is familiar with first-order logic. For a brief review, see Section 2.3.

"James is Fleur's grandfather" can be expressed in the form

$$\text{male(james)} \land \exists_X \text{ parent(james,}X) \land \text{parent}(X\text{,fleur})$$

However, there are partial specifications of relations that cannot be expressed in this language. For example, there is no way to express the fact "James is an ancestor of Fleur," or the fact "The relation between Soames and Fleur is the same as the relation between James and Winifred." To express the first fact, we need to add a new predicate "ancestor(X, Y)". To express the second fact, we need to augment our language with the ability to treat relations as objects in themselves. For instance, we could add the function "relation_of(X, Y)" to our language. We then can express the above fact in the form "relation_of(soames,fleur) = relation_of(james,winifred)."

This treating of relations or properties as objects is known as *reifying*. In order to be able to give a clear semantics to reifications and to the symbols like "relation_of" that describe them, it is necessary to identify the reified entities with some well-defined entity in the microworld. One common technique for achieving this (due to Frege) is to identify properties with the set of objects that have the property, and to identify relations with the set of object tuples satisfying the relation. For example, the property of maleness could be identified with the set of male people: Maleness = {James, Soames, Nicholas, Timothy ... }. The relation of aunthood could be identified with the pair of all aunts with their niece or nephew: Aunthood = { < Winifred, Fleur >, < Ann, Soames >, < Julia, Soames > ... }. We can then define the predicate "holds(R, X, Y)", meaning that relation R holds on persons X and Y, as true just if $< X, Y > \in R$. The function "relation_of(X, Y)" then maps the two persons X and Y to the relation that holds between them. (If X and Y are related in two different ways, relation_of(X, Y) denotes their most direct relation, according to some particular criterion of directness.)

We can also use the formal language to express general facts about the microworld, and we can interpret certain commonsense inferences in the domain as inferences from these facts. For example, consider the old riddle:

> Brothers and sisters have I none,
> But that man's father is my father's son.

One can frame the drawing of the conclusion, "That man is my son," as an inference from the riddle and plausible axioms, as shown in Table 1.1.

Table 1.1 Proof in the Family Microworld

Definition D.1: A brother is a different male with the same parent.
$$\forall_{X,Y} \; brother(X,Y) \Leftrightarrow$$
$$[\; X \neq Y \wedge male(X) \wedge \exists_Z \; parent(Z,X) \wedge parent(Z,Y)]$$

Definition D.2: A sister is a different female with the same parent.
$$\forall_{X,Y} \; sister(X,Y) \Leftrightarrow$$
$$[\; X \neq Y \wedge female(X) \wedge \exists_Z \; parent(Z,X) \wedge parent(Z,Y)]$$

Definition D.3: A father is a male parent.
$$\forall_{X,Y} \; father(X,Y) \Leftrightarrow [\; parent(X,Y) \wedge male(X)]$$

Definition D.4: A son is a male child.
$$\forall_{X,Y} \; son(X,Y) \Leftrightarrow [parent(Y,X) \wedge male(X)]$$

Axiom A.1: Everyone is either male or female.
$$\forall_X \; male(X) \vee female(X)$$

Fact F.1: Brothers and sisters have I none.
$$\neg(\exists_Z \; brother(Z,\text{me}) \vee sister(Z,\text{me}))$$

Fact F.2: That man's father is my father's son.
$$\exists_{U,V} \; father(U,\text{that}) \wedge father(V,\text{me}) \wedge son(U,V)$$

Fact F.3. That man is male.
$$male(\text{that})$$

Prove: That man is my son.
$$son(\text{that},\text{me})$$

Step S.1: Someone with the same parent is either a brother, a sister, or self.
$$\forall_{X,Y,Z} \; [\; parent(X,Y) \wedge parent(X,Z)\;] \Rightarrow$$
$$[\; brother(Y,Z) \vee sister(Y,Z) \vee Y = Z\;]$$
Proof: D.1, D.2, A.1

Step S.2: If a parent of mine has a son, then that is me.
$$\forall_{X,Y} \; [\; parent(X,\text{me}) \wedge son(Y,X)\;] \Rightarrow Y = \text{me}$$
Proof: D.4, S.1, F.1

Step S.3: I am that man's parent.
$$parent(\text{me},\text{that}).$$
Proof: D.3, S.2, F.2

Step S.4: That man is my son.
$$son(\text{that},\text{me}).$$
Proof: S.3, D.4, F.3

One simple knowledge structure for this domain is a labeled graph, with nodes denoting individual people, labeled with their name and sex, and with arcs representing parenthood and marriage (Figure 1.2). It is easy to devise graph search procedures to answer queries such as "Who are Soames's aunts?" or "What is the relation between Winifred and Fleur?" and to verify that these procedures are correct in terms of the definition of the data structure and the properties of these relations. Such an implementation has the advantage of simplicity and ease of use, but it is limited in its capacity to express partial information. For instance, it is not possible in this implementation to record the fact "Sarah is either married to Martin or to Jimmy." By contrast, the fact is easily expressed in our formal language.

married(sarah,martin) ∨ married(sarah,jimmy)

If the application of the reasoning program demands the manipulation of facts such as this, therefore, some more powerful data structure must be used. One possibility would be a direct representation of the above formal sentence as a string of symbols.

One potential source of ambiguity in using an implementation like the labeled graph of family relations is the question of completeness. Can one assume that the nonexistence of an arc means that no such relation holds or not? In the family graph, for example, if there is no "married" arc attached to a person's node, does that mean that the person is definitely unmarried? or that he or she is definitely not married to any of the other people in the graph, but may be married to someone not in the graph? or does it not offer any such constraint? Similarly, if there is an arc indicating that Fleur is the child of Soames, but there is no other parenthood arc from Soames, does that mean that Fleur is definitely Soames's only child? Certainly, one cannot assume that the graph shows everyone's parents; otherwise the graph would have to be infinite. Depending on the application, one may choose to decide this question either way, but it is important to be clear which choice is made, and to interpret the inferences made by the system in light of the decision. Under any choice, the expressive power of the graph is limited in one respect or another. If the graph must show every child of each individual, then there is no way to express a fact like "Fleur has children" if the number of children is not known. If the graph need not show every child, then there is no way to express a fact like "Fleur has no children."

There are definitely costs to giving precise definitions to the representations used in AI systems. First, doing so can be a lot of hard work, as this book will amply illustrate. If the inferences to be performed have limited scope, then it may be easier to code them up intuitively,

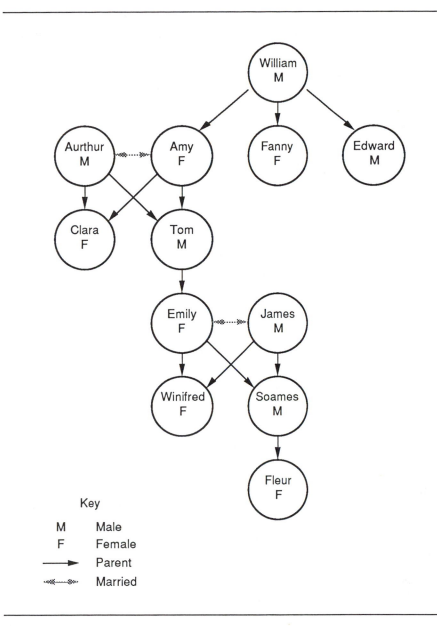

Figure 1.2 Family trees

and rely on the empirical success of the program as justification. Second, using a precisely defined representation may make it harder to express vague concepts (Section 1.7) or to establish a correspondence between the representation and natural language text (Section 1.4). Third, the use of precise definitions for concepts relies on a distinction between analytic knowledge (knowledge that is true by definition) and synthetic knowledge (knowledge that is true by virtue of the external world), a distinction that has been philosophically in ill repute for the last 40 years or so [Quine 1953].

Finally, it is not clear how to use precisely defined representations in the context of a program that learns concepts incrementally. For example, a friend of mine was under the impression, when she was a child, that ponies were young horses; she learned, in the eighth grade, that they are a small breed of horse. A computer program that did this would use a symbol PONY to represent the concept of ponies; start with the definition "PONY is a young horse"; and change to the definition "PONY is a breed of small horse." But, in our view of representation, it is hard to understand why this is progress. Is it the symbol PONY that has changed its meaning? If so, the change seems perfectly arbitrary, since PONY is an internal symbol that could just as well be G0011. In what respect is it "better" for PONY to represent ponies than young horses? Is it the concept of PONY that has changed its meaning? To say so would seem to introduce a peculiar distinction between a concept, on the one hand, and the meaning of the concept, on the other.[4] All this is not to say that the program is not behaving reasonably; just that it is difficult to explain its behavior under the view we have taken of concepts.

1.3   Implementation

Since the bottom line in AI research is the construction of intelligent programs, it is reasonable to ask how formal domain theories like those we discuss here will help us in the actual programming. This question of the relation of theory to practice is difficult in many fields; it is particularly difficult in AI, where basic techniques and method-

---

[4] Another possible suggestion is that the definition of the symbol PONY is, from first to last, "Any creature called a "pony" by the English-speaking community," and that the program goes from the belief of the (synthetic) fact that ponies, so defined, are young horses to the belief that they are a small breed of horse. Aside from the fact that this makes concepts subordinate to language, this solution can be objected to on two grounds: (a) This will do for an individual, but how do we explain what happens when the community finds that it has been mistaken about ponies? (b) This definition breaks down if we discover we have made a mistake about the word. If we discover that the word is actually "ponay" then we are left believing nothing.

ology are still very much in a state of development. We can, however, point out a number of possible connections:

1. The axioms of the domain may be used directly in symbolic form as input to a theorem prover[5] or other domain-independent inference engine. The inferences made by the inference engine from the axioms would then constitute part or all of the reasoning performed by the AI program. The achievement of such a direct link between a logical theory and a working program is one of the central ideals of logic programming. At present, however, the techniques of domain-independent inference are too weak to work efficiently on theories as complex as those we will consider.

2. The theory can be used to verify the correctness of an AI program. The theoretical justification of a domain-specific AI program must rest on a precise theory of that domain. "Theoretical justification" is, of course, a broad category [DeMillo, Lipton, and Perlis 1979], which may range from a fully symbolic proof, based on the semantics of the programming language, to an argument, based on an understanding of the program and the domain.

At some future date, it may be possible to automate the verification or even the construction of AI programs based on formal specifications of the domain and of the purpose of the program.

3. The formal characterization of a domain may allow the application of known mathematical results to solve particular problems, or to determine their difficulty.

4. The knowledge structures used in the program may be based on the formal theory. As discussed in Section 1.2, the familiarity of commonsense domains makes it particularly easy to abuse notation in AI programs and to use a single symbol in different ways that are not quite mutually consistent. A formal definition of the meaning of the symbols is very helpful in avoiding this kind of bug. For this purpose, the key part of the formal theory is the definition of the microworld and the semantics of the symbols. The construction of an axiomatic system is less important.

5. Logical analysis of the domain often serves to uncover peculiarities or anomalies that a programmer may at first overlook in writing code. In particular, a logical analysis is a good way to determine what information is needed to support a given conclusion, and what kinds of assumptions are reasonable and necessary in reasoning about given domain. For example, in designing a system that will reason about

---

[5] A theorem prover is a domain-independent program that performs deductive inference from information expressed as a set of formulas in some logical notation. Resolution theorem provers and Prolog interpreters are two types of theorem provers.

knowledge and belief, it is generally wise to determine what kinds of problems of referential opacity (Section 2.5) will arise in the particular application, and to decide how they can be dealt with, at an early stage.

6. After an AI program has been written, a *post hoc* logical analysis may aid in debugging, understanding, presenting, and extending it. The logical analysis may reveal some flaw in the program's reasoning or some inconsistency in the assumptions that it makes about the microworld that could lead to a bug. It may reveal some gap in the program's reasoning that could easily be filled in a natural extension. It can help separate central features of the program from peripheral features and control issues from object-level issues. It can help clarify the scope and limits of the program by explicitly defining the microworld and the class of inferences involved.

In this book we look in detail at a number of existing programs: MERCATOR (Section 6.2.3) and TOUR (Section 6.2.4), which maintain cognitive maps; NEWTON (Section 6.2.6), ENVISION (Section 7.1), and QP (Section 7.2), which make physical predications; and TWEAK (Section 9.1.1) and RAP (Section 9.4.1), which are planners. We also look at a number of knowledge structures that have been developed and applied primarily in the context of programs rather than in the abstract, including qualitative differential equations (Section 4.9), occupancy arrays (Section 6.2.1), constructive solid geometry (Section 6.2.2), and configuration spaces (Section 6.2.5).

1.4 The Role of Natural Language

People have developed many flexible, broad, powerful schemes for expressing and communicating commonsense facts; namely, the natural languages. How AI theories of commonsense reasoning should use natural language concepts is an important question, but a difficult and highly disputed one.

There is widespread agreement that AI programs should not use full natural language text as a knowledge-representation language. Natural language cannot be easily manipulated algorithmically. It is full of ambiguities. Its meaning is context dependent. Its syntax is extremely complex, and strongly dependent on semantics. Its connectives (prepositions, articles, and conjunctions) are remarkably vague and unsystematic. There are few powerful rules of inference on natural language strings. Moreover, natural language is notoriously ineffective at transmitting certain types of information, notably spatial information. (A picture is worth a thousand words.)

Thus, AI representations should be very much systematized as compared to natural language. The question is, how radical should this systematization be? At the one extreme are those theorists who form their representations by starting with natural language text, simplifying syntax and connectives, and resolving ambiguities. At the other extreme are those who construct their representations like a mathematical notation, analyzing the knowledge necessary for a problem in terms as abstract as possible.

There are several practical and theoretical arguments in favor of basing representation on natural language. The first of these is simply one of ease. We describe commonsense situations and we assert commonsense rules in natural language. It is relatively easy to "transliterate" these descriptions and rules into a fixed syntax, and it is hard to develop a language that is better or more precise, particularly in domains where no precise scientific language is available. In a related way, knowledge engineers who are trying to encode expert knowledge generally extract the basic domain primitives from spoken and written protocols. There is not much else one can do.

Second, a major function of commonsense inference systems is to interact with natural language systems. Obviously, the automatic translation of natural language to an internal representation is easier if the internal representation is close to the natural language. More importantly, we must be able to represent anything sensible that appears in the text. If a natural language term is vague or ill defined, then any representation of its content will likewise be vague and ill defined. (See [Hobbs 1985c].)

Third, several important philosophical schools argue in various ways (not wholly compatible) that beliefs and mental states are inextricably tied up with natural language. It has been argued that any representation scheme ultimately draws its meaning from natural language [Wittgenstein 1958]; or that beliefs can be reasonably ascribed only to creatures that use language [Davidson 1975]; or that the particular forms of a native natural language influence the basic structure of thought [Whorf 1956]; or that, since natural language terms are not precisely definable, the representation of natural language text must be in terms of primitives very close to the text [Fodor 1975]. If any of these philosophical arguments is correct, then it is inherently futile to look for a language-independent system of representation. (Many of the philosophers who make these arguments would claim that any attempt at artificial intelligence is inherently futile.)

Despite these arguments, my opinion is that the study of AI representations should not be focused on the representation of natural language text. I feel that natural language text is a poor starting point for thinking about representation; that natural language is too vague and too ill defined, even when rationalized, to allow systematic forms of inference; and that the tailoring of representations to natural language text can lead to an emphasis on extremely subtle issues of modality, reference, and context, while avoiding "nuts and bolts" issues such as spatial and physical reasoning.

1.5 The Role of Logic

No issue has been more debated in knowledge representation than the proper role of logic. Extreme logicists maintain that almost all intelligent functions can be characterized as deductions from some set of axioms, and can be carried out by a sufficiently well-crafted general-purpose theorem prover. Extreme antilogicists maintain logic is wholly irrelevant, either as a notation or as a theory of inference. There are also many possible intermediate positions. It is not possible here to present the various sides of this debate in any detail. References to some of the most important papers on the issue are given at the end of the chapter. Here, we will just point out some of the central issues. Our own position should be clear from our discussion of methodology in Section 1.2.

The debate over logic deals with the role of "theorem provers" in programs and the role of formalisms (formal ontologies, languages, and semantics) in AI theories. The ultimate questions to resolve are, is an AI program likely to be largely a theorem prover, or to contain a theorem prover as a small component, or not to contain anything that looks anything like a theorem prover? and to what degree should the representations in an AI program be given formal definitions? The following issues have been particularly important in the debate:

- How much intelligent reasoning can be characterized or approximated as deduction?

- Can formal theories of inference be extended to cover nondeductive inference?

- Does intelligent reasoning require the full power of logical inference?

- It is possible to do arbitrary computation using a theorem prover. Is this relevant?

- Are formal representations useful even if inferences are not formally characterized?

- Is it useful to characterize the inferences carried out in an AI program independently of the procedures to carry them out? Is it possible to separate domain knowledge from control knowledge?

- Must AI deal with vague concepts? If so, does that make logic irrelevant?

The arguments over the role of logic in commonsense reasoning are orthogonal to the arguments over the role of language. AI researchers have taken all combinations of positions. For instance, Hobbs [1985c] uses natural language primitives in a predicate calculus syntax. Montague semanticists [Montague 1974] have combined logic and natural language constructs in an even stronger form, by interpreting natural language as a formal logic. Much of the work on natural language processing has used natural language terms for representation, but has not attempted to give precise definition, for either the terms or the syntax of their representational scheme. (Wilks [1976] explicitly claims that it would be a mistake to attempt precise definitions.) Much of the work in spatial, temporal, and physical reasoning has used a precise, logical language and ignored the relevant natural language constructs. Work on representing narrative, particularly that of Schank and his students [1975, 1977], has used a system of abstract primitives that are language independent, but which are defined informally rather than logically; this work uses neither natural language nor logic as a basis. Connectionist systems use no symbolic representations at all.

The choice of methodology often depends on domain. Work in complex, poorly structured domains, like many expert systems domains, tends to use natural language terms, since they are available, and to avoid formal definitions, since they are hard to formulate. Work in simple, highly structured domains, such as simple physics and temporal reasoning, tends to avoid natural language, which is ambiguous and convoluted, and to use logical definitions, since precision is relatively easy to attain.

To some extent, these issues reflect similar issues in the philosophy of language and epistemology. The view that theories should be formal and language independent derives ultimately from the example of mathematics, and was argued by Bertrand Russell [1940] and related philosophers ([Carnap 1967]; [Ayer 1946]). The view that theories should be informal and based on natural language is related to the "ordinary language" philosophy of Austin [1961] and Wittgenstein [1958]. The view that natural language can be associated with a logical structure is particularly associated with Richard Montague [1974].

1.6 Incomplete and Uncertain Knowledge

There is a great gap to be bridged between the rigidity of a computer program and the flexibility of human reasoning. One aspect of this flexibility is the broad scope of human common sense discussed at the beginning of the chapter. Another aspect is the human ability to deal with partial and uncertain information. Very little of the knowledge that you use in daily life is precise or complete, and very little is certain. You know that the water in the tea-kettle will come to a boil soon after you turn the knob on the stove, but you do not know how soon it will boil, how hot the flame is, or how much liquid is in the kettle. This is incompleteness. Moreover, you cannot be entirely sure that the water will boil at all; the stove may be broken, or someone may come and turn it off, or the kettle may be empty. This is uncertainty. Similar considerations apply in all commonsense domains. You may have good reason to believe that your niece will be pleased if you send her flowers for her birthday. But you may not know whether she would prefer roses or irises (incompleteness) and it is possible that she hates either flowers, or her birthday, or you.

The use of partial information is critically important for several reasons. First, there are many cases where exact information is expensive or impossible to attain. Vision systems can deliver exact information only at great cost, or in very restricted environments. An intelligent creature that makes use of a practical vision system must therefore be able to cope with partial information as to the positions, shapes, and types of objects it sees. Complete information about the psychology of another person cannot be obtained at any cost; in fact, it is not clear that such a concept makes any sense. Again, decisions must be based on incomplete information. Second, even when the information is available, it may be too complicated to use. If you drive a car off a cliff, what happens? Well, if exact specifications of the car have been obtained from the manufacturer, and the cliff has been carefully surveyed, it may be possible to calculate the result very precisely. But the calculation will be long and difficult, and quite pointless if all you want to know is that you should not go over the cliff as a shortcut to the bottom. Third, it is often useful to do generic reasoning about whole classes of similar, but not quite identical cases. Suppose that you are putting up a chicken-wire fence to keep the chickens out of the asparagus, and you want to be sure that none of your chickens can get through it. Even if you happen to know the exact proportions of each chicken, you do not want to do a separate calculation for each one, establishing that it cannot go through your fence. You want to be able to determine that no chicken can go through the fence, by reasoning about the general characteristics of chickens.

The use of uncertain information is necessary when some important datum derives from some unreliable source. This can be an imperfect sensor, or an unreliable informant, or an uncertain rule. Uncertain rules, in turn, must often be used to supplement incomplete knowledge with plausible, but uncertain, guesses. If we see a car coming down the street, we infer the presence of a driver. This inference is not certain, but it is generally correct, and it is necessary to plan sensible action.

The representation of incomplete knowledge in various domains is one of the focal issues of this book. The central technique is to find predicates that express useful partial information. Disjunction and existential quantification also serve to express partial information. The representation and use of uncertain information is discussed in Chapter 3. Elsewhere in this book, we largely avoid the use of uncertain information.

1.7 Vagueness

In some respects, the concepts of commonsense knowledge are *vague,* in a sense that goes beyond uncertainty and incompleteness. Many categories of common sense have no well-marked boundary lines; there are clear examples and clear nonexamples, but in between lies an uncertain region that we cannot categorize, even in principle. For example, the concepts of the various species would seem to be necessary in a commonsense understanding of the natural world. Yet, as we know, since species evolve one from another, there cannot be any clear line dividing them; by traveling down and up the evolutionary chain, we can turn a dog into a cat in nearly continuous steps. There would be no way to decide at what precise point the ancestors of dogs cease to be dogs, as one goes back in time, even if we knew everything about these proto-dogs. In the same way, there is no way to define the exact line, to the inch, that marks the boundary of the Rocky Mountains; there is no maximum numbers of hairs permitted to a man who is bald; there is no telling, to the second, when a person ceases to be a child. All these terms — "dog," "Rocky Mountains," "bald," "child," — are vague.

From a theoretical point of view, this vagueness is extremely difficult to deal with, and no really satisfactory solutions have been proposed. The difficulties are made vivid by an ancient paradox called the "Sorites" (meaning "heap"). If you have a heap of sand, and you take away one single grain of sand, you will obviously still have a heap of sand. But therefore, by induction, you can take away all the sand, and still have a heap, which is absurd. Like the other terms above, "heap" is vague; there is no specific minimum number of grains that a heap can contain.

Often, we can treat vagueness of this kind in the same way as incompleteness. Though inadequate theoretically, this works in many practical cases. Suppose that "bald" did refer to some specific number of hairs on the head, only we did not know which number. We know that a man with twenty thousand hairs on his head is not bald, and that a man with three hairs on his head is bald, but somewhere in between we are doubtful. Under this analysis, the statement "Sam is bald" is no more problematic than "Sam has fewer hairs than John." In either case, sometimes we will be sure that it is true, sometimes we will be sure that it is false, and sometimes we will be uncertain. But despite this uncertainty, "bald" is a precise concept just as "the number of hairs on John's head" is a precise concept (at some specific moment), despite the fact that we do not know this number. Under this account the basic step of the Sorites paradox applied to baldness, "If a man is not bald, then losing one hair will not make him bald," becomes merely a plausible, not a necessary inference, just as, "If a man has more hairs than John then he will still have more hairs after losing one" is true in most, but not all, cases. It seems very likely that this account will prove inadequate for some purposes, since it is unquestionably wrong — "bald" is *not* a precise but undetermined concept; it is a vague concept — but it is not clear where it breaks down. In any case, this analysis is all we need for the purposes of this book. (Another technique for dealing with vague concepts is fuzzy logic [Zadeh 1987].)

1.8 Indexicals

Particular problems arise with indexicals, words like "I," "here," "now," and "this." The meaning of these words and the truth of sentences containing these words depend entirely on the circumstances of their use. Formal theories have therefore in general avoided these concepts by replacing sentences like "I am hungry now" with *eternal* sentences such as "Ernie Davis is hungry at 3:30, April 12, 1987."[6] However, this is not quite adequate for AI systems. An AI system must at some level

---

[6]An alternative approach is to construct a theory of meaning that builds in circumstance [Barwise and Perry 1982].

be able to distinguish between itself and other systems, and between the present moment and other moments. If the robot comes to believe "At time T a truck is bearing down on P," then what it must do and how hard it must think depends critically on whether T is the present moment, and on whether P is itself.

The approach we advocate for a theoretical analysis is that inference should be done in terms of eternal sentences. The robot's knowledge of its own identity and of the present moment should be programmed into the interfaces between the sensors and the knowledge base, the interfaces between the knowledge base and the effectors, and the control structure that chooses focuses for inference. For example, if the visual sensors of George, the robot, detect a truck bearing down on it, the visual interpretation system, consulting George's internal clock,[7] will enter the sentence, "A truck is bearing down on George at 1:37, March 5" into the knowledge base. The inference control structure will note that the time is the present and George is himself, and that therefore this should be given high priority for inference. The inference engine will then deduce the conclusions, "George is in danger at 1:37, March 5," "George should flee at 1:37, March 5," and "George's wheels should roll rapidly backwards at 1:37 March 5." At this point, the effector control, finding a statement about what George's effectors should do at the present moment, will set the wheels rolling. (This is discussed further in Section 5.13.)

Of course, this is a very much idealized model, and in practice one would want to short-circuit a lot of this. Reflexes in humans, for example, amount to a direct short circuit from the sensors to the effectors with no involvement of the knowledge base. A lot of the low-level planning for converting active current plans into effector actions may be carried out without any explicit representation either of the time or of the robot, since these inferences are only needed for planning the robot's own immediate motions, and are not entered in a permanent knowledge base.

1.9 Commonsense Reasoning in Artificial Intelligence

As we have argued above, all parts of artificial intelligence — vision, natural language, robotics, planning, learning, expert systems — must, sooner or later, make use of commonsense knowledge and commonsense reasoning techniques. Indeed, commonsense reasoning

---

[7]The robot need not have a chronometer that gives it times like "1:37, March 5." All it needs is the ability to give names, such as "t1045" to times, and to mark these extralogically as the current moment.

is so closely bound up with these other subfields that it is by no means clear that it forms an independent domain of inquiry. Certainly we do not make any strong distinction in common parlance: One might well say of a person who consistently adopted semantically strange readings of natural language sentences, or who could not use context to interpret what he saw, or who could not plan his way out of a paper bag, or who did not learn from experience, that he did not have any common sense.

In fact, it seems clear that there is no sharp demarcation line between common sense and these other AI domains, either theoretical or psychological.[8] Nonetheless, for the purposes of research, it does seem possible and useful to delimit a certain area of study. We are studying "consensus reality" [Lenat 1988], knowledge and reasoning available to the overwhelming majority of people in our culture past early childhood; thus, not expert knowledge. Once this knowledge is acquired at a young age, it is fairly stable; thus, we can more or less ignore learning. This knowledge is held by people of many different countries; thus, it does not include knowledge of any particular language, though it would include knowledge about languages generally, such as that people communicate in language. The use of sensors and effectors at the low-level involves a wholly different class of computational techniques; thus we can ignore low level vision and robotics, though probably not high-level vision and robotics. We are studying types of reasoning that seem easy, not those requiring substantial conscious effort; thus, we can ignore sophisticated planning, though not elementary planning.

1.10 Philosophy

Warm yourself by the fire of the wise, but beware lest you burn yourself with their coals, for their bite is the bite of a jackal, and their sting is the sting of a scorpion, and their hiss is the hiss of a serpent, and all their words are burning coals.

Mishnah Avot, 2.15

---

[8]Another possibility could be that there is no general-purpose commonsense reasoning; each separate task domain — vision, natural language processing, robotics, and so on — uses its own separate body of commonsense knowledge and its own inference procedures. We would argue that the basic knowledge of the external world required in all these tasks overlaps sufficiently to make it worthwhile to study the manipulation of this knowledge independently of the particular tasks involved.

The most important external influence on AI theories of common-sense reasoning has been twentieth-century analytical philosophy. Most of our basic analytical tools, particularly formal logics, and much of our analysis of specific domains, particularly time, action, and mind, were developed by philosophers and mathematical logicians. If an AI researcher wants to develop a representation for a commonsense domain, he should certainly take the time to check out what the philosophers have said.

However, he must be prepared to be disappointed. He is likely to find that the philosophers and logicians have nothing to say about the issues that seem key to him, and have focused instead on issues and examples that to him seem trivial, far-fetched, or irrelevant. Simply, AI and philosophy have substantially different objectives and methodologies; they work, so to speak, on different wavelengths.

A central difference between the two fields is that AI looks for useful answers to practical problems, while philosophy looks for ultimate answers to fundamental problems. Accordingly, AI theories must be detailed and specific to the level of implementing systems that solve particular problems. However, they need not stand up under all conceivable criticisms; they need merely be adequate for the problems to which they are addressed. In contrast, philosophical theories are often quite vague, but they are expected to be absolutely valid without exception or counterexample. For this reason, much work in AI, such as describing the expected sequence of events in a restaurant, seems entirely trivial to philosophers, while much work in philosophy seems to AI people to be either uselessly vague or focused on weird counterexamples.

Consider, for example, the problems associated with a "natural kind" term such as "cat." The major philosophical problem associated with such words is to determine what we mean when we use such a word. What is presupposed by the use of "cat"? Under what, if any, circumstances, would we be justified in deciding that "cat" is, in fact, a meaningless word, and that therefore all our previous beliefs about cats were likewise meaningless? Conversely, if we found out that cats were quite a different kind of entity than we had previously believed, how would our previous uses of the word have obtained this meaning? Such questions lead naturally to the construction of hypothetical queries like, "If, on some unexplored island, we find a race of creatures that are exactly like our cats, but have a wholly different evolutionary heritage, would they be cats?"[9]

---

[9]Note that the question is not "Would we then (after finding them) call them cats?" which could be a question about how we change language in response to discoveries. The question is "When we now say 'cat', do we mean to include such hypothetical creatures?"

From the AI point of view, the primary problem is what kinds of commonsense information do we have about cats? The overwhelming bulk of this information (probably) relates to the superficial, sensory properties of cats: what they look, sound, feel, and smell like. Then there are much smaller bodies of information regarding the internal structure, behavior, and origin of cats. Which of these properties, if any, constitute the defining characteristics of a cat is very rarely of practical importance. Our problem is to represent and manipulate all of this very mundane and obvious information about cats. The philosophers have not addressed such issues. The philosophical issues, though possibly of great ultimate importance in formulating theories of concept learning, are not of immediate concern to AI research.

1.11 Mathematics and Commonsense Reasoning

The other major external influence on formal theories of commonsense reasoning is mathematics. In the theories of quantities and geometrical space, mathematical theories are so rich that the problem for us is one of selecting, and to a small degree amplifying, the available tools, rather than originating new theories. The fundamental theories of logic and set theories also owe as much to mathematics as to philosophy. In other commonsense domains, particularly domains involving mental activity, there is very little math that bears on our problems.

There are, however, two important differences between the mathematical mindset and the mindset of research in commonsense reasoning. First, mathematics is driven by abstraction; it looks for common abstract structures that underlie seemingly very different phenomena. It is one of the glories of mathematics that phenomena as different as small-arc pendulums, masses on springs, LRC circuits, and time-varying populations can all be characterized by the same kinds of differential equations. In commonsense theories, by contrast, while it is important that structural similarities exist between representations in different domains so that analogies can be constructed and applied, it is equally important that the concrete, individual aspects be kept in sight. If two very different kinds of things look the same in your theory, then you have abstracted some important issues away. Things that are commonsensically different should be described by a different kind of commonsense theory. (This argument is contested in [Hobbs 1987].)

The need to make this fine distinction is itself a significant contribution of philosophical study.

Another mathematical goal that is not generally carried over to AI is that of axiomatic parsimony. Mathematicians like to find the smallest, weakest set of independent axioms that will give the desired results. Partly, this is a matter of mathematical aesthetics; partly, a desire to make theories as general as possible; partly, a desire to make the axioms as self-evidently true and consistent as possible. None of this matters in AI. Knowledge bases in commonsense domains will, in any case, have so many axioms (many of them just stating contingent facts like "John loves Mary") that nothing will make them aesthetically appealing, or self-evidently true. Generality hardly matters, since AI systems are resolutely focused on the specific.

1.12 References

General: As of the date of writing, this is, as far as I know, the only book-length general survey of commonsense reasoning in AI. [Davis 1987a] surveys the field in a short article. [Charniak and McDermott 1985] gives a good introduction to the area in Chapters 1, 6, and 7. [Genesereth and Nilsson 1987] has several relevant chapters on logic, plausible reasoning, knowledge and belief, and planning. Several important collections of papers in the area have been published. [Hobbs and Moore 1985] is a collection of state-of-the-art research papers in various commonsense domains. The introductory chapter, by Hobbs, is an excellent overview of current research in the area. [Brachman and Levesque 1985] is a collection of classic papers on knowledge representation and commonsense reasoning. These papers tend to be at a more abstract and general level than this book. [Brachman, Levesque, and Reiter 1989] contains the proceedings of a recent conference on knowledge representation.

The necessity for commonsense reasoning in AI was first put forward by John McCarthy in "Programs with Common Sense," in 1959. This paper, and its successor, "Situations, Actions, and Causal Laws," [McCarthy 1963] are still very much worth reading. [Lifschitz and McCarthy 1989] is a collection of papers by McCarthy on commonsense reasoning and artificial intelligence.

The CYC program [Lenat et. al. 1986] is an ambitious project to encode the contents of an encyclopedia in a computer system for intelligent data retrieval. The results of this project are not yet available for evaluation.

Vagueness: The only theory that claims to deal with vagueness adequately is Zadeh's [1963, 1987] fuzzy logic.

Methodology: Many papers have discussed the role of logic in AI, and the issue is still hotly debated. Some of the most significant papers are [McCarthy 1959, 1963], [McCarthy and Hayes 1969], [Minsky 1975], [Hayes 1977, 1978] [McDermott 1978a, 1987a], [Newell 1981], and [Moore 1982]. The use of natural language constructs in representational systems has been much less discussed; [Wilks 1976], [McDermott 1976], and [Hobbs 1985a, 1987] are relevant. The methodology advocated in Section 1.4 here is distilled from [Hayes 1977, 1978] and [McDermott 1978a].

One methodological issue not discussed here is the use of multiple microworlds in an AI program. See [Hobbs 1985b], [de Kleer 1986], and [Addanki et al. 1989].

Philosophy: Discussions of philosophy in the AI literature, and vice versa, mostly discuss philosophy's view of AI as a theory of mind, rather than AI's view of philosophy as providing analyses of commonsense concepts. Particular successful adaptations of philosophical ideas in AI will be found throughout the text and will not be enumerated here. The philosophical discussions of "natural kinds" mentioned may be found in [Putnam 1962] and [Kripke 1972] among other places. Early attempts at a logical analysis of statements about external reality are to be found in the works of Bertrand Russell [1903], A. J. Ayer [1946], and Rudolf Carnap [1967], among others. It may be noted that the "commonsense school" of philosophy was concerned with the defense of common sense rather than its analysis, and so contributed little if anything relevant to our enterprise. Attempts to find common ground between philosophical and AI research have led to some peculiar discussions; see, for example, [Pylyshyn 1987].

Architectures: In this book, we omit any discussion of domain-independent architectures for reasoning. We list here a few references on particularly well-known theories. [Reichgelt in preparation] is a general survey of the area. [Charniak et al. 1988] is a textbook that covers a large range of reasoning architectures implemented in LISP. Logic programming is discussed in [Kowalski 1979] and [Wos et al. 1984]. Semantic networks, and their relation to logical representations, are discussed in [Woods 1975], [Schubert 1978], and [Brachman 1985]. Frame-based programming systems are discussed in [Bobrow and Winograd 1977].

Other: [Geertz 1983] is an interesting discussion of common sense from an anthropological perspective. The major study of the developmental psychology of common sense is the work of Piaget; see, for example, [Piaget 1951].

Chapter 2
Logic

Let us admit what all idealists admit: that the nature of the world is hallucinatory. Let us do what no idealist has done: let us look for the unrealities that confirm that nature. We shall find them, I believe, in the antinomies of Kant and in Zeno's dialectic.

"The greatest sorcerer [writes Novalis memorably] would be the one who bewitched himself to the point of taking his own phantasmagoria for autonomous apparitions. Would not this be true of us?"

I believe that it is. We (the undivided divinity that operates within us) have dreamed the world. We have dreamed it strong, mysterious, visible, ubiquitous in space and secure in time; but we have allowed tenuous, eternal interstices of injustice in its structure so we may know that it is false.

Jorge Luis Borges, "Avatars of the Tortoise," Other Inquisitions

To express knowledge about particular domains, we need to develop languages, define their meaning, and describe what kinds of inferences they allow. It turns out that several basic issues in defining languages, semantics, and inference techniques are important in many different domains of application. It makes sense, therefore, to address these questions once and for all abstractly. That is, we will look first for a general schema for defining languages that handles these common basic issues elegantly and effectively; we can then use this schema to define a particular language for a particular domain. Such a schema is called a *logic*.

The best known logics, and the most often used, are propositional logic and classical first-order logic. We assume that the reader is familiar with these; Sections 2.2–2.3 provide a brief review. Besides these standard logics, however, a number of nonstandard logics have been proposed for use in AI. These nonstandard logics typically modify the standard logics in two ways. First, they allow sentences that say something about other sentences; this is the subject of Sections 2.5–2.8. Second, they deal with uncertain and tentative information; this is the subject of Chapter 3.

2.1 Logical Systems and Languages

A *language* is a collection of meaningful strings, called *sentences*. A *logical system* (or simply *logic*) is a method for defining languages and their meanings. A logic consists of

- A set of *logical symbols*.

- A characterization of the possible *nonlogical symbols* that can be defined, and the types of meanings they can be given.

- *Syntactic rules* for constructing meaningful sentences out of logical and nonlogical symbols.

- A characterization of *proofs*.

- *Semantic rules* for determining the meaning of a sentence, using the syntax of the sentence, and the meanings of the constituent nonlogical symbols.

The structure of a logic is roughly analogous to that of a programming language.[1] The logical symbols correspond to the reserved words or symbols of the programming language. The nonlogical symbols correspond to user-defined identifiers (variable names, function names, and so on). The syntactic rules for constructing a sentence in a logic are analogous to the syntactic rules for constructing a program in the programming language. The semantic rules that define the meaning of a sentence are weakly analogous to semantic rules that define what a program does. Ordinary programming languages have no analogue of an inference rule or an axiom.

In the logics we will study, symbols are *atomic*; the particular sequence of characters that compose them are not significant. (By con-

---

[1]Historically, of course, programming languages were developed later than logical notation.

trast in natural language, the form of a word often carries semantic information.) Naturally, we will use symbols that resemble English words of related meaning. When we need to name an individual object of a particular type, we will often give it a name consisting of the type followed by a number or letter; thus, a chair might be named by the symbol "chair34" or "chairb".

A *proof* is a syntactic structure; it is made of symbols organized according to specific rules. The *hypotheses* and *conclusion* of a proof are sentences that occupy a distinguished position in the proof; if there is a proof of a conclusion from a set of hypotheses, then it is legitimate to infer the conclusion given the hypotheses. Proofs may take many different forms, depending on the particular logic. For example, in an *axiomatic* logic, the logic specifies a set of logical axioms and a set of inference rules, which allow a sentence ϕ to be derived from a set of sentences Γ. A proof is then a sequence of sentences such that each sentence is either a logical axiom, or is a hypothesis, or is derivable from previous sentences via some inference rule.

An *interpretation* for a language $\mathcal{L}$ is a definition of each of the non-logical symbols of the language in terms of some domain. A *semantics* for a logic is a definition of the truth (or other characteristic) of sentences in a language in the logic in terms of the interpretation. If $\mathcal{I}$ is an interpretation of $\mathcal{L}$ and ϕ is a sentence in $\mathcal{L}$ that is true in $\mathcal{I}$, we write $\mathcal{I} \models \phi$ (read "$\mathcal{I}$ satisfies ϕ" or "$\mathcal{I}$ is a model for ϕ"; the symbol $\models$ is called the "double turnstile.") Similarly, if $\mathcal{Q}$ is a set of interpretations, and ϕ is true in all the interpretations in $\mathcal{Q}$, we write $\mathcal{Q} \models \phi$. We often identify a set of sentences Ψ with the set of all interpretations in which all the sentences of Ψ are true. Under this identification, we can write $\Psi \models \phi$ to mean that, for any interpretation $\mathcal{I}$, if $\mathcal{I}$ is a model for all the sentences in Ψ, then $\mathcal{I}$ is also a model for ϕ.

If ϕ is true in all interpretations whatever, then we write $\models \phi$; such a ϕ is said to be *universally valid*. A universally valid sentence is thus one that is true purely by virtue of the logic, independent of what interpretation is given to the language.

The above concept of satisfying a model is a *semantic* concept; it relates to the meaning of a sentence. There is an analogous syntactic concept, based on the idea of a proof. If there is a proof of ϕ from hypotheses Ψ, then we write $\Psi \vdash \phi$ (read "ϕ is derivable from Ψ." The symbol $\vdash$ is called the single turnstile.) If ϕ is derivable without any hypotheses, then we write $\vdash \phi$. A set of hypotheses Ψ is inconsistent if, for some sentence ϕ, both ϕ and its negation[2] can be proven from Ψ.

The semantic concept of validity and the syntactic concept of provability are connected by the logical properties of soundness and completeness. A logic is sound if its proof theory preserves truth; if the sentences in Ψ are true in an interpretation $\mathcal{I}$ and ϕ can be inferred from Ψ, then ϕ is also true in $\mathcal{I}$. In other words, a logic is sound just if, for all Ψ and ϕ, $\Psi \vdash \phi$ implies that $\Psi \models \phi$. A logic is complete if any valid conclusion can be proven; that is, for any Ψ and ϕ, $\Psi \models \phi$ implies $\Psi \vdash \phi$. In a complete logic, the proof system is strong enough to derive any conclusions that are necessarily valid, given a set of axioms. Godel's completeness theorem proves that the predicate calculus is complete.

The term "complete" is also used in a different sense in logic. An axiom system is said to be complete if, for any sentence ϕ in the language, it is either possible to prove ϕ or to prove the negation of ϕ. Thus, completeness of an axiom system means that the axioms are strong enough to characterize every sentence as provably true or false. Completeness of a logic means that the proof theory can extract all the necessary consequences out of a set of axioms. Godel's incompleteness theorem proves that the standard axioms of arithmetic are incomplete.(More precisely, Godel's theorem shows that any recursively enumerable, consistent, axiomatization of arithmetic is incomplete [Nagel and Newman 1958].)

The presentation of an axiom system may enumerate each individual axiom, or it may use an *axiom schema* to generate a class (generally infinite and recursively enumerable) of axioms. An axiom schema is specified by giving some rule that allows us to distinguish members of the class from nonmembers. For example, we may specify the axiom schema "For any sentences ϕ and ψ, the sentence '$\phi \land \psi \Rightarrow \phi$' is an axiom." This axiom schema asserts that any sentence of the given form is an axiom: thus, "can_fly(pigs) $\land$ 1+1=2 $\Rightarrow$ can_fly(pigs)" is an axiom. For another example, the principle of mathematical induction on the integers is an axiom schema.[3] It has the following form: For any formula $\alpha(X)$ with one free variable X, the following is an axiom:

$$[\alpha(0) \land [\forall_N \, \alpha(N) \Rightarrow \alpha(N+1)]] \Rightarrow \forall_N \, \alpha(N)$$

---

[2]This definition assumes that the concept of negation is part of the logic. An alternative definition that avoids this assumption is Ψ is inconsistent if all sentences can be proven from Ψ.

[3]Strictly speaking, this is not the full principle of mathematical induction, but it is the closest one can come in a first-order schema.

Thus, for example, taking $\alpha(X)$ to be $X < X + 1$, we may construct the axiom

$$[(0 < 0 + 1) \wedge [\forall_N \, N < N + 1 \Rightarrow (N + 1) < (N + 1) + 1]] \Rightarrow \forall_N \, N < N + 1$$

Statements about a logical language, whether phrased formally or informally, are said to be *metalinguistic* or to be in a *metalanguage*. For example, any axiom schema, such as the one given above, "For any sentences, ϕ and ψ, the sentence '$\phi \wedge \psi \Rightarrow \phi$' is an axiom," is a metalinguistic statement; it is a sentence about certain sentences in the formal language; it is is not in the language itself. The formal language itself is often called the *object language*. A *theory* is a collection of sentences in an object language, together with all the consequences of those sentences. The base sentences of the theory, from which other sentences are deduced, are called *proper axioms,* as distinguished from the *logical axioms,* which hold for all theories in all languages in this logic.

2.2   Propositional Calculus

The propositional calculus (also called "propositional logic" or "sentential logic") describes how sentences can be combined using Boolean operators. The logical symbols of this theory are the Boolean operators: $\neg$ (not), $\wedge$ (and), $\vee$ (or), $\Rightarrow$ (implies), $\Leftrightarrow$ (if and only if) and $\dot{\vee}$ (exclusive or).   Parentheses and brackets are used for grouping. The nonlogical symbols, called "sentential constants," denote atomic sentences; we will here use lower-case letters. For example, p might be the proposition "Hydrogen is lighter than oxygen," q might be the proposition "All ducks are fish," and r might be the proposition "Roger Maris hit sixty-one home runs in 1961."

A sentence in the propositional calculus is defined recursively as follows:

DEFINITION 2.1   *A string ϕ is a sentence if and only if*

a. ϕ is a sentential constant; or

b. ϕ has one of the following forms: $\neg\psi$; $(\psi \wedge \zeta)$; $(\psi \vee \zeta)$; $(\psi \Rightarrow \zeta)$; $(\psi \Leftrightarrow \zeta)$; $(\psi \dot{\vee} \zeta)$; where ψ and ζ are (recursively) sentences.

Thus, given the sentential constants p, q, and r, sentences include "$(p \lor \neg q)$", "$((p \Leftrightarrow q) \Rightarrow (\neg p \dot{\lor} r))$", and so on.

(Note on notation: In this book, we will often leave out some parentheses, with the convention that $\neg$ has higher priority than $\lor$, $\land$, and $\dot{\lor}$, which have higher priority than $\Rightarrow$ or $\Leftrightarrow$. Thus "$\neg p \land q \Rightarrow r$" is interpreted as "$((\neg p \land q) \Rightarrow r)$". Also we use "running" sequences of $\Leftrightarrow$ and $\dot{\lor}$. Thus "$p \Leftrightarrow q \Leftrightarrow r$" means that all three sentences p, q, and r have the same truth value, rather than being equivalent to "$(p \Leftrightarrow q) \Leftrightarrow r$". Similarly "$p \dot{\lor} q \dot{\lor} r$" means that exactly one of p, q, and r is true, rather than being equivalent to "$(p \dot{\lor} q) \dot{\lor} r$." Such sequences of $\Leftrightarrow$ or $\dot{\lor}$ should be considered as constituting a single operator on the propositions connected, rather than a collection of operators. Thus, strictly speaking it would be better to write "equivalent(p, q, r)" or "exactly_one(p, q, r)", but the other notation is standard and more readable.)

The domain of the propositional calculus consists of the two truth values TRUE and FALSE. Given a set of sentential constants S, an interpretation for S is a mapping from S to the values TRUE and FALSE. For example, if $S = \{p, q, r\}$, then one interpretation $\mathcal{I}$ would be the mapping $\mathcal{I}(p)$=TRUE; $\mathcal{I}(q)$=FALSE; $\mathcal{I}(r)$=FALSE. The semantics of the propositional calculus then defines how an interpretation $\mathcal{I}$ is extended from the sentential constants to all the constants in the language. This is done according to the following recursive rule:

DEFINITION 2.2 *Let S be a set of sentential constants and let $\mathcal{I}$ be an interpretation over S. Then*

- *$\mathcal{I}(\neg \phi)$=TRUE if $\mathcal{I}(\phi)$ = FALSE and TRUE otherwise.*

- *$\mathcal{I}(\phi \lor \psi)$=TRUE if either $\mathcal{I}(\phi)$=TRUE or $\mathcal{I}(\psi)$=TRUE; otherwise it is FALSE.*

- *$\mathcal{I}(\phi \land \psi)$=TRUE just if both $\mathcal{I}(\phi)$=TRUE and $\mathcal{I}(\psi)$=TRUE;*

- *$\mathcal{I}(\phi \Rightarrow \psi)$=TRUE just if either $\mathcal{I}(\phi)$=FALSE or $\mathcal{I}(\psi)$=TRUE;*

- *$\mathcal{I}(\phi \Leftrightarrow \psi)$=TRUE just if $\mathcal{I}(\phi)$ is the same as $\mathcal{I}(\psi)$; and*

- *$\mathcal{I}(\phi \dot{\lor} \psi)$=TRUE just if one but not both of $\mathcal{I}(\phi)$ and $\mathcal{I}(\psi)$ is TRUE.*

At first glance, Definition 2.2 would seem to be no more than a tautologous translation of the formal symbols for Boolean connectives into the corresponding English words. In fact, however, it is more than that; it allows us to establish a correspondence between a string of symbols such as $\neg(p \vee \neg q)$ and the semantic objects TRUE and FALSE, given the truth of the sentential constants. The form of the definition establishes important constraints on the meaning of the Boolean connectives; the truth of a complex sentence depends *only* on the truth values of its components and on nothing else. Thus, for example, there is no way in the propositional calculus of expressing relations between sentences such as "ϕ is the same sentence as ψ" or "ϕ can be proven from ψ." In particular, the material implication $\phi \Rightarrow \psi$ means only that either ϕ is false or that ψ is true; it signifies no further connection between the two sentences. Readers who are still unconvinced that there is anything to the semantic definition 2.2 are asked to suspend judgment until they have seen the more complex semantics in Sections 2.3.2 and 2.7.1.

There are several ways of defining sound and complete inference systems for the propositional calculus. The easiest method for verifying proofs by hand is to use truth tables. However, to define this formally as a proof system involves giving a syntactic characterization of a truth table as a system of symbols, which is messy though not difficult. Table 2.1 shows an axiomatic inference system for the predicate calculus, and Table 2.2 shows some sample proofs.

A universally valid sentence in the propositional calculus is called a *tautology*; an inference in the propositional calculus is called a *tautological* inference.

The propositional calculus is rarely adequate for inference in AI domains. The only inferences it legitimates are the moving of Boolean operations around fixed sentences. This is sufficient to solve some combinatorial problems in fixed domains. For instance, the propositional calculus is adequate for the formulation and solution of puzzles like "Jones, Smith, and Robinson are a fireman, an engineer, and a conductor, not necessarily in that order. Jones owes the fireman $30. The conductor's wife never allows him to borrow money. Smith is a bachelor. Who has what job?" But most useful inferences involve applying a general rule to a specific case, which is beyond the power of the propositional calculus. Nonetheless, it deserves mention because it forms the basis for first-order logic, and because it offers an elementary testing ground for developing logical theories. When alternative forms of logic are studied, they are generally developed first as extensions to propositional calculus, and only later as extensions to first-order logic.

Table 2.1 Axioms for the Propositional Calculus

Axioms: For any sentences α, β, γ, any of the following sentences is an axiom:

PROP.1. $\alpha\Rightarrow(\beta\Rightarrow\alpha)$

PROP.2. $(\alpha\Rightarrow(\beta\Rightarrow\gamma))\Rightarrow((\alpha\Rightarrow\beta)\Rightarrow(\alpha\Rightarrow\gamma))$

PROP.3. $(\neg\alpha\Rightarrow\neg\beta)\Rightarrow((\neg\alpha\Rightarrow\beta)\Rightarrow\alpha)$

(As an aid in reading these axioms, note that $\alpha\Rightarrow(\beta\Rightarrow\gamma)$ means the same as $(\alpha\wedge\beta)\Rightarrow\gamma$.)

Definitional equivalences: (These axioms serve only to define the other Boolean operators in terms of implication and negation. They can be omitted if we restrict our language to have only negation and implication.)

PROP.4. $(\alpha\Leftrightarrow\beta)\Rightarrow(\alpha\Rightarrow\beta)$

PROP.5. $(\alpha\Leftrightarrow\beta)\Rightarrow(\beta\Rightarrow\alpha)$

PROP.6. $(\alpha\Rightarrow\beta)\Rightarrow((\beta\Rightarrow\alpha)\Rightarrow(\alpha\Leftrightarrow\beta))$

PROP.7. $(\alpha\vee\beta)\Leftrightarrow(\neg\alpha\Rightarrow\beta)$

PROP.8. $(\alpha\wedge\beta)\Leftrightarrow\neg(\alpha\Rightarrow\neg\beta)$

PROP.9. $(\alpha\dot\vee\beta)\Leftrightarrow(\alpha\Leftrightarrow\neg\beta)$

Rule of inference (Modus Ponens): For any two sentences ϕ and ψ, ψ may be inferred from the two sentences ϕ and $\phi\Rightarrow\psi$.

Proof: A proof of theorem ϕ from hypotheses Ψ is a sequence of sentences ending in ϕ such that each sentence is either

- An element of Ψ; or

- An axiom; or

- Inferrable from earlier sentences in the proof via modus ponens.

Table 2.2 Proof in the Propositional Calculus

Note: The proof proper is just the sequence of sentences. The justifications on the side are just comments to aid the reader.

Given { }: To prove: $p \Rightarrow p$

No.	Step	Justification
1.	$p \Rightarrow ((p \Rightarrow p) \Rightarrow p)$	PROP.1: $\alpha{=}p$; $\beta{=}(p \Rightarrow p)$.
2.	$(p \Rightarrow ((p \Rightarrow p) \Rightarrow p)) \Rightarrow$ $((p \Rightarrow (p \Rightarrow p)) \Rightarrow (p \Rightarrow p))$	PROP.2: $\alpha{=}p$; $\beta{=}(p \Rightarrow p)$; $\gamma{=}p$.
3.	$(p \Rightarrow (p \Rightarrow p)) \Rightarrow (p \Rightarrow p)$	Modus Ponens: (1) and (2).
4.	$p \Rightarrow (p \Rightarrow p)$	PROP.1: $\alpha = \beta =p$
5.	$p \Rightarrow p$	Modus Ponens: (4) and (3).

Given { $p \wedge q$ }: To prove: q

No.	Step	Justification
1.	$p \wedge q$	Given.
2.	$(p \wedge q) \Leftrightarrow \neg(p \Rightarrow \neg q)$.	PROP.8: $\alpha =p$; $\beta =q$.
3.	$((p \wedge q) \Leftrightarrow \neg(p \Rightarrow \neg q)) \Rightarrow$ $((p \wedge q) \Rightarrow \neg(p \Rightarrow \neg q))$	PROP.4: $\alpha{=}(p \wedge q)$; $\beta{=}\neg(p \Rightarrow \neg q)$
4.	$(p \wedge q) \Rightarrow \neg(p \Rightarrow \neg q)$	Modus Ponens: (2) and (3).
5.	$\neg(p \Rightarrow \neg q)$	Modus Ponens: (1) and (4).
6.	$\neg(p \Rightarrow \neg q) \Rightarrow (\neg q \Rightarrow \neg(p \Rightarrow \neg q))$	PROP.1: $\alpha{=}\neg(p \Rightarrow \neg q)$; $\beta{=}\neg q$.
7.	$\neg q \Rightarrow \neg(p \Rightarrow \neg q)$	Modus Ponens: (5) and (6).
8.	$\neg q \Rightarrow (p \Rightarrow \neg q)$	PROP.1: $\alpha{=}\neg q$; $\beta{=}p$.
9.	$(\neg q \Rightarrow \neg(p \Rightarrow \neg q)) \Rightarrow$ $((\neg q \Rightarrow (p \Rightarrow \neg q)) \Rightarrow q)$	PROP.3: $\alpha{=}q$; $\beta{=}(p \Rightarrow \neg q)$.
10.	$(\neg q \Rightarrow (p \Rightarrow \neg q)) \Rightarrow q$	Modus Ponens: (7) and (9).
11.	q.	Modus Ponens: (8) and (10).

2.3 Predicate Calculus

The predicate calculus, also called first-order logic, is by far the most important and commonly used logical system. We will use this logic for most of our domain theories. It is known that the predicate calculus is sufficiently powerful for classical mathematics.

The predicate calculus extends propositional calculus in two directions. First, it provides an inner structure for atomic sentences; these are viewed as expressing relations between things. Second, it gives us the means to express, and reason with, generalizations; we can say that a certain property holds of all objects, of some object, or of no object.

2.3.1   Syntax of Predicate Calculus

The logical symbols of predicate calculus are the Boolean operators of propositional logic, the quantifiers ∀ (for all) and ∃ (there exists), the comma, the open and close parentheses, and an infinite collection of variable symbols.   Nonlogical symbols are divided into three kinds: constant symbols, function symbols, and predicate symbols.   Associated with each function symbol and predicate symbol is a positive integer, fixing the number of arguments that the symbol may take. In this book, we will use strings with italicized upper-case letters, such as "A," "$X1$," or "$THE\_DAY\_THE\_WORLD\_STOOD\_STILL$," as variables, and strings with lower-case letters, such as "john," "father_of," and "impossible_to_get_started," as nonlogical symbols.

The following definitions are used to define the first-order language $\mathcal{L}$ with a given set of nonlogical symbols.

DEFINITION 3.1   *The string τ is a* term *if one of the following holds:*

a. *τ is a constant symbol; or*

b. *τ is a variable symbol; or*

c. *τ has the form $\beta(\tau_1, \tau_2 \ldots \tau_k)$ where β is a k-place function symbol, and each of the τ_i is a term.*

DEFINITION 3.2   *The string ϕ is a* formula *of $\mathcal{L}$ if one of the following holds:*

a. *ϕ has the form $\gamma(\tau_1, \tau_2 \ldots \tau_k)$, where γ is a k-place relation, and each of the τ_i is a term. (These are called atomic formulas.)*

b. *ϕ has one of the following forms: $\neg\psi$; $(\psi \wedge \zeta)$; $(\psi \vee \zeta)$; $(\psi \Rightarrow \zeta)$; $(\psi \Leftrightarrow \zeta)$; $(\psi \veebar \zeta)$; where ψ and ζ are (recursively) formulas.*

c. *ϕ has the form $\exists\mu\psi$ or $\forall\mu\psi$, where μ is a variable symbol and ψ is a formula.*

DEFINITION 3.3   *An occurrence of a variable μ within a formula ϕ is* bound *if it is within an occurrence in ϕ of a formula of the form $\exists\mu\psi$ or $\forall\mu\psi$. An occurrence that is not bound is* free. *(We speak of free occurrences, rather than free variables, because in a formula like* *"(female(X) ∨ ∃X male(X))" the first occurrence of* X *is free, and the second is bound.)*

DEFINITION 3.4 *A formula* ϕ *is* closed *if every occurrence of a variable in* ϕ *is bound. Otherwise, it is* open *in the variables that appear free. A* sentence *is a closed formula.*

For example, suppose that our language contains the constant symbols "john" and "mary"; the one-place function "father_of"; the two-place function "common_ancestor_of"; the one-place relations "male" and "female", and the two-place relation "married". Then we can use the above definitions to classify strings such as the following:

Terms: "john", "father_of(john)", "common_ancestor_of(mary,$SOMEONE$)",
    "common_ancestor_of(father_of(X), common_ancestor_of(Y,mary))"

Atomic formulas: "male(X)", "female(john)", "married(Y,father_of(Z))",
    "male(common_ancestor_of(X,john))"

Complex formulas: "¬male(john)", "(female(Y) ⇒ female(mary))",
    "∀PP (married(PP, QQ) ∨ male(father_of(PP)))"

Closed formulas: "female(john)," "(married(john,mary) ∨ ∃X (male(X))),"
    "¬∃QQ∀PP (married(PP, QQ) ∨ male(father_of(PP)))"

Some standard notational conventions will be followed in this book. We will use open formulas as independent sentences with the convention that free variables are considered to be universally quantified with the widest possible scope. Variables are displayed subscripted next to the quantifier that binds them. When the same quantifier occurs several times in succession, they are collapsed into one. In using mathematical symbols that are standardly written between their arguments rather than before, (infix, rather than prefix), we will adopt mathematical convention, rather than insist on forms like +(1,X) or $\in (X, S)$. Thus we may write "∃$_{X,Y}$ $X + Y < P + Q$" as an alternative notation for "∀P∀Q∃X∃Y $< (+(X,Y),+(P,Q))$". Quantifiers are taken to have the lowest possible priority, and therefore the largest scope possible in the sentence; they apply until the end of the sentence or until the close of a bracket. For example, the sentence "∃$_X$ p(X) ⇒ p(a)" is read as "∃$_X$ [p(X) ⇒ p(a)]" and not as "[∃$_X$ p(X)] ⇒ p(a)".

There are many ways of defining proof systems in the predicate calculus. The most useful of these, for the purpose of actually writing down proofs, is natural deduction, illustrated in the chapter appendix. Resolution, with Skolemization, is a proof system that is relatively efficient to implement and control, but it is complex and unintuitive. Table 2.3 displays an axiomatic proof system for the predicate calculus.

This system is not particularly easy to use, either in hand construction of proofs or in computation, but it has the advantage of brevity.

DEFINITION 3.5 *Let α be any formula. A formula β is a closure of α if (i) β consists of α preceded by some number of universal quantifiers with variables; and (ii) β is closed. Example: the formula $\forall_A \forall_B \forall_C \exists_X p(X, A) \vee q(C, A)$ is a closure of $\exists_X p(X, A) \vee q(C, A)$.*

2.3.2 Tarskian Semantics

The semantics for first-order logic is called Tarskian semantics, after the logician Alfred Tarski. As in propositional calculus, we begin by defining a domain $\mathcal{D}$ for the formal language; we then state how an interpretation can relate the nonlogical symbols to the domain; lastly, we describe how the truth of sentences is built up out of the meanings of the nonlogical symbols. The semantics of the propositional calculus uses only two semantic entities: the truth values TRUE and FALSE. The predicate calculus, by contrast, needs a richer interpretation, with a universe of objects, tuples of objects, and sets of tuples of objects. We will interpret relations holding on terms as statements that a certain tuple of objects is an element of a certain set of tuples. As with the propositional calculus, the definition of the semantics will at first look almost circular and tautologous, but in fact imposes substantial and important constraints on the meaning of the language. In particular, the use of set theory as a basis for the interpretation means that the language is sensitive only to the *extensional* properties of its symbols; that is, to the entities or sets that they describe and not to the form of the description. Moreover, we can use our understanding of set theory to analyze properties of the logic; for example, to prove that first-order logic is sound and complete.

(Note: the remainder of Section 2.3.2 involves rather abstract logic. It may be omitted without loss of continuity. In the rest of this book, only the end of Section 2.7.1 depends on a detailed understanding of Tarskian semantics.)

A domain $\mathcal{D}$ for a first-order language is a set of entities or individuals. A constant symbol denotes an individual in $\mathcal{D}$. A k-place predicate symbol γ denotes an *extensional relation* Γ, which is a set of k-tuples of elements in $\mathcal{D}$ (a subset of $\mathcal{D}^k$). For example, the predicate "married" in its standard interpretation denotes the extensional relation MARRIED, which is just the set of all pairs of married people: MARRIED = { < Douglas Fairbanks, Mary Pickford >, < Mary Pickford, Dou-

Table 2.3 Axioms for First-Order Logic

For any formulas α, β, γ, any closure of any of the formulas FOL.1 — FOL.5 is an axiom:

FOL.1 $\alpha \Rightarrow (\beta \Rightarrow \alpha)$

FOL.2 $(\alpha \Rightarrow (\beta \Rightarrow \gamma)) \Rightarrow ((\alpha \Rightarrow \beta) \Rightarrow (\alpha \Rightarrow \gamma))$

FOL.3 $(\neg \alpha \Rightarrow \neg \beta) \Rightarrow ((\neg \alpha \Rightarrow \beta) \Rightarrow \alpha)$

FOL.4 $(\forall \mu (\alpha \Rightarrow \beta)) \Rightarrow (\forall \mu \alpha \Rightarrow \forall \mu \beta)$

FOL.5 $\alpha \Rightarrow \forall \mu \alpha$ where μ does not appear free in α

FOL.6 Let α and β be formulas that are identical, except that each free occurrence of the variable μ in α is replaced in β by the term τ. τ is a term that is free of μ in α; that is, no free occurrences of μ in α are within the scope of any quantifier $\forall \nu$ or $\exists \nu$, where ν is a variable occurring in τ. Then any closure of the formula $\beta \Rightarrow \exists \mu \alpha$ is an axiom.

For example, the sentence "outfielder(mickey_mantle) $\Rightarrow \exists X$ outfielder(X)" is an axiom, with $\mu = X$ and $\tau =$ mickey_mantle. The condition that τ must be free of μ in α is needed to block invalid axioms like

$$\forall_Y \, Y < Y + 1 \Rightarrow \exists_X \forall_Y Y < X$$

which is of a similar form, with $\mu = X$ and $\tau = Y + 1$

Definitional equivalences: Any closure of the following formulas is an axiom:

FOL.7 $(\alpha \Leftrightarrow \beta) \Rightarrow (\alpha \Rightarrow \beta)$

FOL.8 $(\alpha \Leftrightarrow \beta) \Rightarrow (\beta \Rightarrow \alpha)$

FOL.9 $(\alpha \Rightarrow \beta) \Rightarrow ((\beta \Rightarrow \alpha) \Rightarrow (\alpha \Leftrightarrow \beta))$

FOL.10 $(\alpha \vee \beta) \Leftrightarrow (\neg \alpha \Rightarrow \beta)$

FOL.11 $(\alpha \wedge \beta) \Leftrightarrow \neg (\alpha \Rightarrow \neg \beta)$

FOL.12 $(\alpha \dot\vee \beta) \Leftrightarrow (\alpha \Leftrightarrow \neg \beta)$

FOL.13 $(\forall \mu \alpha) \Leftrightarrow (\neg \exists \mu \neg \alpha)$

Rule of inference (Modus Ponens): For any two formulas ϕ and ψ, ψ may be inferred from the two formulas ϕ and $\phi \Rightarrow \psi$.

Proof: A proof of theorem ϕ from hypotheses Ψ is a sequence of sentences ending in ϕ such that each sentence is either

- An element of Ψ; or

- An axiom; or

- Inferrable from earlier sentences in the proof via Modus Ponens.

glas Fairbanks >, < Queen Victoria, Prince Albert > ... } A k-place
function symbol β denotes an extensional total function Θ from $\mathcal{D}^k$ to
$\mathcal{D}$; a set of $k + 1$-tuples, whose last element depends functionally on
the first k elements. This condition of functional dependence means
that any k-tuple of elements in $\mathcal{D}$ — that is, any element of $\mathcal{D}^k$ —
appears as the first k elements of exactly one $k + 1$-tuple in the set
Θ. For example, the function symbol "father_of" denotes the function
FATHER_OF, which is the set of pairs of each person with his or her
father: FATHER_OF = { < Cain, Adam >, < Elizabeth I, Henry VIII
> ... }.

An interpretation $\mathcal{I}$ for a language $\mathcal{L}$ associates each of the constant
symbols in $\mathcal{L}$ with an element of $\mathcal{D}$; each of the k-place function symbols with a function from $\mathcal{D}^k$ to $\mathcal{D}$; and each of the k-place predicate
symbols with a k-place relation on $\mathcal{D}$, a subset of $\mathcal{D}^k$. For instance,
let $\mathcal{L}$ contain constant symbols "john" and "mary"; function symbol
"father_of"; and predicate symbol "married". One interpretation for $\mathcal{L}$
would map "john" onto some particular John Doe; "mary" onto Mary
Roe; "father_of" onto the actual FATHER_OF function; and "married"
onto the actual MARRIED relation. Many other interpretations are
possible; for instance, there is an interpretation that maps "mary" onto
Thutmose III, "john" onto Lizzie Borden, "father_of" onto the function
mapping each person to the oldest descendant of his paternal grandfather, and "married" onto the relation between shoe salesmen and their
customers. Given a symbol α and an interpretation $\mathcal{I}$, we use the notation $\alpha^{\mathcal{I}}$ to mean the value that $\mathcal{I}$ associates with the symbol α. Thus
"john$^{\mathcal{I}}$" is the person John Doe; "father_of$^{\mathcal{I}}$" is the actual FATHER_OF
function; and so on.

Defining the semantics of $\mathcal{L}$ is a little tricky, because the significance
of a variable in a term depends on how the variable is quantified, which
is specified in a context external to the term itself. We therefore cannot
use a simple recursive definition, building up the interpretation from
inside to outside, as we did for propositional logic. Rather, our definition proceeds in two stages. First, we define the meaning of atomic
formulas with no variables or quantifiers. This is a straightforward
recursive definition from inside to outside: the denotation of a complex
term is defined in terms of the denotation of the function symbol and
the denotation of its arguments; and the truth of an atomic formula is
defined in terms of the meanings of the predicate and its arguments.
Second, we define the meaning of complex sentences. The truth of
quantified sentences is defined in terms of substitutions: The formula
$\forall_{\mu} \alpha$ is true if α holds for all potential substitutions for μ; the statement $\exists_{\mu} \alpha$ is true if α is true for some potential substitution for μ. The

truth of a Boolean combination of sentences is defined as a Boolean combination of the truths of its components.

DEFINITION 3.6 *A ground term is a term containing no variables. A ground formula is a formula containing no variables, free or bound.*

DEFINITION 3.7 *If τ is a ground term in $\mathcal{L}$ and $\mathcal{I}$ is an interpretation of $\mathcal{L}$, then there is an individual $u \in \mathcal{D}$ that is denoted by τ under $\mathcal{I}$. We write $u = \tau^{\mathcal{I}}$. We determine the denotation of τ as follows:*

a. *If τ is a constant symbol α, then τ denotes the individual that $\mathcal{I}$ associates with the symbol. $\tau^{\mathcal{I}} = \alpha^{\mathcal{I}}$.*

b. *Otherwise, τ has the form $\beta(\tau_1 \ldots \tau_k)$. In this case, the denotation of τ is the result of applying the extensional function that $\mathcal{I}$ associates with β to the denotations of $\tau_1 \ldots \tau_k$.*

$$< \tau_1^{\mathcal{I}} \ldots \tau_k^{\mathcal{I}}, \tau^{\mathcal{I}} > \in \beta^{\mathcal{I}}$$

DEFINITION 3.8 *Let $\phi = \gamma(\tau_1 \ldots \tau_k)$ be an atomic ground sentence. $\phi^{\mathcal{I}}$=TRUE under interpretation $\mathcal{I}$ just if the relation $\gamma^{\mathcal{I}}$ holds on the objects $\tau_1^{\mathcal{I}} \ldots \tau_k^{\mathcal{I}}$; that is, if the tuple $< \tau_1^{\mathcal{I}} \ldots \tau_k^{\mathcal{I}} >$ is an element of $\gamma^{\mathcal{I}}$. Otherwise, $\phi^{\mathcal{I}}$ = FALSE.*

Definitions 3.7 and 3.8 just formalize the natural interpretation of ground terms and formulas. For example, let $\mathcal{I}$ map the constant "isaac" onto Isaac (the Biblical patriarch), the function symbol "father_of" onto the real function FATHER_OF, and the predicate "male" onto the one-place relation of being male. Then the denotation of "isaac" is Isaac; the denotation of "father_of(isaac)" is the image of Isaac under the mapping FATHER_OF, namely Abraham; and the sentence "male(father_of(isaac))" is true, because the tuple $<$ Abraham $>$ is an element of the relation MALE.

We next define the truth of complex closed formulas. Boolean operators are handled just as in propositional logic:

DEFINITION 3.9 *Let $\mathcal{I}$ be an interpretation of $\mathcal{L}$, and let ϕ and ψ be closed formulas in $\mathcal{L}$. Then*

a. *Let $\zeta = \neg\phi$. Then $\zeta^{\mathcal{I}}$=TRUE just if $\phi^{\mathcal{I}}$=FALSE; otherwise $\zeta^{\mathcal{I}}$=FALSE.*

b. Let $\zeta = \phi \vee \psi$. Then $\zeta^{\mathcal{I}}$=TRUE just if either $\phi^{\mathcal{I}}$=TRUE or $\psi^{\mathcal{I}}$=TRUE; otherwise $\zeta^{\mathcal{I}}$=FALSE.

The remaining Boolean operators are handled similarly, as in Definition 2.2.

The treatment of quantifiers is trickier, as we mentioned above. Intuitively, we would like to say that a formula $\exists\mu\alpha$ is true just if there is some value τ that makes α true when τ is substituted for μ. For example, the formula "$\exists_X X + X = X \cdot X$" is true because when 2 is substituted for X, we get the true sentence "$2 + 2 = 2 \cdot 2$." However, it would not be correct to demand that this substituted value be a ground term in $\mathcal{L}$, since there may be objects in the domain $\mathcal{D}$ that are not named by any term in $\mathcal{L}$. (In fact, $\mathcal{L}$ may have no constant symbols whatever, in which case there are no ground terms.) Rather, what we want to say is that $\exists\mu\alpha$ is true if there is some object u in $\mathcal{D}$ such that, if u were given the name δ, then the result of substituting δ for μ in α would be a true sentence. That is what the next two definitions do. Definition 3.10 formalizes the notion of adding a new constant symbol δ to denote object u. Definition 3.11 then uses that to define the meaning of a quantified sentence in terms of the sentences in an extended language with new constants substituted

We assume that there exists an infinite collection of symbols that are not used in the language $\mathcal{L}$, and that are therefore available for use as new constant symbols.

DEFINITION 3.10 *Let $\mathcal{I}$ be an interpretation of language $\mathcal{L}$ with domain $\mathcal{D}$. Let u be any member of $\mathcal{D}$, and let δ be a symbol not in $\mathcal{L}$. Then we define $\mathcal{L} \cup \delta$ to be the first-order language containing all the symbols in $\mathcal{L}$ and also containing δ, used as a constant symbol. We define $\mathcal{I} \cup (\delta \rightarrow u)$ to be an interpretation of $\mathcal{L} \cup \delta$ with domain $\mathcal{D}$ with the following properties:*

- *For each symbol $\alpha \in \mathcal{L}$, $\alpha^{\mathcal{I}\cup(\delta\rightarrow u)} = \alpha^{\mathcal{I}}$*

- *$\delta^{\mathcal{I}\cup(\delta\rightarrow u)} = u$*

DEFINITION 3.11 *Let $\mathcal{I}$ be an interpretation of language $\mathcal{L}$ with domain $\mathcal{D}$. Let δ be a symbol not in $\mathcal{L}$. For any formula α, let $\alpha(\mu/\delta)$ be the formula that is just like α, except that δ has been substituted for every free occurrence of μ. (This can easily be defined formally by recursion over the form of α.)*

Table 2.4 Axioms of Equality

EQL.1 For any term τ and variable μ, any closure of the formula $\exists_\mu \mu = \tau$ is an axiom.

EQL.2 Let τ and ω be terms, and let $\alpha(\mu)$ be an open formula with free variable μ. For any term π, let $\alpha(\mu/\pi)$ be the result of substituting π for every free occurrence of μ in α. Then any closure of the formula $\tau = \omega \Rightarrow (\alpha(\mu/\tau) \Rightarrow \alpha(\mu/\omega))$ is an axiom.

---

a. *Let the closed formula ζ have the form $\exists\mu\alpha$. Then $\zeta^{\mathcal{I}}=TRUE$ just if there is some element $u \in \mathcal{D}$ such that*

$$\alpha(\mu/\delta)^{\mathcal{I}\cup(\delta \to u)} = TRUE$$

b. *Let the closed formula ζ have the form $\forall\mu\alpha$. Then $\zeta^{\mathcal{I}}=TRUE$ just if, for every element $u \in \mathcal{D}$, it is the case that*

$$\alpha(\mu/\delta)^{\mathcal{I}\cup(\delta \to u)} = TRUE$$

2.3.3 Other Issues in First-Order Logic

Equality: First-order logic is often augmented by the equality relation $X = Y$. The equals sign may be considered as just a particular nonlogical predicate symbol, described by axioms EQL.1 and EQL.2 below, or it may be considered an additional logical symbol, whose meaning is fixed in the semantics: If τ_1 and τ_2 are ground terms, then the sentence $\tau_1 = \tau_2$ is true in an interpretation just if τ_1 denotes the same thing as τ_2. Table 2.4 shows the two additional axiom schemas that are needed to handle inference on equality.

As is standard, we will use the notation $X \neq Y$ to mean that X is not equal to Y, and we will string equal signs in expressions like $X = Y = Z = W$ as an abbreviation for $(X = Y) \wedge (Y = Z) \wedge (Z = W)$. We will also use the k-place predicate "distinct($X_1 \ldots X_k$)" to assert that the objects $X_1 \ldots X_k$ are all pairwise distinct. Thus, we have the definition

$$\text{distinct}(X_1 \ldots X_k) \Leftrightarrow X_i \neq X_j \text{ for all } i \neq j$$

Limited quantification: An often useful device in predicate calculus is to qualify a quantified variable by limiting the class of values that it can take. We would like to express "Every positive number has a positive square root" as $\forall_{X>0} \exists_{Y>0} Y \cdot Y = X$. Such expressions can be incorporated as simple syntactic sugar[4] for ordinary predicate calculus. In general, "Any X satisfying $\phi(X)$ also satisfies $\psi(X)$" can be translated "For any X, if $\phi(X)$ then $\psi(X)$." "There exists an X satisfying $\phi(X)$ that satisfies $\psi(X)$" can be translated "There exists an X such that both $\phi(X)$ and $\psi(X)$." Thus, the above sentence is equivalent to

$$\forall_X X > 0 \Rightarrow \exists_Y Y > 0 \land Y \cdot Y = X$$

Partial functions: In our definition of the domain of an interpretation, we assumed that all functions are total; that they were defined on every individual in the domain. Frequently, we would like to use partial functions that are defined only on certain individuals. For example, in the domain of family relationships, we might like to define a function "spouse" that maps a married person to his or her spouse, and which is undefined on unmarried persons. However, this leads to complications. For example, if Anne is unmarried, we would like to say "$\neg \exists_X X =$spouse(Anne)", which contradicts axiom EQL.1 above.

One way to handle this is to replace all function symbols by relation symbols. For example, instead of defining "spouse(X)" as a function, we can define "spouse(X, Y)" as a relation, and add an axiom that for any particular X, there is only one Y who is the spouse.

$$\forall_{X,Y,Z} [\text{ spouse}(X, Y) \land \text{spouse}(X, Z)] \Rightarrow Y = Z$$

An alternative way to handle this formally is to add an additional element $\bot$ (read "undefined" or "bottom") to the universe, and to say that all terms that intuitively are undefined formally have a value of $\bot$; any function with argument $\bot$ evaluates to $\bot$; no predicate holds on $\bot$; and any quantified variable μ is implicitly understood to have the qualification $\mu \neq \bot$. Thus, the above sentence translates to "$\neg \exists_{X \neq \bot} X =$spouse(anne)."

Sorted logics: Partial functions are particularly common when a theory must express facts about many different sorts of things. In such a theory, functions will generally be defined only on arguments of the proper sort. For example, if we had a theory with times, places, and objects, then we might have a function "midpoint(X, Y)" that mapped two places X and Y to their midpoint; a function "where(O, T)," which

---

[4]Syntactic sugar: A departure from or extension of the standard syntax of a language that increases readability but not expressive power. "Excessive syntactic sugar leads to cancer of the semi-colons." (Alan Perlis)

is the place where object O is at time T; and so on. We would not wish to apply "midpoint" to an object and a time, or "where" to two places. Most of the theories that we will discuss use individuals of various sorts in this way.

Sorted logics are helpful in expressing such theories. Sorted logics are very much like typed programming languages. A fixed set of sorts is defined at the outset. Each constant symbol and each quantified variable symbol is declared to be of a particular sort; each relational symbol is declared to take arguments of a particular sort; and each function is declared to take arguments of a particular sort and to return a value of a particular sort. Formally, this can all be viewed as syntactic sugar, which can be expanded to pure predicate calculus by adding the function "sort_of(X)" mapping an entity X to its sort; adding names for the sorts as constant symbols; and adding a few new axioms and a few new clauses to existing axioms to reflect the sort declarations. In the example above, we would add "place", "time", and "object" as constants representing the separate sorts. We would express the declaration of the sort of the "where" function with the two following axioms:

sort_of(O)=object $\land$ sort_of(T)=time $\Rightarrow$ sort_of(where(O, T))=place.

[sort_of(O) $\neq$ object $\lor$ sort_of(T) $\neq$ time] $\Rightarrow$ where(O, T) = $\perp$.

A function or predicate symbol may be *polymorphically* sorted; that is, it may take arguments of different sorts. For example, we will want the predicate $X < Y$ to be defined whenever X and Y are elements of the same quantitative sort, but not to be defined if X and Y have different sorts (comparing weights to lengths). This corresponds to type overloading of function symbols in programming languages; it is not a problem as long as the sort of any term can be determined given the sorts of the arguments.

We will use sorted logics in a fairly informal way. We will define sorts, and we will declare the sorts of our nonlogical symbols. We will declare the sorts of quantified variables implicitly by the predicates and functions that take them as arguments. A common habit in AI papers is to declare the sorts of variables implicitly by the first letter of the variable symbol (shades of FORTRAN); however, we will be using too many different sorts in this book to do that. However, we will slough over the difficult issues in developing a full theory of sorts, such as using hierarchies of sorts, and combining sorts with set theory. The chapter reference list cites some systematic studies of sorted logics.

Common errors: There are a number of errors in writing first-order formulas that often trap beginning students.

One common error is to reverse the translations of limited quantification discussed above: to represent "All crows are black" in the form "$\forall_X$ crow$(X) \wedge$ black(X)" or to represent "Some crows are black," in the form "$\exists_X$ crow$(X) \Rightarrow$ black(X)." One way to avoid this is to keep in mind what these incorrect forms actually mean. The first form "$\forall_X$ crow$(X) \wedge$ black(X)" is equivalent to "$[\forall_X$ crow$(X)] \wedge [\forall_X$ black$(X)]$"; i.e. "Everything in the world is both a crow and is black." The second form, "$\exists_X$ crow$(X) \Rightarrow$ black(X)" is equivalent to "$\exists_X \neg$crow$(X) \vee$ black(X)", which is equivalent to "$[\exists_X \neg$crow(X) $] \vee [\exists_X$ black$(X)]$"; i.e., "Either there is something that is not a crow, or there is something that is black," which is true but uninteresting. Actually, if you ever find yourself writing a formula of the form "$\exists_X \alpha(X) \Rightarrow \beta(X)$", you have almost certainly made a mistake; this formula will be true as long as there is something in the universe satisfying $\neg\alpha(X)$.

A common error in looking for a representation for a sentence like "If something is a crow, then it is black" is to suppose that the use of the word "something" indicates that an existential quantifier should be involved. One is thus led to try the representation "$\exists_X$ crow$(X) \Rightarrow$ black(X)", which, as we have seen, means something quite different, or, worse yet, "$[\exists_X$ crow$(X)] \Rightarrow$ black(X)", which is not even a closed formula. (If the free variable is taken to be universally quantified, as in our convention, then this means "If there exists a crow, then everything is black.") The problem here arises from the English, which is misleading. What this sentence means is "Anything that is a crow is also black," or "For all things, if it is a crow then it is black"; the correct representation is "$\forall_X$ crow$(X) \Rightarrow$ black(X)".

Another error is to read too much into the material implication $p \Rightarrow q$. Keep in mind that *all* this means is that either p is false, or q is true. It does not mean that q can be derived from p; or that q is true as a result of p; or that q is true after p is true; or that q would be true if p were true. For example, suppose we wish to represent the rule "A sure sign of appendicitis is that, if you push on the right side of the abdomen, then there will be pain on release." The temptation is to represent this statement as a biconditional between having appendicitis and the implication, "If you push, then there will be pain on release."

appendicitis$(X) \Leftrightarrow$
[push(rightside(abdomen(X))) $\Rightarrow$ release_pain(X)]

(These primitives are bogus, of course, but the mistake we are discussing can be made even in a reasonable language that includes the temporal relations involved.) The forward implication here

appendicitis(X) $\Rightarrow$
[push(rightside(abdomen(X))) $\Rightarrow$ release_pain(X)]

is correct. If X has appendicitis, then if you push his abdomen, he will have pain. The backwards implication, however,

[push(rightside(abdomen(X))) $\Rightarrow$ release_pain(X)] $\Rightarrow$
appendicitis(X)

is not correct. The antecedent "push(rightside(abdomen(X))) $\Rightarrow$ release_pain(X)" is true whenever you don't push on the abdomen. This rule, therefore, states that anyone whose abdomen is not pushed has appendicitis. The correct form for this implication is that, if the abdomen is pushed and there is pain, then there is appendicitis.

[push(rightside(abdomen(X))) $\land$ release_pain(X)] $\Rightarrow$
appendicitis(X)

The two correct formulas above can be combined into a single rule as follows:

push(rightside(abdomen(X))) $\Rightarrow$
[release_pain(X) $\Leftrightarrow$ appendicitis(X)]

If you push on the abdomen, then pain occurs just if there is appendicitis.

The misuse of the implication sign is even more common in modal theories (see Section 2.7).

2.4 Standard First-Order Notations and Theories

At this point, we introduce a number of standard logical and mathematical notations used in first-order theories. We expect that the reader is familiar with the concepts and notations introduced below. We go through them to fix notation and to show how they fit into formal first-order theories.

Unique existence: The notation $\exists^1_\mu \, \alpha(\mu)$, where μ is a variable symbol and $\alpha(\mu)$ is a formula with the free variable μ, means "There exists a unique μ for which α holds." It may translated into the form

$$\exists_\mu \, \alpha(\mu) \land \forall_\nu (\alpha(\nu) \Rightarrow \nu = \mu)$$

The definite descriptor: If $\alpha(\mu)$ is a first-order formula with a free variable μ that is true of exactly one individual, then the notation

$\iota(\mu)\alpha(\mu)$ is a term that denotes that unique individual. For example, the tallest building in the world is denoted

$$\iota(X)\ (\text{building}(X) \wedge \forall_Y\ (\text{building}(Y) \Rightarrow \text{height}(X) \geq \text{height}(Y)))$$

We will use expressions of the form $\iota(\mu)\alpha(\mu)$ as ordinary terms in predicate calculus formulas. We can view the use of this expression in a sentence as syntactic sugar for a more complex sentence that asserts that some unique object has the property α, and that the rest of the statement is true of that object. In general, a formula of the form "$\beta(\iota(\mu)\alpha(\mu))$," where α is an open formula and β is a predicate symbol (possibly with other arguments as well), is syntactic sugar for

$$[\exists^1_\mu \alpha(\mu)] \wedge \forall_\mu \alpha(\mu) \Rightarrow \beta(\mu)$$

For instance, the sentence

$$\text{wrote}(\iota(X)\ \text{wrote}(X, \text{ivanhoe}), \text{waverley})$$

(meaning "The person who wrote Ivanhoe wrote Waverley") is syntactic sugar for the sentence

$$\exists^1_X\ \text{wrote}(X, \text{ivanhoe})\ ] \wedge$$
$$[\forall_X\ \text{wrote}(X, \text{ivanhoe}) \Rightarrow \text{wrote}(X, \text{waverley})\ ]]$$

Note that if no one or more than one person had written Ivanhoe, then the sentence would be false. In that case, the term "$\iota(X)\ \text{wrote}(X, \text{ivanhoe})$" would be considered to be undefined (equal to $\bot$).

Sets: The notations of set theory will often be useful.[5] The basic nonlogical symbol here is the membership relation $X \in S$. We also use the standard set constructor notation $\{X \mid \alpha(X)\}$, where $\alpha(X)$ is a first order formula, meaning "The set of all X such that $\alpha(X)$." For example $\{I \mid I > 1\}$ is the set of all numbers greater than 1. The notation $\{X \mid \alpha(X)\}$ may be defined using the iota notation above:

$$\{X \mid \alpha(X)\} = \iota(S)[\forall_X\ X \in S \Leftrightarrow \alpha(X)]$$

The best known axioms for set theory are the Zermelo-Frankel axioms. However, since these use a universe containing only sets, which are therefore ultimately built up purely from the null set, they are not quite suitable for describing sets of other kinds of things. We therefore

---

[5] Of course, we have already been using sets and tuples in defining Tarskian semantics. That, however, was at the metalevel, where we are describing the language. Here we are dealing with the object-level theory of sets, where we talk about sets in a first-order language.

Table 2.5 Axioms of Set Theory with Ur-Elements

SET.1 $[set(S1) \land set(S2) \land [\forall_X X \in S1 \Leftrightarrow X \in S2]] \Rightarrow S1 = S2.$
(Extensionality: A set is determined by the elements it contains.)

SET.2 $\neg set(U) \Rightarrow \neg X \in U.$
(Ur-elements contain no elements.)

SET.3 $\forall_{X,Y} \exists_S \forall_Z Z \in S \Leftrightarrow [Z = X \lor Z = Y].$
(Given any two entities X and Y, there is a set $S = \{X, Y\}$.)

SET.4 $\forall_Z \exists_W \forall_Y [Y \in W \Leftrightarrow \exists_{X \in Z} Y \in X.]$
(Arbitrary union: For any set Z there exists a set W which is the union of all the sets in Z.)

SET.5 $\forall_Z \exists_P \forall_X X \in P \Leftrightarrow [\forall_{Y \in X} Y \in Z]$
(Powerset: For any set Z there exists a set P whose elements are just the subsets of Z.)

SET.6 Let $\alpha(\mu)$ be an open formula in the language $\mathcal{L}_s$. Then the following is an axiom:
$\forall_B \exists_C \forall_X X \in C \Leftrightarrow [X \in B \land \alpha(X)].$
(Comprehension: For any property α, there is a set C containing all the elements satisfying α within some larger set B.)

SET.7 $set(\emptyset) \land \forall_X \neg X \in \emptyset.$
(Definition of the empty set.)

---

use a modification, called set theory with ur-elements; an ur-element being any entity that is not a set. We assume that we start with a universe of ur-elements, and a first-order language $\mathcal{L}_0$ for describing ur-elements. We construct a language $\mathcal{L}_s$, which contains $\mathcal{L}_0$ together with the constant symbol $\emptyset$ and the two predicate symbols: $X \in S$ (X is an element of S) and $set(S)$ (S is a set.) Table 2.5 shows the axioms that we shall use in this set theory.

The two critical axioms here are the axiom of extensionality, which asserts that all that matters to the identity of a set are the elements it contains, and the axiom of comprehension, which (roughly) states that one can define a set corresponding to any given property. Unfortunately, Russell's paradox shows that it is incorrect to state the axiom of comprehension with quite that degree of generality; rather, the comprehension axiom must be restricted in some way. The restriction chosen here is to say that given any large set B, we can construct

Table 2.6 Boolean Operators on Sets

$$S1 \cup S2 = \{\ X \mid X \in S1 \vee X \in S2\ \}$$
$$S1 \cap S2 = \{\ X \mid X \in S1 \wedge X \in S2\ \}$$
$$S1 - S2 = \{\ X \mid X \in S1 \wedge \neg(X \in S2)\ \}$$
$$S1 \subseteq S2 \Leftrightarrow \forall_X\ [X \in S1 \Rightarrow X \in S2]$$

a set containing all the elements of B with any given property. The remaining axioms SET.3 — SET.5 exist primarily in order to allow us to construct suitably large sets. Other axioms commonly given for set theory, such as the axiom of infinity, the well-foundedness axiom, and the axiom of choice, are less important for our purposes.

In order to use the comprehension axiom to construct interesting (infinite) sets of ur-elements, we must start with some large sets of ur-elements. One possible approach is to postulate that there is a set containing all ur-elements. In this book, we will assume that for each sort of entity, there is a set containing all entities of that sort.

We augment our language of sets with the standard union, intersection, and set difference functions, and with the subset predicate. Definitions are given in Table 2.6.

Sets are particularly useful for reifying properties: If it is necessary to treat a property as an entity in its own right, one can identify the entity as the set of all objects with the property. The comprehension axiom guarantees that such a set exists. Note that this technique does not make it possible to discriminate between two properties that hold on exactly the same objects. (Lambda abstraction is often used for this purpose instead of set theory. The expressive power is essentially the same.)

Tuples: The k-tuple of the individuals $X_1 \ldots X_k$ is written "tuple $(X_1 \ldots X_k)$" or "$< X_1 \ldots X_k >$." Various functions on tuples, such as appending two tuples, will be introduced as needed.

Operators with arbitrarily many arguments: The "tuple" function just defined and the "distinct" predicate defined in Section 2.3.3 technically violate the definition of the predicate calculus, which requires that every function and predicate symbol take some fixed number of arguments. Such operators may be fitted into first-order logic in either of the following two ways:

1. Redefine the syntax and semantics of the predicate calculus to allow it.

2. For each such operator O, define a collection of operators $O_1, O_2 \ldots$, each with a specific number of arguments. Consider any use of the operator O to be syntactic sugar for the appropriate specialized operator O_k; and consider any general axiom stated for the operator O with any number of arguments to be an axiom schema for each separate specialized operator. For example, we would replace the predicate "distinct$(X_1 \ldots X_k)$" by the separate predicates "distinct$\_2(X_1, X_2)$", "distinct$\_3(X_1, X_2, X_3)$" $\ldots$

Recursive definitions: Recursive definitions of relations and functions are common in math and computer science. For example, the predicate "ancestor(X, Y)", meaning X is an ancestor of Y, might be defined as the transitive closure of the relation "parent(X, Y)" in the following rules:

ancestor(X, X).
Everyone is (in a trivial sense) his own ancestor.

ancestor$(X, Y) \wedge$ parent$(Y, Z) \Rightarrow$ ancestor(X, Z).
If X is an ancestor of Y and Y is a parent of Z then X is an ancestor of Z.

Such recursive definitions of relations do not completely characterize the relation; they permit many different possible alternative interpretations. For instance the axioms above are consistent with interpreting "ancestor(X, Y)" as a predicate that is true if X is an ancestor of Y or if X is Cary Grant and Y is Queen Elizabeth I (who had no children). It is still true of this new relationship that everyone is an ancestor of themselves, and that if X is an ancestor of Y and Y is a parent of Z then X is an ancestor of Z.

Some of these false interpretations can be ruled out by turning the recursive definition into a biconditional. We can say "X is the ancestor of Y if and only if $X = Y$ or X is the ancestor of some Z who is the parent of Y."

ancestor$(X, Y) \Leftrightarrow$
$[\, X = Y \vee [\, \exists_Z$ ancestor$(X, Z) \wedge$ parent$(Z, Y) \,]\,]$

This new axiom rules out the interpretation of "ancestor(X, Y)" as ANCESTOR $\cup \{\, <$ Cary$\_$Grant, Elizabeth$\_$I $> \}$. However, it does not rule out all false interpretations. For instance, assuming that everyone has a parent, it is consistent with the interpretation that "ancestor(X, Y)" holds between all pairs of people, or with the interpretation that "ancestor(X, Y)" holds if either X is an ancestor of Y, or X is Cary Grant and Y is an ancestor of Elizabeth I.

Intuitively, we want to impose the condition that the predicate holds only in the cases where it has to hold, by virtue of the definition.[6] This cannot be done using just first-order axioms connecting "parent" and "ancestor". It can be done using set theory. We consider sets of pairs of people. We define set S to be "ancestor-like" if it satisfies the recursive condition: S contains every pair of a man with himself, and, if S contains the pair $< A, B >$, and B is the parent of C, then S contains the pair $< A, C >$. We then define the relation ancestor(X, Y) as holding just if the pair $< X, Y >$ is an element of all ancestor-like sets.

$$\text{ancestor}(X, Y) \Leftrightarrow$$
$$[\, \forall_S \, [[\forall_A \, < A, A >\in S] \land$$
$$[\forall_{A,B,C} [< A, B >\in S \land \text{parent}(B, C) \Rightarrow \, < A, C >\in S]] \Rightarrow$$
$$< X, Y >\in S]$$

However, this precise characterization of recursive definitions is, in practice, too complicated to be useful in a mechanical theorem prover.

2.5 Operators on Sentences

The predicate calculus gives us great facility to make all kinds of statements about individuals. It does not give us a framework in which to make statements about sentences; the only things one can do with sentences are to combine and negate them with Boolean operators, and to close a formula containing a variable by adding a quantifier. By contrast, in English there are many ways in which one sentence can contain another:

"It is doubtful whether the project will succeed."

"I believe that Ford was one of our greatest presidents."

"If the burglar had been a stranger, the dog would have barked."

"I knocked at the door because the bell was broken."

The relations between the embedded sentences "The project will succeed," "Ford was one of our greatest presidents," "The burglar was a stranger," "The dog barked," "I knocked at the door," and "The bell was

---

[6]Looking ahead to the nonmonotonic logics to be presented in Chapter 3, we may observe that applying the closed-world assumption to the predicate "ancestor" will not give the correct results; we should like our definition to make it possible to deduce that Cary Grant was not a descendent of Elizabeth I, but to remain agnostic on the unknown question of whether Cary Grant was a descendent of Homer. Rather, we wish to circumscribe the predicate "ancestor", holding "parent" fixed.

broken," and the complete sentences that contain them are different from those provided by the predicate calculus. An attempt to express these directly in the predicate calculus leads to trouble. If the sentence "The ball is on the table" is expressed as "on(ball1, table1)", using "on" as a predicate, then it will be syntactically incorrect to express "I believe that the ball is on the table" as "believe(me,on(ball1,table1))" using a predicate "believe", since predicates can take as an argument only a term, not a sentence like "on(ball1,table1)".

Therefore, a formal language that expresses sentences such as these must either eliminate the embedding of sentences by using a structure substantially different from the English; or provide a system in which some or all sentences may be systematically associated with primitive individuals; or extend the predicate calculus by providing additional operators on sentences. Each of these approaches may be useful under different circumstances.

Our aim in this section is to discuss general techniques for dealing with operators on sentences. The detailed analysis of particular operators will be left to the chapters dealing with their particular domains. In particular, temporal operators will be discussed further in Chapter 5 and the belief and knowledge operators will be discussed further in Chapter 8. We use as illustrations operators that are important in commonsense reasoning, rather than those which have been most studied in logic and philosophy. In particular, we do not use the operators "Necessarily ϕ" and "Possibly ϕ," since these have not been much used in AI domain theories. We will restrict attention to operators that have only one sentential argument (though possibly other arguments that are not sentences). Thus we will here exclude operators, like "ϕ because ψ" or "ϕ until ψ" that take two sentences as arguments.

There are a number of important formal properties of an operator $O(\phi)$, which largely determine the general properties of the representation.

1. Is it potentially necessary to apply the operator to all types of sentences, or only to some limited type of sentences? In particular, is the operator self-embedding; that is, is it sometimes necessary to apply the operator to sentences involving the operator itself? For example, the operator "X believes that ϕ" can potentially be applied to any kind of sentence; virtually any kind of sentence (except those that are necessarily false) can be believed. In particular, this operator is self-embedding; "Sue believes that Jim believes that she wants to go home" is the simplest way to express that particular fact. By contrast, it is reasonable to restrict the range of the operator "At time t, ϕ" to sentences ϕ that express the occurrence of an

event or the state of the world. This operator is not directly self-embedding; "On January 1, 1976, it was true that on November 22, 1963, Oswald shot Kennedy," is either meaningless or equivalent to "On November 22, 1963, Oswald shot Kennedy."

2. Does the operator commute with the existential and universal quantifiers? That is, is $O(\exists_X \alpha(X))$ equivalent to $\exists_X O(\alpha(X))$ and likewise for $\forall_X$? If so, then any sentence can be transformed to one in which the operator O is applied only to quantifier-free formulas, which, as we shall see, is a substantial simplification. For example, the operator "X knows that ϕ" does not commute with the quantifiers: "John knows that some people live in Schenectady" is not the same as "There are some people who John knows live in Schenectady." The operator "At time t, ϕ" does commute with the existential quantifier if the world is restricted so that things do not come in and out of existence. For example, if the set of objects in a domain is fixed, then "At 5:00, some object was inside the box" is equivalent to "There exists some object that was inside the box at 5:00."

If an operator O does not commute with the existential operator, then the rule "$\alpha(\tau) \Rightarrow \exists_\mu \alpha(\mu)$" may not hold if α is a formula involving O and τ is a complex term. For example, we do not wish the statement "John knows that the oldest inhabitant of Schenectady lives in Schenectady" to imply the statement "There is some person who John knows lives in Schenectady."

3. Does the operator commute with the Boolean operators? That is, is $O(\phi \vee \psi)$ equivalent to $O(\phi) \vee O(\psi)$, and is $O(\neg\phi)$ equivalent to $\neg(O(\phi))$? For example, the operator "X knows that ϕ" does not commute with the Boolean operators; "John knows that it is not raining" is not equivalent to "It is false that John knows that it is raining." (The first implies the second but not vice versa.) The operator "At time t, ϕ" does commute with the Boolean operators. "On January 1, 1979, Bush was not president" is equivalent to "It is false that on January 1, 1979, Bush was president." Note that any operator that commutes with the Boolean operators must obey the rules of contradiction and of excluded middle: For any sentence ϕ, either $O(\phi)$ or $O(\neg\phi)$, but not both.

4. Can equal terms be substituted for one another? That is, if $X = Y$ and $O(\alpha(X))$, is it necessarily true that $O(\alpha(Y))$? A context where such substitutions may be made is said to be "referentially transparent"; one where substitution may fail is said to be "referentially opaque." For example, "X knows that ϕ" is referentially opaque: "Oedipus knows that he is married to Jocasta" is not equivalent

to "Oedipus knows that he is married to his mother," even though Jocasta is Oedipus' mother. "It is true that ϕ" is referentially transparent: "It is true that Oedipus is married to his mother" follows necessarily from "It is true that Oedipus is married to Jocasta" and "Jocasta is Oedipus' mother."

5. Is the operator closed under the rules of inference? That is, if $O(\phi_1), O(\phi_2) \ldots O(\phi_k)$ and ψ is a consequence of $\phi_1 \ldots \phi_k$, is it necessarily true that $O(\psi)$? (This property is called "consequential closure.") For example, "At time t, ϕ" is consequentially closed; if, on September 15, all members of the cabinet met with the president, and, on September 15, Henry Kissinger was a member of the cabinet, then it follows that, on September 15, Kissinger met with the president. The operator "X said 'ϕ'" is not closed under inference; from the facts "John said 'All members of the cabinet are meeting with the president,'" and "John said 'Kissinger is a member of the cabinet,'" it does not follow that "John said 'Kissinger is meeting with the president.'" Note that, if an operator is referentially transparent and commutes with the quantifiers and the Boolean operators, then it is necessarily closed under inference.

6. How useful is it to quantify over sentences? That is, is there problem-specific information[7] that is most naturally expressed in the form $\exists_\phi \, \alpha(\phi)$ or $\forall_\phi \alpha(\phi)$, where α is a formula involving O? For example, it is often useful to quantify over sentences in the context "John said 'ϕ,'" as in "John gave a speech," or "All of John's answers were correct."

In evaluating these properties for a particular operator in a particular problem domain, it is advisable to be somewhat forgiving, and to ask "Can the logical system give useful results despite having such and such properties?" rather than "Ideally, should the operator have such and such properties?" For example, it is clear that in a complete theory, belief would not be closed under inference; it simply is not true that people believe all the logical consequences of their beliefs. However, as we shall discuss in Section 8.2.1, for many purposes it is acceptable and useful to take belief as closed under inference; in many applications it leads to a simple, powerful theory with many desirable properties and only a few unnatural consequences.

---

[7]Problem-independent information of this form can be expressed in the metalanguage as axiom schemas.

2.6 Extensional Operators

An operator O on sentences is said to be *extensional* if the answers to questions (1) through (5) all indicate a simple structure: that is, O applies only to a limited class of sentences, and, in particular, does not self-embed; it commutes with the quantifiers and the Boolean operators; it is referentially transparent; and it is closed under inference. There are a number of straightforward techniques for expressing facts involving extensional operators in first-order logic.

Probably the most important extensional operator in commonsense domains is the temporal operator "At time t, ϕ." We have discussed each of the required properties of this operator in the previous section, except referential transparency. Referential transparency, the principle that equal terms may be substituted one for another, is somewhat problematic for the temporal operator. If we are not careful applying the principle, we may legitimate such erroneous inferences as "Bush is the president; in 1965, the president was a Democrat; therefore, in 1965, Bush was a Democrat."[8] The problem here is the term "the president," which denotes different things at different times. Therefore, we will begin our discussion by considering only *time-invariant* terms like "Bush," which signify the same thing under all circumstances. Further on, we will see how *time-varying* terms, like "the president" can be handled.

Let us start with a fact like "At 12:00, either the ball was on the table, or everything was in the box." The naive translation to a logic-like notation

true_in(t1200, on(ball1, table1) $\lor \forall_X$ in(X, box1))

is not correct in the syntax of predicate calculus. However, we can translate the sentence to a more tractable equivalent form using the fact that all logical operators commute with the temporal operator. Thus, the above English sentence is equivalent to "Either the ball was on the table at 12:00 or, for all X, X was in the box at 12:00," which we might write

true_in(t1200, on(ball1, table1)) $\lor \forall_X$ true_in(t1200, in(X, box1))

---

[8]The use of English sentences here is confusing, because English can use the same term to denote either a constant or a time-varying object. The clues for disambiguation are often subtle or nonexistent. For example, "In 1965, the president was a Democrat" is (in its default reading) a true sentence about Lyndon Johnson, while "The president was a Democrat in 1965" is a false statement about George Bush (as of the time of writing). An interesting case is the difference between "the king," which may refer either to the time-varying office-holder or to a constant individual, and "His Majesty," which always refers to the individual.

In general, we can always move the temporal operator "inside" sentences so that it is always applied directly to atomic formulas. (Note: this translation is being done purely at the conceptual level, not at the formal level. We do not yet have any formal notation. We are massaging our concepts so that they can be easily expressed in a formal notation.)

We do not yet have first-order logic. In first-order logic, the expression "true_in(t1200, on(ball1, table1))" is not a valid sentence if "on" is a predicate symbol. There are two natural approaches. The first is to change symbols such as "on" to be predicates with three arguments: the two objects and the time. "on(X, Y, T)" will mean that X is on Y at time T. Thus we can write our initial sentence

on(ball1, table1, t1200) $\lor$ $\forall_X$ in(X, box1, t1200)

This is legitimate predicate calculus.

The other approach legitimates the notation "true_in(t1200, on(ball1, table1))" by positing that "on" is a function symbol rather than a predicate symbol, so that "on(ball1, table1)" is a term rather than a sentence. The problem here is semantics: What does the term "on (ball1, table1)" denote? To answer this, we introduce a new type of individual, a "state of affairs," into our ontology. The term "on(ball1, table1)" then denotes the state of affairs of ball1 being on table1. The predicate "true_in(T, S)" thus relates a time T to a state of affairs S, and asserts that the state of affairs S obtains at time T. We can therefore write the original sentence

true_in(t1200, on(ball1, table1)) $\lor$ $\forall_X$ true_in(t1200, in(X, box1))

If a concrete definition is desired, we can use the device of extensionalizing, and say that a "state of affairs" is a set of times: namely, the set of times when (conceptually) the state of affairs obtains. For example, "on(ball1,table1)" denotes the set of times when ball1 is on table1. Under this reading, "true_in(T, S)" is just notation for $T \in S$.

The most obvious difference between the two approaches is aesthetic. The "extra argument" approach forces us to add a somewhat unappealing extra argument to every predicate in the language describing a state of affairs or event. The "state of affairs" approach requires a somewhat mysterious extension of the ontology.

The "state of affairs" approach has the technical advantage that it makes it possible to quantify over states, to predicate properties of states, and to construct more complex terms involving states. As we shall see in Chapters 5 and 9, this expressive power can be useful for more complex temporal reasoning. For example, it allows us to express a plan like "Hammer the nail until the head is flush with the board" as the first-order term "repeat(hammer(nail1), flush(head(nail1),board7))". This representation depends critically on the state of affairs "The head of the nail is flush with the board" being a first-order entity. (See Section 5.11.)

So far, we have excluded time-varying terms, whose values change with time, such as "the president of the U.S." We cannot yet express the statement "In 1965, the president of the U.S. was a Democrat," using "president of the U.S." as a term. There are two ways to extend our system to fix this. The first is to add a time argument to time-varying functions. Thus, we would define the function "president(C,T)" as mapping a country C and a time T onto a person. We can then write

> in_party(president(usa, t1965), democrat, t1965)

using the predicate "in_party" with an extra time argument, or we can write

> true_in(t1965, in_party(president (usa, t1965), democrat))

using "in_party" as a function to states of affairs. Similarly, the fact "The current (1990) president was a Republican in 1965" may be expressed

> in_party(president(usa, t1990), republican, t1965)

> or as

> true_in(t1965, in_party(president(usa, t1990), republican))

The second technique explicitly uses terms that denote a "time-varying individual" or *fluent*; that is, a function from time to individuals. In this system, "president(usa)" denotes the extensional function that maps points of time into the person who was president at that time. A general function "value_in(T, F)" takes an instant of time T and a fluent F and denotes the value of F at time T. In this approach, the fact "In 1965, the president was a Democrat" could be written

> in_party (value_in(t1965, president(usa)), democrat)

> or as

> true_in(t1965, in_party(value_in(t1965, president(usa)), democrat))

Note that, in any of the above notations, once we have defined a concept like "on" or "in_party" or "president" to designate a time-dependent relationship or thing, we cannot ever use the same concept in a time-independent way. The connection to time is built into the semantics. Thus, for instance, we cannot express "The ball is on the table" timelessly as "on(ball1, table1)"; we must include an explicit mention of the time or times referred to. Similarly, "Bush is the president" is not correctly represented as "bush = president(usa)" but as "bush = president(usa, t1990)" or "bush = value_in(t1990, president(usa))." This explicit reference to time blocks erroneous inferences like "Bush is the president; in 1965, the president was a Democrat; hence, in 1965, Bush was a Democrat." "The president" in the first clause is represented "value_in(t1990, president(usa))," while "the president" in the second clause is represented "value_in(t1965, president(usa))."

These techniques can be used with any extensional operator, not just with the temporal operator. Let $O(X_1 \ldots X_k, \phi)$ be an extensional operator with sentential argument ϕ and nonsentential arguments $X_1 \ldots X_k$. The arguments $X_1 \ldots X_k$ enter into representations of O in exactly the same way as the time variable enters into the representations discussed above. Let ϕ have the form $\alpha(\tau_1 \ldots \tau_m)$; for example, if ϕ were "on(ball1, table1)", α would be "on", τ_1 would be "ball1", and τ_2 would be "table1". A sentence involving O can be represented in a first-order language in two ways:

1. Change α so that it takes $X_1 \ldots X_k$ as extra arguments in addition to $\tau_1 \ldots \tau_m$.

2. Construe $\alpha(\tau_1 \ldots \tau_m)$ as a term A whose value is a "state of affairs" over the X_i. Construe the formula $O(X_1 \ldots X_k, A)$ as asserting that the state A holds on the tuple $< X_1 \ldots X_k >$. In the temporal example, X_1 would be the time instant, and A would be a temporal state, such as "on(ball1,table1)".

The definition of "fluents" over the parameter $X_1 \ldots X_k$ is analogous.

2.7 Modal Logic

In some commonsense domains, virtually all facts can be expressed in terms of extensional operators. When this is possible, as it is in physical domains, then the "first-orderizing" techniques of the previous section yield straightforward and tractable representations. Unfortunately, it seems that some types of commonsense knowledge, particularly commonsense theories of mind, unavoidably require operators that are not extensional: operators that do not commute with quantifiers, or are referentially opaque. Incorporating these in a logic requires more powerful tools; how much more powerful depends on whether quantification over sentences is allowed. Information that does not require quantification over sentences can be expressed using modal logic or structures of possible worlds, the subjects of this section. Quantification over sentences requires the use of syntactic operators, the subject of Section 2.8.

A modal logic augments predicate calculus (sometimes propositional calculus) with a number of operators, called modal operators, that take sentential arguments. As usual, the logic defines the syntax of sentences using these operators, a set of logical axioms, a set of inference rules, and a semantics. We will first discuss the syntactic aspects of typical modal logics, and then discuss their semantics.

We will confine our discussion in this section to logics that contain a single modal operator $L(\phi)$ and its dual $M(\phi) \equiv \neg L(\neg \phi)$. L and M have only the one sentential argument ϕ and no other arguments. (Later in this book, we will look at more complicated modal operators and at logics that combine several modal operators.) In the most extensively studied modal logics, $L(\phi)$ is the operators "ϕ is necessarily true" and $M(\phi)$ is the operator "ϕ is not necessarily false" or, equivalently, "ϕ is possible." However, necessity and possibility have not been extensively applied to commonsense reasoning. Instead, we will use some less abstract operators as examples of L, particularly "I now know that ϕ," "I now believe that ϕ," and "ϕ is true at all times." The duals of these may easily be seen to be "I do not now know that ϕ is false," "I do not doubt ϕ", and "There is some time when ϕ is true." (In the context of the operator "ϕ is true at all times," we will here interpret the simple sentence ϕ as meaning "ϕ is true now." In Section 5.12, we will study a temporal modal logic which gives a different interpretation to sentences without temporal operators.) Our aim here, as throughout this chapter, is to study logical techniques rather than to analyze specific domains; we will study theories of knowledge and belief in greater depth in Chapter 8.

The syntax of modal logic is the same as the syntax of ordinary predicate calculus, except that modal operators may be applied to any formula.

DEFINITION 7.1 *A formula in a language with modal operators L and M is one of the following:*

  i. A predicate calculus atomic formula;

  ii. Either $\neg\phi$, $\phi \vee \psi$, $\phi \wedge \psi$, $\phi \Rightarrow \psi$, $\phi \Leftrightarrow \psi$, or $\phi \dot\vee \psi$ where ϕ and ψ are formulas.

iii. Either $\exists_\mu \phi$ or $\forall_\mu \phi$ where μ is a variable and ϕ is a formula.

iv. Either $L(\phi)$ or $M(\phi)$ where ϕ is a formula.

DEFINITION 7.2   *A sentence is a formula with no free variables.*

The following are sample sentences:

$\forall_X \exists_Y$ loves(X, Y).

L [on(ball1, table1) $\wedge$ $\forall_X$ (in$(X$,box1$)$ $\Leftrightarrow$ $X =$top1$)$]

$L(\neg\exists_X \, L(\text{spy}(X)))$

The first is simply predicate calculus; our language includes all predicate calculus sentences. If $L(\phi)$ is taken to be the operator "I know that ϕ," then the second means "I know both that the ball is on the table and that the top is the only thing in the box." The third means "I know that there is no one whom I know to be a spy."

Different modal operators satisfy differents sets of axioms. However, most modal logics that have been studied draw their axioms from a fairly small set of standard axioms. Table 2.7 lists some of these axioms.

We will discuss each of these axioms and inference rules in turn.

Axioms MODAL.1, MODAL.2, and MODAL.3 together with modus ponens bring all of predicate calculus with equality into modal logic. Axiom MODAL.1 also ensures that tautologies of the propositional calculus still hold, even when the propositions contain modal operators. Axiom MODAL.3 specifically bars the substitution of equal terms in modal contexts, in order to achieve referential opacity. Axiom MODAL.2 similarly bars the use of existential abstraction from modal contexts. These axioms always hold, whatever the modal operators.

Axiom MODAL.4 states that existential abstraction can be performed in modal contexts if the term being abstracted is a constant symbol. For example, we can infer "There is some particular person who John knows lives in Schenectady" from "John knows that Clyde lives in Schenectady."

Axioms MODAL.5 and MODAL.6 allow all standard inferences (all inferences not involving the rule of necessitation) to be carried out within the scope of the modal operator. MODAL.5 asserts that L applies to all the logical axioms, and MODAL.6 asserts that the inference

Table 2.7 Axioms of Modal Logic

MODAL.1 (Predicate calculus) Axiom schemas FOL.1 through FOL.5, FOL.7 through FOL.12, and EQL.1 of first-order logic with equality are axiom schemas of modal logic. Where these schemas refer to "sentences" or "formulas," all the sentences or formulas of the modal language are included.

MODAL.2 (Existential abstraction, in nonmodal contexts): Any instance of axiom schema FOL.6, where the sentences have no modal operators, is an axiom of modal logic.

MODAL.3 (Substitution of equals, in nonmodal contexts): Any instance of axiom schema EQL.2, where the sentences have no modal operators, is an axiom of modal logic.

MODAL.4 (Existential abstraction of constants[9] in modal contexts): Let a be a constant symbol, let μ be a variable, let $\alpha(\mu)$ be a formula, and let $\alpha(\mu/a)$ be a formula identical to $\alpha(\mu)$, except that a is substituted for every free occurrence of μ. Any closure of the formula $\alpha(\mu/a) \Rightarrow \exists_\mu \alpha(\mu)$ is an axiom. Note that this axiom applies when the formula α contains modal operators, but it does not apply to substitution of complex terms, other than constant symbols.

MODAL.5 If ϕ is a logical axiom, then $L(\phi)$ is an axiom.

In the remaining axioms, let ϕ and ψ be formulas, and let μ be a variable. Then any closure of the following formulas may be an axiom:

MODAL.6 (Consequential closure) $(L(\phi) \wedge L(\phi \Rightarrow \psi)) \Rightarrow L(\psi)$.

MODAL.7 (Veridicality) $L(\phi) \Rightarrow \phi$.

MODAL.8 $L(\phi) \Rightarrow M(\phi)$.

MODAL.9 $L(\phi) \Rightarrow L(L(\phi))$.

MODAL.10 $M(\phi) \Rightarrow L(M(\phi))$.

MODAL.11 (Barcan axiom). $\forall_\mu L(\alpha) \Rightarrow L(\forall_\mu \alpha)$

MODAL.12 $L(\forall_\mu \alpha) \Rightarrow \forall_\mu L(\alpha)$

MODAL.13 (Definitional equivalence) $M(\alpha) \Leftrightarrow \neg L(\neg \alpha)$

There are two rules of inference generally used:

Modus Ponens: From ϕ and $\phi \Rightarrow \psi$, infer ψ.

Necessitation: From ϕ infer $L(\phi)$.

---

[9] In theories that allow constant symbols to be non-rigid designators, this axiom must be restricted to constants that represent rigid designators. See Section 2.7.1.

rule modus ponens can be performed within the scope of the modal operator. From these two axioms follows the general principle of consequential closure: If $L(\phi_1)$, $L(\phi_2)$ ... $L(\phi_k)$ and ψ is a logical consequence of $\phi_1 ... \phi_k$ then $L(\psi)$ must hold. In particular, L applies to all logical and mathematical theorems. This principle is plausible for operators like "Necessarily ϕ" or "At all times, ϕ"; all logical truths are necessarily true, and true at all times. It is not plausible for operators "I know that ϕ" or "I believe that ϕ"; people do not know all the logical consequences of their knowledge and they do not know all mathematical theorems. (More on this point in Section 9.3.) Despite this implausibility, axioms MODAL.5 and MODAL.6 are part of virtually every modal logic, since it seems to be impossible to get either interesting logical conclusions or a coherent semantics without them (see Section 2.7.1).

Axioms MODAL.7 and MODAL.8 relate the strengths of $L(\phi)$, ϕ, and $M(\phi)$. Axiom MODAL.7 requires that $L(\phi)$ implies ϕ, from which it follows logically that ϕ implies $M(\phi)$. Axiom MODAL.8 is weaker, requiring only that $L(\phi)$ implies $M(\phi)$, with no connection to the truth value of ϕ. Axiom MODAL.7 is appropriate to operators like "I know that ϕ," "Necessarily ϕ," and "ϕ is true at all times"; it is reasonable to posit that anything that is known is true, that anything that is necessarily true is in fact true, and that anything that is always true is true at the current moment. The equivalent form $\phi \Rightarrow M(\phi)$ gives the assertions that anything that is true cannot be known to be false, that anything that is true must be possible, and that anything true at the current moment is true at some time. Axiom MODAL.8 is appropriate to operators like "I believe that ϕ," "It is obligatory that ϕ," or "ϕ will be true at all future times". It is reasonable to posit that, if ϕ is believed true, it is not believed false; that if it is obligatory that ϕ be true, then it cannot also be obligatory that ϕ be false; and that, if ϕ is true at all future times, then it cannot be false at all future times.

MODAL.9 and MODAL.10 relate to iterated modalities. MODAL.9 states that $L(\phi)$ implies $L(L(\phi))$, or, equivalently, that $M(M(\phi))$ implies $M(\phi)$. With knowledge, this is the principle, "If I know ϕ then I know that I know ϕ." MODAL.9 is plausible for knowledge and for most other modal operators. In combination with MODAL.7, MODAL.9 implies that iterated L's are equivalent to a single L and that iterated M's are equivalent to a single M. MODAL.10 together with MODAL.6 implies that any string of iterated modal operators is equivalent to the innermost; for example, $L(M(L(L(M(\phi)))))$ is equivalent to $M(\phi)$. This principle is plausible like an operator like "It is always true that ϕ"; if the statement "At all times, it is true that at some times it is true that ϕ," means anything at all, it can only mean the same thing as "At some times it is true that ϕ." The rule "If I do not believe ϕ then I believe that I do not believe it" is often plausible (though note that, combined with the rule of consequential closure, it leads to very strong results); the rule "If I do not know ϕ, then I know that I don't know it" is much less plausible, but occasionally useful. MODAL.10 is demonstrably false for the operator "Provably ϕ"; it is known that there are statements that are unprovable, but which cannot be proven to be unprovable.

Axiom MODAL.11 (known as the "Barcan" axiom, after the philosopher Ruth Barcan Marcus) asserts that, if a modality applies to every instance of a proposition, then it applies to the universal generalization. For example, let L be the operator "John knows that ϕ," and let α be the formula "If X is a rhinoceros then X has a horn." Then the Barcan formula $\forall_X L(\alpha) \Rightarrow L(\forall_X \alpha)$ means that, if you know about each X in the world that either it is not a rhinoceros or it has a horn, then you know the proposition "For all X, if X is a rhinoceros, then it has a horn." For psychological operators, such as "know" or "believe" this seems to be a safe inference for most α, since it is very rare to know something about every individual in the world without knowing the general rule. (This argument may not be valid in a sorted logic.) However, there are a few exceptions. Let $\alpha(N)$ be the formula "If N is an integer, then T does not halt after N steps" where T is a Turing machine that never halts. Then it follows from the law of consequential closure that one knows every instance of $\alpha(N)$; however, it may not be true that one knows the general rule.[10]

MODAL.12 is the converse of MODAL.11. It states that if L holds on a general rule, then it holds on every instance. It follows from consequential closure that $L(\forall_\mu \alpha(\mu)) \Rightarrow L(\alpha(\tau))$ for any ground term τ. Axiom MODAL.12 is a slightly stronger statement. MODAL.12 is taken as axiomatic in any system that accepts consequential closure. (Many modal logics allow formulas with free variables to be axioms in their own right, and adopt the inference rule of universal generalization, "Infer $\forall_\mu \phi$ from ϕ." In such a logic, MODAL.12 follows directly from consequential closure.)

MODAL.13 is just the definition of the modal operator M in terms of L. It is an axiom in all modal logics.

The inference rule of necessitation, "From ϕ infer $L(\phi)$" is rather curious. The intention is, essentially, to replace axiom MODAL.5 with a slightly stronger statement; all logical theorems are necessarily true. In a theory without proper axioms, ϕ can be inferred as true only if it is a logical theorem, so this rule will be legitimate. It is not, of course,

---

[10]Thanks to Larry Manevitz for pointing out this example to me.

legitimate in a theory with proper axioms; we do not want to infer "Necessarily, John is bald," from the proper axiom, "John is bald." Modal logics are often formulated without considering proper axioms; AI, however, is primarily concerned with theories that do have proper axioms.

Thus, the original motivation behind this inference rule disappears in the AI context. Nonetheless, the inference rule is still useful for some operators even in theories with proper axioms. For example, it is reasonable to infer either "I know that ϕ" or "I believe that ϕ" from ϕ. That is, if you somehow have gotten ϕ into your knowledge base, then you can infer that you know ϕ or that you believe it. On the other hand, there are many operators where the inference rule is obviously false for proper axioms; for instance, there is no inference from "ϕ is true now" to "ϕ is always true."

It should be noted that the logical literature on modal logic generally accepts the necessitation rule without question. This does not invalidate the use of modal logics for operators where the rule does not apply, but it does mean that standard theorems must be used with some caution.

The necessitation rule $\phi \vdash L(\phi)$ is by no means equivalent to the implication "$\phi \Rightarrow L(\phi)$", which is never true for a useful operator L. "$\phi \Rightarrow L(\phi)$" is the truth-value relation "Either ϕ is false or $L(\phi)$ is true"; applied to the "Know" operator, for example, it would state "I know all true sentences." In general, if $\phi \Rightarrow L(\phi)$, then, since $L(\phi) \Rightarrow \phi$, by MODAL.3, it follows that ϕ is equivalent to $L(\phi)$; i.e., the L operator is useless. The difference between the implication and the inference rule is that the implication $\phi \Rightarrow \psi$ means that ψ is true whenever ϕ is true, while the inference $\phi \vdash \psi$ means only that ψ is true whenever ϕ may be inferred, a much stronger condition.

The use of the necessitation rule and the restrictions placed on existential abstraction (axiom MODAL.4) make the construction of proofs in modal logic substantially different than in first-order logic. In general, one has to be careful using intuitions built up in ordinary logic; they may lead to invalid results. In particular, the following standard proof techniques of FOL are not valid in modal logic:

- Discharging: If $\phi \vdash \psi$ — that is, ψ may be proven from the hypothesis ϕ — then infer $\phi \Rightarrow \psi$.

- Splitting: If $\phi \vdash \psi$ and $\zeta \vdash \psi$, infer that $\phi \lor \zeta \vdash \psi$. An example where this fails in modal logic: For any sentence "p", $p \vdash L(p)$ (necessitation), so $p \vdash (L(p) \lor L(\neg p))$ (MODAL.1). Similarly, $\neg p \vdash L(\neg p)$ and so $\neg p \vdash L(p) \lor L(\neg p)$. But it is not the case that $(p \lor \neg p) \vdash L(p) \lor L(\neg p)$.

As mentioned above (Section 2.3.3), in modal contexts it is particularly easy to overinterpret material implication $p \Rightarrow q$ as meaning more than just "p is false or q is true"; such a mistake can lead to bad trouble. For example, let $L(\phi)$ be the modal operator "ϕ is provable," and suppose we wish to express the statement "If ψ follows from ϕ and ϕ is provable, then ψ is provable." The temptation is to express the first clause of this rule "ψ follows from ϕ" as the implication "$\phi \Rightarrow \psi$", and so to express the rule as the axiom schema

$$[[\phi \Rightarrow \psi] \wedge L(\phi)] \Rightarrow L(\psi)$$

But this rule is wrong. The sentence "$\phi \Rightarrow \psi$" does not mean "ψ follows from ϕ"; it means only that ψ is true or ψ is false.

Various sets of the above axioms on modal logics have been singled out for study by logicians. The best known are the systems "T", which contains MODAL.1-8 and the rule of necessitation; "S4", which adds MODAL.9 to T; and "S5", which adds MODAL.10 to S4.[11]

A sample proof in modal logic is given in Table 8.3 at the end of Section 8.2.2.

2.7.1 Possible-Worlds Semantics

The meaning of a first-order language is defined in terms of a Tarskian semantics. An interpretation for the language is an association of each constant, function, and predicate symbol in the language with an individual, mapping, or set in the world. The semantics then specifies the meaning of every term in the language, and the truth conditions for every sentence.

There is no simple way to extend a Tarskian semantics to define the meaning of modal operators. A Tarskian semantics is inherently incapable of distinguishing between two terms that refer to the same object or between two sentences with the same truth value. For example, there is no way of defining a Tarskian semantics so that "He knows that the shortest spy is the shortest spy" and "He does not know that Ralph Ortcutt is the shortest spy" are both true, given Ralph Ortcutt is indeed the shortest spy. "Ralph Ortcutt" and "The shortest spy" will both map to the same individual, and either term can be substituted for the other in any sentence. It is not even possible to fix things so

---

[11] This nomenclature is purely historical. "T" was introduced in [Feys 1937], and given its name in [Sobocinski 1953]. "S4" and "S5" were introduced and named in [Lewis and Langford 1932]. Lewis and Langford also introduced systems named S1, S2, and S3, and subsequent papers have defined and named slews of other systems; but none of these has become as popular.

that "He knows that snow is white" and "He does not know that President Harding's middle name was Gamaliel" are both true, given that both embedded sentences are true.

The semantics for modal languages requires a more complex type of model, known as a Kripke structure (after Saul Kripke). A Kripke structure consists of a collection of *possible worlds,* connected by *accessibility* relations. Each possible world represents one way that the world could possibly be; it is one complete model of the language without modal operators. Thus, each world specifies the truth or falsehood of every nonmodal sentence in a consistent way. The real world is one particular possible world.

The modalities are incorporated in the accessibility relations. There is a separate accessibility relation for each modal operator with nonsentential arguments. Thus, there is an accessibility relation corresponding to the modal operator "John believes ϕ"; a relation corresponding to the operator "Mary believes ϕ"; a relation corresponding to the operator "John knows ϕ"; and so on. The semantics for the modal operators L and M are given by the following rules:

- $L(\phi)$ is true in a world $\mathcal{W}$ iff ϕ is true in all worlds accessible from $\mathcal{W}$.

- $M(\phi)$ is true in a world $\mathcal{W}$ iff ϕ is true in some world accessible from $\mathcal{W}$.

For example, let $L(\phi)$ be the operator "John believes ϕ." We define the following accessibility relation $\mathcal{A}$ between possible worlds: $\mathcal{W}_1$ is accessible from $\mathcal{W}$ just if $\mathcal{W}_1$ is consistent with all the beliefs that John holds in $\mathcal{W}$. One can imagine taking John, as he is in the world $\mathcal{W}$, and showing him other worlds one by one. If he finds something in a world that violates his beliefs, then that world is not accessible; if everything in the world looks reasonable, then the world is accessible. When we are done, any statement that John believes true will be true in all accessible worlds; any statement that he believes false will be false in all accessible worlds; any statement about which he has no opinion will be true in some worlds and false in others. Thus, the statements that are true in all worlds are just those that he believes, as stated in the rule above. See Figure 2.1.

Using the above rule, we can translate iterated modal operators into chains of accessibility relations. For example, "Mary knows that John believes that taking vitamin C prevents cancer" translates to "If a world $\mathcal{W}_1$ is accessible from the real world via Mary's knowledge, then in $\mathcal{W}_1$ it is true that John believes that taking vitamin C prevents cancer." This, in turn, translates to "If $\mathcal{W}_1$ is accessible from the real

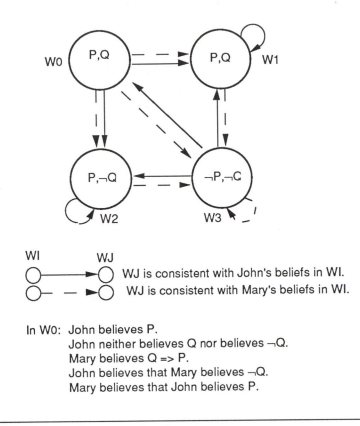

WI   WJ

WJ is consistent with John's beliefs in WI.
WJ is consistent with Mary's beliefs in WI.

In W0: John believes P.
        John neither believes Q nor believes ¬Q.
        Mary believes Q => P.
        John believes that Mary believes ¬Q.
        Mary believes that John believes P.

Figure 2.1 Possible worlds

world via Mary's knowledge, and W_2 is accessible from W_1 via John's
belief, then it is true in W_2 that taking vitamin C prevents cancer."

This kind of semantic definition helps clarify where the formal properties of the modal logic "come from." In this semantics, the operator
$L(\phi)$ is essentially a universal quantifier over accessible worlds, and
$M(\phi)$ is an existential quantifier; and their formal properties in the
logic are similar to the properties of the quantifiers. Thus, for example, the facts that $L(\phi)$ does not commute with negation, disjunction,
or existential quantification — "John knows that it is not raining"
is not equivalent to "It is false that John knows that it is raining";
"John knows that it is either raining or sunny" is not equivalent to
"Either John knows it is raining or he knows that it is sunny"; "John
knows that there are citizens of Mozambique" is not equivalent to

"There are people who John knows are citizens of Mozambique"; — are explained by the corresponding facts about the universal quantifier: $\forall_\mu \neg\alpha(\mu)$ is not equivalent to $\neg\forall_\mu \alpha(\mu)$; $\forall_\mu (\alpha(\mu) \vee \beta(\mu))$ is not equivalent to $(\forall_\mu \alpha(\mu)) \vee (\forall_\mu \beta(\mu))$; $\forall_\mu \exists_\nu \alpha(\mu,\nu)$ is not equivalent to $\exists_\nu \forall_\mu \alpha(\mu,\nu)$.

(Note: the remainder of Section 2.7.1 involves rather abstract logic. It may be skipped without loss of continuity. It is necessary to read Section 2.3.2 before reading this section.)

To express this semantics formally, we change the interpretation function to take two parameters: the sentence or term being interpreted, and the possible world referred to. A constant symbol always refers to the same entity in all possible worlds (see Section 2.7.3), but function and relation symbols may change their extension. For example, if Rosamond is married to Lenny in one possible world but not in another, then the extension of the relation "married_to" includes the pair $<$ rosamond, lenny $>$ in the first, but not in the second. We will write $\mathcal{I}(\gamma, \mathcal{W}_i)$ to mean the meaning of the nonlogical symbol γ in the world $\mathcal{W}_i$ under interpretation $\mathcal{I}$; this is an individual, function, or relation, depending on whether γ is a constant symbol, function symbol, or relation symbol. We then define the concept "ϕ is true in world $\mathcal{W}_i$ under interpretation $\mathcal{I}$." If ϕ is a sentence without a modal operator, ϕ is true in $\mathcal{W}_i$ just if it satisfies the usual Tarskian definition, relative to the interpretations of its symbols in $\mathcal{W}_i$. If ϕ is a sentence of the form $\mathrm{L}(\psi)$, then ϕ is true in a world just if ψ is true in all accessible worlds. Correspondingly, a sentence $\mathrm{M}(\phi)$ is true in world $\mathcal{W}_i$ just if ϕ is true in some accessible world $\mathcal{W}_j$. The truth value of a compound sentence is defined in the usual way.

We will now give a formal definition of the semantics of modal logic with dual modal operators $\mathrm{L}(\phi)$ and $\mathrm{M}(\phi)$.

DEFINITION 7.3   *A Kripke structure consists of four elements:*

a. *A set of possible worlds, $\mathcal{W}$.*

b. *A binary relationship on the worlds $\mathcal{A}(\mathcal{W}_i, \mathcal{W}_j)$, read "$\mathcal{W}_j$ is accessible from $\mathcal{W}_i$". $\mathcal{A}$ has the property that, for any world $\mathcal{W}_i$, there exists at least one world $\mathcal{W}_j$ such that $\mathcal{A}(\mathcal{W}_i, \mathcal{W}_j)$. This condition is called "seriality."*

c. *A distinguished world $\mathcal{W}_0 \in \mathcal{W}$ (the real world).*

d. *A domain of individuals $\mathcal{D}$.*

DEFINITION 7.4   *Let $\mathcal{L}$ be a modal language, let Γ be the set of nonlogical symbols in $\mathcal{L}$, and let $\mathcal{K} = < W, \mathcal{A}, W_0, \mathcal{D} >$ be a Kripke structure. An interpretation $\mathcal{I}$ of $\mathcal{L}$ over $\mathcal{K}$ is a function with two arguments: a symbol $\gamma \in \Gamma$ and a world $W_i \in W$. The function $\mathcal{I}$ has the following properties:*

a. *If γ is a constant symbol, then there exists some individual $d \in \mathcal{D}$ such that, for all worlds $W_i \in W$, $\mathcal{I}(\gamma, W_i) = d$.*

b. *If γ is a k-place function symbol, then for each world $W_i \in W$, $\mathcal{I}(\gamma, W_i)$ is an extensional function from $\mathcal{D}^k$ to $\mathcal{D}$.*

c. *If γ is a k-place predicate symbol, then for each world $W_i \in W$, $\mathcal{I}(\gamma, W_i)$ is an extensional relation on $\mathcal{D}^k$.*

Note that this definition creates a strong distinction between constant symbols, which always represent the same individual, and 0-place function symbols, which may denote different individuals in different possible worlds.[12]   What exactly is meant by "the same individual in different possible worlds" is a subtle issue that we will address in Section 2.7.3.

We extend the interpretation $\mathcal{I}$ to complex terms and sentences using the following definitions.

DEFINITION 7.5   *Let τ be a complex ground term in $\mathcal{L}$ of the form $\beta(\tau_1 \ldots \tau_k)$. Let $\mathcal{I}$ be an interpretation of $\mathcal{L}$, and let W_i be a possible world. $\mathcal{I}(\tau, W_i)$, read "the denotation of τ in world W_i," is the image of the denotations of $\tau_1 \ldots \tau_k$ under the function $\mathcal{I}(\beta, W_i)$.*

$$< \mathcal{I}(\tau_1, W_i) \ldots \mathcal{I}(\tau_k, W_i), \mathcal{I}(\beta(\tau_1 \ldots \tau_k), W_i) > \in \mathcal{I}(\beta, W_i)$$

DEFINITION 7.6   *Let ϕ be a ground atomic formula $\gamma(\tau_1 \ldots \tau_k)$ in $\mathcal{L}$, where γ is a predicate symbol. $\mathcal{I}(\phi, W_i) = TRUE$ just if the relation $\mathcal{I}(\gamma, W_i)$ holds on the objects $\mathcal{I}(\tau_1, W_i) \ldots \mathcal{I}(\tau_k, W_i)$; that is, if*

$$< \mathcal{I}(\tau_1, W_i) \ldots \mathcal{I}(\tau_k, W_i) > \in \mathcal{I}(\gamma, W_i)$$

---

[12]Some formulations of possible-worlds semantics (e.g., [Moore 1980] and [Genesereth and Nilsson 1987]) allow constant symbols to be specified as either rigid designators, which denote the same individual in all possible worlds, or as nonrigid designators, which may denote different things in different possible worlds. I am not aware of any advantages of this approach.

DEFINITION 7.7 *Let ϕ be a sentence in $\mathcal{L}$ of the form "$\neg\psi$" or "ψ op ζ", where "op" is a Boolean operator. $\mathcal{I}(\phi, \mathcal{W}_i)$=TRUE if the truth-value conditions associated with the Boolean operator in Definition 2.2 hold for the two truth values $\mathcal{I}(\psi, \mathcal{W}_i)$ and $\mathcal{I}(\zeta, \mathcal{W}_i)$.*

DEFINITION 7.8 *For any interpretation $\mathcal{I}$, object $u \in \mathcal{D}$, and symbol $\delta \notin \mathcal{L}$, define $\mathcal{I}^{\delta \to u}$ as in Definition 3.10:*

a. *Let ϕ be a sentence in $\mathcal{L}$ of the form $\forall_\mu \alpha(\mu)$.*
   Then $\mathcal{I}(\phi, \mathcal{W}_i)$=TRUE just if $\mathcal{I}^{\delta \to u}(\alpha(\mu/\delta), \mathcal{W}_i)$=TRUE for every $u \in \mathcal{D}$.

b. *Let ϕ be a sentence in $\mathcal{L}$ of the form $\exists_\mu \alpha(\mu)$.*
   Then $\mathcal{I}(\phi, \mathcal{W}_i)$=TRUE just if $\mathcal{I}^{\delta \to u}(\alpha(\mu/\delta), \mathcal{W}_i)$=TRUE for some $u \in \mathcal{D}$.

DEFINITION 7.9

a. *Let ϕ be a sentence in $\mathcal{L}$ of the form $L(\psi)$.*
   Then $\mathcal{I}(\phi, \mathcal{W}_i)$=TRUE just if $\mathcal{I}(\psi, \mathcal{W}_j)$=TRUE for every $\mathcal{W}_j$ such that $\mathcal{A}(\mathcal{W}_i, \mathcal{W}_j)$.

b. *Let ϕ be a sentence in $\mathcal{L}$ of the form $M(\psi)$.*
   Then $\mathcal{I}(\phi, \mathcal{W}_i)$=TRUE just if $\mathcal{I}(\psi, \mathcal{W}_j)$=TRUE for some $\mathcal{W}_j$ such that $\mathcal{A}(\mathcal{W}_i, \mathcal{W}_j)$.

DEFINITION 7.10 *A sentence ϕ in $\mathcal{L}$ is true (simply) if it is true in $\mathcal{W}_0$.*

All of the modal axioms MODAL.1–MODAL.11, except MODAL.7, MODAL.9, and MODAL.10, follow necessarily from this possible-worlds semantics. Consider, for example, MODAL.6, the law of consequential closure, $L(\phi) \wedge L(\phi \Rightarrow \psi) \Rightarrow L(\psi)$. In a possible-worlds semantics, this amounts to saying "If ϕ is true in all accessible worlds, and $\phi \Rightarrow \psi$ is true in all accessible worlds, then ψ is true in all accessible worlds." $\phi \Rightarrow \psi$ is true in a world just if either ϕ is false or ψ is true. Thus, the axiom is clearly true. Similar simple arguments can be made to justify the other axioms. Moreover, this collection of axioms, together with the inference rules of modus ponens and necessitation, is complete for this possible-worlds semantics; that is, if a sentence is true in all structures of possible worlds, then it is provable from the axioms [Kripke 1963a].

The truth of MODAL.7, MODAL.9, and MODAL.10 depends on particular constraints placed on the accessibility between worlds. MODAL.7, the axiom $L(\phi) \Rightarrow \phi$, states that if ϕ is true in all worlds accessible from a world $\mathcal{W}_i$, then it is true in $\mathcal{W}_i$ itself. This is justified if every world is accessible from itself; i.e. if the accessibility relation is reflexive. To interpret MODAL.9, the axiom $L(\phi) \Rightarrow L(L(\phi))$, we observe that $L(\phi)$ means that ϕ is true in all worlds accessible from $\mathcal{W}_i$, and that $L(L(\phi))$ means that $L(\phi)$ is true in all worlds $\mathcal{W}_j$ accessible from $\mathcal{W}_i$, and hence that ϕ is true in any world $\mathcal{W}_k$ such that $\mathcal{W}_k$ is accessible from $\mathcal{W}_j$ and $\mathcal{W}_j$ is accessible from $\mathcal{W}_i$. Hence, the axiom $L(\phi) \Rightarrow L(L(\phi))$ will be true if $\mathcal{A}(\mathcal{W}_i, \mathcal{W}_j)$ and $\mathcal{A}(\mathcal{W}_j, \mathcal{W}_k)$ imply $\mathcal{A}(\mathcal{W}_i, \mathcal{W}_k)$; that is, the accessibility relation is transitive. In a similar way, axioms MODAL.10 and MODAL.7 are together justified if the accessibility relationship is an equivalence relation.

2.7.2 Direct Use of Possible Worlds

Thus far we have used possible worlds as a metalevel theory, to give a coherent semantics to a modal language. However, it is often possible to eliminate the modal language altogether, and to use an object-level language that directly refers to possible worlds and their accessibility relations. This allows us to capture the content of modal sentences in a first-order language to which we can apply standard computational techniques for first-order inference.[13] The resultant language looks very much like the extensional languages discussed in Section 2.6, with the addition of the "accessibility" relation. However, the relation of the representation to the original sentence operator is more complex here. In the theories discussed in Section 2.6, the "possible worlds" entered as a simple argument. "The ball was on the table at noon" was represented as "on(ball1, table1, t1200)" or "true_in(t1200, on(ball1, table1))." In the theories we will discuss here, we capture modal operators such as "believe" using quantification over accessible worlds. "John believes that the ball is on the table" becomes "The ball is on the table in all worlds accessible via John's belief." Introducing a first-order predicate "bel_acc($A, W0, W1$)", meaning that world $W1$ is accessible from world $W0$ relative to the beliefs of A, we can represent this either as,

$$\forall_{W1} \text{ bel\_acc(john,w0,}W1) \Rightarrow \text{on}(W1, \text{ball1, table1})$$

or

---

[13] The construction described in this section was first developed in [Moore 1980]. Moore used an "extra argument" notation, while we shall use a "state of affairs" notation.

$\forall_{W1}$ bel_acc(john,w0,$W1$) $\Rightarrow$ true_in($W1$, on(ball1, table1))

For example, consider the sentential operator "X believes that ϕ." Let $\mathcal{L}$ be a modal language with some nonlogical symbols and the modal operator "X believes that ϕ." Let $\mathcal{L}_0$ be the first-order language over domain $\mathcal{D}_0$ with all the nonlogical symbols of $\mathcal{L}$. The equivalent language of possible worlds $\mathcal{L}_p$ will involve the following:

i. The individuals in the universe must include

    a. People (the first argument of the "believes" operator).

    b. All individuals in $\mathcal{D}_0$.

    c. Possible worlds. The symbol w0 represents the real world.

    d. States of affairs over possible worlds. Extensionally, we can view a state of affairs as just a set of possible worlds; those in which the state obtains.

    e. Fluents over possible worlds. Extensionally, we can view a fluent as a function from possible worlds to individuals in $\mathcal{D}_0$.

ii. The nonlogical symbols of $\mathcal{L}_p$ include the following:

    a. All constant symbols of $\mathcal{L}_0$ are constant symbols of $\mathcal{L}_p$.

    b. Any function symbol of $\mathcal{L}_0$ is a function symbol of $\mathcal{L}_p$. Its meaning, however, is changed. The value of the term "father_of(john)" is no longer a person; it is the fluent that denotes, in each world, the father of John in that world. The father of John in a particular world W is value_in(W,father_of(john)). In particular, John's real father is value_in(w0,(father_of(john))). The function "father_of(X)" thus represents a function whose argument X is either a person (such as "john") or a fluent from possible worlds to persons (such as "mother_of(bob)"), and whose value is a fluent from possible worlds to persons.

    c. Each relation symbol of $\mathcal{L}_0$ becomes a function symbol of $\mathcal{L}_p$. An atomic formula of $\mathcal{L}_0$, like "on(block1,table)", is a term of $\mathcal{L}_p$. It denotes the state of affairs in which the block is on the table. To say that the block is on the table in some particular world W, we write "true_in(W,on(block1,table))." In particular, to say that the block is really on the table, we write "true_in(w0,on(block1,table))".

    d. The function "value_in(W, F)" takes a fluent F from possible worlds to entities, and a possible world W, and returns the value of F in W. For instance, "value_in(W,father_of(john))" is John's father in world W.

    e. The relation "true_in(W, A)" means that the state of affairs A obtains in possible world W. For instance, "true_in(W,on (block1,table))" means that the block is on the table in world W.

    f. The relation bel_acc(P, W_1, W_2) means that W_2 is accessible from W_1 in the beliefs of P.

    g. The constant symbols "w0" represents the real world.

Any statement in the modal logic can be translated into this new language, using the possible worlds semantics for the modal logic. For example, the statement "John believes that Mary believes that all tall people have tall fathers" becomes

$$\forall_{W1,W2} \text{ bel\_acc(john,w0,}W1) \land \text{bel\_acc(mary,}W1,W2) \Rightarrow$$
$$\forall_X [\text{ true\_in}(W2,\text{tall}(X)) \Rightarrow$$
$$\text{true\_in}(W2,\text{tall(value\_in}(W2,\text{father\_of}(X))))]$$

2.7.3 Individuals and Modality

The difficult and dubious parts of modal logic lie in the treatment of constant symbols and quantified variables inside the scope of modal operators. A thorough treatment of this topic involves many difficult technical and philosophical issues. Within the scope of this chapter, we can only point out some of the important issues involved.

Cross-world identification: One strength of a possible-worlds semantics is that it greatly clarifies the interrelation of quantifiers and modal operators. "John believes that someone wrote Waverley" means "In each accessible world, there exists a person who wrote Waverley." "There is someone whom John believes to have written Waverley" means "There exists an individual who, in every accessible world, wrote Waverley." The difference between the two reduces to a difference in the ordering of quantifiers. In the first form, often called *"de dicto"* modality, the author of Waverley may vary from one world to the next; in the second, called *"de re"* modality, the same person wrote Waverley in all worlds.

This notion of "the same entity in all possible worlds" is a fundamental part of the possible worlds semantics. In particular, our definition of an interpretation required that any constant symbol represent a fixed entity in all possible worlds. This is necessary if we are to perform existential abstraction over constant symbols, to deduce "There is someone whom John believes to have written Waverley" from "John believes that George IV wrote Waverley."

But, though the formal properties of the idea are clear, it is not at all clear what it means. It can be hard enough, even in principle, to identify "the same thing" over time and circumstance; how are we to do so over the range of imaginable universes? Indeed, one can easily dream up situations in which the question of identity becomes obviously unanswerable or meaningless. If Mrs. Bonaparte's oldest child had been a girl, would she have been Napoleon? If France had invaded Germany in 1938 in response to the Anschluss, would that have been World War II? If the Founding Fathers had decided to place the national capital on the banks of the Connecticut River, would that city be Washington, D.C.? These problems seem silly, but they are hard to avoid in developing this kind of logic.

There is another, more subtle kind of problem with this notion. If objects are to be identified across possible worlds, then we must distinguish between *rigid designators*, terms whose denotation does not change from one world to the next, and *nonrigid designators,* terms that denote different objects in different possible worlds. For example, in the sentence "John believes that Scott wrote Waverley," the term "Scott" is a rigid designator. Therefore this sentence implies the *de re* modal statement, "There is someone whom John believes wrote Waverley," which we are glossing as "Waverley was written by a single person in every world consistent with John's belief," that single person being Scott. By constrast, in the sentence "John believes that the author of Waverley wrote Waverley," the term "the author of Waverley" is a nonrigid designator. Therefore, this sentence does not imply the above *de re* sentence; John's beliefs (as far as we have specified them) are consistent with any of a number of people having written Waverley. The sentence "John believes that the author of Waverley wrote Waverley" implies only the *de dicto* sentence "John believes that someone wrote Waverley."

However, in practice, this distinction between rigid and nonrigid designators seems to be very hard to make, and, often, not worth making. Consider the following scenario: One morning you get an anonymous letter, threatening to publish compromising photographs. The letter is followed by a phone call. You meet with the blackmailer face to face and make appropriate arrangements. Some months later, you see a photograph of the blackmailer, identified as Ralph Norbertson, in the paper. The question is, at what point can you claim to have a rigid designator that denotes this man? That is, at what point can you make statement of *de re* knowledge about him, like "There is someone who I know sent me a blackmailing letter?" It seems clear that there is no dividing line, no clear criterion for distinguishing how much and what kind of contact is needed for *de re* knowledge. But, unfortunately, it makes a great deal of difference in terms of the logic. If we grant that you have *de re* knowledge of the blackmailer after seeing him face to face, and that you have *de re* knowledge of your long lost brother, and it happens that the blackmailer is your brother, then it follows logically that you know that the blackmailer is your brother.

Changing domains: It is often desirable to make the very existence of objects subject to modal operators. It seems natural to represent "I don't know whether the United States has a prime minister" or "The Eiffel Tower has not always existed" as "¬ L($\exists_X X$ =prime_minister (usa))" and "M(¬$\exists_X X$ =eiffel_tower)".

In other words, we would like to allow different worlds to contain different objects. The prime minister of the U.S.A. does not exist in the real world, but she exists in worlds consistent with my knowledge. The Eiffel Tower exists in the possible worlds of the 1980s but not in the possible worlds of the 1780s. However, in our semantics, we required that all possible worlds have the same domains. The formula M(¬$\exists_X X = \tau$) is provably false for any term τ.

It is fairly easy to change the semantics of modal logic to allow varying domains. In the new semantics, each world has associated with it a particular domain of individuals, which is a subset of the universe of individuals. An interpretation maps a constant symbol a onto an individual u. In any particular world $\mathcal{W}_i$, a denotes u if u is an element of the domain of the world; otherwise, a has no denotation in the world. In each world a function symbol represents a partial function over the domain of that world. Terms involving nonexistent objects are nonexistent; atomic formulas involving nonexistent objects are false. Quantified formulas are true in a world if they are true of each individual in that world. However, the axiomatization needed for this logic is more complex than that of Table 2.7 above.

2.8 Syntactic Theories

There are facts in commonsense domains that seem to involve quantifying over sentences. For example, one would like to express the fact "John knows something that Bill doesn't" in the form "$\exists_P$ know(john, P) ∧ ¬ know(bill, P)," or the fact "George said something about taxes" as "$\exists_P$ said(george, P) ∧ about(P, taxes)". Quantification of this kind is beyond the expressive power of first-order modal logic and possible-worlds semantics. Certain kinds of quantification can be expressed within "higher order" logics, which we will not discuss. (See, for example, [Andrews 1986].) The most general and powerful technique for dealing with facts of this kind is the use of a *syntactic* theory, a first-order theory incorporating strings that represent sentences and other metalevel entities.[14] Syntactic theories, however, have a severe drawback: It can be hard to give them a consistent axiomatization. Section 2.8.2 will discuss this difficulty.

Besides allowing quantification over sentences, syntactic theories are also useful for expressing metalevel properties of descriptions of entities, such as computational properties. For example, we must use a syntactic theory to express facts such as, "Archie knows the primes up to 200," where what is meant is that he knows some explicit enumeration of the primes, expressed as sequences of digits.

The difference between syntactic theories and modal theories is roughly analogous to the difference between direct quotation ("John said, 'I am hungry'"), and indirect quotation ("John said that he was hungry"). Any kind of sayable or writable string may be embedded in direct quotation, while only meaningful sentences may be embedded in indirect quotation. "John said 'Arglebargle glumph'" is meaningful, while "John said that arglebargle glumph" is not. Purely syntactic predicates, which relate only to the form of the utterance, may be used of the object of a direct quotation; one can say "John said something that began with an 'I' and ended with a 'y'." As we shall see, similar things can be done in syntactic theories. However, there is one important difference between quotation and other operators on sentences that weakens this analogy. Any fact about an indirect quotation acquires its truth by virtue of some fact about a direct quotation. If "John said that he was hungry" is true, then there is some particular string that John said; there is some sentence ϕ such that "John said 'ϕ'" is true. There is no reason to believe that this property holds of other operators on sentences such as "believes." (See Sections 8.2 and 9.4.)

2.8.1 Strings

We start with some finite alphabet of characters. We will denote a single character by prefixing a colon; thus :a, :b, :X, :∃, and :: are constant symbols that denote the particular character. The alphabet includes all the characters we use in constructing first-order sentences: the upper and lower-case letters, the digits, the logical symbols, the

---

[14]In logic texts, it is common to use numbers to represent sentences rather than strings, so that metatheoretic statements can be interpreted as statements of integer arithmetic. The mapping of sentences to numbers was introduced by Kurt Gödel, in proving the incompleteness of arithmetic. Where the metatheory of arithmetic is not involved, the string representation of sentences is considerably more readable than the numeric representation.

parentheses, and also the colon itself. Other standard characters can be added to the alphabet as desired. A *string* is a finite tuple of characters; for example tuple(:C, :a, :t) is the string "Cat". A *syntactic theory* (also called a theory of quoted strings) is a first-order theory that allows strings as a sort of individual, provides certain standard functions and relations on strings characterized by standard axioms, and provides some axioms or axiom schemas that relate the strings that represent sentences to the sentences they represent.

We abbreviate tuples of characters using the symbols $\prec \succ$ as string delimiters. For example, $\prec$Cat$\succ$ is an alternate notation for tuple(:C, :a, :t). It should be emphasized that this is merely a notational convenience (syntactic sugar) and that it can always be expanded to the "tuple" notation. Quotation marks can be embedded; in this case, the meaning of the inner quotation is derived by expanding it into "tuple" notation. For example, the string $\prec$length($\prec$Cat$\succ$)=3$\succ$ is equivalent to $\prec$length(tuple(:C, :a, :t))=3$\succ$, which is equivalent to the tuple of 25 characters

tuple(:l, :e, :n, :g, :t, :h, :(, :t, :u, :p, :l, :e,
    :(, ::, :C, :,, ::, :a, :,, ::, :t, :), :), :=, :3)

Quotation marks create a context that is completely opaque regarding substitution under equality. For example, from the statements length($\prec$bush$\succ$)=4 and bush=president(usa), we are certainly not entitled to deduce length($\prec$president(usa)$\succ$) = 4; the length of the string $\prec$president(usa)$\succ$ is 14. Substitutivity fails because the sentence "length($\prec$bush$\succ$) = 4" contains no reference to Bush, and, in fact, no use of the symbol "bush", but merely uses of the characters :b, :u, :s, and :h, as can be seen if we rewrite it

length(tuple(:b, :u, :s, :h)) = 4

Our interest is in strings that spell out first-order terms or formulas; these we will call *meaningful* strings. Meaningful strings are built up by combining meaningful symbols. We define a string as *symbolic* if it spells out a nonlogical symbol (constant function, or predicate symbol), a variable symbol, a Boolean operator, or a quantifier. Thus, $\prec$mary$\succ$, $\prec X2\succ$, $\prec \wedge \succ$, and $\prec\exists\succ$ are symbolic; the strings $\prec X \wedge \exists\succ$, $\prec)\succ$, and $\prec$f(X)$\succ$ are not symbolic. We introduce the function "apply($O, A1, \ldots, Ak$)", which constructs a meaningful string expressing the application of operator symbol O to meaningful strings $A1, \ldots, Ak$. It is possible for O to be a function or predicate symbol and $A1 \ldots Ak$ to spell out terms; or for O to be a Boolean operator and for $A1$ and $A2$ to spell out formulas; or for O to be a quantifier, $A1$ to be a variable symbol, and $A2$ to spell out a formula.

Table 2.8 Use of the "apply" Function

---

apply(≺parent≻, ≺marion≻, ≺$X2$≻) = ≺parent(marion,$X2$)≻.
apply(≺ > ≻, ≺1000≻, apply(≺ + ≻, ≺200≻, ≺34≻)) =
≺1000 > 200 + 34≻.
apply(≺ ∧ ≻, ≺p(A)≻, ≺¬q(b)≻) = ≺p(A) ∧ q(b))≻.
apply(≺∃≻, ≺X≻, ≺ father(marion, X)≻) =
≺∃X father(marion,X)≻.

Table 2.8 gives some examples of the use of the "apply" function. Table 2.9 enumerates a number of nonlogical symbols useful in a syntactic theory.

The operators "is_symbol," "is_meaningful," "is_constant," "is_term," "is_sentence," "apply," and "subst" are called *syntactic* operators. Their truth can be computed merely from knowing the forms of the arguments, and the nonlogical symbols of the language. They can be fully axiomatized in a standard way. The operators "denotes," "true," and "name_of" are *semantic* operators. Determining their truth requires knowing the meaning of the language and the state of the world.

In addition to these object-level relations, a central concept is that of an object-level string *spelling out* a metalevel construct. We will not give a formal definition, as that would require formalizing the metalanguage, but the meaning should be obvious: The object-level string ≺father_of(john)≻ (= tuple(:f, :a, :t . . .)) spells out the metalevel term "father_of(john)"; the object-level string ≺X=f(X)≻ spells out the metalevel formula "X=f(X)", and so on.

We can now add any operator on sentences that we like by treating it as an operator on strings. The properties of the operator are specified in terms of particular axioms for that operator; no particular properties are imposed *a priori*. The result is a very flexible language for talking about sentences.

For example, we can introduce the operator "know(A, S)" meaning that person A knows sentence S. We can then express "John knows something that Bill doesn't" as

$\exists_S$ know(john,S) ∧ ¬know(bill,S)

This is now legitimate, since S ranges over strings.

Table 2.9 Nonlogical Symbols for a Syntactic Theory

- is_symbol(S) is a predicate meaning that string S is a symbolic string.

- is_meaningful(S) is a predicate meaning that string S is meaningful (a term or sentence).

- is_constant(S) is a predicate meaning that the string S is a constant symbol in the language. For example, is_constant(≺john≻) is true; is_constant(≺father_of(john)≻) is false.

- is_term(S) is a predicate meaning that the string S is a term in the language. For example, is_term(≺father(X)≻) is true, while is_term(≺)∃cat≻) is false.

- is_sentence(S) is a predicate meaning that the string S is a sentence in the language. For example, is_sentence(≺elephant(clyde)≻) is true while is_sentence(≺father(John)=≻) is false.

- apply($O, A1, \ldots Ak$) is a function that gives the string consisting of the operator O applied to arguments $A1 \ldots Ak$.

- subst($SNEW, SVAR, SOLD$) is a function that gives the result of substituting the term string $SNEW$ for every genuine free occurrence of the variable string $SVAR$ (that is, every occurrence outside quantifiers or embedded quotation marks) in the formula string $SOLD$. For example,

    subst(≺john≻, ≺X≻, ≺loves(X,father(X))≻) =
    ≺loves(john, father(john))≻

  It is straightforward to define "subst" in terms of "is_symbol" and "apply".

Table 2.9 Nonlogical Symbols for a Syntactic Theory (Continued)

- dbl_quote(S) is a function that adds a level of quotation to a string. For example,

  dbl_quote(≺cat≻) = dbl_quote(tuple(:c, :a, :t)) =
  ≺≺cat≻≻ = ≺tuple(:c, :a, :t)≻ =
  tuple(:t, :u, :p, :l, :e, :(, ::, :c, :,, ::, :a, :,, ::, :t, :))

  Note that the argument to dbl_quote must be a string. If "bill" is a constant symbol denoting the person Bill, then "dbl_quote(bill)" is a meaningless expression. We cannot have dbl_quote(bill) be the string ≺bill≻, because, since "bill" is an ordinary constant symbol, it can always be replaced by equal terms. That is, if "dbl_quote" were a function that applied to bill and bill=father(john) were true, then dbl_quote(bill) would have to be equal to dbl_quote(father(john)).[15]

- denotation(S) is a function mapping a string expressing a ground term S into the object that S denotes. Thus, if John's father is Bill, then the following is true:

  denotation(≺bill≻) = denotation(≺father_of(john)≻) =
  bill = father(john)

- true(S) means that the string S is a true sentence. For example, true(≺1+1=2≻) is true.

- name_of(X) maps an object X onto a constant denoting X.

  constant(name_of(X)) ∧ denotation(name_of(X)) = X

We can express the fact, "John knows the name of the capital of Massachusetts" as

$\exists_S$ is_constant(S) ∧
know(john,apply(≺ = ≻, ≺capital(massachusetts)≻, S))

This is true, because for the value S=≺boston≻, which is a constant symbol, the value of the "apply" term becomes ≺capital(massachusetts) =boston≻, which John knows to be true. The requirement that the string be a constant means that the statement would not be true if John only knew the statement ≺capital(massachusetts) = capital (massachusetts)≻. (A more readable notation will be introduced in Section 8.2.3.) Constant strings thus play a role in syntactic theories similar to the role of rigid designators in modal theories (Section 2.7.3). The problems connected with rigid designators can be directly addressed in syntactic theories by using a variety of syntactic predicates, depending on the circumstance.

In this way, we can express operators on sentences, where the sentences may be quantified over with any definable criterion. In some ways, this often feels like too much power; the language is so expressive that it gives no constraints. In possible-worlds semantics, the interpretation of an operator on a sentence is related to the meaning of the sentence; the operator is true if the sentence is true in certain accessible worlds. In a syntactic theory, there is not any necessary relation between the interpretation of operators and their meaning. We can perfectly well define operators on strings that, by themselves, are completely meaningless. For instance, we can define an operator "shmow(X, P)" that is true just if X knows P written backwards, and, moreover, the letters occurring in P are in alphabetical order. Moreover, it can be argued that using a logic grounded in the theory of strings eliminates one of the major advantages of defining an extensional semantics. A Tarskian or possible-worlds semantics for a domain without quotation allows us to forget about the syntactic structure of proofs, and reason about the objects, functions, and relations of the domain directly. By using a theory of quotation, we must return to worrying about the details of string manipulation.

Others find syntactic theories more intelligible than modal theories. The concepts of possible worlds and of accessibility are rather metaphysical, in the pejorative sense; and the reduction of modality to possible worlds often seems strained. It seem strange (to me) to say that John knows that Clyde is an elephant by virtue of the nature of Clyde in other possible worlds, rather than by virtue of something about John in this world. (By contrast, it seems reasonable to say that "Yesterday, it rained" is true by virtue of the state of the world at a different time, or that "If Barney had known French, he would have understood the lecture" is true by virtue of a hypothetical world (or worlds) in which Barney did know French.) The idea that John knows that Clyde is an elephant by virtue of a relation between John and the string ≺elephant(clyde)≻ seems comparatively clear: the string is somehow encoded in his brain. (See Section 8.2.)

2.8.2 Paradoxes of Self-Reference

Syntactic theories suffer from a very serious problem. It is easy to construct contradictions in them. These contradictions arise from the combination of self-referential sentences and terms — sentences and terms that refer to strings that embed them — with axioms that relate strings to their meanings.

The axioms are, in themselves, very plausible. We would like to say that the predicate "true" applies to the quoted form of a sentence just if the sentence is true. For example the sentence "true(≺parent(john, bill)≻)" is true just if "parent(john,bill)" is true. This is, after all, what we mean by "true." We can express this as follows:

Axiom Schema of Truth: Let P be a string that spells out the sentence ϕ. Then

$$\text{true}(P) \Leftrightarrow \phi$$

is an axiom.

Thus, for example,

$$\text{true}(\prec\text{parent(john,bill)}\succ) \Leftrightarrow \text{parent(john,bill)}$$

is an axiom.

In the same way we would like to assert that the quoted forms of terms denote the object that the terms mean. That is, if T is a string that spells out term τ, then "denotation$(T)=\tau$" is an axiom. For example,

$$\text{denotation}(\prec\text{father\_of(john)}\succ) = \text{father\_of(john)}$$

is an axiom.

The problem is that we can construct sentences that assert that their own quoted form is false, and terms that are described in terms of their own failure to denote. Standard examples of these in English are "This sentence is false" and "The smallest number not describable in fewer than twelve English words." The first of these is called the *liar sentence*. It is not consistent, either to suppose that the sentence is true or to suppose that it is false.

We cannot directly translate the above liar sentence into first-order logic, since logic has no equivalent of the demonstrative "this," used self-referentially. However, a syntactic theory does allow us to construct a term τ that denotes a string that spells out a sentence containing τ. In this way, we can construct a sentence ϕ that can be shown to be equivalent to $\neg\text{true}(\phi)$. A syntactic notation allows us to create such a sentence; a sentence ϕ that asserts $\neg\text{true}(P)$, where P spells out ϕ. The sentence below is an example.

¬ true(subst(≺≺¬ true(subst(dbl_quote(X1),≺X1≻, X1)))≻≻,
      ≺X1≻,
      ≺¬(true(subst(dbl_quote(X1),≺X1≻,X1)))≻≻))

Using the axiom schema of truth and the definitions of subst and quote, one can easily derive a contradiction. If the liar sentence above is true, then it must be false; if it is false, it must be true. (The casual reader may take this on faith. The more dedicated reader may enjoy figuring out how this works (Exercise 2.9).)

Sentences of similar structure can be created for any operator on sentences. We can construct a sentence that says, in effect, "John believes that he does not believe this," "John knows that he does not know this," "John says that he does not say this," and so on. If sufficiently strong axioms are asserted about the operator, it may be possible to use these to derive a contradiction. It should be noted that the paradoxes rely as much on the axioms governing the operator as on the self-referential sentences. There is, for instance, nothing paradoxical about someone standing up and saying, "I am not speaking this sentence"; he is simply obviously lying. No contradiction can be derived because there are practically no axioms whatever that govern what a person can speak.

(Digression: A more interesting example is the predicate "ϕ is provable." Let T be a first-order theory of quoted strings containing syntactic operators such as concat and subst, but no semantic operators. Then, since proof is a purely syntactic notion, it is possible to define the predicates "proof(P, A)", meaning "String P is a proof of string A in T," and the predicate "provable(A)", meaning "String A can be proven in T." Using a construction like that above, it is possible to construct a string P such that

a. P spells out a sentence ϕ

b. The sentence "$\phi \Leftrightarrow \neg$provable($P$)" is provable in T.

Furthermore, we can prove in the metatheory that if string A spells out sentence α and A is provable, then α is true. However, the sentence "provable(A) $\Rightarrow \alpha$" need not be provable in T. Thus, since in the metatheory we have shown that $\phi \Leftrightarrow \neg$provable($P$) and that provable($P$) $\Rightarrow \phi$, we can conclude that ϕ is true but not provable in T. There is no contradiction, since this argument is a proof in the metatheory, not in T.

The argument above is the second part of Godel's incompleteness theorem. The first, and more difficult, part is the number theory necessary to show that the syntactic definitions we need to define provability and to construct the self-referential sentence can all be mirrored in the language of arithmetic. End of digression.)

These contradictions can only be resolved either by dropping the axiom of truth or, more extremely, by abandoning two-valued logic. Various ways of doing these have been proposed. (See References.) A natural proposal is to say that the axiom schema only applies to ordinary sentences, not to paradoxical sentences. The problem is that it is not, in general, possible to determine which sentences are paradoxical; it may, in fact, depend on external facts about the world. For example, the sentence "Either this sentence is false or Paris is the capital of France" is not paradoxical, but true; while the sentence "Either this sentence is false, or Rome is the capital of France" is paradoxical. For another example, "THE FIRST QUOTED SENTENCE PRINTED IN BLOCK CAPITALS IN *REPRESENTATIONS OF COMMONSENSE KNOWLEDGE* IS FALSE" is paradoxical, but it would not be if we had inserted an innocuous sentence in block capitals earlier. Thus, we cannot, in general, determine whether a sentence is an instance of the axiom of truth, or whether it is an invalid attempt to apply this schema to a paradoxical sentence. We could restrict the axiom schema so that it applies only to sentences that can be easily determined syntactically not to be paradoxical, but this results in a very limited theory.

In practice, this may not make very much difference to AI programs. An AI program might plausibly run for a long time applying the axiom of truth without worrying and never run into self-referential sentences. However, this is not very satisfying. There is no useful way to define logical consequence in an inconsistent logic; hence, there is no way to use this logic to verify that an inference engine is behaving reasonably. Having a fundamental flaw like this in a logic is worrisome, like carrying a loaded grenade; you never know when it might go off. Moreover, sentences that, taken literally, are self-referential do come up, from time to time, even in the most innocuous contexts. A magazine article on pasta contained the following sentence: "Once you have made pasta that is neither mushy nor rubbery and you have experimented with the ways different shapes and thicknesses combine with different sauces ... the end of this sentence is not 'you'll never accept substitutes.'" Or they may be brought up with malice aforethought. There was an episode of Star Trek in which a malignant computer suffered a nervous breakdown when it was presented with a liar sentence. We would wish our programs to be immune to this sad fate.

2.9 Appendix A: Natural Deduction

Natural deduction is a proof system for first-order logic that generates proofs that are, in their structure, relatively close to the kinds of proofs written by human theorem provers, and therefore relatively readable. Numerous minor variants of natural deduction exist. The one presented below is adapted from [Mates 1972]; it contains nine rules of inference and no logical axioms.

Two features of natural deduction are particularly notable. First, in a natural deduction proof it is possible to assume one fact ϕ, deduce a new fact ψ from ϕ, and then conclude the material implication $\phi \Rightarrow \psi$ from the fact that $\phi \vdash \psi$. This inference is formalized in the rule of discharging. Such an argument can be used, for example, in proofs by contradiction: To show that ϕ is true, assume $\neg\phi$, show that that leads to a contradiction, and conclude that ϕ must be true. Second, it is possible in natural deduction to use a new constant symbol "locally" to represent an object with a given property. This reflects such forms in informal proofs as "Let p be a prime number." In natural deduction, we can make assumptions such as "p is a prime number" and see where it leads us. If we can conclude some other property of p — for example, that $X^p \equiv X \bmod p$ for all X, — then we can conclude that this property holds for all prime numbers. Moreover, if we know that there exist prime numbers, then we can conclude that there are numbers with the above property. To do this, we must, of course, use constants that are not used elsewhere in the proof. Moreover, we may need arbitrarily many constants. We therefore assume that the language has an infinite collection of constants that we can draw on. These types of inference are formalized in the rules of universal generalization and existential specification.

The structure of a proof in natural deduction is more complicated than in the axiomatic proof theory considered earlier. In order to carry out the discharging inference, in which we assume ϕ, derive ψ, and infer $\phi \Rightarrow \psi$, we must keep track of all the assumptions that underlie any given step of the proof. We therefore define a proof step as follows:

DEFINITION A.1 *Let $\mathcal{L}$ be a first-order language. A proof step S over $\mathcal{L}$ is a triple consisting of*

   i. A sentence in $\mathcal{L}$, denoted "content(S)".

  ii. A label of the step, denoted "label(S)". We will use integers as labels, but any type of symbol may be used.

iii. The set of the labels of the assumptions underlying S, *denoted "assumptions(S)".*

DEFINITION A.2 *A proof structure is a sequence of proof steps, no two of which have the same label.*

We now define the various types of inference. In all the definitions below, S, I, J, K are proof steps and P is a proof structure.

DEFINITION A.3 Axiom. S *can be inferred in proof structure* P *from hypotheses* Γ *as an* axiom *if*

i. *content(S)* $\in \Gamma$.

ii. *assumptions(S)*=$\emptyset$.

DEFINITION A.4 Assumption. S *can be inferred in* P *as an assumption if assumptions(S) = { label(S) }. Note that there is no constraint on the content of S; any sentence can be taken as an assumption.*

DEFINITION A.5 Tautology. S *can be inferred from steps* $I_1 \ldots I_k$ *in* P *by the rule of tautology if*

i. *Steps* $I_1 \ldots I_k$ *precede* S *in* P.

ii. *content(S) is a tautological (propositional calculus) consequence of content(I_1) ...content(I_k);*

iii. *assumptions(S)* $= \cup_{i=1\ldots k}$ *assumptions(I_i).*

DEFINITION A.6 Discharge. S *can be inferred from* I *and* J *in* P *through the rule of discharge (conditionalizing) if the following hold:*

i. P *contains* I, J, *and* S *in that order (though not necessarily consecutively).*

ii. *Let content(I)=ϕ and content(J)=ψ. Then content(S)=$\phi \Rightarrow \psi$.*

iii. *assumptions(S) = assumptions(J) − { label(I) }.*

DEFINITION A.7 Universal Specification. *S can be inferred from I in P by the rule of universal specification if the following hold:*

  i. I precedes S in P.

  ii. There is an open formula α, a variable μ, and a ground term τ such that content(I) = $\forall_\mu \alpha(\mu)$ and content(S) = $\alpha(\mu/\tau)$.

  iii. assumptions(S) = assumptions(I).

DEFINITION A.8 Universal Generalization. *S can be inferred from I in P by the rule of universal generalization if there is an open formula α, a variable μ, and a constant symbol β such that the following hold:*

  i. I precedes S in P.

  ii. content(I) = $\alpha(\mu/\beta)$; content(S)=$\forall_\mu \alpha(\mu)$.

  iii. assumptions(S)=assumptions(I).

  iv. The constant β does not appear in $\alpha(\mu)$ or in the content of any assumption of I.

  v. The constant β does not appear in the content of any axiom in P.

DEFINITION A.9 Existential Generalization. *S can be inferred from I in P by existential generalization if*

  i. I precedes S in P.

  ii. content(I) = $\alpha(\mu/\tau)$ and content(S) = $\exists_\mu \alpha(\mu)$, for some formula α, variable μ, and term τ.

  iii. assumptions(S) = assumptions(I).

DEFINITION A.10 Existential Specification. *S can be inferred from I, J, K in P by existential specification if there is a formula α, a constant symbol β, and a variable symbol μ such that*

  i. I, J, K, S occur in that order (not necessarily consecutively) in P.

  ii. content(I) = $\exists_\mu \alpha(\mu)$; content(J) = $\alpha(\mu/\beta)$.

  iii. content(S) = content(K)

iv. β *does not appear in content($\mathcal{I}$), in content($\mathcal{K}$), or in the content of any assumption of $\mathcal{K}$ other than $\mathcal{J}$.*

v. β *does not appear in the content of any axiom in $\mathcal{P}$.*

vi. *assumptions($\mathcal{S}$) = assumptions($\mathcal{I}$) $\cup$ assumptions($\mathcal{K}$) $-$ { label($\mathcal{J}$) }*

DEFINITION A.11 Quantifier Exchange: $\mathcal{S}$ *can be inferred from $\mathcal{I}$ in $\mathcal{P}$ by quantifier exchange if*

i. $\mathcal{I}$ *precedes $\mathcal{S}$ in $\mathcal{P}$.*

ii. *There is a formula α and variable μ such that either*

    a. *content($\mathcal{S}$) = $\forall_\mu \alpha$; content($\mathcal{I}$) = $\neg\exists_\mu \neg\alpha$;*
    b. *content($\mathcal{S}$) = $\forall_\mu \neg\alpha$; content($\mathcal{I}$) = $\neg\exists_\mu \alpha$;*
    c. *content($\mathcal{S}$) = $\exists_\mu \alpha$; content($\mathcal{I}$) = $\neg\forall_\mu \neg\alpha$; or*
    d. *content($\mathcal{S}$) = $\exists_\mu \neg\alpha$; content($\mathcal{I}$) = $\neg\forall_\mu \alpha$.*

iii. *assumptions($\mathcal{S}$) = assumptions($\mathcal{I}$)*

Finally, we can define a proof.

DEFINITION A.12 *A proof of conclusion ϕ from hypotheses Γ is a proof structure in which every step can be inferred either as an axiom of Γ, as an assumption, or via one of the rules of tautology, discharge, universal specification, universal generalization, existential specification, existential generalization, or quantifier exchange.*

Strictly speaking, the rules of existential specification and existential generalization are redundant; any theorem can be proven without recourse to these rules.

Table 2.10 shows an example of a proof.

2.10 References

[Turner 1984] surveys many of the logics used in AI.

[Genesereth and Nilsson 1987] contains an excellent introduction to first-order logic addressed to the student of AI. As a textbook for

Table 2.10 Proof in Natural Deduction

Givens:

$\forall_P$ vegetarian$(P) \Leftrightarrow [\forall_X$ eats$(P, X) \Rightarrow \neg$meat$(X)]$
(A vegetarian is someone who does not eat any meat.)

$\exists_P \forall_X$ eats$(P, X) \Rightarrow [$tomato$(X) \vee$ carrot$(X)]$
(There is someone who eats only tomatos and carrots.)

$\forall_X$ tomato$(X) \Rightarrow \neg$meat(X).
(Tomatoes are not meat.)

$\forall_X$ carrot$(X) \Rightarrow \neg$meat(X).
(Carrots are not meat.)

To prove: $\exists_X$ vegetarian(X). (There exists a vegetarian.)

Label	Content	Assumptions	Justification
1.	$\exists_P \forall_X$ eats$(P, X) \Rightarrow$ [tomato$(X) \vee$ carrot$(X)]$	{ }	Axiom
2.	$\forall_X$ eats$(p1,X) \Rightarrow$ [tomato$(X) \vee$ carrot$(X)]$	{ 2 }	Assumption
3.	eats$(p1,x1) \Rightarrow$ [tomato$(x1) \vee$ carrot$(x1)$]	{ 2 }	Universal Spec. (2)
4.	eats$(p1,x1)$	{ 4 }	Assumption
5.	tomato$(x1) \vee$ carrot$(x1)$	{ 2,4 }	Tautology (3,4)
6.	$\forall_X$ tomato$(X) \Rightarrow \neg$meat(X)	{ }	Axiom
7.	tomato$(x1) \Rightarrow \neg$meat$(x1)$	{ }	Universal Spec. (6)
8.	$\forall_X$ carrot$(X) \Rightarrow \neg$meat(X)	{ }	Axiom
9.	carrot$(x1) \Rightarrow \neg$meat$(x1)$	{ }	Universal Spec. (8)
10.	[tomato$(x1) \vee$ carrot$(x1)] \Rightarrow \neg$meat$(x1)$	{ }	Tautology (7,9)
11.	$\neg$meat$(x1)$	{ 2,4 }	Tautology (5,10)
12.	eats$(p1,x1) \Rightarrow \neg$meat$(x1)$	{ 2 }	Discharge (4,11)
13.	$\forall_X$ eats$(p1,X) \Rightarrow \neg$meat(X)	{ 2 }	Universal Gen. (12)
14.	$\forall_P$ vegetarian$(P) \Leftrightarrow [\forall_X$ eats$(P, X) \Rightarrow \neg$meat$(X)]$	{ }	Axiom
15.	vegetarian$(p1) \Leftrightarrow [\forall_X$ eats$(p1,X) \Rightarrow \neg$meat$(X)]$	{ }	Universal Spec. (14)
16.	vegetarian$(p1)$	{ 2 }	Tautology (13,15)
17.	$\exists_P$ vegetarian(P)	{ 2 }	Existential Gen. (16)
18.	$\exists_P$ vegetarian(P)	{ }	Existential Spec. (1,2,17)

further study of first-order logic I recommend [Mates 1972]. (In particular, [Mates 1972] has an extensive discussion of the translation of English sentences to first-order logic.) The axioms given here for propositional and predicate calculus are slightly modified from [Genesereth and Nilsson 1987]. The definition of Tarskian semantics and the natural deduction system described in Appendix A, Section 2.9, are adapted from [Mates 1972].

Sorted logics are discussed in [Cohn 1985] and [Walther 1985].

[Halmos 1960] is a readable introduction to set theory. The only discussion of set theory with ur-elements that I have found is [Barwise 1975]; this, however, is an advanced text requiring a great deal of background. [Zadrozny 1989] presents a new, less constraining set theory that he argues is more suitable to commonsense reasoning.

Extensional operators have been used in AI logics of time since [McCarthy 1959]. [Hobbs 1985c] is a general discussion of extensional operators; Hobbs proposes that it should be possible to create an entity corresponding to any atomic sentence.

[Hughes and Cresswell 1968] is a standard text on modal logic. Unfortunately, the logic presented there uses neither constant symbols nor proper axioms, so it required some modification for its presentation here. (The uninterest of modal logicians in theories with proper axioms is indicated by the fact that modal logic with proper axioms was first proven complete in [McDermott 1982b].) Possible-worlds semantics for modal logic was introduced in [Kripke 1963a, 1963b]; these used a possible-worlds semantics in which different worlds could have different domains of individuals. Higher order modal logics are discussed in [Gallin 1975]. Modal logics of knowledge and belief were developed in [Hintikka 1962]. Hintikka's logic of knowledge was extended in [Moore 1980] to incorporate a representation for action. Moore also introduced the idea of translating the modal logic into a first-order logic over possible worlds. Other AI applications of modal logic include [Appelt 1982] and [Shoham 1988].

For higher order logics, see [Church 1956] and chapter 5 of [Andrews 1986].

There is a large philosophical literature dealing with the status of *de re* modalities and rigid designators. The best known work is probably [Kripke 1972]; see also [Burge 1977] [Dennett 1981], [Goodman 1961], [Kaplan 1968], [Moore, 1980], and [Quine 1969]. Possible-worlds interpretations for counterfactual sentences are discussed in [Lewis 1973]. [Ginsberg 1986] discusses applications of counterfactuals to AI.

The theory of quoted strings is discussed in [Genesereth and Nilsson 1987, chap. 10], though in the context of the metalanguage rather than in the object language. AI theories that have used syntactic operators include [Perlis 1985], [Konolige 1982], [Haas 1983], and [Morgenstern 1988]. [Tarski 1956], [Kripke 1975], [Gupta 1982], and [Barwise and Etchemendy 1987] are analyses of the liar paradox. [Hofstadter 1979] and [Hofstadter 1985] are entertaining popular books that explore problems of self-reference and related issues. [Smullyan 1978] is one of a number of collections of puzzles on the same theme. [Kaplan and Montague 1960] discusses analogues of the liar paradox with the operators "know" and "believe".

Situation logic, presented in [Barwise and Perry 1982], is an alternative approach to the problems discussed in this chapter.

2.11 Exercises

(Starred problems are more difficult.)

1. Express the "Jones, Smith, and Robinson" puzzle in section 2.2 in the propositional calculus.

2. (a) Given the hypothesis $\neg\neg p$, prove p, using axioms PROP.1 — PROP.7 of the propositional calculus.

   (b) * Given the hypothesis p, prove p ∨ q, using axioms PROP.1 — PROP.7.

3. Consider a domain consisting of people, books, and copies of books (volumes). Let $\mathcal{L}$ be a sorted first-order language with "person", "book", and "volume" as sorts, and with the following nonlogical symbols:

   Constants: sam, barbara, tolstoy, joyce.
   Predicates: owns(P, V) — Person P owns volume V.
               author(P, B) — Person P wrote book B.
               copy(V, B) — Volume V is a copy of book B.

   Express each of the following statements as a sentence in $\mathcal{L}$ (you need not include the conditions to enforce correct sorting):

   i. Sam owns a copy of every book that is either by Tolstoy or Joyce.

   ii. All the volumes that Barbara owns are copies of books by Tolstoy.

iii. If Barbara owns a copy of a book, then Sam owns a copy of the same book.

iv. There is some book that Sam owns but Barbara doesn't.

v. Every author owns a copy of each of his own books.

4. Consider the following "proof" of sentence (iv) in Exercise 2.3 from (i) and (ii): Sam owns all books by Joyce (from (i)) and Barbara owns only books by Tolstoy (from (ii)). Therefore any book by Joyce is owned by Sam but not by Barbara. Therefore Sam owns some book that Barbara doesn't.

   (a) What background assumptions does this proof rely on? Express these as sentences in $\mathcal{L}$.

   (b) Using the natural deduction system described in Section 2.9, Appendix A, give a proof of (iv) from (i), (ii), and the additional assumptions in (a).

5. Define the modal operator "knows(X, ϕ)", to mean "X knows that ϕ." In a modal language containing this operator, the language defined in Exercise 2.3, and the constant "ulysses" (the name of a book), express the following sentences.

   (a) Sam knows that Joyce is the author of Ulysses.

   (b) Barbara knows that Sam owns a copy of every book by Joyce.

   (c) There is a book B by Tolstoy such that Barbara knows that she owns a copy of B.

   (d) Everyone knows that there is no book by Tolstoy with no copies owned by anyone.

   (e) Sam knows that everyone knows that Joyce is the author of Ulysses.

   (f) Someone knows that Sam owns a copy of a book that he himself (the someone) wrote.

6. Express each of the sentences in Exercise 2.5 in terms of a possible-worlds semantics

7. * Express each of the sentences in Exercise 2.5, treating "know(X, ϕ)" as a syntactic operator. (Note: This exercise will be much easier after Chapter 8 has been covered.)

8. Show that axiom MODAL.10 (Section 2.7) is true in any Kripke structure in which accessibility of possible worlds is an equivalence relation.

9. * Show that the liar sentence in Section 2.8.2 asserts its own false-
    hood. Note the difference between the term dbl_quote($X1$), which
    contains the symbol $X1$ and is therefore changed by the subst, and
    the term $\prec X1 \succ$, which does not contain the symbol X1, only the
    characters :X and :1, and is therefore unchanged by the subst.

Plausible Reasoning

Talking of those who denied the truth of Christianity, he [Dr. Johnson] said, "It is always easy to be on the negative side. If a man were to deny that there is salt on the table, you could not reduce him to an absurdity. Come, let us try this a little further. I deny that Canada is taken, and I can support my denial by pretty good arguments. The French are a much more numerous people than we; and it is not likely that they would allow us to take it. 'But the ministry have assured us, in all the formality of the Gazette, that it is taken.' — Very true. But the ministry have put us to an enormous expense by the war in America, and it is their interest to persuade us that we have got something for our money. 'But the fact is confirmed by thousands of men who were at the taking of it.' — Ay, but those men have still more interest in deceiving us. They don't want that you should think the French have beat them but that they have beat the French. Now suppose you should go over and find that it is really taken, that would only satisfy yourself; for when you come home we will not believe you. We will say, you have been bribed. — Yet, Sir, notwithstanding all these plausible objections, we have no doubt that Canada is really ours. Such is the weight of common testimony. How much stronger are the evidences of the Christian religion?"

Boswell's Life of Johnson, July 14, 1763

The logics outlined in the previous chapter describe how rules of universal validity can be applied to facts known with absolute certainty to deduce other facts known with absolute certainty. Unfortunately, few of the rules that we use in everyday life are universally true, and few, if any, of our beliefs are completely certain to the degree that we cannot imagine them being overthrown given sufficient contrary evidence. (Possible candidates for certain belief include mathematical theorems, statements true by definition, and our knowledge of our own current mental state.) Therefore, deduction does not adequately characterize commonsense inference; we need also a description of how plausible, provisional conclusions may be drawn from uncertain or partial evidence.

A great variety of issues arises in the study of plausible inference. There are many different functions that a theory of plausible inference may serve; there are many types of complications that it involves. The problems to be addressed, the centrality of the problems that are addressed, and the interrelations between problems vary widely from one theory to the next. Below, we enumerate some prominent issues in plausible inference. The items on the list are not intended to be disjoint, independent, or exhaustive.

Representing degree of belief: I am entirely certain that there is train service between New York and New Haven, because I have taken this train dozens of times. I would guess that there is train service between Portland, Oregon and Seattle, Washington, because they are major cities fairly close together. It would be useful to be able to represent the difference in my strength of belief in these two statements, reflected in the phrases "entirely certain" and "would guess."

Evaluating the strength of arguments: I would guess that there is probably train service between Portland and Seattle, because they are large cities close together. This is a fairly weak argument. If I called train information, and they told me that there was no train, then that would be stronger evidence, and I would take that argument as overriding the first. This evidence could be counteracted in various ways; for example, if I called the same information number, and was told that there was no train service between New York and New Haven, which I know to be false, then I would lose faith in the train information and be in a state of doubt about whether there was a train. If I went to the Portland station and took the train to Seattle, then that would be overwhelming evidence that there was such a train; it would take very powerful counterevidence, which would explain how I was deceived, to shake my faith then. We would like our theory to provide a calculus in which we can calculate and compare the strengths of such arguments.

Applying rules of general but not universal validity: Standard logic justifies the use of universally quantified rules; rules that are always true without exception. Much commonsense inference relies on applying *default* rules that hold in general but not always. For instance, in the above example, we use a rule like "If two cities are large and close together, then they are likely to be connected by train." In reasoning that I can call my wife from the office, I use rules like "My phone generally works" and "My wife is generally home at six o'clock." These rules sometimes fail, but they are usually valid.

Avoiding the enumeration of all the conditions on a rule: It often happens that a plausible commonsense rule, when examined closely, has an almost unlimited number of possible types of exceptions. The problem of dealing with all these potential exceptions is known as the *qualification* problem. For example, a rule like "To find out how my stocks are doing, I can buy a newspaper at the newsstand and read it" should really read "To find out how my stocks are doing, I can buy a paper at the newsstand and read it, as long as the newspaper is in English, and I can find some light, and no lunatic passerby tears the newspaper from my hands, and the newspaper is not a fake distributed so as to spread disinformation, and I don't go blind or mad, and the editor of the newspaper has not decided to stop printing the stock prices, and ..." It would probably be impossible to state all the necessary conditions; it would certainly be impossible to verify them each time you wanted to read a newspaper. What you would like is to state the rule "To find out how my stocks are doing, I can buy and read a newspaper, unless something strange happens," where the "unless" clause is not to be verified unless there is substantial reason to worry about some particular anomaly.

Inference from the absence of information: It is often reasonable to infer that a statement ϕ is false from the fact that one does not know ϕ to be true, or from the fact that it is not stated to be true in a problem statement. Such an inference can take a number of forms:

1. The statement ϕ may be unlikely given other facts that I know. For example, if I hear of an animal or infer the existence of one, and I do not know that it is an albino, I am probably safe in assuming that it is not one, since albinism is a rare condition.

2. I may have reason to believe that, if ϕ were true, I would have learned about ϕ. For example, I know that Mark Twain was never governor of New York, not because I have ever read that he was not, nor because I know all the governors, nor because I know everything that Mark Twain ever did, but just because I may safely presume that I would have heard about it if he had been. This is called an *autoepistemic* inference [Moore 1985].

3. If another person is communicating facts to me, it may be a convention that, if ϕ were true, he should have communicated it. For example, if I find the statement "There are more than half a million people in Boston" in an article, I am probably safe in concluding that there are fewer than a million people, since otherwise the author of the article should have written "More than a million." Such conventions are known as Gricean conditions [Grice 1957].

Limiting the extent of inference: Many intuitively appealing sets of axioms have the property that the first few inferences all seem to be reasonable and to have reasonable conclusions, but that, as the inferences get further and further from the starting axioms, the conclusions seem less and less sensible, and they eventually end up in pure nonsense. The "Sorites" paradox has this form: If you have a heap of sand then you will still have a heap of sand after taking away one grain; hence, by induction, if you take away all the sand, you still have a heap. No single application of the rule is very objectionable, but too many together lead to trouble. The "consequential-closure" problem (Section 8.2) is similar: It is often useful to postulate that, if a person knows that p is true and he knows that p implies q, then he knows q. Certainly it would be strange to encounter a man who knew that Socrates was a man and that all men are mortal but really did not know that Socrates was mortal. Unfortunately, if we accept the axiom, then we can show that everyone knows all mathematical theorems, since they can be proven in this way one step at a time from the axioms. Again, no single application of the rule is troublesome. A way around these problems is to cast them as plausible rather than certain inferences, and to construct a theory in which chaining plausible inferences together leads to rapidly less plausible conclusions.

Inference using vague concepts: Inferences that involve reasoning near the boundaries of a vague concept are often uncertain. For instance, given that a man is tall, it is a safe inference that he is more than four feet tall, but it is a questionable inference that he is more than six feet tall. The theory of fuzzy logic [Zadeh 1987] addresses such issues.

Finding expected utility: Often, we are faced with choosing between actions whose consequences are uncertain. In such a case, we would like to guide our actions in terms of reasonable combinations of the likelihoods of the various outcomes with their desirability. For example, we would like to be able to reason that in Britain it is generally worthwhile carrying an umbrella, while in Arizona it is not generally worthwhile, using our knowledge of the cost of carrying the umbrella, the cost of getting caught without it in the rain, and the likelihood of rain.

Inferring an explanation: Commonsense reasoners try to explain the reasons underlying their observations. If I observe that the street is wet, I infer that it rained. On the presentation of other evidence, I may adopt another explanation. For instance, if I observe that the sidewalk is not wet, I may decide instead that the street cleaners have been by. A distinctive characteristic of explanations is that generally only one explanation at a time is needed. Wet streets can be evidence either for rain or for street cleaners, but not for both; external evidence in favor of one, such as seeing overcast skies or the street-cleaning truck, will generally be taken as reducing the likelihood of the other, even though they are not, in fact, incompatible. [Pearl 1988]

Schema-based inference: Many useful commonsense concepts correspond to large systems of relations that are instantiated in many separate instances in the world. For example, the concept of a house involves both physical relationships between many different physical components (walls, windows, floors, doors, ...) and functional relations, such as being inhabited. A visit to the doctor involves a structure of events and scenes (waiting in the waiting room, seeing the nurse, ...). Such concepts are called *schemas* or *frames*. A schema is represented as a collection of *slots*, which are characteristic variables, and the relations on these slots. The entity corresponding to a slot in an instantiation of a schema is called the *filler* of the slot. Fillers may be atomic entities or they may themselves be schemas.

There are at least four different kinds of inferences involved in the use of a schema (called *schema application*):

1. Schema identification: From finding a number of the fillers of slots satisfying appropriate relations and properties, infer the presence of the schema. For example, from seeing an

outer wall, windows, and roof in their customary arrangement, infer that these are part of a house. From seeing a man waiting in a doctor's waiting room, infer that he is a patient waiting to see the doctor.

2. Slot prediction: Predict that the instance of the schema contains fillers of the slots. For example, predict that there is a kitchen in the house; predict that the patient at the doctor's office will be asked to take off his clothes.

3. Filler identification: Identify a real-world entity as a filler of a slot. For example, identify the real kitchen as filling the "kitchen" slot; identify a particular act of writing a check as filling the "pay doctor" slot.

4. Relation prediction: Predict that the relations defined on the slots will hold on the specific fillers. For example, predict that the walls of the house support the roof; predict that the patient's taking off his clothes will come after he has been brought to an inner room.

In general, these inferences are plausible rather than certain. An office building may look like a house from the outside; a house may lack a kitchen; a patient may write any number of other checks while at the doctor's; the roof of a house may be supported by some structure other than the walls. These are default inferences, generally valid but not always.

Analogy: If A is similar to B in some ways then it may be reasonable to assume that it is similar in other related ways as well. For example, if you meet a man who pronounces the words "car," "idea," and "fear" in the same way as your next-door neighbor, you may assume that he will also have the same pronunciation of "tire."

Inferring a general rule from examples: People are always on the lookout for general rules that encapsulate their observations. If I get sick to my stomach after eating a Brazil nut for the first time, I might construct the general rule "Brazil nuts do not agree with me." If I meet four graduates of Pretentious U., and all four are unbearable, I might construct the general rule "All graduates of Pretentious U. are unbearable." No such inferences are sound; they can be overthrown either by bringing a counterexample (an experience of eating a Brazil nut without trouble; a charming graduate) or bringing a better alternative explanation. For example, if I observe that everyone else I know also had stomach trouble this week, whether or not they ate the nut, I may conclude that the trouble was due to a contagious stomach disease.

AI researchers and logicians have constructed a number of theories that address the above issues. Section 3.1 discusses various nonmonotonic logics, including default logic and circumscription. Sections 3.2 and 3.3 discuss probability theory. Analogy and generalization are not discussed here.

In subsequent chapters of this book, we will not, in fact, use any of these formal theories. Rather, on the rare occasions where we discuss plausible inference, we will either describe a narrow domain-specific inference rule, or we will use a bogus notation, "plausible(ϕ, ψ)", meaning "Given ϕ, it is a plausible inference that ψ is true, in the absence of contradictory evidence," and we will leave it open how this rule can, in fact, be reasonably defined and applied.

3.1 Nonmonotonic Logic

3.1.1 Nonmonotonicity

A major difference — arguably, the defining difference — between sound deductive inference and plausible inference is monotonicity. Deductive inference is monotonic in the following sense: If a sentence ϕ is a valid conclusion from a set of sentences Γ, and Γ is a subset of Δ, then ϕ is a valid conclusion from Δ. Symbolically, if $\Gamma \subseteq \Delta$ and $\Gamma \vdash \phi$ then $\Delta \vdash \phi$; if $\Gamma \models \phi$ then $\Delta \models \phi$. Plausible inference does not have this property; inferences are made provisionally, and they may be withdrawn if more evidence contravening them comes along.

(The statement is sometimes made that classical probability theory, such as we will discuss in Section 3.2, is a monotonic theory. This is true at the metalevel; the statement "Given Γ, ϕ has probability x" does not change its truth. But, by the same token, the statements of nonmonotonic logic are monotonic at the metalevel; the statement "Given Γ, ϕ is a plausible inference" does not change its truth. At the object level, probability theory is nonmonotonic. The statement ϕ may become more or less likely as increasing evidence is accumulated.)

This nonmonotonicity has profound consequences for theories of plausible inference. Monotonicity is deeply built into standard logic, both in the syntactic concept of a proof, and in the semantic concept of semantic consequence; a theory of plausible inference must therefore alter or ignore these basic concepts. In standard systems of proof, the validity of a proof step depends only on particular steps being earlier in the proof or in the set of hypotheses. Adding additional axioms to the hypothesis set cannot invalidate a proof step. Therefore, a proof of statement ϕ from axioms Γ is also a proof of ϕ from any Δ containing Γ. The axioms of Γ are also axioms of Δ, and any inferences valid in proofs from Γ are also valid in proofs from Δ. In nonmonotonic theories, an inference may require the absence as well as the presence of information; it may therefore be valid in Γ and invalid in Δ. Thus, an inference may involve the entire structure of the theory as a whole, not just some particular set of axioms in the theory.

Similarly, in the standard concept of semantic consequence, ϕ follows from Γ ($\Gamma \models \phi$) just if every model $\mathcal{M}$ that satisfies Γ also satisfies ϕ. This definition gives us the monotonicity property. Suppose that $\Gamma \models \phi$ and that $\Delta \supset \Gamma$. By the definition of consequence, if $\mathcal{M}$ is a model satisfying Γ, then $\mathcal{M}$ satisfies ϕ. Clearly, any model that satisfies Δ must also satisfy Γ, since Γ is a subset of Δ. Therefore any model satisfying Δ also satisfies ϕ, which is our definition of $\Delta \models \phi$. Therefore to describe plausible inference in terms of models, we will either have to change the definition of a model satisfying a statement, or our definition of semantic consequence, or both.

The nonmonotonicity of plausible inference invalidates many types of inference familiar from ordinary logic; one must be careful about applying one's logical intuitions. For example, in deductive logic, if r follows from q and q follows from p then r follows from p. In plausible inference, this does not hold. Let p be the sentence "John is a naturalized U.S. citizen," let q be the sentence "John is a U.S. citizen," and let r be the sentence "John was born in the U.S." Then q is a plausible (indeed, a necessary) inference from p, and r is a plausible inference from q, but r is not a plausible inference from p. Similarly, in standard logic, if it is possible to infer a statement "$\alpha(\gamma)$" from a hypothesis set that contains "$\beta(\gamma)$" but no other mention of the constant symbol γ, then it is possible to infer "$\forall_X \beta(X) \Rightarrow \alpha(X)$." In plausible inference this close connection between universal generalization and reasoning from partial knowledge does not hold. It may be plausible to infer "John was born in the U.S." from "John is a U.S. citizen," but that does not legitimate the inference "Every U.S. citizen was born in the U.S."

A nonmonotonic logic is an extension of standard logic that supports some types of plausible inferences. Nonmonotonic logics address the problems of the nonmonotonicity of plausible inference, and of inference from the absence of information; they do not, typically, allow the expression of the degree of belief, the comparison of strengths of arguments, or the weakening of an argument under many inference steps.

3.1.2 Domain-Independent Rules

3.1.2.1 Domain Closure

One basic type of inference often used in problem solving is to assume that the entities specified in the problem are the only entities, or the only entities of a given sort, that are relevant to its solution. For example, the initial conditions of a blocks-world problem might be given by specifying that block A is on block B and blocks B and C are on the table. The problem solver should then assume that blocks A, B, and C are the only blocks relevant to the problem, and that, in particular, there are no other blocks on block A. The missionaries and cannibals problem may specify "There are three missionaries, three cannibals, and a boat"; to address the problem one must assume that there are no other people, and no other ways to cross the river.

The ultimate justification of this inference depends on the source of the information. If the problem was given as a natural language communication, then it is an application of a Gricean rule: The person formulating the problem should give all the relevant information, so if there were another block, he should have mentioned it. If the table was seen, then it can be inferred that any other blocks would have been seen as well. However, in all these cases, the inference takes the same form, and can be handled in the same way.

This kind of inference is called the *domain-closure assumption*. It can be formalized as follows: Given a theory T, assume that the only objects that exist are those named by ground terms in the language of T; that is, constant symbols and the application of function symbols to constant symbols. Thus, in a blocks-world problem where the only constant symbols were "table", "a", "b", and "c", and where there are no function symbols, the domain-closure assumption specifies that these were the only objects; i.e.,

$$\forall_X X = \text{a} \lor X = \text{b} \lor X = \text{c} \lor X = \text{table}$$

In a problem in family relations, if the constants are "betty" and "mordred" and the function symbols are "father_of(X)", "mother_of(X)", and "common_ancestor(X, Y)", then the assumption specifies that the only objects are made by composing these functions with these constants, in terms such as "betty", "father_of(mordred)", "common_ancestor (mother_of(betty), mordred)", and so on. This assumption cannot be written in a first-order formula.

The domain-closure assumption is nonmonotonic, since if T is augmented with axioms that use new constant or function symbols, then the assumption becomes weakened to allow terms made from these.

The assumption is often applied only to entities of certain sorts. For instance, in planning problems, it might be reasonable to suppose that all the relevant physical objects have been explicitly named, but not that all instants of time or points of space have been named. In this case, the domain-closure assumption could be applied only to physical objects.

The assumption depends only on the symbols used in T, not on the content of the theory T. In fact, the assumption yields powerful consequences even when applied to a vacuous theory, such as one with the single axiom "f(a) = f(a)". Applying the domain-closure assumption to this theory has as a consequence the assumption that the only entities are a, f(a), f(f(a)), and so on.

If there are no function symbols in the language and only finitely many constant symbols "a", "b", and "c", then the domain-closure assumption is completely stated in the axiom

$$\forall_X \ X = a \lor X = b \lor X = c$$

Thus, a proof of ϕ from T with the domain-closure assumption can take the following form:

1. Verify that no function symbols appear in T and that the only constant symbols are "a", "b", and "c". Increment the theory T by adding the axiom

$$\forall_X \ X = a \lor X = b \lor X = c$$

2. Verify that there is a proof of the standard sort of ϕ from the augmented version of T.

Step (1) is not a proof step of an ordinary kind. It is a nonmonotonic operation; if additional axioms are added to the starting version of T, the domain-closure axiom may be weakened by allowing the possibility of other constant values.

For example, let T contain the following axioms:

1. on(a,b).
2. on(b,table).
3. on(c,table).
4. $on(X, Y) \land Y \neq Z \Rightarrow \neg on(X, Z)$. ($X$ can only be on one object at a time.)
5. $\neg on(table, X)$. (The table is not on anything.)
6. $clear(X) \Leftrightarrow \forall_Y \neg on(Y, X)$. (An object is clear if nothing is on it.)

   7. distinct(a,b,c,table).

Monotonically, $\mathcal{T}$ does not support the inference "clear(a)", since these axioms do not rule out the possibility that there is some other block "d" on "a." However, we can derive this result through the domain-closure inference. Since the only constant symbols in $\mathcal{T}$ are "a," "b," "c," and "table," and since there are no function symbols, the domain-closure axiom allows us to add the axiom

   $DC.$ $\forall_X X = a \lor X = b \lor X = c \lor X = \text{table}$

We can then prove the desired result as follows:

From [1], [4], and [7] infer

   8. ¬on(a,a)

From [2], [4], and [7] infer

   9. ¬on(b,a)

From [3], [4], and [7] infer

   10. ¬on(c,a)

From [5] infer

   11. ¬on(table,a)

From [DC], [8], [9], [10], and [11], infer

   12. ¬on(X,a)

From [12] and [6] infer

   13. clear(a).

If there are function symbols in the language, then the effect of the domain-closure assumption cannot be expressed in any first-order axiom, or, indeed, in any recursive axiom schema. (Proof: Adding the domain-closure assumption to the standard axioms of the integers is sufficient to rule out nonstandard models of those axioms and restrict the model to the "standard" integers. But there is no complete recursive axiomatization of the integers.) Thus, there is no complete categorization of proof using the domain-closure assumption. We can, however, categorize various limited classes of proofs. For example, suppose that the constant symbols of $\mathcal{T}$ are "a" and "b", and the function symbols are "f" and "g". Then, clearly, the domain-closure assumption entails the following axiom:

$$\forall_X X = a \lor X = b \lor \exists_Y X = f(Y) \lor X = g(Y)$$

Thus, any proof from T together with the above axiom is a valid proof from T with the domain-closure assumption.

If the starting theory has at least one constant symbol, and it is fully Skolemized — that is, all existentially quantified variables are replaced by Skolem constants or terms — then the set of terms is the Herbrand universe of the theory, and the domain-closure assumption is guaranteed to be consistent. If the theory contains sentences with existential quantifiers, then the domain-closure assumption may not be consistent.

For example, consider the theory T with the following axioms:

1. $\exists_X p(X)$

2. $\neg p(a)$

Since the only constant symbol is "a" and there are no function symbols, the domain-closure assumption is

3. $\forall_X X = a$

However, [3] is obviously inconsistent with [1] and [2].

3.1.2.2 Closed-World Assumption

In the domain-closure assumption, we postulate that all the entities relevant to a given problem are mentioned in the problem statement. Similarly, it is often reasonable to assume that all the significant relations between entities in the problem are given in the problem statement. If we identify a significant relation as one that has a predicate symbol, and a significant entity as one named by a ground term, then we can formalize this assumption as follows: Let T be a theory, and let ϕ be a ground atomic formula — that is, a formula without variables or Boolean connectives, including negation. If ϕ cannot be inferred from T, then nonmonotonically infer $\neg \phi$.

For example, using the closed-world assumption in the above blocks-world problem enables us to simplify the starting theory by eliminating several axioms. Let T have the following axioms:

1. on(a,b).

2. on(b,table).

3. on(c,table).

We now apply the closed-world assumption to T. Since "on(a,a)" is clearly not a consequence of T, by the closed-world assumption, we can add the axiom "¬on(a,a)". Similarly, since "on(b,a)", "on(c,a)", and "on(table,a)" are not consequences of T, we can add the axioms "¬on(b,a)", "¬on(c,a)", and "¬on(table,a)". We now make the domain-closure assumption

DC. $\forall_X X = $ a $\lor X = $ b $\lor X = $ c $\lor X = $ table

From these axioms, we can infer directly that nothing is on block a.

14. $\forall_X \neg\text{on}(X, \text{a})$

This is not quite the conclusion we arrived at before. We would like to use 14 to infer "clear(a)" from the definition of "clear". Here, however, there is a difficulty. Let T_2 be a theory containing [1], [2], and [3] as above and also axiom [6] defining clear:

6. $\text{clear}(X) \Leftrightarrow \forall_Y \neg\text{on}(Y, X)$

On the one hand, the closed-world assumption and domain closure justify [14] in the same way as before, and by combining [14] with [6] we can infer "clear(a)." However, we can also apply the closed-world assumption to T_2 in a different way: Since T_2 certainly does not by itself imply "clear(a)", therefore the closed-world assumption justifies the inference "¬clear(a)".

In short, the closed-world assumption, applied across the board, is inconsistent for the theory T_2. The solution, therefore, is not to apply it across the board, but to specify that it applies to some predicates but not others. In this example, we would wish to apply it to the predicate "on(X, Y)", but not to the predicate "clear(X)". In reasoning about people at a party, it might be reasonable to apply the closed-world assumption to predicates that describe who is at the party, but not to predicates that describe their personal relations.

The closed-world assumption is noncomputable in the general case, since the statement "p(a) cannot be derived from T" is noncomputable.

The closed-world assumption restricted to the equality predicate is known as the (nonmonotonic) *unique-names assumption*. The unique-names assumption asserts that two distinct terms t_1 and t_2 may be assumed to be unequal unless they are demonstrably equal. In our blocks-world example, the unique-names assumption is equivalent to the axiom "distinct(a,b,c,table)."

It is suggestive of the power of these nonmonotonic inference rules that, if we start with the constant symbol 0 and the function symbol s(X) for the successor function, and no proper axioms at all, and we apply the domain-closure assumption and the unique-names assumption, the result is the complete theory of the integers. The unique-names assumption asserts that the terms 0, s(0), s(s(0)), and so on, are all distinct. The domain-closure assumption asserts that these terms comprise all the integers.

All domain-independent types of nonmonotonic inference depend strongly on particular syntactic features of the language used; if the language is changed to some logically equivalent form, the nonmonotonic inferences may all be changed. Domain closure depends on the use of particular constant and function symbols. The closed-world assumption depends on the use of particular predicate symbols. For example, we may formulate a blocks-world theory, either using the predicate "on(X, Y)" or using the predicate "off(X, Y)." The content of the two theories will be exactly equivalent. However, the effect of applying the closed-world assumption will be exactly opposite. Similarly, we may formulate a theory of families, either using a function symbol "father_of(X)" or with a predicate symbol "father(Y, X)." The content of the two theories will be equivalent, if, in the latter case, we include an axiom stating that each person has exactly one father. $\forall_X \exists_Y^1 \text{father}(Y, X)$. However, the domain-closure assumption can be effectively applied only to the first, while the closed-world assumption can be applied only to the second.

It should be noted that it is possible to have an algorithm whose behavior depends on the absence of some data structure but that can nonetheless be justified purely in terms of a monotonic logic. It all depends on the conventions for interpreting the data structure in terms of the logic. For example, consider an algorithm that computes least-cost paths in a weighted graph. The algorithm is nonmonotonic with respect to the data structure; if you add additional edges of lower cost, the algorithm will arrive at a different answer. Whether this algorithm represents nonmonotonic inference depends on the meaning of the graph, and the meaning of the answer. If the graph is defined as meaning just that the edges it records exist, and the answer is intended to be the exact cost of the least-cost path, then the algorithm is performing the nonmonotonic inference that other edges do not exist. If, however, the graph is defined as containing all relevant edges — that is, if the input would be considered incorrect, not merely incomplete, if there turned out to be other edges — then the inferences of the algorithm are entirely sound. The data structure has merely encoded the completeness statement, "No other edges exist besides these," in an implicit rather than explicit form. The inference is truly nonmonotonic only if there are circumstances under which this reading of the data structure can be overruled. Likewise, if the answer is taken to be the cost of an inexpensive path, rather than necessarily the cost of the least expensive path, then the inference is monotonic, however the graph is interpreted.

3.1.3 Circumscription

Plausible inference often has the form "Assume that as few objects as possible have a particular property." The closed-world assumption, discussed above, is a simple form of this inference; we assume that the only atomic ground formulas that are true are those that can be proven within the theory. However, we often want to apply this assumption to nonground formulas as well. For example, the default assumption "Assume that eggs are fresh" can be phrased as "Assume that the class of rotten eggs is as small as possible." Given this default assumption, we would like to be able to assume that all the eggs in the box we are carrying are fresh. However, unless we have a constant symbol for each egg in the box, the closed-world assumption will not support this conclusion. Instead, we can use the method of *circumscription*.

The rotten eggs example above turns out to involve some subtleties, so we will start with a simpler example. Let us suppose that we know that kangaroos and opossums are marsupials, and we know that very few animals are marsupials. We know that cats are neither kangaroos nor opossums. We would like to infer by default that cats are presumably not marsupials.

Our basic theory T consists of the following axioms:

1. $\forall_X$ kangaroo$(X) \Rightarrow$ marsupial(X)

2. $\forall_X$ opossum$(X) \Rightarrow$ marsupial(X)

3. $\forall_X$ cat$(X) \Rightarrow \neg($kangaroo$(X) \vee$ opossum$(X))$

We want to force the set of marsupials to be as small as possible, consistent with the theory T. We can formulate this requirement as follows: Let $\alpha(X)$ be any possible property of X that would satisfy the axioms on "marsupial" in T. Then the real marsupials should not be a proper superset of α; otherwise, we could reduce the class of marsupials to α, and still satisfy the axioms of T. That is to say, if α satisfies the conditions

$\forall_X$ kangaroo$(X) \Rightarrow \alpha(X)$
$\forall_X$ opossum$(X) \Rightarrow \alpha(X)$

then it cannot be the case that all α's are marsupials and that some marsupials are not α's. We can write this rule as the axiom schema

4. $[\forall_X \text{ kangaroo}(X) \Rightarrow \alpha(X) \wedge \forall_X \text{ opossum}(X) \Rightarrow \alpha(X)\ ] \Rightarrow$
   $\neg[\forall_X \alpha(X) \Rightarrow \text{marsupial}(X) \wedge \exists_X \text{ marsupial}(X) \wedge \neg \alpha(X)\ ]$

or, equivalently,

5. $[\forall_X \text{ kangaroo}(X) \Rightarrow \alpha(X) \wedge$
   $\quad \forall_X \text{ opossum}(X) \Rightarrow \alpha(X) \wedge$
   $\quad \forall_X \alpha(X) \Rightarrow \text{marsupial}(X)\ ] \Rightarrow$
   $\quad \forall_X \text{ marsupial}(X) \Rightarrow \alpha(X)$

The above statement is true of every property α. In a second-order logic, we can quantify over all α, and state the axiom

$\quad \forall_\alpha\ [\ \forall_X \text{ kangaroo}(X) \Rightarrow \alpha(X) \wedge$
$\quad\quad \forall_X \text{ opossum}(X) \Rightarrow \alpha(X) \wedge$
$\quad\quad \forall_X \alpha(X) \Rightarrow \text{marsupial}(X)\ ] \Rightarrow$
$\quad\quad \forall_X \text{ marsupial}(X) \Rightarrow \alpha(X)$

In a first-order logic, we can assert formula 5 as an axiom schema, applying to each open formula α. Since we have not discussed higher-order logic, we will take this approach. (Using higher-order logic has some technical advantages [Genesereth and Nilsson 1987].)

Formula 5, above, is known as the *circumscriptive* axiom schema. The *circumscription* of theory T in the predicate "marsupial", written CIRC[T;marsupial]) is the theory T with the circumscriptive axiom schema added.

We can easily show that the only marsupials are kangaroos or opossums in the circumscribed theory. Pick $\alpha(X)$ to be the formula "kangaroo(X) $\vee$ opossum(X)". Substituting this formula for α in the axiom schema gives the axiom

6. $[\forall_X \text{ kangaroo}(X) \Rightarrow [\text{kangaroo}(X) \vee \text{opossum}(X)] \wedge$
   $\quad \forall_X \text{ opossum}(X) \Rightarrow [\text{kangaroo}(X) \vee \text{opossum}(X)] \wedge$
   $\quad \forall_X [\text{kangaroo}(X) \vee \text{opossum}(X)\ ] \Rightarrow \text{marsupial}(X)\ ] \Rightarrow$
   $\quad \forall_X \text{ marsupial}(X) \Rightarrow \text{kangaroo}(X) \vee \text{opossum}(X)$

Of the three implications in the antecedent of axiom 6, the first two are trivial, and the third is just a restatement of axioms 1 and 2 of T. Therefore, the antecedent of the implication is true, which means that the consequent is also true. Thus we have the formula

7. $\forall_X \text{ marsupial}(X) \Rightarrow [\ \text{kangaroo}(X) \vee \text{opossum}(X)\ ]$

i.e., all marsupials are kangaroos or opossums. Using this and axiom 3 of T, it follows directly that no cats are marsupials.

We have thus shown that formula 7 above, which states that all marsupials are either kangaroos or opossums, is a consequence of the circumscriptive axiom schema 5. In fact, 7 is equivalent to 5; that is, if $\mathcal{F}$ is a theory containing T and formula 7, then all instances of axiom schema 5 are true in $\mathcal{F}$. (Exercise 6: Prove this.) Thus, in this case, circumscribing the theory has the effect of adding a single first-order axiom. This is not true in all cases of circumscription, but it is true in many important cases.

If we extend T by telling it about some other marsupials, then we change the circumscriptive axiom. For example, let $\mathcal{W}$ be the theory containing axioms 1, 2, and 3 of T, together with axiom 8, asserting that all koala bears are marsupials.

8. $\forall_X$ koala$(X) \Rightarrow$ marsupial(X)

Then the circumscription of $\mathcal{W}$ in "marsupial" adds the axiom schema,

9. $[\ \forall_X$ kangaroo$(X) \Rightarrow \alpha(X) \wedge$
   $\forall_X$ opossum$(X) \Rightarrow \alpha(X) \wedge$
   $\forall_X$ koala$(X) \Rightarrow \alpha(X) \wedge$
   $\forall_X \alpha(X) \Rightarrow$ marsupial$(X)\ ] \Rightarrow$
   $\forall_X$ marsupial$(X) \Rightarrow \alpha(X)$

Substituting the formula "kangaroo$(X) \vee$ opossum$(X) \vee$ koala(X)" for $\alpha(X)$ in axiom schema 9, we can infer the conclusion,

10. marsupial$(X) \Leftrightarrow [$ kangaroo$(X) \vee$ opossum$(X) \vee$ koala$(X)\ ]$

Note that by strengthening the theory T to $\mathcal{W}$, we have weakened the circumscriptive axiom schema, and therefore have weakened the conclusions that can be drawn. We can no longer deduce that cats are not marsupials, unless we have an additional axiom that no cats are koala bears.

We can describe this technique formally as follows: Let T be a finite theory and let $\mu(X)$ be a predicate symbol appearing in T. (X can be a single variable or a tuple of variables.) For any open formula $\alpha(X)$, let $T[\mu/\alpha]$ be the theory formed from T by replacing every occurrence of μ by α. Then we define the circumscription of T in μ, CIRC[T, μ] as the theory T together with the axiom schema

$$[T[\mu/\alpha] \wedge [\forall_X \alpha(X) \Rightarrow \mu(X)]] \Rightarrow [\ \forall_X \mu(X) \Rightarrow \alpha(X)\ ]$$

where $\alpha(X)$ is any open formula. (In this formula, the antecedent $T[\mu/\alpha]$ guarantees that α has all the properties that μ must have; the antecedent $\forall_X \alpha(X) \Rightarrow \mu(X)$ guarantees that α fits within μ; the consequent $\forall_X \mu(X) \Rightarrow \alpha(X)$ guarantees that μ fits inside α. Thus, the formula may be read "If α is any property that satisfies the theory T, and that fits inside μ, then α must just be μ." Thus, μ must be a minimal set satisfying T.)

As mentioned above, as T is strengthened, the antecedent of the circumscription axiom schema is strengthened, and the axiom as a whole is weakened.

The original inference (7) that, if X is a marsupial then it is either a kangaroo or an opossum, can only be used in the backward direction, to infer that something that is known not to be a kangaroo or opossum may be presumed not to be a marsupial. It cannot be used to deduce that something that is known to be a marsupial should be presumed to be either a kangaroo or an opossum, for, if the theory is extended to include other marsupials, the circumscriptive axiom will change. For example, if we add to the theory T the statement that Pete is a marsupial, the circumscriptive axiom will become

11. $[\forall_X \text{ kangaroo}(X) \Rightarrow \alpha(X) \wedge$
  $\quad \forall_X \text{ opossum}(X) \Rightarrow \alpha(X) \wedge$
  $\quad \alpha(\text{pete}) \wedge$
  $\quad \forall_X \alpha(X) \Rightarrow \text{marsupial}(X)] \Rightarrow$
  $\quad \forall_X \text{ marsupial}(X) \Rightarrow \alpha(X)$

or, equivalently,

12. $\forall_X \text{ marsupial}(X) \Leftrightarrow$
  $\quad [\text{kangaroo}(X) \vee \text{opossum}(X) \vee X = \text{pete}]$

Note, also, that, in order to apply the circumscriptive axiom 5 to deduce that a given animal is not a marsupial, it is necessary to know that it is not a kangaroo or opossum. One cannot deduce that it is not a marsupial if one is completely ignorant about the animal. We can get around this limitation by circumscribing over the three predicates "marsupial(X)", "kangaroo(X)", and "opossum(X)". Circumscription in parallel is a straightforward extension of circumscription over a single predicate. Consider the theory T_2 containing the following axioms:

2.1. $\forall_X \text{ kangaroo}(X) \Rightarrow \text{marsupial}(X)$
2.2. $\forall_X \text{ opossum}(X) \Rightarrow \text{marsupial}(X)$
2.3. kangaroo(kanga)
2.4. opossum(george)

We require that the extension of the predicates "marsupial", "kangaroo", and "opossum" be as small as possible. To do this, we use three variable properties α, β, and γ, and require that, if α, β, and γ satisfy the theory T_2 when substituted for "marsupial", "kangarooo", and "opossum", then they cannot be strict subsets of the desired predicates. The resultant axiom schema is

2.5. $[\ [\ \forall_X \ \beta(X){\Rightarrow}\alpha(X) \ ] \land [\ \forall_X \ \gamma(X){\Rightarrow}\alpha(X) \ ] \land \beta(\text{kanga}) \land$
    $\gamma(\text{george}) \land$
    $[\ \forall_X \ \alpha(X) \Rightarrow \text{marsupial}(X) \ ] \land$
    $[\ \forall_X \ \beta(X) \Rightarrow \text{kangaroo}(X) \ ] \land$
    $[\ \forall_X \ \gamma(X) \Rightarrow \text{opossum}(X) \ ] \ ] \Rightarrow$
    $[\ [\ \forall_X \ \text{marsupial}(X) \Rightarrow \alpha(X) \ ] \land$
    $[\ \forall_X \ \text{kangaroo}(X) \Rightarrow \beta(X) \ ] \land$
    $[\ \forall_X \ \text{opossum}(X) \Rightarrow \gamma(X) \ ] \ ]$

It is easily shown (Exercise 7) that the circumscribed theory, CIRC[T_2; marsupial,kangaroo,opossum], of T_2 together with axiom schema 2.5 is equivalent to the single axiom 2.6.

2.6. $\forall_X \ [\ \text{marsupial}(X) \Leftrightarrow X =\text{kanga} \lor X{=}\text{george} \ ] \land$
    $[\ \text{kangaroo}(X) \Leftrightarrow X =\text{kanga} \ ] \land$
    $[\ \text{opossum}(X) \Leftrightarrow X =\text{george} \ ]$

Let us see what happens when we apply these techniques to the fresh-eggs problem. We wish to infer that any given egg is fresh, unless it is known to be otherwise; that is, within the class of eggs, we wish to maximize the class of those that are fresh. To apply circumscription, we must pose the problem in terms of a predicate to be minimized. We can do this by introducing the new predicate "rotten_egg(X)". We give an axiom stating that an egg that is not a rotten egg is fresh; we can then achieve our goal of making as many eggs as possible fresh by minimizing the extension of "rotten_egg". (Such a predicate is often called an "abnormality" predicate, and given a name such as "ab(X)".)

Thus we start with a single axiom

3.1 $\forall_X \ \text{egg}(X) \land \neg\text{rotten\_egg}(X) \Rightarrow \text{fresh}(X)$

and we circumscribe this theory in "rotten_egg". The result is the axiom schema

3.2. $[\ [\ \forall_X \ \text{egg}(X) \land \neg\alpha(X) \Rightarrow \text{fresh}(X) \ ] \land$
    $[\ \forall_X \ \alpha(X) \Rightarrow \text{rotten\_egg}(X) \ ] \ ] \Rightarrow$
    $\forall_X \ \text{rotten\_egg}(X) \Rightarrow \alpha(X)$

However, this circumscribed theory is equivalent to the axiom

3.3. $\forall_X$ rotten_egg$(X) \iff$ egg$(X) \wedge \neg$ fresh(X)

In other words, all that circumscription has done for us here is to restrict the extension of "rotten_egg" to eggs that are not fresh. Something has gone awry.

The problem is that our formalism treats "egg" and "fresh" symmetrically, while, in reality, we are thinking of them in quite different ways. We can rephrase axiom 3.1 in the form

3.1a. $\forall_X$ [egg$(X) \wedge \neg$fresh(X)] $\Rightarrow$ rotten_egg(X)

There are three ways that we can make the extension of "rotten_egg" as small as possible, while preserving the truth of axiom 3.1a above:

    i. Disallow anything from satisfying "rotten_egg(X)" unless it is an egg that is not fresh.
    ii. Make the extension of "egg" as small as possible within the class of unfresh objects.
    iii. Make the extension of "fresh" as large as possible within the class of eggs.

Simple circumscription, as we have seen, accomplishes only i. In reality, what we primarily want to accomplish is iii. i is irrelevant and ii is misdirected. We can achieve our aim by using circumscription with variable predicates.

In circumscription with variable predicates, we minimize the extension of one predicate (in this case, "rotten_egg"), letting certain other, specified predicates (in this case, "fresh") range over all possible extensions. That is, we choose a value for "rotten_egg" and a value for "fresh" such that the extension of "rotten_egg" is as small as possible, subject to the constraint that the starting theory be true.

Formally, if α and β are predicates that satisfy the given theory when substituted for "rotten_egg" and "fresh" respectively, then the extension of α may not be a proper subset of the extension of "rotten_egg". We state this in the axiom schema

3.4. [[$\forall_X$ egg$(X) \wedge \neg\beta(X) \Rightarrow \alpha(X)$] $\wedge$
     [$\forall_X \alpha(X) \Rightarrow$ rotten_egg(X)]] $\Rightarrow$
     $\forall_X$ rotten_egg$(X) \Rightarrow \alpha(X)$

It is easily shown (Exercise 8) that this axiom schema is satisfied only if all eggs are fresh and none are rotten. Thus, all the eggs in our box may be assumed to be fresh. If we knew of some particular rotten eggs, a similar circumscription would allow us to assume that the only rotten eggs in the world were those known to be rotten.

3.1.4 Default Theory

One basic form of plausible reasoning involves the use of *default* inferences — inferring that an element of a given class has properties characteristic of the class. For example (the standard example in the field), given that Tweety is a bird and that birds can typically fly, infer provisionally that Tweety can fly. This inference is nonmonotonic, since it can be overruled by additional information that Tweety is an ostrich, or is injured, or can't fly.

Reiter [1980a] describes a logic in which rules like "Birds typically can fly" can be stated as a tentative rule of inference. This particular rule is written[1] in the form

$$\frac{\text{bird}(X) : \text{can\_fly}(X)}{\text{can\_fly}(X)}$$

or, inline, as "bird(X) : can_fly(X) / can_fly(X)". The general form of a default inference rule is

$$\frac{\alpha : \beta}{\gamma}$$

The meaning of this rule is, roughly, "If you believe α and you have no reason to doubt β then you are justified in believing γ." The formula α is called the *prerequisite* of the rule; β is the *justification*; γ is the *consequent*. Frequently, default rules take the form "$\alpha : \beta/\beta$", with identical justification and consequent. Such a rule is said to be *normal*; it can be read "α's are typically β's" or "If α then assume β."

Defining the consequences of a theory containing axioms and default rules is tricky, because the condition "no reason to doubt β" has a difficult circularity; whether one has reason to doubt β may depend, circularly, on whether one can apply the rule in which β is a justification. For example, consider a theory containing the two rules "If someone speaks Turkish fluently, then assume that he is a Turkish citizen" and "If someone lives in the U.S., assume that he is a U.S. citizen," and the three facts "Kemal speaks Turkish fluently," "Kemal lives in the U.S.," and "No one is both a Turkish and an American citizen." One way of thinking about this theory would be to deduce

---

[1]See Exercise 11 for an alternative representation of the rule "Birds can typically fly" within Reiter's theory with some technical advantages.

from the first rule that Kemal is Turkish and use that conclusion to establish doubt of the justification "Kemal is an American citizen" and thus block the use of the second rule. The use of the first rule is now legitimated, since there is no reason to doubt that Kemal is Turkish. Alternatively, one can do the reverse: use the second rule to deduce that Kemal is American and thus block the justification of the first rule. Another possibility is to take the disjunction of these two, and conclude that Kemal is either Turkish or American. Or perhaps the best thing under the circumstances is to abstain from concluding anything at all about Kemal's nationality.

In Reiter's logic, either of the first two arguments is valid, but they cannot be combined. Each argument gives a possible way of looking at the world, given these facts and default rules. The view is that the proper use of a default theory T is to find one way of choosing one's belief that is "consistent" with T; if there is more than one such belief set, the reasoner can choose between them arbitrarily. Specifically, one looks for an *extension* $\mathcal{E}$ of T, a set of sentences with the following properties: (i) $\mathcal{E}$ contains the sentences (not the default rules) of T. (ii) $\mathcal{E}$ is closed under ordinary logical inference. (iii) $\mathcal{E}$ contains the conclusions of every applicable default rule in T. A default rule is applicable if $\mathcal{E}$ contains its prerequisite, but does not contain the negation of any of its justifications. (iv) Every sentence in $\mathcal{E}$ can be justified by a finite-length derivation, where each step of the derivation is either an ordinary first-order inference or the application of an applicable default rule.

The catch here is that the definition of "applicable" depends on $\mathcal{E}$ itself. In formulating our definition of an extension, therefore, we start with a set $\mathcal{E}$, use that set to define applicability, and thus a set of conclusions. $\mathcal{E}$ is an extension if this operation brings us back where we started.

Formally, let $\mathcal{L}$ be a first-order language. If S is a set of sentences in $\mathcal{L}$, let Th(S) be the set of first-order consequences of S. We define a default theory to be a pair $< \mathcal{D}, \mathcal{W} >$ where $\mathcal{W}$ is a set of sentences in $\mathcal{L}$ and where $\mathcal{D}$ is a set of inference rules of the form "$\alpha : \beta/\gamma$" where α, β, γ are formulas in $\mathcal{L}$. A default rule Φ' is an instance of rule Φ if Φ' is closed, and some substitution for the variables in Φ gives Φ'.

Let $< \mathcal{D}, \mathcal{W} >$ be a default theory and let $\mathcal{E}$ be any set of sentences in $\mathcal{L}$. For any subset $S \subset \mathcal{E}$, define the function concs($S, \mathcal{D}, \mathcal{E}$) (the conclusions from S using default rules $\mathcal{D}$ in extension $\mathcal{E}$) as follows:

$\text{concs}(\mathcal{S}, \mathcal{D}, \mathcal{E}) = \{ \gamma \mid$ there exists a rule $\Phi' = \alpha : \beta/\gamma$
that is an instance of some rule $\Phi \in \mathcal{D}$
such that $\alpha \in \mathcal{S}$ and $\neg\beta \notin \mathcal{E} \}$

Now, define the sequence $\mathcal{E}_0, \mathcal{E}_1, \ldots$ as follows

$$\mathcal{E}_0 = \mathcal{W}$$
$$\mathcal{E}_{i+1} = \text{Th}(\mathcal{E}_i) \cup \text{concs}(\mathcal{E}_i, \mathcal{D}, \mathcal{E})$$

$\mathcal{E}$ is an *extension* of $< \mathcal{D}, \mathcal{W} >$ if

$$\mathcal{E} = \bigcup_{i=0}^{\infty} \mathcal{E}_i$$

Examples:

1. Let $\mathcal{D} = \{$ bird$(X) :$ can_fly(X) / can_fly$(X) \}$ and
   $\mathcal{W} = \{$ bird(tweety) $\}$.
   Then there is a unique extension $\mathcal{E} = \text{Th}(\{$ bird(tweety), can_fly(tweety) $\})$.
   In this case $\mathcal{E}_0 = \mathcal{W}$; $\mathcal{E}_1 = \text{Th}(\mathcal{W}) \cup \{$ can_fly(tweety) $\}$; $\mathcal{E}_2 = \mathcal{E}$.

2. Let $\mathcal{D} = \{$ bird$(X) :$ can_fly(X) / can_fly$(X) \}$ and
   $\mathcal{W} = \{$ ostrich(ozzie),
   $\qquad \forall_X$ ostrich$(X) \Rightarrow ($bird$(X) \wedge \neg$can_fly$(X)) \}$.
   This has a single extension $\mathcal{E} = \text{Th}(\mathcal{W})$.

3. Let $\mathcal{D} = \{$ bird$(X) :$ can_fly(X) / can_fly(X);
   $\qquad$ sings$(X,$bird_song$) :$ bird(X) / bird$(X) \}$ and
   $\mathcal{W} = \{$ sings(tweety,bird_song) $\}$.
   This has a single extension $\mathcal{E} = \text{Th}(\mathcal{W} \cup \{$ bird(tweety), can_fly(tweety) $\})$.

4. Let $\mathcal{D} = \{$ speak$(X,$turkish$) :$ citizen$(X,$turkey$)$ / citizen$(X,$turkey$)$;
   $\qquad$ lives_in$(X, C) :$ citizen(X, C) / citizen$(X, C) \}$.
   Let $\mathcal{W} = \{$ speak(kemal,turkish),
   $\qquad$ lives_in(kemal,usa),
   $\qquad \forall_X \neg($citizen$(X,$turkey$) \wedge$ citizen$(X,$usa$)) \}$.
   This has two extensions: $\mathcal{E}_A = \text{Th}(\mathcal{W} \cup \{$ citizen(kemal,turkey) $\})$ and
   $\qquad\qquad\qquad\qquad \mathcal{E}_B = \text{Th}(\mathcal{W} \cup \{$ citizen(kemal,usa) $\})$.

5. Let $\mathcal{D} = \{$:B / $\neg$B $\}$ and let $\mathcal{W} = \emptyset$.
   This theory has no extensions.
   Proof: Let $\mathcal{E}$ be any set of sentences, and construct the sequence
   $\mathcal{E}_0, \mathcal{E}_1 \ldots$ according to the above definition. If $\neg$B $\notin \mathcal{E}$, then the
   justification of the default is satisfied, so that B$\in \mathcal{E}_1$, and $\mathcal{E} \neq \cup\mathcal{E}_i$.
   If $\neg$B $\in \mathcal{E}$, then the justification of the rule is denied,
   and B$\notin \mathcal{E}_i$ for any i, so again $\mathcal{E} \neq \cup\mathcal{E}_i$.

3.1.5 Preferred Models

As we discussed above, the monotonicity of standard logic is inherent in its semantics. A theory T has a consequence ϕ if ϕ is true in all models satisfying T. This is an inescapably monotonic idea of consequence, because when we increment T with a new fact ψ, we simply reduce the set of relevant models to a subset; ϕ must still be true in all of them.

How can we get out of this? One approach is to say that T has consequence ϕ if ϕ is true in *most* of the worlds satisfying T. Once we add a new fact ψ, we may select an atypical subset of these models, and most of the models in this subset may not satisfy ϕ. This approach leads to the possible-worlds semantics for probability, which we will discuss in Section 3.2.2. Another approach, which we will study here, is to say that ϕ is a consequence of T if ϕ is true in the *best* models that satisfy T. If T is augmented by a statement ψ, then the class of best models may change. ϕ may be true in the best models of $T \cup \{\psi\}$, though false in the best models of T.

Formally, we define a partial ordering $\mathcal{M}_1 < \mathcal{M}_2$ on models, read "$\mathcal{M}_1$ is preferred to $\mathcal{M}_2$." $\mathcal{M}$ is said to be a *minimal model* of theory T if $\mathcal{M}$ satisfies T, and no other model satisfying T is preferred to $\mathcal{M}$. If the sentence ψ is true in all minimal models of T, then ψ is called a *nonmonotonic consequence* of T relative to the partial ordering "$<$".

For example, the default rule "Typical sonatas have three movements," can be described by saying that model $\mathcal{M}_1$ is preferred to $\mathcal{M}_2$ if every sonata with three movements in $\mathcal{M}_2$ also has three in $\mathcal{M}_1$, but not vice versa. Now, suppose we do not know how many movements are in Beethoven's Opus 111. Our theory thus allows models in which it has three movements and models in which it has other numbers of movements. The former will be preferred — to be precise, for each model $\mathcal{M}_2$ in which Opus 111 has some other number of movements, there will be another model $\mathcal{M}_1$ that agrees with $\mathcal{M}_2$ on all other sonatas but gives Opus 111 the standard three movements. Thus, the statement "Opus 111 has three movements" is true in all minimal models of our theory; it is a nonmonotonic consequence of our theory. If we now find out that Opus 111 has only two movements, then models where it has three movements do not satisfy our new theory; hence, the conclusion is no longer valid.

A number of types of nonmonotonic inference can be described in terms of preferences on models. For example, the effect of circumscription in a predicate μ can correspond to the preference relation $\mathcal{M}_1 < \mathcal{M}_2$ if the extension of μ in $\mathcal{M}_1$ is a proper subset of its extension in $\mathcal{M}_2$, and all other predicate symbols have equal extensions.

3.2   Classical Probability Theory

The oldest and best understood formal theory of plausible reasoning is the classical theory of mathematical probability. Probability theory is a quantitative theory: The probability of a statement given a body of evidence is a real number between 0 and 1.[2] The theory thus provides a straightforward measure of strength of belief. Probability theory consists of two parts. The first part, the theory of probability proper, asserts weak, inviolable constraints relating the probabilities of different statements; for example, the probability of $E \wedge F$ is less than or equal to probability of F. The second part, the theory of statistical inference, gives nonmonotonic suggestions for picking the actual values; for example, if there are n possibilities, and there is no reason to suppose one more likely than another, then assign each of them a probability of $1/n$.

There are several different ways to interpret probability theory. All of them use the same formulas; they differ in what they connect probabilities to. In general, the simpler the interpretation of probabilities, the further the theory is from anything that can be applied to plausible reasoning. In the simplest formulation, probability is just a ratio of the measures of two sets [Kolmogorov 1950; Russell 1948]; the probability of "Brown" given "Cow" is just the number of brown cows divided by the number of cows. In this interpretation, the axioms of probability theory are trivial consequences of the axioms of measures on sets, and the question of deriving the initial value of probabilities does not arise. In a more complex formulation [Mises 1960], probabilities are based on the idea of infinite random sequences of repeatable events. However, plausible reasoning involves reasoning about events that occur only once; the probability that Sam has the measles, or the probability that Clyde is gray. The only obvious sets here are singletons, namely the set of Sam and the set of Clyde, and there is nothing repeatable about the events involved. In AI, therefore, we are obliged to use *subjective* probability theory, in which probabilities are interpreted as the likelihood of particular statements, given a body of evidence. This interpretation is much less concrete and its logical form less clear than the other interpretations; indeed, its legitimacy has been hotly debated back and forth over the last 200 years (see the chapter reference list for citations). Even in using a subjective interpretation of probabilities, it is useful to have the frequency interpretation to refer to, since any general formula of subjective probability can be justified

---

[2]This does not mean that a program or a theory that uses probability theory must assign floating-point numbers as the probability of statements. It just means that probabilities are quantities (real numbers, in the classical theory) that can be described in the languages of quantities discussed in Chapter 4.

in terms of frequencies, and frequencies are a more concrete object of thought than judgments of likelihood.

We will view a theory as having two kinds of statements: unqualified statements about the real world, such as "Clyde is an elephant" or "95% of all elephants are gray," and statements about probabilities, such as "The probability that Clyde is gray is greater than the probability that he is white" or "The probability that Wendy is white is greater if Wendy is a sea gull than if she is an elephant." These probabilities represent a possible judgment of the likelihood of E by a rational agent who knows the given unqualified facts. Our definition of a "rational" agent is just one that assigns probabilities in a way conforming to the rules given below.

Formally, we can define a probabilistic language as follows (this is one method among many): Let $\mathcal{L}_0$ be an object language: this will be the language in which we write the object-level sentences to which we will assign probabilities. These object-level sentences are called *events*.[3] The unqualified part of a theory $\mathcal{T}_0$ is a set of sentences in $\mathcal{L}_0$. We introduce two probability functions: the prior probability of E, relative to $\mathcal{T}_0$, written $P(E)$, and the conditional probability of E given F, relative to $\mathcal{T}_0$, written $P(E \mid F)$. These are partial functions: $P(E \mid F)$ is always undefined if F is known to be false, and it may be undefined if there is no relevant information whatever. (What is the probability that Clyde is gray given the parallel postulate?) E and F, the arguments to P, are events; the function P maps them to a real number in the interval [0,1]. We speak about these probabilities by using them as atomic terms in a first-order language $\mathcal{L}_R$ of real arithmetic. $\mathcal{L}_R$ will typically contain the arithmetic functions plus, minus, times and divide, the order relations $X > Y$, and any other useful arithmetic relations and functions. A *probabilistic sentence*, then, is some sentence in $\mathcal{L}_R$ containing terms of the form $P(E)$ and $P(E \mid F)$ as atomic terms. A *probabilistic theory* is a pair $< \mathcal{T}_0, \mathcal{T}_P >$ where $\mathcal{T}_0$ is a set of sentences in $\mathcal{L}_0$, and $\mathcal{T}_P$ is a set of probabilistic sentences.

Thus, in the above example, $\mathcal{L}_0$ would be language rich enough to express sentences such as "Clyde is an elephant," "Wendy is white," "95% of elephants are gray," and so on. The unqualified theory $\mathcal{T}_0$ would contain "Clyde is an elephant" and "95% of elephants are gray." The terms "P(gray(clyde))", the probability that Clyde is gray, and "P(white(wendy) | seagull(wendy))", the conditional probability that Wendy is white given that she is a sea gull, are probabilistic terms. The sentences "P(gray(clyde)) = .95" and

---

[3] This is quite different from the use of the term *events* in temporal reasoning.

P(white(wendy) | seagull(wendy)) >
P(white(wendy) | elephant(wendy))

are probabilistic sentences, which may be part of the probabilistic component T_P.

The above definition imposes two restrictions that should be noted:

- The definition does not allow quantification into the scope of a probability operator. For example, the definition rules out a sentence such as "$\forall_X$ P(gray(X) | elephant(X)) = 0.95" or "$\exists_X$ P(color(wendy) = X | elephant(wendy)) $\geq$ 0.95" (meaning "There is some particular color that is almost certainly Wendy's color"). Such quantification would require that P be viewed as a modal operator creating an opaque context; we should not want to substitute "the youngest white elephant" for X in the first sentence above, nor to derive the second sentence from the fact "P(color(wendy)=color(wendy) | elephant(wendy)) $\geq$ 0.95" by existential abstraction on "color(wendy)." To simplify our theory, we therefore rule out these sentences. Part of the effect of a universal quantifier can be gotten by using axiom schemas; for example, we might posit the rule "For any constant symbol γ, P(gray(γ) | elephant(γ)) = 0.95."

- The definition does not allow "higher-order" probabilities such as "P(P(gray(clyde)) > .95) = .5" meaning "There is a .5 probability that the probability that Clyde is gray is greater than .95." Such higher-order probabilities can generally be avoided in simple applications of probability theory to plausible reasoning, though they can be useful in a metalevel evaluation of a system that assigns object-level probabilities [Gaifman 1983, 1986]

In any probabilistic theory $T = < T_0, T_P >$ the following axioms must hold:

1. (Closure) If P(E) and P(F) are defined, then P($E \wedge F$), P($E \vee F$), and P($\neg E$) are all defined. If two of the quantities P(E), P(F), and P($E \mid F$) are defined, then the third is also defined, unless P(F) = 0.

2. (Probability of known facts) If $T_0 \vdash E$ then P(E) = 1 and P($\neg E$) = 0. Facts known without qualification have probability 1, and their negations have probability 0. Note that the converse is not the case; a sentence may be given probability 1 without its being provable from the known facts.

3. (Range) $0 \leq$ P(E) ≤ 1. All probabilities are between 0 and 1.

4. (Invariance under equivalence) If $T_0 \vdash (E \Leftrightarrow F)$ then $P(E) = P(F)$. If E and F are known to have the same truth value, then they have equal probabilities.

5. (Conjunction) $P(E \wedge F) = P(E) \cdot P(F \mid E)$. The probability that E and F are both true is the probability that E is true times the probability that F is true given that E is true. This can function as a definition of the conditional probability $P(E \mid F)$, except in cases where $P(F) = 0$.

It should be noted that $P(E \mid F)$ is not the same as $P(F \Rightarrow E) = P(\neg F \vee E)$. The latter term is, in fact, rather useless. If $P(E \mid F)$ is high, then we can legitimately infer E given F. By contrast $P(F \Rightarrow E)$ may be high just because F is very unlikely; if F is found out to be true, E may still be unlikely.

6. (Disjunction) If $T_0 \vdash \neg(E \wedge F)$ then $P(E \vee F) = P(E) + P(F)$. If it is known that E and F cannot both be true, then the probability of the disjunction $E \vee F$ is the sum of the probability of E plus the probability of F.

7. (Belief update) A final meta-axiom does not constrain any particular probabilistic theory; rather, it describes how a rational agent should pass from one theory to another when he establishes some new information. An agent who finds out that event E is true should adopt the previous value of $P(F \mid E)$ as his new value for the prior $P(F)$, and should adopt the previous value of $P(F \mid E \wedge G)$ as his new value of $P(F \mid G)$, assuming that these quantities were previously defined. For instance, suppose you previously calculated that there was a .95 probability that Clyde is gray given that Clyde is an elephant, and a .90 probability that Clyde can do tricks given that Clyde is an elephant and that he is a circus animal. You now find out that Clyde is, indeed, an elephant. You should now believe that there is a .95 prior probability that Clyde is gray, and that there is a .90 probability that he can do tricks given that he is a circus animal.

The expected value of a term is defined as the sum of its possible values times the probability of its having that value.

$$E(T) = \sum_{X_i} P(T = X_i) \cdot X_i$$

A number of important consequences follow directly from these axioms:

8. (Implication) If $\mathcal{T}_0 \vdash E \Rightarrow F$ then $\mathrm{P}(F) \geq \mathrm{P}(E)$

9. (Relativizing rules 3, 5, 6, and 8 to conditional probabilities.)
   a. $0 \leq \mathrm{P}(E \mid F) \leq 1$
   b. $\mathrm{P}(E \wedge F \mid G) = \mathrm{P}(E \mid G) \cdot \mathrm{P}(F \mid G \wedge E)$
   c. If $\mathcal{T}_0 \vdash G \Rightarrow (\neg(E \wedge F))$ then $\mathrm{P}(E \vee F \mid G) = \mathrm{P}(E \mid G) + \mathrm{P}(F \mid G)$
   d. If $\mathcal{T}_0 \vdash G \Rightarrow (E \Rightarrow F)$ then $\mathrm{P}(F \mid G) \geq \mathrm{P}(E \mid G)$

This result is important for establishing the coherence of the update rule (7), since it guarantees that the new probabilities satisfy the axioms of a probability theory.

10. Exhaustive disjoint possibilities. Let $E_1 \ldots E_k$ be a set of events of which it is known that exactly one is true. Such a set of events is known as a *frame of discernment*. The sum of the probabilities of such events must be 1. This applies both to prior probabilities and to probabilities conditioned on some fixed condition F. Formally,

If $\mathcal{T}_0 \vdash E_1 \dot\vee E_2 \dot\vee \ldots \dot\vee E_k$ then

$$\sum_{i=1}^{k} \mathrm{P}(E_i) = \sum_{i=1}^{k} \mathrm{P}(E_i \mid F) = 1$$

11. The probability of a disjunction can be calculated as follows:

$$\mathrm{P}(E \vee F) = \mathrm{P}(E) + \mathrm{P}(F) - \mathrm{P}(E \wedge F)$$

12. Corresponding to modus ponens: $\mathrm{P}(F) \geq \mathrm{P}(E) \cdot \mathrm{P}(F \mid E)$

13. Evidence augmentation: Let $\mathrm{P}(X \mid E) = a$ and let $\mathrm{P}(F \mid E) = b$. Then

$$\frac{a+b-1}{b} \leq \mathrm{P}(X \mid E \wedge F) \leq \frac{a}{b}$$

If b is close to 1, this allows us to compute useful bounds on the effect of learning F on the plausibility of X.

3.2.1   Bayes's Formula

Axiom 5 allows us to reverse the direction of conditional probabilities. If we know $\mathrm{P}(E)$, $\mathrm{P}(F)$, and $\mathrm{P}(E \mid F)$, then by axiom 5,

$$\mathrm{P}(F \mid E) = \frac{\mathrm{P}(E \wedge F)}{\mathrm{P}(E)} = \frac{\mathrm{P}(E \mid F) \cdot \mathrm{P}(F)}{\mathrm{P}(E)}$$

This is called Bayes's formula.

Bayes's formula is often used in reasoning from an observed effect E to an inferred cause F. If we know the prior probabilities of E and F and we know the likelihood that F will occur if E has occurred, then Bayes's formula allows us to compute the likelihood that E occurred given that F occurred. Often, the probability of the effect F is not known directly, but is computed from considering all the possible causes. Let E_1, E_2, $\ldots E_k$ be an exhaustive set of mutually disjoint causes for F; that is, given F we know that exactly one of the E_i must have occurred. Formally,

$$\mathcal{T}_0 \vdash F \Rightarrow (E_1 \dot{\vee} E_2 \dot{\vee} \ldots \dot{\vee} E_k)$$

Using axiom 6 above

$P(F) = P(F \wedge (E_1 \dot{\vee} \ldots \dot{\vee} E_k)) =$
$P((F \wedge E_1) \dot{\vee} \ldots \dot{\vee} (F \wedge E_k)) =$
$P(F \wedge E_1) + \ldots + P(F \wedge E_k) =$
$P(F \mid E_1) P(E_1) + \ldots + P(F \mid E_k) P(E_k) =$
$\sum_{j=1}^{k} P(F \mid E_j) P(E_j)$

Substituting this last expression for $P(F)$ in Bayes's formula above yields the formula

$$P(E_i \mid F) = \frac{P(F \mid E_i) P(E_i)}{\sum_{j=1}^{k} P(F \mid E_j) \, P(E_j)}$$

For example, consider the following situation: Edgar invites Karen to a movie Saturday night, and Karen answers that unfortunately she has a prior engagement. Edgar is now interested in the probability that Karen is politely lying. Let A be the event that Karen answers that she is busy; B, the event that Karen is actually busy; and F, the event that Karen is actually free. Edgar now estimates the prior probabilities as follows:

$P(B) = 0.3$ (She's popular, but he called her on Monday, which is plenty of time.)

$P(F) = 1 - P(B) = 0.7$

$P(A \mid B) = 0.95$ (There was a 1/20 chance that Karen would be so wild about him as to break a previous date.)

$P(A \mid F) = 0.25$ (Edgar has a pretty good opinion of his own attractiveness.)

Applying Bayes's formula, we have

$$P(F \mid A) = \frac{P(A \mid F) \cdot P(F)}{P(A \mid F) \cdot P(F) + P(A \mid B) \cdot P(B)} =$$

$$\frac{0.25 \cdot 0.7}{0.25 \cdot 0.7 + 0.95 \cdot 0.3} = 0.38$$

Not so large as to discourage another call next week.

3.2.2 Possible-Worlds Semantics

There is a natural possible-worlds semantics for probability judgments. A world is described by the events in $\mathcal{L}_0$. We define a measure μ on sets of possible worlds, satisfying the following axioms:

1. For any set X, $\mu(X) \geq 0$.

2. If W and X are disjoint sets of possible worlds, then $\mu(W \cup X) = \mu(W) + \mu(X)$.

We define the probability of an event E as the fraction of worlds satisfying E out of all the worlds satisfying the background theory. Formally, let $\mathcal{U}$ be the set of all worlds that satisfy the background theory, and let $\mathcal{W}_E$ be the subset of worlds that satisfy both the background theory and E. Then

$$P(E) = \frac{\mu(\mathcal{W}_E)}{\mu(\mathcal{U})}$$

The conditional probability $P(E \mid F)$ is defined as the ratio

$$P(E \mid F) = \frac{\mu(\mathcal{W}_E \cap \mathcal{W}_F)}{\mu(\mathcal{W}_F)}$$

It is easily shown that all the above axioms follow from these axioms and definitions, and that, conversely, for any probability distribution satisfying the axioms, there is a corresponding measure μ (just pick the measure to be equal to the probability). In this way, subjective probability can be formally reduced to frequencies.

3.3 Statistical Inference

The above formulas express the necessary properties of a probabilistic theory. They are, however, very weak constraints. In particular, for any body of deterministic knowledge, it is possible to assign all prior and conditional probabilities to be either 0 or 1. Moreover, the axioms above provide little calculus of evidence combination, beyond the weak rule of augmentation (13) given above. If we have n logically independent events X, A, B, C, ..., then the 2^{n-1} quantities

$$P(X), P(X \mid A), P(X \mid B), P(X \mid C), \ldots$$
$$P(X \mid A \wedge B), P(X \mid A \wedge C) \ldots P(X \mid B \wedge C) \ldots$$
$$P(X \mid A \wedge B \wedge C) \ldots$$
$$\ldots$$

can each be assigned an arbitrary value between 0 and 1, and the result will be perfectly consistent with the axioms. To remedy the situation, we have a variety of rules that can used to pick probabilities other than 0 or 1, and to relate conditional probabilities. These are all nonmonotonic rules; they are deduced from a body of information and can be overruled if more information becomes available. For example, suppose an object-level theory T_0 supports the probabilistic sentence P(E)=1/2. The extension $T_0 \cup \{E\}$ supports the sentence P(E)=1 and does not support the sentence P(E)=1/2.

3.3.1 Frequency

The most basic probabilistic heuristic is the principle of relative frequency: If there are N objects with property α, and M of these have property β, then for any term t, P($\beta(t) \mid \alpha(t)$) = M/N, unless we have some additional information about the term t. For example, given that about 51.5% of all people are women, the probability can be taken to be .515 that the next person I see will be a woman. This inference must be changed if I have more information available. For instance, if I know that I am sitting in a class in which there are 17 people other than myself, of whom 3 are women, then the probability is 3/17 = .176 that the next person I see will be a woman.

An important special case of the frequency principle is the principle of equidistribution. Let $\beta(X)$ be the property $X = s$ for some term s. Since there is only one element with this property, namely s itself, the probability P($t = s \mid \alpha(t)$) = $1/N$. Again, the inference is nonmonotonic and rests on the assumption that there is no other information relating t and s. For example, if t and s are the same term then the probability is 1. If t and s are different constants and the unique-names assumption is operative, then the probability is 0.

A much stronger form of the principle of equidistribution is the *principle of indifference:* If the n events $E_1 \ldots E_n$ form a frame of discernment, then, in the absence of other information, each should be assigned probability $1/n$. For example, if it is known that a block is either black, red, blue, or white, then, absent other information, assign probability 1/4 to each possibility. The obvious problem with this principle is that, in general, a given event may belong to many different frames of discernment, of different sizes, and the principle does not indicate which one should be chosen. For example, suppose that we carefully examine the contents of a supermarket. We are then told "Reginald bought one item at the market," and we are asked "What is the probability that he bought a potato?" What is the proper frame of discernment here? Should we assign equal probability to each individual item in the store? or to each category? or to each foot of shelf space? If individual items form the frame of discernment, does a six-pack of beer count as one or six? If categories are the frame of discernment, are Maine and Idaho potatoes two categories or one? It would seem that there is no way to choose without more information; but once more information is available, the problem is changed.

3.3.2 Independence

A key observation in probability theory is that most pairs of events have *nothing whatever* to do with one another, and that knowing one has no effect on the probability of the other. Knowing that one coin toss came up heads does not change the probabilities that another will come up heads; knowing the price of tea in China does not affect the probability that the next president will be a woman. Two such events are said to be *independent*.

Formally, events E and F are independent if $P(E \mid F) = P(E)$. By axiom 5, this is equivalent to the symmetric constraint,

$$P(E \wedge F) = P(E) \cdot P(F)$$

By formula 11, above, this implies the equation,

$$P(E \vee F) = P(E) + P(F) - P(E) \cdot P(F)$$

Thus, given a collection of independent events $E_1, E_2, \ldots, E_k$, and their prior probabilities $P(E_1) \ldots P(E_k)$, we can compute uniquely the probability of any Boolean combination of the E_i. Note that we must know, not only that the E_i are pairwise independent, but that every subset of the E_i is collectively independent; that is, for any set S of the E_i,

$$P(S) = \prod_{E \in S} P(E)$$

This condition of collective independence does not follow from the pairwise independence constraints

$$P(E_i \wedge E_j) = P(E_i) \cdot P(E_j)$$

Thus, the independence assumption is a very powerful tool when it can be applied. Moreover, it is a default assumption; two events may be assumed to be independent unless there is some reason to believe that they are connected. (We can also justify this assumption on the basis of the maximum-entropy principle; see Section 3.3.4 below.) This assumption is enormously valuable in ignoring the masses of irrelevant information always present; if we want to compute the probability that a patient has a heart condition, we are justified in ignoring his name, zodiacal sign, and the color of his eyes as independent of the event of interest. It is less frequently applicable in computing the probability of Boolean combinations, as described above. The problem is that, if the probability of the event $E \wedge F$ is worth computing, it is generally because there is some connection between E and F, and where there is a connection there is often some degree of dependence.

Suppose, for example, that you are expecting twins, and you wish to know the probability that both children will be boys. As a first guess, one might use the principle of indifference to estimate that the probability that a random child will be a boy is 1/2, and then, assuming independence, square this to get 1/4. Of course, this is wrong; fraternal twins are independent but identical twins are not. To get an accurate probability, it is necessary to know the probability that a pair of twins will be identical. If no information on the frequency of identical twins is available, one might use the principle of indifference to guess that the probability is 1/2, which would lead to a probability of 3/8 that both children are boys.

In practice, establishing independence is not simply a default inference; it can be a very difficult enterprise. For example, much of the ongoing debate about the interpretation of the differences in standardized test scores across different segments of the population rests on such questions as whether, for fixed intelligence, test scores are independent of social background; or whether, for fixed conditions of social pressures and expectations, test scores are independent of sex.

3.3.3 Independent Evidence

The independence assumption can also be used in evidence combination. Suppose that we have two events E and F, both of which are evidence for another event X. If we can assume that E and F are independent given X, and that E and F are independent given $\neg X$, then it is easy to compute $P(X \mid E \wedge F)$ from $P(X \mid E)$ and $P(X \mid F)$ as follows:

Let E and F be independent, both with respect to X and with respect to $\neg X$; thus $P(E \wedge F \mid X) = P(E \mid X)\,P(F \mid X)$ and $P(E \wedge F \mid \neg X) = P(E \mid \neg X)\,P(F \mid \neg X)$. By Bayes's formula

1.

$$P(X \mid E \wedge F) = \frac{P(E \wedge F \mid X)P(X)}{P(E \wedge F)}$$

Similarly,

2.

$$P(\neg X \mid E \wedge F) = \frac{P(E \wedge F \mid \neg X)P(\neg X)}{P(E \wedge F)}$$

Dividing formula (1) by (2) yields

3.

$$\frac{P(X \mid E \wedge F)}{P(\neg X \mid E \wedge F)} = \frac{P(E \wedge F \mid X)P(X)}{P(E \wedge F \mid \neg X)P(\neg X)}$$

Using our independence assumptions, we can rewrite this.

4.

$$\frac{P(X \mid E \wedge F)}{P(\neg X \mid E \wedge F)} = \frac{P(E \mid X)P(F \mid X)P(X)}{P(E \mid \neg X)P(F \mid \neg X)P(\neg X)}$$

Let us define the odds on A as the ratio $P(A)/P(\neg A)$. Thus, if $P(A) = 1/4$, then $P(\neg A) = 1 - P(A) = 3/4$ so $\text{Odds}(A) = (1/4)/(3/4) = 1/3$. Analogously, we define $\text{Odds}(A \mid B)$ as the ratio $P(A \mid B)/P(\neg A \mid B)$. Using Bayes's rule

5.

$$\text{Odds}(A \mid B) = \frac{P(A \mid B)}{P(\neg A \mid B)} = \frac{P(B \mid A)P(A)/P(B)}{P(B \mid \neg A)P(\neg A)/P(B)} =$$

$$\frac{P(B \mid A)}{P(B \mid \neg A)} \cdot \text{Odds}(A)$$

so

6.

$$\frac{P(B \mid A)}{P(B \mid \neg A)} = \frac{\text{Odds}(A \mid B)}{\text{Odds}(A)}$$

Let us now define the odds updating function $OU(A \mid B)$ as the ratio $\text{Odds}(A \mid B)/\text{Odds}(A)$, the change that evidence B makes in the odds of A. From (6), we have

7.

$$\frac{P(B \mid A)}{P(B \mid \neg A)} = OU(A \mid B)$$

We can therefore rewrite formula (4) as

8.

$$OU(X \mid E \wedge F) = OU(X \mid E) \cdot OU(X \mid F)$$

For example, suppose that $P(X) = 1/3$, $P(X \mid E) = 2/3$, and $P(X \mid F) = 3/4$. Then $\text{Odds}(X) = 1/2$, $\text{Odds}(X \mid E) = 2$, $\text{Odds}(X \mid F) = 3$; so $OU(X \mid E) = 4$ and $OU(X \mid F) = 6$. Therefore $OU(X \mid E \wedge F) = 24$, so $\text{Odds}(X \mid E \wedge F) = OU(X \mid E \wedge F) \cdot \text{Odds}(X) = 12$, and

$$P(X \mid E \wedge F) = \frac{\text{Odds}(X \mid E \wedge F)}{1 + \text{Odds}(X \mid E \wedge F)} = 12/13$$

(The assumption we have made above that E and F are independent with respect to both X and $\neg X$ is sometimes replaced by the assumption that E and F are independent with respect to both X and the background theory (e.g., [Charniak and McDermott 1985].) This leads to the following combination formula:

$$\frac{P(X \mid E \wedge F)}{P(X)} = \frac{P(X \mid E)}{P(X)} \cdot \frac{P(X \mid F)}{P(X)}$$

There are a number of reasons to prefer the assumption that we have made, leading to formula 8, above. First, intuitively, if E and F are both positive evidence for X, then it seems likely that they are connected, and hence unlikely that they are independent relative to the background. Second, the first formula always gives meaningful results; by contrast, the second can yield values for $P(X \mid E \wedge F)$ that are greater than 1. Third, the first formula is consistent with the maximum-entropy assumption (Exercise 12), while the second is not.

3.3.4 Maximum Entropy

(Note: This section is somewhat difficult mathematically. It may be omitted without loss of continuity.)

Both the rules above, equidistribution and independence, can be derived as special cases of a very general principle called the principle of maximum entropy. There are a number of ways to justify this principle; our approach is relatively simple, though informal.[4] We divide the principle of maximum entropy into two parts:

I. Let $S = \{E_1, E_2, \ldots, E_k\}$ be a set of events forming a frame of discernment. Suppose we know some partial constraints on their probabilities p_i. The values that we should assign to the probabilities p_i are those that give us the least information about which of the events occurs, subject to our constraints.

II. One's ignorance about which event will occur is measured by the *entropy* function $H(S) = -\sum_{i=1}^{k} p_i \, log(p_i)$. Therefore, principle (I) is carried out by picking the p_i so as to maximize the entropy function.

Principle I would seem to be inherently plausible. Since it is an informal statement of a desideratum, there is no way of arguing for it formally, though it is evidence for its reasonableness that it is consistent with equidistribution and independence. Principle II, on the other hand, though formally a definition, is not at all intuitive; its justification will require a brief excursion into information theory. We will develop the formula above in three steps:

1. Consider a process that randomly generates bits. Since there are 2^k different strings of k bits, the probability of any particular set of k bits having a particular value is $1/2^k$. For example, the probability that the first 6 bits will be 101001 is $1/2^6 = 1/64$. Thus, k bits of information have probability $1/2^k$. Inverting this, we may say that an event of probability p has information $log(1/p) = -log(p)$.

2. Let $S = \{E_1 \ldots E_k\}$ be events with probabilities $p_1 \ldots p_k$ forming a frame of discernment. Consider the measure of the information that is gained by finding out which event occurs. The expected value of this information is

$$H(S) = -\sum p_i \, log(p_i)$$

---

[4][Shore and Johnson 1980] gives a derivation of the principle of maximum entropy from a set of invariance principles.

This quantity is called the entropy of the probability distribution.

A fundamental theorem of information theory [Shannon and Weaver 1949] states that if you devise any unambiguous binary code for the events $E_1 \ldots E_k$, then the expected number of bits necessary to specify which event occurred is greater than or equal to $H(S)$; and that there exists a code where the expected number of bits is between $H(S)$ and $H(S) + 1$.

3. Now, suppose that we have a frame of discernment $S = \{E_1 \ldots E_k\}$ and two candidate probability distributions $p_1 \ldots p_k$ and $q_1 \ldots q_k$. Once we find out which event occurred, then we clearly have the same information, under either distribution. Finding out which event occurred will, on average, provide information $H_p(S) = -\sum p_i \, log(p_i)$ if we assign the first distribution, and will provide information $H_q(S) = -\sum q_i \, log(q_i)$ if we assign the second. Suppose that $H_p(S) > H_q(S)$. Since we end up with the same information once we know the event, and we gained more information under p_i than under q_i, we must have started with more information under q_i. That is, the probabilities q_i give us more information for predicting the event before knowing the outcome than the probabilities p_i do. Therefore, if we want to assume we have the least-possible information about the event before it occurs, distribution p_i will be better than q_i. To minimize the prior information, therefore, we should choose the values of p_i that maximize the sum $H_p(S) = -\sum p_i \, log(p_i)$.

The principle of maximum entropy, like the principle of indifference, requires an appropriate choice of frame of discernment for its correct application.

We will now illustrate the power of the principle by using it to derive the principles of equidistribution and of independence. We leave it as an exercise (12) to show that the maximum-entropy assumption justifies combining evidence using the independence assumptions described above.

Equidistribution: Let $E_1 \ldots E_k$ be a frame of discernment, with probabilities $p_1 \ldots p_k$ about which nothing whatever is known. The only constraint, therefore, is the universally applying constraint $\sum p_i = 1$. We want to maximize the entropy function $H(S) = -\sum p_i \, log(p_i)$ subject to this constraint. To simplify the calculations, we will use natural logs for the entropy function rather than base-2 logs; the only effect is to change the magnitude of the entropy (a quantity of no great interest) by a uniform factor of ln2. We find our maximum using the method of Lagrangian multipliers: To maximize $H_p(S)$ subject to the constraint $C(p) = \sum p_i - 1 = 0$, we construct the formula

$$f(p) = H_p(S) + \alpha C(p) = -\sum p_i \ln(p_i) + \alpha \left(\sum p_i - 1 \right)$$

and solve the simultaneous equations

$$\frac{\partial f}{\partial p_i} = 0$$

$$C(p) = 0$$

Performing the differentiations, we get

$$-1 - \ln(p_1) + \alpha = 0$$

$$-1 - \ln(p_2) + \alpha = 0$$

$$\ldots$$

$$-1 - \ln(p_k) + \alpha = 0$$

$$\sum p_i = 1$$

The first k equation implies that all the p_i are equal to $e^{\alpha - 1}$, and therefore all equal to one another: $p_1 = p_2 = \ldots = p_k$. Applying the last constraint gives us $p_1 = p_2 = \ldots = p_k = 1/k$, which is the principle of equidistribution.

Independence: The principle of maximum entropy can be used to show that, given the probability of a collection of events, and lacking any information connecting them, the minimum-information assumption is to assume that they are all independent. We will illustrate with two events; the analysis for k events is analogous, but messier. Suppose that P(A) = a and that P(B) = b. We wish to show that P($A \wedge B$) = P(A) $\cdot$ P(B) = ab.

We construct the frame of discernment $E_1 = A \wedge B$; $E_2 = A \wedge \neg B$; $E_3 = \neg A \wedge B$; $E_4 = \neg A \wedge \neg B$. Let these have probabilities $p_1 \ldots p_4$. Our constraints are as follows:

Frame of discernment: $p_1 + p_2 + p_3 + p_4 = 1$
P(A) = a: $p_1 + p_2 = a$
P(B) = b: $p_1 + p_3 = b$

We therefore construct the function

$$f(p) \;=\; -(p_1 \ln(p_1) + p_2 \ln(p_2) + p_3 \ln(p_3) + p_4 \ln(p_4)$$
$$+\alpha(p_1 + p_2 + p_3 + p_4 - 1) + \beta(p_1 + p_2 - a) + \gamma(p_1 + p_3 - b))$$

The equations to be solved are

1.

$$0 = \frac{\partial f}{\partial p_1} = -1 - \ln(p_1) + \alpha + \beta + \gamma$$

2.

$$0 = \frac{\partial f}{\partial p_2} = -1 - \ln(p_2) + \alpha + \beta$$

3.

$$0 = \frac{\partial f}{\partial p_3} = -1 - \ln(p_3) + \alpha + \gamma$$

4.

$$0 = \frac{\partial f}{\partial p_4} = -1 - \ln(p_4) + \alpha$$

5.

$$p_1 + p_2 + p_3 + p_4 = 1$$

6.

$$p_1 + p_2 = a$$

7.

$$p_1 + p_3 = b$$

Adding equation 2 to 3 and 1 to 4 gives us

$$0 = -2 - \ln(p_2) - \ln(p_3) + 2\alpha + \beta + \gamma = -2 - \ln(p_1) - \ln(p_4) + 2\alpha + \beta + \gamma$$

Canceling common terms, we get, $\ln(p_2) + \ln(p_3) = \ln(p_1) + \ln(p_4)$, or equivalently

8.

$$p_2 p_3 = p_1 p_4$$

From 7, $p_3 = b - p_1$; from 6, $p_2 = a - p_1$. Combining these with 5 gives $p_4 = 1 + p_1 - a - b$. Substituting these in 8 gives

9.

$$(a - p_1)(b - p_1) = p_1(1 + p_1 - a - b)$$

or, simplifying,

10.

$$p_1 = ab$$

which was the desired result.

3.3.5 Sampling

Frequently, it is not feasible or worthwhile to determine the actual incidence of a property in a population. In such cases, it is often possible to estimate the frequency by sampling. A sample of set S is just a subset of S. A sample T of S is *representative* of S with respect to a property α to within a given tolerance if the fraction of elements of T with property α is within tolerance of the fraction of the elements of S with property α. Thus, if you can determine the frequency of α in a representative sample T, you can use it as an estimate of the frequency of α in S as a whole.

Of course, this statement is a useless tautology unless you have some way to find a representative sample without knowing in advance the frequency of α in S. This can be done in various ways. One way is to know that T is representative of S for properties similar to α. For example, if you know that the overall popular vote for president has always been within 2 percentage points of the vote in McMurdo County, then you can treat the county as a representative sample of the country for the next election. Another technique is to divide the population into subgroups of known size along lines believed to be relevant to α, to sample these subgroups, and to weight their significance in proportion to the size of the subgroups. For example, political poll takers are careful to pick a proportional mix of sexes, ages, and income levels in their samples.

The most basic method of getting a representative sample is to take a random sample. Almost all samples of a substantial size are representative to within a small tolerance; therefore, if all different samples have equal probability of being chosen, there is a very large probability of getting a representative sample. In particular, the law of large numbers states the following. Let p be the frequency of α in S, let T be a random sample of S of size n, and let q be the frequency of α in T. Then, for any $\epsilon > 0$

$$\mathbf{P}(|\, p - q \,|> \epsilon) < \frac{p(1-p)}{n\epsilon^2}$$

Thus, by making n large enough, one can make arbitrarily certain that q lies arbitrarily close to p.

We need to reverse this inference; to find the probabilities of frequencies in the overall population given the frequency in the sample. We can do this using Bayes's rule, if we have some prior distribution on the probabilities of frequency in the population. This prior is generally taken to be a uniform distribution, in which all frequencies are equally likely.

The following can be proven: Let T be a random sample of size n, out of a population S whose size is very much greater than n. Assume a prior probability distribution in which all frequencies of property α in S are equally likely. Then, given the further fact that k elements of T have property α, the following statments hold:

1. The most probable frequency of α in S is k/n.

2. The expected frequency of α in S is $(k+1)/(n+2)$.

3. The probability that a randomly chosen element X in S is α is $(k+1)/(n+2)$.

The above theorem rests on the assumption that all samples are equally probable, or at least that the event of an element being in your sample is independent of the event of its having property α. This assumption is an instance of the principle of equidistribution or of independence, and it is therefore the default in the absence of other information. In practice, however, it requires considerable work to attain this condition. If you have access to all the elements of S, and can use a truely random procedure, such as rolling dice, to pick the ones to include in your sample, then you are on safe ground. In most commonsense cases, however, you do not have access to all elements of S; indeed, often you are obliged to be purely passive, and use as your sample those elements of S that happen within your grasp. Whether such a sampling is independent of the property under study depends both on the set S being sampled and the property being sampled for.

The students in your classes may be an adequate sample for determining the incidence of old age among students at the university, or the incidence of left-handedness among the population of the world; they are unlikely to be a valid sample for determining the frequencies of various majors among university students, or the incidence of old age in the world population, or the number of legs among members of the animal kingdom. A large body of statistical theory addresses the question of whether samples are being drawn randomly relative to a given property.

3.3.6 Domain-Specific Knowledge

In many problems, domain-specific knowledge will provide reasonable prior probability distributions, or constraints on such distributions. Examples:

1. Let X be a point in space, let $V1$ be a region in space, and let $V2$ be a subset of $V1$. Then the probability that X is in $V2$ given that X is in $V1$ may be taken to be volume($V2$)/volume($V1$).

2. If you establish some desired condition, and then leave it alone, the probability that it will still hold after time T is a decreasing function of T. A good prior distribution for this probability would be $e^{-T/\lambda}$, where λ is a characteristic time constant.

3. Consider a set of objects that are designed to be as nearly as possible a given length L — for example, nails that are supposed to be one-half inch long. The probability that the actual length of a randomly chosen object is less than $L + \Delta$ is typically given by the integral

$$\int_{-\infty}^{\Delta} e^{-x^2/\epsilon^2} dx$$

where ϵ is a constant length characteristic of the manufacturing process.

4. When someone tells you something that you had no particular reason to believe true or false, your evaluation of the probability of its truth depends largely on your estimation of the reliability of the source. This estimation combines a number of factors including:

   - Has he been correct in the past?
   - Is he likely to know the truth of the matter?
   - Does he have any reason to wish to deceive you?

- Are there reasons that he would be particularly careful in making this statement?

3.3.7   Conclusion

The axioms of probability theory are a solidly justified set of constraints for quantitative evaluations of likelihood. They are, however, rather weak constraints. To get useful results, it is necessary to have additional values or constraints on the prior or conditional probabilities of events. We have seen a number of heuristics for computing such additional information: equidistribution, frequency, independence, maximum entropy, sampling, and domain-dependent knowledge. These heuristics are more delicate and difficult than the axioms; they are nonmonotonic inferences, and the relation on world knowledge is not wholly understood. Nonetheless, when they can be correctly applied, they give us powerful and well-founded techniques for evaluating likelihoods, combining evidence, and calculating expected values. Probability theory has been successfully applied in many different aspects of AI, including expert systems, robotics, planning, and natural-language understanding.

Nonetheless, the problem of finding sufficient constraints or values for probabilistic computations is still difficult and poorly understood for many types of commonsense reasoning. (The corresponding problem for nonmonotonic logics — how nonmonotonic rules are found or justified – is even more obsure.) Let us return, for example, to our example in Section 3.2.1 of Edgar inviting Karen to a movie. Suppose that Edgar has asked Karen out three weeks in a row and been turned down all three times. Edgar is getting discouraged, and wants to compute the probability that, if he asks again this week, he will again be rejected. Let B_i be the event that Karen is actually busy when Edgar asks her on the ith week; F_i, the event that she is actually free; and A_i, the event that she rejects the invitation. Then we are interested in the probability of A_4 given A_1, A_2, and A_3.

If Karen were actually a random process, the estimates of the probabilities were firmly established, and the different invitations were independent trials, then there would be no reason to be discouraged, any more than there is reason to bet on white after a run of red on the roulette wheel. The probability of being rejected this week would be

$$P(A_4 \mid A_1 \wedge A_2 \wedge A_3) = P(A_4) =$$
$$P(A_4 \mid B_4) \cdot P(B_4) + P(A_4 \mid F_4) \cdot P(F_4) =$$

$$0.95 \cdot 0.3 + 0.25 \cdot 0.7 = 0.46$$

But these assumptions do not hold. First, there is good reason to think that the events $A_1 \ldots A_4$ are not independent, relative to fixed B_i and F_i. They are likely to be positively correlated for any of a number of reasons: Karen may be involved with someone else, or she may have some habitual Saturday night activity, or she may dislike Edgar. Second, there is reason to suspect that the action of asking may itself influence the outcome of later trials. Karen may get tired of being bugged; she may deliberately arrange to be busy Saturday night so that she won't have to lie. Contrariwise, she may be impressed by Edgar's persistence, and she may deliberately arrange to leave her Saturday night free so that she can accept his next invitation. Third, however the original prior probabilities were derived, the experiences with Karen suggest that they may be due for revision. The original priors were based on some kinds of estimates (based on sampling, heuristics, or whatever) about how often, in general, young women have booked their Saturdays by Monday; how often they will cancel a previous engagement for a date with Edgar; and how often they will invent a previous engagement in order to avoid a date with Edgar. Perhaps these estimates were wrong to start with.

Edgar must now consider all of these circumstances in trying now to evaluate his prospects for success if he calls again. Where is he to get any kind of estimate of the correlations and dependencies involved here?

Moreover, even supposing that we have found rules for assigning subjective probabilities to events, how are we to determine whether these rules are reasonable? Since each event is a unique occurrence and involves a different prior knowledge state, it is not possible to ask whether the prediction corresponds to the actual frequency. (See, however, [Gaifman 1983].) We could try matching the assigned probabilities to likelihoods as estimated by humans. However, many studies have shown that human subjects judge likelihoods in bizarre ways, which violate the most fundamental laws of probability theory. For example, Daniel Kahneman and Amos Tversky (1982) carried out an experiment in which undergraduate subjects were presented with the following personality sketch: "Linda is 31 years old, single, outspoken, and very bright. As a student she was deeply concerned with issues of discrimination and social justice and also participated in antinuclear demonstrations." The subjects were then asked which of the following statements was more likely: (A) Linda is a bank teller; or (B) Linda is a bank teller who is active in the feminist movement. 86% of the subjects judged the second statement more likely, despite the fact that this violates the basic rule that a more general state (being a bank teller) is never less likely than a more specific state (being a feminist bank teller). (Perhaps more surprisingly, 43% of the psychology graduate students who were given the same question made the same mistake.) It is hard to conceive of a coherent theory of likelihood that would justify this answer.[5] Nonetheless, people continuously carry out plausible reasoning, and they do it well enough to work their way through a very uncertain world. They must be doing something right, but these experiments suggest that it will not be easy to explain what they are doing and why it is adequate.

3.4 References

General: [Turner 1984] is a good introduction to many theories of plausible reasoning.

Nonmonotonic logic: A good starting point is [Genesereth and Nilsson 1987, chap. 6], which gives a more extensive treatment of the issues covered in this chapter. Many of the important early papers on nonmonotonic logic were published together in a special issue of *Artificial Intelligence* [Winograd 1980]. Most of these are reprinted, together with other important papers, in [Ginsberg 1987]. The closed-world assumption was first analyzed in [Reiter 1978]. Domain closure was presented in [Reiter 1980b]. Circumscription was presented in terms of an axiom schema in [McCarthy 1980]; it was re-analyzed in terms of a second order axiom in [Lifschitz 1985]. [McCarthy 1986] is a general discussion of the scope and limits of circumscription. Reiter's default logic was introduced in [Reiter 1980a]. [Etherington and Reiter 1983] studies the connection between default logic and hierarchical inheritance. The minimal model theory was presented in [Shoham 1987]. Other theories of nonmonotonic logic include the

---

[5]There are similar results that indicate that people often perform deductive inference poorly [Johnson-Laird and Wason 1970]. In my opinion, however, the importance of these results to the theory of deductive reasoning is less than the importance of Kahneman and Tversky's results to the theory of plausible reasoning for a number of reasons:

1. We have a complete formal characterization of valid deduction. We do not have a complete theory of the determination of prior and conditional probabilities. It has been often suggested that these ultimately rest on subjective evaluations; these results show that this will be difficult.

2. The negative results on deductive reasoning appear only in rather artificial settings, while the results on likelihood evaluation appear with quite natural questions, such as the experiment cited above.

3. The experiments with likelihood evaluation have the bizarre feature that the wrong answer still seems to have something right about it even after the correct answer has been explained and understood.

NML of [McDermott and Doyle 1980] and [McDermott 1982] and the autoepistemic logic of [Moore 1985b]. Also closely related are the techniques for carrying out nonmonotonic inference in actual programs, such as the "negation as failure" rule of logic programming (analyzed formally in [Lifschitz 1987b]) and various types of data-dependency maintenance [Doyle 1979].

Probability theory: The deepest and most extensive study of the applicability and implementation of probabilistic reasoning in AI systems is [Pearl 1988a]. [Kanal and Lemmer 1986] and [Lemmer and Kanal 1988] are collections of papers on the application of probability and other theories of plausible reasoning to AI. The applicability of probability to AI is a matter of heated debate; see, for example, [Cheeseman 1985], [Charniak 1983]. (This debate is closedly connected with a larger debate about the correct interpretation of probability theory and the legitimacy of subjective probability [Fine 1973].) The particular probabilistic logic described here is close to that of [Grosof, 1988]. The possible-worlds semantics for probability is discussed in [Nilsson 1986]. For the principle of maximum entropy, see [Jaynes 1979]. [Grosof 1988] is a pleasing study of the use of nonmonotonic inference in probabilistic reasoning, particular in deriving independence conditions. [Dawes 1988] discusses how probability theory ought to be used by humans in commonsensical situations, and how far humans are from actually using it.

Schemas: The *locus classicus* for reasoning using schemas is [Minsky 1975]. See also [Kuipers 1975], [Hayes 1979b], [Schank 1982], [Kolodner 1984], and [Charniak 1988].

Other: Other theories of plausible reasoning include Dempster-Shafer theory [Shafer 1976], [Hummel and Landy 1986]; the theory of endorsements [Cohen 1985]; and fuzzy logic [Zadeh 1987], which deals with vagueness as well as uncertainty. Good overviews of these theories may be found in [Turner 1984] and in [Bonissone 1987].

3.5 Exercises

(Starred problems are more difficult.)

1. Let $\mathcal{T}$ contain the following axioms:

    (a) father(joe,sam).
    (b) father(sam,agnes).
    (c) sibling$(X, Y) \Leftrightarrow \exists_Z$ father$(Z, X) \land$ father(Z, Y).
    (d) only_child$(Z) \Leftrightarrow \forall_X$ (sibling$(X, Z) \Rightarrow X = Z$).

(e) ¬father(X, X).

(f) father$(X, Y) \land$ father$(Z, Y) \Rightarrow X = Y$.

Show how the conclusion "only_child(sam)" can be inferred from T by applying domain closure.

2. Let T_2 contain only axioms (a)–(d) of T. Show how we can infer "only_child(sam)" from T_2 by applying the closed-world assumption to the predicate "father" together with the domain-closure assumption.

3. Let T_3 contain the axioms in T together with the seventh axiom

   (g) $\forall_X \exists_Y$ father(Y, X).

   What erroneous conclusion can be drawn if the domain-closure assumption is applied to T_3?

4. Explain the difference between applying the closed-world assumption to a predicate α, and circumscribing in α. Give an example where the two operations give different results.

5. * An important type of plausible inference is default inheritance of properties. A standard example is "If X is a bird, assume that X can fly." Let T contain the following axioms:

   (a) creature$(X) \land \neg ab1(X) \Rightarrow \neg can\_fly(X)$.
   (Typically creatures do not fly. The predicate ab1(X) is an abnormality predicate. Peculiar creatures can fly.)

   (b) bird$(X) \land \neg ab2(X) \Rightarrow can\_fly(X)$. (Typically, birds can_fly.)

   (c) penguin$(X) \Rightarrow \neg can\_fly(X)$. (Penguins cannot fly.)

   (d) penguin$(X) \Rightarrow$ bird$(X) \land ab2(X)$.

   (e) bird$(X) \Rightarrow$ creature$(X) \land ab1(X)$.

   (f) creature(fred).

   (g) bird(wilma).

   (h) penguin(barney).

   Show that we can infer that Wilma can fly but Fred and Barney cannot, by circumscribing over ab1 and ab2 in parallel, letting can_fly vary.

6. * Show that formula 5 in Section 3.2.2 is a consequence of formula 7, for all formulas α.

7. * Show that 2.6 in Section 3.2.2 is equivalent to formula 2.5.

8. Show that formulas 3.1 and 3.4 in Section 3.2.2 together imply the
   formula
   $$\forall_X \text{egg}(X) \Rightarrow \text{fresh}(X)$$

9. Consider the deduction theorem "If $\phi \vdash \psi$ then $\vdash \phi \Rightarrow \psi$."

   (a) Prove that this theorem holds in a theory with circumscription.
   (b) Prove that it holds in a minimal-models theory.
   (c) Prove that it does not hold in Reiter's default logic.

10. * Prove formulas 8, 9b, 10, 11, 13 in Section 3.3 from axioms 1–5.

11. In first-order logic, one can make inferences from disjunction using
    the rule of *splitting*: if $P \vdash R$ and $Q \vdash R$ then $P \lor Q \vdash R$.

    (a) Show that if the default rules "Birds can typically fly" and
        "Bats can typically fly" are written in the forms "bird(X) :
        can_fly(X) / can_fly(X)" and "bat(X) : can_fly(X) / can_fly(X)",
        then splitting fails. The conclusion "can_fly(tweety)" cannot be
        inferred from "bat(tweety) ∨ bird(tweety)", though it can be
        inferred from "bat(tweety)" and from "bird(tweety)".
    (b) Show that the problem in (a) goes away if these default rules
        are written using the axioms "bird(X) ∧ ¬ab(X) ⇒ can_fly(X)"
        and "bat(X) ∧ ¬ab(X) ⇒ can_fly(X)" and the default rule
        ":¬(ab(X)) / ¬ab(X)".
    (c) * Given that P(X | E)=a and P(X | F)=b, show that
        P(X | E ∨ F) ≥ ab / (a+b−ab).

12. * Show that the maximum-entropy assumption justifies the inde-
    pendence assumptions used for evidence combination in Section
    3.3.3. Specifically, show that given values for P(X), P(X | E), and
    P(X | F), the maximum-entropy solution satisfies the equations
    $P(E \land F \mid X) = P(E \mid X) P(F \mid X)$ and $P(E \land F \mid \neg X) = P(E \mid \neg X)$
    $P(F \mid \neg X)$.

    You may use the following outline for the proof:

    (a) Use the frame of discernment
        $E_1 = X \land A \land B.$ $E_2 = X \land A \land \neg B.$
        $E_3 = X \land \neg A \land B.$ $E_4 = X \land \neg A \land \neg B.$
        $E_5 = \neg X \land A \land B.$ $E_6 = \neg X \land A \land \neg B.$
        $E_7 = \neg X \land \neg A \land B.$ $E_8 = \neg X \land \neg A \land \neg B.$
    (b) Show that the desired independence conditions are equivalent
        to the equations $p_1 p_4 = p_2 p_3$ and $p_5 p_8 = p_6 p_7$.
    (c) Set up the constraints $P(X) = x,$ $P(\neg X) = 1 - x,$ $P(X \mid E) = e,$
        $P(X \mid F) = f,$ in terms of the p_i.

(d) Apply the method of Lagrangian multipliers to set up constraints on the value of the p_i that maximize the entropy $-\sum p_i \ln p_i$ subject to the constraints derived in part c, above. Derive the equations in part b from these constraints.

Note: This is not a complete proof, since it does not show that this solution is a maximum rather than a minimum or other point of zero derivative. Do not worry about it.

Chapter 4
Quantities and Measurements

I have figured out for you the distance between the horns of a dilemma, night and day, A and Z. I have computed how far is Up, how long it takes to get Away, and what becomes of Gone. I have discovered the length of the sea serpent, the price of the priceless, and the square of the hippopotamus. I know where you are when you are at Sixes and Sevens, how much Is you have to have to make an Are, and how many birds you can catch with the salt in the ocean — 187,796,132 if it would interest you to know.

James Thurber, *Many Moons*

Consider the following story:

John's boss kept him at the office one evening, and he got home late. He had promised his wife that he would get supper ready in time to watch "Dallas," so he decided to make hamburgers instead of beef stew. He didn't have any ground meat in the house, so he took the car to go to the butcher. The supermarket was closer, but the butcher had superior meat. On the way, he noticed that he was almost out of gas, so he stopped at a gas station. When he got to the butcher's, he saw that the price of ground beef had gone up again, which the butcher explained was due to the rising price of cattle feed. John had been getting more and more frustrated, and he yelled at the butcher for being a thieving scoundrel.

This story has no numbers or mathematics in it. Nonetheless, it is replete with *quantities* — parameters that can take greater or lesser values — and it cannot be understood without some ability to reason about quantities. The quantities in this story include spatial quantities, such as the distance to the butcher and the supermarket; temporal quantities, such as the times at which these various events occur, and the length of time needed to cook hamburgers and stew; physical quantities, such as the amount of ground beef and gasoline; psychological quantities, such as the degree of John's frustration; economic quantities, such as the price of hamburger; and quantities of other categories, such as the quality of meat. Some of these quantities are functions of other quantities; for example, the price of hamburger, the quantity of gasoline, and the distance to the butcher are all functions of time. To assert that the gas will run out before the car reaches the butcher requires comparing the behavior of these two functions.

It is fundamental to mathematics that many aspects of reasoning about quantities are independent of the particular domain involved. For that reason, we will study the representations and reasoning strategies associated with quantities as a whole before entering into their particular applications. Now, of course, mathematicians have been studying quantities for thousands of years, and numerical analysts have been studying computations with quantities for hundreds of years, so we in AI are hardly exploring new ground here. Much of our work has been done for us. Ontological issues have been largely settled for us by the work on foundations of mathematics, which has given solid answers to such questions as "What is a number?," "What is a function?," and "What is an infinite/infinitesimal quantity?" As regards representations, we have an embarrassment of riches in the wealth of mathematical symbols and theories that are available. The problem for the AI researcher is largely to determine which mathematical concepts and techniques are appropriate for his particular application. The common characteristic in AI reasoning about quantities is the focus on rapidly deriving partial, qualitative conclusions from partial input information, rather than deriving very detailed and precise information using lengthy calculations.

In this chapter, therefore, rather than systematically review the foundations of arithmetic, we will consider a series of examples of commonsense quantitative inferences, and examine the representations and inferences used in each.

Table 4.1 Axioms of Ordering

ORD.1. $X < Y \Rightarrow \neg(Y < X)$ (Anti-symmetry)
ORD.2. $X < Y \wedge Y < Z \Rightarrow X < Z$ (Transitivity)
ORD.3. $X < Y \vee Y < X \vee X = Y$ (Totality)

4.1 Order

Examples:

> Brown is a better teacher than Crawford. Crawford is a better teacher than Gay. Infer that Brown is a better teacher than Gay.

> Any French wine is classier than any Rhode Island wine. Infer that Rhode Island Red '83 is not classier than Chateau Lafitte '23.

The most fundamental quantitative relation is the order relation "$X < Y$." (Note that, in mathematical parlance, an "inequality" is always an order relation on terms, though there are, of course, many other possible relations besides equality and ordering.) In domains where assigning exact values is not very meaningful, such as quality of teaching or classiness of wines, order relations are often the only useful quantitative relations.

Table 4.1 shows the axioms of ordering. A partial ordering obeys axioms ORD.1 and ORD.2; a total ordering obeys axiom ORD.3 as well.

A logical sort of entity that is partially or totally ordered is called a *measure space*.[1] For example, "lengths," "masses," or "dates" are measure spaces. It makes sense to ask which of two dates is later, but it makes no sense to ask whether a date is greater than a length. Thus, the relation "$X < Y$", like most of the quantitative relations we will introduce in this chapter, is polymorphically sorted. "$X < Y$" is meaningful just if X and Y are elements of the same measure space.

A collection of atomic ground inequalities can be implemented as a DAG (directed acyclic graph) whose nodes are the ground terms and

---

[1]The term was introduced with this meaning in [Hayes 1978]. This usage differs from the meaning of "measure space" in mathematical analysis.

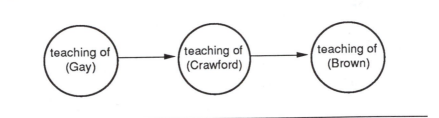

Figure 4.1 Inequalities as a DAG.

whose arcs correspond to inequalities. In our first example above, the nodes would be labeled "teaching_of(brown)", "teaching_of(crawford)", and "teaching_of(gay)", with arcs from Crawford to Brown and from Gay to Crawford (see Figure 4.1). The inequality "$X < Y$" is a consequence of the input if there is an arc from X to Y in the transitive closure of the DAG. This can be determined in time $O(n^2)$ in the worst case, using Dijkstra's algorithm.

4.2 Intervals

Example:

> The first Crusade occurred during the Middle Ages. The Middle Ages predated the Enlightenment. Infer that the first Crusade predated the Enlightenment.

Many natural entities in commonsense reasoning corrsespond to intervals of a measure space, rather than single points. In the above example, the times of the first Crusade, of the Middle Ages, and of the Enlightenment are intervals of time. In reasoning about the temperature measure space, it might be natural to pick out the range of comfortable temperatures, the range of temperature in which water is liquid, and so on.

There are 13 possible order relations between pairs of intervals [Allen 1983]: Interval I is *before* interval J; I *meets* J; I *overlaps* J; I *starts* J; I *finishes* J; I occurs *during* J; I is *equal* to J; and the inverses of these (Figure 4.2). (The names of these relations were picked for a temporal measure space; however, the same basic relations apply to intervals in any measure space.) These relations can be combined according to rules of transitivity. For instance, the inference in the above example can be justified by the rule "If I occurs *during*

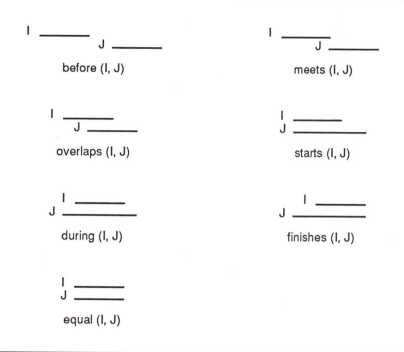

Figure 4.2 Interval relations

J and J precedes K, then I precedes K." (See Exercise 2 for a discussion of the remaining rules.) It is possible to take as primitive just the relation "meet(I, J)" and define all the other relations in terms of it (see Table 4.2).

For many purposes, it is useful to combine "equals", "starts", "during", and "finishes" into a single relation "I is *contained in* J." It is also useful to introduce two partial functions on intervals: The *overlap* of I and J, written "overlap_of(I, J)" is the maximal interval that is contained in both I and J; it is defined only if I overlaps J, I is part of J, or vice versa. The *join* of I and J, written "join(I, J)" is the minimal interval containing I and J; it is defined for all I and J unless I is before or after J.

In some domains, it is reasonable to use both points and intervals. For example, we might want to say that the death of Charlemagne (a point in time) occurred in the Middle Ages, or that the boiling point of alcohol is in the range of temperatures where water is liquid. One method to represent such statements is to treat a point just as an

The heavy line shows the internal I.

Figure 4.3 Interval in a Partial Ordering

interval that does not properly contain any other interval. Another approach, which we will follow here, is to view an interval I just as the set of points that fall in I. Specifically, consider a totally ordered measure space $\mathcal{M}$. An interval I in $\mathcal{M}$ is any set of points in $\mathcal{M}$ such that if $X \in I$, $Y \in I$, and $X < Z < Y$, then $Z \in I$. In this view, the relation of a point falling inside an interval is just set membership. Table 4.2 shows how the other relations between intervals can be expressed in terms of points.

The definition of an interval over partial ordered measure spaces is trickier, but will be important in constructing branching models of time. Here, an interval is defined as a subset I of the measure space such that (i) I is totally ordered and (ii) no point Z between two points of I can be added to I without destroying the total ordering (Figure 4.3). The formulas below give a formal definition, using the predicate "ordered(X, Y)", meaning that X and Y are ordered in their measure space.

$$\text{ordered}(X, Y) \Leftrightarrow [\ X < Y \ \vee \ Y < X \ \vee \ X = Y\ ].$$

$$\text{interval}(I) \Leftrightarrow$$
$$[\ [\ \forall_{X, Y \in I}\ \text{ordered}(X, Y)\ ] \wedge$$
$$[\ \forall_{Z \notin I}\ \forall_{X, Y \in I}\ X < Z < Y \Rightarrow \exists_{P \in I}\ \neg\text{ordered}(Z, P)\ ]].$$

Another fundamental relation between points and intervals is that a point can be the starting point or ending point of an interval. We use the function symbols "start(I)" and "end(I)" to represent the mappings from an interval to its starting and ending points. These can be defined as follows: We define X to be a *lower bound* of interval I if X

is less than or equal to every element of I, and to be an *upper bound* of I if X is greater than or equal to every element of I. Then the start of I is the greatest lower bound for I, if this exists, and the end of I is the least upper bound, if that exists.

lower_bound$(X, I) \Leftrightarrow \forall_{Y \in I} Y \geq X$.

upper_bound$(X, I) \Leftrightarrow \forall_{Y \in I} Y \leq X$.

$X = \text{start}(I) \Leftrightarrow$
lower_bound$(X, I) \wedge \forall_Y$ lower_bound$(Y, I) \Rightarrow Y \leq X$.

$X = \text{end}(I) \Leftrightarrow$
upper_bound$(X, I) \wedge \forall_Y$ upper_bound$(Y, I) \Rightarrow Y \geq X$.

We can now distinguish four possible behaviors of an interval at each of its ends:

- Interval I is *closed* below if start(I) exists and is an element of I. I is closed above if end(I) exists and is an element of I. We use the standard notation $[X, Y]$ to represent the closed interval from X to Y.

  In many applications, it is possible to restrict attention only to closed intervals. In a discrete measure space, all intervals are closed. In any measure space, closed intervals have the property that the overlap or join of two closed intervals is a closed interval. However, in order to perform complementation or set difference in a dense measure space, then it is necessary to go beyond closed intervals. For example, if the bathroom light is turned on during a time interval that is closed above, then it must be off during a time interval that is open below. Moreover, in order to make the standard interval calculus work on a dense interval space containing only closed intervals, it is necessary to disallow closed intervals consisting of a single point, and to define the relation between interval relations and the points they contain in a somewhat different way. See Table 4.2.

- Interval I is *unbounded* below if it has no lower bound; it is unbounded above if it has no upper bound. A theory or algorithm that works correctly for closed intervals can, in many cases, be adapted to work for unbounded intervals by adding the mythic elements ∞ and $-\infty$ as the largest and smallest elements of the measure space, and treating an unbounded interval as a closed interval including these infinite elements. We use the predicates "infinite_on_right(I)" and "infinite_on_left(I)" to characterize intervals that are unbounded above (below).

- Interval I is *open* (but neither closed or unbounded) below if start(I) exists but is not an element of I; it is open above if end(I) exists but is not an element of I. The notation (X, Y) is standardly used for the open interval from X to Y. In a complete measure space, such as the real numbers, all intervals are either closed, open, or unbounded in each direction.

- Interval I is *gapped* below (above) if it has a lower (upper) bound, but no greatest lower bound (no least upper bound). Such intervals can exists in incomplete spaces. For example, the set of rational numbers whose square is less than 2 is gapped above, as is also the set of infinitesimals in a model of the reals with infinitesimals (see Section 4.10). Such intervals do not have an endpoint, and therefore cannot be denoted in terms of their endpoints; special purpose representations must be used. (Topologically, such intervals are both closed and open.)

A significant attraction of using just a pure language of intervals and avoiding references to points is precisely to avoid the hair-splitting issues involved in working out the behavior of the interval at its endpoints. Even where the structure of the measure space guarantees the existence of an endpoint, the concept definition may be vague enough to make the endpoints very questionable entities. For example, if the time line or the temperature scale is taken to have the structure of the real line, then, provably, every bounded interval has an endpoint. Nonetheless, concepts like "the ending instant of the Middle Ages" or "the lower endpoint of the range of comfortable temperatures" are rather dubious, and one would rather avoid formulating inferences in terms of them.

Table 4.2 illustrates the seven possible types of order relations between two intervals. Each entry has the following five parts:

a. The name of a relation $R(I, J)$.

b. The definition of R in terms of "meet" (from [Allen and Hayes 1986]).

c. A definition of R in terms of the quantities in I and J, valid for the space of all intervals over a measure space.

d. A definition of R in terms of the quantities in I and J, valid for the space of closed intervals with more than one point.

e. A definition of R in terms of the endpoints of I and J, valid for the space of intervals that have endpoints.

Table 4.2 Relations Among Intervals

a. before(I, J).
b. $\exists_K$ meets$(I, K) \wedge$ meets(K, J).
c. $\exists_X \forall_{W \in I, Z \in J} W < X < Z$.
d. $\forall_{X \in I, Y \in J} X < Y$.
e. end$(I) <$ start(J).

a. meets(I, J).
b. meets(I, J).
c. $[\forall_{X \in I, Y \in J} X < Y] \wedge \neg \exists_X \forall_{W \in I, Z \in J} W < X < Z$.
d. $[\forall_{X \in I, Y \in J} X \leq Y] \wedge [\exists_X X \in I \wedge X \in J]$.
e. end$(I) =$ start(J).

a. overlaps(I, J)
b. $\exists_{A,B,C,D,E}$ meet$(A, I) \wedge$ meet$(I, D) \wedge$ meet$(D, E) \wedge$
    meet$(A, B) \wedge$ meet$(B, J) \wedge$ meet(J, E).
c. $[\exists_{X \in I} \forall_{Y \in J} X < Y] \wedge [\exists_{Y \in J} \forall_{X \in I} X < Y] \wedge \exists_X X \in I \cap J$.
d. $[\exists_{X \in I} \forall_{Y \in J} X < Y] \wedge [\exists_{Y \in J} \forall_{X \in I} X < Y] \wedge \exists_{X \in I, Y \in J} Y < X$.
e. start$(I) <$ start$(J) <$ end$(I) <$ end(J).

a. starts(I, J).
b. $\exists_{A,B,C}$ meets$(A, I) \wedge$ meets$(I, B) \wedge$ meets$(B, C) \wedge$
    meets$(A, J) \wedge$ meets(J, C).
c. $I \subseteq J \wedge I \neq J \wedge \forall_{Y \in J} \exists_{X \in I} X \leq Y$.
d. $I \subseteq J \wedge I \neq J \wedge \forall_{Y \in J} \exists_{X \in I} X \leq Y$.
e. start$(I) =$ start$(J) \wedge$ end$(I) <$ end(J).

a. equals(I, J).
b. $\exists_{A,B}$ meets$(A, I) \wedge$ meet$(I, B) \wedge$ meet$(A, J) \wedge$ meet(J, B).
c. $I = J$.
d. $I = J$.
e. start$(I) =$ start$(J) \wedge$ end$(I) =$ end(J).

a. during(I, J).
b. $\exists_{A,B,C,D}$ meet$(A, B) \wedge$ meet$(B, I) \wedge$ meet$(I, C) \wedge$
    meet$(C, D) \wedge$ meet$(A, J) \wedge$ meet(J, D).
c. $\exists_{P,Z \in J} \forall_{X \in I} P < X < Z$.
d. $\exists_{P,Z \in J} \forall_{X \in I} P < X < Z$.
e. start$(J) <$ start$(I) <$ end$(I) <$ end(J).

a. finishes(I, J).
b. $\exists_{A,B,C}$ meets$(A, B) \wedge$ meets$(B, I) \wedge$ meets$(I, C) \wedge$
    meets $(A, J) \wedge$ meets(J, C).
c. $I \subseteq J \wedge I \neq J \wedge \forall_{Y \in J} \exists_{X \in I} X \geq Y$.
d. $I \subseteq J \wedge I \neq J \wedge \forall_{Y \in J} \exists_{X \in I} X \geq Y$.
e. start$(J) <$ start$(I) \wedge$ end$(I) =$ end(J).

Definitions c and d give different interpretations of the relations. For example, if I and J are closed intervals and the upper bound of I is equal to the lower bound of J, then I and J overlap according to definition c and meet according to definition d. However, both definitions give the same transitivity rules; for example, it is true in both that, if I meets J and J meets K then I is before K. Definition e is equivalent to d where I and J are closed, but definition e applies to open intervals as well.

4.3   Addition and Subtraction

Examples:

> On Tuesday night, *Gone with the Wind* and *Duck Soup* are both showing on TV. *Gone with the Wind* starts later than *Duck Soup* and takes longer. Infer that *Gone with the Wind* will end later than *Duck Soup*.
>
> Sophy removes a small quantity of flour from a flour bin, and then pours a much larger quantity into the bin. Infer that there is more flour in the bin at the end than at the beginning.

The basic concept in these two examples is that of the *difference* between two quantities, such as the difference between the ending and starting times of a movie, or the difference between two quantities of flour. If X and Y are elements of a measure space $\mathcal{M}$, then the difference between them, $Y - X$, is an element of a measure space $\mathcal{D}$, called the *difference space* of $\mathcal{M}$. The ordering on $\mathcal{M}$ defines a weak partial ordering on the elements of $\mathcal{D}$, as specified by the rule below.

$$X > Y \Rightarrow [X - Z > Y - Z] \wedge [Z - X < Z - Y].$$

For example, if Pooh is more cheerful than Kanga and Kanga is more cheerful than Eeyore, then the difference between Pooh's cheer and Eeyore's is greater than the difference between Pooh's cheer and Kanga's.

Two particularly important classes of measure space are *differential* and *integral* spaces.[2] A measure space $\mathcal{D}$ is a differential space if (a) $\mathcal{D}$ is totally ordered; (b) the difference space of $\mathcal{D}$ is $\mathcal{D}$ itself; and (c) $\mathcal{D}$ satisfies the regularity axioms of Table 4.3. A measure space $\mathcal{M}$ is an integral space if its difference space $\mathcal{D}$ is a differential space but is not equal to $\mathcal{M}$. For example, the space of masses, or of lengths of times, or of quantities of volume, are all differential spaces; the

---

[2]These terms were introduced with these meanings in [McDermott 1980]

Table 4.3 Axioms for Differential Space

DIFF.1. $[X + P = Y] \Leftrightarrow [Y - P = X] \Leftrightarrow [Y - X = P]$. (Definition of addition.)

DIFF.2. $X + (-P) = X - P$. (Definition of unary negation.)

DIFF.3. $X + 0_{\mathcal{D}} = X$. (Identity element.)

DIFF.4. $X + P = P + X$. (Commutativity.)

DIFF.5. $X + (P + Q) = (X + P) + Q$. (Associativity.)

DIFF.6. $X > Y \Leftrightarrow X - Y > 0_{\mathcal{D}}$. (Order preservation.)

---

difference between two masses is a mass, the difference between two time lengths is a time length, the difference between two volumes is a volume. By contrast, the space of clock times is an integral space; the difference between two clock times is a length of time, which is not a clock time.

Let $\mathcal{M}$ be an integral or differential measure space and let $\mathcal{D}$ be the difference space of $\mathcal{M}$. (Note that if $\mathcal{M}$ is differential, then $\mathcal{D} = \mathcal{M}$.) Let X, Y range over elements of $\mathcal{M}$ and let P, Q range over elements of $\mathcal{D}$. Let $0_{\mathcal{D}}$ be the zero point of $\mathcal{D}$. (Each different space has its own zero; usually, we will omit the subscript that distinguishes between them.) Then the axioms of Table 4.3 are satisfied.

We can now formalize our sample inferences. The givens in the first inference can be stated in the following form: Let "igone" and "iduck" be the time intervals in which *Gone with the Wind* and *Duck Soup* are shown. (In Chapter 5, we will introduce more general representations for these and for the constraints used in the second example.) The given constraints are then

> start(iduck) < start(igone)
> end(iduck) − start(iduck) < end(igone) − start(igone)

The conclusion, "end(iduck) < end(igone)", then follows directly from the givens and axioms DIFF.1–DIFF.6. The second example, of the flour bin, is similar.

4.4   Real Valued Scales

Example:

> Sophy has 8-1/2 pounds of flour in a flour bin. She removes 1/4
> pound, and adds 1-3/4 pounds. Infer that Sophy now has 10
> pounds of flour in the bin.

In this example, we use numerical values (8-1/2, 1-3/4, 1/4, 10) together with the unit "pound" to denote different quantities of mass.
The legitimacy of doing this, and of basic calculations in a quantity
space on calculations over the reals, is established in the following
theorem:

THEOREM 4.1 *Let $\mathcal{D}$ be any differential space satisfying the axioms
DIFF.1 — DIFF.6 and also possessing the Archimedean property:*

*(Archimedes) For any $X, Y > 0$ there is an integer N such that $Y <
X + X + \ldots X$ (N times).*

Let U (a unit *quantity) be any positive element of $\mathcal{D}$. Then there is
a function $scale_U(X)$, mapping $\mathcal{D}$ into the real line, with the following
properties:*

1. $scale_U(U) = 1$.

2. $scale_U(X + Y) = scale_U(X) + scale_U(Y)$.

3. $X < Y \Leftrightarrow scale_U(X) < scale_U(Y)$.

Thus, by fixing a standard unit, such as a pound, we can associate
each element of $\mathcal{D}$ with a real number, and we can perform computations on elements of $\mathcal{D}$ by performing the same computations on the
corresponding real numbers. (Note that the scale function may map
$\mathcal{D}$ to some subset of the reals, such as the integers or the rationals.
In that case, it may be possible to use a theory that is either computationally or ontologically simpler than real arithmetic.)

Similarly, given an integral space $\mathcal{M}$ whose difference space has
the Archimedean property, it is possible to choose an arbitrary origin
$O \in \mathcal{M}$ and an arbitrary unit $U \in \mathcal{D}$, and then define a scale in $\mathcal{M}$
where O corresponds to 0 and where U corresponds to a difference of 1.
For example, the Centigrade scale associates temperatures with real
numbers by choosing the origin to be the freezing point of water, and
the unit to one one-hundredth of the difference between the boiling
point and the freezing point of water.

Table 4.4 Axioms of Multiplication

MULT.1. $X \cdot Y = Y \cdot X$.

MULT.2. $X \cdot (Y \cdot Z) = (X \cdot Y) \cdot Z$.

MULT.3. $0 \cdot X = 0$.

MULT.4. $1 \cdot X = X$.

MULT.5. $X > 0 \wedge Y > 0 \Rightarrow X \cdot Y > 0$.

MULT.6. $X \cdot (Y + Z) = X \cdot Y + X \cdot Z$.

4.5   More Arithmetic

Examples:

Four quarts of water weigh twice as much as two quarts.

If dinner at Chez Pierre costs more than $50 per person, and there are at least 20 people in our dinner party, infer that the total bill will be more than $1000.

The reasoning in these two examples requires introducing some further arithmetic relations. The first example involves the relation of multiplication. The multiplication function $X \cdot Y$ takes as arguments two quantities from any two differential quantity spaces, M and N, and returns a quantity from the product space of M and N. If M is the space of dimensionless quantities (pure numbers) then the product space of M and N is just N. Table 4.4 shows the well-known axioms of multiplication.

In axiom MULT.3, the "0" on the left side is the zero point of an arbitrary differential space $\mathcal{M}$; the "0" on the right is the zero point in the product space of $\mathcal{M}$ with the space of X. In axiom MULT.4, "1" is a dimensionless quantity.

We can now state the general rule that the weight of a quantity of pure stuff is equal to its volume times the density of the stuff (under standard conditions).

$\text{pure}(Q, S) \Rightarrow \text{weight}(Q) = \text{volume}(Q) \cdot \text{density}(S)$.

Given this physical rule and the above axioms, we can make our desired inference.

[pure($Q1$,water) $\wedge$ pure($Q2$,water) $\wedge$
volume($Q1$) = 4·quart $\wedge$ volume($Q2$) = 2·quart] $\Rightarrow$
weight($Q1$) = 2· weight($Q2$).

The second example requires reasoning about the arithmetic properties of an underspecified set. To represent this reasoning, we introduce two arithmetic functions over sets. The function "card(S)" or "$| \, S \, |$" gives the cardinality of a finite set S, which is a dimensionless integer. The function "sum_over(S, F)," usually written in the form

$$\sum_{X \in S} F(X)$$

gives the sum of function F over the set S. F must be a function mapping S into a differential space D. Axioms SSUM.1 — SSUM.3 define these functions:

SSUM.1. sum_over($\{X\}, F$) = $F(X)$.

SSUM.2. $A \cap B = \emptyset \Rightarrow$
sum_over($A \cup B, F$) = sum_over(A, F) + sum_over(B, F).

SSUM.3. card(S) = sum_over($S, \lambda(X)(1)$).

(Note: These axioms involve a second-order logic, which allows quantifying over functions.)

From these axioms, we can deduce the basic result needed for our example: if $F(X) > C$ for each $X \in S$, then $\sum_{X \in S} F$ is greater than C times the cardinality of S.[3]

[$\forall_{X \in S}$ value_of(F, X) > C] $\Rightarrow$ sum_over(S, F) > C·card(S).

Further arithmetic operators used in spatial reasoning, such as trigonometric functions, will be introduced in Chapter 6.

---

[3]This proof requires a proof by induction over the cardinality of S, since it applies only to finite sets.

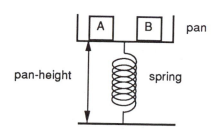

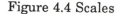

Figure 4.4 Scales

4.6 Parameters; Signs; Monotonic Relations

Example:

Consider the scales shown in Figure 4.4. Suppose that the following constraints are specified:

- The downward force exerted by each block on the pan is the mass of the block times the gravitational constant.
- The force exerted by the spring upward on the pan is proportional to the stiffness of the spring times its compression from its rest length.
- When the scales are at rest, the upward force exerted on the pan by the spring must exactly balance the sum of the downward forces exerted on the pan by the blocks.
- The height of the pan is equal to the rest length of the spring minus its compression.

Suppose that block A is made more massive, but the scales otherwise remain the same. Infer that the rest position of the pan is lowered, using the following line of reasoning: Since the mass of A has increased, the force exerted by A must have increased. Since the mass of B remained the same, the force exerted by B must have remained the same. Therefore, the sum of the forces exerted by the two blocks must have increased. Therefore, the upward force exerted by the spring must have increased. Since the stiffness of the spring has not changed, the compression of the spring must have increased to create this new force. Since the compression of the spring has increased and its rest length has remained the same, the pan must be lower.

The form of the inference above is a common one in physical reasoning. We are comparing situations involving two systems with the same structure but with different values in the input parameters. We specify the direction of the change between the two situations but not its magnitude. The problem is to determine, if possible, the direction of change in the output parameters. Note that we are here only interested in the change in the equilibrium state, when the systems have come to rest; we are not asking how the system goes from one state to the other. (The dynamic behavior of this system will be discussed in Section 4.9. The problem of deriving the above relations from a physical description of the system will be discussed in Section 7.1.)

The above inference can be expressed and carried out without using any concepts or axioms beyond those already discussed in previous sections. However, since this type of inference is particularly common in commonsense reasoning about quantities, it is worthwhile to develop a specialized notation and calculation method for dealing with it. In particular, we would like our formal inference method to resemble the above informal argument in focusing on the increase or decrease in specific quantities from one situation to the next, and to be able to calculate the direction of change in one quantity from the direction of change in related quantities.

To do this, we need to be able to refer to entities such as "the mass of block A," which may correspond to a particular quantity in each different situation. We therefore introduce the ontological sort of a *parameter*. If $\mathcal{M}$ is a measure space, then an $\mathcal{M}$-valued parameter is an entity that associates each situation with a quantity from $\mathcal{M}$; extensionally, the parameter may be viewed as a function from situations to $\mathcal{M}$. (In Chapter 5, we will generalize the concept of a parameter to that of a general fluent.)

We now introduce a number of functions on parameters. The most basic is the function "value_in(S, Q)," introduced in Section 2.6, which maps a situation S and parameter Q to the value that Q takes in S. The function delta$(Q, S1, S2)$ gives the change in Q from $S1$ to $S2$; it is defined by axiom DEL.1 as the difference between Q's values in the two situations. We also introduce arithmetic operations such as addition, subtraction, multiplication, and so on as operators on parameters. These are defined by axiom schema DEL.2: the value of the combination of parameters is equal to the combination of their values.

DEL.1. delta$(Q, S1, S2) = $ value_in$(S2, Q) - $ value_in$(S1, Q)$.

DEL.2. value_in$(S, \alpha(Q1, Q2)) = \alpha($value_in$(S, Q1)$, value_in$(S, Q2))$
where α is any arithmetic operator.

We can now express statements like "A increases in mass" in the form "delta(mass(blocka),s1,s2) > 0." We can now simplify this form still further. We introduce the function symbol "sign(X)," also written "[X]", which maps a quantity X onto its sign. We also introduce three constants: "pos", the interval of positive quantities; "neg", the interval of negative quantities; and "ind", the set of all quantities. (As with the constant 0, we will use the same symbol to represent these intervals in all differential spaces.) Thus, if $X = 0$ then sign(X)=[X] = 0; if $X > 0$ then [X] =pos; if $X < 0$ then [X] =neg. We can then write the above statement in the form "sign(delta(mass(blocka),s1,s2)) = pos". The sign function can be applied to a parameter in the same way as other arithmetic functions; that is, if Q is a parameter, then [Q] is the parameter whose value is always the sign of the value of Q.

A further notational convenience,[4] used in circumstances where we are comparing two fixed situations s1 and s2, is to abbreviate "sign(delta(Q,s1,s2))" in the form ΔQ. Thus, we can express the statement "A increases in mass" in the form Δmass(blockA) = pos. Table 4.5 shows the complete specification for our example problem.

To carry out inferences from the specifications given in Table 4.5, we need rules that will allow us to start with a parameter equation, such as "weight(blocka) = grav_acc · mass(blocka)," combine this with the values "Δmass(blocka) = pos," "Δgrav_acc = 0," and "[grav_acc] = pos," and to conclude "Δweight(blocka) = 0." These rules can be expressed elegantly by splitting them into two parts.

The first part of these inference rules defines the arithmetic operations on the signs pos, 0, and neg, together with the interval ind (indeterminate), which is the interval of all quantities, positive, negative, and zero. The arithmetic combination of two signs is all the possible signs of the combination of values in the signs. For example, pos + pos is pos, because the sum of any two positive quantities is positive; pos + neg is ind, because the sum of a positive quantity and a negative quantity may be positive, zero, or negative, depending on the relative magnitudes of the two quantities. Table 4.6 shows the arithmetic relations on signs.

Two signs $SG1$ and $SG2$ are *compatible*, written "$SG1 \sim SG2$" if there is some quantity in both.[5] Specifically, any sign is compatible with itself, and any sign is compatible with the sign ind. Note that compatibility is not a transitive relation; ind is compatible with both pos and neg, but pos is not compatible with neg. Any equation on

---

[4]In the literature, the notation ∂Q is often used for sign(delta(Q,s1,s2)). We will reserve this, however, to mean the sign of the derivative (see Section 4.7).

[5]In the literature, this is usually written "$SG1 = SG2$"; however, this notation is confusing.

Table 4.5 Problem Specification for Scales

Constants:
blocka, blockb — Two blocks.
s1, s2 — Two situations.

Parameter:
mass(X) — The mass of block X.
weight(X) — Downward force exerted by block X.
blocks_weight — Total downward force exerted by blocks.
spring — Stiffness of the spring.
compression — Compression of the spring.
rest_length — Rest length of the spring.
spring_force — Upward force exerted by spring.
pan_height — Height of pan.
grav_acc — Gravitational accelleration.

Constraints:
weight(X) = grav_acc · mass(X).
blocks_weight = weight(blocka) + weight(blockb).
spring_force = spring · compression.
spring_force = blocks_weight.
pan_height = rest_length − compression.

Parameter values:
[spring] = pos.
[grav_acc] = pos.

Given comparisons:.
Δmass(blocka) = pos.
Δmass(blockb) = 0.
Δspring = 0.
Δrest_length = 0.
Δgrav_acc = 0.

---

quantities can be converted into a corresponding compatibility relation on the signs of the quantities. For example, from the equation $X+Y = P \cdot Q$, it is legitimate to derive the compatibility relation $[X] + [Y] \sim [P] \cdot [Q]$. (See Exercise 4). The converse is not the case; the truth of a compatibility relation does not imply the truth of the corresponding equation.

Table 4.6 Arithmetic of Signs

+	neg	0	pos	ind
neg	neg	neg	ind	ind
0	neg	0	pos	ind
pos	ind	pos	pos	ind
ind	ind	ind	ind	ind

×	neg	0	pos	ind
neg	pos	0	neg	ind
0	0	0	0	0
pos	neg	0	pos	ind
ind	ind	0	ind	ind

−	neg	0	pos	ind
	pos	0	neg	ind

$1/X$	neg	0	pos	ind
	neg	***	pos	ind

The second part of the inference rules defines the relations among the signs of parameters and the signs of their changes using the arithmetic on signs. Table 4.7 shows these rules. Combining these rules, it is straightforward to derive the desired result from the givens of our example of the scales. Table 4.8 shows the inference path.

The inference in our example that the pan will go down if the weight of A is increased does not, in fact, depend on the spring obeying the linear law, "spring_force = spring · compression." For the purposes of this inference, it would be sufficient to know that, for any fixed (positive) value of the spring constant, the force is a strictly increasing function of the compression. The inference in Table 4.8 would go through exactly as before.

To express this formally, we introduce the predicate "monotonic(QD, QI, QF, SN)," meaning that, for any fixed value of the parameter QF, the dependent parameter QD depends monotonically on the independent parameter QI with sign SN. That is, if SN=pos, then QD is monotonically increasing in QI; if SN=neg, then QD is monotonically

Table 4.7 Differences of Arithmetic Functions

SGN.1. $\Delta(P + Q) \sim \Delta P + \Delta Q$

SGN.2. $\Delta(-P) = -\Delta P$

SGN.3a. $\Delta(P \cdot Q) \sim$
         value_in$(S1, [P]) \cdot \Delta Q$ + value_in$(S1, [Q]) \cdot \Delta P$ +
         $\Delta P \cdot \Delta Q$

SGN.3b. If either $[P]$ or $[Q]$ is constant over all situations, then
         $\Delta(P \cdot Q) \sim$
         value_in$(S1, [P]) \cdot \Delta Q$ +
         value_in$(S1, [Q]) \cdot \Delta P$.

decreasing in QI. QD must depend functionally on QI and QF. (It is easy to extend the definition of this predicate to describe parameters that depend on more than two parameters.) We can now replace the constraint "spring_force = spring · compression" in the scales example with the weaker constraint "monotonic(spring_force, compression, spring, pos)," and still derive the same inference as before. Table 4.9 shows the formal definition and some basic properties of monotonic dependence.

Axiom MON.1 is the definition of monotonic dependence. Rules MON.2–MON.5 are straightforward consequences of the definition that are useful for calculations.

4.7 Derivatives

Example:

> Water is pouring slowly into a tank at the top and draining out rapidly at the bottom. The height of water in a tank is an increasing function of the volume. Infer that both the volume and the height of the water in the tank is steadily decreasing.

This inference, like those in the previous section, centers around the concept of parameters such as the volume and height of water. However, it uses this concept in a rather different way. Rather than view a parameter as a function from separate situations representing different hypothetical states of the world, we must now view a parameter as a function from situations from a continuous time line to a quantity space. With this view, we can introduce the concept of

Table 4.8 Applying the Sign Calculus

We can carry out our inference as follows:

From the givens: [grav_acc] = pos; Δgrav_acc = 0;
$\quad\quad$ Δmass(blocka) = pos;
$\quad\quad$ and the rule: weight(X) = grav_acc · mass(X)
Infer: Δweight(blocka) = pos.

From the givens: [grav_acc] = pos; Δgrav_acc = 0;
$\quad\quad$ Δmass(blockb) = 0;
$\quad\quad$ and the rule: weight(X) = grav_acc · mass(X)
Infer: Δweight(blockb) = 0.

From the calculated values: Δweight(blocka) = pos;
$\quad\quad$ Δweight(blockb) = 0;
$\quad\quad$ and the rule: blocks_weight = weight(blocka) +
$\quad\quad$ weight(blockb)
Infer: Δblocks_weight = pos.

From the calculated value: Δblocks_weight = pos;
$\quad\quad$ and the rule: spring_force = blocks_weight
Infer: Δspring_force = pos.

From the calculated value: Δspring_force = pos;
$\quad\quad$ and the givens: [spring]=pos; Δspring=0.
$\quad\quad$ and the rule: spring_force = spring · compression
Infer: Δcompression = pos.

From the calculated value: Δcompression = pos;
$\quad\quad$ and the given: Δrest_length =0;
$\quad\quad$ and the rule: pan_height = rest_length − compression
Infer: Δpan_height = neg

---

the *derivative* of a parameter. The function "deriv(P)," which we will often abbreviate as $\dot{P}$, maps a parameter over a measure space $\mathcal{M}$ to a parameter over the difference space of $\mathcal{M}$. Formally, it is defined in the usual way as the limit of the quotient.

$$\text{value\_in}(S, \text{deriv}(P)) = \lim_{S1 \to S} \frac{\text{value\_in}(S1, P) - \text{value\_in}(S, P)}{S1 - S}$$

Table 4.9 Axioms for Monotonic Dependence

MON.1. monotonic$(QD, QI, QF, SG) \Leftrightarrow$
[$\forall_{S1,S2}$ value_in$(S1, QF)$ = value_in$(S2, QF) \Rightarrow$
[value_in$(S1, QI)$ = value_in$(S2, QI) \Rightarrow$
value_in$(S1, QD)$ = value_in$(S2, QD)$] $\wedge$
[value_in$(S1, QI)$ < value_in$(S2, QI) \Rightarrow$
value_in$(S1, QD)$ $-$ value_in$(S2, QD) \in SG]$

MON.2. monotonic$(QD, QI, QF, SG1) \wedge$
monotonic$(QI, QD, QF, SG2) \Rightarrow$
$SG1 = SG2$

MON.3. [monotonic$(QD, QI, QF, SG) \wedge \Delta QF = 0$] $\Rightarrow$
$\Delta QD \sim \Delta QI \cdot SG$

MON.4. [monotonic$(QD, QI, QF, SG1) \wedge$
monotonic$(QD, QF, QI, SG2)] \Rightarrow$
$\Delta QD \sim \Delta QI \cdot SG1 + \Delta QF \cdot SG2.$

MON.5 [monotonic$(QA, QB, QC, SG1) \wedge$
monotonic$(QB, QC, QA, SG2) \wedge$
monotonic$(QC, QA, QB, SG3)$] $\Rightarrow$
$SG1 \cdot SG2 \cdot SG3$=neg

Table 4.10 shows how our example problem can be formalized using parameters and the derivative function. Table 4.11 shows some of the basic properties of the derivative function, including those needed for our sample inference.

As this example suggests, the sign of the derivative of a parameter is often important in commonsense reasoning, since it indicates whether the parameter is increasing or decreasing at a given point in time. It is therefore common to designate it using the special notation ∂Q=sign(deriv(Q)).

4.8 Mode Transition Networks

Example:

A pendulum oscillates horizontally back and forth around a central lowest point. Infer that the height of the pendulum oscil-

Table 4.10 Inference with Derivatives

Parameters:
inpour	— Rate that the water is pouring in at the top.
outdrain	— Rate that the water is draining out at the bottom.
height_w	— Height of water in the tank.
volume_w	— Volume of water in the tank.

Constraints:

$\forall_S$ value_in(S,inpour) < value_in(S,outdrain).
(The water always drains out faster than it pours in.)

deriv(volume_w) = inpour − outdrain.
(The volume of water in the tank is increased by the pouring in
and diminished by the draining.)

monotonic(height_w,volume_w,pos).
The height of water is an increasing function of the volume.
(There is no other parameter to be fixed, assuming we are speak-
ing of a tank of fixed shape.)

To infer:

$\forall_S$ value_in(S,deriv(height_w)) < 0.
(The height decreases over time.)

Table 4.11 Axioms of Derivatives

DRV.1. deriv($P + Q$) = deriv(P) + deriv(Q)
DRV.2. deriv($-P$) = −deriv(P)
DRV.3. deriv($P \cdot Q$) = Q·deriv(P) + P·deriv(Q)
DRV.4. deriv($1/P$) = −deriv(P)/P^2
DRV.5. [monotonic($P, Q, R, SG1$) ∧ monotonic($P, R, Q, SG2$)] ⇒
        sign(deriv(P)) ∼ $SG1$·sign(deriv(Q)) + $SG2$·sign(deriv(R))

lates down to the lowest point, with two vertical oscillations for
each horizontal oscillation. (see Figure 4.5).

The major new representational problem in this example is how to
describe the behavior of a collection of parameters, such as the horizontal position and the height of the pendulum, over time. A common

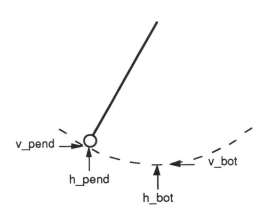

Figure 4.5 Pendulum

solution to this problem proceeds along the following lines: Let Q be a parameter with values in the measure space M. We partition M into a set of exclusive and exhaustive intervals according to some external criterion of significance, and we characterize the value of Q at any given instant by specifying which interval it falls into. If M is a differential space, it is generally divided into the intervals {neg, 0, pos}. If M is an integral space, it is common to choose a number of particularly significant *landmark* values, and to divide the space into the landmark values and the intervals between them. For example, if M is temperature, and Q is the temperature of a quantity of water, one might choose the landmark values to be 32° and 212°, and thus choose the intervals to be {(absolute_zero, 32°), 32°, (32°, 212°), 212°, (212°, ∞)}.

Our example of the pendulum uses two parameters: h_pend, the horizontal position of the pendulum, and v_pend, the vertical position of the pendulum. For characterizing h_pend, we use the landmark value of h_bot, the horizontal position of the bottom of the arc, and we partition the space into the three intervals { (−∞, h_bot), h_bot, (h_bot,∞) }. For characterizing v_pend, we use the landmark value of v_bot, the height of the bottom of the arc, and we partition the space into the three intervals { (−∞,v_bot), v_bot, (v_bot, ∞) }.

Given a particular interval partitition of quantity space M, and a quantity $X \in M$, we extend the notation of Section 4.6, so that $[X]$ now signifies the interval in the partition containing X. It should be kept in mind that this significance of $[X]$ is now relative to some fixed partition, a dependence that is not explicitly shown in the representation.

Given a system of parameters, a *mode* of the system is a particular assignment of intervals to each parameter. For example, the pendulum system has three attainable modes:

M1:   h_pend $\in (-\infty,$h_bot$)$ v_pend $\in ($v_bot$, \infty)$
M2:   h_pend $=$ h_bot   v_pend $=$ v_bot
M3:   h_pend $\in ($h_bot$, \infty)$ v_pend $\in ($v_bot$, \infty)$

If a parameter system changes its mode only finitely many times in a given period, then we can represent its behavior by specifying the sequence of modes it goes through. For example, we can describe one full swing of the pendulum as an occurence of the mode sequence $<$ M1, M2, M3, M2, M1 $>$. To represent phenomena like oscillation, where the system changes modes in some systematic fashion, we can use a *mode transition network*, a finite-state transition network showing which modes can follow which other modes. A mode transition network is a valid representation of a parameter system over a period if the mode sequence executed by the system is a path through the network. Figure 4.6 shows two possible mode transition networks for the pendulum. Note that the second network is correct but not complete. The behavior of the pendulum is a path through the network, but there are paths through the network, such as $<$ M1,M2,M1 $>$, that do not correspond to possible behavior of the pendulum. The first network is both correct and complete; the paths through the network are just the possible behaviors of the pendulum. The first network is thus strictly stronger than the second.

We can now carry out our example inference. The givens to the inference are (i) the transition network for the horizontal position h_pend, corresponding to the statement that the pendulum oscillates; and (ii) the physical constraints "h_pend=h_bot $\Rightarrow$ v_pend $=$ v_bot" and "h_pend $\neq$ h_bot $\Rightarrow$ v_pend $>$ v_bot". Applying these constraints, it is trivial to add the mode of v_pend to the transition network. The new network directly expresses the fact that v_pend oscillates at twice the rate of h_pend. (Admittedly, it would not be easy to automate an inference such as "If h_pend goes through a mode cycle k times in a interval, then v_pend goes through a mode cycle $2k$ times in the same interval," from the network representation.)

Mode sequences are used as representations for other functions than temporal sequences. For example, we may partially characterize the curve in Figure 4.7A by considering it as a function from arc-length to a quadrant of the plane. The mode sequence for the curve would then be the sequence shown in Figure 4.7B (see Section 6.2.6).

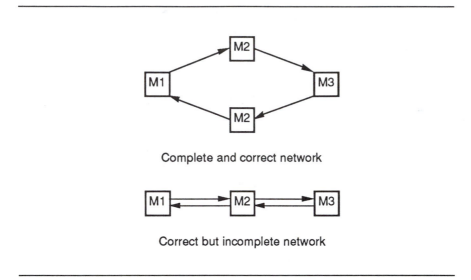

Complete and correct network

Correct but incomplete network

Figure 4.6 Mode Transition Networks

Not all mode sequences are possible for well-behaved functions. If the time line is taken to be real valued and all parameters are real valued and continuous functions, then the mode sequence must obey certain constraints. These constraints are critical when mode transition networks are constructed. To express these constraints elegantly, we must add some additional structure to the representation of mode sequences, and consider their semantics in greater depth.

Let S be a system of parameters with a defined collection of modes. We define a time interval I to be *unimodal* with respect to S if S is in a single mode throughout I. I is maximal unimodal if I is unimodal and no interval properly containing I is unimodal. Clearly, any system of parameters partitions the time line into a collection of disjoint and exhaustive maximal unimodal intervals. We will impose the further condition on our parameter system that any finite duration of time contain only finitely many maximal unimodal intervals; that is, that no parameter changes its mode infinitely many times in any finite interval. In this case, the behavior of the system over any finite time interval may be characterized by a finite mode sequence.

To aid us in stating the restrictions that hold on continuous parameter systems, we augment our representation of mode sequences. An *augmented* mode of the parameter system is a specification, for a given maximal unimodal time interval I, of the following information: (i) the mode of the parameter system; and (ii) the topology of I — is

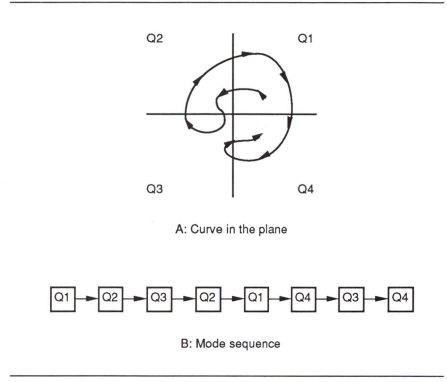

A: Curve in the plane

B: Mode sequence

Figure 4.7 Mode Sequence for Spatial Curve

it unbounded, bounded and open, or bounded and closed above and below? If it is closed both above and below, is it a single point or an interval of finite length? An augmented mode sequence is then a sequence of augmented modes; an augmented mode transition network is a directed graph on augmented modes.

The constraints in Table 4.12 govern any augmented mode sequence for real-valued continuous parameters:

If, as is common, the only closed intervals used in the partition parameter space are single landmark points, then axiom MODE.5 is vacuous.

Axioms MODE.1–MODE.5 can be used to prune substantially the transitions that are possible in a mode transition graph. For example, consider a system of two identical independent pendulums, as shown in Figure 4.8. Each pendulum can be in one of three modes; the system as a whole therefore has nine modes. We are given that, in the starting mode M, pendulum A is left of center, while pendulum B is at the

Table 4.12 Rules for Mode Transitions

Let M and N be successive augmented modes in a mode sequence. For any parameter Q let $[Q]_M$ and $[Q]_N$ be the modes of Q in M and N. Let I_M and I_N be the time intervals of M and N.

MODE.1. (Temporal topology) I_M is bounded above; I_N is bounded below. One of the following two possibilities must hold:

   a. I_M is open above and I_N is closed below.
   b. I_M is closed above and I_N is open below.

MODE.2. (Change) There is some parameter Q such that $[Q]_M \neq [Q]_N$.

MODE.3. (Continuity) For each parameter Q, either $[Q]_M = [Q]_N$ or the intervals $[Q]_M$ and $[Q]_N$ are adjacent in the quantity space of Q.

MODE.4. (Parameter topology) If $[Q]_M \neq [Q]_N$. then the boundary between $[Q]_M$ and $[Q]_N$ is topologically the same as the boundary between I_M and I_N. Specifically:

   a. If $[Q]_M < [Q]_N$, I_M is open above, and I_N is closed below, then $[Q]_M$ is open above and $[Q]_N$ is closed below.
   b. If $[Q]_M < [Q]_N$, I_M is closed above, and I_N is open below, then $[Q]_M$ is closed above and $[Q]_N$ is open below.
   c. If $[Q]_M > [Q]_N$, I_M is open above, and I_N is closed below, then $[Q]_M$ is open below and $[Q]_N$ is closed above.
   d. If $[Q]_M > [Q]_N$, I_M is closed above, and I_N is open below, then $[Q]_M$ is closed below and $[Q]_N$ is open above.

MODE.5. Let M, N, and P be three successive augmented modes and Q a parameter such that $[Q]_N$ is closed at both ends and has finite length (not a single point). If $[Q]_M$, $[Q]_N$, and $[Q]_P$ all have different values, then I_N has finite length.

---

center point. We can restrict the possibilities for the succeeding mode N as follows: By continuity [MODE.3], A cannot be to the right of center in N. This rules out three possible modes as succesors. By the axiom of change [MODE.2], N must be different from M. This rules out another possible successor. By temporal topology [MODE.4],

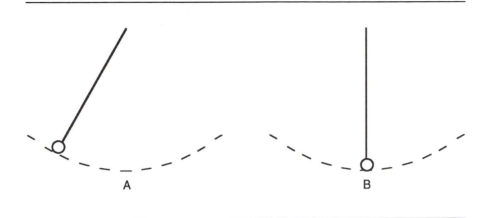

Figure 4.8 Two Pendulums

if pendulum A moves from left of center to center, then $[I]_M$ must be closed above, while if pendulum B moves out of the center then $[I]_M$ must be open above. Therefore, these two types of transitions cannot both occur between M and N, ruling out two more possible successor modes. We are left with three possible successors: A and B are both at the center; A and B are both left of center; and A is left of center while B is right of center.

4.9 Qualitative Differential Equations

Example:

> Consider a block attached to a spring, as in Figure 4.9. When the spring is extended, it exerts an inward force on the block; when it is compressed, it exerts an outward force. No other force acts on the block. Deduce that the block will oscillate back and forth around the rest point of the spring.

The problem here is to derive the behavior of a system of parameters over time, given constraints obeyed by the parameters and their derivatives at each instant of time. These constraints derive in part from the problem specifications and in part from a background knowledge of physics. Specifically, the problem can be formulated as shown in Table 4.13. (We shall discuss how this formulation can be derived from physical specifications in Chapter 7.)

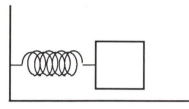

Figure 4.9 Block on a Spring

Table 4.13 Dynamics of the Spring System

Parameters:
x — Position of the block
f — Force exerted on the block by the spring

Atemporal constants:
m — Mass of the block
compress — Interval of compressed spring positions
rest — Rest length of the spring
expand — Interval of expanded spring positions

Constraints:
$f = m\ \ddot{x}$. (Newton's second law: The force is proportional to the acceleration)
[f] = rest − [x]

The givens thus form a system of differential relations; the problem is to solve them to derive a characterization of parameters over time. However, the problem differs from the differential equations in standard calculus courses in that the relation [f]=rest−[x] provide only a weak constraint between the parameters, rather than an exact functional relation. The solution of the problem can therefore at best come up with a partial characterization of the behavior, such as "the block oscillates," rather than a precise functional description. Specifically, the technique we will present will construct a mode transition network, called an *envisionment graph,* for the solutions to the equations.

The basic technique for constructing an envisionment graph for such a system of equations involves the following steps:

1. Translate any higher differential equations into a system of first-order equations by introducing the intermediate derivatives as new variables. In our example, we would convert the equation "$f = \ddot{x}$" to the pair of equations "$f = m \cdot \dot{v}$; $v = \dot{x}$", by introducing the velocity v as a new parameter. All parameters so introduced are derivatives, and so may be characterized in terms of the signs { neg, 0, pos }.

2. Change all equations to relations on the signs or intervals of the parameters. In our example, we would change the two equations introduced in step 1 to the form "$[f] = \partial v$; $[v] = \partial x$." (Recall that ∂Q = sign(deriv(Q)). Note that we have used the fact that the mass m is positive). The constraint "$[f] = \text{rest}-[x]$" is already in the proper form. The resultant equations are called *qualitative differential equations* (QDE's). Often, the problem is presented in the form of a set of QDE's, steps 1 and 2 having been performed implicitly in the problem formulation.

3. Let S be a parameter system containing all the parameters and derivatives from the equations in step 2. Construct all modes of the system consistent with the qualitative differential equations. In the spring example, there are nine such modes; they are listed in Table 4.15.

4. Determine which transitions between modes are possible. The constraints on possible transitions are axioms MODE.1–MODE.5, which apply to all continuous parameter systems, and axioms QDE.1–QDE.2, in Table 4.14 which relate the derivative of a quantity to the change in the quantity. Table 4.16 shows how these rules apply to the spring example; Figure 4.10 shows the final envisionment graph.

One substantial limitation of the analysis, not obvious on cursory examination of Table 4.16 or Figure 4.10, is that it does not establish that the system does not end permanently in state M1, M3, M5, or M7. The problem here is not an inadequacy of the axioms MODE.1–MODE.5 and QDE.1–QDE.2. Rather, it is a consequence of steps 1 and

2 of the solution process, in which the original equations are transformed to qualitative first-order equations. All solutions to the original equations oscillate. The tranformation, however, loses information so as to admit solutions that remain forever in a single state (Exercise 8). Strictly speaking, therefore, it is necessary to consider the higher-order QDE's to infer that the system oscillates [de Kleer and Brown 1984; Kuipers and Chiu 1986]. In practice, however, most systems that use envisionment graphs make the assumption that, if a mode has any transitions out of it, then it will not last forever.

Table 4.14 Axioms for QDE's

Let M, N, and P be successive augmented modes in a mode sequence. For any parameter Q and mode A, let $[Q]_A$ be the mode of Q in A; let ∂Q_A be the sign of the derivative of Q in A; and let I_A be the time interval in A. We will restrict attention in these axioms to partitions of measure spaces into landmark values and the open intervals between them. The analysis of half-open intervals and of closed intervals of finite magnitude is substantially messier.

QDE.1. (Mean value)
   If $[Q]_M < [Q]_N$ and $[Q]_N$ is an open interval, then ∂Q_N=pos.
   If $[Q]_M > [Q]_N$ and $[Q]_N$ is an open interval, then ∂Q_N=neg.
   If $[Q]_M < [Q]_N$ and $[Q]_M$ is an open interval, then ∂Q_M=pos.
   If $[Q]_M > [Q]_N$ and $[Q]_M$ is an open interval, then ∂Q_M=neg.

QDE.2. (Point transitions)
   If $[Q]_N$ is a point interval and ∂Q_N=pos,
   then $[Q]_M < [Q]_N < [Q]_P$ and I_N is a point interval.
   If $[Q]_N$ is a point interval and ∂Q_N=neg,
   then $[Q]_M > [Q]_N > [Q]_P$ and I_N is a point interval.

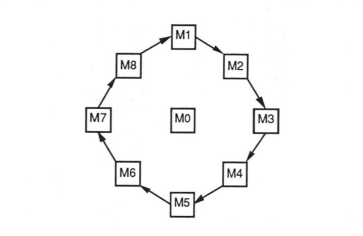

Figure 4.10 Envisionment Graph

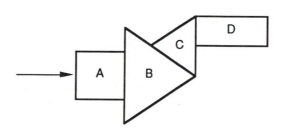

When you push A, it pushes B, which pushes C . . .

Figure 4.11 Instantaneous Sequence of Events

Table 4.15 Modes of the Spring System

Mode	[x]	$[v] = \partial x$	$[f] = \partial v$
M0	rest	0	0
M1	expand	pos	neg
M2	expand	0	neg
M3	expand	neg	neg
M4	rest	neg	0
M5	compress	neg	pos
M6	compress	0	pos
M7	compress	pos	pos
M8	rest	pos	0

4.10 Orders of Magnitude

Examples:

> You weigh a letter and determine that it is less than an ounce and requires only a 25 cent stamp. You therefore plan to affix the stamp, but realize that the stamped letter will weigh more. However, reasoning that the weight of a stamp is negligible as compared to the weight of a letter, you conclude that it will not bring the weight of the letter over the limit.

> A number of blocks placed together are hit from the outside (Figure 4.11). Represent the statement that the shock travels from one block to another in sequence, but that the entire propagation is complete before any of the blocks can move any finite distance.

It is often useful to reason about one quantity being very much larger than another, without being precise about the numerical value of the ratio. Thus, rather than say that the shock wave moves one hundred or one thousand times faster than the blocks do, or that the letter is a hundred times heavier than the stamp, it may be easier, though inaccurate, to suppose that the larger quantity is actually infinite as compared to the smaller.

To make this notion coherent, we need a model of quantities that allow infinite ratios between quantities. Such a model has, in fact, been developed in the last 30 years; it is called the *nonstandard* model of the reals with infinitesimals. It is beyond the scope of this book to

Table 4.16 Constructing an Envisionment Graph for the Scales

M0: No transitions into or out of M0 are consistent with the mean value axiom QDE.1.

M1: By continuity (MODE.3), M1 can be followed only by M0, M2, or M8. By mean value (QDE.1), M1 cannot be followed by M0 or M8. Hence M1 must be followed by M2.

M2: By point transition on parameter v (QDE.2), M2 must be followed by M3, M4, or M5, and must have a point time interval. By continuity (MODE.3), M2 cannot be followed by M5. By topology (MODE.4), M2 cannot be followed by M4. Hence M2 is followed by M3.

M3: By continuity (MODE.3), M3 can be followed only by M0, M2, or M4. By mean value (QDE.1), M3 cannot be followed by M0 or M2. Hence M3 must be followed by M4.

M4: By point transition on parameter x (QDE.2), M4 must be followed by M5, M6, or M7, and must have a point time interval. By continuity (MODE.3), M4 cannot be followed by M7. By topology (MODE.4), M4 cannot be followed by M6. Hence M4 is followed by M5.

M5: By continuity (MODE.3), M5 can be followed only by M0, M4, or M6. By mean value (QDE.1), M5 cannot be followed by M0 or M4. Hence M5 must be followed by M6.

M6: By point transition on parameter v (QDE.2), M6 must be followed by M7, M8, or M1, and must have a point time interval. By continuity (MODE.3), M6 cannot be followed by M1. By topology (MODE.4), M6 cannot be followed by M8. Hence M6 is followed by M7.

M7: By continuity (MODE.3), M7 can be followed only by M0, M6, or M8. By mean value (QDE.1), M7 cannot be followed by M0 or M6. Hence M7 must be followed by M8.

M8: By point transition on parameter x (QDE.2), M8 must be followed by M1, M2, or M3, and must have a point time interval. By continuity (MODE.3), M8 cannot be followed by M3. By topology (MODE.4), M8 cannot be followed by M2. Hence M8 is followed by M1.

---

describe the logical foundations of this theory. (See [Robinson 1965; Davis and Hersh 1972].)

For the purposes of inferences such as those above, it suffices to introduce the concept of one quantity of a differential space being negligible as compared to another. We introduce the predicate $X \ll Y$, which holds if X and Y are positive quantities and X is infinitesimal as compared to Y. The predicate observes the following axioms:

NEG.1. $X \ll Y \Rightarrow 0 < X < Y$.

NEG.2. $[0 < W \leq X \ll Y \leq Z] \Rightarrow W \ll Z$.

NEG.3. $[W \ll Y \wedge X \ll Y] \Rightarrow (W + X) \ll Y$.

NEG.4. $[W \ll X \wedge 0 < Y] \Rightarrow W \cdot Y \ll X \cdot Y$.

NEG.5. $\exists_{X,Y} X \ll Y$.

NEG.6.   Any first-order statement which is true of the standard real numbers and does not involve the symbol $\ll$ is also true of the nonstandard real numbers.

Axiom NEG.3 states that if both W and X are negligible compared to Y, then $W + X$ is likewise negligible. This directly contradicts the Archimedian property of the reals, that by adding any positive quantity X to itself sufficiently often, one can exceed any given quantity Y. Also, the completeness property of the reals, that every nonempty set with an upper bound has a least upper bound, does not hold on the nonstandard line; for any $X > 0$, the set of numbers Y such that $Y \ll X$ does not have a least upper bound. (Neither of these properties can be fully axiomatized in a first-order statement; hence their failure does not contract the axiom schema NEG.5.)

We can now formalize our example of the letter and stamp. We introduce the predicate "close(X, Y)" meaning that $Y - X$ is of negligible magnitude as compared to Y.

$$\text{close}(X, Y) \Leftrightarrow \text{abs}(Y - X) \ll \text{abs}(Y).$$

We now specify that the letter is less than an ounce and not close to an ounce, and that the weight of a stamp is negligible as compared to the weight of the letter. It then follows directly that the letter plus stamp is less than an ounce.

Given: letter < ounce $\wedge$ ¬close(letter,ounce).
          stamp $\ll$ letter.

Infer: stamp + letter < ounce.

4.11 References

General: [Hayes 1978] contains a general discussion of the nature and structure of measure spaces used in commonsense reasoning, particularly physical reasoning. [Davis 1987b] contains a survey of the different kinds of arithmetic primitives needed for various commonsense domains with real-valued measure spaces. [Weld and de Kleer 1989] reprints many of the most significant papers on reasoning about quantities for physical reasoning, including many of the papers cited below on reasoning about collections of arithmetic relations, QDE's, and orders of magnitude.

Intervals: The interval calculus has been studied almost exclusively as a representation for temporal relations. In particular, [Van Benthem 1983] contains a thorough study of the algebraic and topological properties and logical power of various sets of axioms on the ordering of points and intervals. The seminal AI paper on the interval calculus was [Allen 1983], which introduced the 13 relations on intervals that we have used, and presented a transitivity table for combining them. Further studies of the logical and computational properties of the interval calculus include [Vilain and Kautz 1986; Allen and Hayes 1985; Ladkin 1987].

Real-valued scales: The primary issue in incorporating real arithmetic in AI systems has been the organization and maintenance of an efficient system for ground atomic relations. Propagation of exact values and of symbolic terms has been used to solve systems of equations in [Sutherland 1963; Borning 1977; Sussman and Steele 1980]. Waltz propagation on real intervals has been applied to temporal reasoning in [Dean 1984], and to spatial reasoning in [McDermott and Davis 1984] and [Davis 1986]. [Davis 1987b] has a formal analysis of the power of Waltz propagation as applied to different classes of arithmetic relations. [Malik and Binford 1983] advocates the use of the simplex algorithm for the analysis of linear inequalities that arise in AI systems. The ACRONYM system of [Brooks 1981] has a powerful system for solving inequalities that may contain complex algebraic and trigonometric terms for spatial reasoning. The BOUNDER program [Sacks 1987] uses a series of increasingly powerful and increasingly costly techniques for analyzing systems of inequalities; it extends a similar system of Simmons's [1986].

Sign calculus and QDE's: In the AI literature, these two techniques were developed in tandem for qualitative physical reasoning. QDE analysis was used implicitly in the NEWTON program [de Kleer 1975] (see Section 6.2.6.) QDE's and sign arithmetic were first developed as theories in their own right in [de Kleer and Brown 1985],

[Kuipers 1985], and [Williams 1985]. [Kuipers 1986] is a careful and rigorous analysis of the underlying theory. [Struss 1989] studies the limits of sign and QDE analysis. Since then a number of papers have extended the basic theory by using richer information and more powerful analysis techniques. Many of these are collected in [de Kleer and Weld 1989]. Particularly significant are [de Kleer and Bobrow 1984] and [Kuipers and Chiu 1988] which study higher-order QDE equations; [Weld 1986], which shows how QDE techniques can be applied to certain discrete systems; and [Weld 1988a], which analyses qualitatively how the solutions to a differential equations are affected by perturbations to the parameters of the equations. [Sacks 1988] gives a more powerful qualitative analysis of exact differential equations, based on approximating the equations with piecewise linear equations, and categorizing the solutions in terms of transitions between regions of phase space.

Order of magnitude: The theory of nonstandard real analysis was created by Abraham Robinson [1965]; for a popular account, see [Davis and Hersh 1972]. In the AI literature, nonstandard analysis has been applied to the automation of proofs in real analysis in [Ballantyne and Bledsoe 1977]; to the semantics of robotic programming languages in [Davis 1984]; and to physical reasoning in [Raiman 1986]. [Davis 1989b] and [Weld 1988b] describe systems that combine order of magnitude reasoning with QDE's. [Mavrovouniotis and Stephanopoulos 1989] gives a detailed account of an inference engine for order-of-magnitude reasoning, and its application to process engineering.

4.12 Exercises

(Starred problems are more difficult.)

1. Some AI programs (e.g., NOAH [Sacerdoti 1975]) have represented partial orderings using the functions "sequence$(P1, P2, \ldots Pk)$" and "split$(P1, P2 \ldots Pk)$." The function "sequence$(P1 \ldots Pk)$" combines a collection of disjoint partial orderings $P1 \ldots Pk$ by placing them in increasing order; if $i < j$, $Xi \in Pi$ and $Xj \in Pj$ then $Xi < Xj$. The function "split$(P1 \ldots Pk)$" combines disjoint partial orderings $P1 \ldots Pk$ by placing them in parallel; if $Xi \in Pi$, $Xj \in Pj$ and $i \neq j$, then Xi and Xj are unordered. Figure 4.12 shows some examples.

    (a) Give an example of a partial ordering that cannot be represented using "sequence" and "split".

    (b) * Define the functions "sequence" and "split" in a first-order theory that treats partial orderings as first-order entities. In

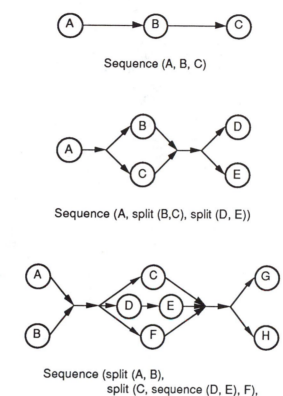

Sequence (A, B, C)

Sequence (A, split (B,C), split (D, E))

Sequence (split (A, B),
        split (C, sequence (D, E), F),
        split (G, H))

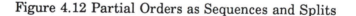

Figure 4.12 Partial Orders as Sequences and Splits

order that these functions are applied only to partial ordering, and not to simple elements, you may use a function "unary_po (X)" that maps an element X to the partial ordering containing only X. You may also assume for simplicity that "sequence" and "split" take exactly two arguments. Thus the partial ordering with $X1$, $X2$, and $X3$ in that order could be written

sequence(sequence(unary_po($X1$),unary_po($X2$)),
                unary_po($X3$))

Use the predicates "ordered($X1, X2, P$)", meaning that $X1$ precedes $X2$ in ordering P, and "element(X, P)", meaning that X is an element of ordering P.

(c) Another representation of partial orderings [Meehan 1975] is to associate a real interval with each element of the partial ordering, and to define X as coming before Y in the ordering if the upper bound of the interval of X is less than the lower bound of Y. For example the labels $X1 \rightarrow [0,1]$, $X2 \rightarrow [2,4]$, $X3 \rightarrow [3,6]$, and $X4 \rightarrow [5,8]$ correspond to the ordering $X1 < X2 < X4$, $X1 < X3$. Give an example of a partial ordering that cannot be represented in this way.

(d) * The representations in parts a and c are "compact," in the sense that they require space linear in the number of elements of the partial ordering. Show that there are more than 2^{cn^2} different partial orderings on n elements, for some constant c. Argue that therefore no compact representation of partial orderings can represent all possible partial orderings.

2. Construct a *transitivity table* for the 13 interval relations discussed in Section 4.2. This is a 13 by 13 table, in which each row is a relation between I and J, each column is a relation between J and K, and the entry is the possible relations between I and K. For example, in the row "during(I,J)" and the column "before(J,K)," the entry is "{ before(I,K) }". Note that some of the entries will not be single valued, if there is more than one possible relation between I and K. For example, in the row "starts(I,J)" and column "starts(K,J)", the entry is "{starts(I,K), $I=K$, starts(K,I)}".

3. Find an efficient ($O(n^2)$) algorithm to solve the following problem: Given a collection of atomic, ground interval constraints, determine whether the constraints are consistent. For example the set {before(a,b), meets(a,c), overlap(c,b)} is consistent; it is satisfied by the interval a=[0,1], b=[2,4], c=[1,3]. The set {before(a,b), meets(a,c), during(c,b)} is inconsistent.

4. Justify the statement in Section 4.6, "Any equation on quantities can be converted into a corresponding compatibility relation on the signs of the quantities. For example, from the equation $X + Y = P \cdot Q$, it is legitimate to infer the compatibility relation $[X] + [Y] \sim [P] \cdot [Q]$."

5. * Justify the axiom MON.5 from Table 4.9.

MON.5. [monotonic$(QA,QB,QC,SG1) \wedge$
monotonic$(QB,QC,QA,SG2) \wedge$
monotonic$(QC,QA,QB,SG3)$] $\Rightarrow$
$SG1 \cdot SG2 \cdot SG3$=neg

6. (a) Find the mode transition network for the function
$f(t) = sin(t)\ sin(2t)$ using the signs of the function and its
derivative.

   (b) Find the mode transition network for the function
$f(t) = sin(t)\ sin(2t)$ using the signs of the function and its first
two derivatives.

7. If we modify the model of the block on the spring in Section 4.9
by adding a damping force proportional to the velocity, then the
equations become,

$f = m\ \dot{v}.$
$v = \dot{x}.$
$[f] = rest - [x] - [v].$

Use the technique of Section 4.9 to construct an envisionment
graph for this problem.

8. (a) * Show that any solution to the qualitative differential equation "$[\ddot{x}] = -[x]$" must oscillate.

   (b) * Show that there are solutions to the pair of first-order QDE's
"$\partial x=v;\ \partial v=-x$" that remain forever in a single mode.

Chapter 5

Time

This thing all things devours:
Birds, beasts, trees, flowers;
Gnaws iron, bites steel;
Grinds hard stones to meal;
Slays king, ruins town,
And beats high mountain down.

J. R. R. Tolkien, *The Hobbit*

Reasoning about time and change is ubiquitous in commonsense reasoning. Very few commonsense problems can be formulated in purely static terms. Temporal reasoning is central in prediction, planning, and most kinds of explanations.

A temporal representation must address a number of issues, depending on the application. In virtually all applications, it must be possible to represent change; the occurrence of events; constraints on the possible states of the world; and causal laws. Many applications require, in addition, the ability to represent quantitative relations among times and durations, to distinguish between past, present, and future, to compare hypothetical courses of events, or to reason about continuous time.

5.1 Situations

The first task of a temporal representation is to represent facts that are temporally limited, such as "At 9:00, John was on the bus," or "From 1789 to 1797, George Washington was president." As we have discussed in Section 2.6, constructs like "At 9:00 ..." or "From 1789 to 1797 ..." are extensional sentence operators. They commute with Boolean operators and with the existential quantifier (subject to a qualification described below), and they do not self-imbed. "At 9:00, Tim was not on the bus" is synonymous with "It is not the case that, at 9:00, Tim was on the bus." "At 9:00, there was someone on the bus" is synonymous with "There is someone who was on the bus at 9:00." "At 10:00, it was the case that, at 9:00 Tim was on the bus" is not a particularly meaningful or useful construction. Therefore, there is a straightforward representation of these statements in a first-order language.

Our representation is based on the use of *situations*. A situation is a snapshot of the universe at an instant. It constitutes one possible way that the world could be at an instant. By considering situations to be entities, we can include them as arguments to first-order predicates and functions.

As discussed in Section 2.6, there are two general techniques for representing time-varying facts using situations. In the first, the situation is made an extra argument to every time-varying relation and time-varying term. For example, to represent the statement "The radio was turned on at 9:00," we would use a predicate "turned_on(O, S)," meaning that appliance O is turned on in situation S. The above statement would then be represented as the sentence "turned_on(radio23, s900)." To represent the sentence, "Kennedy was president of the U.S. at the beginning of 1962," we would introduce the function "president (C, S)" mapping a situation S to the person who was president of country C in S, and we would write the sentence in the form, "kennedy=president (us,s1962)."

The second representational system reifies time-varying terms as *fluents* (a generalization of the "parameters" introduced in Section 4.6) and time-varying relations as *Boolean fluents* or *states*. In the above examples, "turned_on(O)" would be the state of appliance O being turned on, and "president(C)" would be the fluent of the president of country C over time. The predicate "true_in(S, A)" asserts that state A holds in situation S. The statement "The radio was turned on at 9:00" would thus be represented in the form "true_in(s900, turned_on(radio23))." The function "value_in(S, F)" maps a situation S and a fluent F to the value of F in S. The statement "Kennedy was president of the U.S. at the beginning of 1962 would thus be represented "kennedy=value_in(s1962, president(us))."

The second system is less concise than the first, but it is somewhat more expressive, in that it allows fluents to be treated as entities. Thus, it is possible in the second system to apply functions to fluents and to quantify over fluents. For example, we can assert that an object o1 moves continuously using the sentence "continuous(place(o1))". Here "place(o1)" is a fluent, and "continuous(F)" is a predicate taking as its argument a fluent whose value in each situation is a region of space. There are also differences between the two systems when syntax-dependent types of plausible reasoning, such as domain closure, are applied.

Similarly, as discussed in Section 4.6, we can define functions that map fluents into fluents. Frequently, this is done by taking a function defined as mapping atemporal objects to atemporal objects and extending it to a function mapping fluents to fluents; or by taking an atemporal relation on objects and overloading the same symbol to represent a state-valued function on fluents. For example, given a function "centroid(R)" that maps a spatial region R to its centroid, we can extend it to take a region-valued fluent F as argument, and map the fluent F to the trace of the centroid of F over time. Thus, "centroid(place(o1))" would be a fluent that, in each situation, gives the centroid of the object o1 in that situation. Similarly, if "inside($R1, R2$)" is a predicate meaning that region $R1$ is inside region $R2$, we can define a function "inside($F1, F2$)" that maps two region-valued fluents $F1$ and $F2$ to the state of $F1$ being inside $F2$. Thus, "inside(place(o1),place(o2))" would represent the state of object o1 being inside o2. We can define these extensions in the axiom schemas below:

Let $\alpha(\tau_1 \ldots \tau_k)$ be a function on atemporal objects. We extend α to be a function on fluents using the rule:

$\forall_{S,F1\ldots Fk}$ value_in($S, \alpha(F1 \ldots Fk)$) =
$\quad \alpha$(value_in($S, F1$) $\ldots$ value_in(S, Fk))

Let $\beta(\tau_1 \ldots \tau_k)$ be a predicate on atemporal objects. We extend β to be a function from fluents to states using the rule:

$\forall_{S,F1\ldots Fk}$ true_in($S, \beta(F1 \ldots Fk)$) $\Leftrightarrow$
$\quad \beta$(value_in($S, F1$) $\ldots$ value_in(S, Fk))

One relation that we do not wish to extend this way is the equality relation; we wish "$F1 = F2$" to mean the statement that $F1$ and $F2$ are the same fluent rather than denote the state of $F1$ and $F2$ being equal. We introduce the function "eql($F1, F2$)" to map two fluents to the state of their being equal.

true_in(S,eql($F1, F2$)) $\Leftrightarrow$ value_in($S, F1$) = value_in($S, F2$)

The use of these conventions can greatly simplify the expression of temporal statements. For example, the statement "At 8:30, the husband of the prime minister was inside his car," can be represented simply as

true_in(s830, inside(place(husband_of(prime_minister)),
                    place(car_of(husband_of(prime_minister)))))

Without the convention of extending functions to fluents, this would have to be represented,

inside(v(s, place(v(s, husband_of(v(s, prime_minister))))),
       v(s, place(v(s, car_of(v(s, husband_of(v(s, prime_minister)))))))).

(We abbreviate "value_in" as "v" and "s830" as s.)

Situations are ordered. The situations that actually occur are totally ordered; hypothetical situations, to be discussed in Section 5.6, are partially ordered. We can thus use the order relation $S1 < S2$, which we will often write "precedes$(S1, S2)$." The sentence "Kennedy was senator from Massachusetts before he was ever president," can then be represented,

[$\exists_{S1,S2}$ true_in($S1$,senator(kennedy,massachusetts)) $\wedge$
kennedy=value_in($S2$,president(us))] $\wedge$
[$\exists_{S1}\forall_{S2}$ [true_in($S1$,senator(kennedy,massachusetts)) $\wedge$
kennedy=value_in($S2$,president(us))] $\Rightarrow S1 < S2$]

In order to express more detailed arithmetic information about times while maintaining the option of using a partially ordered system of situations, we introduce the measure space of *clock times*. For example, "11:23 A.M., January 9, 1956," is a clock time. The space of clock times is a integral measure space; the corresponding differential space consists of length of time durations, such as "five minutes," "2.451 years," and so on. The fluent "clock_time" associates each situation with a clock time. For example, the statement "The temperature in Detroit dropped 15 degrees within an hour," can be expressed as follows:

$\exists_{S1,S2} S1 < S2 \wedge$
value_in($S2$,clock_time) $-$ value_in($S1$,clock_time) $\leq$ hour $\wedge$
value_in($S1$,temp(detroit)) $-$ value_in($S2$,temp(detroit)) $=$
15 $\cdot$ degree

The order of clock times is postulated to be consistent with the order of situations.

$S1 < S2 \Rightarrow$ value_in(S1,clock_time) $<$ value_in(S2,clock_time).

We can also introduce intervals of situations as entities of the temporal ontology, and apply to them the language of intervals developed in Section 4.2. For example, the sentence "Kennedy was president throughout 1962" may be represented

$S \in$ year_1962 $\Rightarrow$ kennedy=value_in(S,president(us))

In many uses of fluents, it is necessary to allow null values in order to cover times when the fluent did not exist. For example, there was no president of the U.S. in 1620; thus, the term "president(us,s1620)" must denote a null value. Similarly, things that we would like to represent by constants can similarly come into and out of existence. For example, Eisenhower came into existence in 1890 and ceased to exist in 1969. However, if "eisenhower" is used as a constant term, then it denotes something atemporal that is not restricted to this period. In these cases, it is advisable to introduce the predicate "present_in(O, S)," which asserts that entity O was around in situation S. Statements quantifying over objects should then be structured to avoid attributing any time-varying properties to objects in situations where they do not exist.

The states that we have discussed above are state *types*. It is sometimes useful to use state *tokens* instead, or in addition. For example, suppose that Martin has been twice in the USSR. The representation above does not allow us to state properties of the two visits; for example, to state that the first was legal and the second illegal. We need to introduce state tokens instead. A state token is one particular occurrence of a state type. In our example, we would have two state tokens, each of the type "in(martin,ussr)."

We introduce two new nonlogical symbols: "token_of(K, A)", a predicate meaning that token K is of type A, and "time_of(K)", a function mapping token K into the interval during which K took place. (We assume that a state token occurs over an interval; that is, if a state is broken up into pieces, then each piece is to be considered a token in itself.) These are connected to the predicate "true_in(S, A)" through the following axiom:

$$\text{true\_in}(S, A) \Leftrightarrow \exists_K \text{ token\_of}(K, A) \land S \in \text{time\_of}(K)$$

We can now express the statement "Martin's first visit to the USSR was legal, but the second was illegal" as follows:

token_of(visit1, in(martin,ussr)) $\land$
token_of(visit2, in(martin,ussr)) $\land$
before(time_of(visit1), time_of(visit2)) $\land$
legal(visit1) $\land$ ¬legal(visit2).

Another use of state tokens, for physical processes, is discussed in Section 7.2.

5.2 Events

In addition to the value of states and fluents, a temporal language must allow us to describe the occurrence of events, such as "Francois sang the Marseillaise," or "Jake sneezed." Our representation for events is very similar to the representation for states.[1] We introduce two new ontological sorts, the event token and the event type. We extend the predicate "token_of(K, E)" and the function "time_of(K)" to apply to event tokens and types, as well as states. We also introduce the predicate "occurs(I, E)" to mean that an event of type E occurs during time interval I. This is defined by the following axiom:

$$\text{occurs}(I, E) \Leftrightarrow \exists_K \text{ token\_of}(K, E) \wedge I = \text{time\_of}(K)$$

For example, the statement "Francois sang the Marseillaise" can be represented in the sentence "occurs(i23, sing(francois, marseillaise))". The statement "Francois sang the Marseillaise twice" can be represented in the form

$$\exists_{K1,K2} \text{ token\_of}(K1, \text{sing(francois,marseillaise)}) \wedge$$
$$\text{token\_of}(K2, \text{sing(francois,marseillaise)}) \wedge K1 \neq K2$$

The same event token may be a token of more than one type. For instance, a single event token may be an instance of the types "Grace toggles the light switch," "Grace turned out the light," "Grace darkened the room." The statement "Grace darkened the room by toggling the light switch" can thus be partially expressed by stating that a token of both types occurred. (This representation does not indicate the causal direction between the two event types.)

$$\exists_K \text{ token\_of}(K, \text{toggle(grace,switch19)}) \wedge$$
$$\text{token\_of}(K, \text{darken(grace,room24)})$$

It can also happen that one token can be part of another. For instance, we might want to say that Grace's turning out of the light was part of her going to bed. We represent this using the predicate "event_part($K1, K2$)." The statement that Grace turned off the light as part of going to bed is then represented

$$\exists_{K1,K2} \text{ token\_of}(K1, \text{turn\_off(grace,light38)}) \wedge$$
$$\text{token\_of}(K2, \text{go\_to\_bed(grace)}) \wedge$$
$$\text{event\_part}(K1, K2)$$

The event_part relation defines a hierarchy on event tokens. If one token is part of another then it occurs in a subinterval of time.

---

[1] Shoham's [1988] temporal representation makes no distinction whatever.

event_part($K1, K2$) $\Rightarrow$ time_of($K1$) $\subseteq$ time_of($K2$).
[event_part($K1, K2$) $\wedge$ time_of($K1$) = time_of($K2$)] $\Leftrightarrow K1 = K2$.
[event_part($K1, K2$) $\wedge$ event_part($K2, K3$)] $\Rightarrow$ event_part($K1, K3$).

It is often reasonable to consider this hierarchy as reflecting an *abstraction hierarchy* of event types. For example, going to bed is a more abstract event type than turning out a light; hence an event token of the latter may be part of an event token of the former.

5.3 Temporal Reasoning: Blocks World

We will draw many of our examples in this chapter from the simple blocks world illustrated in Figure 5.1. The following rules hold in this world: Blocks are stacked one on top of another, forming towers one block thick. Each tower is based on the table, at a defined horizontal location. The hand can hold one block at a time. If the hand is empty, it can pick up the top block of a tower directly under it (at the same horizontal location). If the hand is holding a block, it can put that block on the top of the tower under it, or, if there are no blocks under it, it can start a new tower. Every block must either be in the hand, on the table, or on top of another block.

The apparatus developed in sections 1 and 2 is sufficient to allow us to axiomatize this blocks world. Table 5.1 shows the nonlogical terms that we will use; Table 5.2 gives some basic axioms of the domain.

Axioms BW.3 through BW.12 are *state coherence* axioms. They constrain the states that can hold simultaneously in a single situation. BW.13 and BW.14 are *precondition* axioms, which specify the states that must hold at the start of an event. Axioms BW.15 through BW.18 are *causal* axioms, which constrain events and states at different times. These particular axioms follow a form that is common for causal axioms: If an event occurs and certain states hold at the beginning of the event, then other states will hold at the end of the event.

Readers who have seen other axiomatizations of the blocks world may notice a number of minor differences in the theory here. The first difference is that we use the three events "pickup", "move", and "putdown" instead of the single macro-operation "puton(X, Y)". This is a purely stylistic change, in order to make a theory with more than one type of event for pedagogical purposes. In planning, it is obviously more sensible to use "puton(X, Y)".

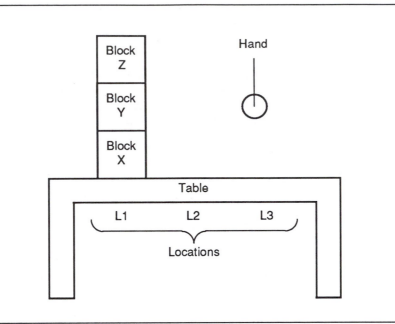

Figure 5.1 Blocks World

The second difference between our theory and others is that we describe the vertical position of blocks using the state "beneath(X, Y)" rather than the state "on(X, Y)." The advantage of "on(X, Y)" over "beneath(X, Y)" is that there are only linearly many "on" relations between blocks, while there may be quadratically many "beneath" relations. The advantage of "beneath(X, Y)" is that it makes it possible to state a more powerful theory. It is possible to define "on" in terms of "beneath"; it is not possible to fully define "beneath" in terms of "on" in a first-order theory. In fact, the state coherence axioms above are complete for finite sets of blocks, in the sense that any arrangement of a finite set of blocks consistent with these axioms is physically possible. This condition is not achievable if "on" is used instead of "beneath."

The third peculiarity of our theory is that it gives separate precondition axioms, which make the precondition a necessary condition of the occurrence of the event. It is more common to include the precondition as part of the antecedent of the conditional of the causal axiom governing the event. If we took this approach here, we would eliminate axioms BW.13 and BW.14, and modify axiom BW.15 to include in its antecedent the condition that the hand be clear.

Table 5.1 Nonlogical Symbols for the Blocks World

Sorts: We indicate the sort of a variable by its first letter. We use the following sorts: physical objects (X or Y), horizontal locations (L), state types (A), fluents (F), event types (E), situations (S), closed intervals (I).

Physical objects:
   hand — Constant
   table — Constant
   block(X) — Predicate: X is a block.

States:
   beneath(X,Y) — X is beneath Y, supporting it directly or
       indirectly.
   clear(X) — State type of block or hand X being clear.
   clear_table(L) — State type of the table being clear at location L.
   under_hand(X) — State type of block X being the top of the tower
       under the hand.

Fluents:
   place(X) — Location of block or hand X.

Events:
   pickup — Constant. Event type of the hand picking up the block
       underneath.
   putdown — Constant. Event type of the hand putting down the
       block that it is holding.
   move(L) — Function. Event type of the
       hand moving to location L.

BW.15′ [occurs(I,pickup) ∧ true_in(start(I),clear(hand)) ∧
       true_in(start(I),under_hand(X))] ⇒
       true_in(end(I),beneath(hand,X))

Axioms BW.17 and BW.18 already have the precondition built into the antecedent, in order to identify the object held in the hand.

   In this new approach, it is undefined what happens if an event occurs when its preconditions are unsatisfied, while in our original

Table 5.2 Blocks-World Axioms

Atemporal Axioms

BW.1. $\overline{\text{block}}(X) \lor X = \text{table} \lor X = \text{hand}$. (Domain closure.)

BW.2. $\neg\text{block}(\text{hand}) \land \neg\text{block}(\text{table}) \land \text{hand} \neq \text{table}$. (Unique names.)

State Coherence Axioms

BW.3 $\neg[\text{ true\_in}(S,\text{beneath}(X, Y)) \land \text{true\_in}(S,\text{beneath}(Y, X))\ ]$.
("Beneath" is antisymmetric.)

BW.4. $[\text{ true\_in}(S,\text{beneath}(X, Y)) \land \text{true\_in}(S,\text{beneath}(Y, Z))\ ] \Rightarrow$
$\text{true\_in}(S,\text{beneath}(X, Z))$.
("Beneath" is transitive.)

BW.5. $[\text{true\_in}(S,\text{beneath}(\text{table},X)) \land \text{true\_in}(S,\text{beneath}(\text{table},Y)) \land$
$\text{value\_in}(S,\text{place}(X)) = \text{value\_in}(S,\text{place}(Y))] \Rightarrow$
$[X = Y \lor \text{true\_in}(S,\text{beneath}(X, Y)) \lor \text{true\_in}(S,\text{beneath}(Y, X))\ ]$.
("Beneath" is a total ordering on blocks in the same place above the table.)

BW.6. $\text{true\_in}(S,\text{beneath}(X, Y)) \Rightarrow$
$[X = \text{table} \lor \text{value\_in}(S,\text{place}(X)) = \text{value\_in}(S,\text{place}(Y))]$.
(If X is beneath Y then either X is the table, or the two are at the same horizontal location.)

BW.7. $\text{block}(X) \Rightarrow$
$\text{true\_in}(S,\text{beneath}(\text{table},X)) \mathbin{\dot{\lor}} \text{true\_in}(S,\text{beneath}(\text{hand},X))]$.
(Every block is above either the hand or the table, but not both.)

BW.8. $[\text{true\_in}(S,\text{beneath}(\text{hand},X)) \land$
$\text{true\_in}(S,\text{beneath}(\text{hand},Y))\ ] \Rightarrow X = Y$.
(There can be only one block in the hand.)

BW.9. $\neg\text{true\_in}(S,\text{beneath}(X,\text{table})) \land \neg \text{true\_in}(S,\text{beneath}(X,\text{hand}))$.
(Nothing is beneath the table or the hand.)

BW.10. $\text{true\_in}(S,\text{clear}(X)) \Leftrightarrow \neg\exists_Y \text{true\_in}(S,\text{beneath}(X, Y))$.
(Definition of clear.)

BW.11. $\text{true\_in}(S, \text{clear\_table}(L)) \Leftrightarrow$
$\neg\exists_X \text{true\_in}(S,\text{beneath}(\text{table},X)) \land L = \text{value\_in}(S, \text{place}(X))$.
(Definition of clear_table.)

BW.12. $\text{true\_in}(S,\text{under\_hand}(X)) \Leftrightarrow$
$[\ \text{block}(X) \land \text{true\_in}(S,\text{clear}(X)) \land \text{true\_in}(S,\text{beneath}(\text{table},X)) \land$
$\text{value\_in}(S,\text{place}(X)) = \text{value\_in}(S,\text{place}(\text{hand}))\ ]$.
(Definition of under_hand.)

Table 5.2 Blocks-World Axioms (Continued)

Preconditions

BW.13. occurs(I,pickup) $\Rightarrow$
[true_in(start(I),clear(hand)) $\wedge$
$\exists_X$ true_in(start(I),under_hand(X))].
(For a pickup to occur, the hand must be clear, and there must
be a block underneath it.)

BW.14. occurs(I,putdown) $\Rightarrow$ $\exists_X$ true_in(start(I),beneath(hand,X)).
(For a putdown to occur, there must be something in the hand.)

Causal Axioms

BW.15. [occurs(I,pickup) $\wedge$ true_in(start(I),under_hand(X))] $\Rightarrow$
true_in(end(I),beneath(hand,X)).
(If the hand executes a pickup, and block X is clear under it, then
X becomes above the hand.)

BW.16. occurs(I,move(L)) $\Rightarrow$ L=value_in(end(I), place(hand)).
(After a move to L, the hand is at L.)

BW.17. [occurs(I,putdown) $\wedge$ true_in(start(I),beneath(hand,X)) $\wedge$
true_in(start(I),under_hand(Y))] $\Rightarrow$
true_in(end(I),beneath(Y, X)).
(If the hand is holding X, and Y is clear underneath, and the
hand executes a putdown, then Y becomes beneath X.)

BW.18. [occurs(I,putdown) $\wedge$ true_in(start(I),beneath(hand,X)) $\wedge$
true_in(start(I),clear_table(value_in(start(I),place(hand))))] $\Rightarrow$
true_in(end(I),beneath(table,X)).
(If the hand is holding X, and the table is clear where the hand
is, and the hand executes a putdown, then the table becomes
beneath X.)

approach, it is demonstrable that the event cannot occur if its preconditions are unsatisfied. This alternative approach has the advantage
of drawing theorem proving and planning very close together. In the
alternative approach, a sequence of events is a feasible way to achieve
a state if it is provable (modulo the frame axioms to be discussed below) that at the end of the occurrence of the events, the state will
hold. Moreover, the backward chaining technique of proving such a
theorem is very close to the means-end analysis used for planning.
In our axiomatization, by contrast, a sequence of events is feasible
if its occurrence is not inconsistent with the axioms. Finding such
a sequence to achieve a given state involves a mixture of backward

chaining through the causal axioms and forward chaining through the precondition axioms.

For example, with our axioms it is possible to prove that, if a pickup occurs in the situation shown in Figure 5.1, then the hand will end up beneath block A, while this is not provable in the alternative system. However, in our system, we can likewise show that, if the pickup occurs in that situation, then the moon is made of green cheese; that is, we can show that the pickup cannot occur.

Nonetheless, we prefer our approach. Our axiom set is strictly stronger and expresses more clearly the relation between events and their preconditions. It allows the reasoner to infer that the preconditions must have held from the knowledge that the event occurred. Also, for tasks other than planning, such as physical reasoning, where one does not directly control the events that occur, being able to infer that a given event cannot occur may be critical. We shall deal with plan feasibility in Section 9.1.

5.4   The Frame Problem and the Ramification Problem

One might suppose that axioms BW.1 through BW.18 would be sufficient to carry out prediction; given the states that hold in a starting situation and a series of events that occur, predict the states that hold in the final situation. For instance, given the starting situation s1 pictured in Figure 5.2A, and given that the events "pickup; move(12); putdown" occur, one would like to predict that the final situation is as in Figure 5.2B. Table 5.3 gives a formal statement of this inference.

An apparently plausible proof can be formulated as follows: From PS1–PS5, BW.6, BW.7, BW.9, BW.10, and BW.12 it follows that blocks A and B are clear and that A is underneath the hand. Hence, by PS6 and BW.15, the hand is beneath block A at the end of i1 after the pickup, which, by PS9, is the beginning of i2. By PS7 and BW.16, the hand will be at location 12 at the end of i2 after the move, which, by PS9 is the beginning of i3. Since block B is at location 12 and is clear, by BW.17 the effect of the putdown is that A will be above B in s4, the end of i4.

Careful analysis, however, shows that this argument is not justified by these axioms, but has a number of gaps, all similar. Throughout the "proof," we have assumed that if an event is not specified to change a state or fluent, then that state or fluent remains the same. But there is nothing in these axioms to justify that assumption. There is no way to show from these axioms that block B will still be at location 12 after

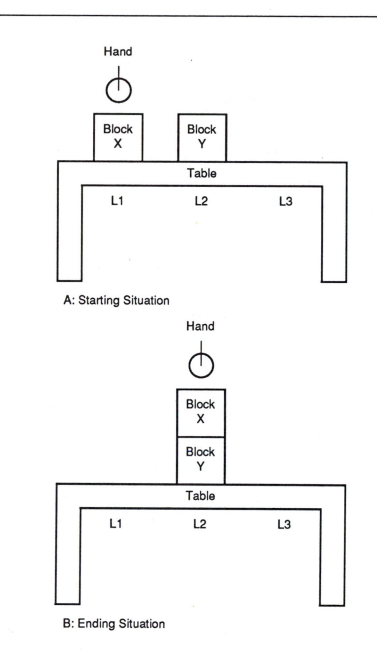

A: Starting Situation

B: Ending Situation

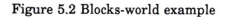

Figure 5.2 Blocks-world example

Table 5.3 Statement of Blocks-World Problem
___

Given:

    PS1. block(X) ⇔ X=a ∨ X=b.
    PS2. value_in(s1, place(a)) = l1.
    PS3. value_in(s1, place(b)) = l2 ≠ l1.
    PS4. value_in(s1, place(hand)) = l1.
    PS5. true_in(s1,clear(hand)).
    PS6. occurs(i1, pickup).
    PS7. occurs(i2, move(l2)).
    PS8. occurs(i3, putdown).
    PS9. s1 = start(i1) ∧ meet(i1,i2) ∧ meet(i2,i3) ∧ s4=end(i3).

To prove:

    value_in(s4, place(a)) = value_in(s4, place(b)) =
    value_in(s4, place(hand)) = l2 ∧
    true_in(s4,beneath(table, b)) ∧ true_in(s4, beneath(b,a))

___

the pickup or after the move or after the putdown, or to show that block A is still above the hand after the move, or to show that block A or the hand are still at l2 after the putdown. This problem of deducing that states and fluents are not changed by events is called the *frame problem* [McCarthy and Hayes 1969]. In a first-order logic, solving the frame problem requires adding additional axioms, known as frame axioms. In the remainder of this section, we will present several ways of formulating frame axioms. In Section 5.5 we will discuss some approaches to the frame problem involving plausible inference.

Solutions to the frame problem must take into account a complementary problem, known as the *ramification* problem. This is the problem of predicting how one state will automatically change when another does, due to some constraint connecting them. In our example, we want to be able to predict that the table will be clear at location l1 after the pickup, since block A is now above the hand, and that block A will be at location l2 after the move, since it is above the hand, and the hand is now at l2. For the latter deduction, note that the desired axioms must specify that it is the state of the hand being beneath the

Table 5.4 Frame Axioms: Framing by Events and Fluents

FRA.1.   occurs(I,pickup) $\Rightarrow$
value_in(start(I),place(X)) = value_in(end(I),place(X)).
(A pick up does not change the horizontal positions of anything.)

FRA.2.   [occurs(I,pickup) $\wedge$
$\neg$true_in(start(I),under_hand(Y))] $\Rightarrow$
true_in(start(I), beneath(X, Y)) $\Leftrightarrow$
true_in(end(I), beneath(X, Y)).

FRA.3.   occurs(I,move(L)) $\Rightarrow$
[true_in(start(I), beneath(X, Y)) $\Leftrightarrow$
true_in(end(I), beneath(X, Y))].

FRA.4.   [occurs(I,move(L)) $\wedge$ hand$\neq Y$ $\wedge$
$\neg$true_in(start(I),beneath(hand,Y))] $\Rightarrow$
value_in(start(I),place(Y)) = value_in(end(I),place(Y)).

FRA.5.   occurs(I,putdown) $\Rightarrow$
value_in(start(I),place(X)) = value_in(end(I),place(X)).

FRA.6.   [occurs(I,putdown) $\wedge$
$\neg$true_in(start(I),beneath(hand,Y))] $\Rightarrow$
true_in(start(I), beneath(X, Y)) $\Leftrightarrow$
true_in(end(I), beneath(X, Y)).

block, rather than the location of the block, that is unchanged by the move event.

In this section, we will consider three general techniques for solving the frame problem in first-order logic. In Section 5.5, we will sketch the issues involved and the difficulties encountered in trying to solve the frame problem using plausible inference.

The most straightforward approach to the frame problem, which we will call "framing by events and fluents," is to add separate frame axioms asserting that a particular category of event type does not change a particular category of state type. In the blocks world, these axioms would assert that a pick up or a put down does not change any horizontal locations, nor any beneath relation except those involving the block picked up or put down, and that a move does not change any beneath relations, nor any horizontal positions except those of the hand and a held block. Table 5.4 shows the formal statement of these axioms.

There are two important problems with this approach. First, it is necessary to state a separate axiom for each combination of a state and an event. If we added the color of a block as a state type and the act of painting a block as an event type, then we would need additional axioms stating that a move, a putdown, and a pickup do not change colors of blocks, and that painting does not change position or beneath relations. Second, these axioms assume implicitly that only one event can occur at a time. For example, in a world where there were two hands that could act simultaneously, we could not use axioms analogous to those of Table 5.4. It would not be correct to say that nothing changes place when a pickup takes place, since the other hand could be moving at the same time.

Another gap in the above axioms is that, as worded above, they do not specify anything of what happens during the events. It would be consistent with these axioms to have blocks flying all over the place during an event, as long as they are back in their proper places by its end. For example, it is not possible to prove from these axioms that block X is never beneath block Y during the course of events in Figure 5.2. This gap can be fixed by adding axioms asserting that every fluent or state that remains constant across the occurrence of an event must remain constant during the event.

FRA.7. [[occurs(I,pickup) $\lor$ occurs(I,move(L)) $\lor$
            occurs(I,putdown)] $\land$
            value_in(start(I),F) = value_in(end(I),F)] $\Rightarrow$
            $\forall_{S \in I}$ value_in(S, F) = value_in(start(I),F).

FRA.8. [[occurs(I,pickup) $\lor$ occurs(I,move(L)) $\lor$
            occurs(I,putdown)] $\land$
            true_in(start(I),A) $\Leftrightarrow$ true_in(end(I),A)] $\Rightarrow$
            $\forall_{S \in I}$ true_in(S, A) $\Leftrightarrow$ true_in(start(I),A).

What happens to fluents that do change in the midst of an event varies with each fluent and event type. For example, it might be reasonable to suppose that in the midst of picking up block X, the objects beneath X are either those beneath X at the start, or the hand. However, it would not be reasonable to suppose that, in the midst of a move, the hand is always at the beginning or ending location. The first supposition would be necessary to show that block X is not above block Y at any time during the pickup in Figure 5.2. To show that block X is never at some distant location L3 at any time during the move would require some richer theory of space and motion.

FRA.9. $[S \in I \wedge [\text{occurs}(I,\text{pickup}) \vee \text{occurs}(I,\text{putdown})]] \Rightarrow$
$[[\forall_{X,Y} \text{ true\_in}(S,\text{beneath}(Y, X)) \Leftrightarrow$
$\text{true\_in}(\text{start}(I),\text{beneath}(Y, X))] \vee$
$[\forall_{X,Y} \text{ true\_in}(S,\text{beneath}(Y, X)) \Leftrightarrow$
$\text{true\_in}(\text{end}(I),\text{beneath}(Y, X))]]$

Note, however, that ramification is no problem in this kind of axiomatization. We do not have to write any axioms about how events affect the "clear" state; that follows automatically from their effect on the beneath state, and the relation between beneath and clear expressed in axiom BW.10.

A second approach to the frame problem, which we call "framing primitive fluents by events," eliminates the proliferation of axioms found in the first. Instead of enumerating for lots of different states and fluents that the event leaves them the same, we use a general statement to assert that only certain specified states and fluents are changed by the event, and (roughly) that all others remain the same. This last description needs some qualification; we do not actually want to specify *all* the states and fluents that might change. In the blocks world we have specified all changes to the beneath state in the causal axioms, and these implicitly specify the changes to the clear state. We do not want to specify separately each change to clear, but to infer it via the definition BW.10. If our language allows us to define arbitrary complex combinations of states and fluents, then there may be infinitely many different states and fluents that change value during an event (e.g., the state of block X being at location l1 and Indianapolis having a greater population than Boston). We should certainly avoid enumerating all these.

The way around these problems is to designate a few states and fluents as *primitive*, as distinguished from the rest, which are *derived*. The primitive states and fluents should be chosen in such a way that, once their values are fixed in a situation, the values of all other significant states and fluents are likewise fixed via the state-coherence axioms. In the blocks world, we may choose the fluents "beneath(X, Y)" and "place(X)" to be primitive. The states "clear(X)", "clear_table(L)", and "under_hand(X)" are derived; their values can be determined, given all values of the beneath and place fluents, together with the domain-closure axiom. Our frame axioms can now be worded to assert that the only primitive fluents or states that change during an event are those specified; all others remain fixed. We also add a unique-names axiom to assert that any two primitive states or fluents with different names are, in fact, unequal. Table 5.5 shows these axioms for the blocks world.

Table 5.5 Frame Axioms: Framing Primitive Fluents By Events

FRB.1.   prim_change(I, F) $\Leftrightarrow$
         [[prim_state(F) $\wedge$ [true_in(start(I),F) $\dot{\vee}$
         true_in(end(I),F)]] $\vee$
         [prim_fluent(F) $\wedge$ value_in(start(I),F) $\neq$
         value_in(end(I),F)]].
         (A primitive change is either a change to the truth value
         of a state or a change to the value of a fluent.)

FRB.2.   prim_state(beneath(X, Y)).
         ("Beneath" is a primitive state.)

FRB.3   prim_fluent(place(X)).
         ("Place" is a primitive fluent.)

FRB.4.   Axiom schema: Let $\alpha(\tau_1 \ldots \tau_k)$ be a function in our lan-
         guage whose range is primitive states or primitive fluents.
         Then the following is an axiom:

$$\forall_{X1\ldots Xk,Y1\ldots Yk}\ \alpha(X1\ldots Xk) = \ldots \alpha(Y1\ldots Yk) \Rightarrow$$
$$[X1 = Y1 \ldots Xk = Yk]$$

   Moreover, if $\beta(\omega_1 \ldots \omega_m)$ is a different function mapping
   onto a primitive state or fluent, then the following is an
   axiom:

$$\alpha(X1\ldots Xk) \neq \beta(Y1\ldots Ym)$$
   In the blocks world, this gives us the following axioms:

   a. beneath($X1, X2$) = beneath($Y1, Y2$) $\Rightarrow$
      [$X1 = Y1 \wedge X2 = Y2$].
   b. place($X1$) = place($Y1$) $\Rightarrow X1 = Y1$.
   c. beneath($X1, X2$) $\neq$ place($Y1$).

   (Unique names: No two beneath states are equal, nor two
   place fluents, nor is any beneath state equal to a place fluent.)

FRB.5.   occurs(I,pickup) $\Rightarrow$

   [$\forall_F$ prim_change(I, F) $\Leftrightarrow$
        [$\exists_{X,Y}$ true_in(start(I),under_hand(X)) $\wedge$
        F=beneath(Y, X)]].
   (The only primitive fluents to change during a pickup are
   the objects beneath the block under the hand.)

Table 5.5 A Modal Temporal Logic (Continued)

FRB.6.   occurs(I,move(L)) $\Rightarrow$

$[\forall_F$ prim_change(I, F) $\Leftrightarrow$
$[F$=place(hand) $\vee$
$[\exists_X$ true_in(start(I),beneath(hand,X)) $\wedge$
F=place(X) $]$ $]$.
(The only primitive fluent to change during a move is the place of the hand and the place of a block held in the hand.)

FRB.7.   occurs(I,putdown) $\Rightarrow$

$[\forall_F$ prim_change(I, F) $\Leftrightarrow$
$[\exists_{X,Y}$ block(X) $\wedge$
true_in(start(I),beneath(hand,X)) $\wedge$
F=beneath(Y, X) $]$ $]$.
(The only primitive fluents to change during a putdown of X are the beneath relations in which X is on top.)

These axioms are a little complex, but they do get around the problem in Table 5.4. We can show, for example, that the truth value of "beneath(blocka, blockb)" does not change during a "move" as follows: By FRB.2, this is a primitive state, so by FRB.1, a change to its truth value over the time of the move is a primitive change. But by FRB.6, during a move, the only primitive change is to place fluents, and by FRB.4, a beneath state is not equal to a place fluent. Hence, the state beneath(blocka,blockb) does not change.

If we now add a new, independent primitive fluent type, such as "color_of(X)", the frame axioms FRB.5, FRB.6, and FRB.7 require no change. In order to infer that a pickup, putdown, or move does not change color_of(X), it is necessary only to add an axiom analogous to FRB.3 stating that color_of(X) is a primitive fluent, and to extend the scope of FRB.4 to assert that color_of(X) is not the same as any beneath state or place fluent. Strictly speaking, the unique-names assumption FRB.4 involves a separate first-order axiom for every pair of primitive state functions. However, these are easily automated, and need not, in practice, be listed explicitly.

There are, however, costs to this approach. First, it forces us to use a language in which we can quantify over fluents and states (either types or tokens), whereas axioms analogous to those of Table 5.4 can be stated in any of the temporal representations we have discussed.

Second, it requires the inference mechanism to reason about equality, implicitly or explicitly. Third, the primitives "prim_state(F)" and "prim_fluent(F)" are not really quite kosher. They do not correspond to anything much in the real world; they are arbitrary distinctions made by us, as theory builders, for the purpose of making axioms cleaner and shorter. As a result, our representation becomes less a description of the relations in the world and more a matter of logic programming.

Framing primitive fluents, like framing fluents and events, rules out the possibility of concurrent events, since it says that only a few states can change whenever an event takes place. It also requires the gap axioms FRA.7, FRA.8, and FRA.9 to specify what happens while the event is going on.

A third way to formulate the frame axioms, "framing primitive events by fluents," is to assert that a given state or fluent type cannot change unless some particular type of event occurs. In the blocks world, we would assert that no beneath relation can change unless a pickup or putdown of the appropriate kind occurs, and that no position changes unless a move occurs. Specifically, if block X becomes above the hand, then X must have been picked up. If X ceases to be above the hand, then X must have been put down. If X was above Y and ceases to be above Y, or if X was not above Y and becomes above Y, then X must have been in the hand some time in between. If the position of the hand changes to L, then the hand must have moved to L. If the position of block X changes to L, then the hand must have moved to L while holding X. In each of these statements, we assert only that some part of the event must occur some time between two situations where the change of state is observed. (The change may occur in the midst of the event itself.) Table 5.6 gives a formal axiomatization of these statements.

These axioms have built into them the gap conditions governing the possible states that hold during an event, since they describe all possible changes in state. We need one axiom for each primitive state or fluent type. The size of the axiom is related to the number of event types that can change the state or fluent, and is independent of the number that leave it unchanged. The size of the axiom set is thus of the same order of magnitude as in framing primitive fluents.

These axioms, unlike those of the first two approaches, are compatible with the possibility of concurrent events. They assert that a change of state occurs only if a given event occurs, but they do not rule out the possibility that many different states can change as a result of many different events occurring at once. Carrying out a frame inference now requires showing, not that the event or events that did occur do not change the state, but that no event occurred that did

---

Table 5.6 Frame Axioms: Framing Primitive Events

FRC.0. intersect$(I1, I2) \Leftrightarrow \exists_{SA,SB \in I1 \cap I2} SA \neq SB$

FRC.1. [$S1 < S2 \wedge \neg$true_in$(S1$,beneath(hand,X)) $\wedge$
  true_in$(S2$,beneath(hand,X))] $\Rightarrow$
  $\exists_I$ intersect$(I, [S1, S2]) \wedge$ occurs$(I$,pickup) $\wedge$
  true_in(start(I),under_hand(X)).
  (If block X becomes above the hand between $S1$ and $S2$,
  then the interval $[S1, S2]$ must intersect with a pickup of X.)

FRC.2. [$S1 < S2 \wedge$ true_in$(S1$,beneath(hand,X)) $\wedge$
  $\neg$true_in$(S2$,beneath(hand,X))] $\Rightarrow$
  $\exists_I$ intersect$(I, [S1, S2]) \wedge$ occurs$(I$,putdown) $\wedge$
  true_in(start(I),beneath(hand,X)).
  (Block X can only cease to be above the hand if a putdown
  of X occurs.)

FRC.3. [$S1 < S2 \wedge$ [true_in$(S1$,beneath(Y, X))
  $\dot{\vee}$ true_in$(S2$,beneath(Y, X))]] $\Rightarrow$
  $\exists_S S1 \leq S \leq S2 \wedge$ true_in$(S$,beneath(hand,X))
  (If some beneath relation involving X on top changes, then
  X must be in the hand some time in between.)

FRC.4. [$S1 < S2 \wedge$ value_in$(S2$,place(hand)) $\neq$
  value_in$(S1$,place(hand))] $\Rightarrow$
  $\exists_{I,L1}$ intersect$(I, [S1, S2]) \wedge$ occurs$(I$,move$(L1)$)
  (The place of the hand can only change, if a move occurs.)

FRC.5. [$S1 < S2 \wedge$ block$(X) \wedge$
  value_in$(S2$,place$(X)) \neq$ value_in$(S1$,place(X))] $\Rightarrow$
  $\exists_{I,L1}$ intersect$(I, [S1, S2]) \wedge$ occurs$(I$,move$(L1))\wedge$
  true_in(start(I),beneath(hand,X))
  (The place of block X can change only if it is held in the
  hand while the hand moves.)

Table 5.7 Nonoccurrence of Extraneous Events

Domain axioms:
$\neg$[occurs($I1$,pickup) $\land$ occurs($I2$,putdown) $\land$ intersect($I1, I2$)]
$\neg$[occurs($I1$,pickup) $\land$ occurs($I2$,move(L)) $\land$ intersect($I1, I2$)]
$\neg$[occurs($I1$,putdown) $\land$ occurs($I2$,move(L)) $\land$ intersect($I1, I2$)]

Problem statement:
[occurs(I, E) $\land$ intersect(I,i1)] $\Leftrightarrow$ E=pickup
[occurs(I, E) $\land$ intersect(I,i2)] $\Leftrightarrow$ E=move(l2)
[occurs(I, E) $\land$ intersect(I,i3)] $\Leftrightarrow$ E=putdown

---

change the state. In our blocks-world example, to show that block Y
never moves using axiom FRC.6, we must show that the hand does
not execute a move while holding Y any time between situations s1
and s4. This consequence does not, however, follow from any of the
axioms we have so far. It is perfectly consistent with our axioms that,
during i1, while the hand is picking up block X, it is simultaneously
moving to l2, picking up Y, and moving Y somewhere else. We must
therefore add additional axioms to rule out these additional events:
either domain axioms that restrict the events that can occur under
given circumstances or axioms in the problem statement that assert
that additional events do not occur. Table 5.7 illustrates these two
kinds of assertions for the blocks world.

We can replace the specific domain rules of Table 5.7 with a general
rule that unequal events do not overlap, together with a unique-names
assumption analogous to FRB.4.

FRC.6.   [occurs($I1, E1$) $\land$ occurs($I2, E2$) $\land$ intersect($I1, I2$)] $\Rightarrow$
           [$E1 = E2 \land I1 = I2$].

FRC.7.   Axiom schema: Let $\alpha(\tau_1 \ldots \tau_k)$ be a function in our language
           whose range is primitive events. Then the following is an
           axiom:

$$\forall_{X1 \ldots Xk, Y1 \ldots Yk} \; \alpha(X1 \ldots Xk) = \ldots = \alpha(Y1 \ldots Yk) \Rightarrow$$
$$[X1 = Y1 \land \ldots \land Xk = Yk].$$

           Moreover, if $\beta(\omega_1 \ldots \omega_m)$ is a different function mapping onto
           a primitive event, then the following is an axiom:

$$\alpha(X1 \ldots Xk) \neq \beta(Y1 \ldots Ym).$$

           In the blocks world, we would have the following axioms:

a. distinct(pickup, putdown, move(L)).

b. move($L1$) = move($L2$) $\Rightarrow$ $L1 = L2$.

This switch in the burden of proof, from tracing the events that do occur to showing that a particular event does not, can make the process of constructing proofs harder; negative statements are generally harder to prove than positive ones. On the other hand, there are many circumstances where we may not know all the events that did occur, but we can limit them. For instance, we may not know the exact motions of the hand during an interval, but we know that it never executed a pickup when over block X, and that block X was not held in the starting scene. In this case, the axioms of Table 5.6 give a straightforward proof that block X remains above the same supports in the same position. It is not possible to justify this conclusion using the first or second approach to the frame problem.

5.5 The Frame Problem as a Plausible Inference

As we have seen, solving the frame problem in a standard logic requires the use of rather constraining or complex axioms. Perhaps the problem is that the inference is not fundamentally a deductive inference, but rather a plausible inference: Assume that a state from a previous situation will persist to a later situation, unless there is some reason to believe that it changes. Here we will sketch some of the problems that arise in applying plausible inference to the frame problem and some methods that have been proposed. We will not explain the technical mechanisms of these methods.

There are at least three different kinds of plausible inference that may be involved in the frame inference:

1. Given causal axioms that describe the changes in state brought about by a given event type, and coherence axioms that describe how states are interconnected in a single situation, infer that any fluent that is not forced to change remains the same. In the blocks world, for example, we would like to describe an nonmonotonic inference rule that could examine the form of causal axioms BW.15– BW.18, determine which fluents are not specifically stated to be changed, and automatically generate one of the above tables of frame axioms, stating that these are not changed. (For this to be in any way feasible, it would be necessary to extend BW.16 to indicate that the position of a held block changes during a move. As the axiom is currently worded, there is no way that such a hypothetical machinery could determine whether the position changes while its

support remains the same, or whether the support changes while
its position remains the same.)

2. Given an enumeration of events occurring during an interval, assume that these (or these and their causal consequences) are the
   only events that occur. For example, given the specification that
   the events "pickup; move(l2); putdown" occur, assume that no other
   events occur at the same time, or in between.

3. Even in cases where it is not reasonable to assume that all events
   are known, assume that no event has occurred to change the state
   in question. For example, if you know that Christine Park was
   your father's boss yesterday, assume that she is still his boss today.
   There are many types of events that could have happened to change
   this — she could have quit or been transferred or promoted or fired,
   or your father could have — and you do not know that any of these
   have not happened, but it is a good guess that they have not. This
   kind of inference depends critically on the length of time that has
   passed, and on the particular state and situation involved. For
   example, if you have not talked to your father about his work for
   20 years, then it is quite likely that his boss has changed in the
   meantime. If you leave your coat in a restaurant, then you are
   likely to find it there five minutes later, but you are not likely to
   find it there 12 months later.

It might seem that all three types of inference could be handled by
a single default rule, "Assume that any state will remain the same,
unless there is reason to suppose that it changes." The time limits in
the third type of inference would then require rules explicitly stating
that a state is likely to change its value after a given time period.
However, applying this rule in this simple form leads to an anomalous result, discovered by Hanks and McDermott [1987], known as the
"Yale Shooting Problem." The problem is as follows: Suppose we are
told that John loads a gun, waits, and then shoots Harry. Our domain
axioms tell us that loading a gun causes it to be loaded, that waiting
has no effects, and that shooting a loaded gun causes the person being
shot at to die. (Table 5.8)

It would seem that we could show, as a default inference, that Harry
is dead at the end of i3 using the following argument: From axioms
YS1, the gun is loaded at the end of i1. Using the frame assumption,
the gun will still be loaded at the end of i2. Therefore, by axiom YS2,
Harry will be dead at the end of i3.

Unfortunately, these axioms justify an alternative argument: Using
the frame inference three times, we can justify the assumptions that

Table 5.8 Yale Shooting Problem

Axioms:

> YS1. occurs(I,load) $\Rightarrow$ true_in(end(I), loaded).
> YS2. [occurs(I,shoot) $\wedge$ true_in(start(I), loaded)] $\Rightarrow$
>   true_in(end(I),dead).

Problem statement:

> occurs(i1,load).
> occurs(i2,wait).
> occurs(i3,shoot).
> meet(i1,i2) $\wedge$ meet(i2,i3).

To prove:

> true_in(end(i3), dead).

John is alive at the end of i1, at the end of i2, and at the end of i3. Therefore, we can infer from YS2 that the gun was unloaded at the end of i2; in short, it became unloaded due to unspecified causes during i2.

There are thus two conflicting ways that we can apply the frame inference. We can use it to infer that the gun remains loaded during i2, or we can use it to infer that John remains alive during i3. The logic gives us no reason to prefer one to the other. Depending on the particular default logic used, the result may be either that the theory has two extensions, or that the theory supports only the disjunction of the two possibilities.

One approach to this problem is to require that the default theory prefer a course of events in which as many changes as possible occur as late as possible [Shoham 1988; Kautz 1986]. For example, in the Yale Shooting Problem we prefer the assumption that John dies to the assumption that the gun becomes unloaded, because the hypothetical death would come later than the hypothetical unloading. However, this kind of inference leads to counterintuitive results in cases where a change is known to have occurred. For example, suppose you park your car, come back two days later, and find, to your surprise, that it is no longer where you parked it. The rule of "change as late as possible" would lead to the conclusion that it was stolen just before you arrived on the scene, which is not reasonable. Many alternative solutions have been discussed in the literature; see the reference section at the end of the chapter for some citations.

5.6   Branching Time

In reasoning about the actions of independent agents, it is often important to distinguish between what they do and what they could do. In particular, it is important that our representation be able to say something about events that are possible but do not take place, and not treat them as merely nonexistent. For example, the statement "Belinda prevented Sidney from reading her diary by burning it" can only be represented in a system in which it makes sense to say that if Belinda had not burned the diary then Sidney might have read it; that is, in a theory that distinguishes between the event of the reading, which might have occurred but did not, and the event of (say) the diary turning into a turtle, which was never in the cards. Similarly, the inference of "Washington was noble" from the fact "Washington did not make himself king at the end of the revolution, though he could have" depends critically on the hypothetical event of Washington making himself king. The inference "Benedict Arnold was noble" from "Benedict Arnold did not make himself king at the end of the revolution" does not hold water, even though Washington's and Arnold's actual actions were the same, as regards making themselves king. In reasoning about such hypothetical events, we must consider their effects; for example, we would be able to make statements such as "If Washington had tried to crown himself, he would have had the support of the Continental Army." (Hypothetical events and branching time are also useful in defining the feasibility of complex plans. See Section 9.1.)

To carry out such reasoning, we must change our model of time from a linear sequence of actual situations to a more complex structure that includes hypothetical situations as well. Hypothetical situations do not occur in isolation; each situation must be part of (at least) one possible chain of events. We define a *chronicle* as one single complete account of the history of a world. The situations in a single chronicle form a fully ordered time line. A situation may appear in more than one chronicle.

We must revise our previous concepts to fit with this new ontology. The space of situations now includes both actual and hypothet-

Table 5.9 Axioms of Chronicles

Sorts: chronicles and intervals (I), situations (S), clock times (T)
Axioms:

BR.1. chronicle(I) $\Leftrightarrow$
   [[$\forall_{S1,S2 \in I} \Rightarrow$ ordered($S1, S2$)] $\wedge$
   [$\forall_{SA \notin I} \exists_{SB \in I} \neg$ordered($SA, SB$)]].
   (A chronicle is a maximal totally ordered set of situations.)

BR.2. $\forall_{I1} \exists_{IC}$ chronicle(IC) $\wedge$ $I1 \subseteq IC$.

   (Every interval is a subset of some chronicle. This is
   provable from the definition of an interval (Section 4.2)
   and BR.1, given the axiom of choice.)

BR.3. $\forall_{T,I}$ chronicle(I) $\Rightarrow \exists_{S \in I}$ value_in(S,clock_time)=T.

---

ical snapshots of the world. The relation "precedes($S1, S2$)" becomes
a partial ordering instead of a total ordering; $S1$ precedes $S2$ if there
is some possible course of events in which $S1$ comes before $S2$. (It is
sometimes useful to further restrict the structure of this partial ordering; for example, to require that it be a forward-branching tree.)
Table 5.9 shows some axioms on chronicles that may be reasonably
posited.

We define the constant symbol "real_chronicle" to represent the chronicle that actually takes place.

The language relating events and states to situations is the same as
before. It must be kept in mind that statements like "true_in(S, A)" or
"occurs(I, E)" no longer carry the implication that state A ever actually
held, or that event E ever actually occurred, unless it is additionally
specified that S and I are part of the real chronicle.

We can now define possible events. An event E is possible in situation S if there is an interval starting in S in which E occurs.

   possible_occur(S, E) $\Leftrightarrow \exists_I$ S=start(I) $\wedge$ occurs(I, E).

For example, we might specify that, in our blocks world, the event
"move(L)" can always occur; that "pickup" can occur if the hand is

Table 5.10 Formulation of Blocks-World Problem

Given:

PS1.   block(X) $\Leftrightarrow$ X=a $\vee$ X=b.
PS2.   value_in(s1, place(a)) = l1.
PS3.   value_in(s1, place(b)) = l2.
PS3.   value_in(s1, place(hand)) = l1.
PS5.   true_in(s1,beneath(table,a)).
PS6.   true_in(s1,beneath(table,b)).

Show:

$\exists_{SE}$ value_in(SE,place(a)) = value_in(SE,place(b)) =
value_in(place(hand)) = l2 $\wedge$
true_in(SE,beneath(b,a)) $\wedge$
true_in(SE,beneath(table,b)) $\wedge$ precede(s1,SE)

---

empty and is above a block; and that "putdown" can occur if the hand is nonempty.

BWP.1.   possible_occur(S,move(L)).
BWP.2.   possible_occur(S,pickup) $\Leftrightarrow$
          true_in(S,clear(hand)) $\wedge$
          $\exists_X$ true_in(S,under_hand(X)).
BWP.3.   possible_occur(S,putdown) $\Leftrightarrow$ $\neg$true_in(S,clear(hand)).

Note that axioms BWP.2 and BWP.3 are strictly stronger than the precondition axioms BW.13 and BW.14, respectively. BW.13 and BW.14 state that the preconditions are necessary conditions for the occurrence of the event; BWP.2 and BWP.3 state that the preconditions are necessary and sufficient conditions for its possible occurrence.

We can use these axioms to show that we can reach the states shown in Figure 5.2B from those in Figure 5.2A. (Table 5.10.)

The proof is straightforward. We use axioms BWP.1–BWP.3 and the axioms governing branching time to show that there exists a chronicle in which the events "pickup," "move(l2)", and "putdown" occur in sequence. We then use the basic blocks-world and frame axioms to show that the specified states hold in the final situation.

We can formalize the concept of prevention as follows: To prevent an event type E is itself an event type EP. EP is a preventing of E in situation S if (i) it is possible in S that E will occur — that is, there are chronicles including S in which E occurs after S; and (ii) after EP occurs, it is impossible that E will occur.

occurs(I,prevent(E)) $\Leftrightarrow$
[[$\exists_{I1}$ precede(start(I),start($I1$)) $\wedge$ occurs($I1, E$)] $\wedge$
[$\neg\exists_{I1}$ precede(end(I),start($I1$)) $\wedge$ occurs($I1, E$)]]

We represent the statement that one event type prevented another by stating that some token of the first was also a token of a preventing of the second. For example, the statement "Belinda prevented Sidney from reading her diary by burning it" is represented in the form:

$\exists_K$ token_of(K,burn(belinda,diary_of(belinda))) $\wedge$
token_of(K,prevent(read(sidney,diary_of(belinda)))).

5.7 The STRIPS Representation

The STRIPS planning program [Fikes and Nilsson 1971] used a representation for events that can often greatly simplify computing whether a given sequence of discrete events is possible, predicting the effect of a sequence of events, and planning a sequence of events that brings about a desired state. In particular, the STRIPS representation gives an elegant solution to the frame problem. The representation we present here is slightly simplified from that used in STRIPS; it combines aspects of STRIPS with aspects of TWEAK [Chapman 1987] (see Section 9.2).

In our representation, a situation is characterized in terms of a set of state types of a restricted form. Each state type is expressed in one of the two forms a_i or $f_i(c_1, \ldots c_k)$ where a_i is a state-type constant, f_i is a state-valued function, and $c_1 \ldots c_k$ are constant symbols. The effect of an event is specified in terms of an *add list*, which enumerates the states that become true when the event takes place, and a *delete list*, which enumerates the states that become false. Also associated with the event is a list of *preconditions*, simple states or their negations that must hold in order for the events to be possible.[2] Any state type

---

[2]The actual STRIPS representation allowed preconditions to be arbitrary first-order sentences, without situational argument, similar to the state propositions in the modal logic described in Section 5.12. This extended the power of the representation, at the cost of requiring potentially arbitrarily difficult theorem proving to verify the possibility of a plan. The simplification of restricting preconditions to be simple states was introduced in later planning programs [Sacerdoti 1975; Chapman 1987].

that is not on the add list or delete list of an event is unaffected by the event. Thus, the frame inference is carried out just by carrying over these unaffected states from one situation to the next.

Given such a representation, many temporal calculations become simple. The situation resulting from a series of events can be calculated by starting with states in the starting situation, and, for each event type, adding the states on the add list and removing those on the delete list. The total time needed for this prediction is at most the sum of the sizes of the add list and delete list of each event involved (Exercise 8). Such a sequence of events is possible if the precondition list of each event is satisfied in the situation where it occurs; this can be computed together with the prediction of the effect in additional time proportional to the sum of the sizes of the precondition list. Planning a sequence of events to satisfy a given goal can be carried out by planning an event with the goal on the add list, and then recursively planning to satisfy the preconditions of the event. (This is an inherently difficult operation — NP-hard — but the representation at least makes it straightforward, if not easy.)

The success of these algorithms depends on two strong conditions on the representation. Every state in an add list, delete list, or precondition list must be represented as an atomic, ground term. Every state type that appears in any precondition list must appear in all relevant add lists and delete lists. It is therefore not generally possible to restrict add and delete lists to contain only primitive states. For example, since it is a precondition of a pickup that the hand be clear, it is necessary that any event that changes whether the hand is clear state that explicitly, and not leave it to be inferred using the state-coherence axioms. Most importantly, the effects and preconditions of each event type must depend only on the event type itself, and not on the situation at the beginning of the event. In many cases, this will require a finer discrimination of event types than the natural categorization of events. This discrimination may be achieved either by dividing up event-type functions into several categories, or by adding formal arguments to them. In other cases, it may require using a new vocabulary of states.

For example, the number of beneath states changed by a pickup or putdown depends on the height of the stack involved. The "beneath" relation is thus unsuited to a STRIPS representation in this domain. We use instead the relation "on(X, Y)", meaning that X is immediately above Y; a pickup or putdown creates only one "on" relation and destroys one. Second, the effects of the blocks-world events "move(L)," "pickup," and "putdown" used above cannot be determined from the event type alone. Whether a move event changes the position of a block, and, if so, which block; and which block has its beneath relations changed by a pickup or putdown depend on which blocks are being held or are under the hand in the starting situation. We must therefore modify the "move" event to discriminate between moving empty, and moving holding a block, and to specify which block, and we must modify "pickup" and "putdown" to specify which block is being picked up or put down, and what was or will be beneath the block. Finally, there is a difference between the forms of the preconditions in putting a block X down on another block Y, and those of the preconditions of putting X down on the table. In the first case, we require the state "clear(Y)"; in the latter, we require the state "clear_table(L)". One way to deal with this difference is to distinguish the event of putting a block on the table from the event of putting it on another block, and making the analogous distinction in picking up. Another approach, which we will follow, is to use a unified state "clear(X, L)", meaning that object X (block or table) is clear at location L. The argument L is, of course, redundant unless X is the table. We will use a different state, "empty_hand," to indicate that the hand is empty. Table 5.11 shows the complete STRIPS representation for the blocks world.

5.8 Situation Calculus

In circumstances where only one event occurs at a time, where time durations do not matter, and where the state of the world during an event does not matter, it is often convenient to model time as a discrete graph, whose nodes are situations, and whose arcs are primitive events. Situation nodes are labeled with the states that hold in the situation. Event arcs are labeled with the event type, and point from the starting situation to the ending situation (Figure 5.3). Extensionally, an event type can be viewed as a function mapping the starting situation to the ending situation. A convenient method to represent this model logically is to use the function "result(S, E)," which takes a starting situation S and an event E, and returns the ending situation. For example, the term "result(s1, pickup)" denotes the situation resulting when a pickup is performed in s1. The term "result(S, E)" should be taken as undefined if event E is not possible in situation S. The "result" function can be used to replace the "occurs" predicate, using the following axiom:

$$\text{end}(I) = \text{result}(\text{start}(I), E) \Leftrightarrow \text{occurs}(I, E).$$

Table 5.11 The Blocks-World in STRIPS

State types:
  place(X, L), on(X, Y), clear(X, L), empty_hand

Events:

  move_free($L1, L2$) (Moving empty-handed from $L1$ to $L2$.)
    Add list: place(hand,$L2$)
    Delete list: place(hand,$L1$)
    Preconditions: empty_hand, place(hand,$L1$).

  carry($X, L1, L2$) (Carrying block X from $L1$ to $L2$)
    Add list: place($X, L2$), place(hand,$L2$),
        clear($X, L2$)
    Delete list: place($X, L1$), place(hand,$L1$),
        clear($X, L1$)
    Preconditions: on(X,hand), place(hand,$L1$).

  pickup(X, Y, L) (Picking block X up off block Y at
        location L)
    Add list: on(X,hand), clear(Y, L)
    Delete list: clear_hand, on(X, Y)
    Preconditions: clear(X, L), on(X, Y), clear_hand,
        place(hand,L)

  putdown(X, Y, L) (Putting block X down on block Y at
        location L)
    Add list: on(X, Y), clear_hand
    Delete list: on(X,hand), clear(Y, L)
    Preconditions: clear(Y, L), on(X,hand),
        place(hand,L)

For example, the blocks-world axiom BW.11, describing the results of a move, can be expressed as follows:

  L=value_in(result(S,move(L)), place(hand)).

  (After a move to L, the hand is at L.)

The statement that event E has precondition A can be expressed by stating that "result(S, E)" is the null value unless A holds in S.

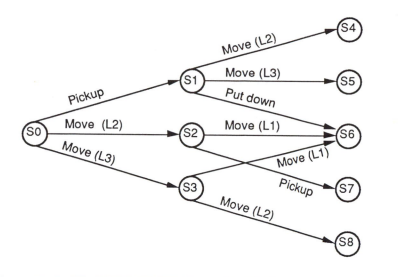

Figure 5.3 Graph of situations and events

result(S,pickup) $\neq \perp \Leftrightarrow$
true_in(S,clear(hand)) $\land \exists_X$ true_in(S,under_hand(X)).

The situation calculus was the earliest temporal representation to be used in AI [McCarthy 1963], and it has been one of the most extensively studied.

5.9 Real-Valued Time

In reasoning about motion and other continuous change in physical quantities, it is generally best to use a continuous model of time. We can adapt the formal apparatus we have developed so far to continuous time simply by specifying that the space of clock times is isomorphic to the reals. The language of real-valued quantities and functions developed in Chapter 4 can then be applied. No further formal symbols or theories are required.

We give two examples to illustrate this type of reasoning. The first is given as an example of reasoning where a continuous model of time is needed, though no exact quantities are mentioned. The second is given as an example of a temporal domain theory of a very different structure than the blocks world described above. Further uses of continuous time are discussed in Chapters 6 and 7.

Example 1: Ian and Tom are running a race, and Ian is currently behind Tom. Show that, if Ian is to win the race, then he must be level with Tom some time between now and the end of the race. Let "place(X)" be the fluent representing the position of person X along the racetrack. We assume, for simplicity, that this position is a one-dimensional measure space. Table 5.12 shows the formal statement of this problem and the axioms needed in its solution.

To prove this, we first show that in situation s1 Tom is short of the finish line. From the problem statement, we know that Tom is never at the finish line. Suppose that Tom were past the finish line in situation s1. Then, by the axiom of continuity, there would have to be a time S between s0 and s1 in which Tom was at the finish line, but this violates the problem statement. Having shown this, we consider the fluent F = place(ian) − place(tom). It is easily shown that this fluent is continuous, that it is negative in s0, and that it is positive in s1. Therefore, it is zero some time in between. In that situation, Ian and Tom must be equally far along.

Example 2: A number of tasks must be carried out on identical processors. The completion of a task requires a fixed length of time, independent of the processor that executes it. A precedence relation is defined on tasks; certain tasks must be completed before others can be started. Each processor can execute only one task at a time. Each task must be executed once. Table 5.13 shows an axiomatization of this domain.

5.10 Complex States and Events

As discussed in Section 5.1, the advantage to representing time-varying facts using state and event types rather than using extra-argument notation is that it gives us the power to use state and event types as arguments to functions and predicates and to quantify over them. To take full advantage of this power, we must be able to name any state or event type that seems convenient. Our vocabulary so far does not allow us to do that. For example, our blocks-world language allows us to represent "the state of block A being beneath block B" as "beneath(a,b)" or to represent the event of picking something up as "pickup"; but it does not give us any way to represent (i) "the state of block A being beneath some other block," or (ii) "the state of the hand being clear when block A is directly underneath it," or (iii) "the event

Table 5.12 Sample Axioms for Continuous Reasoning

Problem statement:

value_in(s0,place(ian)) < value_in(s0,place(tom)) < track_end.
(In situation s0, Ian is behind Tom, who has not
finished the race.)

value_in(s1,place(ian)) = track_end.
(Ian reaches the end of the track in s1.)

$\forall_{S\in[s0,s1]}$ value_in(S,place(tom)) $\neq$ track_end.
(Tom is never at the end of the track between
s0 and s1.)

precedes(s0,s1).
(Situation s0 precedes s1.)

To prove:

$\exists_{S\in[s0,s1]}$ value_in(S,place(ian)) = value_in(S,place(tom)).
(Ian and Tom are the same distance along at some time
between s0 and s1.)

Axioms:

continuous(place(X)).
(People move continuously.)

continuous(F) $\land$ continuous(G) $\Rightarrow$ continuous($F - G$).
(The difference of two continuous fluents is
continuous.)

[continuous(F) $\land$ value_in($S1, F$) < C $\land$
value_in($S2, F$) > C $\land$ precedes($S1, S2$)] $\Rightarrow$
$\exists_{S\in[S1,S2]}$ value_in(S, F) = C
(A continuous fluent F that goes from less than C to
greater than C must be equal to C some time in between.)

Table 5.13 Axioms for Multiprocessor Scheduling

Nonlogical symbols:

task(T) — Predicate. T is a task.
processor(P) — Predicate. P is a processor.
runs(T, P) — Function. Event type of task T running on processor P.
precedence($T1, T2$) — Predicate. Task $T1$ takes precedence over $T2$.
length(T) — Function. The length of time necessary to carry out
　　task T.

Axioms:

- task(T) $\Rightarrow \exists^1_{I,P}$ processor(P) $\wedge$ occurs(I,runs(T, P)).
  (Every task is executed exactly once.)

- [precedence($T1, T2$) $\wedge$ occurs($I1$,runs($T1, P1$)) $\wedge$
  occurs($I2$,runs($T2, P2$))] $\Rightarrow$
  end($I1$) $\leq$ start($I2$).
  (If $T1$ has precedence over $T2$, then $T1$ must be completed before
  $T2$ can be started.)

- [occurs($I1$,runs($T1, P$)) $\wedge$ occurs($I2$,runs($T2, P$)) $\wedge$
  intersect($I1, I2$)] $\Rightarrow$
  $T1 = T2$.
  (A processor P can run only one task at a time.)

- occurs(I,run(T, P)) $\Rightarrow$
  value_in(end(I),clock_time) $-$ value_in(start(I),clock_time) =
  length(T).
  (A task T must run for its length.)

---

of picking up block A," or (iv) "the event of doing a pickup followed by a putdown." Of course we can define new primitives for these particular cases, but we would like a uniform technique that allows us to name them, without forever introducing new primitives and new axioms to define them.

The language of Section 6.3 does allow us to state that any of these states held in a given situation, or any of these events occurred in an interval, using complex sentences. We can assert that state (i) (block

A being beneath some other block) held in situation s0 in the formula

$\exists_Y$ block(Y) $\land$ true_in(s0,beneath(a,Y))

We can assert that event (iii) (picking up block A) occurred in interval i0 in the formula

occurs(i0,pickup) $\land$ true_in(end(i0),beneath(hand,a))

However, this language does not allow us to attribute a property directly to one of these states or events. If, for example, we have a predicate "intermittent(A)" that holds on states A, there is no way that we can apply it to the state of block A being beneath some block. Indeed, our axioms do not even guarantee that there is any such state type as "Block A being under some block."

In the following sections, we will look at some solutions to this problem. This section describes the use of set theory for this purpose; Section 5.11 describes control structures, which are useful functions for naming complex events; and Section 5.12 describes the use of modal logics.

One solution to these problems, which also gives an elegant extensional interpretation of state and event types, is to identify a state A with the set of situations in which A holds and to identify an event E with the set of intervals during which E occurs.[3] Similarly, a general fluent is associated with a function from the space of situations to the particular domain of the fluent. Under this identification, the axiom of comprehension on sets guarantees the existence of any state or event type whose constituent situations or intervals can be described in any first-order formula; and set-constructor notation gives us the means to name them. We can name the state and event types (i–iv) above as follows:

i. { S | $\exists_Y$ block(Y) $\land$ true_in(S,beneath(a,Y)) }

ii. { S | true_in(S,clear(hand)) $\land$ true_in(S,underhand(a)) }

iii. { I | occurs(I,pickup) $\land$ true_in(end(I),beneath(hand,a)) }

iv. { join($I1, I2$) | occurs(II,pickup) $\land$
    occurs($I2$,putdown) $\land$ meet($I1, I2$) }

The basic Boolean operators on sets correspond to useful operations on state and event types. A situation is an element of a state if the

---

[3]To the best of my knowledge, this was first proposed in [McDermott 1982a]. McDermott [1985] later withdrew his proposal, under pressure, I believe, from a school of thought hostile to sets.

Table 5.14 Blocks-World State Coherence Axioms: Set Notation

New nonlogical symbol:
   always — Constant. Set of all situations.

Blocks-World State Coherence Axioms:

BW.3. $\text{beneath}(X, Y) \cap \text{beneath}(Y, X) = \emptyset$.

BW.4. $\text{beneath}(X, Y) \cap \text{beneath}(Y, Z) \subseteq \text{beneath}(X, Z)$.

BW.5. $X \neq Y \Rightarrow$
   $(\text{beneath}(\text{table}, X) \cap \text{beneath}(\text{table}, Y) \cap$
   $\text{eql}(\text{place}(X), \text{place}(Y)))\ \subseteq$
   $(\text{beneath}(X, Y) \cup \text{beneath}(Y, X))$.

BW.6. $X \neq \text{table} \Rightarrow \text{beneath}(X, Y) \subseteq \text{eql}(\text{place}(X), \text{place}(Y))$.

BW.7a. $\text{block}(X) \Rightarrow \text{beneath}(\text{table}, X) \cup \text{beneath}(\text{hand}, X) = \text{always}$.

BW.7b. $\text{block}(X) \Rightarrow \text{beneath}(\text{table}, X) \cap \text{beneath}(\text{hand}, X) = \emptyset$.

BW.8. $[\text{beneath}(\text{hand}, X) \cap \text{beneath}(\text{hand}, Y) \neq \emptyset\ ] \Rightarrow X = Y$.

BW.9. $\text{beneath}(X, \text{table}) = \text{beneath}(X, \text{hand}) = \emptyset$.

---

state holds in the situation. The intersection of two states $A1 \cap A2$ is the state where both states hold; the union $A1 \cup A2$ is the state where one or the other holds; the complement $\sim A1$ is the state where $A1$ does not hold. We can thus rewrite formula (ii) above in the cleaner form "clear(hand) $\cap$ underhand(a)." Similarly, we can rewrite state-coherence axioms as set theoretic relations on the states involved. For example, Table 5.14 shows a rewriting of blocks-world axioms BW.3–BW.9.

Similar correspondences apply to events. An interval is an element of an event type if the event occurs in the interval. The intersection of two events $E1 \cap E2$ is the event of both $E1$ and $E2$ starting and ending simultaneously; the union of two events $E1 \cup E2$ is the event of either $E1$ or $E2$ occurring. The complementation operator, however, does not give a very useful construct; the complement of the set of intervals in which E occurs is the set of intervals that do not exactly correspond to a single occurrence of E. To represent the nonoccurrence of event type E, we introduce the function "nonoccurrence(E)." The nonoccurrence of E takes place in interval I if E does not occur in any subinterval of I.

$$\text{occurs}(I, \text{nonoccurrence}(E)) \Leftrightarrow \neg \exists_{I1} \; I1 \subseteq I \wedge \text{occur}(I1, E)$$

5.11 Control Structures

It is often convenient to reason about complex structures of events built up out of simple events. For example, in our blocks world, we might want to show that we can transfer all the blocks in location l1 to location l2 by repeating the sequence "move(l1); pickup; move(l2); putdown," until the table is clear at l1. In physical reasoning, we might want to describe the action of an ideal pendulum as "Swinging back and forth with constant amplitude."

A natural set of constructs to use in formulating such descriptions are analogous to the statement level control structures used in ALGOL-type programming languages: sequences, conditionals, and loops.[4] For example, the plan above for moving blocks from l1 to l2 could be represented in the form

```
while(~clear_table(l1),
sequence(move(l1), pickup, move(l2), putdown))
```

The eternally swinging pendulum could be described in the form

```
while(always, sequence(swing(pend1,−x), swing(pend1,x)))
```

where "x" represents the furthest horizontal displacement of the swing.

Formally, we define the following functions, mapping event types and state types to event types:

- sequence($E1, E2, \ldots, Ek$) — Events $E1$ through Ek occur in sequence.

- cond($A, E1, E2$) — If state type A holds, then $E1$ occurs, else $E2$ occurs.

---

[4]"Purer" approaches to programming languages, such as functional programming or logical programming, are less suited to apply to events. Pure programming languages generally try to avoid the use of side effects. By contrast, side effects are central in reasoning about events.

Table 5.15 Axioms on Compound Events

CE.1.   sequence($E1, E2$) =
$\qquad$ { join($I1, I2$) | $I1 \in E1 \land I2 \in E2 \land$ meets($I1, I2$)}

CE.2.   sequence($E1, E2, \ldots Ek$) = sequence($E1$, sequence($E2 \ldots Ek$))

CE.3.   cond($A, E1, E2$) =
$\qquad$ { I | $I \in E1 \land$ start(I) $\in A$ } $\cup$ { I | $I \in E2 \land$ start(I) $\notin A$ }

CE.4.   null = { $[S, S]$ }
CE.5.   while(A, E) = cond(A, sequence(E, while(A, E)), null)
CE.6. $I \in$ while(A, E) $\Rightarrow$
$\qquad$ [bounded(I) $\Rightarrow$ end(I) $\notin A$] $\land$
$\qquad$ [$\forall_{S \in I}$ $S \neq$ end(I) $\Rightarrow \exists_{IS}$ $S \in IS \land IS \in E \land$ start(IS) $\in A$.]

- while(A, E) — Event E repeats as long as A holds at the beginning of an iteration.

Table 5.15 shows the definitions of these constructs.

Axioms CE.1, which defines the sequence of two actions, CE.2, which recursively defines the sequence of k actions, and CE.3, which defines a conditional, are straightforward. Axiom CE.4 defines the null action as occurring in any instantaneous interval, for use in axiom CE.5. Axioms CE.5 and CE.6 give two separate characterizations of the while loop. CE.5 defines a while loop constructively in the recursive form, "If A holds, then first do E, and next execute the loop while(A, E); else halt." CE.6 gives a nonconstructive characterization of the occurrence of the loop "while(A, E)" during the interval I in terms of the following constraints: (i) If I is bounded, then A is false at the end of I; and (ii) Every situation S in I, except possibly the last, is part of some iteration of E; that is, part of an interval IS such that E occurs in IS, and such that A is true at the beginning of IS.

Axiom CE.5, being constructive, is more useful in expanding a while loop into a sequence of events in a given situation. However, its recursive structure makes it difficult to prove general theorems in contexts where it is hard to rule out infinite loops. For example, it is consistent with axiom CE.5, that the occurrence of a loop like "while(place(a,l1), sequence(pickup,putdown))" should consist of an infinite loop of pickups and putdowns, following arbitrary motions of the hand. Axiom

CE.6 rules out this kind of interpretation, not by eliminating the possibility of infinite loops, but by constraining the hand to keep on picking up and putting down even after the infinite loop, as long as the termination condition of the while loop is not met.

The following examples illustrate how the axioms of Table 5.14 can be used to verify that such a structure of events can achieve a situation with specified properties.

Example 1: Show that the hand will be at location L after the occurrence of the event "Move to L unless the hand is at L." This event is represented "cond(eql(place(hand),L), null, move(L))." (Since L is a constant rather than a fluent, the term "eql(place(hand),L)" constitutes an abuse of notation of a mild and familiar kind.) The formal statement of the fact that this will succeed in getting the hand to L is

$I \in$ cond(eql(place(hand),L),null,move(L))) $\Rightarrow$
value_in(end(I),place(hand)) = L

Proof by cases: Either the hand is at L at the start of I or it is not. If it is, then, by CE.3, the occurrence of the conditional is equivalent to the occurrence of its first branch, the null event. Therefore, by CE.4, the end of I is the same as the start of I. If the hand is not at L, then, by CE.3, the occurrence of the conditional is the occurrence of the second branch, the move to L. By axiom BW.16, the hand is at L after a move to L.

Example 2: Show that the event

while(~clear_table($L1$),
        sequence(move($L1$), pickup, move($L2$), putdown))

has the effect of moving all the blocks at $L1$ to $L2$, assuming that it terminates. (We cannot prove that it terminates, because that may be false if there are infinitely many blocks at $L1$, and the condition that there are only finitely many cannot be stated without great extensions to the language.) The formal statement is

[$I \in$while(~clear_table($L1$),
            sequence(move($L1$), pickup, move($L2$), putdown)) $\wedge$
    value_in(start(I),place(X)) = $L1 \wedge$ block(X) $\wedge$ bounded(I)] $\Rightarrow$
    value_in(end(I),place(X)) = $L2$

Proof: It follows from axiom CE.6 that every situation in the interval I is part of an occurrence of the event type "sequence(move($L1$), pickup,move($L2$),putdown)". Hence, by axioms CE.1 and CE.2, every situation is part of an occurrence of one of the events, "move($L1$)", "pickup", "move($L2$)", or "putdown". By the axioms of Table 5.7, it follows that no event of any other type occurred during this interval. Since I terminates, it follows from axiom CE.6 that the table is clear at $L1$ at the end of I; that is, by the blocks-world axioms, there are no blocks at $L1$ at the end of I. Therefore, if block X was at $L1$ at the beginning of I, it must have moved during I. By frame axiom FRC.4, block X can only change its position from $L1$ if it is held, and the hand moves from $L1$. But we have shown that the only moves away from $L1$ are moves to $L2$, which cause block X to be at $L2$. A similar analysis shows that, once block X is at $L2$, it cannot afterward move away from $L2$. Therefore, X will be at $L2$ when the loop is complete.

Axioms CE.1 through CE.6 exhibit some anomalies that should be kept in mind. The first, already noted, is that they do not rule out the possibility of a loop executing infinitely many iterations in finite time, and then going on to execute some more iterations. The second is that they behave badly with instantaneous events. In particular, a loop whose body is an instantaneous event is a rather strange concept. Unfortunately, they also make it necessary to include instantaneous events as possibilities: There is no other interpretation of a while loop whose continuation condition is violated in the start scene.

Another useful event operator is the concurrency operator "concurrent $(E1, \ldots, Ek)$," asserting that events $E1$ through Ek occur concurrently. The formal definition is simple: Events $E1 \ldots Ek$ occur during I if each event Ei starts at the beginning of I, and I continues until the last is finished.

CE.7. occurs(I,concurrent($E1 \ldots Ek$)) $\Leftrightarrow$
        $\exists_{I1 \ldots Ik}$ occurs($I1, E1$) $\wedge \ldots \wedge$ occurs(Ik, Ek) $\wedge$
        start(I) = start($I1$) = $\ldots$ = start(Ik) $\wedge$
        end(I) = max(end($I1$) $\ldots$ end(Ik))

The frame problem becomes more difficult in reasoning about concurrency. So far, all our solutions to the frame problem have been based on the assumption that only one event occurs at a time; this was either explicitly stated or built into the frame axioms. Once we allow concurrent actions, this assumption obviously cannot be used. However, if we have a plan including concurrent events, we do want to assert that only the events specified occur. In a world with several hands, if we specify the occurrence of the event "concurrent(pickup(hand1), move(hand3,l2))," we want to rule out the possibility that hand2 is doing something else at the same time. But ruling this out requires some care, since this concurrent statement may be just part of a larger plan that does specify that the hand2 be executing a plan.

One way to solve this problem is to invoke the nonmonotonic closed-world assumption on the predicate "occurs." We can solve this problem in a monotonic logic as follows: We view a compound event type as involving a number of occurrences of primitive events. A compound event occurs if all its primitive components occur. A compound event occurs exclusively in interval I if its primitive components are the only primitive events that occur during that interval. Table 5.16 shows an axiomatization of this theory.

5.12 Modal Temporal Logic

(Note: This section depends on Section 2.7.)

An alternative approach to temporal representations is to view temporal operators, such as "true_in" and "occurs", as modal operators taking propositions as arguments, rather than as first-order symbols. In such a language, we can write expressions like "true_in(s100, $\forall_B$ block(B) $\Rightarrow$ beneath(table,B))," or "cond($\exists_X$ beneath (table,X), putdown, null)" without any embarrassment.

There are many different ways to define modal temporal logic; the one we will illustrate was chosen to be close to our first-order language above. Our language will contain three different kinds of formulas: state propositions, event propositions, and anchored propositions. These correspond, respectively, to the state types, event types, and propositions of our first-order theory. State propositions and event propositions "float" without a specific temporal reference. For example, "The table is clear" or "Every block is clear" would be state propositions; "The hand moves to the location of block A" would be an event proposition. Anchored propositions are fixed in time, either because they are timeless, such as "Block A is not equal to block B," or because temporal references are fixed, such as "In situation s1, every block was clear" or "In interval i2, the hand moved to the location of block A."

A state proposition occurring at top level in a knowledge base is interpreted as meaning that the state holds in all situations; a top-level event proposition is interpreted as meaning that the event occurs in all intervals. (In Section 2.6, we discussed temporal modal logics where a top-level state proposition is interpreted as meaning that the proposition is true now. We do not adopt this interpretation here because it is unsuitable for a knowledge base that persists over time.)

Table 5.17 shows the recursive definition of the type of a complex formula. This logic can be axiomatized by specifying how a formula in

Table 5.16 Axioms for Primitive-Event Components

New predicates:

primitive(E) — E is a primitive event type.

primitive_component(KP, KC) — Event token KP is a primitive component of event token KC.

occurs_exclusively(K) — Event token K constitutes all that happens during its time period.

Axioms:

EP.1.　occurs_exclusively(K) $\Leftrightarrow$
　　　　[$\forall_{EP,KP}$ [primitive(EP) $\wedge$ token_of(KP, EP)] $\Rightarrow$
　　　　　　intersect(time_of(KP),time_of(K)) $\Leftrightarrow$
　　　　　　primitive_component(KP, K)]
　　　　(A compound event K occurs exclusively if the only primitive events that occur during its time are its components.)

EP.2.　[token_of(K, E) $\wedge$ primitive(E)] $\Rightarrow$
　　　　[primitive_component(KP, K) $\Leftrightarrow$ $KP = K$]
　　　　(Base case: A primitive event is its own primitive component.)

EP.3.　[token_of(K,sequence($E1, E2$)) $\Rightarrow$
　　　　$\exists_{K1,K2}$ token_of($K1, E1$) $\wedge$ token_of($K2, E2$) $\wedge$
　　　　　time_of(K) = join(time_of($K1$), time_of($K2$)) $\wedge$
　　　　　$\forall_{KP}$ primitive_component(KP, K) $\Leftrightarrow$
　　　　　　　[primitive_component($KP, K1$) $\vee$ primitive_component($KP, K2$)]
　　　　(The primitive components of sequence($E1, E2$) are the primitive components of $E1$ together with the primitive components of $E2$.)

EP.4.　token_of(K,cond($A, E1, E2$) $\Rightarrow$
　　　　[[true_in(start(time_of(K)),A) $\wedge$ token_of($K, E1$)] $\vee$
　　　　[$\neg$true_in(start(time_of(K)),A) $\wedge$ token_of($K, E2$)]]
　　　　(The occurrence of a conditional is the occurrence of the appropriate branch.)

EP.5.　while(A, E) = cond(A,sequence(E,while(A, E)), null)
　　　　(Same as CE.5. Adequate when loops are provably finite, as discussed above. It is difficult to modify axiom CE.6 to give an enumeration of primitive components.)

EP.6.　token_of(K,concurrent($E1, E2$)) $\Rightarrow$
　　　　$\exists_{K1,K2}$ token_of($K1, E1$) $\wedge$ token_of($K2, E2$) $\wedge$
　　　　　start(time_of(K)) = start(time_of($K1$)) = start(time_of($K2$)) $\wedge$
　　　　　end(time_of(K)) = max(end(time_of($K1$)),end(time_of($K2$)) $\wedge$
　　　　　[$\forall_{KP}$ primitive_component(KP, K) $\Leftrightarrow$
　　　　　　[primitive_component($KP, K1$) $\vee$
　　　　　　　primitive_component($KP, K2$)]]
　　　　(The primitive components of concurrent($E1, E2$) are the primitive components of $E1$ together with the primitive components of $E2$.)

---

this language can be translated into one that would be acceptable in our first-order language. The translation rules are simple: Booleans and quantifiers commute with "true_in" and "occurs"; "true_in" and "occurs" are redundant when applied to anchored propositions; "value_in" is redundant when applied to an anchored term; a fluent argument inside a state predicate inside "true_in(S,.)" can be replaced by its value in S; a fluent argument inside an event predicate inside "occurs(I,.)" can be replaced by its value at the start of I. All the rules of the predicate calculus apply, except that existential abstraction and universal specification can be applied only to anchored terms and not to fluents (Exercise 9). The inference rule of necessitation is used to translate a stand-alone state or event to the statement that that state always holds. Table 5.18 gives a formal description of this modal logic.

We can augment the above logic with a variety of additional modal operators. *Tense* logic introduces a number of state modal operators that characterize a situation in terms of states that hold in its future or past. For instance, we can define operators "future(ϕ)," meaning that ϕ will always be true in the future; "past(ϕ)," meaning that ϕ was always true in the past; "some_future(ϕ)," meaning that ϕ will be true at some point in the future; and "some_past(ϕ)," meaning that ϕ was true at some point in the past. Table 5.19 shows how these may be formally defined in terms of "true_in." (Standard tense logics use only tense operators like these; they do not use the "true_in" operator. The logic provides rules for combining these operators, such as "some_past(ϕ) $\Rightarrow$ future(some_past(ϕ)).")

Dynamic modal operators allow events and states to be combined in complex structures. For example, we could define a modal operator "after(θ, ϕ)," which takes as arguments a state θ and an event ψ, and returns the state of just having completed ϕ after a situation where θ held.

true_in(S,after(θ, ϕ)) $\Leftrightarrow$
$\exists_I$ end(I)=S $\wedge$ true_in(start(I),θ) $\wedge$ occurs(I, ϕ)

Similarly, the control structures defined in Section 5.11 can all be defined as modal operators that take events and states as arguments and return events. The operator "sequence(ϕ_1, ϕ_2)" maps two events to an event; "cond(θ, ϕ_1, ϕ_2)" maps a state θ and two events, ϕ_1, ϕ_2, to an event; "while(θ, ϕ)" maps a state θ and event ϕ to an event.

Modal language allows many statements to be expressed more compactly and in a form closer to English. Table 5.20 illustrates the expression of some of the blocks-world axioms in terms of the operators we have defined above.

Table 5.17 Syntax of Modal Temporal Logic

1. Each predicate and sentential constant is designated as either a
   state, event, or anchored type. Examples: "block(X)" is anchored;
   "beneath(X, Y)," "clear(X)," "clear_table(L)," and "under_hand(X)"
   are states; "pickup," "putdown," and "move(L)" are events.

2. Each function and constant is designated as either anchored or a
   fluent. Examples: "hand" and "table" are anchored; "place(X)" is a
   fluent.

3. A term is anchored if it is either:

   (a) A variable. Example: "X".
   (b) An anchored constant. Example: "hand".
   (c) An anchored function applied to anchored terms. (No examples
       in our blocks-world language.)
   (d) A term of the form "value_in(S, T)" where S is a situation.
       Example: "value_in(s1,place(X))".

   Any other term is a fluent. Example: "place(hand)" is a fluent.

4. A state formula is either:

   (a) An atomic formula with a state predicate.   Example:
       "beneath(X,blocka)".
   (b) An atomic formula with an anchored predicate or equality ap-
       plied to arguments, at least one of which is a fluent. Example:
       "place(blocka) = place(hand)" is a state. (Note that this is con-
       trary to the convention established in the first-order theory,
       where $F1 = F2$ is a proposition and eql($F1, F2$) is a state.)
   (c) The Boolean combination of two state formulas or of a state
       formula with an anchored formula.
       Example: "block(X) $\Rightarrow$ beneath(table,X)".
   (d) A quantifier applied to a state.
       Example: "$\forall_X$ block(X) $\Rightarrow$ beneath(table,X)".

Table 5.17 Syntax of Modal Temporal Logic (Continued)

5. An event formula is either:

   (a) An atomic formula with an event predicate.   Example: "pickup," "move(place(O))". If an event predicate is given a fluent argument, we assume that the argument is "evaluated" at the beginning of the event. Thus, "move(place(blocka))" is the event of moving to where block A is at the start of the move.

   (b) The Boolean combination of two event formulas or of an event formula with an anchored formula.   Example: "true_in(s0,$L \neq$ place(blocka)) $\land$ move(L)".

   (c) A quantifier applied to an event formula.   Example: "$\exists_L$ move(L)".

6. An anchored formula has one of the following forms:

   (a) An anchored predicate applied to anchored terms.   Example: "block(X)".

   (b) The form "true_in(S, A)" where S is a situation and A is a state. Example: "true_in(s1,beneath(X, Y))."

   (c) The form "occurs(I, E)" where I is an interval and E is an event.
   Example: "occurs(i0,pickup)".

   (d) A Boolean operator or quantifier applied to anchored formulas. Example: "$\forall_I$ occurs(I,pickup) $\Rightarrow$
   true_in(start(I), $\exists_X$ under_hand(X))."

7. A Boolean combination of a state formula with an event formula is not syntactically valid.

5.13 Tracking the Present Moment

So far, our representations have viewed all situations as equal *sub specie aeternis*. Obviously, an intelligent creature must be able to distinguish between the present situation from the past and the future. The present and immediate past and future almost always deserve considerably more attention than the distant past or future. Perceptions reflect the present and immediate past; actions must be appropriate to the present and immediate future.

Table 5.18 A Modal Temporal Logic

MTIME.1. Any tautology of the propositional calculus is an axiom.

MTIME.2. If α and β are anchored formulas, then any closure of

$$[\forall_\mu \alpha \wedge \forall_\mu \alpha \Rightarrow \beta] \Rightarrow \forall_\mu \beta$$

is an axiom.

MTIME.3. If τ is an anchored term, and $\alpha(\mu)$ is a formula with free variable μ, then any closure of $\alpha(\mu/\tau) \Rightarrow \exists_\mu \alpha(\mu)$ is an axiom.

MTIME.4. For any formulas ϕ and ψ and Boolean operator O, any closure of the formulas below is an axiom:

   true_in$(S, \phi$ O $\psi) \Leftrightarrow$ true_in(S, ϕ) O true_in(S, ψ).
   occurs$(I, \phi$ O $\psi) \Leftrightarrow$ occurs(I, ϕ) O occurs(I, ψ).

(Booleans commute with true_in and occurs.)

MTIME.5. For any formula ϕ, variable μ, and quantifier Q, any closure of the formulas below is an axiom:

   true_in$(S, \mathbf{Q}_\mu \phi) \Leftrightarrow \mathbf{Q}_\mu$ true_in(S, ϕ).
   occurs$(I, \mathbf{Q}_\mu \phi) \Leftrightarrow \mathbf{Q}_\mu$ occurs(I, ϕ).

(Quantifiers commute with true_in and occurs.)

MTIME.6. If ϕ is an anchored proposition then

   true_in$(S, \phi) \Leftrightarrow \phi$.
   occurs$(I, \phi) \Leftrightarrow \phi$.

(True_in and occurs are redundant applied to an anchored proposition.)

MTIME.7. If τ is an anchored term then value_in$(S, \tau) = \tau$.
(Value_in is redundant applied to anchored terms.)

MTIME.8. For any predicate symbol β and terms $\tau_1 \ldots \tau_k$,

   true_in$(S, \beta(\tau_1 \ldots \tau_k)) \Leftrightarrow$
   true_in$(S, \beta($value_in$(S, \tau_1), \ldots$ value_in$(S, \tau_k)))$.

(A predicate holds on fluent arguments just if it holds on the values of the fluents at the anchoring time.)

5.18 A Modal Temporal Logic (Continued)

MTIME.9. For any predicate symbol β and terms $\tau_1 \ldots \tau_k$,

  occurs$(I,\beta(\tau_1 \ldots \tau_k)) \Leftrightarrow$
  occurs$(I,\beta(\text{value\_in}(\text{start}(I),\tau_1), \ldots \text{value\_in}(\text{start}(I),\tau_k)))$.

(An event term with fluent arguments occurs just if the event term with the values of the arguments at the start of the anchoring interval occurs.)

MTIME.10. For any function symbol β and terms $\tau_1, \ldots \tau_k$,

  value_in$(S,\beta(\tau_1 \ldots \tau_k)) =$
  value_in$(S,\beta(\text{value\_in}(S, \tau_1),$
  $\ldots$ value_in$(S, \tau_k)))$.

(The value in S of a term involving fluents is equal to the value in S on the same term with the fluents replaced by their values in S.)

Inference rules:

Modus ponens: From α and $\alpha \Rightarrow \beta$ infer β.

Necessitation:

  If ϕ is a state proposition, then $\phi \vdash \forall_S \text{true\_in}(S, \phi)$.
  If ϕ is an event proposition, then $\phi \vdash \forall_I \text{occurs}(I, \phi)$.

Table 5.19 Tense Operators

true_in$(S,\text{future}(\phi)) \Leftrightarrow \forall_{S1 > S} \text{true\_in}(S1, \phi)$.
true_in$(S,\text{past}(\phi)) \Leftrightarrow \forall_{S1 < S} \text{true\_in}(S1, \phi)$.
true_in$(S,\text{some\_future}(\phi)) \Leftrightarrow \exists_{S1 > S} \text{true\_in}(S1, \phi)$.
true_in$(S,\text{some\_past}(\phi)) \Leftrightarrow \exists_{S1 < S} \text{true\_in}(S1, \phi)$.

It would seem, however, that the distinguishing of the present cannot be part of the logical structure of the temporal representation, because which situation is the present continually changes. Time moves on while reasoning is carried out, or if no reasoning is taking place.

Table 5.20 Some Modal Blocks-World Axioms

BW.3. $\neg$(beneath$(X, Y) \wedge$ beneath(Y, X).

BW.4.   [beneath$(X, Y) \wedge$ beneath$(Y, Z)] \Rightarrow$ beneath(X, Z).

BW.5.   [beneath(table,X) $\wedge$ beneath(table,Y) $\wedge$
         place(X) = place(Y)] $\Rightarrow$
         [$X = Y \vee$ beneath$(X, Y) \vee$ beneath(Y, X)].

BW.15.   after(under_hand(X),pickup) $\Rightarrow$ beneath(hand,X).

BW.16.   after(true, move(L)) $\Rightarrow$ L=place(hand).

BW.17.   after(beneath(hand,X) $\wedge$ under_hand(Y), putdown) $\Rightarrow$
         beneath(Y, X).

BW.18.   after(beneath(hand,X) $\wedge$ clear_table(place(hand)),
               putdown) $\Rightarrow$
         beneath(table,X).

The continual change to the present therefore cannot be the result of an inferential process.

The following architecture can be used for programs that must track the present moment while doing significant temporal reasoning. The basic knowledge base is a time line, with no indication of past, present, or future. The program maintains a nonlogical pointer to the current situation in the time line (or, more realistically, to the latest situation known to be in the past.) The perceptions received by the system, which can include feedback from the effectors or readings from a clock, are each tagged as belonging to a particular situation or interval on the time line. As soon as a perception is incorporated into the time line, the system updates the "now" pointer to indicate that this perception is in the past. The control mechanisms for the effectors are hard-wired to carry out the actions planned for the present moment; the control mechanism for the inference engine is hard-wired to focus its energy on the present moment. ([Subramanian and Woodfill 1989] studies an alternative approach in which "now" is used as a formal primitive, and the knowledge base is continually updated.)

Many programs use a knowledge base that describes only the current situation without temporal markings. Such an architecture is fine for reasoning about the present, but it cannot be used for any substantial temporal reasoning. A program with a time line may find it useful, for purposes of efficiency, to maintain a description of the present as an adjunct knowledge base.

5.14 References

Situations were introduced as an AI temporal representation in an early paper on commonsense reasoning by McCarthy [1963]. Green [1969] used the situation calculus in his QA3 planner. McCarthy and Hayes [1969] gave a detailed presentation of the situation calculus and a discussion of the frame problem. Hayes [1978] suggested using histories — chunks of space-time — as an alternative to situations. McDermott [1982a] modified the situation calculus to deal with continuous, forward-branching time; the presentation in this chapter is largely based on this work. Allen [1984] developed a temporal ontology based on the use of intervals, rather than situations. [Shoham 1985b] is an interesting discussion of the requirements of a temporal theory. [Subramanian and Woodfill 1989] discusses the use of the temporal indexical "now."

The STRIPS representation was developed in [Fikes and Nilsson 1971]. [Lifschitz 1987c] gives a logical analysis of this representation.

There is a large body of work on the frame problem, and on solving the frame problem using default logic, particularly since the Yale Shooting Problem was discovered [Hanks and McDermott 1987]. Particularly significant are [Shoham 1988], [Lifschitz 1987a], [Kautz 1986], [Dean and Kanazawa 1988], [Morgenstern and Stein 1988], [Morris 1988], [Shoham and McDermott 1988], and [Baker 1989]. [Brown 1987] is a collection of technical papers on this subject. [Pylyshyn 1987] contains papers by AI researchers, cognitive scientists, and philosophers discussing the frame problem from a broad perspective.

Implementations of temporal reasoning engines are discussed in [Kahn and Gorry 1977], [Vilain 1982], [Vere 1983], and [Dean 1985].

The reification of event tokens was proposed by Davidson [1967]. Modal logic was first applied to temporal logic by Prior [1967]; see also [Rescher and Urquhart 1971] and [van Benthem 1983]. Of related interest is dynamic logic, which has been developed for the formal analysis of computer programs; see [Pratt 1976] and [Harel 1979].

5.15 Exercises

(Starred problems are more difficult.)

Problems 1–6 can all be carried out using only the simple notation of Sections 5.1–5.4 of first-order logic without set theory, without control structures, and without branching time. The student should be thoroughly familiar with the expressive power of this language before going on to these more advanced notations.

1. Consider the following microworld: There are light bulbs, sockets, and switches. Each socket is controlled by exactly one switch; each switch controls exactly one socket. The following states are significant: A light bulb may be in a socket; a light bulb may be shining or dark; a light bulb may be working or burned out; a switch may be on or off. The following events are significant: A switch may be turned on or off; a light bulb may be inserted or removed from a socket; a light bulb may burn out.

    (a) Describe the light bulb domain in a temporal logic.
    (b) Describe the light bulb domain in the STRIPS representation.

2. Axiomatize the game of Tic-Tac-Toe. You may assume that a predicate "line($Q1, Q2, Q3$)," asserting that the three squares $Q1$, $Q2$, and $Q3$ lie in a row, is available. Your axiomatization should allow the following statements to be expressed: (i) If square Q contains a mark in one situation, it has the same mark in all later situations; and (ii) If the board is as shown in Figure 5.4, then, whatever O plays, X can win on the next turn.

3. * Axiomatize the game of GHOST. You may assume that the following nonlogical symbols are already defined:

    word(W) — Predicate: holds if string W is an English word

    add_letter(W, X) — Function: Maps string W and letter X onto the string that results when X is added at the end of W.

    initial_string($W1, W2$) — Predicate: Holds if word $W1$ is an initial string of word $W2$.

    null — Constant. The null string. next_player(P, L) — Function: L is a list of players in order. P is a player. next_player(P, L) is the player who plays after P, according to list L.

drop_player(P, L) — Function: L and P are as above. drop_player(P, L) is the list L with player P removed.

single_list(P) — Function: Maps player P onto the list containing only P.

Include the following features: Each player takes turns adding one letter to the end of the string. A player loses a round, and gains a point, when he completes a word. A player who has five points has lost the game, and drops out. A player wins when all other players have dropped out.

4. Axiomatize the blocks world with multiple hands, assuming that only one hand can act at a time.

5. * Axiomatize the blocks world with multiple hands that can act simultaneously.

6. You are trying to get from the train station to the public library. To do this, you must take the number 43 bus from the station to downtown, and then take the number 31 bus from downtown to the public library. The number 43 bus comes every 5 minutes, and takes between 12 and 15 minutes to go from the station to downtown. The number 31 bus comes every 15 minutes, and takes between 15 and 20 minutes to go from downtown to the library.

   (a) Formalize this information in an axiomatic system. Show that your axiomatization supports the inference "It will take between 27 and 55 minutes to go from downtown to the library."

   (b) Add the facts that the 31 bus leaves downtown on the hour, quarter-past, half-past, and quarter-of, and that you arrive at the train station at two minutes to twelve. Show that your axiomatization supports the conclusion "The arrival at the library will either be between 12:30 and 12:35 or between 12:45 and 12:50."

7. * In our representation of branching time, we distinguish only what actually happened as particularly significant. All other possible situations and chronicles are treated as equally hypothetical. For this reason, our representation does not allow us to speak of what *would* have happened under particular circumstances, as opposed to what *could* have happened. For example, we would like to say that Nixon would not have resigned in 1974 if Watergate had not been discovered, though, of course, he could have in any case. Show how such concept can be represented by defining — for each situation, real and hypothetical — the "realest" chronicle of that situa-

tion; that is, the chronicle that would occur if that situation came about.

8. In this problem, we will discuss efficient implementation of prediction, using the STRIPS representation of events. A prediction problem will be specified by giving the relevant states that hold in the starting situation and the sequence of event types that occur. In the algorithms we are looking for, there will a certain amount of initial processing when the problem is presented. The system is then equipped to answer quickly queries of the form "Does state A hold in situation S?" Assume that no coherence axioms are needed to answer these queries; the relevant states are all listed in the original situation description or in the add lists and delete lists of the events.

Let k be the number of states that hold in the initial situation. Let c_A be the number of times that state A changes its value in the course of the events that occur. Let C be the sum of the sizes of the add lists and delete lists over all the events that occur.

(a) Give an algorithm to determine whether state A holds in the final situation S in expected constant O(1) time, using initial processing with expected time $O(k + C)$. (Hint: Since all states are atomic and ground, one can hash directly on the name of a state type.)

(b) * Assuming that the intermediate situations are numerically ordered, give an algorithm to determine whether state A holds in situation S in expected time $O(log(c_A))$, using initial processing with expected time $O(k + C)$.

9. * In the modal logic of Section 5.12, show that applying existential abstraction and universal specification to fluents will lead to incorrect results.

Chapter 6

Space

He bound him onto a swift camel and brought him into the desert. Three days they rode, and then the captor said, "O king of time and crown of the century! In Babylon you lured me into a labyrinth of brass cluttered with many stairways, doors, and walls; now the Almighty has brought it to pass that I show you mine, which has neither stairways to climb, nor doors to force, nor unending galleries to wear one down, nor walls to block one's way."

Jorge Luis Borges, "The Two Kings and their Two Labyrinths"

In the animal kingdom as a whole, spatial reasoning is probably the most common and basic form of intelligence. Nearly all animals have some control over their movements, and any but the simplest local criteria for choosing a motion requires some spatial knowledge of the environment. Flatworms can be taught to turn right or left; honey bees find their way around large areas and communicate their knowledge; many migratory creatures, such as salmon, navigate their ways across oceans. The common human habit of converting problems of all kinds into spatial terms (drawing a diagram or graph) suggests that, for people, spatial reasoning is a particularly powerful and accessible mode of cognition.

In everyday cognition, spatial reasoning serves three primary functions:

- *High-level vision*: The process of interpreting vision draws on a large body of knowledge about the shapes, positions, and motions of objects.

- *Physical reasoning*: The behavior of most physical systems depends strongly on their spatial layout. Changes to spatial layout form a large part of the behavior of physical systems. General common-sense physical reasoning requires a rich geometric vocabulary and a strong spatial reasoner.

- *Route planning*: The problem of getting from one place to another, or of moving another object from one place to another, is critical for any mobile creature. A large part of this problem is the spatial reasoning involved in retrieving a path leading from the source to the destination. (It should be noted that there are other aspects to the route-planning problem. The hard part of planning to get to the top of Mount Everest or to get supplies to the eastern front is not the spatial reasoning.)

Other cognitive tasks draw on spatial reasoning to a lesser degree. Natural-language processing must use spatial reasoning in dealing with scene descriptions and route instructions. Spatial analogies are used for problem solving of all kinds.

A major part of all these applications, especially route planning, is the construction and maintenance of a *cognitive map*. A cognitive map is a knowledge structure that describes the spatial layout of an environment; it keeps track of what things are where. Thus, a cognitive map encodes the same type of information as a cartographical map. Typical kinds of information recorded might include "The red block is on the blue block," "Looking south from New Haven you can see Long Island," "Oklahoma has a long thin panhandle on the west," "Land elevation increases steadily going west through Nebraska," and "There is no salt at this end of the table." There are, however, two key differences between cartographical and cognitive maps. On the one hand, a cartographical map is constrained to represent most of its information pictorially, so that people can read it easily, while a cognitive map may use any data structure that supports efficient routines. On the other hand, a cognitive map must in general deal much more deeply with the problems of approximation and of partial knowledge. Someone who is drawing a cartographical map generally chooses a certain uniform level of accuracy and completeness for his map, gathers his information to that level, and makes sure that his map reflects that information. Occasionally, cartographical maps indicate uncertainty, by marking an area "Terra incognita" or by marking uncertainty tolerances on the positions of objects, but these are exceptions, rather than the general rule. A cognitive map, by contrast, must record information gathered catch-as-catch-can by a creature whose primary interest is probably not the gathering of spatial information, through a variety of modes: direct perception, particularly vision; natural language; and physical inference. Such information will tend to vary widely in its precision and its completeness; some regions will be known well, others only sketchily. The design of a cognitive map must therefore reflect both the kinds of information to be retrieved from the map and the kinds of information available in constructing the map.

In many applications, a cognitive map must be combined with a temporal knowledge base to record facts about spatial relations over time and about motion, such as "Jane used to be only four feet tall," "There were no rabbits in Australia before 1800," "Eric crossed the border from Spain to France in October," "The bus is coming down the street at 10 miles an hour," and "I will reach the corner before the bus."

The state of the art in spatial reasoning, like that in quantitative reasoning, is at a rather different level than in most of the other domains we study in this book. Almost any particular sound commonsense inference in spatial reasoning can be expressed and proven as a theorem of Euclidean geometry using well-known mathematical terminology and axioms. (This does not apply to plausible spatial inference. Characterizing these is an open problem.) Thus, there are few ontological problems in spatial reasoning. The space of commonsense reasoning may almost always be taken to be Euclidean space,[1] and the sorts of entities needed to be standard geometric sorts such as points, vectors, mappings, and regions. Likewise, there are essentially no representational or axiomatic problems, in the sense of new concepts that need a formal definition, or axiomatic systems that need to be formulated or evaluated.

Nonetheless, choosing a language for a particular type of spatial reasoning can be trickier than it appears at first glance. Precisely because spatial representations appear so straightforward, a variety of ambiguities can be hidden under the rug in a representation, to make trouble at a later date. We give two examples:

1. *Shape*: Many cognitive maps approximate the complex shapes of real-world features in terms of an idealized simple geometry. In such cases, it is often possible to find two quite different legitimate representations for the same actual shape (Figure 6.1). It is therefore important to define the sense of approximation involved, so that sound rules for matching can be found. Consider, for example, the following approximation criteria for two-dimensional shapes:

    i. The approximation boundary is everywhere close to the real boundary. ("Close" and "small" in these criteria are to be interpreted relative to the diameter of the approximating shape.)

---

[1] There has been some interesting research on the use of nonstandard geometries in commonsense reasoning [Fleck 1987].

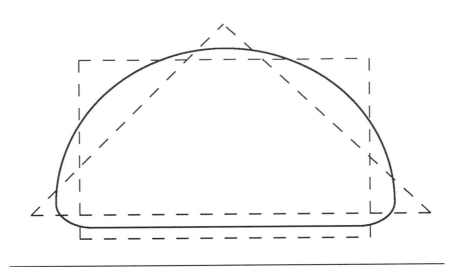

Figure 6.1 Two representations for a single shape

   ii. The real boundary is everywhere close to the approximation.

   iii. There is a continuous one-to-one function from the approximation interior onto the real interior that moves points only a small amount.

   iv. The area of the symmetric difference between the two regions is small.

   v. The tangent to the approximation is close to the tangent to the real boundary at some nearby point.

Different approximation criteria lead to different evaluations of correctness. For example, in Figure 6.2, example A satisfies criteria (i), (iv), and (v); B satisfies (ii); C satisfies (i), (ii), (iii), and (v); D satisfies (iv); E satisfies (i), (ii), (iii), and (iv); and F satisfies (i), (ii), (iv), and (v).

2. *Individuation of objects*: In a cognitive map that enumerates discrete objects, two questions arise about the significance of the enumeration. The first question is essentially the validity of a closed-world assumption on objects. Can it be assumed that any object that is in the area shown in the map and that can be detected by the sensors is represented in the map? If so, precisely how do we delimit the area within which the closed-world assumption applies, and the class of objects to which it applies? If the assumption does

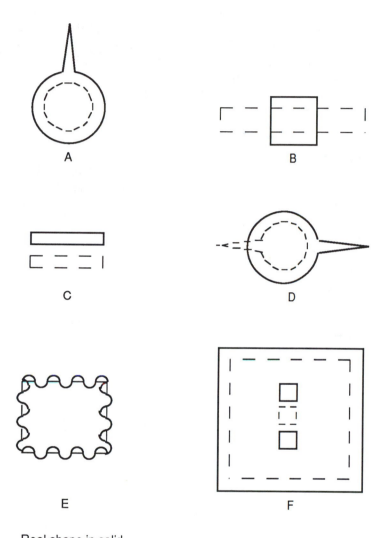

Real shape in solid.
Approximation in dotted line

Figure 6.2 Criteria of approximation

not apply in a blanket way, is there any particular way to represent the fact that an area is clear of all objects, or of all objects of a given type? Is it ever possible to infer soundly from a map that a given area is clear of objects of a given type?

The second question is essentially the validity of the unique-names assumption. Can we assume that two separate object descriptions in the map correspond to two different real-world objects? If only separated parts of an object have been perceived, must their representations in the map be identified as being definitely the same object? or possibly the same object?

How the semantics of a map should decide these issues of shape approximation and object individuation depends on the type of information available and the use being made of the information. For example, if the smooth motion of an object is important in some application, then its surface properties will likewise be important, and the semantics of the representation must constrain them. Another example: if the robot often sees only parts of objects due to occlusion, the map should allow the separate representation of two separated parts of an object.

Even when all problems of ontology and representation have been addressed for a given class of spatial problems, it is generally very difficult to design a useful spatial inference module. The very richness of geometric theory makes it essentially hopeless to expect useful results from applying a general-purpose geometric theorem prover to arbitrarily constructed sentences in a geometric language. (Programs that do geometrical theorem proving such as [Gelernter 1963], [Wing and Arbab 1985], [Chou 1986] are not, in general, suitable for commonsense reasoning applications, such as cognitive map maintenance, particularly in view of the typically large size of the knowledge base involved.) It is generally necessary to restrict very tightly the kind of information allowed in a knowledge base and the kinds of inferences to be made, and then to devise special-purpose algorithms to perform these inferences. Even so restricted, many simple geometric problems are computationally intractable, and must be addressed by approximate algorithms or heuristics.

In view of the state of the field, this chapter will focus on illustrating specific representations and methods of inference rather than giving general principles. In Section 6.1, we will illustrate how a number of specific commonsense inferences can be represented and justified. In Section 6.2, we will look at the knowledge structures used in a number of actual spatial reasoning programs.

Table 6.1 Sorts of Geometric Entities

Sort	Notation	Example
Points	Bold face	$\mathbf{P}$
Lengths	Tildes	$\tilde{L}$
Directions	Hats	$\hat{D}$
Coordinate systems	Script letters	$\mathcal{C}$
Mappings	Greek capitals	Φ
Regions	Double letters in bold	$\mathbf{PP}$

We will use a number of geometric sorts in this chapter:

- *Points*: These are the fundamental components of our ontology. A point is an atomic location in space. The space as a whole is a set of points.

- *Measures*: Lengths, areas, and volumes. Each of these is a differential measure space. Area is length squared; volume is length cubed.

- *Directions*: A direction can be viewed as a point on the unit sphere.

- *Coordinate systems*: A right-handed orthogonal coordinate system consists of an origin (a point), a unit length, and a triple of mutually orthogonal axis directions. Let $\mathbf{P}$ be a point, and let $\mathcal{C}$ be a three-dimensional coordinate system, with origin $\mathbf{O}$, unit length $\tilde{L}$, and axis directions $\hat{E}_1$, $\hat{E}_2$, and $\hat{E}_3$. Then the function "coordinates($\mathbf{P}$,$\mathcal{C}$)" gives the triple of real numbers $< p_1, p_2, p_3 >$ satisfying the equation

$$\mathbf{P} = \mathbf{O} + p_1 \cdot \tilde{L} \cdot \hat{E}_1 + p_2 \cdot \tilde{L} \cdot \hat{E}_2 + p_3 \cdot \tilde{L} \cdot \hat{E}_3$$

- *Mappings*: A mapping is a function from the space to itself.

- *Regions*: A region is a set of points.

We distinguish the sort of variable and constant symbols by conventions of typography and diacritical marks as shown in Table 6.1.

Figure 6.3 Example Scenario: Calvin and his socks

6.1 Spatial Inferences: Examples

In this section, we will show how a number of commonsense spatial inferences can be stated and justified in terms of Euclidean geometry. Our purpose is to illustrate both the range of geometric issues that arise even in relatively simple scenarios, and also the ontological, representational, and inferential adequacy of Euclidean geometry in dealing with these issues.

Our examples all relate to the scenario illustrated in Figure 6.3. Calvin is downstairs, barefoot; his socks and shoes are in a closed bureau drawer upstairs.

6.1.1 Set Operations on Regions

Given that Calvin is inside the living room, and that the living room is disjoint from the bedroom, infer that Calvin is not in the bedroom.

This involves only Boolean operations on point sets. Let **cc** be the region occupied by Calvin; let **ll** be the living room; let **bb** be the bedroom. Then the givens are represented **cc** $\subset$ **ll** (Calvin is in the living room) and **ll** $\cap$ **bb** $= \emptyset$ (The living room is disjoint from the bedroom). From these, together with the implicit constraint **cc** $\neq \emptyset$ (Calvin is nonempty), the conclusion **cc** $\not\subset$ **bb** (Calvin is not in the bedroom) follows directly.

6.1.2 Distance

Given that Calvin is less than 100 feet from the nearest point of the bedroom, that the bedroom is less than 40 feet in diameter, and that the socks are inside the bedroom, deduce that Calvin is less than 140 feet from the socks.

We express this inference using the Euclidean distance function "dist(**A,B**)," mapping two points **A** and **B** to a length. The distance function obeys the metric axioms:

dist(**A,A**) = 0.
dist(**A,B**) = dist(**B,A**).
dist(**A,B**) $\leq$ dist(**A,C**) + dist(**C,B**). (Triangle inequality)

We define the distance between two regions as the distance between their closest points.

dist(**PP,QQ**) = glb{dist (**P,Q**) | **P** $\in$ **PP**, **Q** $\in$ **QQ**}

We also introduce the function "diameter(**PP**)," mapping a region **PP** to the maximum distance between two points in **PP**.

diameter(**PP,QQ**) = lub{ dist(**P1,P2**) | **P1,P2** $\in$ **PP** }

Returning to our example, let **ss** be the region occupied by the socks. We can formalize the constraints as follows:

Calvin is less than 100 feet from the bedroom.	dist(**cc,bb**) $\leq$ 100
The bedroom is less than 40 feet in diameter.	diameter(**bb**) $\leq$ 40
The socks are in the bedroom.	**ss** $\subset$ **bb**
(Implicit.) The socks are nonempty.	**ss** $\neq$ $\emptyset$

Applying the triangle inequality and the above definitions to these constraints, it follows directly that Calvin is less than 140 feet from the socks.

$$\text{dist}(\mathbf{cc,ss}) \leq 140$$

6.1.3 Relative Position

Consider the situation shown in Figure 6.4. Calvin is standing at the doorway of the bedroom. We model the information provided him by his sensors as constraints on the distance from objects to his visual reference point, the angle intercepted by objects at the reference point, and the relative orientations of objects. Calvin also knows from previous experience that the bureau is a 30- by 12-inch rectangle with one-inch sides, and that the socks form a two-inch-radius circular ball

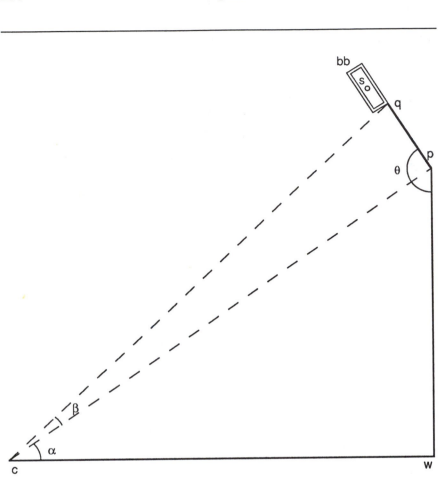

Figure 6.4 Geometry of bedroom

inside the bureau. (For this example, we will assume that the bureau
drawer and socks are exactly these ideal shapes. We also restrict
this problem to two dimensions. We will loosen these assumptions in
Section 6.1.4.) What can Calvin deduce about the distance from his
reference point to the socks?

Expressing this problem requires a number of standard geometric
primitives to describe angles, coordinate systems, and shapes. These
are illustrated in Table 6.2. We also need topological primitives to
describe the relations between the socks and the bureau drawer: The
socks are *inside* the drawer, but they do not *overlap* the material of

Table 6.2 Primitives for Relative Position Example

Angles:

angle(**X,Y,Z**) — Function. Angle from ray **X–Y** to **Z–Y**.

colinear(**X,Y,Z**) — Predicate. **X,Y,Z** are on the same line in that order.

Coordinate systems:

origin($\mathcal{C}$) — Function. Origin of coordinate system $\mathcal{C}$.

unit_length($\mathcal{C}$) — Function. Unit length of $\mathcal{C}$

x_axis($\mathcal{C}$) — Function. Positive x direction in $\mathcal{C}$.

direction(**X,Y**) — Function. Direction from **X** to **Y**.

Shapes:

rectangle($\mathcal{C}, IX, IY$) — Function. The rectangular region of every point whose x coordinate in $\mathcal{C}$ is in IX and whose y coordinate is in IY.

circle(**O**,$\tilde{L}$) — Function. The circle of center **O** and radius $\tilde{L}$.

Topological:

inside(**II,RR**) — Predicate. **II** is an inside of closed box **RR**.

is_inside(**AA,BB**) — Predicate. **AA** is inside **BB**. if **AA** is a subset of some inside of **BB**.

overlap_reg(**AA,BB**) — Predicate. Regions **AA** and **BB** overlap.

---

the drawer. We may define these as follows. A bounded region **RR** is a *closed box* if the complement of **RR** has more than one connected component. Necessarily, one of these components will be unbounded; the rest will be bounded. The unbounded component is the *outside* of **RR**; any bounded component is an *inside*. Two regions **AA** and **BB** overlap if their interiors intersect.

Table 6.2 enumerates the new primitives needed in this problem. Table 6.3 shows the constants in this problem. Table 6.4 shows the input constraints.

Table 6.3 Constants for Relative-Position Example

c,w,p,q,s	—	points as in Figure 6.4.
bb	—	the region occupied by the material of the bureau.
ss	—	the region occupied by the socks.
α	=	angle(**w,c,p**).
β	=	angle(**p,c,q**).
θ	=	angle(**q,p,w**).
$\tilde{d}$	=	dist(**w,c**).
$\tilde{f}t$	—	standard foot.
$\tilde{i}n$	—	standard inch.
$\mathcal{B}$	—	frame of reference aligned with bureau with origin at **q**.

The calculation involves four parts. The first step is to determine that the bureau drawer has a unique inside, rectangle($\beta, [1, 29], [1, 11]$). (β is a coordinate system with an origin **q**, a unit length of an inch, and an x axis oriented along the direction from **p** to **q**.) This can be established from four observations: (a) The region **bb** includes the four edges from $< 1, 1 >$ to $< 29, 1 >$ to $< 29, 11 >$ to $< 1, 11 >$ back to $< 1, 1 >$. Therefore any point in the polygon enclosed by these edges is either an element of **bb** or inside **bb**. The interior of this polygon is just rectangle($\beta, [1, 29], [1, 11]$). (b) The region **bb** does not include any points inside rectangle($\beta, [1, 29], [1, 11]$). (c) The region **bb** does not include any points not in rectangle($\beta, [0, 30], [0, 12]$). Hence, any such point is in the outside of **bb**. (d) Any point that is not outside rectangle($\beta, [0, 30], [0, 12]$) and not inside rectangle($\beta, [1, 29], [1, 11]$) is in **bb**. The desired result follows directly from these facts.

The second inference in our calculation is that the center of the socks **s** is located somewhere in rectangle($\beta, [3, 27], [3, 9]$). From the first step, we know that **s** is somewhere in rectangle($\beta, [1, 29], [1, 11]$). From the shape description of the drawer and the socks, it is easily determined that, if the x coordinate of **s** were less than 3 or greater than 27, or if the y coordinate were less than 3 or greater than 9, then the socks and the drawer would overlap. Since they cannot overlap, the result follows.

The third step is to use the constraints on lengths and angles to fix bounds on the distance between the point **s** and the point **c**. We will do this using as reference a coordinate system $\mathcal{C}$ with origin **c**, unit

Table 6.4 Constraints in Relative-Positions Example

$\tilde{d}/\tilde{ft} \in [20, 25]$.
$\tilde{ft} = 12 \cdot \tilde{in}$.

angle($\mathbf{p}$,$\mathbf{w}$,$\mathbf{c}$) = $\pi/2$.
$\alpha \in [30°, 40°]$.
$\beta \in [5°, 10°]$.
$\theta \in [145°, 160°]$.

origin($\mathcal{B}$) = $\mathbf{q}$.
unit_length($\mathcal{B}$) = $\tilde{in}$.
x_axis($\mathcal{B}$) = direction($\mathbf{p}$,$\mathbf{q}$).

bb = rectangle($\mathcal{B}$, [0,30],[0,1]) $\cup$ rectangle($\mathcal{B}$, [0,1],[0,12]) $\cup$
   rectangle($\mathcal{B}$, [0,30],[11,12]) $\cup$ rectangle($\mathcal{B}$, [29,30],[0,12]).
ss = circle($\mathbf{s}$,2 $\cdot$ $\tilde{in}$).
is_inside(**ss**,**bb**).
¬overlap_reg(**ss**,**bb**).

---

length of a foot, and x axis aligned along the line $\mathbf{c}$–$\mathbf{w}$. For any point
$\mathbf{a}$ and coordinate system $\mathcal{F}$ let $\mathbf{a}_{x,\mathcal{F}}$ be the x coordinate of $\mathbf{a}$ relative to
$\mathcal{F}$ and $\mathbf{a}_{y,\mathcal{F}}$ be the y coordinate. The equations in Table 6.5 can then
be derived from standard trigonometric rules.

The problem now is to find bounds on the expression in Table 6.5,
given the constraints on the parameters. As it happens, in this example, the distance attains its maximum and minimum values over
this region at extremes of the parameters. (Since these functions are
nonlinear, this is not true in general.) The minimum value of the dis-
tance is 22.3 feet, attained when $\tilde{d} = 20$, $\alpha = 30°$, $\beta = 5°$, $\theta = 145°$,
$\mathbf{s}_{x,\mathcal{B}} = 3$, and $\mathbf{s}_{y,\mathcal{B}} = 9$. The maximum value of the distance is 36.4
feet, attained when $\tilde{d} = 25$, $\alpha = 40°$, $\beta = 10°$, $\theta = 160°$, $\mathbf{s}_{x,\mathcal{B}} = 27$, and
$\mathbf{s}_{y,\mathcal{B}} = 3$.

The final step of this calculation is to determine that the distance
from Calvin to the socks is 2 inches less than the distance from Calvin
to the center $\mathbf{s}$. This follows directly from the definition of a circle as
the locus of all points within the radius of the center. The final answer,

Table 6.5 Equations for Relative-Positions Example

$$\text{dist}(\mathbf{p},\mathbf{c}) = \frac{\tilde{d}}{\cos}(\alpha)$$

$$\text{angle}(\mathbf{c},\mathbf{p},\mathbf{q}) = \theta + \alpha - \pi/2$$

$$\text{angle}(\mathbf{c},\mathbf{q},\mathbf{p}) = 3\pi/2 - (\theta + \alpha + \beta)$$

$$\text{dist}(\mathbf{c},\mathbf{q}) = \text{dist}(\mathbf{p},\mathbf{c}) \cdot \sin(\text{angle}(\mathbf{c},\mathbf{p},\mathbf{q}))/\sin(\text{angle}(\mathbf{c},\mathbf{q},\mathbf{p})) =$$

$$\frac{\tilde{d}\cos(\theta + \alpha)}{\cos(\alpha)\cos(\theta + \alpha + \beta)}$$

$$\mathbf{q}_{x,c} = \text{dist}(c,q)\cos(\alpha + \beta) = \frac{\tilde{d}\cos(\theta + \alpha)\cos(\alpha + \beta)}{\cos(\alpha)\cos(\theta + \alpha + \beta)}$$

$$\mathbf{q}_{y,c} = \text{dist}(\mathbf{c},\mathbf{q})\sin(\alpha + \beta) = \frac{\tilde{d}\cos(\theta + \alpha)\sin(\alpha + \beta)}{\cos(\alpha)\cos(\theta + \alpha + \beta)}$$

$$\mathbf{s}_{x,c} = \mathbf{q}_{x,c} - \frac{\tilde{in}}{\tilde{ft}} \cdot (\mathbf{s}_{x,B} \cdot \sin(\theta) - \mathbf{s}_{y,B} \cdot \cos(\theta)) =$$

$$\frac{\tilde{d}\cos(\theta + \alpha)\cos(\alpha + \beta)}{\cos(\alpha)\cos(\theta + \alpha + \beta)} - (1/12 \cdot \mathbf{s}_{x,B} \cdot \sin(\theta) - \mathbf{s}_{y,B} \cdot \cos(\theta))$$

$$\mathbf{s}_{y,c} = \mathbf{q}_{y,c} - \frac{\tilde{in}}{\tilde{ft}} \cdot (\mathbf{s}_{x,B} \cdot \cos(\theta) + \mathbf{s}_{y,B} \cdot \sin(\theta)) =$$

$$\frac{\tilde{d}\cos(\theta + \alpha)\sin(\alpha + \beta)}{\cos(\alpha)\cos(\theta + \alpha + \beta)} - 1/12 \cdot (\mathbf{s}_{x,B} \cdot \cos(\theta) + \mathbf{s}_{y,B} \cdot \sin(\theta))$$

$$\text{dist}(\mathbf{c},\mathbf{s}) = \sqrt{\mathbf{s}_{x,c}^2 + \mathbf{s}_{y,c}^2} \cdot \tilde{ft}$$

therefore, is that the distance from the reference point **c** to the socks is between 22.1 and 36.2 feet.

6.1.4 Containment and Fitting

Assume that a shoe is 10 inches long, 4 inches wide, and 3 inches high, and that the bureau drawer is 12 inches deep, 8 inches high, 30 inches wide, and 1 inch thick. Infer that a shoe can fit in the drawer. In this example, by contrast with the previous one, we will work with three dimensions. Further, we will not assume that the shapes of the objects involved correspond exactly to an ideal; rather we give only approximate bounds of the regions that they fill.

First, we must give a precise interpretation to the two concepts of the inside of a bureau drawer, and of an object fitting in a space. "Inside" here means something different than in the previous section, since the drawer does not topologically separate its inside from its outside. In this case of a container with an opening on top, the meaning is something like the following: Region **RR** is inside container **CC** if one could put a horizontal "lid" onto **CC**, and **RR** would be enclosed by the lidded container.

Formally, we define a region **XX** to be an open box with opening **SS** and inside **II** if **SS** is a horizontal planar surface; **XX** ∪ **SS** is a closed box; and **II** is the inside of **XX** ∪ **SS** but not of **XX** by itself. (Figure 6.5). The formal definitions below use the predicates "planar(**PP**)" and "horizontal(**PP**)" (of a planar surface **PP**) with their standard interpretations.

open_box(**XX,PP,II**) ⇔
[planar(**PP**) ∧ horizontal(**PP**) ∧ inside(**II, XX** ∪ **PP**)].

inside_open_box(**II,XX**) ⇔ $\exists_{PP}$ open_box(**XX,PP,II**).

Object O fits in region **RR** if there is a physically possible placement of O that is a subset of **RR**. In the case of a rigid object like a shoe, the physically possible placements of O are all congruent to one another (without reflection). We can therefore characterize the regions that can potentially be occupied by the shoe by characterizing the region the shoe occupies in some standard position, and then stating that it may occupy any congruent shape. The statement that the shoe fits inside the drawer is then interpreted as "There is some subset of the inside of the drawer that is congruent to the standard shape of the shoe." To represent this, we introduce the predicate "congruent(**AA,BB**)," with a narrowed interpretation that excludes reflections.

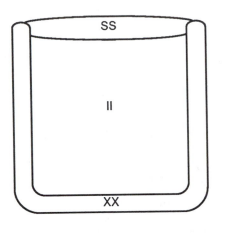

Figure 6.5 Inside of an open box

Next, we formalize the information given about the shoes and the drawer. Let **hh** and **dd** be the regions occupied by the shoes and the drawer in some arbitrary configuration. The statement about the dimensions of the shoe can be stated by asserting that the shoe lies within the box $< [0,10],[0,4],[0,3] >$ in some coordinate frame with inch unit. Formally,

$$\exists_{\mathcal{C}} \; \text{unit\_length}(\mathcal{C}) = \tilde{in} \wedge \textbf{hh} \subset \text{rectangle}(\mathcal{C}, [0,10], [0,4], [0,3])$$

The description of the drawer is more complicated, since we have to specify more than just its outer limits. There are several ways of formalizing the description above; our formalization will assert that the material of the drawer lies entirely within an inch on the inside of the horizontal sides and bottom of a shell of the specified dimensions. Specifically, let $\mathcal{D}$ be a reference frame for the drawer in a standard position, with opening on top. Let **ddb0** be a 30-by-12-by-8-inch box containing the shelf. Let **ddb1** be the sides and bottom of this box; that is, the boundary of the box minus the top. Then we assert that (i) the shelf is contained within **ddb0**; (ii) all of the shelf is within an inch of **ddb1**; (iii) every point of **ddb1** is within an inch of some point of the shelf; and (iv) the shelf is simply connected; that is, there are no holes through it (Figure 6.6). Introducing the functions "z_coor(**P**,$\mathcal{C}$)" and "simply_connected(**RR**)" with their natural interpretations, we can formalize the constraints as follows:

unit_length($\mathcal{D}$) = $\tilde{in}$.

Side View (Y-Z plane)

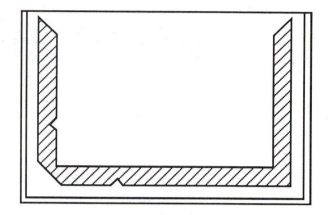

ddb0 - solid rectangle
ddb1 - doubled edges of ddb0
dd - hatched region

Figure 6.6 Shape of shelf

ddb0 = rectangle($\mathcal{D}$, [0,30], [0,12], [0,8]).
ddb1 = boundary(**ddb0**) − { **P** | z_coor(**P**, $\mathcal{D}$) = 8 }.
dd ⊂ **ddb0**.
$\forall_{\mathbf{P} \in \mathbf{dd}}$ dist(**P**,**ddb1**) < $i\tilde{n}$.
$\forall_{\mathbf{P} \in \mathbf{ddb1}}$ dist(**P**,**dd**) < $i\tilde{n}$.
simply_connected(**dd**).

It is easily shown from these constraints that the drawer is an open box with an inside of at least 28 by 10 by 7, and that, therefore the shoe fits inside the drawer.

$\exists_{II,HH1}$ inside_open_box(**II, dd**) $\wedge$ **HH1** ⊂ **II** $\wedge$ congruent(**HH1,hh**)

6.1.5 Abutment and Overlapping

When Calvin is wearing his socks, they cover the whole surface of his foot.[2] Therefore, his feet do not directly touch his shoes while he is wearing his socks.

In order to describe two objects meeting in space, we introduce the function "boundary(**AA**)", giving the boundary of region **AA**. We also use the function "abut(**AA,BB,FF**)", meaning that **AA** and **BB** abut on surface **FF**. Formally, abut(**AA,BB,FF**) holds if **AA** and **BB** do not overlap, but their boundaries have a non-null intersection, and **FF** is that intersection.

abut(**AA,BB,FF**) ⇔
[¬overlap_reg(**AA,BB**) ∧
boundary(**AA**) ∩ boundary(**BB**) = **FF** ≠ ∅]

To prevent the sock from being a planar surface, which would allow the shoe to touch the foot right through the sock, we require that all the physical objects involved be *regular*. A regular region is "three-dimensional" throughout; it does not reduce to a two-dimensional surface or a one-dimensional curve anywhere. (Formally, a region is regular if it is equal to the closure of its interior.)

One might think that the constraint that the sock abuts the whole foot on its entire outer surfaces, together with the physical constraints that the shoe and sock cannot overlap and must be regular, would be sufficient to support the conclusion that the shoe cannot abut the foot. However, such a conclusion would not be valid, as Figure 6.7 illustrates.

Therefore, we must weaken the conclusion to state that the shoe cannot abut the foot in an extended region. (An alternative is to strengthen the premises to assert that the sock has no such thin points.) To express this, we introduce the predicate "two_d(**FF**)", which means that **FF** is the union of separated two-dimensional surfaces. (One possible formal definition is that **FF** has zero volume but nonzero area.) Our conclusion is now that the shoe does not abut the foot in any face.

Tables 6.6 and 6.7 show the formalization of the problem and its solution.

---

[2]This is not exactly realistic, since socks do not directly cover the inner surfaces of the toes. The assumption more accurately describes a skin-tight glove.

Table 6.6 Axioms for the Shoe-Sock Example

Geometric Axioms

- The boundary of a regular shape is two dimensional

  regular(**XX**) $\Rightarrow$ two_d(boundary(**XX**))

- If the union of two regions **BB** and **CC** is two dimensional, then either **BB** or **CC** is two dimensional. (We assume that all sets involved are measurable.)

  two_d(**BB** $\cup$ **CC**) $\Rightarrow$ [two_d(**BB**) $\vee$ two_d(**CC**)]

- Let **AA**, **BB** and **CC** be regular; let **BB** abut **AA** in **FF** and let **CC** abut **AA** in **GG**. If **FF** $\cap$ **GG** is two dimensional, then **BB** overlaps **CC**. (Figure 6.8)

  [regular(**AA**) $\wedge$ regular(**BB**) $\wedge$ regular(**CC**) $\wedge$
  abut(**BB,AA,FF**) $\wedge$ abut(**CC,AA,GG**) $\wedge$ two_d(**FF** $\cap$ **GG**)]
  $\Rightarrow$ overlap_reg(**BB,CC**)

Physical Axioms

- A solid object is regular.

  solid(X) $\Rightarrow$ regular(value_in(S,place(X)))

- Two solid objects do not overlap.

  solid(X) $\wedge$ solid(Y) $\wedge$ $X \neq Y \Rightarrow$
  $\neg$overlap_reg(value_in(S,place(X)),value_in(S,place(Y)))

Table 6.7 Specifications for the Shoe-Sock Example

Constants

s1   — A situation where Calvin is wearing his sock
foot   — the foot
sock   — the sock
shoe   — the shoe
ankle   — the ankle
ff1   — the region occupied by the foot
ss1   — the region occupied by the sock
hh1   — the region occupied by the shoe
aa1   — the region occupied by the ankle
oo1   — the outer surface of the foot

Problem Specifications

- Definitions of the point sets.

  ff1 = value_in(s1,place(foot)).
  ss1 = value_in(s1,place(sock)).
  hh1 = value_in(s1,place(shoe)).
  aa1 = value_in(s1,place(ankle)).

- Unique names: The sock, shoe, foot, and ankle are distinct.

  distinct(sock,shoe,foot,ankle).

- The sock, shoe, foot, and ankle are solid objects.

  solid(sock) $\wedge$ solid(shoe) $\wedge$ solid(foot) $\wedge$ solid(ankle).

- The sock covers the entire outer surface of the foot.

  oo1 $\subset$ boundary(**ss1**).

- The boundary of the foot consists of its outer surface and the face where it abuts with the ankle.

  $\exists_{AA}$ abut(**ff1**,**aa1**,**AA**) $\wedge$ **AA** $\cup$ **oo1** = boundary(**ff1**).

Conclusion

- The shoe does not abut the foot in a face.

  abut(**hh1**,**ff1**,**FF**) $\Rightarrow \neg$two_d(**FF**).

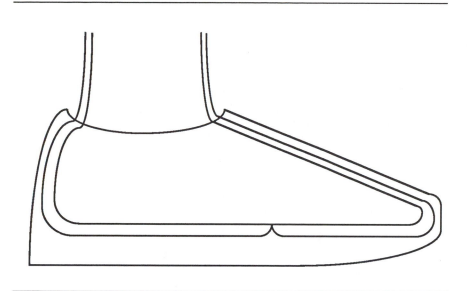

Figure 6.7 Contact through a thin point

6.1.6 Motion

(Note: This section depends on Chapter 5.) The only opening of the bedroom is the doorway. Infer that Calvin must go through the doorway to get from the living room to the bedroom.

The major concepts to be represented here are that of the opening of a region, and that of going through a region. The first is straightforward, given the concepts we have already developed. A region **OO** is an opening of the barrier **BB** into the interior region **II** iff **II** is an inside of the closed box **BB** ∪ **OO**, but **II** is not an inside of **BB** by itself.

opening(**OO,BB,II**) ⇔ inside(**II,BB** ∪ **OO**) ∧ ¬inside(**II,BB**)

The constraint in our problem is then that the doorway is the only opening into the bedroom through a solid barrier. Formally, let **ww** be the doorway. Our constraint is that there is a region **XX**, corresponding to the walls, ceiling, and floor of the bedroom, such that the doorway is an opening through **XX** into the bedroom.

$\exists_{XX}$ regular(**XX**) ∧
$\qquad \forall_S$ **XX** ⊂ value_in(S,place(house)) ∧ opening(**ww,XX,bb**)

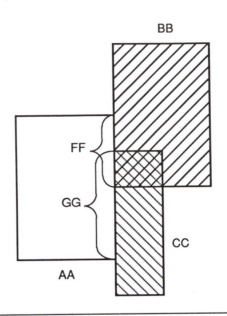

Figure 6.8 A common extended abutment implies an overlap

The second concept we need is that of an object going through a region. This is not (as far as I know) a standard geometrical term, and it is technically somewhat tricky. The formal definition is given in Appendix B of this chapter. Here, we will just introduce the event "goes_through(**FF**, **PP**)" meaning that fluent **FF** goes through region **PP**. For this example, we need the following axiom on this predicate: Let **FF** be a continuous fluent whose values are regular regions (such as "place(O)"); let **XX** be a regular region; and let **OO** be an opening through barrier **XX** into interior space **II**. If **FF** goes from outside **XX** into **II** without ever overlapping **XX**, then **FF** must go through **OO**.

[continuous(**FF**) $\wedge$ opening(**OO**,**XX**,**II**) $\wedge$ regular(**XX**) $\wedge$
value_in(start(I),**FF**) $\subset$ outside(**XX** $\cup$ **OO**) $\wedge$
value_in(end(I),**FF**) $\subset$ **II** $\wedge$
$\forall_{S \in I}$ regular(value_in(S,**FF**)) $\wedge$
$\neg$overlap_reg(value_in(S,**FF**),**XX**)] $\Rightarrow$
goes_through(**FF**,**OO**)

Now, given that Calvin and the house are two distinct solid objects, it can be shown that Calvin must go through the doorway to go from outside the room to inside it.

6.1.7 Surface Differential

Infer that Calvin cannot open the bureau drawer without touching the handle.

The inference here involves the following steps: Calvin can move the drawer out of the bureau only by exerting a net force on it with a positive component in the outward direction. The force exerted by Calvin on the drawer at any point of contact between him and the drawer is normal to the surface of the drawer and directed into the material of the drawer. Therefore, to push the drawer out of the bureau, Calvin must make contact with the drawer at some point where the surface normal into the material of the drawer is directed away from the bureau. Though there are a number of such areas on the surface of the drawer, the only such area that is accessible to Calvin's hand when the drawer is closed is the inner surface of the handle. Therefore, Calvin must touch the inner surface of the handle in order to open the drawer.

We will not give a detailed formalization of this inference. The bulk of the inference process is showing that the other surfaces of the drawer with the proper orientation are not accessible to Calvin, an inference which is involved but not deep. The major new primitive needed is the predicate "surf_norm(**PP,X**)," which gives the surface normal pointing outward from a solid region **PP** at point **X**. **X** must be on the boundary of **PP**, and must be a point where the boundary is smooth.

6.1.8 Other Predicates

Other situations require the use of still further types of spatial predicates. The curvature of two-dimensional curve **PP** at point **X** will be important in the characterization of a roller-coaster track discussed in Section 6.2.6. The volume of a three-dimensional region, denoted "volume(**RR**)," will be used in Section 7.4 to characterize the quantity of a liquid. A spatial description of a textured object such as a sieve, a sponge, a golf ball, or a fur coat must be in terms of the density of a certain kind of feature. Many natural objects such as clouds, mountain tops, and rivers have characteristic irregularities of shape, which can be represented in terms of fractals. A representation of a shape of a tree should express the fact that its upper part is tree structured in the graph-theory sense. (Excuse the nonpun.) The arboreal trunk is the graphical root; the arboreal branches are the graphical intermediate nodes, getting smaller as one gets further in the graph from

																		K	K	K	K		
																		K			K		
																K	K	K	K	K	K	K	
															K	K	K	K	K	K	K	K	
									K					K	K	K	K	K	K	K	K	K	
			C	C	C	C	C		K	K				K	K	K	K	K	K	K	K	K	
	C	C	C	C	C	C	C			K	K			K	K	K	K	K	K	K	K	K	
	C		C	C	C	C	C				K	K		K	K	K	K	K	K	K	K	K	
	C		C	C	C	C	C					K	K	K	K	K	K	K	K	K	K	K	
	C	C	C	C	C	C	C							K	K	K	K	K	K	K	K	K	
			C	C	C	C	C							K	K	K	K	K	K	K	K	K	
			C	C	C	C	C							K	K	K	K	K	K	K	K	K	
			C	C	C	C	C							K	K	K	K	K	K	K	K	K	

Figure 6.9 An occupancy array

the root, and connected to their parent nodes by biological branching; and the arboreal leaves are the graphical leaves.

6.2 Knowledge Structures

In this section we will discuss the spatial representations used in a number of actual AI programs. We have, in some cases, simplified or modified the actual representation for the sake of clarifying the presentation.

6.2.1 Occupancy

One of the simplest of all spatial representation schemes is the spatial occupancy array. In an occupancy array A, the element $A[I, J]$ corresponds to the square $[I, I+1] \times [J, J+1]$ in a fixed coordinate system. The array element holds a list of the objects that occupy its square. (Figure 6.9). (For efficiency of retrieval, it may be efficient to associate a list of the squares occupied with the representation of the object.)

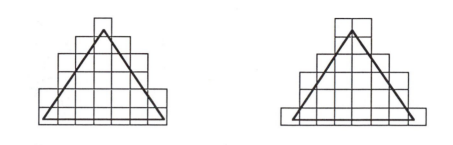

Figure 6.10 Matching shapes in a simple occupancy array

Occupancy arrays have a number of attractive features. They are easy for a programmer to visualize, to interpret, and to interface to graphics systems. They are similar to the pixel representation of an image that forms the input to most vision systems. Certain computations, such as checking intersection or performing translations are easily performed and easily adapted to parallel implementations. Furthermore, there is a large body of psychological experiments on visualization whose results have been interpreted as indicating that two-dimensional occupancy arrays are used in human spatial reasoning. However, as we shall see, in their simplest form, they are rather inflexible and inexpressive. In the following, we will consider a number of limitations and propose schemes for extending the representation to remove them; unfortunately, these extensions also tend to complicate the representation and make it harder to use.

Almost all actual implementations of occupancy arrays use the Boolean labeling indicated above; a square is either occupied by an object or unoccupied. They do not, in general, distinguish between fully and partially occupied squares. Rather, the functions that operate on the representation generally use an implicit assumption that cells on the boundary of the region may be fully or partially occupied, but those in the interior must be fully occupied. For example, a routine designed to match a given shape against a typical template would be tolerant of changes of one tile more or less on the exterior, since these can arise just as a result of the exact position of the shape with respect to the grid, but would be intolerant of changes in the interior. (Figure 6.10)

This assumption, however, means that the system is incapable of accurately representing shapes where interior squares are not wholly filled, or that if such shapes are represented, the functions may give incorrect answers. For example, if the system were asked whether the two shapes represented in Figure 6.11A intersect, it would an-

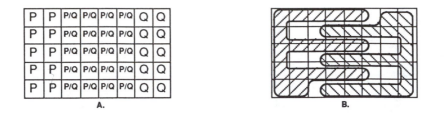

Figure 6.11 False evaluation of intersection

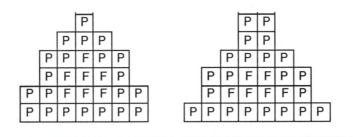

Figure 6.12 Occupancy array with partial/full occupancy

swer "Yes"; as Figure 6.11B shows, however, this need not be correct. We have therefore three options: (i) to exclude by fiat objects such as those in Figure 6.11B that have complex behavior on a scale comparable to the grid size; (ii) to refuse to accept queries such as "Do two objects intersect?" requiring that the query be posed instead as "Do the two objects come within the grid size of one another?"; and (iii) to distinguish between squares that are partially occupied from those that are fully occupied. Since the first two are necessarily very restrictive, we will here explore only the third. Figure 6.12 shows this representation applied to the sample figures of Figure 6.10.

The representation must be further extended in order to compute motions of an object. Suppose that we start with a shape such as is illustrated in Figure 6.13, and we specify that the object translates one-half a grid length to the right. How, then, shall we label squares 1 and 7 in the result? Square 1 may either be partially occupied or empty; 7 may be partially occupied or full. It therefore seems expedient to add these labels to the representation, and also the label "Don't know," meaning that the square may be full, partial, or empty.

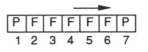

Figure 6.13 Loss of knowledge due to motion

Figure 6.14 Disjunction in occupancy arrays

Our representation now has seven possible labels for each square and object; full, partial, empty, full or partial, partial or empty, or don't know. The operations on the representations, however, are qualitatively very much the same as in the initial simple representation. Functions like the intersection of two objects can still be computed cell by cell; all that is needed is a table specifying how to compute the combinations of labels on the cell. (Exercise 1.)

Motion raises another issue that is more troublesome. Suppose, as in Figure 6.14, we start with an object that partially occupies cell 1, and we move it half a cell length to the right. Now, cell 1 may be either empty or partial, and cell 2 may be either empty or partial. However, they cannot both be empty. Thus, we should add a disjunction, "Either cell 1 is partial or cell 2 is partial," to our individual cell labels. However, the cost of computing with such constraints is so large (problems become NP-hard) and the information expressed is in general so weak, that these are not generally worth including.

With or without the use of disjunctive constraints, the motion of a shape is almost always accompanied by a substantial loss of information. If a series of k rotations is applied incrementally to a single cell, in the end there will be on the order of k^2 cells that cannot be labeled "Empty." (Figure 6.15). One method to avoid this problem in computing the results of motions is to represent a region as a pair of an ideal, time-invariant shape, represented as an occupancy array, and a rigid mapping (Figure 6.16). The mapping corresponds to the change in position of the object; it is recomputed each time the object moves. This

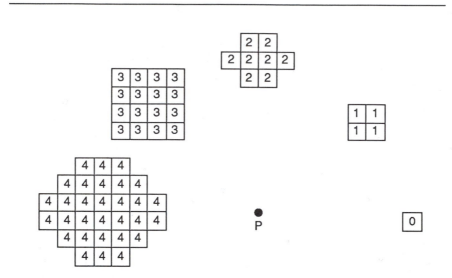

Incremental rotations of 45° applied to square 0 around point **P**.

Figure 6.15 Rotation applied to a Occupancy Array

representation relies on the fact that the compositions of two rigid mappings is a rigid mapping and is easily computed. Appendix A of this chapter discusses effective representations for rigid mappings. To perform operations that require an occupancy-array representation of the actual spatial region occupied at a given time, the rigid mapping is applied to the time-invariant shape; since this is a single motion, the loss of information is as small as possible.

Another serious problem with occupancy arrays is that they can be very space inefficient. If the features of interest are spread out over a region of diameter D and you need to represent details of size δ, then you need an array of size D^2/δ^2 in two dimensions and of size D^3/δ^3 in three dimensions. This space requirement can often be overcome by the use of quad trees or oct trees. A quad tree is a tree of squares, structured by containment. Squares that lie entirely inside or entirely outside an object are leaves of the tree; they are not further decomposed. A square is decomposed to smaller squares only if the object partly overlaps the square (Figure 6.17). Analogously, an oct tree decomposes three-dimensional space into a hierarchy of labeled cubes.

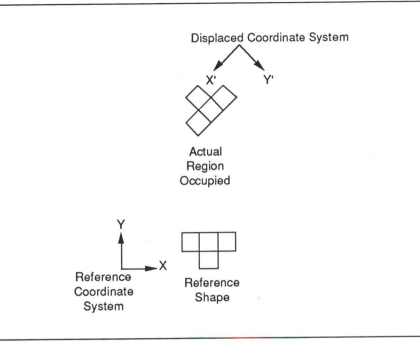

Figure 6.16 Occupancy Array and Rigid Mapping

The most serious limitation of occupancy arrays is their clumsiness at expressing partial knowledge. Frequently, an intelligent creature may know two separate areas in detail, while knowing only roughly the relative positions of the two objects. For example, suppose that Frederick knows the position of his socks in his bureau drawer to within three inches, and the position of his stapler on his office desk to within three inches, but knows the relative position of his office from his home only to within a quarter of a mile and knows nothing at all about their relative orientation. Then Frederick's knowledge cannot be represented in a single occupancy array or quad tree. If the positions of the office and the house are represented with the appropriate uncertainty, all knowledge about the position of the stapler will be washed out. Instead, we will need a number of occupancy arrays, one for each area and scale of information, and these arrays will be related by partial constraints. At this point, however, any query that involves combining information across different maps will involve primarily computing with the constraints connecting the maps, which vitiates most of the advantages of the representation.

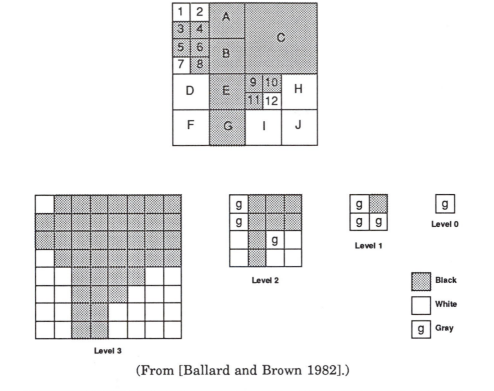

(From [Ballard and Brown 1982].)

Figure 6.17 Quad tree

In short, occupancy arrays can be an effective representation when the level of precision of information is more or less constant, and global knowledge is not much less precise than local information. In other circumstances they are inadequate, and must be augmented with other knowledge structures.

6.2.2 Constructive Solid Geometry

Constructive solid geometry (CSG) is another basic system for representing shapes. In CSG, a complex shape is described as the combination of shapes in different positions. For example, Figure 6.18 illus-

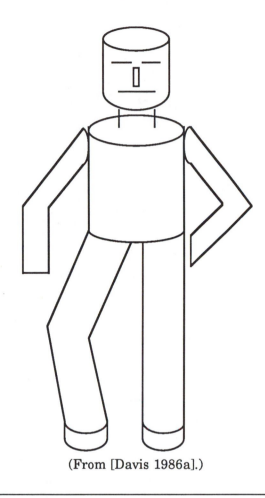

(From [Davis 1986a].)

Figure 6.18 A human as the union of cylinders

trates the representation of a human figure as the union of a collection of cylinders. CSG is a typical example of a *volumetric* representation.

A CSG language contains a number of composition operators, a vocabulary of primitive shapes, and a system for describing relative position. In simple CSG systems, the only composition operator may be forming the union of two regions. More complex systems may include the intersection and set difference operations as well. (Technically, since intersection and set difference can lead to regions that are not normal, the operations used in CSG are generally intersection or set

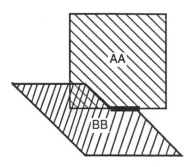

The intersection of the closed regions AA and BB includes both the cross-hatched region and the heavy-lined edge. Normalization drops the dangling edge.

Figure 6.19 Normalized set operations

difference followed by a normalization procedure (Figure 6.19). The normalization of region **RR** is the closure of the interior of **RR**.)

What primitive shapes are used in a CSG system depends on which shapes occur naturally in the domain in question. In dealing with tools, the natural primitives are shapes that are easy to manufacture, such as prisms and cylinders. In dealing with natural objects, a popular choice as primitive is the *generalized cylinder,* the volume generated by sweeping a shape along a central axis. Each generalized cylinder is described in terms of its cross section, its axis, and its sweeping rule. Each of these may be chosen from a fixed vocabulary of primitive values with numerical parameters. For instance, the cross section may be a circle or a polygon; the axis may be a straight line or a circular arc; and the sweeping rule may be constant, linear contraction, or two different linear contractions in orthogonal directions. With each generalized cylinder is associated a coordinate system; the cylinder occupies a standard position and orientation within its own coordinate system. Figure 6.20 shows a variety of generalized cylinders.

The position of a given shape in a region can be described using the strategies for expressing rigid mappings given in Appendix A of this chapter.

The quantities used in the shape or position description may be represented as exact quantities or as constrained parameters. Such constraints can be used either to represent partial knowledge of the

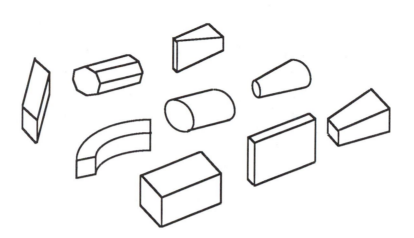

(From [Brooks 1981]).

Figure 6.20 Generalized Cylinders

exact parameter values or to represent generic shapes that may vary within the constraints. Table 6.8 shows part of a representation for the human body of Figure 6.18.

A disadvantage of this method for relating the positions of regions is that the available information often relates to the positions of the boundaries of objects, rather than the positions of their reference points. For example, the distance or angle between the two closest boundaries of two objects is often perceptually evident or inferrable from physical behavior. Expressing this information about object boundaries in terms of constraints on rigid mappings may lead to ugly formulas that are difficult to use.

For a volumetric representation to be used as an approximation for shapes that do not conform exactly to its ideals (i.e., that are not perfect combinations of primitive shapes), a definition of the type and degree of approximation should be provided in the semantics of the representation. Otherwise, there is no way to specify that any given volumetric representation does not correspond to any arbitrary other shape; it might just be a very bad approximation. In practice, this sense of approximation is not generally specified, but is defined only operationally.

Table 6.8 CSG Generic Shape

---

human = head $\cup$ neck $\cup$ torso $\cup$
         ru_arm (right upper) $\cup$ rl_arm $\cup$ lu_arm $\cup$ ll_arm $\cup$
         right_thigh $\cup$ right_shin $\cup$ left_thigh $\cup$ left_shin.

/* cylinder($\tilde{L}, \tilde{R}, \mathcal{F}$) is the right circular cylinder of length $\tilde{L}$ and radius $\tilde{R}$, positioned so that the axis is aligned on the z axis of $\mathcal{F}$ and the center of the bottom face is the origin of $\mathcal{F}$ */

torso = cylinder(torso_height,torso_radius,torso_frame).
torso_height $\in$ overall_height $\cdot$ [.25, .4].
torso_radius $\in$ torso_height $\cdot$ [.25, .5].

ru_arm = cylinder(upper_arm_length, upper_arm_radius,
                ru_arm_frame).

upper_arm_length $\in$ torso_height $\cdot$ [.6,.9].
upper_arm_radius $\in$ upper_arm_length $\cdot$ [.1,.2].

/* Position of arm relative to torso. The origin of the arm frame is placed slightly inside the torso, to avoid unsightly gaps when the arm bends. See Appendix A of this chapter for an explanation of the Z-Y-Z Euler angles */

coordinates(origin(ru_arm_frame), torso_frame) =
1/scale(torso_frame) $\cdot$ $<$ torso_radius $-$ upper_arm_radius, 0,
              torso_height $-$ upper_arm_radius $>$.

z_y_z_euler(ru_arm_frame, torso_frame) = $< \theta_1, \theta_2, \theta_3 >$.
$\theta_1 \in [0, \pi/4]$.
$\theta_2 \in [0, 4\pi/3]$.
$\theta_3 \in [-2\pi/3, 4\pi/3]$.

6.2.3 Boundary Representation

Information about the relations between the boundaries of objects, such as discussed above, can be expressed most easily in a boundary-based representation. In this section, we discuss a two-dimensional boundary representation used in the MERCATOR program [Davis 1986a]. MERCATOR is designed to simulate how a robot could put together a cognitive map in two dimensions by traveling through a region and using a vision system.

The most notable characteristic of the MERCATOR representation is its use of three well-defined types of partial knowledge:

- Partial knowledge of dimension, direction, and angle, both in the shapes of single objects and in the relative positions of objects.

- Partial knowledge of the shapes of objects. The fine detail of the shape of an object may be unknown if the object has been seen only from a considerable distance.

- Partial knowledge of the extent of an object. If an object has been partially occluded, then the knowledge base must record what has been seen without overconstraining the unseen part.

In order to deal with these three issues, MERCATOR uses a two-level representation. The first level consists of a grid of points connected by edges. Partial knowledge of dimensions and directions is expressed through constraints on the lengths and directions of the edges. MERCATOR uses a particularly simple form of constraint: interval bounds on the measurements of length and direction relative to a fixed coordinate system. The second level relates the shape of objects to the grid of edges. The known part of the boundary of an object is approximated by a chain of edges; the approximation is a tag indicating the maximum deviation of the real boundary from its approximation. If parts of an object have not been seen, then the chain of approximating edges does not form a closed cycle.

Formally, the second level of representation, relating the approximation of the boundary to its real position, is expressed using the predicate

$$\text{tolerance}(\mathbf{CC}, << \mathbf{EE1}, \tilde{D}_1 >, \ldots, < \mathbf{EEk}, \tilde{D}_k >>),$$

The predicate "tolerance" takes as arguments a directed curve $\mathbf{CC}$ and a tuple of pairs $< \mathbf{EEi}, \tilde{D}_i >$, where $\mathbf{EEi}$ is a directed edge and $\tilde{D}_i$ is a distance. The predicate is true if there is a direction-preserving, continuous, one-to-one function from the union of the $\mathbf{EEi}$ to $\mathbf{CC}$ such that no point in $\mathbf{EEi}$ is moved by more than $\tilde{D}_i$.

Table 6.9 and Figure 6.21 illustrate the MERCATOR representation.

MERCATOR uses this same representation both for the simulated visual input and for the permanent cognitive map. MERCATOR must therefore address three problems: first, to match the objects in the visual input with objects in the known map; second, to incorporate the new information in the visual input into the cognitive map; and third, to use the cognitive map to retrieve spatial information. Due to the richness of the representation and the inherent complexity of two-dimensional space, it is demonstrably computationally infeasible to develop complete algorithms for these tasks. Even reasonable heuristic algorithms tend to be quite involved.

Table 6.9 MERCATOR Representation

Grid of edges:
dist(**a,b**) ∈ [10,15] · foot.
dist(**b,c**) ∈ [20,30] · foot.
dist(**b,e**) ∈ [10,15] · foot.
dist(**c,d**) ∈ [11,17] · foot.
dist(**c,f**) ∈ [12,18] · foot.
dist(**e,f**) ∈ [12,16] · foot.
dist(**e,j**) ∈ [8,12] · foot.
dist(**f,g**) ∈ [12,18] · foot.
dist(**g,h**) ∈ [9,15] · foot.
dist(**h,i**) ∈ [13,19] · foot.
dist(**i,j**) ∈ [12,16] · foot.

($\hat{x}$ below is a standard reference direction.)

angle(**b-a**,$\hat{x}$) ∈ [20°, 35°].
angle(**c-b**,$\hat{x}$) ∈ [0°, 5°].
angle(**e-b**,$\hat{x}$) ∈ [80°, 90°].
angle(**d-c**,$\hat{x}$) ∈ [15°, 40°].
angle(**f-c**,$\hat{x}$) ∈ [120°, 130°].
angle(**f-e**,$\hat{x}$) ∈ [−10°, 0°].
angle(**j-e**,$\hat{x}$) ∈ [80°, 90°].
angle(**g-f**,$\hat{x}$) ∈ [95°, 110°].
angle(**h-g**,$\hat{x}$) ∈ [70°, 85°].
angle(**i-h**,$\hat{x}$) ∈ [175°, 185°].
angle(**j-i**,$\hat{x}$) ∈ [280°, 305°].

(dboundary(**RR**) below is the boundary of region **RR**, directed counterclockwise around **RR**.
dedge(**X,Y**) is the directed edge from **X** to **Y**.)

tolerance(dboundary(road),
         << dedge(**a,b**), 1.5 · foot >, < dedge(**b,c**), 1.2 · foot >,
                                  < dedge(**c,d**), 0.6 · foot >>).

tolerance(dboundary(road),
         << dedge(**d,c**), 1.2 · foot >, < dedge(**c,b**), 1.2 · foot >,
                                  < dedge(**b,a**), 0.5 · foot >>).

tolerance(dboundary(lake),
         << dedge(**e,f**), 2.5 · foot >, < dedge(**f,g**), 1.8 · foot >,
          < dedge(**g,h**), 1.8 · foot >, < dedge(**h,i**), 2.5 · foot >,
          < dedge(**i,j**), 2.5 · foot >, < dedge(**j,e**), 1.5 · foot >>).

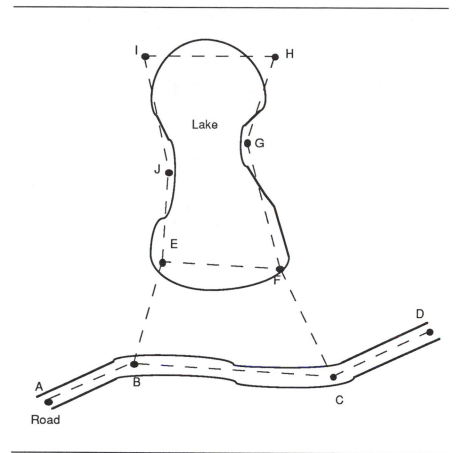

Figure 6.21 MERCATOR representation

For example, to compute tight bounds on the distance between two points **U** and **V** in the first-level grid, given the constraints on edges in the graph, is demonstrably NP-hard. MERCATOR uses the following heuristic: Find a path of edges from **U** to **V**, and evaluate the distance from **U** to **V** under randomly chosen values for the lengths and orientations of the edge satisfying the constraints. To find the distance between two polygons in the grid, MERCATOR uses a heuristic search to pick out likely candidates for the closest pairs of vertices and edges, and then uses a similar Monte Carlo search to evaluate the distance between each candidate vertex-edge pair. To find bounds on the distance between two objects (or, more exactly, between the known parts of two objects), MERCATOR finds the distance between their approximating polygons, then adds in an uncertainty corresponding to the sum of the accuracies of the two approximations.

Two particular omissions in the MERCATOR representation should be noted. First, the language of constraints used — interval bounds on lengths and directions of edges — is not powerful enough to express many common states of partial knowledge. There is no way in such a representation to express the statement that a given quadrilateral is a square of unknown dimensions, or of unknown orientation, since each side of the square must be allowed to vary independently within the specified bounds. This defect could be remedied, in either of two ways. One way would be just to allow symbolic constraints of a more complex form, such as a constraint "length(**EE**) = length(**FF**)" for two edges **EE** and **FF**. The other would be to use multiple coordinate frames. We could then describe a square of unknown size and orientation by saying that it is a square of size 1 in some coordinate frame, but that the unit length and orientation of that frame are only partially known. (This approach is used in [McDermott and Davis 1984].) Of course, either of these extensions would make the problems of computing values from a map even more difficult.

A second omission in the MERCATOR representation is that it offers no way to express absence information. A cognitive map in MERCATOR never rules out, explicitly or implicitly, the possibility of any number of other objects being anywhere they choose. MERCATOR always allows the possibility that it may have overlooked objects of any kind, and it is not aware of restrictions on the positions of objects, such as the rule that solid objects may not overlap. Therefore, if the matcher of MERCATOR is given two maps, such as in Figure 6.22, which disagree entirely except for two matching objects, the matcher will not conclude that they represent two different places. Rather, it will conclude that the matching objects are in fact the same, and that the remaining objects were just overlooked on one occasion or the other.

6.2.4   Topological Route Maps

Most land travel over extended distances is carried out on well-defined roads, which are very long and thin. The primary knowledge needed for planning routes for such travel is the incidence relations between roads and places: which roads meet, where they meet, and which places lie on which roads. It is considerably less important to know distance or angle relations; one should distinguish between a ten-minute ride and a three-hour ride, or between a gentle left turn and a hard

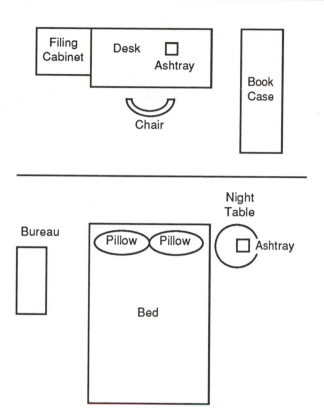

Absent other information, MERCATOR will identify the two ashtrays, and will create a composite containing all the objects from both rooms, freely overlapping one another.

Figure 6.22 Maps matched by MERCATOR

right, but precise measurements are not generally needed. Global spatial knowledge is often entirely superfluous; it is notorious that people can travel from point **a** to point **b** for years, and still have only vague or mistaken notions of their relative positions. The TOUR program [Kuipers 1978] was designed for performing assimilation and inference on such information about incidence relations.

TOUR uses three ontological sorts of entities: places, which are points; paths, which are directed curves; and regions. There is also a single mobile robot; the robot is the only thing that moves over time.

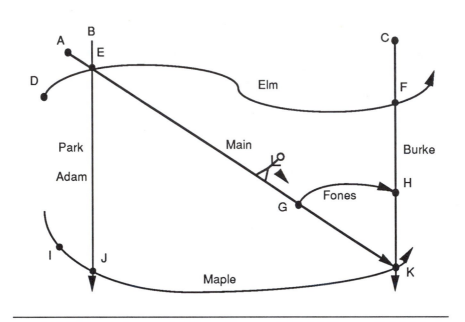

Figure 6.23 World state in TOUR

The state of the robot is defined by its position, which is a place, and its orientation, which is a path and a direction on the path. Figure 6.23 shows a typical world state. A TOUR cognitive map is a collection of atomic, ground formulas, together with a state function that tracks the current position of the robot. Table 6.10 lists the primitives used by TOUR; Table 6.11 gives the TOUR representation of the world state of Figure 6.23.

The TOUR program simulates the assimilation of a cognitive map through the execution of these actions. The robot starts out knowing nothing about the relations in the world. It is given a series of executable actions to carry out. When it executes a "go" command, it can add its destination on the path traveled, in the proper direction from its source. When it executes a "turn" command, it finds itself on a new path, which it can record as meeting the star of its current place. TOUR does not support the assimilation of region information.

Table 6.10 Primitives in TOUR

Static, spatial predicates:

on_path($PP, X_1, X_2, \ldots, X_k$) —
Places X_1 through X_k occur in that order on path PP.

star($X, < PP_1, S_1 >, < PP_2, S_2 > \ldots < PP_k, S_k >$) —
Paths PP_1 through PP_k all meet at place X; moreover, the directed paths PP_i with sense S_i occur in counter-clockwise order around X. S_i is a Boolean, indicating forward or backward direction.[3]

border(RR , PP , S) —
Path PP is on the border of region RR. S is a Boolean, indicating whether the forward direction on PP goes clockwise or counter-clockwise around RR.

$X \in RR$

$RR1 \subset RR2$

State function:

robot(X, PP, S) —
The robot is now at place X oriented along path PP in the direction indicated by Boolean S.

Events:

go_forward — The robot moves to the next place along current path.

turn(R) — Turn to next path at current place. R is a Boolean, indicating clockwise or counter-clockwise rotation.

---

[3]The actual TOUR program indicated the angle of the various paths, and the angle of rotation in the "turn" action described below.

Table 6.11 World State in TOUR

path(**main, a, e, g, k**).
path(**elm, d,e,f**).
path(**maple, i,j,k**).
path(**adam, b,e,j**).
path(**burke,c,f,h,k**).
path(**fones,g,h**).

star(e, < **elm, +** >, < **adam, −** >, < **main, −** >,
    < **elm, −** >, < **adam, +** >, < **main, +** >).
star(f, < **elm, +** >, < **burke, −** >, < **elm, −** >, < **burke, +** >).
star(g, < **main, +** >, < **fones, +** >, < **main, −** >).
star(f, < **burke, +** >, < **burke, −** >, < **fones, −** >).
star(j, < **maple, +** >, < **adam, −** >, < **maple, −** >, < **adam, +** >).
star(k, < **maple, +** >, < **burke, −** >, < **main, −** >,
    < **maple, −** >, < **burke, +** >).

border(**maple, park**, +).
border(**adam, park**, −).
border(**elm, park**, −).

robot(**g, main**,+).

6.2.5   Configuration Spaces

In reasoning about the motion of hard objects among hard obstacles, it is sometimes helpful to view the problem in terms of a *configuration space*. A *configuration* is a positioning of all the mobile objects in the problem, and a configuration space is the space of all such configurations. The dimensionality of the configuration space is the total number of degrees of freedom of the objects. k separate objects in two space determine a $3k$-dimensional configuration space (two dimensions of translation and one of rotation for each object), while k objects in three space determine a $6k$-dimensional configuration space (three of translation and three of rotation). Two objects connected by a pin joint in two dimensions have, together, four degrees of freedom: three determining the translation and rotation of the first, and one determining the angle of the joint (Figure 6.24). They are thus described in a four-dimensional configuration space.

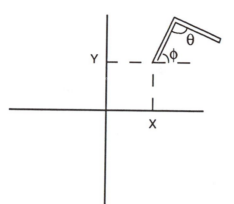

The configuration space of the pair of jointed rods has four dimensions: x, y, , ϕ and θ

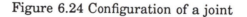

Figure 6.24 Configuration of a joint

Using a configuration space thus reduces a complex state description to a single point, at the cost of imposing a complex, high-dimensional space. The space is rather complex because some of its dimensions correspond to rotations and are therefore cyclical.

The configuration space is divided into physically attainable regions, where the actual objects do not overlap, and physically unattainable regions, where they do. All physical behavior must take place in the physically attainable regions. For example, a feasible motion of the objects from one positioning to another corresponds to a continuous path in configuration space from the starting point to the ending point through the physically attainable region.

If **RR** is the region occupied by an object O in some standard position, and C is a configuration of O, then we will denote the region occupied by O in C as "image(C, **RR**)." In this book, we will use this only in the case where O is a rigid object, so that the configuration C is a rigid mapping in space.

Configuration spaces are easiest to use and most effective when the problem is structured so that the configuration space has relatively few dimensions. This can happen if the motion of the mobile objects is restricted by some external constraint to a few degrees of freedom. An example is a pair of meshed gears that are each pinned so that they

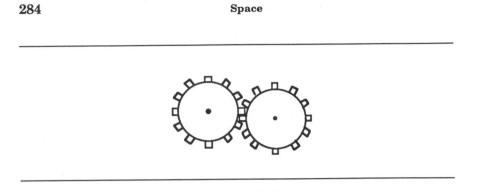

Figure 6.25 Meshed gears

can only rotate around their axes. The relative position of the gears is completely determined by their two orientations, and the relevant configuration space describes the pairs of orientations that do not cause them to overlap (Figure 6.25). Another example is in the analysis of jointed objects such as robots: A configuration space analysis focuses attention on the actual configurations that the robot can attain, rather than all conceivable combinations of positions of its parts.

The dimension of the configuration space can also be reduced if the mobile object has some kind of continuous symmetry so that movements in the symmetry group can be ignored. An example is a circular disk moving in two space around obstacles. The configuration space of the disk is two dimensional, since it is invariant under rotations. This configuration space is the set of positions of the center of the disk. The unattainable regions have the shape of the obstacles, swollen by the radius of the disk (Figure 6.26).

Configuration spaces are particularly useful in reasoning about rigid objects in circumstances where their physical behavior depends on their shapes and positions, and is independent of such issues as velocity and mass. Consider, for example, a collection of blocks on a table that move only when they are pushed. Suppose that the motion of one block is controlled by an external force, and we wish to determine the motions of the remaining blocks. This behavior can be calculated from the configuration space as follows: If the motion of the controlled block lies in the interior of the space, then the other blocks remain motionless. If the motion of the controlled block will bring it into the area of the space forbidden by the other blocks, then the configuration as a whole moves along the boundary of the forbidden area, in a way that the control block executes its specified motion (Figure 6.27).

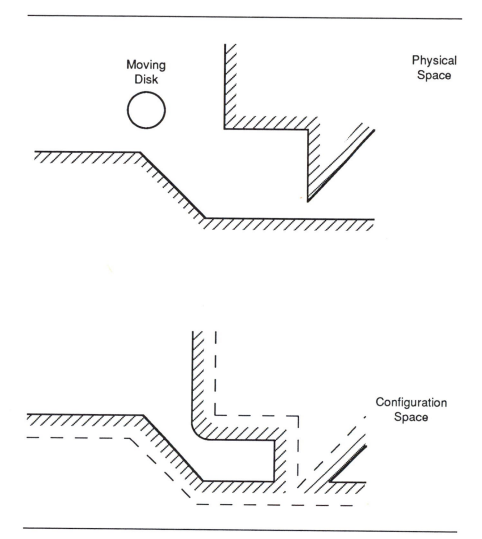

Figure 6.26 Configuration space of a disk

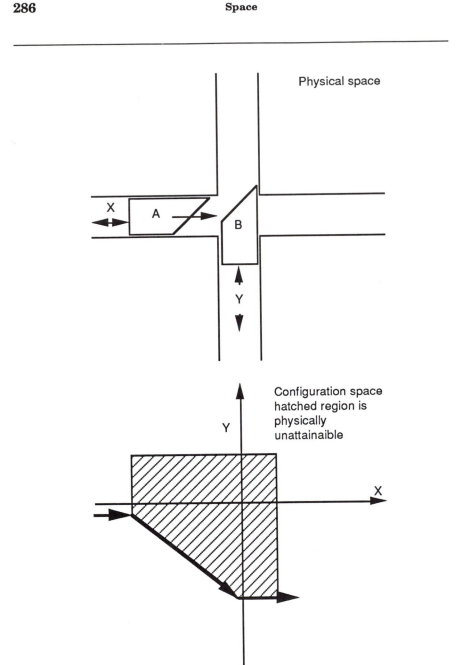

If block A is pushed to the right, the configuration follows the marked path through configuration space.

Figure 6.27 Configuration space in quasi-static environments

6.2.6 The Roller Coaster

NEWTON [de Kleer 1975] is a program that predicts the behavior of a cart on a roller-coaster track from qualitative information about the shape of the track. The cart is assumed to move without friction under the force of gravity. The problem is to predict how the velocity and position of the cart will change over time. The cart is not securely held to the track, so it is possible that the cart may fall or fly off the track. NEWTON will predict that the cart comes off the track, but does not attempt to guess its further fate.

In a complete model, we would have to consider the cart and the track as three-dimensional objects, that may be in contact over some extended region. (Figure 6.28). However, for the purposes of qualitative reasoning, we may make some radical simplifications. We assume that we can ignore the third dimension, and describe the entire system in terms of a world with one horizontal and one vertical dimension. We assume that the interactions between the cart and the track depend only on the boundary of the track; hence, we can model the track as a curve in two dimensions, with a distinguished clockwise direction around it. (The two-dimensional representation of the track may cross itself; the two corresponding parts of the three-dimensional track would be slightly displaced in the third dimension at the cross point.) The cart is assumed to be small enough (compared to any shape features of the track) that the shape of the cart is irrelevant and the contact between the cart and the track can be approximated as a single point. Therefore, we can describe the state of the cart simply by specifying the location of the contact point and requiring that the cart lies on the outside of the track rather than inside it. Whether these approximations can be validly made for a particular cart and track is outside the scope of NEWTON's theory.

Two forces affect the behavior of the cart relative to the track: the gravitational force and the centrifugal force. The gravitational force is always constant, and directed vertically downward. The centrifugal force is always directed along the normal to the track. Where the curvature is positive (the track curves up toward the cart), the centrifugal force points inward to the track; where it is negative, the centrifugal force points outward, away from the track. The magnitude of the centrifugal force is proportional to the square of the velocity of the cart times the curvature of the track.

We can summarize the effect of these two forces in the following two rules:

1. The acceleration of the cart along the track is proportional to the component of gravity in the direction tangent to the track. (The

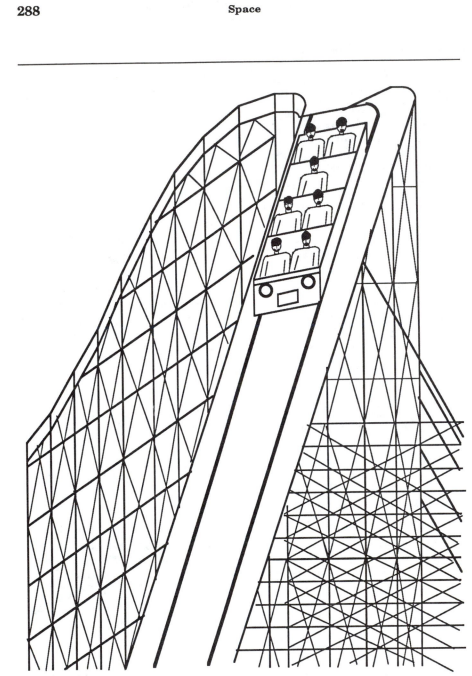

Figure 6.28 Cart on a roller coaster

centrifugal force is always normal to the track.) If the forward direction of the track is uphill, then the cart will accelerate backward; if it is downhill, the cart will accelerate forward.

2. The force holding the cart on the track is the sum of the centrifugal force plus the component of gravity in the direction normal to the track. If this sum is positive or zero, the cart will stay on the track; if it becomes negative, the cart will fall or fly off the track.

Reasoning about the behavior of the cart therefore requires some specification of the shape of the track, including its tangent and curvature at each point, and the history of position and velocity of the cart along the track over time. In NEWTON, the shape of the track is represented as an ordered sequence of segments. For each segment, we record the quadrant of the forward tangent direction, the sign of the curvature, and whether the segment is an isolated point or is a curve of finite length. (See Figure 6.29 and Table 6.12.) The segments are chosen so that the quadrant of the tangent direction and the sign of the curvature have a single value over the segment.[4]

Directions are divided into eight quadrant values: Up, Right, Down, Left, Up-Right, Up-Left, Down-Right, Down-Left (abbreviated U, R, D, L, UR, UL, DR, DL). We will call the first four "point directions," and the last four "range directions." (Figure 6.30)

This representation for curves is analogous to the representation of temporal parameters discussed in Section 4.8. Here, the independent variable, corresponding to time, is arc length; the dependent variables, corresponding to parameters, are curvature and direction.

We specify the position of the cart at an instant in terms of the segment of the curve where it is located. We specify its velocity as going forward on the curve, going backward, or standing still. A state of the cart is specified by giving the position of the cart and its velocity. We also label each state with an indication of whether it persists for finite time or whether it occurs only for an instant. For example, the starting state of the cart illustrated in Figure 6.29 is specified as being in SEG4, with a positive velocity; the state lasts for finite time. The special state "FELL_OFF" is terminal.

The task of the NEWTON program is thus to characterize the possible sequences of states of the cart, given the shape description of the track and some starting state of the cart. The output of the program is expressed in terms of a *mode transition graph*, which shows which states can follow other states. As discussed in Section 4.9, any pos-

---

[4] The actual NEWTON program supported a richer representation with metric information about height, which allowed some ambiguities in behavior to be resolved.

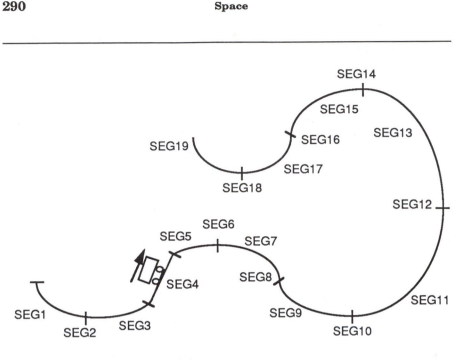

Figure 6.29 Track in NEWTON

sible behavior of the system must correspond to a path through the graph; the converse is not true.

There are two problems to be solved: (1) Determine whether a shape description of the track is consistent; and (2) Find the behavior of the cart. We will consider each of these in turn.

The shape description of the track must satisfy the following geometrical constraints:

A.1. Continuity. The quadrant of the tangent must change continuously, going from one range in the circle of quadrants to a neighboring range (Figure 6.30). The sign of the curvature must change continuously; to go from negative to positive curvature or vice versa, it must go through zero.

A.2. Mean-value theorem. The curvature is the derivative of the tangent angle; hence, changes in the tangent must be in the direction indicated by the curvature. Specifically:

   i. If the tangent direction changes from a point direction to the neighboring range in the counterclockwise (clockwise) direction, then the curvature in the second segment must be positive (negative).

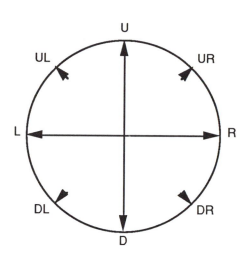

Figure 6.30 Quadrants of directions

ii. If the tangent direction changes from a range direction to the
neighboring point in the counterclockwise (clockwise) direction, then the curvature in the first segment must be positive
(negative).

A.3. A segment with a point direction and nonzero curvature must
occupy only a point and it must border a segment with a range
direction on both sides. A segment with a range direction and a
nonzero curvature must have finite length.

A.4. (Topology of change.) It is impossible that one segment should
have nonzero curvature and a point tangent direction and that
an adjacent segment have zero curvature and a range tangent
direction.

Any sequence of segments obeying these constraints is a valid shape
description. Note that, if two segments appear consecutively, at least
one must be of finite length.

We can now describe the dynamics of the system using qualitative
differential equations, as described in Section 4.9. Let **PP** be the
direction curve of the track; let $\mathbf{X}(T)$ be the arc length coordinate
of the cart along the track; and let $V(T)$ be the derivative of $\mathbf{X}(T)$.
Then the acceleration of the cart along the track is proportional to the

Table 6.12 Qualitative Representation of the Track in Figure 6.29

Segment	Tangent	Inward Normal	Curvature	Length
SEG1	DR	DL	POS	Finite
SEG2	R	D	POS	Point
SEG3	UR	DR	POS	Finite
SEG4	UR	DR	ZERO	Finite
SEG5	UR	DR	NEG	Finite
SEG6	R	D	NEG	Point
SEG7	DR	DL	NEG	Finite
SEG8	DR	DL	ZERO	Point
SEG9	DR	DL	POS	Finite
SEG10	R	D	POS	Point
SEG11	UR	DR	POS	Finite
SEG12	U	R	POS	Point
SEG13	UL	UR	POS	Finite
SEG14	L	U	POS	Point
SEG15	LD	UL	POS	Finite
SEG16	LD	UL	ZERO	Point
SEG17	LD	UL	NEG	Finite
SEG18	L	U	NEG	Point
SEG19	UL	UR	NEG	Finite

component of the forward tangent in the downward direction. This can be stated in the following pair of qualitative differential equations:

$$\partial X = V$$
$$\partial V = -[\text{ direction}(\text{tangent}(\mathbf{PP}, \mathbf{X})) \cdot \hat{k}]$$

where tangent($\mathbf{PP}, \mathbf{X}$) is the forward tangent to the curve $\mathbf{PP}$ at $\mathbf{X}$, and $\hat{k}$ is the vertical direction.

These equations are adequate as long as the cart stays on the track. If the cart were attached to the track, like a bead on a wire, they would be a full specification of the behavior. We can extend the system to consider the possibility that the cart may fall off the track as follows: As stated above, the cart will fall off if the sum of the centrifugal force with the component of gravitational force in the direction normal into the track becomes negative. If both of these terms are negative, or one is negative and the other zero, then the sum must be negative; if one is negative and the other positive, then the sum could be negative, zero, or positive. The sign of the centrifugal force is equal to the sign of the curvature. Therefore, we can formulate the following rule:

Falling off: The cart may fall off at point **X** if and only if either normal(**PP**, **X**) has a component vertically down or if curvature(**PP**, **X**) is negative and V is nonzero. The cart must fall off if normal(**PP**, **X**) has a component vertically down, and either V is zero or curvature (**PP**, **X**) is not positive.

By combining these special falling-off transitions with the transitions generated in solving the above QDE's, we can find the behavior of the cart.

For example, the cart in Figure 6.29 starts in a state, which we call ST4a, in which it is located in SEG4 with a positive velocity. Since the tangent to SEG4 is upward and to the right, the acceleration must be negative. Since the inward normal to the track is downward and to the right, the force of gravity pushes it onto the track. Since the curvature of the track is zero, the centrifugal force is zero. Therefore, the cart cannot fly off the track. Two transitions out of ST4a are possible. The velocity may carry the position to the next segment. Then the cart will be on SEG5 with positive velocity; this is state ST5a. Alternatively, the acceleration may bring the velocity to zero. Then the cart will still be on segment SEG4 with zero velocity; this is state ST4b.

In state ST5a, the acceleration of the cart on the track is negative, since the forward tangent to SEG5 is upward to the right. Since the inward normal is downward and to the right, the gravitational force tends to hold the cart on the track. However, since the curvature of the track is negative, the centrifugal force tends to push the cart off the track. If the velocity of the cart is large, so that the centrifugal force is large, or if the slope of the track is large, so that the component of gravity pushing toward the track is small, then the centrifugal force may overcome gravity, and the cart will fly off the track. Otherwise, there are three possible transitions: either the velocity will carry the cart onto segment SEG6, or the acceleration will bring the velocity to zero, or both will happen simultaneously (Figure 6.31).

By continuing this type of analysis, one can create the complete envisionment graph for the behavior. (Exercise 3). The transition graph allows many different possible behaviors: the cart may oscillate in the first valley, in the second valley, or between the two valleys; it may fly off on the hill, or fall off in the overhang (SEG11, SEG12, and SEG13). If it makes it to the inverted hill (segment SEG17), then it must fall off.

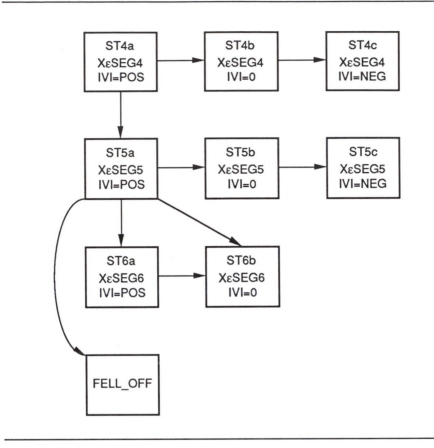

Figure 6.31 State transitions in NEWTON

6.3   Appendix A: Coordinate Transformations

As we have seen in Sections 6.1.3, 6.2.1, and 6.2.2, it is often convenient to describe spatial information in terms of coordinates in a
specially chosen coordinate system. There are a number of purposes
that may be served by such a representational strategy:

- It may simplify description and calculation. For example, the inequalities that describe a solid right cylinder are very much simpler
  in a coordinate system aligned with the axis of the cylinder than
  in other coordinate systems.

- If the shape moves rigidly through space over time, then the motion
  of the object can be described by having its coordinate system move

and the shape of the object remain constant relative to its own coordinate system. The motions of a coordinate system are much simpler and easier to describe than the transformations of a region.

- The information available to an intelligent creature is often precise on a local scale and much less precise on a global scale. In such a case, it may be effective to use a collection of local coordinate systems.

In order to use this strategy, we must have a language for expressing the relations between one coordinate system and another, and for computing with these relations. This appendix presents a number of ways to do this.

Formally, a *coordinate system* in n-space is a triple $C =< \mathbf{O}, \tilde{L}, \hat{D}D >$, where $\mathbf{O}$ is the origin (a point), $\tilde{L}$ is the unit length, and $\hat{D}D$ is the frame of axis directions, an n-tuple $< \hat{D}_1 \ldots \hat{D}_n >$ of mutually perpendicular directions, ordered with the "right-hand" orientation. Fixing a coordinate system gives a standard way of naming points, lengths, and directions:

Let $C =< \mathbf{O}, \tilde{L}, < \hat{D}_1 \ldots \hat{D}_n >>$ be a coordinate system in n-space. We define the measure of length $\tilde{M}$ in C, "measure($\tilde{M}, C$)," to be the real number $\tilde{M}/\tilde{L}$. The product $\tilde{L} \cdot \hat{D}$ is defined as the vector with length $\tilde{L}$ and direction $\hat{D}$. Finally, we define the coordinates of a vector $\vec{V}$ in C to be the unique n-tuple of real numbers $c_1 \ldots c_n$ such that

$$\vec{V} = c_1 \cdot \tilde{L} \cdot \hat{D}_1 + \ldots + c_n \cdot \tilde{L} \cdot \hat{D}_n$$

We define the coordinates of a point $\mathbf{A}$ in C, "coordinates($\mathbf{A}, C$)," to be equal to the coordinates of the vector $\mathbf{A} - \mathbf{O}$. In this representation, addition and subtraction of vectors and points can be carried out place by place.

There are a number of ways of using coordinate systems to specify a direction $\hat{E}$. One approach is to use the directional cosines: that is, the projections of $\hat{E}$ on the coordinate axes. Formally, we define the direction cosines of direction $\hat{E}$, written "dir_cosines($\hat{E}, C$)," to be the coordinates of $\tilde{L} \cdot \hat{E}$. Another approach is to represent $\hat{E}$ in terms of the angle between $\hat{E}$ and the coordinate axes. In two dimensions, only one angle is needed; we define "angle($\hat{E}, C$)" to be the angle between $\hat{E}$ and the x axis of C. In three dimensions, two angles are needed. There are a number of ways to choose these angles. One typical approach is to use the co-latitude of $\hat{E}$, which is the angle between $\hat{E}$ and the z axis, and the longitude of $\hat{E}$, which is the angle between the x axis and the x–y projection of $\hat{E}$ (Figure 6.32).

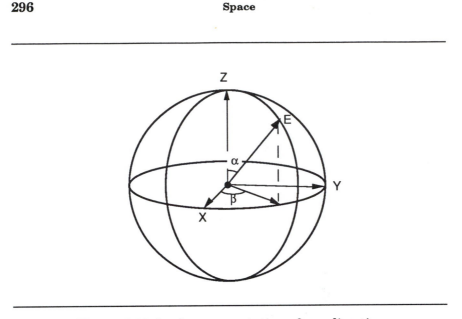

Figure 6.32 Angle representations for a direction

The relation between two frames $\mathcal{C}$ and $\mathcal{F}$ can be represented by characterizing the elements of $\mathcal{F}$ — its origin, unit length, and frame of axis directions — in terms of $\mathcal{C}$. The unit and origin are straightforward; the unit is given by its measure and the origin by its coordinates. There are, however, a number of ways of representing the axis directions, each with strengths and weaknesses.

The first method is to represent the frame of axis directions of $\mathcal{F}$ in terms of the directional cosines of each direction. Let $\mathcal{C}$ and $\mathcal{F} = \langle \mathbf{O}, \tilde{L}, \langle \hat{D}_1, \hat{D}_2 \rangle \rangle$ be two two-dimensional coordinate frames. Let coordinates$(\mathbf{O}, \mathcal{C}) = \langle O_1, O_2 \rangle$; let measure$(\tilde{L}, \mathcal{C}) = L$; let dir_cosines $(\hat{D}_1, \mathcal{C}) = \langle D_{11}, D_{12} \rangle$; and let dir_cosines$(\hat{D}_2, \mathcal{C}) = \langle D_{21}, D_{22} \rangle$. The transformations from $\mathcal{F}$ to $\mathcal{C}$ obey the following rules:

For any length $\tilde{M}$, measure$(\tilde{M}, \mathcal{C}) = L \cdot$measure$(\tilde{M}, \mathcal{F})$.

For any direction $\hat{E}$, let dir_cosines$(\hat{E}, \mathcal{F}) = \langle E_1, E_2 \rangle$. Then
dir_cosines$(\hat{E}, \mathcal{C}) = \langle D_{11}E_1 + D_{21}E_2, D_{12}E_1 + D_{22}E_2 \rangle$

For any point $\mathbf{P}$, let coordinates$(\mathbf{P}, \mathcal{F}) = \langle P_1, P_2 \rangle$. Then

$$\text{coordinates}(\mathbf{P}, \mathcal{C}) = \langle O_1 + L(D_{11}P_1 + D_{21}P_2),$$
$$O_2 + L(D_{12}P_1 + D_{22}P_2) \rangle$$

The last two transformations above can be written more concisely and clearly in matrix notation. Let us identify any pair of numbers with the corresponding column array.

$$< X_1, X_2 >= \left[\begin{array}{c} X_1 \\ X_2 \end{array} \right]$$

Let dir_cosines$(\hat{D}D, \mathcal{C})$ be the square array of direction cosines

$$\text{dir\_cosines}(\hat{D}D, \mathcal{C}) = \left[\begin{array}{cc} D_{11} & D_{21} \\ D_{12} & D_{22} \end{array} \right]$$

Then the above formulas may be expressed as follows:

dir_cosines$(\hat{E}, \mathcal{C})$ = dir_cosines$(\hat{D}D, \mathcal{C}) \cdot$ dir_cosines$(\hat{E}, \mathcal{F})$

coordinates$(\mathbf{P}, \mathcal{C})$ = coordinates$(\mathbf{O}, \mathcal{C})$ +
    measure$(\tilde{L}, \mathcal{C}) \cdot$ dir_cosines$(\hat{D}D, \mathcal{C}) \cdot$ coordinates$(\mathbf{P}, \mathcal{F})$

The rule for coordinate transformations above uses a matrix multiplication and a vector addition. These two can be collapsed into a single matrix multiplication. This reduction involves adding an additional fictional dimension. We represent a two-dimensional point $\mathbf{P}$ in coordinate frame $\mathcal{C}$ by a column array of three elements: the two coordinates of $\mathbf{P}$ in $\mathcal{C}$ and the number 1.

$$\text{coor1}(\mathbf{P}, \mathcal{C}) =< \text{coordinates}(\mathbf{P}, \mathcal{C}), 1 >$$

We represent the coordinate transformation from $\mathcal{C}$ to $\mathcal{F}$ by the three-by-three array:

$$K = \left[\begin{array}{ccc} LD_{11} & LD_{21} & O_1 \\ LD_{12} & LD_{22} & O_2 \\ 0 & 0 & 1 \end{array} \right]$$

The transformation from coordinate system $\mathcal{F}$ to $\mathcal{C}$ can now be represented just as multiplying by the matrix K.

$$\text{coor1}(\mathbf{P}, \mathcal{C}) = K \cdot \text{coor1}(\mathbf{P}, \mathcal{F})$$

If the matrix above is considered as a representation for the transformation from $\mathcal{F}$ to $\mathcal{C}$, then the composition of transformations can be computed as the product of matrices, and the inversion of a transformation can be computed as the inverse of the matrix.

Three-dimensional coordinate transformations can be handled analogously.

The advantage of this representation is the simplicity of the above formulas. The disadvantages arise from the fact that it is highly redundant. The representation uses four numbers to represent a two-dimensional rotation, which is a one-parameter space, and nine numbers to represent a three-dimensional rotation, which is a three-parameter space. This redundancy means that the numbers used here are mutually constrained. If exact values are known, then there is no problem. However, if only partial information is available, then reasoning with this information will involve incorporating these built-in constraints, either explicitly or implicitly. This complicates both the representation of partial information and calculations with it. It is therefore worth considering alternative representations for rotations, based on angles. These simplify the representation of rotations, at the cost of complicating the transformation equations. Here, we must consider the two-dimensional case, which is quite easy, separately from the three-dimensional case, which is difficult.

In two dimensions, the rotation from coordinate frame $\mathcal{C}$ to $\mathcal{F}$ can be represented by the angle between their x directions, which we denote "angle($\mathcal{F}, \mathcal{C}$)". Let "angle($\hat{E}, \mathcal{C}$)" be the angle between the direction $\hat{E}$ and the x axis of $\mathcal{C}$. We then have the following simple equations:

$$\text{angle}(\hat{E}, \mathcal{F}) + \text{angle}(\mathcal{F}, \mathcal{C}) = \text{angle}(\hat{E}, \mathcal{C}) \bmod 2\pi.$$

$$\text{angle}(\mathcal{G}, \mathcal{F}) + \text{angle}(\mathcal{F}, \mathcal{C}) = \text{angle}(\mathcal{G}, \mathcal{C}) \bmod 2\pi.$$

$$\text{angle}(\mathcal{F}, \mathcal{C}) = - \text{angle}(\mathcal{C}, \mathcal{F}) \bmod 2\pi$$

Moreover, uncertainty in the amount of a rotation can be represented in simple interval constraints, such as angle($\mathcal{F}, \mathcal{C}$) $\in [20°, 30°]$.

Overall, the coordinate transformation from $\mathcal{F}$ to $\mathcal{C}$ is represented in terms of four real numbers: The coordinates $< O_1, O_2 >$ of the origin of $\mathcal{F}$ in $\mathcal{C}$; the angle α between $\mathcal{F}$ and $\mathcal{C}$; and the scale change L. The transformation formula is as follows: Let $< P_1, P_2 >$ be the coordinates of point $\mathbf{P}$ in $\mathcal{F}$. Then

$$\text{coordinates}(\mathbf{P}, \mathcal{C}) = < O_1 + L \cdot P_1 \cos(\alpha) - L \cdot P_2 \sin(\alpha),$$
$$O_2 + L \cdot P_1 \sin(\alpha) + L \cdot P_2 \cos(\alpha) >$$

Thus, computing coordinate transformation requires computing trigonometric functions. Similarly, computing angles given coordinate or distance information requires computing inverse trigonometric functions. By contrast, all calculations with directional cosines are algebraic.

The elegance of angles as representations for two-dimensional directions and rotations relies on a few particular properties of these spaces. None of these properties hold in three dimensions; hence, the representation of three-dimensional rotations and directions is necessarily clumsier and more complicated.

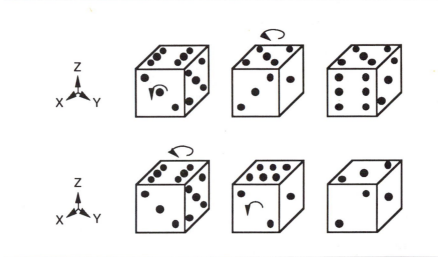

Figure 6.33 Noncommutativity of three-dimensional rotations

- Rotations do not commute. The result of a 90° rotation around the x axis followed by a 90° rotation around the z axis is not equal to the result of the same rotations in the opposite order (Figure 6.33).

- The three-parameter space of rotations is not isomorphic to the two-parameter space of directions. In particular, there is not a unique rotation that maps one direction $\hat{D}$ into another $\hat{E}$; there is a class of such rotations.

- There is no mapping that preserves congruence, either from the plane to the space of three-dimensional directions, or from three space to the space of three-dimensional rotations. Therefore, no technique for naming directions in terms of two real parameters, or for naming rotations in terms of three real parameters, can treat all points uniformly; any naming will treat some points and some areas differently from others. (This last point can be made more strongly in topological terms: Any continuous mapping from two space to the space of three-dimensional directions, or from three space to the space of three-dimensional rotations, must have topological singularities.)

These properties suggest strongly that any representation for three-dimensional directions and rotations will have some inelegancies. There are a number of ways of choosing three angles associated with a rotation as the representation of the rotation. For example, any three-dimensional rotation has a fixed axis that remains unchanged. A rotation can therefore be represented by giving the colatitude and longitude of the direction of the axis of rotation, and the angular amount of the rotation. Similar representations can be derived by writing a rotation as the composition of three rotations of variable angles around fixed axes. For example, let $\Psi_Z(\alpha)$ be the rotation by angle α around the z axis, and let $\Psi_Y(\beta)$ be the rotation by angle β around the y axis. It is then a fact that any rotation can be decomposed in the form $\Psi_Z(\alpha) \cdot \Psi_Y(\beta) \cdot \Psi_Z(\gamma)$ for some angles α, β, γ. The triple $< \alpha, \beta, \gamma >$ are known as the Z-Y-Z Euler angles of the rotation. (Figure 6.34)

Such angle-based systems have the advantage that, with practice, they can be easily visualized (at least as compared to the nine directional cosines). Moreover, they lend themselves to certain types of physical calculations; the Euler angles, for example, are useful in calculating the energy of objects that are radially symmetric. However, for pure geometric calculations, they are mostly horrible. To determine the image of an arbitrary direction under a rotation described in terms of a three-axis system, or to compose two rotations described in a three-axis system, it is generally necessary to compute many trigonometric and inverse trigonometric functions; in effect, to translate from the axis-system to the directional cosines and then translate back.

Another technique for representing three-dimensional rotations is to use *quaternions*. Quaternions are less compact than the above angle representations, having one redundant parameter, but they are much easier to compute with. A quaternion is a triple of four numbers, $< a, b, c, d >$, generally written $a + b\mathbf{i} + c\mathbf{j} + d\mathbf{k}$. (The symbols $\mathbf{i}, \mathbf{j}, \mathbf{k}$ here are particular quaternion constants, rather than geometrical points.) Quaternions may be added and multiplied according to the following rules: Let $P = a + b\mathbf{i} + c\mathbf{j} + d\mathbf{k}$. Let $Q = w + x\mathbf{i} + y\mathbf{j} + z\mathbf{k}$. Then

$$
\begin{aligned}
P + Q &= (a + w) + (b + x)\mathbf{i} + (c + y)\mathbf{j} + (d + z)\mathbf{k} \\
PQ &= (aw - bx - cy - dz) + \\
&\quad (ax + bw + cz - dy)\mathbf{i} + (ay - bz + cw + dx)\mathbf{j} + \\
&\quad (az + by - cx + dw)\mathbf{k}
\end{aligned}
$$

This complicated rule for multiplication can be derived from the following simpler axioms:

   i. Multiplication is associative. $P(QW) = (PQ)W$.

   ii. Multiplication distributes over addition on either side.
     $(P + Q)W = PW + QW$.
     $W(P + Q) = WP + WQ$.

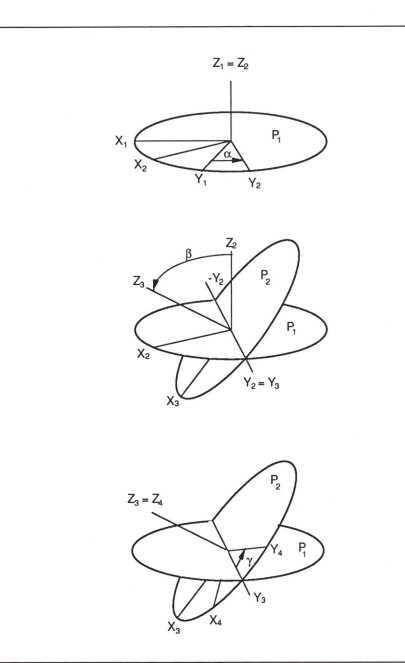

Figure 6.34 Euler angles. $P_1 = X_1 - Y_1$ plane. $P_2 = X_3 - Y_3$ plane.

iii. The quaternion $a+0\mathbf{i}+0\mathbf{j}+0\mathbf{k}$ is identified with the scalar a. Multiplication of a quaternion by a scalar is commutative. $Pa = aP$.

iv. $\mathbf{i}^2 = \mathbf{j}^2 = \mathbf{k}^2 = -1$.

v. $\mathbf{ij} = -\mathbf{ji} = \mathbf{k}; \mathbf{jk} = -\mathbf{kj} = \mathbf{i}; \mathbf{ki} = -\mathbf{ik} = \mathbf{j}$.

As part v makes evident, multiplication of quaternions is not commutative.

Let $P = a + b\mathbf{i} + c\mathbf{j} + d\mathbf{k}$. We define conj($P$),the conjugate of P, to be $a - b\mathbf{i} - c\mathbf{j} - d\mathbf{k}$.

We may now apply quaternion arithmetic to directions as follows. Let $< P_1, P_2, P_3 >$ be the coordinates of point $\mathbf{P}$ in coordinate frame $\mathcal{F}$. Identify $\mathbf{P}$ with the quaternion

$$\text{quat}(\mathbf{P}, \mathcal{F}) = 1 + P_1\mathbf{i} + P_2\mathbf{j} + P_3\mathbf{k}$$

Let $\mathcal{C}$ be a coordinate frame with the same origin and unit length as $\mathcal{F}$, so that they differ only by a rotation Φ. Let $\hat{N}$ be the direction that is fixed under Φ; let $< N_1, N_2, N_3 > = \text{dir\_cosines}(\hat{N}, \mathcal{C})$, and let θ be the amount of Φ. We map the rotation to the quaternion

$$\text{quat}(\mathcal{F}, \mathcal{C}) = \cos(\theta/2) + \sin(\theta/2)(N_1\mathbf{i} + N_2\mathbf{j} + N_3\mathbf{k})$$

Then the following identities hold:

a. $\text{quat}(\vec{V}, \mathcal{C}) = \text{quat}(\mathcal{F}, \mathcal{C}) \cdot \text{quat}(\vec{V}, \mathcal{F}) \cdot \text{conj}(\text{quat}(\mathcal{F}, \mathcal{C}))$.

b. $\text{quat}(\mathcal{G}, \mathcal{C}) = \text{quat}(\mathcal{G}, \mathcal{F}) \cdot \text{quat}(\mathcal{F}, \mathcal{C})$.

That is, we can carry out a rotation of a coordinate system in terms of multiplication by quaternions. Proofs of these equations can be found in [Bottema and Roth 1979, chap. 13].

6.4   Appendix B: Going Through

In this appendix, we formally define the event of a fluent **FF** "going through" a surface **PP**. The primary purpose in this discussion is to illustrate the technique and issues that arise in characterizing topological properties of motion.

Let **PP** be a smooth surface homeomorphic to a closed disk. For the purposes of our discussion here, references to the "boundary" and "interior" of **PP** will not be taken relative to the containing three-dimensional space (in which all of **PP** is on the boundary). Rather, by

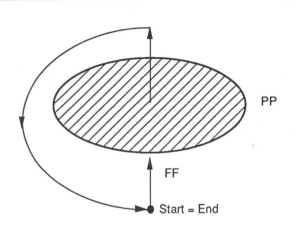

Figure 6.35 Going through and coming back

the boundary of **PP**, we mean the curve that forms the edge of **PP**; formally, the image of the boundary of the unit disk in two dimensions, under some homeomorphism between the disk and **PP**. The interior of **PP** is all points not in the boundary. **FF** is restricted to be a continuous fluent whose value at each time instant is a regular region. (We will give the definition for three-dimensional space; the definition for a two-dimensional object going through a curve is analogous.)

Note that whether **FF** goes through **PP** cannot be determined from the starting and ending positions of the fluent. In fact, **FF** may go through **PP** and yet start and end in the same position. (Figure 6.35).

We begin with the following definition: Let **PP** be as above. A region **RR** is a *divided neighborhood* of **PP** if (i) **RR** is a connected open set in the three-dimensional space; (ii) **RR** contains the interior of **PP**, but not the boundary of **PP**; and (iii) the difference **RR − PP** consists of two connected components (Figure 6.36). It is easily seen that we can assign labels "positive" and "negative" to the components of all divided neighborhoods of **PP** in a consistent way; that is, so that the positive components of any two divided neighborhoods intersect with each other, as do their negative components.

Let **X** be a point-valued fluent. We say that **X** threads **PP** once positively during the time interval $[T_0, T_1]$ if there is a divided neighborhood **NN** of **PP** satisfying the following conditions.

1. value_in$(T_0, \mathbf{X})$ is in the negative component of **NN**.

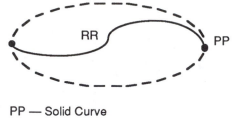

PP — Solid Curve
RR — Interior of dotted curve

Figure 6.36 Divided neighborhood

2. value_in$(T_1, \mathbf{X})$ is in the positive component of **NN**.

3. For all $T \in [T_0, T_1]$, value_in$(T, \mathbf{X})$ is in **NN**.

We say that **X** threads **PP** negatively during $[T_0, T_1]$ if, for some divided neighborhood, **X** goes from the positive to the negative components of **NN**, while always staying in **NN**. We say that **X** does not thread **PP** if, for some divided neighborhood **NN**, **X** stays in **NN** during I and starts and ends in the same component of **NN**. (Note that this includes, as a special case, cases where **X** does not intersect **PP** at all during I.)

Note that these events are mutually exclusive during a single interval I; that is, if **X** threads **PP** positively in I, then it does not thread **PP** negatively in I, or fail to thread **PP** in I. However, any of these event types may be occur within any of the others; for example, it is possible for **X** to thread **PP** positively in I, but to thread **PP** negatively in some subinterval $I2$ of I. (Figure 6.37).

Now, let **PP** and **X** be as above, and let $[A, B]$ be a time interval such that neither value_in$(A, \mathbf{X})$ nor value_in$(B, \mathbf{X})$ are in **PP**. Assume further that **X** does not intersect the boundary of **PP** during the interval $[A, B]$. It can be shown that it is possible to break up the interval $[A, B]$ into a finite sequence of subintervals $[A_0 = A, A_1], [A_1, A_2] \ldots [A_{k-1}, A_k = B]$ such that in each interval $[A_i, A_{i+1}]$, exactly one of the following holds:

a. **X** threads **PP** once positively in $[A_i, A_{i+1}]$.

b. **X** threads **PP** once negatively in $[A_i, A_{i+1}]$.

c. **X** does not thread **PP** in $[A_i, A_{i+1}]$.

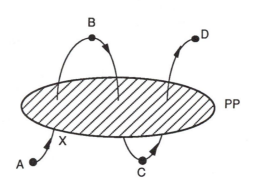

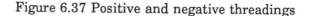

X threads PP positively between A and D but negatively between B and C

Figure 6.37 Positive and negative threadings

Assign the number 1 to intervals of type (a), -1 to intervals of type (b), and 0 to intervals of type (c). Add up all these numbers to get a total k (which may be positive, zero, or negative). Then we say that **X** threads **PP** positively k times in the interval $[A, B]$. It can be shown that this total k is the same for any subdivision of $[A, B]$ satisfying conditions (a) – (c).

Finally, let **FF** be a region-valued fluent. We say that **FF** goes through **PP** k times positively during I if the following holds: Let **X** be a continuous point-valued fluent. Moreover, let **X** stay in the interior of **FF** during I; that is, for any situation S in I, value_in(S,**X**) is an interior point of value_in(S,**FF**). Then X threads **PP** k times positively.

6.5 References

General: [McDermott 1987b] is a survey of work on commonsense spatial reasoning. [Fleck 1987] presents an alternative spatial topology for use in commonsense reasoning. [Randell and Cohn 1989] discuss and axiomatize a variety of topological and metrical operators.

Cognitive maps: Several research projects have addressed the problem of constructing and using cognitive maps. Kuipers' TOUR program [1977, 1978] and Davis's MERCATOR program [1986a] are described in the text. Lavin's DYNAVU [1979] constructs a map of a landscape of Gaussian hills rising above a plane from simulated visual input, recording the coordinates and height of the peaks with some measure of uncertainty. Rowat's UTAK [1981] constructs a cognitive map of a two-dimensional layout of objects and uses it to plan the manipulation of objects. It used an occupancy array. McDermott's SPAM [McDermott and Davis 1984] creates a three-dimensional map from a series of symbolic constraints. SPAM uses multiple frames of references, whose relative positions are partially specified by interval bounds on length ratio, origin coordinates, and angles between coordinate axes. Figures are represented as unions and differences of cylinders with spherical endcaps. The NX program [Kuipers and Levitt 1988] constructs a cognitive map consisting of a collection of perceptually distinguishable places, with sensory-motor rules for getting from one to another, from simulated sonar input. Moravec [1988] uses a bit-map representation of space, with cells labeled by probability of occupancy.

Closely related is the problem of reconstructing a spatial arrangement from constraints. Ambler and Popplestone [1975] study combining constraints derived from coplanarity of faces of given polyhedra.

Physical reasoning: Some work on physical reasoning has studied geometric features important in physics. Much of this is discussed further in Chapter 7. De Kleer's NEWTON [1975], discussed in Section 6.2.6, represented curves in two dimensions with a distinguished vertical dimension in terms of the signs of their derivatives and the relative heights of distinguished points. He used this representation to find the behavior of a point object moving on such a curve. [Forbus 1979] considered a similar two-dimensional world where the ground is a polyline whose edges are specified in terms of the sign of the normal and the relative heights of their endpoints. He used this representation to find a physically meaningful decomposition of free space into regions bounded by the ground and horizontal and vertical lines, and to determine the behavior of elastic balls moving in this world. [Hayes 1978] studied representations for the shapes of containers of liquids in a three-dimensional space with a distinguished vertical. Hayes's representations combined physical properties with spatial properties; the spatial aspects of his representations mostly relate to topology and the vertical dimension. [Davis 1988] discussed a variety of spatial concepts necessary for qualitative descriptions of the dynamics of solid objects; in particular, differential surface properties. [Shoham 1985] analyses the differential motions possible for rigid objects constrained by other rigid objects in two dimensions. Recent work on the kinematics of mechanisms ([Gelsey 1987; Joskowicz 1987]) has been largely concerned with finding the extended motions possible to a piece or collection of pieces in a three-dimensional mechanism. Faltings [1987a,b] discusses the use of configuration space in the analysis of mechanisms and gives a thorough analysis of the configuration space of pairs of polygonal objects, each with one degree of freedom, such as pairs of interlocking gears.

One physical-reasoning problem that has been studied in great depth is the "piano movers" problem: how to move an object around obstacles from a starting to an ending position. Heuristics for various forms of this problem are discussed in [Brooks 1982], [Thorpe 1984] and [Wallace 1984]. The problem has also been studied extensively from the point of view of computational geometry; [Schwartz Sharir, and Hopcroft, 1987] contains many important papers in this area.

Natural language: The interpretation of spatial information in natural-language text has been a central part of a number of AI programs, including [McDermott 1974], [Boggess 1979], [Novak 1977], [Riesbeck 1980], [Waltz 1980], and [Retz-Schmidt 1988].

Vision and robotics: Much of the work in spatial reasoning in AI has been done in the contexts of vision and of robotics. Vision research in this area is mainly concerned with representing figures and shapes so that they can be easily matched against images. [Ballard and Brown 1982] contains a fine survey of this research. The CSG representation discussed in Section 6.2.2 is modeled on that used by Brooks [1981], who applied constructive solid geometry to visual recognition. Robotics has mostly worked on the problem of determining the figure occupied by a manipulator, given joint positions, and of finding a method of getting a manipulator or an entire mobile robot with contents into a desired configuration. This research is surveyed in [Craig 1986].

Other computer science: Spatial reasoning is also central in other areas in computer science, particularly computer-aided design, computer graphics, and computational geometry. Of these, computer-aided design is the closest in its interests to AI. [Requicha 1980] surveys representations of three-dimensional figures, and [Requicha 1983] deals with questions of tolerances. Computational geometry seeks to find very efficient algorithms for geometrical problems; like most work in algorithms, it tends to focus more on issues of efficiency rather than expressiveness. [Hoffmann 1990] surveys shape representations from the point of computational geometry. As mentioned above, [Schwartz, Sharir, and Hopcroft 1987] contains many important papers on the piano-movers problem.

Psychology: Spatial reasoning has been studied extensively by cognitive psychologists, possibly because of the ease of designing experiments. [Piaget and Inhelder 1967] studies the development of spatial reasoning in children. [Downs and Stea 1973a] surveys psychological studies of cognitive mapping. [Downs and Stea 1973b] is a collection of articles on spatial reasoning generally. [Tversky 1981] presents some interesting results on characteristic errors in cognitive maps. The nature of mental imagery has been the subject of substantial debate among cognitive scientists. The "pro-imagery" side is argued in [Kosslyn 1980]; the "anti-imagery" side is argued in [Pylyshyn 1984] and [Hinton 1979].

6.6 Exercises

(Starred problems are more difficult.)

1. Consider an occupancy-array spatial representation in which each region is marked in each cell with one of the following labels: F (full), P (partial), E (empty), FP (full or partial), EP (empty or partial, or DK (don't know).

   (a) Boolean operation on regions can be carried out cell by cell. That is, it is possible to compute functions like the intersection of two regions **AA** and **BB** by looping through each cell X in the array, and computing the intersection of **AA** and **BB** on X. To do this we would use rules like "If **AA** is full in X, and **BB** is full or partial in X, then A intersection B is full or partial in X." Such rules can be displayed in a table of **AA** values by **BB** values; the above rule would place "FP" as the value in the "F" row and "FP" column. Construct such tables for the intersection, union, and complementation operations.

   (b) Do the tables constructed in part a satisfy De Morgan's laws? Do they have the property that union can be distributed over intersection, and vice versa? Do they observe the law of associativity?

   (c) Describe an algorithm that takes as input two regions **AA** and **BB** and determines whether **AA** is a subset of **BB**. (Note: The answer can be "True," "False," or "Maybe.")

   (d) * Describe an algorithm that takes as input two regions **AA** and **BB** and returns upper and lower bounds on the minimal distance between **AA** and **BB**. Your algorithm should return a lower bound that is as tight as possible, given the information, and an upper bound that is within one grid length of the best-possible upper bound, given the information.

(e) *** Give an algorithm that gives a tight upper bound on the minimal distance between two regions. (Note: If you solve this problem, please inform the author of this book.)

2. Let **AA,BB,CC,DD** range over connected, bounded, regular, non-empty regions in the X-Z planes. We wish to define the concept of **AA** being "above" **BB**, and we have a number of desirable properties and proposed definitions. Let x(**P**) and z(**P**) be the x and z coordinates of point **P**.

Definitions:

(a) **AA** is above **BB** if, for every point **A** in **AA** and **B** in **BB**, z(**A**) > z(**B**).

(b) **AA** is above **BB** if, for every point **A** in **AA**, there is a point **B** in **BB** such that z(**A**) > z(**B**).

(c) **AA** is above **BB** if, for every point **B** in **BB** there is a point **A** in **AA** such that z(**A**) > z(**B**) and x(**A**) = x(**B**).

(d) **AA** is above **BB** if z(**A**) > z(**B**) for every point **A** in **AA** and **B** in **BB** such that x(**A**) = x(**B**).

Axioms:

W. If **AA** is above **BB** then **BB** is not above **AA**.

X. If **AA** is above **BB** and **CC** is a subset of **AA**, then **CC** is above **BB**.

Y. If **AA** is above **BB** and **DD** is a subset of **BB**, then **AA** is above **DD**.

Z. If **AA** is above **BB**, then, if **AA** is "moved downward" without intersecting **BB**, then the result of that motion is above **BB**. Formally, if **AA** is above **BB** and, for all $t \in [0, k]$, **AA** $- t\hat{z}$ is disjoint from **BB**, then **AA** $-k\hat{z}$ is above **BB**.

(a) State which of these axioms are true under which of these definitions.

(b) Can you find a definition of "above" that satisfies all these properties? Can you find such a definition that at all corresponds to the standard meaning of "above"?

3. Find the complete transition graph for the attainable states of the cart on the track in Figure 6.29.

4. Extend the CSG representation of a human in Table 6.8 by adding the right upper leg and its position relative to the torso. The constraints you give should have some distant relation to the variation possible for a human being and the range of positions that a human can achieve. Do not worry about achieving any great degree of precision; the representation is too crude to achieve it.

5. Figure 6.1 shows a shape approximated by two different polygons. Show how these two approximations can be expressed in the MER-CATOR representation.

6. * Using the information in Table 6.9, find a lower bound on the distance between the lake and the road. (Your demonstration of the lower bound need not be rigorously complete. The lower bound need not be tight, but it should be greater than two feet.)

Chapter 7
Physics

I know people who would not deposit a nickel and a dime in a cigarette-vending machine and push the lever even if a diamond necklace came out. I know dozens who would not climb into an aeroplane even if it didn't move off the ground. In none of these people have I discerned what I would call a neurosis, an "exaggerated" fear; I have discerned only a natural caution in a world made up of gadgets that whir and whine and whiz and shriek and sometimes explode.

James Thurber, "Sex ex Machina," in *Let Your Mind Alone!*

To act effectively and flexibly, to take advantage of opportunities and to avoid dangers, an intelligent creature must understand the behavior of the physical world. In particular, it must understand how its own actions will affect the world.

The kind of knowledge required for sensible behavior can be quite different from scientific theories. In general, it is not necessary nor even useful to incorporate the most complete theories of modern physics into a robotics program. On the one hand, these theories deal with phenomena far outside the scope of ordinary experience. On the other hand, though it is probably true that any valid statement about the commonsense physical world is, in principle, a consequence of these underlying theories, deriving a useful commonsense inference from fundamental physical laws, or even stating boundary conditions for a commonsense problem in terms of fundamental physical properties, is wholly impractical. A commonsense physical reasoning system should deal with concepts more or less at the level of everyday discourse.

The theories that we will study in this chapter are all grounded in scientific theories; they are approximations to scientific truth. The physical theories that can be elicited from the man on the street are, apparently, substantially different. (See, for example [McCloskey 1983].) We have chosen to ignore these, first, because correct theories are presumably more useful, and, second, because correct theories are more uniform, better known, more easily specified, and less prone to internal inconsistency. Also, since the man on the street can, generally, accept physical reality without continual surprise, the predictions of the true physical laws must be largely compatible with his beliefs in most situations. (There are exceptions, such as gyroscopes, even among simple physical situations.)

In their daily lives, human beings deal with myriads of different types of physical substances and interactions. AI theories of physical reasoning do not yet begin to reflect this range of phenomena; so far, they have studied only a rather small number of different areas. Often the choice of an area for study has been based on a perceived potential for practical application, rather than on centrality or interest for commonsense reasoning. This chapter, necessarily, follows the existing research in its choice of topics.

7.1 The Component Model

A divide-and-conquer strategy that is often useful in analyzing physical systems, particularly man-made devices, is to view the system as a whole as composed of separate components connected together. The behavior of the system can then be analyzed by studying the behaviors of the components, each of which is presumably simpler than the overall system, and determining how these behaviors interact. This kind of analysis is easiest and most effective if the assemblage has the following properties:

- The device is assembled out of a set of components, which are connected together. What components are used, and how they are connected together, is invariant over time.

- The instantaneous state of the assemblage can be characterized by the values of a number of one-dimensional *parameters*. (We rule out devices where two- or three-dimensional motion is important, except where each dimension of motion can be handled independently.)

- Each component has a fixed number of *ports*. Components interact only by being connected at ports.

- Each parameter is associated with one port of one component. The behavior of a component is entirely characterized in terms of constraints that it imposes on values of parameters at its various ports. The behavior of a connection is entirely characterized in terms of constraints that it imposes on the ports that it joins.

The best examples of such systems are electronic devices, which, however, are at best marginally objects of a commonsense understanding. The model may also be applied, less well, to other types of devices such as hydraulic systems, heat-transfer systems, and simple mechanical devices. Our description of the component model is based on the well-known ENVISION program [de Kleer and Brown 1985].

An important objective in analyzing such systems is the principle of "No function in structure" [de Kleer and Brown 1985]. That is, the component and connection descriptions, which constitute the input description of the system (structure), should be given in a form that is independent of properties of the overall system. This objective is rarely fully achievable in a component analysis, except for electronic devices, but it can be partially achieved if the specified descriptions apply across a large range of devices that use the component. For example, a description of a switch that specifies that current flows through a switch just if the switch is closed would violate "No function in structure" badly, since there are many closed switches with no current flow, such as a switch in a circuit with no power source, or a closed switch in series with an open switch. A description that specifies that a switch prohibits current flow if it is open and prohibits voltage difference if it is closed would be valid for most standard uses of a switch, and so would observe the "no function in structure" principle. The account will not serve for nonstandard uses of a switch — e.g., as a paperweight, or to cast a shadow, or to create an electric arc by placing it almost closed. No description of an object in terms of constraints among ports will cover all of its possible physical behaviors.

As an example of component-based analysis, consider the simple scale shown in Figure 7.1. In this scale, the height of the needle varies with the mass in the pan. The relation is controlled by the two springs. For the purposes of this example, we will assume that, within the operating range of the scales, the slope of the lever is small enough that the horizontal displacement of the ends can be ignored.

We divide the scales into five components: A weight with two ports, one for the gravitational force and one for the support; a lever with two ports; a base with one port; and two springs, each with two ports. Each port has two parameters associated: its height and the vertical force exerted on the component at the port. (In a substantial violation

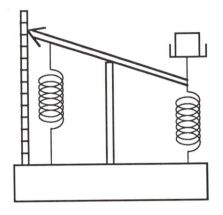

Figure 7.1 Scale

of "no function in structure," our models of springs and lever presume that the springs are vertical and that the lever is nearly horizontal.) The component models are as follows: The port of the base is at a constant height. The force on the two ends of the lever are equal. The heights of the two ends of the lever are constrained by the fact that their midpoint is a fixed fulcrum of constant height, so that the sum of their heights is constant. The forces exerted on the spring at each of its ports are equal in magnitude and opposite in direction, and the difference in height between the two ports is an increasing function of the difference in the forces. (The sign is not reversed, because we are considering the force exerted on the spring rather than the force exerted by the spring.) The weight obeys Newton's laws: The total force on the weight is equal to its mass times its vertical acceleration. The total force on the weight is equal to the gravitational force, which is considered one port, plus the force exerted on the weight by its support, which is considered another port.

The following rules apply to connections:

- All ports at a connection must have equal heights.

- The sum of the forces exerted on all the ports at a connection must be zero.

The system is at rest (in equilibrium) when all parameter values are constant. In particular, the acceleration of the weight must be zero.

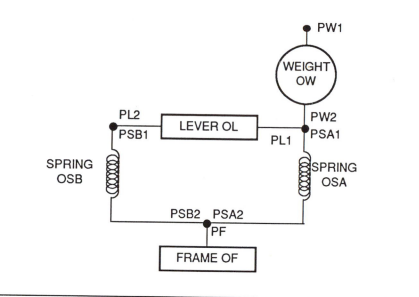

Figure 7.2 Schematic of scale

Figure 7.2 shows an abstract component diagram of the scale. Table 7.1 shows the primitives used in representing the scale. Table 7.2 gives an axiomatization of the physical laws involved. Table 7.3 shows a specific description of the scale. Table 7.4 shows the equations that govern the scale; these can be derived straightforwardly from the axioms and problem statement.

If we restrict attention to situations where the system is at rest, so that all derivatives are zero, then the last equation in Table 7.4 becomes, "f_w = mg."

There are a number of ways that these equations can be used for physical inference:

Exact solution: If the properties of the springs are stated exactly, rather than merely specifying that the expansion of the spring is an increasing function of the force applied, then the equations can be solved exactly. For example, suppose it is specified that the springs are linear; that is, they are governed by the rule

spring$(O, P1, P2) \Rightarrow$
   $(1/2) \times$ (force_on$(P1)$ − force_on$(P2)$) =
   spring_const$(O) \times$ (height$(P1)$ − height$(P2)$ − rest_length(O))

Table 7.1 Primitives for Scales

Sorts: Ports, components, heights, forces, situations, and fluents.

Atemporal:

grav_acc	—	Constant. Acceleration of gravity.
mass(O)	—	Function. Mass of weight O.
base_height(O)	—	Function. Height of frame O.
center_height(O)	—	Function. Central height of lever O.
frame(O, P)	—	Predicate. Object O is a frame with port P.
weight($O, P1, P2$)	—	Predicate. Object O is a weight with ports $P1$ and $P2$.
lever($O, P1, P2$)	—	Predicate. Object O is a lever with ports $P1$ and $P2$.
spring($O, P1, P2$)	—	Predicate. Object O is a spring with ports $P1$ and $P2$.
connection($P1, P2 \ldots Pk$)	—	Predicate. Ports $P1 \ldots Pk$ are connected.

Fluents:

height(P)	—	height of port P.
force_on(P)	—	force exerted on port P.

Let k_a = spring_const(osa); k_b = spring_const(osb); l_a = rest_length(osa); and l_b = rest_length(osb). The above constraint gives us the equations

$$\tfrac{1}{2}(f_{sa1} - f_{sa2}) = k_a \cdot (x_w - x_f - l_a)$$

$$\tfrac{1}{2}(f_{sb1} - f_{sb2}) = k_b \cdot (x_b - x_f - l_b)$$

Solving the above equations algebraically, together with those of Table 7.4, we can derive that the height of the arrow obeys the equation

$$\ddot{x}_b = g - \frac{1}{m}((k_a + k_b)x_b - (k_a + k_b)h_f + k_a l_a - k_b l_b - 2k_a h_{lf})$$

If the system is at rest, the arrow is at height

$$x_b = x_{rest} = h_f + \frac{1}{k_a + k_b}(mg + k_b l_b + 2k_a h_{lf} - k_a l_a)$$

Otherwise, the arrow executes a motion of form

$$x_b(t) = x_{rest} + a \sin(\omega t + t_0)$$

Table 7.2 Axioms for Scales

Component Rules

SC1. weight$(O, P1, P2) \Rightarrow$
value_in$(S,$force_on$(P1)) =$ mass$(O) \times$ grav_acc.

SC2. weight$(O, P1, P2) \Rightarrow$
mass$(O) \times$ deriv(deriv(height$(P2))) =$
$$\text{force\_on}(P1) + \text{force\_on}(P2).$$

SC3. spring$(O, P1, P2) \Rightarrow$
monotonic(height$(P1)$ − height$(P2)$,
force_on$(P1)$ − force_on$(P2)$, pos).

SC4. spring$(O, P1, P2) \Rightarrow$ force_on$(P1) = -$force_on$(P2)$.

SC5. frame$(O, P) \Rightarrow$ value_in$(S,$height$(P)) =$ base_height(O).

SC6. lever$(O, P1, P2) \Rightarrow$
value_in$(S,$height$(P1))$ − center_height$(O) =$
center_height(O) − value_in$(S,$height$(P2))$.

SC7. lever$(O, P1, P2) \Rightarrow$ force_on$(P1) =$ force_on$(P2)$.
(The lever has arms of equal length.)

Connection Rules

SC8. connection$(P1 \dots Pk) \Rightarrow$ height$(P1) = \dots =$ height(Pk).

SC9. connection$(P1 \dots Pk) \Rightarrow$ force_on$(P1) + \dots +$ force_on$(Pk) =$
0.

Table 7.3 Problem Description of Example Scale

weight(ow,pw1,pw2).
lever(ol,pl1,pl2).
frame(of,pf).
spring(osa,psa1,psa2).
spring(osb,psb1,psb2).
connection(pw2,pl1,psa1).
connection(pl2,psb1).
connection(psa2,psb2,pf).

Table 7.4 Equations of Scales

Define the following constants and fluents:
Constants: (See Figure 7.3)

m = mass(ow).
g = grav_acc.
h_l = center_height(ol).
h_f = base_height(of).
h_{lf} = $h_l - h_f$. (Height of the lever above the frame.)

Fluents:

x_w = height(pw2) = height(psa1) = height(pl1).
x_f = height(pf) = height(psa2) = height(psb2).
x_b = height(pl2) = height(psb2).
f_w = force_on(pw2).
f_{sa1} = force_on(psa1).
f_{sa2} = force_on(psa2).
f_{sb1} = force_on(psb1).
f_{sb2} = force_on(psb2).
f_l = force_on(pl1) = force_on(pl2).
f_f = force_on(pf).

Then we have the following relations:

$f_l + f_{sa1} + f_w = 0$.
$f_l + f_{sb1} = 0$.
$f_{sa2} + f_{sb2} + f_f = 0$.
$f_{sa1} = -f_{sa2}$.
$f_{sb1} = -f_{sb2}$.
$x_f = h_f$.
$x_b - h_l = h_l - x_w$.
monotonic($x_w - x_f, f_{sa1} - f_{sa2}$, pos).
monotonic($x_b - x_f, f_{sb1} - f_{sb2}$, pos).
$m \ddot{x}_w = f_w - mg$.

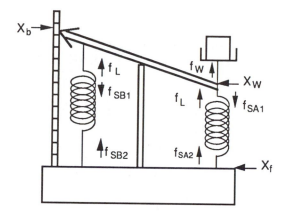

Figure 7.3 Constants of scale

where $\omega = \sqrt{(k_a + k_b)/m}$ and "a" and "t0" depend on the initial values of motion.

Perturbation of equilibrium: If the exact properties of the springs are not known, or if they obey a complex nonlinear equation, then it may be impossible or impractical to find closed-form solutions like those above, or even to find numerical values. However, it is still possible to extract various types of qualitative information. One type of qualitative inference is to calculate how the equilibrium state changes with a change to the constant parameters of the problem. For example, we can calculate how the rest position of the arrow is affected by a change in the mass. Suppose that the mass of the weight increases, and that all the other parameters of the system — the spring constants and lengths, the heights of the base and the lever, and the gravitational field — remain constant. Assuming the equilibrium state, where $\ddot{x}_w = 0$, and applying axioms SGN.1–SGN.3 of Table 4.6 governing the Δ operation, we obtain the following relations:

$\Delta f_l + \Delta f_{sa1} + \Delta f_w \sim 0.$
$\Delta f_l + \Delta f_{sb1} \sim 0.$
$\Delta f_{sa2} + \Delta f_{sb2} + \Delta f_f \sim 0.$
$\Delta f_{sa1} \sim -\Delta f_{sa2}.$

$$\Delta f_{sb1} \sim -\Delta f_{sb2}.$$
$$\Delta x_f \sim 0.$$
$$\Delta x_b + \Delta x_w \sim 0.$$
$$\Delta x_w - \Delta x_f \sim \Delta f_{sa1} - \Delta f_{sa2}.$$
$$\Delta x_b - \Delta x_f \sim \Delta f_{sb1} - \Delta f_{sb2}.$$
$$0 \sim \Delta f_w - \Delta m$$

The last equation above relies on the facts that the gravitational acceleration constant, grav_acc, is positive. Given these equations, it is easy to show that, if Δm is positive, then Δx_b is likewise positive. (Exercise 1)

Qualitative dynamic equations: It is also possible to use these partial constraints to derive a qualitative description of the dynamic behavior of the system, for fixed values of the constant parameters. Differentiating and applying sign operations to the equations in Table 7.4, we obtain the following qualitative equations:

$$\text{sign}(f_l) + \text{sign}(f_{sa1}) + \text{sign}(f_w) \sim 0.$$
$$\text{sign}(f_l) + \text{sign}(f_{sb1}) \sim 0.$$
$$\text{sign}(f_{sa2}) + \text{sign}(f_{sb2}) + \text{sign}(f_f) \sim 0.$$
$$\text{sign}(f_{sa1}) \sim - \text{sign}(f_{sa2}).$$
$$\text{sign}(f_{sb1}) \sim - \text{sign}(f_{sb2}).$$
$$\partial x_f \sim 0.$$
$$\partial x_b + \partial x_w \sim 0.$$
$$\partial x_w - \partial x_f \sim \partial f_{sa1} - \partial f_{sa2}.$$
$$\partial x_b - \partial x_f \sim \partial f_{sb1} - \partial f_{sb2}.$$
$$\partial x_w \sim \text{sign}(f_w).$$

We may use algebraic techniques to reduce the above relations to the following:

$$\partial^2 x_b \sim -\text{sign}(f_w).$$
$$\partial f_w \sim \partial x_b.$$

These equations thus have the same form as those analyzed in Section 4.9. Using the techniques discussed there, we can show that the height of the arrow follows the state transition illustrated in Figure 4.11; that is, it oscillates, regardless of the exact properties of the springs involved. (We have discussed some limitations on this conclusion in Section 4.9)

The ENVISION program carries out qualitative analyses of equilibrium perturbation and of dynamic behavior; it does not find exact quantitative solutions.

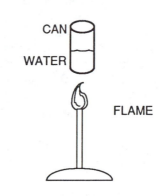

Figure 7.4 Boiling water in a can

7.2   Qualitative-Process Theory

As we have seen, the component model analyzes a complex physical system in terms of the questions "What are the pieces of the system?," "How does each piece constrain the parameters associated with it?," and "How are the pieces connected?" An alternative method, called *qualitative process* (QP) theory [Forbus 1985], focuses instead on the questions "What processes take place in the system?," "How do these processes influence system parameters?," and "How do the processes interact?" Consider, for example, a closed can of water suspended over a lit Bunsen burner (Figure 7.4). We would like to determine that heat flows from the burner through the can to the water, and that the water first becomes hotter until reaching its boiling point, then it boils and turns to vapor, then it continues to get hotter until reaching the temperature of the flame (or bursting the can). To analyze this system in terms of components constraining parameters at ports would be unnatural. Also, by focusing exclusively on the relations between parameters, the component model would entirely avoid facts such as the boiling of the water, which seem to be central to a commonsense understanding of the system behavior.

The central concept in Forbus's analysis[1] is that of a *process*. An individual process is a state token of a particular type. The process is said to be *active* during the time interval in which it takes place. The significant properties of a process are its *preconditions* and its *influences*. The preconditions of a process are states that must hold

---

[1] We simplify Forbus's theory and depart from his terminology in some respects.

if the process is to be active. (In some circumstances, it is useful to distinguish between the initiating conditions, which must hold for the process to start, and the sustaining conditions, which must hold for the process to continue. For example, a fire requires an external spark as an initiating condition, but not as a sustaining condition.) The influences of a process are the effects it has on parameters.

For example, consider the process of a heat flow from object A to object B. A sufficient precondition for heat flow is that A and B are thermally connected, and the temperature of A is greater than the temperature of B. Necessary preconditions are that A and B are thermally connected and that the temperature of A is greater than or equal to the temperature of B. (Heat can flow from one object to another of equal temperature if there is an external heat flow into the first. Consider, for example, flow between the two levels of a double boiler when both levels are boiling.) The influences of the heat flow are to reduce the heat of A and to increase the heat of B.

Besides characterizing processes, a QP theory must describe the connections between parameters. Parameters are divided into two types. Parameters of the first type are directly influenced by processes. The time derivative of such a parameter is equal to the sum of the influences of all processes on the parameter. In our example, the parameter "heat of A" is directly influenced by the heat flows into and out of A. Parameters of the second type are affected directly by other parameters; they are affected by processes only indirectly, through other parameters. In our example, the parameter "temperature of A" is directly affected by the parameter "heat of A" and only indirectly by the heat-flow process. QP theory expresses relations between parameters using statements of qualitative proportionality. Parameter $R1$ is qualitatively proportional to parameter $R2$, written $R1 \propto_{Q+} R2$, if an increase in $R2$ will cause an increase in $R1$, other things being equal. $R1$ is negatively qualitatively proportional to $R2$, written $R1 \propto_{Q-} R2$, if an increase in $R2$ will cause a decrease in $R1$, other things being equal. In our example, QP theory would specify that temperature(A) is qualitatively proportional to heat(A).

(Neither of the ideas in the previous paragraph — distinguishing between directly and indirectly affected parameters, and the definition of qualitative proportionality — have sound foundations in actual physics. Consider a piston containing gas. In such a system it is possible to control either the volume, by fixing the position of the piston, or the pressure, by putting a weight on the piston, or some function of the volume and pressure, by attaching a spring to the piston. Similarly, one can control either the temperature, by bringing it into thermal equilibrium with a heat reservoir of fixed temperature, or the heat, by

Table 7.5 Nonlogical symbols for Qualitative-Process Theory

Sorts: Situations (S), processes (P), process types (A), parameters (Q). Formally, processes and process types are just special cases of state tokens and state types. A parameter is a fluent into a quantity space.

Nonlogical symbols:

active(S, P)	—	Predicate. Process P is active in situation S. Equivalent to "$S \in$ time_of(P)."
process(P, A)	—	Predicate. P is a process of type A. Equivalent to "token_of(P, A)."
influence(P, Q)	—	Function. Influence of process P on parameter Q. A fluent onto the differential space, "Units of Q per unit time."
$P1 \propto_{Q+} P2$	—	Predicate (at least syntactically). $P1$ is qualitatively proportional to $P2$.
$P1 \propto_{Q-} P2$	—	Predicate. $P1$ is negatively qualitatively proportional to $P2$.

insulating the system. Thus, which parameters are directly affected and which are indirectly affected depends on circumstances. The relations between parameters similarly depends on circumstances. For example, if the pressure is held constant, then temperature and volume increase together, while if heat is held constant (adiabatic expansion), then temperature increases as volume decreases. Asking whether the temperature is an increasing or decreasing function of volume is somewhat like asking whether the area of a rectangle is an increasing or decreasing function of the length of its longer side. If the length of the shorter side is held constant, then the area is increasing; if the perimeter of the rectangle is held constant, then the area is decreasing.)

We now have all the representational equipment to express the example of the water in the can. Table 7.5 shows nonlogical symbols and axioms for QP theory. Tables 7.6 and 7.7 give the axioms neeeded for the particular example. Table 7.8 gives the particular problem statement.

Table 7.6 Nonlogical Symbols for Heat Flow Example

Sorts: Situations (S), processes (P), process types, states, fluents, temperature, heat, mass, objects (O). Temperature, heat, and mass are parameters. Objects, for the purpose of this example, are rather artificial constructs; they are collections of stuff, of uniform composition and uniform temperature, which at any instant may be gaseous, liquid, or solid, depending on the temperature.

Atemporal properties:

boiling_point(O)	—	Function. Boiling temperature of object O.
freezing_point(O)	—	Function. Freezing temperature of object O.
mass(O)	—	Function. Mass of object O.

Parameters:

temperature(O)	—	Function. Fluent of temperature of object O.
heat(O)	—	Function. Fluent of heat of object O.
solid_mass(O)	—	Function. Fluent of the mass of the solid part of O.
liquid_mass(O)	—	Function. Fluent of the mass of the liquid part of O.
gas_mass(O)	—	Function. Fluent of the mass of the gaseous part of O.

State type:

thermally_connected($O1, O2$).	—	Function. State of $O1$ being thermally connected to $O2$.

Processes types:

heat_flow($O1, O2$)	—	Function. Process type of a heat flow from $O1$ to $O2$.
boiling(O)	—	Function. Process type of object O boiling.

Table 7.7 Axioms for Heat-Flow Example

Process Definition for Heat Flow

HF1. [true_in(S,thermally_connected(OS,OD)) $\wedge$
value_in(S,temperature(OS)) >
value_in(S,temperature(OD))] $\Rightarrow$
$\exists_P$ process(P,heat_flow(OS,OD)) $\wedge$ active(S,P).
(Sufficient precondition for heat flow: If source OS is thermally connected to destination OD and OS is hotter than OD, then heat will flow from OS to OD.)

HF2. [process(P,heat_flow(OS,OD)) $\wedge$
active(S,P)] $\Rightarrow$
[$OS \neq OD$ $\wedge$ true_in(S,thermally_connected(OS,OD)) $\wedge$
value_in(S,temperature(OS)) $\geq$
value_in(S,temperature(OD))].
(Necessary preconditions for heat flow: For heat to flow directly from OS to OD, they must be thermally connected and OS must be at least as hot as OD.)

HF3. [token_of(P,heat_flow(OS,OD)) $\wedge$ active(S,P)] $\Rightarrow$
[value_in(S,influence(P,heat(OS))) < 0 $\wedge$
value_in(S,influence(P,heat(OD))) > 0]
(Influences of heat flow.)

Process Definition for Boiling

HF4. [value_in(S,liquid_mass(OB)) > 0 $\wedge$
value_in(S,temperature(OB)) = boiling_point(OB) $\wedge$
process($P2$,heat_flow(OS,OB)) $\wedge$ active($S,P2$)]$\Leftrightarrow$
$\exists_P$ process(P,boiling(OB)) $\wedge$ active(S,P).
(Preconditions for boiling: An object OB will boil if it is partially liquid and is at its boiling point and there is heat flow into OB.)

HF5. [process(P,boiling(OB)) $\wedge$ active(S,P)] $\Rightarrow$
[influence(P,liquid_mass(OB)) < 0 $\wedge$
influence(P,gas_mass(OB)) > 0.]
(Influences of boiling: It reduces the liquid mass of OB and increases its gaseous mass.)

Qualitative Proportionality

HF6. temperature(O) $\propto_{Q+}$ heat(O)

Table 7.7: Axioms for Heat-Flow Example (Continued)

State Coherence Axioms

HF7. value_in(S,solid_mass(O)) > 0 $\Rightarrow$
      value_in(S,temperature(O)) $\leq$ freezing_point(O).
      (An object can exist in solid form only below its freezing
      point.)

HF8. value_in(S,liquid_mass(O)) > 0 $\Rightarrow$
      freezing_point(O) $\leq$ value_in(S,temperature(O)) $\leq$ boiling_point(O).
      (An object can exist in liquid form only between its freezing
      and boiling points.)

HF9. value_in(S,gas_mass(O)) > 0 $\Rightarrow$
      boiling_point(O) $\leq$ value_in(S,temperature(O)).
      (An object can exist in gaseous form only above its boiling
      point.)

HF10. value_in(S,solid_mass(O)) + value_in(S,liquid_mass(O)) +
      value_in(S,gas_mass(O)) = mass(O) > 0.
      (The sum of the solid, liquid, and gaseous parts of an object
      is equal to the total mass of the substance, which is positive
      and time-invariant.)

HF11. value_in(S,solid_mass(O)) $\geq$ 0 $\wedge$
      value_in(S,liquid_mass(O)) $\geq$ 0 $\wedge$
      value_in(S,gas_mass(O)) $\geq$ 0.
      (No masses are less than zero.)

Table 7.8 Problem Specification for Heat-Flow Example

Constants: oflame, owater, s0, i0.

infinite_on_right(i0) ∧ start(i0) = s0.
(i0 is an infinite interval beginning with s0.)

$\forall_{S \in i0}$ true_in(S, thermally_connected(oflame,owater)).
(The water is always thermally connected to the flame.)

$\forall_{S \in i0}$ value_in(S,temperature(oflame)) > boiling_point(owater).
(The flame is always above the boiling point of water.)

freezing_point(owater) < value_in(s0, temperature(owater)) <
                 boiling_point(owater).

(The water temperature starts between its freezing point and
its boiling point.)

Given process characterizations and qualitative proportionalities, as
in Table 7.7, and the boundary conditions of a physical situation, as
in Table 7.8, it is possible to predict the behavior of the system. This
involves the following algorithm:

Algorithm 7.1: Prediction in QP Theory

1. Determine what processes have their preconditions satisfied and
   are therefore active. If no processes are active, then halt.

2. Determine the influences of these processes.

3. Determine the direction of change of the parameters. First, determine the change in each directly influenced parameter by summing
   the influences of the active processes. Then determine the change
   in indirectly influenced parameters by using the qualitative proportionalities in topological sort order. If the direction of change is
   ambiguous, then consider all combinations of possibilities disjunctively.

4. Extrapolate the changes to the parameters to predict which quantity conditions will change first, causing the beginning or end of
   a process. If it is ambiguous which change occurs first, then con-

sider all possibilities disjunctively. If no such change can occur, then halt.

5. Compute the state of the world at the transition point computed in (4). Go to 1.

Algorithm 7.1 above is very similar to the techniques discussed in Section 4.9 for solving qualitative differential equations. However, it involves three types of nonmonotonic inference. First, a closed-world assumption is applied to the predicate "active(S, P)"; that is, we assume that the only processes that are active in a given situation S are those that we have proven. Second, the use of a qualitative proportionality $P1 \propto_Q P2$ in step (3) assumes that any parameter relevant to $P1$ whose change has not been calculated is constant. Third, the algorithm makes the assumption, discussed in Section 4.9, that if a quantity-valued fluent approaches a value, then it will eventually attain the value.

Table 7.9 shows how this algorithm behaves on the heat-flow example.

7.3 Rigid Solid Objects

Perhaps the most common area of commonsense physical reasoning is the interactions of solid objects. Solid objects are involved in most terrestrial natural phenomena and in nearly every man-made artifact. They are familiar to every human from infancy and fairly well understood by childhood. So natural and familiar is solid-object behavior that it was long believed to be the fundamental type of physical behavior; hence, the efforts of physicists from the Greek atomists through the beginning of this century to explain physical phenomena of all sorts in mechanistic terms.

In reasoning about solid objects, it is often possible to assume that the class of solid objects and the shape of each solid object remains fixed. That is, the solid objects involved are not created, destroyed, broken, bent, or worn down. If so, we can define a time-invariant function, "shape(O)," mapping an object O to the region that it occupies in some standard position. The fluent "place(O)" is the region occupied by O in each situation; since O is rigid, place(O) is always congruent to shape(O). The fluent "position(O)" is the rigid mapping that maps shape(O) to place(O).

Table 7.9 Prediction in QP Theory

First iteration:

1. Active process: From HF1, infer that there is a heat flow ph1 from oflame to owater active in s0.

2. From HF3, infer that ph1 has a positive influence on the heat of owater and a negative influence on the heat of oflame.

3. Applying the closed-world assumption on influences, infer that the heat of owater increases and the heat of oflame decreases. From HF6, infer that the temperature of owater increases and the temperature of oflame decreases. (This is not true, of course, of an actual flame, but it will not affect the remainder of the prediction. A richer theory of flames could block this nonmonotonic inference (see Exercise 2). The inference would be valid if we immersed the can in a high-temperature bath, rather than putting it over the flame.)

4. By extrapolating the changes, we can see two possible changes in the quantity conditions. First, the temperature of the flame and of the water could become equal, which might bring an end to the heat flow. Second, the temperature of the water might reach its boiling point, which would cause a boiling process to begin. However, due to the boundary condition that the temperature of the flame is always above the boiling point of water, we can determine that the second transition always takes place before the first. Hence, we can define a new situation s1, in which the temperature of owater is at its boiling point.

5. In s1, the temperature of owater is equal to the boiling point of water. All other relations remain the same as in owater.

Table 7.9: Prediction in QP Theory (Continued)

Second iteration:

1. Active processes: From HF1, infer that the heat flow ph1 from oflame to owater continues. (See Exercise 3 for a discussion of this inference.) From HF4, infer that there is a boiling process pb1 active in s1.

2. From HF3, the heat flow ph1 has a positive influence on the heat of owater and a negative influence on the heat of oflame. From HF5, the boiling has a positive influence on the gaseous mass of owater and a negative influence on its liquid mass.

3. Applying the closed-world assumption on influences, we infer that the heat of owater increases, the heat of oflame decreases, the liquid mass of owater decreases, and the gaseous mass decreases. Applying HF6, we infer that the temperature of oflame decreases. We would also infer that the temperature of owater increases, except that we can show that it cannot, since, by HF8, its temperature cannot exceeed its boiling point unless its liquid mass is zero. Therefore, we conclude that, due to the change from liquid to gas, HF6 does not apply. (To make the blocking of this inference more direct, it may be advisable to add the qualitative proportionality "temperature(O) $\propto_{Q-}$ gaseous_mass(O)." Note that this rule will only be invoked during a boiling (or condensing) process, since those are the only times that the gaseous mass changes.)

4. By extrapolating the changes we can see two possible changes. Either the temperature of the flame will reduce to the point where it is no longer higher than the water, bringing the heat flow to an end, or the liquid mass of the water will reach zero, bringing the boiling to an end. Again, the boundary conditions rule out the first event. We can thus predict that at the next transition situation, s2, the liquid mass of owater will be zero.

5. In s2, the liquid mass of owater is zero and (by HF7 and HF10) the gaseous mass is equal to the total mass. All other relations remain as in s1.

Table 7.9: Prediction in QP Theory (Continued)

Third iteration:

1. In s2, the only active process is the heat flow ph1.

2. The heat flow hf1 has a positive influence on the heat of owater and a negative influence on the heat of oflame (HF1).

3. As above, we infer nonmonotonically that the heat of owater and its temperature increase, while the heat and temperature of oflame decrease. (HF6.)

4. The only possible transition is that the temperature of the water and the flame become equal, possibly bringing the heat flow from oflame to owater to an end.

5. In s3, the temperatures of oflame and owater become equal. All other relations are as in s2.

Fourth iteration:

1. In s3, the heat flow ph1 may or may not continue (HF1, HF2). If it does not, then the system has reached stasis. If it does, we continue as follows:

2. The influence of the heat flow is to raise the heat of owater and decrease the heat of the flame.

3. Applying the closed-world assumption, we infer that the heat of owater increases and the heat of oflame decreases. From HF6, we would infer that the temperature of owater increases and the temperature of oflame decreases. If this happened, however, the heat flow would immediately halt, by HF2. Therefore, we can infer that as long as the heat flow continues, the temperatures of owater and oflame must be equal. If the heat flow ever stops, then since there are no active processes, the temperatures will still remain the same.

4. No further transitions are possible.

The basic constraints on solid objects are that they are rigid, they move continuously, and two objects do not overlap. We further assume that all objects are regular and connected. Axioms SO.1–SO.5 express these formally.

SO.1. value_in(S,place(O)) =
image(value_in(S,position(O)),shape(O)).
(Relation of position and place.)

SO.2. rigid_mapping(value_in(S,position(O))).
(Objects are rigid.)

SO.3. continuous(position(O)).
(Objects move continuously over time.)

SO.4. $O1 \neq O2 \Rightarrow$
¬overlap_reg(value_in(S,place($O1$)), value_in(S,place($O2$))).
(Two distinct objects do not overlap in the same situation.)

SO.5. regular(shape(O)) $\land$ connected(shape(O)).
(Objects are regular and connected.)

A *kinematic* analysis of a system of solid objects is one that uses only the above properties. Thus, it considers only how the geometry of the solid objects involved causes them to block each other's motion or to push one another into position, and ignores issues such as mass, forces, energies, friction, and so on. Kinematic analysis by itself is sufficient to establish inferences like the following: (Figure 7.5)

A. If the topmost gear in Figure 7.5A is rotated clockwise, the other objects will move as shown. (We assume that the gears are pinned at their centers to a fixed frame.)

B. The gear in Figure 7.5B cannot move.

C. An object cannot go from inside to outside a closed box.

D. A hanger on a pole cannot move directly downwards.

Formalizing statements such as those above involves only enumerating the objects involved and specifying their shapes, their positions, and the constraints on their motions. Kinematic analysis is then just determining the class of motions consistent with these boundary conditions and the constraints SO.1–SO.5. We have discussed a number of techniques for such analysis, including topological reasoning and the use of configuration spaces, in Sections 6.1.6 and 6.2.5. For example, the statement C can be formalized as follows:

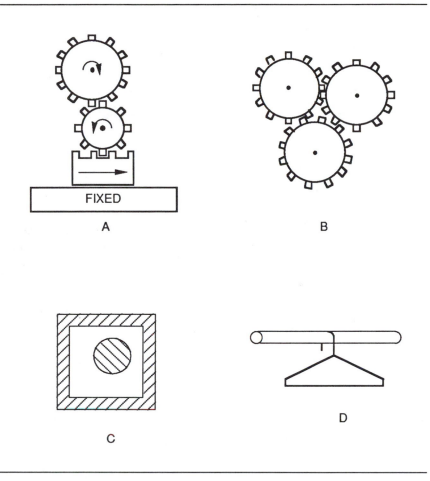

Figure 7.5 Kinematic systems

[precedes($S, S1$) $\wedge$
is_inside(value_in(S,place($O2$)), value_in(S,place($O1$)))] $\Rightarrow$
is_inside(value_in($S1$,place($O2$)), value_in($S1$,place($O1$)))]

This follows directly from the geometric rule that, if a continuous fluent over regular regions goes from inside a box to outside it, then it
must at some point overlap the box.

Another example: We can show that gear B will rotate if gear A
rotates in Figure 7.5A, by constructing the configuration space for the
two gears and establishing that, for any path P through the permitted
region of the space, if A rotates on P, then B rotates as well.

There are, however, many aspects of solid-object behavior that are
not captured in a kinematic analysis. For example, consider the following inferences (Figure 7.6):

E. A block sitting on a table will remain motionless. A block dropped
   on a table will come to rest near where it was dropped.

F. If you lift a table at one end, it will rotate around the farther legs.

G. A round wheel will roll easily; a square wheel will not.

H. A garden rake placed in an umbrella stand is likely to knock it
   over. A rake placed against a piano may fall, but it will not knock
   the piano over.

Kinematic analysis supports none of these conclusions; any other continuous rigid motion that does not bring objects into collision is equally
consistent with the constraints of kinematics. These inferences require a *dynamic* analysis, involving masses, forces, and related concepts.

The standard theory of solid-object dynamics is Newtonian mechanics. The central new concept is that of a force. In most problems,
three types of forces are needed: the gravitational force, which may
be taken, within a local terrestrial environment, to be uniformly downward; constraint forces, which enforce the constraint that solid objects
do not overlap; and frictive forces, which act to reduce the sliding between objects. Force is related to motion by two differential equations:
Force equals mass times linear acceleration, and torque equals the moment of inertia times angular acceleration. Collisions must be handled
separately by conservation of energy and momentum.

In order to avoid a theory in which all objects are in free fall, it is
necessary to define certain objects as being fixed in space. We introduce the predicate "fixed(O)," satisfying the axiom that fixed objects
do not move.

$$\text{fixed}(O) \Rightarrow \exists_P \forall_S \text{ value\_in}(S, \text{position}(O)) = P.$$

It is often useful to introduce the *ground* as a special fixed object
occupying an infinite surface below all other objects.

We now present Newtonian mechanics for a very restricted domain,
in which there is only one mobile point object moving among fixed
obstacles. This radical simplification enables us to avoid the messy
issues involved in variable orientations and the associated issues of
angular velocity, angular momentum, and torque; extended contact
between objects; and collisions among collections of mobile objects.

Figure 7.6 Dynamic systems

(More on these below.) We denote the space occupied by the obstacle as "obstacle," and we posit that it is regular and smooth. Table 7.10 shows the nonlogical symbols involved in the theory. (The physical symbols are all constants, owing to the restricted nature of the domain. We also introduce some new geometric symbols.) Table 7.11 gives the axioms that govern the behavior of the object.

From the rules in Table 7.11 it is possible (though not easy) to prove the following two useful rules: (i) Reduction of energy: The mechanical energy of the object never increases. (ii) Attainment of rest: The object eventually reaches a state of rest, unless there is an infinitely deep hole, or the coefficient of friction is zero.

PO.17. energyp = massp × grav_acc × height(placep) +
$\qquad$ 1/2 massp × velocityp · velocityp.
$\qquad$ (Definition of the fluent "energyp", mechanical energy of the object.)

Table 7.10 Nonlogical Symbols for Point-Object Dynamics

Sorts: Mass (a quantity space), spatial sorts, states, situations, forces (vectors with dimension mass times distance over time squared).

Physical:

obstacle	—	Spatial region occupied by the obstacle.
massp	—	Mass of the point object.
coeff_fricp	—	Coefficient of friction of the object against the obstacle (dimensionless quantity).
restitutionp	—	Coefficient of restitution of the object colliding with the obstacle (dimensionless quantity).
placep	—	Place of the object (fluent).
velocityp	—	Velocity of the object (fluent).
contact	—	State of contact between the object and the obstacle.
collision	—	State of a collision between the object and the obstacle.
forcep	—	Total force exerted on object (fluent).
fricp	—	Frictive force exerted on object (fluent).
normalp	—	Normal force exerted on object (fluent).
grav_acc	—	Acceleration of gravity.

Geometric and quantitative:

surf_norm(**RR, P**)	—	Function. Surface normal out of **RR** at boundary point **P**.
smooth(**RR**)	—	Predicate. Region **RR** has a smooth boundary.
mag(V)	—	Function. Magnitude of vector V.
low_limit(F)	—	Function. Let F be a fluent. low_limit(F) is likewise a fluent. The quantity value_in(S,low_limit(F)) is the limit of F as time approaches S from below (previous times).
high_limit(F)	—	Function. Fluent analogous to low_limit.
perp_comp($V1, V2$)	—	Function. Component of vector $V1$ in direction perpendicular to $V2$. perp_comp($V1, V2$) = $V1 - (V1 \cdot V2)V2/\text{mag}(V2)$.

Table 7.11 Axioms for the Dynamics of a Point Object

Kinematics: PO.1–PO.3 are analogous to SO.3–SO.5 but modified to suit the requirements of a point object.

PO.1. continuous(placep).
   (The object moves continuously over time.)

PO.2. ¬value_in(S,placep) ∈ interior(obstacle).
   (The object is never inside the obstacle.)

PO.3. regular(obstacle) ∧ smooth(obstacle).
   (The obstacle is regular and smooth.)

PO.4. velocityp = deriv(placep).
   (Definition of velocity.)

Dynamics:

PO.5. ¬true_in(S,collision) ⇒ value_in(S,forcep) =
   massp × value_in(S,deriv(deriv(placep))).
   (Newton's second law: F=ma.)

PO.6. forcep = −grav_acc × massp × $\hat{k}$ + fricp + normalp.
   (The forces are gravity, friction, and the normal force.)

PO.7. true_in(S,contact) ⇔ value_in(S,placep) ∈ boundary(obstacle).
   (Definition of contact.)

PO.10. ¬true_in(S,contact) ⇒
   value_in(S,fricp) = value_in(S,normalp) = 0.
   (Frictive and normal forces only apply when the object is in contact with the obstacle.)

PO.11. parallel(value_in(S,normalp),
         surf_norm(obstacle,value_in(S,placep))).
   (The normal force is always parallel to the surface normal at the contact point.)

PO.12. perpendicular(value_in(S,fricp),
             surf_norm(obstacle,value_in(S,placep))).
   (The frictive force is always perpendicular to the surface normal at the contact point.)

PO.13. mag(value_in(S,fricp)) ≤ coeff_fricp × mag(value_in(S,normalp)).
   (The magnitude of the frictive force is always less than or equal to the magnitude of the normal force times the coefficient of friction.)

PO.14. [value_in(S,velocityp) ≠ 0 ∧ true_in(S,contact)] ⇒
   [mag(value_in(S,fricp)) =
   coeff_fricp × mag(value_in(S,normalp)) ∧
   parallel(value_in(S,fricp), −value_in(S,velocityp))].
   (If the object is moving against an obstacle, then the magnitude of the friction is equal to the magnitude of the normal force times the coefficient of friction, and it is directed opposite to the velocity.)

7.11 Axioms for the Dynamics of a Point Object (Continued)

PO.15 true_in(S,collision) $\Leftrightarrow$
       [true_in(S,contact) $\wedge$
       ¬perpendicular(value_in(S,low_limit(velocityp)),
                            surf_norm(obstacle,value_in(S,placep))].
       (A collision is taking place just if the object is in contact with the
       obstacle, and the limit of velocity from before is not tangent to the
       obstacle.)

PO.16. [true_in(S,collision) $\wedge$
        N=surf_norm(obstacle,value_in(S,placep))] $\Rightarrow$
        [value_in(S,high_limit(velocityp)) $\cdot$ N =
        $-$restitutionp $\cdot$ value_in(S,low_limit(velocityp)) $\cdot$ N $\wedge$
        perp_comp(value_in(S,high_limit(velocityp)),N) =
        perp_comp(value_in(S,high_limit(velocityp)),N)].
        (Rule of collisions: The velocity in the direction of the surface
        normal is reversed and reduced by the coefficient of restitution.
        The velocity tangential to the surface is unchanged.)

PO.18. precedes($S1, S2$) $\Rightarrow$
        value_in($S1$,energyp) $\geq$ value_in($S2$,energyp).
        (Energy never increases.)

PO.19. [infinite_on_right(I) $\wedge$ coeff_fricp $\neq$ 0 $\wedge$
        [$\exists_H \forall_P$ height($\mathbf{P}$) $< H \Rightarrow \mathbf{P} \in$ obstacle]] $\Rightarrow$
        $\exists_{S \in I} \forall_{S2 \in I}$ precedes($S, S2$) $\Rightarrow$
                      value_in(S,placep) = value_in($S2$,placep).
        (The object eventually reaches a state of rest.)

These rules can be used to solve a variety of problems. A simple
problem is shown in Figure 7.7: The object is dropped from within
a steep funnel. We wish to show that it must eventually exit the
bottom of the funnel. The proof is as follows: Geometrically, since the
object cannot enter the interior of the obstacle (PO.2), it must either
exit the top, exit the bottom, or stay inside forever. To exit the top,
it would have to go higher than it is at the start, which (by PO.17)
would mean that it has more energy than at the start, which is ruled
out by (PO.18). If it stays inside forever, then, by (PO.19), it must
eventually come to a state of rest. By (PO.15) and (PO.5), the net forces
on it then must be zero. By (PO.6) this means that the frictive and
normal forces must counteract the gravitational force. However, using
(PO.11), (PO.12), and (PO.13), which assert that the normal force is
parallel to the surface normal, the frictive force is perpendicular, and

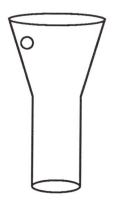

Figure 7.7 Point object in a funnel

the frictive force is at most the coefficient of friction times the normal force, we can show geometrically that this balancing of forces can only hold if the slope of the surface is less than the coefficient of friction. Thus, by showing from the geometric specifications of the funnel that, at any point of the surface that the object can reach, the slope is too great, we can conclude that the object cannot come to rest inside. The only remaining possibility is that it exits the bottom.

Another example of the use of the above theory is in deriving the rules used for a point object on a track in the NEWTON program, discussed in Section 6.2.6. We will illustrate with the derivation of the following rule: The object cannot stay on a curve (or surface) at a point where the curve is convex and has a normal with a downward component. The proof runs as follows: We wish first to show that the object must undergo an acceleration with a positive component in the direction of the surface normal. By (PO.11), the normal force on the object (if any) is parallel to the surface normal; by (PO.12), the frictive force is perpendicular to the surface normal, so that it is irrelevant; by hypothesis, the surface normal is pointing downward, so the gravitational force, which is nonzero and points downward, also has a positive component. By (PO.6) the net force is the sum of these, and therefore has a positive component in the direction of the surface normal. By (PO.5), therefore, the acceleration has a positive component in the direction of the surface normal. However, it is possible to show geometrically that a motion on a curve can have an acceleration with a positive component in the direction of the surface normal only if the curve is concave at that point. Since the curve is convex, the object cannot stay on it.

The full theory of Newtonian mechanics extends the above toy theory to handle multiple extended objects. The complete theory has the strengths that it is correct (to the extent that rigid objects exist at all) and that it is complete: It gives a prediction for any situation. Moreover, no alternative is available; no one has described a commonsense dynamic theory of solid objects that is anywhere near complete. However, Newtonian mechanics has substantial problems as a theory of commonsense reasoning. First, it is in several respects contradictory to a naive understanding of solid objects. This is partly because some actual behaviors of solid objects, such as gyroscopic motion, are strongly counterintuitive even when they are directly perceived, and partly because inertial motion, which is the default in Newtonian theory, is very much the exception in terrestrial environments, owing to the ubiquity of friction, air resistance, and other dissipative forces.

Second, axiomatizing the complete theory of Newtonian dynamics, including friction and collisions, for extended objects is surprisingly complex (see [Kilmister and Reeve 1966; Davis 1988a]). A number of sticky issues arise, including the following: (i) Forces between objects may be applied at a point, on a curve, or across a face (Figure 7.8). The dimensionality of the force at a point depends on which of these holds: (ii) The analogue to rule (PO.19) above, that an isolated system with no source of energy will eventually reach a state of rest, is frequently useful in commonsense reasoning. Unfortunately, this rule is not true for extended objects, unless we include forces such as air resistance, which are hard to quantify. (iii) Newtonian physics is generally deterministic; that is, given the shapes and material properties of the objects involved and their positions and velocities in a starting situation, all future events are determined. There are, however, a variety of circumstances, involving friction or collisions, in which the theory becomes nondeterministic, allowing more than one possible behavior. (iv) Collisions are particularly difficult to analyze within the idealization of inelastic objects, particularly in cases where the collision involves more than two objects, or where the objects collide over some extended surface. The standard rules given in mechanics textbooks for approximating the effects of a collision using the coefficients of restitution of the objects involved are hard to apply to extended objects and, in any case, are adopted more for reasons of theoretical elegance than of close approximation to the truth [Kilmister and Reeves 1966, p. 189]. (By contrast, Coulomb's law of friction, though also an approximation, is very nearly valid across a large range of circumstances.)

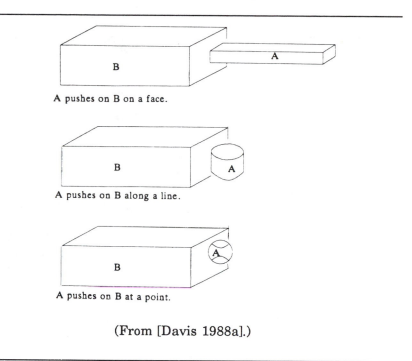

A pushes on B on a face.

A pushes on B along a line.

A pushes on B at a point.

(From [Davis 1988a].)

Figure 7.8 Varying dimensionality of force

Thirdly, though Newtonian physics is, no doubt, in principle sufficient to support any correct commonsensical inference, in practice it
is often necessary to augment Newton's laws with more specialized
heuristics. Consider the following statement: "If object O is dropped
from rest onto a flat horizontal surface from height h, then O will
come to rest on the surface not far from the vertical projection of
its release point, unless either O is very elastic or O rolls well." It
seems likely that, once the vague terms in this statement have been
suitably tightened, this statement is true and a consequence of Newtonian dynamics. However, proving it as a theorem from Newton's
laws seems to be very difficult. (Usual techniques for dealing with
differential equations are not applicable because of the collisions involved.) Given a particular object description, starting position, and
starting height, it is possible to simulate its behavior using the laws
of Newtonian physics by predicting each state of collision, rolling and
sliding in sequence; but the general result cannot be established by
such simulations. It is currently an open question how to formulate
such rules effectively for commonsense reasoning.

Thus, there is currently no qualitative theory of solid-object dynamics that supports efficient inference of commonsensically obvious facts. The Reference section at the end of the chapter lists some preliminary studies.

7.4 Liquids

It is even harder to develop a commonsense theory of liquids than a theory of solids. First, the scientific theory of fluid mechanics is further from commonsense understanding, mathematically enormously more difficult, and scientifically much less complete than Newtonian mechanics. (Basic questions, such as the nature and cause of turbulence are still not wholly solved.) Second, the ontology of liquids is much less clear than the ontology of solids, since liquids are not divided into discrete objects, but combine and divide freely. Conversely, many persistent liquid entities such as the Mississippi River do not consist of a constant body of substance but are constantly depleted and refilled.

The foundations of a commonsense theory of liquids were developed by Pat Hayes [1979]. Our discussion here derives from Hayes's, though it is more limited and differs in details.[2] The central idea is that, rather than think about individual pieces of liquid that move around, as we do with solids, we think about regions of space, and ask how much liquid they contain. Thus, we introduce the fluent, "liquid_in(**RR**)", which is the volume of liquid in region **RR** in each situation. (We will assume throughout that we are dealing with only one type of liquid, so as to avoid the difficult problems of treating mixtures.) We also define the predicate "solid(O)" meaning that O is a solid object. This fluent obeys the following axioms:

LI.1. (Additivity) $\textbf{RR1} \cap \textbf{RR2} = \emptyset \Rightarrow$
      liquid_in(**RR1** $\cup$ **RR2**) = liquid_in(**RR1**) + liquid_in(**RR2**).

LI.2. (Bounds) $0 \leq$ value_in(S,liquid_in(**RR**)) $\leq$ volume(**RR**).

LI.3. (Nonmixing with solids) solid(O) $\Rightarrow$
      value_in(S,liquid_in(value_in(S,place(O)))) = 0.

---

[2]There are two major differences: (i) Hayes uses a nonstandard spatial topology, while we use Euclidean geometry. (ii) Hayes studies transitions between different states of liquids using *histories*, which are chunks of space-time. We will not consider such transitions, and therefore will not use histories.

The amount of liquid in a region **RR** changes as a result of flows into and out of **RR** and of phase changes — melting, freezing, evaporation, and condensation — of material inside **RR**. In our discussion here, we will ignore phase changes and treat only flows. Under this assumption, a conservation law states that the change to the amount of liquid in **RR** is equal to the total flow into **RR**. We can express this as follows: Let "flow_through(**FF**)" be a fluent representing the rate of liquid flow outward through directed surface **FF** in each situation. Let the function "dboundary(**RR**)" give the outward-directed boundary of region **RR**. We can state the basic properties of flow as follows.

LI.4. deriv(liquid_in(**RR**)) = −flow_through(dboundary(**RR**)).
(Conservation of mass: The change in liquid contained is equal to minus the total outward flow.)

LI.5. **FF1** ∩ **FF2** = ∅ ⇒
flow_through(**FF1** ∪ **FF2**) =
flow_through(**FF1**) + flow_through(**FF2**).
(Flow is additive over faces.)

LI.6. [solid(O) ∧ **FF** ⊂ value_in(S,place(O))] ⇒
value_in(S,flow_through(**FF**)) = 0.
(There is no flow through a solid face.)

It follows directly from these axioms that a region with solid boundaries always has a constant amount of liquid, and that the change of liquid of a region with a number of openings is equal to the net flow through the openings.

In order to express the fundamental dynamic rules governing the behavior of liquids, we need to define some additional geometric and physical concepts. We introduce the following nonlogical symbols: The constant length "thin" is the maximum thickness of liquid wetting a surface. (This distance is, in reality, dependent on a number of factors, particularly the material of the liquid. We ignore this.) The predicate "bulk(**RR**,$\tilde{D}$)", read "Region **RR** is bulk with thickness $\tilde{D}$," holds if, for each point **P** in **RR**, there is a sphere **SS** of radius $\tilde{D}$, such that **P** is in **SS** and **SS** is a subset of **RR** (Figure 7.9). The function "filled_liquid(**RR**)" is the state of region **RR** being filled with liquid. The function "empty(**RR**)" is the state of region **RR** being empty of either liquid or solids. The function "liquid_at_rest(**RR**)" is the state of all liquid in **RR** being motionless and having zero acceleration (to exclude the case of a liquid at the top of a fountain.) The function "solid_coating(**RR**,$\tilde{D}$)" is the state of all points in **RR** being within distance $\tilde{D}$ of a solid object. Axioms LI.7–LI.11 give the formal definition of these symbols.

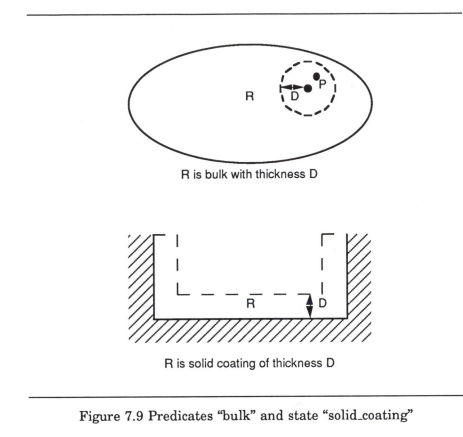

R is bulk with thickness D

R is solid coating of thickness D

Figure 7.9 Predicates "bulk" and state "solid_coating"

LI.7. bulk$(\mathbf{RR},\tilde{D})$ ⟺ $\forall_{P \in RR} \exists_{Q \in RR}$ **P** ∈ sphere$(\mathbf{Q},\tilde{D})$ ⊂ **RR**.
(Definition of bulk.)

LI.8. true_in(S,filled_liquid$(\mathbf{RR})$)) ⟺
value_in(S,liquid_in$(\mathbf{RR})$)) = volume$(\mathbf{RR})$.
(Definition of filled_liquid.)

LI.9. true_in(S,empty$(\mathbf{RR})$)) ⟺
[value_in(S,liquid_in$(\mathbf{RR})$)) = 0 ∧
[$\forall_O$ solid(O) ⟹ **RR** ∩ value_in(S,place(O))) = ∅]] .
(Definition of empty.)

LI.10. true_in(S,liquid_at_rest$(\mathbf{RR})$)) ⟹
$\forall_{FF \subset RR}$ value_in(S,flow_through$(\mathbf{FF})$)) = 0.
(If the liquid in **RR** is at rest, then there is no flow through
any face contained in **RR**.)

LI.11. true_in(S,solid_coating$(\mathbf{RR},\tilde{D})$)) ⟺
$\forall_{P \in RR}$ $\exists_O$ solid(O) ∧ distance(**P**,value_in(S,place(O)))) < $\tilde{D}$.
(Definition of solid coating.)

We can now express some simple laws of the dynamics of liquids. We will consider only liquid in bulk and liquid wetting a surface; we exclude such other states as absorbed in an absorbent material or spread about as mist. The following rules are then plausible:

LI.12. Liquid at rest must either be in bulk or wetting a surface.
[true_in(S,filled_liquid(**RR**)) $\wedge$
true_in(S,liquid_at_rest(**RR**))] $\Rightarrow$
$\exists_{RRB,RRC}$ **RR=RRB** $\cup$ **RRC** $\wedge$ bulk(**RRB**,thin) $\wedge$
true_in(S,solid_coating(**RRC**,thin)).

LI.13. A liquid in bulk at rest can border the air only at a horizontal surface.
[bulk(**RR**,thin) $\wedge$ true_in(S,filled_liquid(**RR**)) $\wedge$
true_in(S,liquid_at_rest(**RR**)) $\wedge$
true_in(S,empty(**RR2**)) $\wedge$ abut(**RR,RR2,FF**)] $\Rightarrow$
$\forall_{P \in FF}$ surf_norm(**RR,P**) = $\hat{k}$.

LI.14. If, after time $S0$, there is no flow into or out of region **RR**, and no solid object moves in **RR**, then the liquid in **RR** will eventually come to rest. (We introduce the state function, "motionless(O).")
[[$\forall_{S>S0}$ [$\forall_F$ **FF** $\subseteq$dboundary(**RR**) $\Rightarrow$
          value_in(S,flow_through(**FF**)) = 0] $\wedge$
[[$\forall_O$ solid(O) $\wedge$ value_in(S,place(O)) $\cap$ **RR** $\neq \emptyset$] $\Rightarrow$
true_in(S,motionless(O))]] $\Rightarrow$
$\exists_{S1>S0}$ $\forall_{S>S1}$ true_in(S,liquid_at_rest(**RR**)).

These rules are not strictly true. For example, the surface of a contained liquid is not perfectly horizontal, due to surface tension; in the scenario of the last rule, the liquid could be scattered as a mist if it encounters sufficiently violent collisions, like a waterfall on rocks. However, they are reasonable initial approximations.

Using the above axioms we can establish results such as the following: Let O be a solid object with an internal spherical cavity of radius $\tilde{R}$ containing liquid of volume V. Let $\tau =$thin. Then, if O is motionless and $V > 4\pi\tilde{R}^2\tau$, then after sufficient time, there will be a puddle of volume at least $V - 4\pi\tilde{R}^2\tau$ at the bottom of the cavity. (Figure 7.10)

The proof is as follows: Since the cavity is the inside of O, which is a closed box, any face of the cavity must border on O. Therefore, by LI.6, there can be no liquid flow into or out of the cavity, and by axiom SO.4, no solid object can come inside the cavity. By LI.4, the quantity of liquid in the cavity must remain constant. Morover, the antecedents of LI.14 are satisfied, so the liquid must attain a state of rest inside the cavity. By LI.11, when the liquid is in a state of rest, it

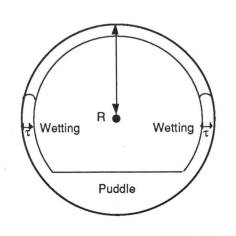

Figure 7.10 Liquid in a cavity

must all be either wetting a surface or in bulk. Since the solid surface
bounding the cavity has area $4\pi R^2$, the maximum quantity that can be
wetting the surface is $4\pi R^2 \tau$. Therefore, the remainder of the liquid,
of quantity $V - 4\pi R^2 \tau$, must be in bulk. However, by LI.12, liquid at
rest in bulk can border empty space only below a horizontal surface.
By a geometrical argument, this remaining liquid must lie in a puddle
at the bottom of the cavity.

7.5   Physical Agents

So far, our theories have considered only the behaviors of inanimate
objects. In many important applications, however, it is necessary to
reason about physical interactions involving intelligent agents. In particular, an intelligent creature will generally be interested in how it
can affect the world, and how the world can affect it. To address the
first question, a physical theory must supply a language for describing
the *actions* of an autonomous agent and a theory of how these action
affect the world. We will not here address the question of reasoning about the impact of the world on an agent, though we will touch
on it indirectly in Sections 8.7 and 9.3.5, which deal with perception
and the adoption of goals by an agent. (The conceptual dependency
(CD) representation of human actions [Schank 1975] will be consid-

ered separately in Appendix 10.A, since it combines physical, mental, and interpersonal reasoning.)

Given any physical theory of inanimate objects, such as those we have considered so far in this chapter, it is possible to extend the theory to include agents and actions as physical entities and physical events that are only weakly constrained by physical law. For example, in a component theory, we could model an agent as a component with ports, and an action as a relation among the port parameters that is enforced at the will of the agent. Thus, in the scales example, we could add an agent as a component with a port attached to the weight side of the lever, and specify that it executes actions such as "Move the lever down at a constant rate" or "Apply a force of 50 pounds until the height of the port reaches 2 feet; thereafter, hold the height constant there." It is then possible to use the component model to predict the behavior of the system, given this action. Similarly, in a process model, we could model an agent as a process and an action as a trace of its influences over time. In a kinematic theory of solid objects, we could model an agent as a solid object, and an action as a trace of its position over time. In a dynamic theory of solid objects, we could model an agent as a solid object, and an action as a time-varying relation between its position and the forces it applies to objects in contact.

7.6   References

General: [Weld and de Kleer 1989] is a very comprehensive collection of papers on qualitative physics, including most of the papers cited below. Hayes's paper "The Naive Physics Manifesto" [1978] was the first extensive discussion of commonsense physical reasoning. It advocates the development of logical theories that express commonsense physical intuition. [Gentner and Stevens 1983] is a collection of papers on psychological and historical aspects of physical reasoning.

Component model: Our description of the component model is based on the well-known paper [de Kleer and Brown 1985], which describes the ENVISION program. The "No function in structure" principle is discussed there. Also of interest are the papers by Kuipers [1985] and Williams [1985]. Component-based analyses for electronic systems have been studied in [Sussman and Steele 1980] and [Davis, R. 1983]; both papers discuss the use of a hierarchical analysis of systems. An alternative approach to component analysis, based on combining small components together into larger components of known behavior, is considered in [Bylander and Chandrasekaran 1985]. [Rieger

and Grinberg 1977] was a relatively early attempt at a component
analysis of a complex device (a flush toilet); however, the underlying
theory was never very clearly developed, and the component descriptions did not satisfy the "No function in structure" principle.

Qualitative process theory: Qualitative process theory was first
developed by Forbus [1985]. [Forbus 1989] discusses an improved version of the program. [Forbus 1986] applies QP theory to the problem of
interpreting a given time sequence of measurements. Also of interest
is the discussion of processes in [McDermott 1982a].

Solid objects kinematics: [Shoham 1985a] considers the motions
possible for an object abutting obstacles. [Faltings 1987a] and [Falt-
ings 1987b] analyze in detail the kinematics of two-dimensional mechanisms composed of parts each with one degree of freedom. [Joskowicz
1987] studies the kinematics of a system that has few degrees of freedom by virtue of the interaction of its components. [Joskowicz and
Addanki 1988] uses a kinematic analysis to solve problems of design.
[Gelsey 1987] proposes a number of special-case heuristics to increase
the efficiency of the analysis. The possibility of a qualitative kinematics is denied in [Forbus et. al. 1987]; this is disproved, at least in part,
by [Faltings, et. al. 1989], which exhibits such a qualitative characterization of kinematics, based on the topology of the configuration
space. [Gelsey 1989] discusses the construction of kinematic models
of varying degrees of detail of a physical system from its geometrical specifications, and the use of the kinematic model in prediction.
Closely related is the work on the "piano-movers" problem; citations
are given in the Reference section for Chapter 6.

Solid object dynamics: Though, as mentioned in the text, there
is no thorough treatment of solid-object dynamics, there are many
partial studies. [Fahlman 1974] gives an algorithm for determining
the stability of a collection of polyhedral blocks. NEWTON [de Kleer
1975], discussed in Section 6.2.6, predicts the behavior of a point object sliding on a constraint. MECHO [Bundy 1978] uses force analysis and conservation laws to solve a variety of problems in closed
form. FROB [Forbus 1979] extends NEWTON by predicting the behavior of a point object flying among fixed constraints. WHISPER
[Funt 1980] simulates dynamical systems using an occupancy-array
representation. Davis [1988a] argues that formulations of dynamics
in terms of differential equations are not adequate for many commonsense problems, and presents a first-order theory for dynamics that,
in some cases, avoids the use of differential equations. Nielsen [1988]
presents a system that does qualitative dynamical reasoning. Also of

interest are works in robotics (e.g., [Mason 1986; Peshkin and Sanderson 1987; Wang 1986]) that study exact solutions to restricted classes of dynamical problems.

Liquids: Our discussion of reasoning about liquids derives from [Hayes 1979]. Other papers of interest include [Schmolze 1986] and [Collins and Forbus 1987]; both of these combine a theory of liquids with a theory of processes.

Other domains: [Doyle 1989] applies a rich component model to the problem of guessing the structure of a device, such as a pressure gauge for tire, from observations of its behaviors. [Bunt 1985] discusses the problems in giving semantics to "mass" nouns; since these are generally associated with physical substances, many of the issues discussed are important for physical reasoning.

Causality: We have deliberately avoided discussing causality in the text, because there is no consensus in the AI community as to whether, where, and how causality should enter into physical theories. Various approches to causality can be found in [Rieger and Grinberg 1977; McDermott 1982a; Allen 1984; de Kleer and Brown 1985; Iwasaki and Simon 1986; de Kleer and Brown 1986; Shoham 1988; and Pearl 1988b]. [Shoham 1988] also has an extensive review of the philosophical literature on the subject.

7.7 Exercises

(Starred problems are more difficult.)

1. Verify the algebraic manipulations used to derive the various solutions to the scale equations in Section 7.1.

2. * Construct a QP model of the process of burning. Use your model to determine the behavior of the sample system of a can of water over a candle flame.

3. * In our sample trace of the qualitative process algorithm we wrote (second iteration, step 1), "From HF1, infer that the heat flow hf1 from oflame to owater continues." Actually, the axiom HF1 only supports the conclusion that there is some heat flow, not that it is necessarily the same heat flow. In fact, it is consistent with the axioms that there should be more than one heat flow, or that the identity of the heat flow(s) changes every instant.

(a) Show that the prediction we derive for the example does not depend on any of these unwarranted assumptions and, in fact, can be derived from the axioms.

(b) In view of part a, it might seem that it would be more natural not to try to distinguish process tokens, and just use process types, such as "the state of heat flowing from oflame to owater." Rewrite the theory in this way.

(c) Under what circumstances will it be useful to use process tokens rather than process types?

(d) Augment the original theory with axioms that guarantee that, in the heat-flow example, there is a single heat-flow process and a single boiling process.

4. Show that the remaining rules used in NEWTON (Section 6.2.6) can be derived from our axiomatization of point-object dynamics, together with the suitable geometric theorems.

Chapter 8
Minds

It was in none other than the black, memorable year 1929 that the indefatigable Professor Walter B. Pitkin rose up with the announcement that 'for the first time in the career of mankind, happiness is coming within the reach of millions of people.' Happy living, he confidently asserted, could be attained by at least six or seven people out of every ten, but he figured that not more than one in a thousand was actually attaining it. However, all the external conditions required for happy living were present, he said, just waiting to be used. The only obstacle was a psychological one. Figuring on a basis of 130,000,000 population in America and reducing the Professor's estimates to round numbers, we find that in 1929 only 130,000 people were happy, but that between 78,000,000 and 91,000,000 could have been happy, leaving only 52,000,000, at the outside, doomed to discontent. The trouble with all the unhappy ones (except the 52,000,000) was that they didn't Know Themselves, they didn't understand the Science of Happiness, they had no Technique of Thinking. Professor Pitkin wrote a book on the subject; he is, in fact, always writing a book on the subject. So are a number of other people. I have devoted myself to a careful study of as many of these books as a man of my unsteady eyesight and wandering attention could be expected to encompass. And I decided to write a series of articles of my own on the subject, examining what the Success Experts have to say and offering some ideas of my own, the basic one of which is, I think, that man will be better off if he quits monkeying with his mind and just lets it alone.

James Thurber, *Let Your Mind Alone!*

It is to the advantage of a thinking creature to be aware of thought and to be able to reason about it. If it has to interact with other thinking creatures, then reasoning about their mental processes is often necessary to understand and predict their behavior. Even if the creature is alone, stranded on a desert island, the ability to reason about its own mental life will be valuable. A Robinson Crusoe robot will need to make plans involving the gaining and maintaining of knowledge, such as "If I want to learn my way around the island, I should go to the top of the big hill," or "If I want to avoid being eaten, I should keep a close watch."

A commonsense mental theory is in many ways harder to formulate than a physical theory. We have no "correct" theory to draw on. The fundamental natures of basic psychological phenomena such as thinking, perceiving, reasoning, and believing are very little understood, despite the efforts of psychology, philosophy, neurophysiology, and AI. Natural language provides a vocabulary that is rich but vague and ambiguous. Our intuitions are often strong, but they are hard to systematize. Moreover, the mental life and its relation to behavior are notoriously lawless. We can almost never make certain predictions about an individual. Even if a prediction is in practice essentially certain, it often seems intuitively that freedom of choice rules out absolute certainty. Whatever rule we put forward, no matter how qualified — say, "If a man is hungry, and there is food set before him ready to be eaten, and he is able to eat it immediately, and he plans to eat it immediately, and he has no reason not to eat it immediately, and he has nothing else on his mind, and he is aware of all this, then he will eat it" — it can be objected that, though a likely conclusion, it is not certain, since he can always act capriciously and not eat it.

Our commonsense understanding of the life of the mind is rich and complex. Consider the following passage from "Ali Baba" in the *Arabian Nights:*

> Cassim rose early in the morning and set out with ten mules laden with great chests, which he planned to fill. He followed the road which Ali Baba had told him. When he came to the door, he pronounced the words "Open Sesame" and it opened. When he was in, it shut again. In examining the cave, he was astonished to find much more riches than he had supposed from Ali Baba's story. He was so fond of riches that he could have spent the whole day in feasting his eyes with so much treasure, if the thought that he came to carry some away with him had not hindered him. He laid as many bags of gold as he could carry away by the entrance. When at last he came to open the door, his thoughts were so full of the great riches he should

possess that he could not think of the necessary word. Instead of "Open Sesame," he said, "Open Barley," and was very much amazed to find that the door did not open, but remained fast shut. He named several sorts of grain — all but the right one — and the door would not open.

Cassim had never expected such an accident. He was so frightened at the danger he was in that the more he endeavored to remember the word "Sesame," the more his memory failed. He had as much forgotten it as if he had never heard it in his life. He threw down the bags with which he had laden himself, and walked hastily up and down the cave without the least attention to the riches that were around him.

The passage is straightforward, with no surprising or deep psychological insights, and with no mention of the really mysterious aspects of human minds, such as dreaming, consciousness, or intuition. Nonetheless, it presumes a complex theory of mind. Understanding this episode requires knowledge about belief, perception, memory, failures of memory, character traits, goals, plan formation and execution, emotions, and the interactions between all of these. Only a small part of this knowledge has to date been incorporated in formal theories. We do not, at this time, know how to represent most of the knowledge involved in this passage.

One way to avoid some of these problems and complexities is to take our thinkers to be AI programs, or, rather, idealized models of AI programs, rather than people or animals. Here, we can construct a precise underlying theory, we can have definite laws, and issues of free will do not trouble us. We will adopt this device from time to time in our discussion. However, it has the obvious danger of leading us to a consistent dreamworld, in which our theories will be good to describe the behavior of robots constructed according to those very theories, and nothing else.

Our theory of mind will be constructed along the following lines. Certain physical objects — namely, living animals of certain species, including humans, and, possibly, autonomous intelligent robots — are *agents* who have a mental life. We characterize the mental life of an agent in terms of the variations of mental states over time and the occurrence of mental events.

There are many different types of mental states. An agent may hold a proposition to be more or less certainly true; he may be sure of a proposition, believe it, be unsure of it, doubt it, or be sure that it is false. He may hold a proposition to be more or less desirable; he may hope for it, be indifferent to it, or fear it. He may have intentions

ation about the external world; reasoning, in which he combines his

existing beliefs to form a new belief; deciding, in which he adopts an

and changing emotional state. Some of these mental events are delib-

Some of the features of mental lives differ from one agent to another,

and from one period of an agent's life to another. These features are

categorized in terms of psychological traits; we say that an agent is

Models such as these are called "folk psychological" models. Though

they are fairly natural, every part of them has been challenged. It has

been argued that "mental life" is just a category one imposes on things

in order to generate certain kinds of explanations, and that therefore

it could sometimes be correct to ascribe mental states to an entity

of a sort that is not generally viewed as a single agent, such as a

thermostat or the nation of France [Dennett 1978, chap.1]. It has

with the use of language, and can only be correctly ascribed to crea-

(e.g., [Skinner 1971]) argue that mental states and events are illegit-

such as Leibniz, have claimed that the physical world does not actu-

and propositions is the matter of intense debate, both as to its nature

and its existence. Regardless of the validity of these objections and al-

be the most suitable for the formal expression of commonsense knowl-

edge of psychology, and we will focus almost exclusively on this model.

(An alternative model from [Rosenschein and Kaelbling 1986] will be

We will study only limited parts of the model discussed above. This

chapter is concerned only with the mental states of knowledge and

---

[1] It may be consoling to observe that some of the worst philosophical knots in this domain do not have to be addressed in a commonsense theory. In particular, it seems that we can ignore the "mind-body" problem of how mental states relate to states of the brain.

belief, and the events that affect them. In Sections 1 through 5 of this chapter, we present an idealized model of knowledge and believing at a single moment of time, without considering temporal change. In Section 6, we extend this model to include change in state. In Section 7, we present a representation for perceptions. In Section 8, we consider the consequences of dropping the idealizations of our model. Chapter 9 deals with goals, intentions, decisions, and actions. We will not consider emotions or psychological traits in this book; see the Reference section in this chapter for citations.

8.1 Propositional Attitudes

Many important mental states are *propositional attitudes,* relations between the agent and various propositions about the world. For example, Anne sees that it is raining, she hopes that the sun will come out, she fears that the cellar will flood, she believes that her husband knows that the attic window is open. Here, "sees," "hopes," "fears," and "believes" are types of attitudes; "It is raining," "The sun will come out," "The cellar will flood," and "Anne's husband knows that the attic is open," are propositions. As the last example shows, the statement of a propositional attitude may itself be a proposition.

A propositional attitude is a relation between an agent and a proposition: "Anne sees that it is raining," expresses the relation "sees" between Anne's current mental state and the proposition "It is raining." (As mentioned above, we will ignore the temporal aspects of propositional attitudes until Section 8.6.) Statements of propositional attitudes are an opaque context; they are not invariant under substitution of equal terms. For example, "Oedipus believed that Jocasta was the queen" is not equivalent to "Oedipus believed that his mother was the queen," even though Jocasta was his mother.[2] In Chapter 2 we presented three techniques for representing opaque operators with sentential arguments. In modal logics, first-order logic is extended by the introduction of modal operators as logical symbols. In a possible-worlds representation, the sentential operator is replaced by quantification over a particular class of possible worlds. In syntactic representations, the embedded sentence is replaced by a string that expresses that sentence. The sentential operator is an ordinary first-order predicate, which takes a string as an argument.

---

[2]Barwise and Perry [1982] point out that there is an extensional use of "see," in which one may say, "Oedipus saw his mother talk to Antigone," even if Oedipus did not know the woman was his mother.

8.2 Belief

A basic propositional attitude is to believe that a proposition is true. The conscious behavior of a rational agent is essentially guided by his beliefs and his goals. He acts in a manner that would satisfy his goals if his beliefs were true.[3] In particular, even if an agent's beliefs are false — that is, they do not correspond to reality — still, his deliberate actions will, in the main, correspond to his beliefs, rather than the actual reality. Therefore, an account of an agent's beliefs is critical for understanding him, particularly if these beliefs are false or incomplete in some significant manner. We use a two-place operator, "believe(A, ϕ)," to mean that agent A believes proposition ϕ. In a modal theory, this is a modal operator; in a syntactic theory, it is a two-place predicate. For the time being, we will consider only beliefs of which the agent is quite confident; we will consider uncertain beliefs in Section 8.4.

It is hard to define exactly what constitutes belief in people. We generally infer a fellow human's beliefs from considering his actions, including his speech, by judging what he might reasonably believe, given what he has learned and perceived; and by assuming that he believes what most people believe, or what most people similar to him believe. These general criteria do not amount to any useful formal definition. We therefore take belief in people to be a primitive relation.

It is possible to be much more specific about what an AI program "believes." Indeed, a major theme of this book is that an AI program should be written and conceptualized so that one can say very precisely what the program believes. An AI program of the kind we have been advocating has a knowledge base that encodes all its beliefs, and the meaning of this knowledge base is firmly defined by semantic definitions. Thus, we can determine what an AI program believes just by printing out its knowledge base and interpreting it according to the semantics. We will adopt this as our model of belief, keeping an eye out from time to time to make sure that its consequences are not violently divergent from our feelings about human belief.

There is still an ambiguity, however. Let us say that our knowledge base is written as transparently as possible, as a collection of assertions, and that the program has some inference engine for answering queries from this knowledge base. There are three possible definitions of what the program believes:

---

[3]We ignore, of course, many kinds of erratic behavior, e.g., meaningless acts, self-destructive acts, and uncontrolled acts.

i. *Explicit belief*: The program believes anything that is explicitly in the knowledge base.

ii. *Derivable belief*: The program believes anything that the inference engine can derive in a retrieval.

iii. *Implicit belief*: The program believes anything that could be inferred in principle via sound deduction from the knowledge base.

Which is the real belief? It would seem that if the purpose of attributing belief is to predict behavior, then derivable belief (ii) would be best. The program will act on the basis of those facts that it can derive for itself. With realistic inference engines, however, derivable belief is very difficult to characterize, since it depends not only on the state of the knowledge base, but also on the circumstances of the query. For example, an inference engine may allocate different amounts of time to queries, depending on circumstances; whether a result can be derived may depend on the time available. Moreover, these circumstances may change during the process of derivation, possibly even as a result of that process. Constructing a plausible model of an inference engine is thus very difficult. (See Section 8.8 for further discussion.) Taking explicit belief as a primitive does not avoid this problem. In almost all cases, some model of inference must be included; otherwise the theory will be impossibly simple-minded. An intelligent agent should be able, under appropriate circumstances, to go from "This is a tiger" and "Tigers are dangerous" to "This is dangerous," or else it hardly deserves the name of intelligent.

The use of implicit belief as a primitive greatly simplifies the problem of characterizing an inference engine. Implicit belief obeys the principle of *consequential closure:* An agent implicitly believes any fact that deductively follows from his belief. In effect, we approximate the real inference engine with an idealized inference engine capable of drawing any deductive inference arbitrarily quickly. The resultant theory is an approximation of rationality that is simple and elegant. It is sometimes unrealistically powerful. An agent cannot fail to grasp any of the implications of his beliefs. In particular, all agents know all mathematical theorems. Worse, an agent cannot have beliefs that are implicitly contradictory without believing everything. Moreover, deductive inference leaves the set of implicit beliefs unchanged; implicit belief therefore cannot be used to model the action of deductive inference. Reasoning about students learning, or about mathematicians researching, therefore requires a model of explicit belief. Conversely, true rationality implies a great deal more than just competence in deduction. We assume that a rational agent will be able to find reasonable explanations and generalizations, and to make and revise plausible inferences, as well as making logically sound deductions.

Consequential closure is taken as an axiom of most modal logics. As discussed in Section 2.7.1, it is a necessary consequence of a possible-worlds semantics. Thus a modal logic with a possible-worlds semantics can describe only implicit belief; where a more verisimilar theory of belief is needed, a syntactic theory must be used.

8.2.1 Axioms for Belief

We begin our formalization of belief by considering a variety of axioms and inference rules describing the beliefs of an agent at an instant. Table 8.1 shows a number of axiom schemas for belief expressed in a modal language, together with the corresponding axioms on possible worlds. Table 8.2 shows some possible inference rules applying to belief, some deductive and others plausible. (Further on in this chapter, Table 8.4 will show these axioms expressed in terms of possible worlds, and Table 8.5 will show them expressed in syntactic terms.) It is not necessary to use all these axioms and rules together in a theory of belief; rather, Tables 8.1 and 8.2 should be viewed as a smorgasbord, from which one extracts a subset of axioms suitable to a given application.

We can divide the axioms and rules of Tables 8.1 and 8.2 into three general categories. BEL.1, BEL.2, BEL.9, and BEL.14 discuss the closure of belief under logical or plausible inference. BEL.3, BEL.4, BEL.5, BEL.6, BEL.11, and BEL.13 state weak forms of the principle of veridicality. BEL.7, BEL.8, BEL.10, and BEL.12 characterize introspection. We examine each of these categories in turn.

Logical closure: Implicit belief, by definition, is closed under logical implication. This property is expressed in rules BEL.1 (consequential closure), BEL.2 (belief in the axioms), and BEL.9 (general consequential closure). These rules are part of most modal logics of belief, including any modal logic with a possible-world semantics. Consequential closure is not plausible for explicit belief. BEL.9 is a useful shortcut, not an independent rule; any instance of BEL.9 can be proven from BEL.1 and BEL.2.

BEL.14 extends BEL.1 to cover plausible inference. If we know that A believes that ψ is a plausible inference from ϕ, and we know that A believes ϕ, then, in the absence of contradictory evidence, we may plausibly infer that A believes ψ. In Section 10.3.2, we will give an example of an inference that uses this rule.

Table 8.1 Axioms of Belief

In all of the following, ϕ and ψ are metalinguistic symbols, ranging over all sentences in the modal language. A is an object-language variable ranging over agents. (This table omits the analogues of MODAL.1–MODAL.4, MODAL.11, and MODAL.12, which describe the interface between the modal operator and the predicate calculus.)

BEL.1.   Consequential closure: Implicit belief is closed under *modus ponens*.

$$\forall_A \ (\text{believe}(A, \phi) \wedge \text{believe}(A, \phi \Rightarrow \psi)) \Rightarrow \text{believe}(A, \psi).$$

BEL.2.   Belief in the axioms: An agent believes the axioms of logic and of belief.

If ϕ is a logical axiom or an axiom of belief,
then $\forall_A \ \text{believe}(A, \phi)$.

BEL.3.   Consistency: No one believes a statement and its negation.

$$\forall_A \ \neg(\text{believe}(A, \phi) \wedge \text{believe}(A, \neg\phi)).$$

BEL.4.   Privileged access: If an agent believes that he believes ϕ, then he does, in fact, believe ϕ.

$$\forall_A \ \text{believe}(A, \text{believe}(A, \phi)) \Rightarrow \text{believe}(A, \phi).$$

BEL.5.   Axiom of coherence: If an agent believes that he does not believe ϕ, then he does not believe ϕ.

$$\forall_A \ \text{believe}(A, \neg\text{believe}(A, \phi)) \Rightarrow \neg\text{believe}(A, \phi).$$

BEL.6.   Axiom of arrogance: An agent believes that all his beliefs are true.

$$\forall_A \ \text{believe}(A, (\text{believe}(A, \phi) \Rightarrow \phi)).$$

BEL.7.   Positive introspection: If an agent believes ϕ, then he believes that he believes ϕ.

$$\forall_A \ \text{believe}(A, \phi) \Rightarrow \text{believe}(A, \text{believe}(A, \phi)).$$

BEL.8.   Negative introspection: If an agent does not believe ϕ, then he believes that he does not believe ϕ.

$$\forall_A \ \neg\text{believe}(A, \phi) \Rightarrow \text{believe}(A, \neg \ \text{believe}(A, \phi)).$$

Table 8.2 Inference Rules for Implicit Belief

In all the following rules, the notation $\phi \vdash_A \psi$ means that, if agent A finds sentence ϕ in his knowledge base, then he is entitled to conclude ψ.

Deductive Rules

BEL.9.   General inference rule of consequential closure: An agent believes any logical consequence of his beliefs.

   If ($\phi_1, \phi_2, \ldots \phi_k \vdash \psi$) monotonically, then the statement
   $$\forall_A \; [\text{believes}(A, \phi_1) \wedge \text{believes}(A, \phi_2) \wedge \ldots \wedge$$
   $$\text{believes}(A, \phi_k)] \Rightarrow \text{believes}(A, \psi)$$
   is true.

BEL.10.   Necessitation: An agent who has ϕ in his knowledge base may conclude that he himself believes ϕ.

   $\phi \vdash_A \text{believe}(A, \phi)$.

BEL.11.   Optimism. An agent may infer ϕ from the fact that he himself believes ϕ.

   $\text{believe}(A, \phi) \vdash_A \phi$.

Nonmonotonic Inference

BEL.12.   Inference of ignorance: If an agent cannot infer ϕ, he may infer that he does not believe ϕ.

   $(\nvdash_A \phi) \vdash_A \neg\text{believe}(A, \phi)$.

BEL.13.   Principle of charity: Any belief of any agent is likely to be true.

   $\text{plausible}(\text{believe}(A, \phi) \; \phi)$.

BEL.14.   Consequential closure on plausible inference: If A believes that ψ is a plausible inference from ϕ, and A believes ϕ, then it is plausible to infer that A believes ψ.

   $\text{plausible}(\text{believe}(A, \text{plausible}(\phi, \psi)) \wedge \text{believe}(A, \phi),$
   $\text{believe}(A, \psi))$.

Weak veridicality: Unlike many modal operators, belief does not obey the rule of veridicality $O(\phi) \Rightarrow \phi$; beliefs may be false. However, there are a number of weaker statements that are worth considering as axioms on belief:

BEL.3. (Consistency) No one believes a statement and its negation; an agent's beliefs are internally consistent. This sets a lower limit on sanity. This axiom, in its literal reading, is fairly plausible as a statement about explicit belief; an inference engine can easily ensure that ϕ and $\neg\phi$ are not both in a knowledge base simultaneously. In a theory of implicit belief, where the principle of consequential closure holds, it is both highly implausible — it is not possible for an agent to ensure that his beliefs are internally consistent — and utterly necessary — an agent whose beliefs are internally inconsistent implicitly believes any statement at all. This is an axiom in most modal logics.

BEL.4. (Privileged access) An agent's beliefs about his own beliefs are correct; if he believes that he believes ϕ, then he is right. This is a special case of a more general principle of privileged access, that people's beliefs about their own mental states are correct. The principle is much debated in philosophy (see the Reference section at the end of this chapter), and one can think of cases where it seems to be wrong, such as a neurotic who believes he loves his mother while he actually hates her; but in most commonsense situations, it is quite plausible. Axiom BEL.4 characterizes an agent who carries out the inference rule of optimism, BEL.9. It is a strictly weaker consequence of the axiom of arrogance, BEL.6.

BEL.5. (Coherence) If a person believes that he does not believe ϕ, then he does not believe ϕ.

$$\forall_A \text{ believe}(A, \neg\text{believe}(A, \phi)) \Rightarrow \neg\text{believe}(A, \phi).$$

This is the principle of privileged access applied to nonbelief. It is logically equivalent to "No one ever believes, both that ϕ is true and that he doesn't believe it."

$$\forall_A \neg\text{believe}(A, \phi \wedge \neg\text{believe}(A, \phi))$$

This is true in any reasonable model of belief; a person who believed that ϕ was true but that he didn't believe it would be seriously confused. It is a strictly weaker consequence of the axiom of positive introspection BEL.7, together with the axiom of consistency, BEL.3.

BEL.6. (Arrogance) An agent believes that all his beliefs are true. Note the difference between this and the axiom of privileged access, BEL.4. The axiom of privileged access states that if a person believes that he believes a particular statement ϕ, then he does, in fact, believe ϕ. This axiom makes the stronger statement that every person believes of every statement ϕ that, if he believes ϕ, then ϕ is true. Whether this is true in a theory of implicit belief depends rather subtly on exactly what is meant by "implicit."

BEL.11. (Inference rule of optimism) If agent A deduces that he believes ϕ, then he can add ϕ to his knowledge base. This inference rule is not sound; there are many cases where A will believe false things, and, therefore, believe(A, ϕ) will be true and ϕ will be false. However, it is a *safe* rule in the following sense: If this rule ever takes an agent from a true premise to a false conclusion, then he could have gotten to that conclusion in any case. For "believe(M, ϕ)" is only true (by definition) if ϕ can be inferred from the statements in the knowledge base; and if there is some way that ϕ can be inferred, then we could have used that means to infer it. This inference rule essentially represents the agent's trust in his own rationality.

BEL.13. (Principle of charity) Any belief of an agent is likely to be true.[4] (Note that this inference can be performed by agents other than A.) This seems like a very strong claim and one's natural instinct is to refute it by enumerating all the stupid and wrong things that people do believe. This, however, is probably an illusion, due to the salience of wrong beliefs. The neighborhood crank who believes in astrology and UFO's is a fount of colorful false beliefs; one tends to forget that these few errors are greatly overbalanced by tremendous numbers[5] of true beliefs: the belief that his name is Sam Jackson, the belief that he has a bathroom on the second floor, the commonsense axioms in this book, and so on. This principle cannot generally be adopted as a certain inference; in domains where it can, it is more reasonable to talk of "knowledge" than of "belief." (See Section 9.5.) It is, however, quite a strong plausible inference.

The principle of charity is important in a theory of communication. The basis of communication is that, if A tells something to B, B will generally believe it. Why should B believe it? It seems plausible

---

[4] The principle of charity is discussed in [Wilson 1959], and in [Davidson 1974], among other places. Davidson views it as a necessary truth: If an agent's beliefs are not mostly true, then we have no way of saying that the agent is rational, no way of reasonably ascribing any beliefs to him, and no way to determine the contents of his beliefs.

[5] Not that there is any obvious way of individuating or counting separate beliefs.

that B reasons as follows: Most utterances are sincere; hence A probably believes what he says. Most beliefs are true; hence what A said is probably true.[6] (See Section 10.3.2.)

Introspection: The last group of rules allows an agent to determine his own beliefs by examining the contents of his knowledge base, and allows an external reasoner to predict the results of such introspection on the part of the agent.

BEL.7. (Positive introspection) If an agent uses the rule of necessitation, BEL.10, then he can be characterized by an external observer as obeying the law of positive introspection: If he believes ϕ, then he believes that he believes ϕ, since he can deduce that he believes ϕ via necessitation. This is an optional axiom in modal logic.

BEL.8. (Negative introspection) If an agent does not believe ϕ, then he believes that he does not believe ϕ. This characterizes an agent who reliably uses the inference of ignorance. It is often a useful axiom. We need something of the kind to predict that agents will sometimes answer "I have no idea" to queries, or will realize that they have to go seek information. In general, however, it is implausible, since an agent does not believe a statement only if it does not follow from anything that he knows, and this is uncomputable, in general. The difficulty is more than theoretical. This axiom is hard to use in practical problems, since it is hard to show that an agent does not believe ϕ, except by showing that he believes $\neg\phi$. The point is illustrated by a well-known example of John McCarthy's.

- A. "Is the President sitting down or standing up at this moment?"
- B. "I haven't the faintest notion."
- A. "Think harder."

How is it that B knows that thinking harder won't get him anywhere?

BEL.10. (Necessitation) If an agent finds ϕ as an assertion in his knowledge base, then he is justified in concluding that he believes ϕ. As we discussed in Section 2.7, this inference rule cannot be turned into a material implication; the axiom schema $\phi \Rightarrow$

---

[6] This argument is flawed, since the class of beliefs uttered is by no means a representative sample of the class of beliefs. There are biases in both directions. On the one hand, utterances generally deal with interesting beliefs, which are more likely to be wrong than uninteresting beliefs. (Sam Jackson is more likely to talk about UFOs than to tell you where his bathroom is.) On the other hand, responsible speakers tend not to utter uncertain beliefs, and certain beliefs tend to be more reliable than uncertain beliefs.

believe(A, ϕ) would mean that A believes all true facts, and is not valid. However, whenever it is applied it will be valid, since it can only be applied when ϕ is part of the knowledge base; that is, when A does, in fact, believe ϕ. In fact, it has the curious strength that, whenever it is applied, the conclusion believe(M, ϕ) will be true whether or not the assumption ϕ is true. Necessitation is taken as an axiom in most systems of modal logic, though not usually with this interpretation.

BEL.12. (Inference of ignorance) If an agent cannot infer a fact ϕ from his knowledge base, then he may infer that he does not believe ϕ. This type of inference is central to the nonmonotonic autoepistemic inference [Moore 1985b]. It is a problematic rule in a number of respects. The antecedent of the inference is in general uncomputable. It makes the logic nonmonotonic, since the presence of one inference depends on the absence of another. It introduces a circularity into the concept of inference, which may result in there being either no consistent and logically closed set of implicit beliefs for the agent, or many different such sets.

Rules BEL.3, BEL.4, BEL.5, BEL.11, and BEL.13 are plausible in a theory of explicit belief. The rest of the axioms are inappropriate, as, in general, they imply the agent believes infinitely many statements.

As an example of the use of these rules consider the following problem: Harry says "Anyone who believes that all Libras are judicious also believe that all Capricorns are promiscuous. But not all Capricorns are promiscuous." We assume that Harry is speaking sincerely, and therefore believes what he is saying. We wish to infer that Harry does not believe that all Libras are judicious. (Our axioms do not justify the conclusion "Harry believes that not all Libras are judicious.")

We can formalize this as follows: Let pl be the proposition, "All Libras are judicious," and let pc be the proposition "All Capricorns are promiscuous." Our starting assumptions are "believe(harry, $\forall_A$ believe(A,pl) $\Rightarrow$ believe(A,pc))" and "believe(harry, ¬pc)". We wish to infer "¬believe(harry,pl)." Table 8.3 shows the justification of this inference in a modal logic containing the above axioms. The logic uses an axiomatic proof theory, based on the axioms of predicate calculus, the above modal axioms of belief, tautological inference, and the necessitation inference rule, as in Section 2.7. (Tautological inferences are left implicit in the proof below.)

Table 8.3 Proof Using the Modal Theory of Belief

No.	Step	Justification
1.	believe(harry,∀$_A$ believe(A,pl) ⇒ believe(A,pc))	Given
2.	believe(harry, believe(harry,pl) ⇒ believe(harry,pc))	Consequential closure from 1.
3.	believe(harry,pc) ⇒ ¬believe(harry,¬pc)	Consistency (axiom).
4.	believe(harry, believe(harry,pc) ⇒ ¬believe(harry,¬pc))	Belief in the axiom 3.
5.	believe(harry, believe(harry,pl)) ⇒ ¬believe(harry,¬pc))	Consequential closure from 2 and 4.
6.	believe(harry, believe(harry,¬pc)) ⇒ ¬believe(harry,pl))	Consequential closure from 5.
7.	believe(harry, ¬pc)	Given.
8.	believe(harry, believe(harry, ¬pc))	Positive introspection from 7.
9.	believe(harry, ¬believe(harry,pl))	Consequential closure from 8 and 6.
10.	¬believe(harry,pl)	Coherence from 9.

8.2.2 Possible Worlds

As discussed in Section 2.7.2, it is possible to express propositions with a modal operator in a language of possible worlds. To apply this technique to belief, we introduce possible worlds as primitive entities in our ontology. A possible world is one particular way that the world could be. The real world is denoted by the constant w0. Any atomic proposition that could potentially be believed or disbelieved must be viewed as a Boolean fluent over possible worlds. As with temporal fluents, we will use the predicate "true_in(W, P)" to mean that state P holds in world W. For example, the sentence "true_in(w6,blond(michelle))" means that Michelle is blond in world w6. (We will also use the function "value_in(W, F)" for fluents that are not Boolean.) We express propositions about belief using an accessibility relation between possible worlds, "bel_acc($A, W1, W2$)". This relation, read "World $W2$ is accessible from world $W1$ relative to the beliefs of A," means that $W2$ is consistent in all respects with the beliefs that A holds in $W1$; any fact that A believes in $W1$ is actually true in $W2$. Facts about which A has no beliefs in $W1$ may go either way in $W2$; if A neither believes nor disbelieves ϕ in $W0$ then there will be accessible worlds in which ϕ is true and accessible worlds in which ϕ is false. We can thus state that A believes a sentence ϕ by stating that the corresponding fluent holds in all possible worlds.

For example, the statement "Ralph believes that Michelle is blond" may be expressed

$\forall_{W1}$ bel_acc(ralph,w0,$W1$) $\Rightarrow$ true_in($W1$,blond(michelle)).

Belief in compound sentences can be expressed by compounding the consequents of such implications. For example, the sentence "Ralph believes that either Michelle or Agnes is blond" can be expressed

$\forall_{W1}$ bel_acc(ralph,w0,$W1$) $\Rightarrow$
[true_in($W1$,blond(michelle)) $\vee$ true_in($W1$,blond(Agnes))].

This should be distinguished from the stronger statement, "Either Ralph believes that Michelle is blond, or he believes that Agnes is blond" which is expressed,

[$\forall_{W1}$ bel_acc(ralph,w0,$W1$) $\Rightarrow$ true_in($W1$,blond(michelle))] $\vee$
[$\forall_{W1}$ bel_acc(ralph,w0,$W1$) $\Rightarrow$ true_in($W1$,blond(agnes))].

The statement "Ralph believes that someone is blond" is expressed in the form

$\forall_{W1}$ bel_acc(ralph,w0,$W1$) $\Rightarrow$ $\exists_X$ true_in($W1$,blond(X)).

Statements of imbedded belief can be expressed by chaining together accessibility relations. For example, the statement "Ralph believes that Michelle believes that Agnes is blond" is equivalent to "If world $W1$ is accessible from w0 relative to Ralph, then in $W1$ Michelle believes that Agnes is blond," which, in turn, is equivalent to "If $W1$ is accessible from w0 relative to Ralph, then, if $W2$ is accessible from $W1$ relative to Michelle, then Agnes is blond in $W2$."

[$\forall_{W1,W2}$ bel_acc(ralph,w0,$W1$) $\wedge$ bel_acc(michelle,$W1,W2$)] $\Rightarrow$
true_in($W2$,blond(agnes)).

In this way, any sentence in the modal language of belief can be translated into the language of possible worlds.

Axioms BEL.1, of consequential closure, and BEL.2, that the agent believes all axioms, must hold in all possible-worlds systems. The remaining axioms of belief enumerated in Table 8.1 correspond to constraints on the structure of belief-accessibility relations. For example, axiom BEL.7 of positive introspection, "believe(A, ϕ) $\Rightarrow$ believe(A, believe(A, ϕ))," corresponds to the constraint that the accessibility relation be transitive,

$$\forall_{A, W1, W2, W3} \, [\, \text{bel\_acc}(A, W1, W2) \wedge \text{bel\_acc}(A, W2, W3) \,] \Rightarrow$$
$$\text{bel\_acc}(A, W1, W3).$$

It is easily shown that the axiom of positive introspection is true if the accessibility relation is transitive. Suppose that in $W1$, A does not believe that he believes that ϕ. Translated into the language of possible worlds, this means that in $W1$ there is an accessible world $W2$ in which A does not believe ϕ; that is, there is a world $W2$ accessible from $W1$ such that there is a world $W3$ accessible from $W2$ such that ϕ is false in $W3$. If transitivity holds, then $W3$ is accessible from $W1$. Thus, there is a world accessible from $W1$ in which ϕ is false; that is, in $W1$, A does not believe ϕ. We have shown that if A does not believe that he believes ϕ, then he does not believe ϕ, which is just the contrapositive of the axiom of positive introspection.

It is also possible, though much more difficult, to establish the reverse relation between the modal axiom and the constraint on possible worlds: If $\mathcal{T}$ is a modal theory that obeys the axiom of positive introspection, and also the axioms BEL.1, consequential closure, and BEL.2, belief in the axioms, then there is a model of $\mathcal{T}$ in which the accessibility relation is transitive [Kripke 1975].

Table 8.4 shows the translation of all the axioms for belief into constraints on accessibility relations.

8.2.3 Syntactic Formulation

Expressing the axioms of Section 8.2.1 in a language of strings and syntactic operators involves some slightly subtle considerations. In particular, the correct manipulation of quantified variables within strings requires care. For example, suppose we want to express the axiom "For all N and A, if N is the address of A, then A believes that N is the address of A." We will assume that addresses are strings of characters such as ≺59_Turnover_Place≻. Keeping in mind that, in a syntactic theory, the object of a proposition must be a quoted string, a naive guess at a representation would be,

i. $\forall_{N, A} \, \text{address}(N, A) \Rightarrow \text{believe}(A, \prec\text{address}(N, A)\succ)$.

From this, and the statement, "Oscar's address is 59 Turnover Place," the conclusion should follow that "Oscar believes that his address is 59 Turnover Place."

ii. believe(oscar, ≺address(≺59_Turnover_Place≻,oscar)≻).

Table 8.4 Axioms of Belief in Terms of Possible Worlds

BEL.1.	(Consequential closure)
	True in any possible-worlds semantics.
BEL.2.	(Belief in the axioms)
	True in any possible-worlds semantics
BEL.3.	(Consistency)
	$\forall_{A,W0}\exists_{W1}$ bel_acc$(A, W0, W1)$.
BEL.4.	(Privileged access)
	$\forall_{A,W0,W1}$ bel_acc$(A, W0, W1) \Rightarrow$ $\exists_{W2}$ [bel_acc$(A, W0, W2) \wedge$ bel_acc$(A, W2, W1)$].
BEL.5.	(Coherence)
	$\forall_{A,W0}\exists_{W1}$ bel_acc$(A, W0, W1) \wedge$ [$\forall_{W2}$ bel_acc$(A, W1, W2) \Rightarrow$ bel_acc$(A, W0, W2)$].
BEL.6.	(Arrogance)
	$\forall_{A,W0,W1}$ bel_acc$(A, W0, W1) \Rightarrow$ bel_acc$(A, W1, W1)$.
BEL.7.	(Positive introspection)
	$\forall_{A,W0,W1,W2}$ [bel_acc$(A, W0, W1) \wedge$ bel_acc$(A, W1, W2)$] $\Rightarrow$ bel_acc$(A, W0, W2)$.
BEL.8.	(Negative introspection)
	$\forall_{A,W0,W1,W2}$ [bel_acc$(A, W0, W1) \wedge$ bel_acc$(A, W0, W2)$] $\Rightarrow$ bel_acc$(A, W1, W2)$.

However what actually follows from rule i is that Oscar believes ≺address(N, A)≻, which is either meaningless, or means that everything is everyone's address. The problem, as discussed in Section 2.8, is that there is no connection between the quantified variables N and A outside the quotation marks, and the substring ≺N≻ and ≺A≻ inside the quotation marks. The quoted string does not use the symbols N or A, just the characters $: N$ and $: A$.

What we actually want to say is the following: If N is A's address, then A believes a string of the form "address (< N inside string delimiters >, < name of A >)" where the name of the agent and the address are inserted in the proper place. To express this, we use three functions introduced in Section 2.8. The function "name_of(X)" maps any entity X to a constant string that denotes X. Thus, if Oscar is the father of Harriet, the following is true: name_of(oscar) = name_of(father_of(harriet)) = ≺oscar≻. The function "dbl_quote(P)" takes a string P as an argument, and returns a string with an additional level of quotation. For example, dbl_quote(≺oscar≻) = ≺≺oscar≻≻. (For the interpretation of this notation in terms of tuples of characters, see Section 2.8). The function "apply$(O, A1 \ldots Ak)$" takes as arguments a string O, which spells out an operator, and strings $A1 \ldots Ak$, which spell out operands; it denotes the string that spells out the application of the operator to the operands.

We can now state the rule i correctly:

i' $\forall_{A,N}$ address$(N, A) \Rightarrow$
   believe(A, apply(≺address≻, dbl_quote(N), name_of(A))).

Thus, if A is oscar and N is ≺59_Turnover_Place≻, then dbl_quote(N) = ≺≺59_Turnover_Place≻≻ and name_of(A) = ≺oscar≻. The arguments to the apply are thus, ≺address≻, ≺≺59_Turnover_Place≻≻, and ≺oscar≻, and the value of the apply is ≺address(≺59_Turnover_Place≻, oscar)≻, which is what was desired.

We can compress the notation with some syntactic sugar. Note that any string within string delimiters that is not a simple symbol can be rewritten as the application of an operator string to operand strings; thus,

≺$1 + 1 = 2$≻ = apply(≺ $=$ ≻, ≺$1 + 1$≻, ≺2≻) =
apply(≺ $=$ ≻, apply(≺ $+$ ≻, ≺1≻, ≺1≻), ≺2≻)

We adopt the following convention: Let T be a string within string delimiters, and let S be a substring of T. If S is surrounded in T by down arrows ↓, then S itself, rather than its quoted form, is made an argument to the apply function. If S is surrounded by at signs

@, then name_of(S) is made an argument of the apply function. If S is surrounded by exclamation points !, then dbl_quote(S) is made an argument of the apply function.[7] Thus, we can write the above rule more concisely as

$$\forall_{A,N} \ address(N, A) \Rightarrow believe(A, \prec address(!N!, @A@) \succ).$$

or, equivalently,

$$\forall_{A,N} \ address(N, A) \Rightarrow$$
$$believe(A, \prec address(\downarrow dbl\_quote(N)\downarrow, \downarrow name\_of(A)\downarrow) \succ)$$

Table 8.5 shows how the axioms and inference rules for belief given in modal form in Tables 8.1 and 8.2 can be rewritten in syntactic form. We assume that every agent knows a name for himself. (The modal axioms implicitly make the corresponding assumption that every agent knows a rigid designator for himself.)

As discussed in Section 2.8.2, syntactic theories allow the construction of self-referential sentences and sentences that deny themselves. It is often possible to use such sentences to show that a small set of natural axioms on the sentential operators is inconsistent. In particular, in a syntactic theory we can construct a sentence of the form "I do not believe this sentence." Using this sentence, we can show that a syntactic theory of belief is inconsistent if it contains the axiom of consequential closure, BEL.1, the axiom of knowledge of the axioms, BEL.2, and the axiom of coherence, BEL.5. (Exercise 8.3).

8.3 Degree of Belief

Beliefs are held with greater and lesser degrees of certainty. We can incorporate degrees of certainty within our model by introducing a two-place modal function, "d_belief(A, ϕ)," which maps an agent A and a proposition ϕ into a degree of belief, which is a quantity. Thus, the sentence

$$d\_belief(john, grey(clyde)) > d\_belief(john, elephant(clyde))$$

---

[7]Readers familiar with LISP will recognize this as analogous to the quasi-quote macro. As in LISP, the interpretation of anti-quote marks inside several layers of string delimiters is a potential area for ambiguity. On the half-dozen or so occasions that this arises in the text, I will indicate the scoping of the anti-quote marks by an explicit comment. Except in one place, the scoping is always to the innermost string delimiters. Ultimately, one would need systematic conventions to deal with this horrible problem.

Table 8.5 Rules for Belief: Syntactic Form

In these rules, A is an object-level variable ranging over agents, and P and Q are object-level variables ranging over strings that spell out sentences. ϕ is a metalevel variable ranging over sentences, for use in axiom schemas and inference rules. BEL.9–BEL.14 below are inference rules. BEL.2 is an axiom schema. BEL.1 and BEL.3–BEL.8 are simple axioms, single first-order sentences.

BEL.1. (Consequential closure)

$\forall_{A,P,Q}$ (believe$(A, P) \wedge$ believe$(A, \prec\downarrow P\downarrow\Rightarrow\downarrow Q\downarrow\succ)) \Rightarrow$
believe(A, Q).

BEL.2. (Belief in the axioms)

If ϕ is a logical axiom or an axiom of belief, and string P spells out ϕ, then $\forall_A$ believe(A, P) is an axiom.

BEL.3. (Consistency)

$\forall_{A,P}$ ¬(believe$(A, P) \wedge$ believe$(A, \prec\neg\downarrow P\downarrow\succ))$.

BEL.4. (Privileged access)

$\forall_A$ believe$(A,\prec$believe$(@A@, !P!)\succ) \Rightarrow$ believe(A, P).

BEL.5. (Coherence)

$\forall_{A,P}$ believe$(A,\prec\neg$believe$(@A@, !P!)\succ) \Rightarrow \neg$believe$(A, P)$.

BEL.6. (Arrogance)

$\forall_{A,P}$ believe$(A, \prec$believe$(@A@, !P!) \Rightarrow \downarrow P\downarrow\succ)$.

BEL.7. (Positive introspection)

$\forall_{A,P}$ believe$(A, P) \Rightarrow$ believe$(A,\prec$believe$(@A@, !P!)\succ)$.

BEL.8. (Negative introspection)

$\forall_{A,P}$ ¬believe$(A, P) \Rightarrow$ believe$(A, \prec\neg$ believe$(@A@, !P!)\succ)$.

Table 8.5: Rules for Belief: Syntactic Form (Continued)

BEL.9. (General inference rule of consequential closure)

If ($\phi_1, \phi_2, \ldots \phi_k \vdash \psi$) monotonically, strings $P_1 \ldots P_k$ spell out $\phi_1 \ldots \phi_k$ respectively, and Q spells out ψ, then the statement

$\forall_A$ [believes$(A, P_1) \wedge \ldots \wedge$ believes(A, P_k)] $\Rightarrow$ believes(A, Q).

BEL.10. (Necessitation)

If string P spells out sentence ϕ, then $\phi \vdash_A$ believe(A, P).

BEL.11. (Optimism)

If string P spells out sentence ϕ, then believe$(A, P) \vdash_A \phi$.

BEL.12. (Inference of ignorance.)

If string P spells out sentence ϕ, then $(\nvdash_A \phi) \vdash_A$ $\neg$believe(A, P).

BEL.13. (Charity)

If string P spells out sentence ϕ, then plausible(believe(A, P), ϕ).

BEL.14. (Consequential closure on plausible inference)
If A believes that Q is a plausible inference from P, and A believes P, then it is plausible to infer that A believes Q.

plausible(believe$(A, \prec$plausible$(\downarrow P \downarrow, \downarrow Q \downarrow)\succ) \wedge$
        believe(A, P),
        believe(A, Q))

---

means that John is more sure that Clyde is grey than that he is an elephant. (In a syntactic theory, the second argument would be a string spelling out a sentence.)

Degrees of belief are generally assumed to be governed by a calculus of uncertainty like those of Chapter 3. For example, if we assume that agents follow a probabilistic model in assigning degrees of belief, we can state the following axioms:

DBEL.1.   d_belief$(A, \phi) \in [0,1]$.

DBEL.2.   If $\vdash \phi$ then d_belief$(A, \phi) = 1$ and d_belief$(A, \neg\phi) = 0$.

DBEL.3.   If $\vdash \phi \Leftrightarrow \psi$ then d_belief$(A, \phi) = $ d_belief(A, ψ).

DBEL.4.   If $\vdash \phi \Leftrightarrow \neg\psi$ then
$$\text{d\_belief}(A, \phi \vee \psi) = \text{d\_belief}(A, \phi) + \text{d\_belief}(A, \psi).$$

We can then interpret the unquantified belief predicate "believe (A, ϕ)" as meaning certain belief:

$$\text{believe}(A, \phi) \Leftrightarrow \text{d\_belief}(A, \phi) = 1.$$

Axioms BEL.1, BEL.2, and BEL.3 on "believe(M, ϕ)" then follow directly from DBEL.1–DBEL.4 above. Note that we are still assuming a perfectly rational agent with consequential closure here; we are merely allowing him to be unsure of certain things.

How to assign values to embedded statements of belief is not altogether clear. The axiom of privileged access suggests, perhaps, that one's beliefs about one's own beliefs should always be certain. If so, we can reasonably adopt the following axioms:

DBEL.5.   d_belief$(A,$ d_belief$(A, \phi) = X) \in \{0, 1\}$.
(An agent is always perfectly sure of his own beliefs.)

DBEL.6.   d_belief$(A,$ d_belief$(A, \phi) = X) = 1 \Rightarrow$ d_belief$(A, \phi) = X$.
(An agent is always right about his own beliefs. Privileged access.)

DBEL.7.   d_belief$(A, \phi) = X \Rightarrow$ d_belief$(A,$ d_belief$(A, \phi) = X) = 1$.
(An agent always knows his own beliefs. Positive introspection.)

8.4 Knowledge

For an agent to succeed in accomplishing his goals reliably, he must have adequate knowledge of the relevant issues. Having incorrect beliefs about the issues is often worse than useless. Therefore, predicting the success or failure of an agent at a task generally requires reasoning about his knowledge. In particular, predicting our own future successes or failures requires reasoning about our own knowledge. If we find that our knowledge is likely to be inadequate, we may desire to increase it before we address the task. (There is a very good case to be made that knowledge is a more important concept than belief.

For instance, the word "know" is much more frequently used than the word "believe," or any of its synonyms.)

Like believing a fact, knowing a fact is a propositional attitude, a relation between an agent and a proposition. Knowledge is a stronger relation than belief. If an agent knows a fact, then the fact is true, and he believes it. For example, the statement "Naomi knows that tigers are fierce" implies that tigers are, indeed, fierce and that Naomi believes that tigers are fierce. Not all true belief, however, is knowledge. To know a fact requires having some good reason for believing it. An agent should try to act only on beliefs of his that are true; his best policy to achieve this is to act on beliefs that he holds for good reasons. If a gambler believes that he will win the Lottery and he does win it, we do not say that he knew he would win, because he had no reason for his belief, and consequently his belief did not justify his action. However, it is very difficult to state what constitutes good reason for a belief. (It is also not certain that all true beliefs with good reason are considered knowledge; [Gettier 1963] brings some counterexamples.) Therefore, we treat "know" and "believe" as separate primitive propositional attitudes, connected by the axioms in Table 8.6 below.

Knowledge is generally taken to be a less fundamental concept than belief. Unlike belief, knowledge is not a "pure" psychological predicate; it depends on the state of the outer world, not just on the mental state of the agent.[8] For that reason, it is belief, rather than knowledge, that is critical for predicting actions. If John wants a Coke, and he believes that there is a Coke in the refrigerator, then he will go to the refrigerator. It does not matter whether his belief is true or not, until the moment when he can find out whether it is true. Similarly, the principle of privileged access, that an agent's beliefs about his own mental states are correct, does not apply to the mental state of knowledge; it is not the case that, if John believes that he knows that there is a Coke in the refrigerator, then he does know that there is a Coke in the refrigerator.

However, there is another viewpoint in which knowledge is more fundamental. Suppose we have before us a system that seems to be intelligent, but in which we cannot find anything that looks like a knowledge base or like a declarative representation of propositions. When it "does things right" — when its actions are appropriate to whatever goals we attribute to it — then it is reasonable to say that it had knowledge about those aspects of the world that made its actions right. For example, if a robot stops at the edge of a cliff, then it seems

---

[8]This is a more tenuous distinction than it might appear. It is not clear to what extent belief is independent of the external world. See [Dennett 1981], [Marcus 1986] and [Putnam 1975].

Table 8.6 Axioms of Knowledge

KNOW.1. (Consequential closure) [know$(A, \phi) \wedge$ know$(A, \phi \Rightarrow \psi)] \Rightarrow$ know(A, ψ).

KNOW.2. (Knowledge of axioms) If ϕ is a logical axiom or an axiom of knowledge, then know(A, ϕ) is an axiom.

KNOW.3. (Veridicality) know$(A, \phi) \Rightarrow \phi$.

KNOW.4. (Positive introspection) know$(A, \phi) \Rightarrow$ know$(A,$know$(A, \phi))$.

KNOW.5. (Negative introspection) $\neg$know$(A, \phi) \Rightarrow$ know$(A,\neg$know$(A, \phi))$.

KNOW.6. (Necessitation) $\phi \vdash_A$ know(A, ϕ)

---

reasonable to say that it knew that it should not go further. With more evidence, we may be more detailed and say that it knew that there was a cliff there, and it knew that it could not survive going over a cliff. However, the attribution of false beliefs to a robot that goes over a cliff is much harder. Did it think there was no cliff there? Or did it think it could go over cliffs with impunity? Or was it suicidal? Or was it not behaving rationally at all? This kind of consideration (among others) has led to the development of a quite different theory of mental states from our "folk psychological" model.[9]

Reflecting considerations such as these, an alternative definition of knowledge has been put forward by Rosenschein and Kaelbling [1986]. Here, a multistate machine is said to know proposition P when it is in state S, if, whenever the machine is in state S, P is true. Belief in this theory is defined as uncertain knowledge: The machine, in state S, believes P with certainty α if the probability of P, given that the machine is in S, is equal to α. A limitation of this model is that it makes it hard to give a semantics to embedded knowledge, to changing knowledge, or to knowledge of anything other than the current state of the world.

Table 8.6 enumerates some possible axioms governing the knowledge of a single agent in a modal language. These are largely analogous to the axioms of belief that we have presented above in Table 8.1. Table 8.7 enumerates axioms that relate knowledge to belief.

---

[9]These considerations are also related to those that led Davidson to claim that the principle of charity is a necessary property of belief (Section 8.2.1).

Table 8.7 Axioms Relating Knowledge and Belief

KB.1.　　　(Knowledge is belief) If A knows ϕ then A believes ϕ.

　　　　　　$\text{know}(A, \phi) \Rightarrow \text{believe}(A, \phi)$.

KB.2.　　　(Positive introspection: A) If A believes ϕ, then A knows that he believes ϕ.

　　　　　　$\text{believe}(A, \phi) \Rightarrow \text{know}(A, \text{believe}(A, \phi))$.

KB.3.　　　(Positive introspection: B) If A believes ϕ then A believes that he knows ϕ.

　　　　　　$\text{believe}(A, \phi) \Rightarrow \text{believe}(A, \text{know}(A, \phi))$.

KB.4.　　　(Negative introspection) If A does not believe ϕ, then A knows that he does not believe ϕ.

　　　　　　$\neg\text{believe}(A, \phi) \Rightarrow \text{know}(A, \neg\text{believe}(A, \phi))$.

KB.5.　　　(Arrogance) A believes that, if he believes ϕ, then he knows ϕ.

　　　　　　$\text{believe}(A, \text{believe}(A, \phi) \Rightarrow \text{know}(A, \phi))$.

Axioms KNOW.1 and KNOW.2 establish that knowledge is closed under deductive implicature. These axioms thus describe implicit knowledge; applied to explicit or derivable knowledge, they lead to the same problems as applied to explicit or derivable belief. Axiom KNOW.3 is an intrinsic part of the definition of knowledge. Note that it subsumes the analogues for knowledge of axioms BEL.3–BEL.6 and rules, BEL.11 and BEL.13. Axiom KNOW.4 is analogous to axiom BEL.7 and quite as plausible. By contrast, axiom KNOW.5, asserting that agents have the power of negative introspection on their knowledge, is very strong. For that reason, negative introspection is not generally adopted in theories of knowledge that aim at any degree of psychological verisimilitude, though it can be useful in characterizing certain closed worlds in which the agent's beliefs may be incomplete but cannot be mistaken. For example, in reasoning about a card game, player A can reason that if player B does not know who holds the queen of spades, then B will know that he does not know it. Rule KNOW.6 of necessitation, if interpreted as applying to all statements in the knowledge base of the agent, is similarly incompatible with the agent's holding false beliefs and must likewise be restricted to closed worlds.

Axiom KB.1, that knowledge is belief, is part of the definition of knowledge, as discussed above. Axioms KB.2 and KB.3 are slight strengthenings of axiom BEL.7, of positive introspection on belief; KB.4 is a strengthening of BEL.8, negative introspection on belief; KB.5 is a strengthening of BEL.6, the axiom of arrogance. Note that if we were to define knowledge to be exactly true belief, so that KB.1 was a biconditional, then KB.2 and KB.3 would be equivalent to BEL.7, KB.4 would be equivalent to BEL.8, and KB.5 would be equivalent to KB.6.

We have stated the axioms above as axiom schemas in a modal logic where "know(M, ϕ)" is a modal operator. It is straightforward to convert these to a syntactic notation, in the style of Section 8.2.3. Note that a syntactic theory that contains the axioms of veridicality, consequential closure, and knowing the logical axioms can be shown to be formally inconsistent, using the self-referential sentence "I know that this sentence is false."

It is also possible to translate our modal language of knowledge to a language of possible worlds using a relation "know_acc $(A, W1, W2)$," meaning that world $W2$ is compatible with everything that agent A knows in world $W1$. Axioms KNOW.1 and KNOW.2 hold in any such possible-worlds structure. Axiom KNOW.3 corresponds to the statement that every world is accessible from itself. The translations of axioms KNOW.4 and KNOW.5 are exact analogues of the translations of axioms BEL.7 and BEL.8 given in Table 8.1. By combining the two accessibility relations "bel_acc" and "know_acc," it is possible to express sentences involving both knowledge and belief. For example, axiom KB.1, that if A knows ϕ then A believes ϕ, can be expressed in the axiom "bel_acc$(A, W1, W2) \Rightarrow$ know_acc$(A, W1, W2)$." (If $W2$ is consistent with A's beliefs, then it is consistent with A's knowledge.) The translations of KB.2 and KB.3 are left as exercises.

8.5 Knowing Whether and What

Often, we must express the proposition that another agent has knowledge that we ourselves do not. Since we do not have the knowledge in question, we cannot specify in detail what that knowledge is; we can only give a partial description. Examples:

1. Alfred knows whether Sacramento is the capital of California.

2. Sarah knows what is the capital of California.

3. Charles knows how to get to Sebastian's house.

4. Karen knows how to play the piano.

5. Gil knows a lot about the Bronze Age.

In this section, we will discuss representations for propositions like 1, in which an agent knows whether a fact is true, and 2, in which an agent knows the value of a term. In Section 9.3.2 we will discuss the representation of propositions like 3, where "knowing how" can be thought of as knowing a collection of facts that describe a route to Sebastian's house. Representing propositions like 4, where "knowing how" is not obviously a matter of knowing some collection of sentences, or propositions like 5, which involve the notion of a fact being "about" an entity, is very difficult and is not dealt with in this book. ([Ryle 1949] and [Polanyi 1958] discuss the relation of "knowing how" to "knowing that." [Morgenstern 1988] discusses the formal representation of "knowing how.")

We begin by considering these representational problems in a modal language. We introduce the modal operators "know_whether(A, ϕ)," meaning that agent A knows whether ϕ is true, and "know_val(A, τ)," meaning that A knows the value of term τ. Thus, sentences 1 and 2 could be expressed in the forms

know_whether(alfred, sacramento=capital(california))

know_val(sarah, capital(california))

(Like "know" and "believe," "know_whether" and "know_val" are modal operators that create an opaque context for their second argument. The above sentences are not equivalent to "know_whether(alfred, sacramento=sacramento)" or "know_val (sarah, sacramento)".)

We may now consider how these operators are related to "know". In the case of "know_whether" the relation is obvious and unproblematic: A knows whether ϕ is true if he either knows ϕ or he knows $\neg\phi$.

KW.1. $\forall_A$ know_whether$(A, \phi) \Leftrightarrow [$know$(A, \phi) \lor$ know$(A, \neg\phi)]$.

The relation between "know_val" and "know" is generally taken to be the following: An agent knows the value of a term T if he knows some sentence of the form "$C = T$" where C is a constant.[10] This (not by coincidence) fits perfectly with the conventional reading of sentences containing a modal operator within the scope of a quantifier: If O(ϕ) is a modal operator, then the sentence "$\exists_X$ O$(\alpha(X))$" is taken to be true if (roughly) the sentence "O$(\alpha(C))$" is true for some constant C. (More precisely, $\exists_X$ O$(\alpha(X))$ is true if there is an object δ such that, if a new constant symbol C is defined to denote δ, then the sentence "O$(\alpha(C))$" is true. See Section 2.7.1.) We can then state the definition of know_val in the following axiom schema:

KW.2. For any term τ, the sentence "know_val$(A, \tau) \Leftrightarrow \exists_X$ know$(A, X = \tau)$" is an axiom.

Corresponding approaches to expressing sentences involving knowing the value of a term can be formulated in possible worlds and in syntactic approaches. In a language of possible worlds, we say that A knows the value of T if T is the same object in all accessible worlds. For example, if Sarah knows that the capital of California is Sacramento, then in all accessible worlds the capital of California is Sacramento; if Sarah is uncertain whether the capital is Sacramento or Los Angeles, then in some accessible worlds it is Sacramento and in others it is Los Angeles. We thus express the sentence "Sarah knows what the capital of California is" in the formula

$\exists_X \forall_{W1}$ know_acc(sarah,w0,$W1$) $\Rightarrow$
X=value_in($W1$,capital(california)).

In the above formula, "capital(california)" is a fluent over possible worlds.

In a syntactic language, we say that Sarah knows what the capital of California is if she knows some string of the form "< name of the capital of California > =capital(california)." In our notation, we would write this as

$\exists_X$ know(sarah,$\prec$@X@=capital(california)$\succ$).

We can thus define knowing the value of a term as a syntactic relation between an agent and a string that spells out the term.

---

[10] Or a rigid designator. As discussed in Section 2.7.1, we can identify rigid designators with constant symbols without loss of generality.

KW.2. $\text{know\_val}(A, T) \Leftrightarrow \text{know}(A, \prec @T@ = \downarrow T \downarrow \succ)$.

Any of these notations will support basic inferences about "knowing what". For example, given that Sacramento is the capital of California, and that Sarah knows what the capital of California is, we can use any of these theories to infer that Sarah knows that Sacramento is the capital of California. (Exercise 7).

Universal quantification outside the scope of a modal operator is interpreted similarly. For example, the sentence "Archie knows all the states of the U.S." can be expressed

(1) $\forall_X$ state(X,us) $\Rightarrow$ know(archie, state(X,us)).

In a possible-worlds semantics, this is expressed

(2) $\forall_X$ true_in(w0,state(X,us)) $\Rightarrow$
     [$\forall_{W1}$ know_acc(archie,w0,$W1$) $\Rightarrow$
     true_in($W1$,state(X,us))].

In a syntactic theory, it is expressed

(3) $\forall_X$ state(X,us) $\Rightarrow$ know(archie,$\prec$state(@X@,us)$\succ$).

Given any of these facts, and the fact "state(alabama,us)," it is possible to prove that Archie knows that Alabama is a state. Note that the above formulas do not specify that Archie knows that the 50 states are all there are; they will remain true if Archie also believes that Guam is a state. (See Exercise 8.)

In general, the above techniques provide mechanisms for making statements of the form "A knows what the τ is" for one particular meaning of "knowing what." The meaning of "knowing what" will depend on the kind of description chosen to be viewed as a rigid designator in the modal theory, or a name in the syntactic theory. For example if we agree that a street address is a rigid designator for a location, then "Sam knows where Jessica lives," expressed

$\exists_X$ know(sam, lives_at(jessica,X))

means that Sam knows the street address. If we agree that a pair of coordinates in a standard reference frame are a rigid designator for a place, then the same sentence means that Sam knows the coordinates of where Jessica lives. Note that we cannot have street addresses and coordinates both be rigid designators, unless we are willing to posit that whenever a street address is known, a coordinate is also known, and vice versa.

In a syntactic theory, we can get around this by introducing a variety of characterizations of descriptions of objects. For example, if we have functions street_address(X) mapping a place to its street address, and coordinates(X) mapping a place to its coordinates, then we can distinguish between the two types of knowledge in the two formulas,

$\exists_X$ know(sam,≺lives_at(jessica,↓street_address(X)↓)≻)
$\exists_X$ know(sam,≺lives_at(jessica,↓coordinates(X)↓)≻)

This flexibility is a major advantage of a syntactic theory over a modal or possible-worlds theory.

8.6 Minds and Time

An agent's beliefs and knowledge deal with time and change over time.

To incorporate time into a modal or syntactic language of knowledge and belief is a straightforward application of the techniques of Chapter 5. We convert knowledge and belief into time-varying states either by adding a situational argument to the operators "know" and "believe" or by defining state functions "knowing(A, ϕ)" and "believing(A, ϕ)." Time can be incorporated in the propositional or string argument of know or believe in any of our previous notations. For example, "At 9:00, Warren knew that he was cold and hungry" can be represented in any of the following forms (among others).

know(warren, cold(warren,s900) ∧
    hungry(warren, s900), s900).
    (Temporal: Extra argument. Knowledge: Modal)

true_in(s900,knowing(warren,
                  ≺true_in(s900,cold(warren)) ∧
    true_in(s900,hungry(warren))≻)).
    (Temporal: State type. Knowledge: Syntactic.)

know(warren,cold(warren)) ∧ hungry(warren),s900).
    (Temporal: Modal. Knowledge: Modal)

Having added this temporal component to knowledge and belief, it is necessary to rewrite the previous axioms and rules BEL.1–BEL.14 and KNOW.1–KNOW.8. For the most part, this is a straightforward adding of a single, universally quantified, situational variable to the axiom, and using it wherever a situational argument is needed. For example, the modal axiom of positive introspection on belief becomes

$$\forall_{S,A} \text{ believe}(A, \phi, S) \Rightarrow \text{believe}(A, \text{believe}(A, \phi, S), S)$$

A couple of slightly subtle points may be noted:

- The rules BEL.10, BEL.11, BEL.12, and KNOW.7, where the inference was previously restricted by the agent involved, must be rewritten to be restricted by both the agent and the situation. For example, the rule of necessitation, BEL.10, previously written "$\phi \vdash_A \text{believe}(A, \phi)$," must be rewritten "$\phi \vdash_{A,S} \text{believe}(A, \phi, S)$," meaning that if the agent A finds ϕ in his knowledge base at time S, then he may infer that he believes ϕ at time S.

- In syntactic sentences with imbedded belief states, the internal sentence must use the *name* of the situation, a somewhat problematic concept, particularly since in a continuous model there are uncountably many situations. We take the following view: A name of a situation may contain a real number or a symbol with some real-valued parameter (e.g., a line of a given length). The agent can then coin a name for each situation in turn.

An additional operator that is useful for reasoning about knowledge is that of an agent A knowing the current value of a fluent F in a situation S. We represent this using the operator "know_fluent(A, F, S)". For example, the statement "In s800, Reuben knew the time" is represented "know_fluent(reuben, clock_time, s800)". Under the assumption that an agent always knows a name for a situation, this can be defined as follows:

know_fluent(A, F, S) $\Leftrightarrow$
[know_val(A,value_in(S, F),S) $\lor$
know_whether(A,true_in(S, F),S)]

In a possible-worlds semantics, this is expressed by stating that the fluent F has the same value in all accessible worlds.

Table 8.8 shows a number of plausible axioms constraining knowledge and belief over time that suggest themselves. These, like the previous axioms governing knowledge and belief at an instant, are somewhat idealized, particularly axiom BT.1, stating that an agent who knows something never forgets it. We assume further that all agents know these axioms, in accordance with axiom KNOW.2.

Axiom BT.1, in particular, is useful for predicting that the agent will be able to predict his own future knowledge. For example, Table 8.9

Table 8.8 Axioms of Belief and Knowledge Over Time

In all the axiom schemas below, ϕ is a metalevel variable, ranging over "anchored" sentences; that is, sentences without temporal indexicals.

BT.1. An agent who knows ϕ in a situation knows ϕ in all later situations.

$[\text{know}(A, \phi, S1) \wedge \text{precede}(S1, S2)] \Rightarrow \text{know}(A, \phi, S2).$

BT.2. If A believes ϕ, then he believes that he will always believe ϕ.

$\text{believe}(A, \phi, S1) \Rightarrow$
$\text{believe}(A, \forall_{S2} \text{ precede}(S1, S2) \Rightarrow \text{believe}(A, \phi, S2), S1).$

BT.3 If A believes that he will believe ϕ in the future, then he believes ϕ now.

$\text{believe}(A, \exists_{S2} \text{ precede}(S1, S2) \wedge \text{believe}(A, \phi, S2), S1) \Rightarrow$
$\text{believe}(A, \phi, S1)$

---

shows how we can use this to infer that if an agent knows the physics of the blocks world, knows the starting state, and knows that he can trace what is happening, then he can predict that he will know the final state.

In general, however, there are serious problems in formulating a theory in which an agent's future beliefs and knowledge can be predicted. It is difficult to find any reasonable causal or frame axioms on an agent's beliefs. There are also difficulties in constructing a theory that allows an agent to make predictions without assuming that the agent knows of all the events that occur [Morgenstern 1989].

8.6.1 Situations and Possible Worlds

The situation-based theory of time and the possible-worlds semantics for belief and knowledge use two different types of possible worlds. A temporal situation is a snapshot of the world at a given instant; an epistemically possible world is a way in which the world could possibly be. In combining these two logics, it is necessary to connect these two concepts. Moore [1980] has shown that identifying epistemically

Table 8.9 Sample Inference of Agent's Knowledge of the Future

_____

Given:

The above axioms of knowledge.

Daniel knows all the axioms of the blocks world (Table 5.2).

In situation s0, Daniel knows all "beneath" and "place" fluents.
$\forall_{X,Y}$ know_fluent(daniel,beneath(X, Y),s0).
$\forall_X$ know_fluent(daniel,place(X),s0).

Daniel knows that he knows all the blocks.
know(daniel, $\forall_X$ block(X) $\Rightarrow$ know(daniel,block(X),s0), s0).

Daniel knows that he will know whatever events occur when they are done.
know(daniel,$\forall_{I,E}$ occur(I, E) $\Rightarrow$
know(daniel,occur(I, E),end(I)), s0).

Daniel knows that either a pickup, a putdown, or a move occurs in the interval [s0,s1].
know(daniel, occur([s0,s1],pickup) $\lor$ occur([s0,s1],putdown) $\lor$
$\exists_L$ occur([s0,s1], move(L)),
s0).

Infer:

Daniel knows now that in s1 he will still know all beneath relations.
know(daniel,
$\forall_{X,Y}$ know_whether(daniel,beneath(X,Y), s1), s0).

Sketch of the proof: Daniel knows in s0 that in situation s1 he will know what event has occurred in [s0,s1] (Given). By KNOW.1, he knows axiom BT.1, that he will still know everything in s1 that he knows now. In particular, in s0 he knows that in s1 he will still know the positions of all the blocks in s0 and the axioms governing the blocks world. The positions of the blocks in s1 follow logically from their positions in s0, the event in [s0,s1], and the axioms of the blocks world. Hence, applying consequential closure to Daniel's knowledge in s1, it follows that in s1 he will know the positions of the blocks in s1. Since, by KNOW.1, Daniel knows in s0 that his knowledge in s1 obeys consequential closure, it follows, by consequential closure on his knowledge in s0, that he knows in s0 that he will know in s1 where all the blocks are.

_____

possible worlds with temporal situations gives a theory that is elegant and powerful. (The language we construct below is slightly more expressive than Moore's, which represented time using the situation calculus in the narrow sense (Section 5.8).)

We presume a set of parallel chronicles and an accessibility relation between situations. Situation $S2$ is accessible from $S1$ relative to A if $S2$ is consistent with everything that A knows in $S2$. If an agent knows different things in situation s1 than he does in s2, then different worlds will be accessible to him in s1 than in s2.

Knowledge about the past and the future is expressed as statements about the chronicles containing accessible situations. For example, the sentence "Eva knows that Columbus was alive in 1492" is interpreted "In every chronicle containing a situation compatible with Eva's knowledge, Columbus was alive in 1492."

$\forall_{S1}$ know_acc(eva,s0,$S1$) $\Rightarrow$
$\qquad \exists_{S2}$ precedes($S2, S1$) $\land$ true_in($S2$,alive(columbus)) $\land$
$\qquad$ value_in($S2$,clock_time) $\in$ year_1492.

Here, s0 is the current real situation; $S1$ is any situation which, so far as Eva knows, might be the current situation; and $S2$ is some situation in the same chronicle as $S1$ in 1492 when Columbus was alive (Figure 8.1).

Axioms BT.1–BT.3 can be expressed as constraints on the interrelations on temporal precedence and knowledge accessibility. For example, axiom BT.1, that knowledge is never lost, corresponds to the following constraint: If $S1A$ precedes $S2A$ in chronicle A, and $S2B$ is knowledge accessible from $S2A$, then there is a situation $S1B$ that is knowledge-accessible from $S1A$ and that precedes $S2B$ in chronicle B (Figure 8.2).

$\forall_{S1A,S2A,S2B}$ [precedes($S1A, S2A$) $\land$ know_acc($A, S2A, S2B$)] $\Rightarrow$
$\qquad \exists_{S1B}$ precedes($S1B, S2B$) $\land$ know_acc($A, S1A, S1B$).

We may justify this formulation as follows: Assume that the above constraint holds. Suppose that A does not know ϕ in $S2A$. Then there is a knowledge-accessible situation $S2B$ in which ϕ is false. If $S1A$ precedes $S2A$ then, by the above constraint, there is a situation $S1B$ that is knowledge accessible from $S1A$ and that precedes $S2B$. Since ϕ is a time-independent sentence, and ϕ is false in $S2B$, ϕ must also be false in $S1B$. Thus, A does not know ϕ in $S1A$. We have thus shown that, if A does not know ϕ at a later time, then he does not know ϕ at an earlier time, which is just the contrapositive of the axiom of memory. The expression of the remaining rules BT.2 and BT.3 in a possible-worlds semantics is left to the reader (Exercise 4b).

8.7 Perceptions

Perceptions are the interface that allows the mind to gain information about the external world; they are the ultimate source of most beliefs. Despite their importance, however, there has been little work to date at developing a commonsense theory of the senses. (The detailed models of the senses provided by vision and other sensory research do not enter into a commonsense understanding.) We will discuss some of the issues involved, and briefly sketch a possible theory.

Consider the following quotation:

> Suddenly, there was the momentary gleam of a light in the direction of the ventilator, which vanished immediately, but was succeeded by a strong smell of burning oil and heated metal. Someone in the next room had lit a dark lantern. I heard a gentle sound of movement, and then all was silent once more, though the smell grew stronger. For half an hour I sat with straining ears. Then suddenly another sound became audible — a very gentle, soothing sound, like that of a small jet of steam escaping continually from a kettle. The instant that we heard it, Holmes sprang from the bed, struck a match, and lashed furiously with his cane at the bell-pull.
>
> "You see it, Watson?" he yelled. "You see it?"
>
> But I saw nothing. At the moment when Holmes struck the light, I heard a low, clear whistle, but the sudden glare flashing into my weary eyes made it impossible for me to tell what it was at which my friend lashed so savagely. I could, however, see that his face was deadly pale and was filled with horror and loathing. (Sir Arthur Conan Doyle, "The Adventure of the Speckled Band," *Adventures of Sherlock Holmes.*)

Understanding this passage involves a rich theory of perception. First, the reader must be able to connect Watson's and Holmes's perceptions to their mental state. Watson infers that a dark lantern has been lit from seeing the light and smelling the oil and the heated metal of the dark lantern. Watson cannot identify the source of the steam-like sound; Holmes, presumably, has identified it. Whatever Holmes has seen is the source of his horror. Second, the reader must connect the perceptions to the physics of the external world. Holmes lights a match in order to be able to see, and Watson sees Holmes by the light he has lit. Third, the reader must know something about the actual sensors; in particular, if one's eyes are used to the dark and are suddenly exposed to bright light, one may be temporarily unable to see in the direction of the light. An adequate commonsense theory must deal with all these issues.

A representation for statements about perception, which allows the expression of simple rules connecting the physics of the perceivable neighborhood to the knowledge gained through perception, may be developed in a modified possible-worlds semantics on the following lines: We define a *behavior* to be a possible history of the *physical* world over time. We define a *layout* to be a possible instantaneous snapshot of a behavior. Behaviors and layouts are thus analogous to intervals and situations respectively, except that they do not incorporate nonphysical aspects of the world. In particular, agent's beliefs and knowledge are not aspects of a layout. We define a predicate "$pc(A, L0, L1)$," read "Layout $L1$ is perceptually compatible with layout $L0$ relative to agent A," meaning that layout $L1$ is consistent with everything that A can perceive in $L1$. We define the function "$layout(S)$" as giving the physical layout in situation S. The statement that A perceives the value of a fluent F is expressed by asserting that F has the same value in every compatible layout. For example, the statement that in situation s0 Caroline sees that the cat is on the sofa is represented

$$\forall_{L1} \ pc(caroline,layout(s0),L1) \Rightarrow \text{true\_in}(L1,on(cat15,sofa8)).$$

(We extend "true_in" and "value_in" to layouts in the obvious way.)

The power of a perceptor are expressed by giving necessary conditions for two layouts to be perceptually compatible; its limits are expressed by giving sufficient conditions. Consider, for example, a robot "r2d2" with sonar. The statement that the robot can always perceive whether or not there is a solid object within distance d0 of it can be represented by stating that two layouts are compatible only if either both have an object within distance d0, or neither does.

$$\forall_{L1,L2} \ pc(r2d2,L1,L2) \Rightarrow$$
$$[[\ \exists_X \ solid(X) \ \wedge$$
$$\text{value\_in}(L1,distance(place(r2d2),place(X))) < d0 \ ] \Leftrightarrow$$
$$[\ \exists_X \ solid(X) \ \wedge$$
$$\text{value\_in}(L2,distance(place(r2d2),place(X))) < d0 \ ]].$$

The statement that the robot can never perceive an object more than distance d1 can be expressed by saying that, if two layouts have identical objects within distance d1, then the two are perceptually compatible.

$$\forall_{L1,L2} \ [\ \forall_X \ [\text{value\_in}(L1,\text{distance}(\text{place}(\text{r2d2}), \text{place}(X))) < \text{d1} \ \lor$$
$$\text{value\_in}(L2, \text{distance}(\text{place}(\text{r2d2}),\text{place}(X))) < \text{d1} \ ] \Rightarrow$$
$$\text{value\_in}(L1,\text{place}(X)) = \text{value\_in}(L2,\text{place}(X)) \ ] \Rightarrow$$
$$\text{pc}(\text{r2d2},L1,L2).$$

Perceptions are connected to knowledge by the rules that an agent who perceives ϕ knows ϕ and knows that he perceives ϕ. These rules are expressed in the following axioms.

PERC.1. $\text{know\_acc}(A, S1, S2) \Rightarrow \text{pc}(A,\text{layout}(S1), \text{layout}(S2))$.

PERC.2. $[\ \text{know\_acc}(A, S1, S2) \land \text{pc}(A,\text{layout}(S2), L3)] \Rightarrow$
            $\text{pc}(A, \text{layout}(S1), L3)$.

Similarly, we represent the perception of an event by defining a compatibility relation "$\text{bpc}(A, B1, B2)$" on behaviors. Behaviors $B1$ and $B2$ are compatible relative to agent A if, as far as A can see during I in $B1$, the world might be going through $B2$. Using the function "$\text{behavior}(I)$" mapping an interval I to its behavior, we can represent a sentence like "In interval i0, Hector saw the rabbit eat the carrot" in the form,

$$\forall_{B1} \ \text{bpc}(\text{hector}, \text{behavior}(\text{i0}), B1) \Rightarrow$$
$$\text{occurs}(B1,\text{eat}(\text{rabbit1}, \text{carrot1})).$$

8.8   Realistic Models of Mind

Once we drop the idealization of complete and error-free reasoning and perception, we enter *terra incognita*. As mentioned at the beginning of this chapter, the actual commonsense theory of mind is very rich, and only very limited and preliminary formal models of this theory have been constructed. The most we can do, at this stage, is to discuss a few of the prominent issues that come up in this theory.

1. A complete commonsense theory of mind must include all mental activities of which we are naturally aware. This does not mean that the commonsense theory of mind need include all of cognitive psychology, because we are only aware of the high-level structure of these activities, not of their fine detail. Thus, a commonsense theory of vision need not contain any account of the mechanisms of vision, because these mechanisms are not known to common sense.

(If they were, vision research would be a lot easier.) What the commonsense theory needs is high-level characterizations; rules such as "Familiar objects can generally be recognized." Note that we could have a complete algorithmic theory of vision without having identified these rules. The two problems are quite separate.

2. Mental activities, including deductive inference, generally take perceptible amounts of time. Therefore, these should be considered a type of event and connected by causal theories.

3. Since beliefs are not closed under logical implication, possible-worlds and standard modal theories are out of the question, and syntactic theories must be used.[11] It is not even reasonable to require that beliefs be logically consistent, since logical consistency is noncomputable. It may be reasonable, however, to demand some level of coherence; to require, for example, that if a person at one time believes both P and $\neg P$, then he will try to resolve this conflict.

4. Mental events are sometimes deliberately planned. One may plan to think about a problem, or to pursue some particular line of thought, or to remember some particular item. Not all mental events can be planned, or one ends in an infinite regress [Haas 1986]

5. To reason about agents that can forget something and then remember it later, we must use a model with at least two different knowledge bases of different functionalities. One knowledge base, short-term memory, contains the beliefs of which the agent is currently aware; the other, long-term memory, contains everything that he has known. Remembering is the event of a proposition in long-term memory coming to short-term memory. Note that it is possible to be aware in short-term memory that one knows a fact in long-term memory but not in short-term memory; for example, Cassim in the Ali Baba story is aware that he knows the password in long-term memory, but he can't remember it. This means that propositions in the two knowledge bases must be able to refer to the knowledge bases. Common sense includes a fair amount of knowledge about the interactions between the two knowledge bases. For example, the Ali Baba story quoted at the beginning of the chapter relies on the knowledge that distraction and terror make remembering difficult. The climax of *The Prince and the Pauper* rests on

---

[11] The theories proposed in [Levesque 1984] and [Fagin and Halpern 1985], which are not closed under logical implication, combine aspects of modal and syntactic approaches.

the common observation that an event can be remembered if the course of events leading up to it is rehearsed.

6. The varying knowledge and mental powers of different people, or of the same person over different times, can be categorized in general terms within a commonsense theory. "Cassandra knows a lot of differential geometry." "Richard has perfect pitch." "Edmund is very gullible." "Elaine has an excellent memory, but no sense of direction."

7. It is sometimes possible and useful to state a rule of the form "If ϕ were true, then A would know ϕ"; for example, "If Bob had an older brother, then he would know about it." Generally, this rule is used to infer that, since A does not know ϕ, ϕ must be false. Such rules are derived from general knowledge about what A may be presumed to have learned. We know that most siblings get to be known as part of the family circle, and that, in the rare cases where they are not, they will usually be spoken of from time to time. If Bob had been born when his parents were relatively old, and it was known that his parents had many skeletons in the closet that they never discussed, then the inference rule might not apply. The background knowledge that lies behind rules like this has not been much studied.

8.9 References

One could spend several lifetimes reading the philosophy of mind. Most of the central issues in the theory of knowledge can be found in the Platonic dialogue *Theatatus*. I personally have found Bertrand Russell's *Human Knowledge: Its Scope and Limits* [1948] extremely enlightening. [Ryle 1949] raises many interesting and difficult issues in the theory of mind; his approach is totally at variance with the approach taken here. The articles on "Epistemology, History of" and on "Knowledge and Belief" in the *Encyclopedia of Philosophy* are good general surveys.

The classic works on the modal theories of knowledge and belief were written by Hintikka [1962, 1969]. This modal theory of knowledge was applied to AI and related to the theory of temporal situations by Moore [1980, 1985a]. Moore [1980] also gives a first-order axiomatization of a scheme to translate between modal representations and possible-worlds representations. [Halpern and Moses 1985] reviews the modal theories of knowledge and belief, and adduces complexity results in the propositional theory. Levesque [1984] examines a weakened modal logic of explicit belief that avoids the assumption of consequential closure; extensions of this approach are studied in [Fagin and Halpern 1985]. [McCarthy et al. 1978] was an early AI work on the modal theory of knowledge. [Halpern 1986] and [Vardi 1988] are collections of research papers on formal theories of knowledge.

Syntactic theories of belief and knowledge were studied by Kaplan and Montague [1960], who showed that these theories lead to paradoxes of self-reference. See also [Thomason 1980] for a discussion of these paradoxes. The model of belief as membership in a knowledge base was put forward in [Moore and Hendrix 1982]. Konolige [1982] and Haas [1983] have used syntactic theories to construct models of limited inference engines that lack consequential closure. Morgenstern [1988] has used a syntactic theory of knowledge with consequential closure to achieve a flexible language for describing knowledge preconditions for plans (see Chapter 9). Konolige, Haas, and Morgenstern each propose a possible solution to the paradoxes of self-reference. The syntax used in Section 8.2.3 follows Morgenstern, with minor notational variants.

The axioms of knowledge and belief discussed in the text are mostly culled from modal logic; see, for example, [Hughes and Cresswell 1968]. The principle of charity is discussed in [Davidson 1974]. [Rosenschein and Kaelbling 1986] presents the alternative model of knowledge and belief discussed in Section 9.5. The axiom of arrogance is presented in [Kaplan and Montague 1960]. [Moore 1985b] discusses the inference of ignorance, and the inference "Since A does not know ϕ, ϕ must be false." The principle of privileged access is discussed in [Kripke 1972]

[Hintikka 1962], [Moore 1980] and [Moore 1985a] discuss quantification in modal theories of knowledge. [Haas 1982] and, particularly, [Morgenstern 1988] discuss the partial specification of propositions in syntactic theories.

The relation between possible-worlds semantics for knowledge and situation semantics for time is studied in [Moore 1980] and [Moore 1985a]. [Morgenstern 1989] discusses the difficulties of integrating theories of knowledge with solutions to the frame problem.

[Gettier 1963] argues that "Justified true belief" is not an adequate definition of knowledge. [Putnam, 75], [Dennett 1981], and [Marcus 1986] bring arguments that suggest that what an agent may be said to believe depends on his relation to the external world, as well as his internal state.

There is little of substance on commonsense theories of perception. Conceptual dependency theory [Schank 1975] included ATTENDing a sensor as a primitive act, which could be causally connected to mental events. The theory of layouts sketched above is developed in [Davis 1988, 1989].

There are no very detailed unidealized models of mind. [Konolige 1982] gives general schemes for limiting the power of an inference engine. [Haas 1983] shows how inference may be treated as an event; [Haas 1986] extends this to show how it can be treated as a planned action. [Thomason 1987] discusses a number of interesting aspects of belief, and presents a partial model. The use of a two-level theory of memory is an old idea in cognitive psychology. It was used in conceptual dependency theory [Schank 1975] with the primitive act MTRANS to transfer information from one to the other, but then it fell out of interest. [Kube 1985] deals with a number of interesting issues in this theory.

For formal theories of emotion, see [Schank and Abelson 1977]; [Roseman 1979], [Lehnert 1980], [Dyer 1983], and [Sanders 1989].

8.10 Exercises

(Starred problems are more difficult.)

1. Represent the following sentences (i) in a modal language; (ii) in a language of possible worlds; and (iii) in a syntactic language. For this exercise, ignore the temporal component of these sentences. (Also ignore the fact that, in English, "*A* does not know ϕ" is always interpreted to mean that ϕ is true, despite *A*'s ignorance. For the purposes of all the exercises in this chapter, treat "*A* does not know ϕ" as meaning no more than "It is false that *A* knows ϕ.")

   (a) Jack knows that he lives in Hertfordshire.
   (b) Jack believes that Algernon does not know that Jack lives in Hertfordshire.
   (c) Algernon knows where Jack lives.
   (d) Jack does not know that Algernon knows where Jack lives.

2. Represent the following sentences (i) in a modal language; (ii) in a language of possible-worlds; and (iii) in a syntactic language. Be sure to represent the temporal component of these sentences.

   (a) In situation s1, Algernon knew that Jack lived in Hertfordshire.
   (b) In situation s2, Jack did not know that Algernon had already been at his house for an hour.

(c) In situation s3, Jack did not believe that Algernon would remain at his house for a week.

(d) In situation s4, Jack knew that Cecily had not ever believed that Algernon was dead.

3. Show how the following inferences can be carried out (i) in a modal logic; (ii) in a logic of possible worlds; and (iii) in a syntactic logic. (You may ignore the temporal component.)

(a) Given: Lord Bracknell does not know where Gwendolen is.
Infer: Lord Bracknell does not know that Gwendolen is in Hertfordshire.

(b) Given: Algernon knows that Aunt Augusta believes that Bunbury is sick.
Infer: Aunt Augusta does not know that Bunbury is not sick.

4. *

(a) For each of the axioms BEL.3, BEL.4, BEL.5, BEL.6, and BEL.8 show that, if the possible-worlds axiom in Table 8.4 holds, then the corresponding modal axiom in Table 8.1 holds.

(b) Express axioms BT.2 and BT.3 in the language of possible-worlds.

5. * Show that a syntactic theory is inconsistent if axioms BEL.1, BEL.2, and BEL.5 hold, and the sentence "I do not believe this sentence" can be constructed.

6. * Show that the axiom of arrogance (BEL.6) is strictly stronger than the axiom of privileged access (BEL.4) by exhibiting a possible-worlds structure in which the axiom of privileged access holds but the axiom of arrogance does not. (Hint: All you need are two worlds and one atomic formula.)

7. Given that Sacramento is the capital of California and that Sarah knows what the capital of California is, show that Sarah knows that Sacramento is the capital of California (a) in a possible-worlds theory; and (b) in a syntactic theory.

8. * Represent the statement "Archie knows exactly what the states of the U.S. are" in a formal sentence ϕ. Given ϕ and the fact "state(alabama,us)," it should be possible to infer that Archie knows that Alabama is a state; given ϕ and the fact "¬state(guam,us)," it should be possible to infer that Archie knows that Guam is not a state. ϕ should not contain the names of all 50 states. (Hint: Use set theory.)

Chapter 9

Plans and Goals

Groucho: You say you're going to go to everyone in this house and ask them if they took the painting. Suppose nobody in the house took the painting.

Chico: Go to the house next door.

Groucho: That's great. Suppose there isn't any house next door.

Chico: Well, then, of course, we got to build one.

Animal Crackers

At the bottom line, knowledge and reasoning are valuable insofar as they enable a creature to accomplish its goals through appropriate action. Finding such appropriate actions in a complex world often requires forethought; the creature must think through a course of action before executing it. Carrying out such forethought effectively under a range of circumstances requires the ability to represent and reasoning about one's plans and goals explicitly. Similarly, understanding or predicting the behavior of another intelligent creature requires reasoning about its plans and goals.[1] Accordingly, *plan construction*, the task of finding a plan to accomplish a goal, has been the most extensively studied application of commonsense reasoning. *Motivation analysis*, the task of inferring an agent's goals and plans from his actions, has also been much studied as a major component of understanding narrative text.

---

[1] These statements may seem to be truisms, but they have been debated. The behaviorists [Skinner 1971], of course, rejected them entirely. More recently, Agre and Chapman [1987] have argued that intelligent behavior consists largely of "situated activity," actions performed in direct response to situations, with little long-term planning.

Humans deal with many different types of plans and goals, and they reason about them in many different ways. The following examples illustrate some of these issues that a complete theory of plans and goals must address:

1. It is raining outside, and you have to bring a book home from the library without getting it wet. Infer that you can do this by carrying the book inside a plastic bag. This is a problem of plan construction. The goal is a conjunction of the physical state, "The book is at home," with the physical constraint, "At no time is the book wet." The plan is a description of a physical action. Note that an efficient planner will not plan the route home step by step; it will use general knowledge that it will be able to get home on foot while keeping the book protected.

2. Elly tells you that she is planning to travel to Bosnia via Herzogovinia. You know that the two countries went to war this morning and that there is no way of getting into Bosnia. Infer (a) that Elly does not know about the war; and (b) that Elly will have to drop or postpone her goal of going to Bosnia.

3. Joe is at his workshop. He has to build a desk, but his only record of the dimensions is at home. His customers, who are the only people who know the dimensions, are out of town. Infer that Joe will have to go home to get the dimensions. The problem here is to infer the actions of an agent from his goals. It is similar to plan construction, but, while the problem in plan construction is to find some plan satisfying the goal, here the problem is to characterize all plans that satisfy the goal. (All such plans involve going home.) The constraint here arises because of an informational requirement of a plan. In order to build the desk properly, he must know the desired dimensions.

4. The only thing that you know how to cook is oatmeal, and it is getting monotonous. Infer that one possible plan is to buy yourself a cookbook and learn some recipes. This is a plan-construction task. The goal has a complex structure: to satisfy your hunger at regular intervals in the future, subject to the constraint that the types of food vary sufficiently. To carry this out, it is necessary to know many different ways of preparing food. This requirement can be satisfied by using a cookbook.

5. Ed is driving at a leisurely pace up a one-lane highway. Matilda drives up close behind him and honks. Ed pulls over to the shoulder. Infer that Ed has inferred that Matilda is in a hurry and wants to pass, and that he has courteously cooperated. This is a problem

of motivation analysis: Given an agent's actions, infer his motives. Note that this problem involves reasoning about communication and cooperation between agents.

6. On a dark night, your horse refuses to cross a familiar bridge. Infer that the horse may sense that there is something wrong with the bridge. Here we are inferring something about the mental state of an agent in order to connect its actions with its goals. The goal-plan structure here has some particular points of interest. The underlying goal is one of preventing, or at least postponing, a state (death) rather than achieving one. The plan inferred consists of not doing an action rather than doing it. The plan is adopted in response to a particular circumstance (the bridge being washed out) rather than generated when the goal is adopted.

Most of the work on planning in AI has focused on problems of search, particularly the problem of finding a successful plan given a starting state and a goal. This search problem has generally been studied in the context of rather simple ontologies for plans, in order to concentrate on the search problems. By contrast, we will focus in this chapter on the ontological and representational issues that arise in reasoning about plans and goals.

9.1 Plans as Sequences of Primitive Actions

Many AI planners operate under the following assumptions:

1. The situation calculus model of time as a branching, discrete structure is appropriate. That is, only one primitive event occurs at a time, and the states of the world in the middle of events are unimportant.

2. There is only one agent, and the only events are his actions.

3. A goal is a desired state of the world.

4. All relevant aspects of the world are known to the planner from the start.

Under these circumstances, the execution of a plan will consist of the performance of a sequence of primitive actions. A plan is a complex event type. A *complete* plan description specifies a sequence of particular primitive actions; a *partial* plan description is a set of constraints on sequences of actions. A planning program is given a goal and a description of a starting situation; its task is to find a sequence of actions that will be feasible in the starting situation and will terminate in a situation satisfying the goal.

Figure 9.1 illustrates three plans that accomplish the goal "Send Mr. Jones his bill." In plan A the sequence of actions is fully determined. In plan B the order is underdetermined; the printing of the bill can come before or after the printing of the address label, the sticking of the address label, or the stamping of the envelope. In plan C both the order of the actions and the binding of certain variables is underdetermined. A is a complete plan description; B and C are partial plans. B and C can be converted to complete plans by finding some total ordering obeying the partial ordering and some binding of the variables satisfying the restrictions.

There are two significant advantages to using partial plans. First, it may be worthwhile to leave certain decisions until execution time, since the best choice may be determined by minor considerations that do not arise until execution. For example, there is probably no point in deciding in advance which envelope or which label to use; one may as well just let the agent pick up the most convenient one. Second, in forming the plan, it is often easier to control a search through the space of partial plans than through a space of complete plans. By looking at partial plans, one can concentrate on constraints on the plan that are known to hold, thus avoiding arbitrary choices that are later found to be incorrect. Such a planner, which searches through a space of partial plans, is known as a "nonlinear" planner. We will present the details of one particular nonlinear planner in Section 9.2.

We introduce three fundamental predicates on plans and goals in this restricted model. A plan may be *feasible* in a given situation; it may *lead to* a given goal; and it may be a *valid* way to accomplish a given goal in a situation. These can be easily defined for complete plans using a branching temporal ontology. Plan P is feasible in situation S if P occurs in some interval starting in S. P leads to G if G is true following any execution of P. P is a valid plan to accomplish G in S if P is feasible and P leads to G.

PL.1. $\text{true\_in}(S,\text{feasible}(P)) \Leftrightarrow \exists_{S2} \text{ occurs}([S,S2],P)$.

PL.2. $\text{true\_in}(S,\text{leads\_to}(P,G)) \Leftrightarrow$
$[\ \forall_{S2} \text{ occurs}([S,S2],P) \Rightarrow \text{true\_in}(S2,G)\ ]$.

PL.3. $\text{true\_in}(S,\text{valid}(P,G)) \Leftrightarrow$
$[\text{true\_in}(S,\text{feasible}(P)) \wedge \text{true\_in}(S,\text{leads\_to}(P,G))]$.

However, these definitions PL.1, PL.2, and PL.3 can lead to counterintuitive results when applied to partial plans. Consider, for example, the partial plan shown in Figure 9.2, consisting of two unordered

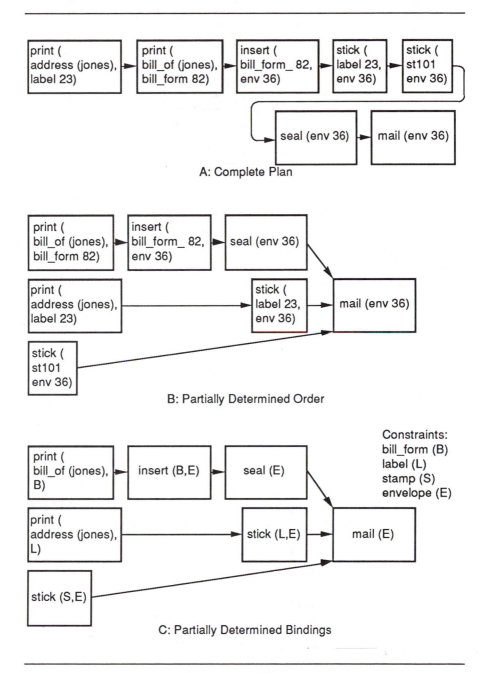

A: Complete Plan

B: Partially Determined Order

C: Partially Determined Bindings

Figure 9.1 Partially determined bindings

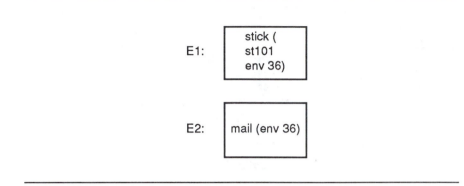

E1:

stick (
st101
env 36)

E2:

mail (env 36)

Figure 9.2 Invalid partial plan

events: ($E1$) Put stamp ST101 on envelope ENV36; ($E2$) Mail envelope ENV36. We would like to say that this is not a valid plan for the
goal of having the envelope posted because if $E2$ is executed first, then
there is no way to execute $E1$. However, it does satisfy our definition
of validity; it can occur in the starting situation, and, if it does occur,
then the goal is satisfied. In fact, if we view plans as event types and
event types as sets of intervals, then this plan is exactly equivalent to
the plan "First put the stamp on; then mail the envelope," since there
are no intervals in which the reverse order occurs. In other words, axiom PL1 characterizes whether it is possible that events corresponding
to the plan occur. With partial plans, this is not a sufficient condition
to establish that the plan is feasible.

The simplest way around this difficulty is to change the way in
which the causal theory treats impossible events. Rather than say
that an event cannot occur if its preconditions are unsatisfied, we will
say that if it does occur, it results in a distinguished impossible state,
which we will call "twilight_zone." The following changes must be
made to the causal theory to accommodate this approach:

- Replace each precondition axiom, "Event E can only occur if its
  preconditions are satisfied," with the weaker axiom "If E occurs
  and its preconditions are unsatisfied, then E leads to the twilight
  zone." For example, in the blocks-world axioms of Table 5.2, we
  would replace axiom BW13 by the new axiom

    [occurs(I,pickup) $\land$ ¬true_in(end(I),twilight_zone)] $\Rightarrow$
    [true_in(start(I),clear(hand)) $\land$
    $\exists_X$ true_in(start(I),under_hand(X))].

- For each causal axiom governing event type E, add the preconditions of E and the statement that the start state is not the twilight zone to the antecedents of the axiom, and add the statement that the final situation is not the twilight zone to its consequences. For example, axiom BW15 would be changed to

$$[\text{occurs}(I,\text{pickup}) \land \text{true\_in}(\text{start}(I),\text{clear}(\text{hand})) \land$$
$$\text{true\_in}(\text{start}(I),\text{under\_hand}(X)) \land$$
$$\neg\text{true\_in}(\text{start}(I),\text{twilight\_zone})] \Rightarrow$$
$$[\text{true\_in}(\text{end}(I),\text{beneath}(\text{hand},X)) \land$$
$$\neg\text{true\_in}(\text{end}(I),\text{twilight\_zone})].$$

- Add the rule that one cannot escape the twilight zone.

$$\text{true\_in}(\text{start}(I),\text{twilight\_zone}) \Rightarrow \text{true\_in}(\text{end}(I),\text{twilight\_zone}).$$

- Add the rule that the twilight zone cannot really come about.

$$S \in \text{real\_chronicle} \Rightarrow \neg\text{true\_in}(S,\text{twilight\_zone}).$$

We can now modify our definition of feasibility to apply to partial plans in a more reasonable way: A plan is feasible if it does not lead to the twilight zone. (Note: For certain powerful representations of partial plans, this definition leads to counter-intuitive results.)

PL1.a. $\text{true\_in}(S,\text{feasible}(P)) \Leftrightarrow$
$$[\forall_{S2} \text{ occurs}([S,S2],P) \Rightarrow \neg\text{true\_in}(S2,\text{twilight\_zone})].$$

A complete plan can be verified by chaining forward in time, step by step. Beginning with the starting situation S, for each action of the plan in turn, verify that the preconditions of the action are satisfied in the situation where the action is to be done, and use the causal theory to predict the situation that will follow the action. When the effects of the last action have been computed, verify that the goal holds in the final situation.

Reasoning about partial plans can be more difficult. This is the subject of the next section.

9.1.1 TWEAK—a Nonlinear Planner

David Chapman's TWEAK program [1987] is a nonlinear planner. It is simple and somewhat limited in scope, but its construction is exceptionally clean and well analyzed. We present it here as an example of the use of nonlinear representations for plans in plan construction.

TWEAK uses a representation of action slightly modified from the STRIPS representation (see Section 5.7). A state type is represented either in the form $p(c_1 \ldots c_k)$ or in the form $\sim p(c_1 \ldots c_k)$, where p is a state function, $c_1 \ldots c_k$ are constants, and $\sim$ represents state negation. The only state-coherence axiom is that $p(c_1 \ldots c_k)$ and $\sim p(c_1 \ldots c_k)$ cannot hold simultaneously. The causal structure of an event type is defined by its effects and its preconditions, each of which is a set of state types. For example, the event type "puton(a,b,c)" (Put a onto b from c) would have effects { clear(c), on(a,b), ~clear(b) ~on(a,c)} and preconditions { clear(a), clear(b), on(a,c) }. An event template is like an event except that free variables may be used instead of constants. An event template may also contain constraints stating that two variables are unequal. For example, the event template "puton(X, Y, Z)" is defined to have effects { clear(Z), on(X, Y), ~clear(Y), ~on(X, Z) }, preconditions { clear(X), on(X, Z), clear(Y) }, and constraints { $X \neq Y$, $Z \neq Y$, $X \neq Z$ }.

The definition of the event template corresponds to a causal axiom that, if the preconditions and constraints hold in the starting situation, and the event takes place, then the effects will hold in the final situation. Also implicit is a frame axiom, stating that any state not on the effects list is not changed by the action. For example, the above definition of the event type "puton(X, Y, Z)" corresponds to the axioms

$$\forall_{S,S1,X,Y,Z} \; [\; \text{true\_in}(S,\text{clear}(X)) \land \text{true\_in}(S,\text{on}(X, Z)) \land$$
$$\text{true\_in}(S,\text{clear}(Y)) \land$$
$$X \neq Y \land Z \neq Y \land X \neq Z \land$$
$$S1 = \text{result}(S,\text{puton}(X, Y, Z)) \;] \Rightarrow$$
$$[\text{true\_in}(S1,\text{clear}(Z)) \land \text{true\_in}(S1,\text{on}(X, Y)) \land$$
$$\neg\text{true\_in}(S1,\text{clear}(Y)) \land \neg\text{true\_in}(S1,\text{on}(X, Z))].$$

$$\forall_{S,X,Y,Z,A} \; [\; \neg\text{true\_in}(S, A) \land$$
$$\text{true\_in}(\text{result}(S,\text{puton}(X, Y, Z)), A)] \Rightarrow$$
$$[A = \text{clear}(Z) \lor A = \text{on}(X, Y) \lor A = \text{~clear}(Y) \;].$$

(In the second formula above, the variable A ranges over primitive state types and their negations.)

A trace of a plan is a linear sequence of variable-free events. Let AA_i be the set of states that hold at the start of event E_i; let EE_i be the set of effects of E_i, and let $\sim EE_i$ be the set of negations of states in EE_i. Then AA_{i+1}, the set of states that hold at the end of E_i, may be computed as $AA_{i+1} = (AA_i \cup EE_i) - \sim EE_i$. For uniformity of description, we treat the starting situation of a planning problem as the effects of an initial event *START* with no preconditions, and treat the goal as the preconditions of a final event *GOAL* with no effects. A trace is feasible if every precondition of each event E_i is satisfied at its start; that is, each precondition of E_i is an element of AA_i.

A plan in TWEAK consists of a collection of partially or fully instantiated event templates, called *steps*. The plan structures the steps in a partial temporal ordering and records constraints on the bindings of the variables in the steps (Figure 9.3). A variable can be constrained to be equal or to be unequal to another variable or to a constant. Constants with distinct names are assumed to be unequal.

A plan subsumes a trace if the events in the trace correspond to the templates in the plan for some linear ordering consistent with the partial ordering of the plan and for some binding of variables consistent with the constraints in the plan. A plan is consistent if it subsumes at least one trace. (The ordering constraints must constitute a partial ordering, and the binding constraints must be consistent.) A plan is feasible if every trace subsumed by the plan is feasible. Given a consistent plan, it is possible to find a trace that it subsumes by finding bindings for the variables that satisfy the constraints, and by doing a topological sort on the steps. (We assume that all variables range over an infinite set of possible values. If so, it is trivial to satisfy the binding constraints, using a greedy algorithm. If variable bindings are restricted to a finite set, then the problem of satisfying the bindings becomes NP-complete, and the conditions for the correctness of the plan, below, are no longer necessary and sufficient.)

The central question in evaluating TWEAK plans, then, is what is needed to guarantee that a given precondition of an event is satisfied at its starting situation. In order to answer this, we introduce some additional technical terms. A step $E1$ *achieves* a state A under a binding if some effect of $E1$ is equal with A under the binding. $E1$ *necessarily* achieves A if it achieves A under all bindings consistent with the constraints. $E1$ *possibly* achieves A if it achieves A under some binding consistent with the constraints. A step $E1$ necessarily *establishes* a precondition A of step E if $E1$ necessarily achieves A, and $E1$ is constrained to occur before E. $E1$ possibly establishes a precondition A of step E if $E1$ possibly achieves A, and $E1$ is allowed to occur before E. A step $E1$ (necessarily / possibly) *clobbers* precondition A of step E if $E1$ (must / may) occur before E and $E1$ (necessarily / possibly) achieves the negation of A.

Chapman shows in his analysis that the following conditions are necessary and sufficient to guarantee that a precondition A of step E will be satisfied:

Effects are shown under the event.
Preconditions are shown above the event.

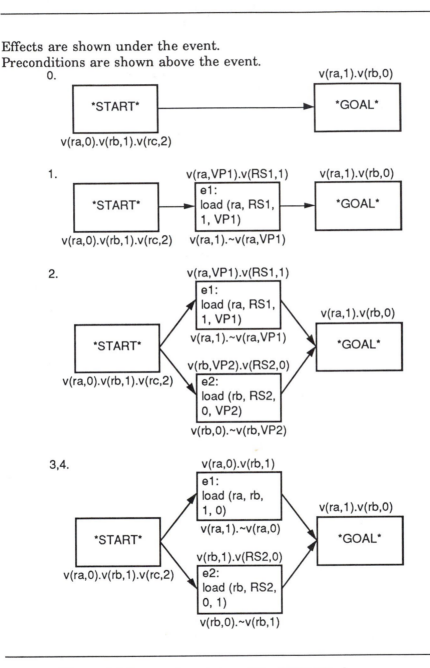

Figure 9.3 Successive states of the TWEAK planner

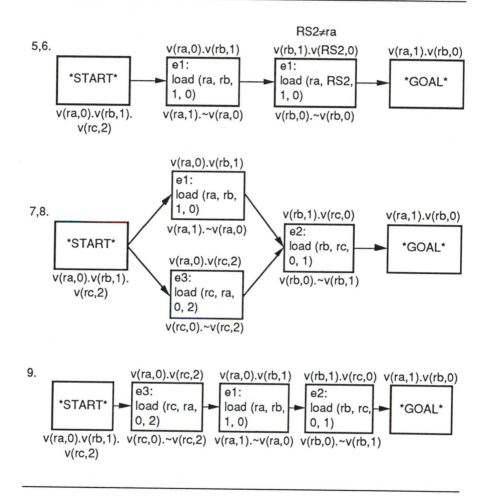

Figure 9.3 Successive states of the TWEAK planner (Continued)

Precondition A of step E is satisfied in all traces of the plan iff:
i.) There exists a step $E1$ that necessarily establishes A.
ii.) For each step C that possibly clobbers A, there exists a step W (called a *white knight*) that comes between C and E such that, for any allowable binding, if C achieves $\sim A$, then W achieves A.

Using this condition, Chapman presents the following algorithm for constructing TWEAK plans:

Algorithm 9.1: TWEAK Algorithm

Input: The effects of step *START* and the preconditions of step *GOAL*. *START* is constrained to precede *GOAL*.

Output: A feasible TWEAK plan including *START* and *GOAL*.

repeat until no changes occur in an iteration
    for each step E do
        for each precondition A of E do
            begin (1) if A is not established then either
                (1.a) Find some step $E1$ in the plan that possibly
                      establishes A. Add temporal constraints so that
                      $E1$ precedes E and binding constraints so that
                      $E1$ necessarily achieves A; or
                (1.b) Find an event template $E1$ that possibly achieves A.
                      Add $E1$ to the plan, constrained to precede E,
                      with bindings constrained so that $E1$ achieves A;
            (2) for each possible clobberer C of A do either
                (2.a) constrain C to follow E; or
                (2.b) Add binding constraints so that C does not
                      achieve $\sim A$; or
                (2.c) Find a step W in the plan that possibly achieves A.
                      Constrain W to come between C and E.
                      Add binding constraints so that W achieves A
                      for every binding under which C achieves $\sim A$; or
                (2.d) Find an event template W that possibly achieves A.
                      Constrain W to come between C and E.
                      Add binding constraints so that W achieves A
                      for every binding under which C achieves $\sim A$.

Chapman gives the following names to the various plan operators:

1.a: Simple establishment
1.b: Step addition
2.a: Promotion
2.b: Separation of variables
2.c: White knight insertion
2.d: White knight addition

For each precondition of every step, either (1.a) or (1.b) must be performed, if it is not established, and either (2.a), (2.b), (2.c), or (2.d) must be accomplished for each of its clobberers, if any. The choice between different possible modifications is performed nondeterministically, either by backtracking or by parallel search. (In Chapman's implementation, it was performed using breadth-first search with data-dependency maintenance, so as to achieve completeness and efficiency.) It can be shown that this algorithm is complete. That is, given any feasible trace T with no pointless steps — i.e., where every step satisfies some precondition of a later step — there is a plan subsuming T that the above algorithm will find for some choice of modification operators.

In general, there may be several ways of carrying out the operation "Add binding constraints so that W achieves A for every binding under which C achieves $\sim A$" in (2.c) and (2.d). For example, suppose that A is the state p(a), that C achieves $\sim$p(X), and that W achieves p(Z). The condition can be achieved either by adding a constraint that $Z =$a or by adding a constraint that $X = Z$. (It can also be achieved by adding a constraint that $X \neq$a, but that case reduces to separation of variables; the white knight is unnecessary.)

For example, consider register swapping, a problem that is beyond the capacity of the STRIPS planning system. The primitive states in this system have the form "value(R, V)", meaning that register R has value V. The events have the form "load(RD, RS, VN, VP)", the action of loading new value VN from source register RS to destination register RD, overwriting the previous value VP in RD. The preconditions of the event "load(RD, RS, VN, VP)" are { value(RS, VN), value(RD, VP) }. The effects of the event are { value(RD, VN), $\sim$value (RD, VP) }. There are constraints $RS \neq RD$, $VP \neq VN$. Let *START* have the effects { value(ra,0), value(rb,1), value(rc,2) } and let *GOAL* have the preconditions { value(ra,1), value(rb,0) }. Table 9.1 shows one series of operations that brings TWEAK to success (Figure 9.3).

Note that the only links between components of this plan are binding constraints between variables and precedence relations between steps. In particular, the concept of one state being a *subgoal* of another plays no significant part in this view of planning.

Table 9.1 Register Swapping in TWEAK

1. To achieve the precondition value(ra,1) of *GOAL*, add the step e1=load(ra,$RS1$,1,$VP1$) between *START* and *GOAL*. (Step addition)

2. To achieve the precondition value(rb,0) of *GOAL*, add the step e2=load(rb,$RS2$,0,$VP2$) between *START* and *GOAL*. (Step addition)

3. To achieve the preconditions value($RS1$,1) and value(ra,$VP1$) of e1, use the effects of *START* by binding $RS1$ to rb and $VP1$ to 0. (Simple establishment)

4. To achieve the precondition value(rb,$VP2$) of e2, use the effects of *START* by binding $VP2$ to 1. (Simple establishment)

5. The effect ~value(rb,1) of e2 is now a potential clobberer of precondition value(rb,1) of e1. Therefore, promote e2 to come after e1. (Promotion)

6. The effect ~value(ra,0) of e1 now potentially clobbers the precondition value($RS2$,0) of e2. Therefore, impose the constraint $RS2 \neq$ra.

7. To establish the precondition value($RS2$,0) of e2, add the step e3=load($RS2$,$RS3$,0,$VP3$) before e2. (Step addition)

8. To achieve the preconditions value($RS2$,$VP3$) and value($RS3$,0) of e3, use the effects of *START* with the bindings $RS2$=rc,$VP3$=2, $RS3$=ra. (Simple establishment)

9. The effect ~value(ra,0) of e1 now potentially clobbers the precondition value(ra,0) of e3. Therefore, promote e1 to come after e3. (Promotion)

The plan is now complete. It contains the three actions, load(rc,ra,0,2), load(ra,rb,1,0), load(rb,rc,0,1), in sequence.

9.2 Extensions

We now consider a number of simple extensions to the theory developed so far. These extensions involve only fairly straightforward changes to the ontology, the representation, or the axiomatics of planning, but they may make the search problem very much more difficult.

Goals of maximizing an objective: Many natural goals, such as "Build a tower as high as possible" or "Make as much money as possible," have no fixed criterion of success, but can be achieved to greater and lesser degree. Such a goal may be represented by a fluent rather than a state. A plan achieves a goal to degree D if the goal has value D when the plan is complete. We replace the Boolean state "valid(P, G)" with the fluent "success(P, G)". Formally, P is guaranteed to succeed to degree D in goal G in situation S if D is the minimum value of G after P occurs starting in S. We replace axiom PL2 above by the new rule:

PL2A. value_in$(S,\text{success}(P, G)) \geq D \Leftrightarrow$
[true_in$(S,\text{feasible}(P)) \wedge$
$\forall_I\ S=\text{start}(I) \wedge \text{occurs}(I, P) \Rightarrow \text{value\_in}(\text{end}(I), G) \geq D$].

Many complex goals can be handled in this format, by encoding the entire goal in a single complex fluent. For example, the goal "Bring all the blocks to $L1$ as quickly as possible" can be expressed as maximizing a fluent whose value is $-\infty$ if the blocks are not all at $L1$, and $-$clocktime if the blocks are all at $L1$.

Interaction with external events: Events other than the agent's own actions may be relevant to the achievement of the goal. These external events may either aid or hinder the agent. Consider, for example, the following plan for preparing tea:

Fill the kettle with water;
Put the kettle on the stove;
Turn on the burner;
Get the tea cup from the shelf;
Put the tea bag in the cup;
Turn off the burner;
Put on a kitchen glove;
Pour the water from the kettle into the tea cup.

The success of this plan depends on the event of the water becoming hot while it is on the stove. The need to put on a glove before pouring the water is due to the event of the kettle becoming hot. Representing such plans requires a model in which external events can occur.

Once external events are admitted, it becomes important for an agent to distinguish his own actions, which are dependent on his will, from other events, which are not. A plan can contain only the agent's own actions; these may give rise to other significant events, such as the water becoming hot in the above example. (Multiagent plans will be discussed in Section 10.2.) We introduce the function "actor_of(E)" mapping an event E onto the agent, if any, who performs E. The actions of agent A are often represented in the form "do(A, ACT)," where ACT is an action type. For example, the term "do(linda,puton(kettle1,stove8))" would be the event of Linda putting the kettle on the stove. We have the general axiom "actor_of(do(A, ACT)) = A".

An integral part of such plans is waiting for external events to bring about a desired result. We introduce three waiting actions: "wait_until(Q)," the action of waiting until state Q becomes true; "wait_while(E)," the action of waiting while event E takes place; and "wait(T)," the action of waiting for a time duration of length T. These may be defined as follows:

occurs(I,do(A,wait_until(Q))) $\Leftrightarrow$
[$\forall_{S \in I}$ true_in(S, Q) $\Leftrightarrow$ S=end(I)].

occurs(I,do(A,wait_while(E))) $\Leftrightarrow$
$\exists_{I1}$ end($I1$)=end(I) $\wedge$ occurs($I1, E$).

occurs(I,do(A,wait(T))) $\Leftrightarrow$
value_in(end(I),clock_time) $-$ value_in(start(I),clock_time) = T.

These axioms do not by themselves specify that the actor do anything or abstain from doing anything while he is waiting. Therefore, to reason deductively about the effect of a plan containing a "wait" action, it will generally be necessary to add axioms that assert that the only actions executed by the agent concurrently with a "wait" are those specified as concurrent in the plan. (See Section 5.11 for a discussion of how this is done.)

Goals over chronicles: Some natural goals, such as "Eat a turkey dinner," "Travel by boat to the Orient," or "Talk to everyone at the party," are not states or fluents that hold in a single final situation, but, rather are characteristics of a whole chronicle or interval. Such goals can be viewed as complex event types. We assert that goal G is accomplished in interval I in the formula "occurs(I, G)." Therefore, a plan P is valid for goal G in situation S if P is feasible in S and, for each interval I starting in S in which P occurs, there is an interval $I1$ with the same ending time as I in which G occurs.

P2B. true_in(S,valid(P, G)) $\Leftrightarrow$
[true_in(S,feasible(P)) $\wedge$
$\forall_I$ [start(I) = S $\wedge$ occurs(I, P)] $\Rightarrow$
$\exists_{I1}$ [end($I1$)=end(I) $\wedge$ occurs($I1, G$)].

A planner that reduces a goal involving complex events to a plan consisting of primitive events is known as a *task-reduction* planner. Such a planner constructs plans by combining task-reduction rules — rules stating how one action can be carried out in terms of other actions — with the techniques discussed in Section 9.1 for achieving precondition states. For example, the task "Give A a medical checkup" can be reduced to the conjunction of the tasks "Check A's temperature," "Check A's blood pressure," "Check A's weight," with no particular temporal ordering (Table 9.2). Each of these subtasks can be further reduced; for example "Check A's temperature" can be reduced to the sequence of steps "Sequence: (1) Place thermometer in A's mouth; (2) Wait three minutes; (3) Remove thermometer from mouth; and (4) Read temperature from thermometer." These substeps have preconditions and effects that the planner must reason about in the same way as the state-achievement planners discussed in Sections 9.1 and 9.2. For example, the step "Place thermometer in A's mouth" has preconditions that both the thermometer and A are available. It has the effect that A's mouth is occupied by a thermometer. The planner must be able to reason that it is not possible to have the patient drink or speak in between steps (1) and (3) of the temperature taking.

The operation of task reduction starts with relatively abstract descriptions of tasks and gradually makes the descriptions more concrete, ending with primitive robotic operations. However, the planner cannot as a whole consistently move down through levels of abstractions because achieving a precondition to a concrete goal may involve much planning at more abstract levels. Consider, for example, the planning involved in achieving the concrete goal "Walk on the moon" or, often, in achieving the goal "Make love to X."

Note that once planning is complete execution can proceed using only the primitive operations at the bottom level of the reduction; no reference to the higher-level tasks is needed. The task-reduction structure is now needed only in case of something unexpected occurring, which requires replanning. (See Section 9.3.3.)

Goals of prevention: In a world with external events, many of the most important goals are those of preserving a state rather than achieving it, or, more generally, of preventing a harmful state or event. The archetype of such goals is the goal of avoiding death or destruction (strictly speaking, this goal is one of postponement rather than of pre-

Table 9.2 Task-Reduction Axioms

Define the predicate "occurs_in(I, E)" (E occurs some time during I) by the axiom

$$\text{occurs\_in}(I, E) \Leftrightarrow \exists_{I1 \subset I} \text{ occurs}(I1, E).$$

occurs_in(I,checkup(A)) ⇔
[occurs_in(I,temperature_check(A)) ∧
  occurs_in(I,blood_pressure_check(A)) ∧
  occurs_in(I,weight_check(A))].

occurs(I,temperature_check(A)) ⇔
$\exists_{TH}$ thermometer(TH) ∧
    occurs(I,sequence(insert(TH,mouth(A)),
                  wait(3 · minute),
                  remove(TH,mouth(A)),
                  read_temperature(TH))).

---

vention). Formally, these are a type of goal over chronicles; however, it is worthwhile to consider them independently on account of their frequency and importance. Some of these goals, such as "Stay alive," are always present, and plans are constructed to guarantee them whenever it seems that they will be jeopardized by the expected course of events. Others, such as "Avoid going to sleep (during a lecture)" are temporally limited; they arise in response to certain circumstances, and may disappear after time. The axioms that govern these goals are, on the whole, more concerned to describe the circumstances that threaten the goals and the actions that remove these threats, rather than the actions that achieve the goals and their preconditions.

Resource and timing constraints: Plans must often be carried out within constraints on resources and time. For example, carrying out a building project might involve constraints such as "The cost for supplies must not exceed $700," "At any instant, the total electric power used by active machines must not exceed 1250 watts," "It is necessary to wait a day between applying coats of paint to an object," "Power tools can only be used in the daytime," and so on. Formally, these can all be expressed as properties of the chronicle involved so that these constraints can all be incorporated as part of a goal over a chronicle. Computationally, even very simple constraints of this kind tend to make the difficulties of finding a satisfactory plan much greater. Techniques for dealing with such constraints have been studied within operations research; the problem of incorporating these techniques into AI planners is a subject of current research.

Repeated goals: If it is expected that a goal, or a collection of similar goals, will often be repeated in the future, it may be worthwhile performing a relatively expensive operation that simplifies the performance of all the goals together. For example, an agent who knows that he will have to travel 30 miles every day may decide to invest in a car. Such planning is known as *goal subsumption* [Wilensky 1978].

Concurrent actions: If an agent is capable of performing more than one action at once, then he should be able to take advantage of this capacity in his plans. However, unless the actions are physically quite independent, it is not, in general, possible to predict either the feasibility or the effects of performing two actions together from knowing their properties singly. Rather, a rich physical model must be used that describes the interactions of the two activities. Little work has been done on such models.

9.3 Plans and Goals as Mental States

In the previous section we considered plans and goals purely as abstract physical constructs. Such a view is appropriate as a model for a single agent who is given a single goal from on high, and who must find a plan to accomplish his goal using just the information in his knowledge base. To go beyond this limited scenario, we must view plans and goals as mental constructs: aspects of an agent's mental state. Such a view will allow an intelligent creature to represent facts about the plans and goals of other creatures, and about his own plans and goals at different times. Such representations are needed to express theories that address questions like the following:

- How are beliefs and knowledge related to plans and goals? In particular, what information is required in order to carry out a specified plan?

- What is the life cycle of a goal or a plan? How are goals and plans adopted, maintained, achieved, modified, or abandoned?

- What goals are characteristic of humans?

The first problem in formalizing plans and goals as mental states is that, like knowledge and belief, having a plan P or a goal G is not an extensional operator. In particular, the goal and plan operators are referentially opaque. Consider the following three sentences:

1. Oedipus has the goal of killing the traveler who is attacking him.

2. The traveler attacking Oedipus is his father.

3. Oedipus does not have the goal of killing his own father.

It is possible for all three statements to be true, as long as Oedipus does not know that the traveler is his father.

We will get around these problems by treating goals and plans as operators over quoted strings. We introduce three primitives. The predicate "goal(A, G, S)" means that, in situation S, agent A has the goal denoted by the quoted string G. The predicate "plan(A, P, S)" means that in situation S, A plans to carry out plan P. The function "deliberate(A, E)" denotes the event of agent A carrying out the action described by string E deliberately. (Like "plan" and "goal", "deliberate" is an opaque operator. Oedipus deliberately killed the stranger but did not deliberately kill his own father, even though the two were the same.) Thus, the statement that, in situation s0, Oedipus had the goal of being king of Thebes is represented

    goal(oedipus,≺eql(oedipus,king_of(thebes))≻,s0)

The statement that Oedipus had the goal of knowing who killed Laius is represented

goal(oedipus,
    ≺{ S | $\exists_X$ know(oedipus, ≺$\exists_I$ end(I) < s0 ∧
                          occur(I,kill(@X@,laius))≻, S)
               }≻,
    s0).

(Note: The @ signs around X in the above formula are scoped to the inner set of string delimiters.)

The statement that Oedipus deliberately married Jocasta is represented as

    occur(i0,deliberate(oedipus,≺do(oedipus,marry(jocasta))≻)).

An alternative solution to the problem of referential opacity is to treat a goal as a state ranging over possible worlds, and to treat a plan or a deliberate action as an event type ranging over possible chronicles. Thus, the statements "Oedipus deliberately married Jocasta," "Oedipus did not deliberately marry his mother," and "Jocasta was Oedipus' mother," are represented

$\exists_I$ occur(I,deliberate(oedipus,do(oedipus,marry(jocasta)))).
$\neg\exists_I$ occur(I,deliberate(oedipus,do(oedipus,

marry(mother_of(oedipus)))))).
jocasta = value_in(w0, mother_of(oedipus)).

These three statements are mutually consistent because the "mother_of" function is made dependent on the possible world; Jocasta is Oedipus' mother in this world, but not in every possible world.

These primitives, together with the primitives of knowledge and belief, are the basic concepts in the theory of plans and goals as mental states. We will develop this theory in four parts. The first part describes what an agent knows or believes about his own plans and goals. The second describes what an agent needs to know in order to carry out his plans. The third describes how an agent gains, carries out, and abandons goals and plans. The last part of the theory describes what goals a human agent is likely to have.

9.3.1 Knowledge of Plans and Goals

A number of plausible axioms governing an agent's knowledge of his own plans and goals may be proposed:

KPG.1. Positive introspection: If A has a plan or a goal then he knows about it. If A performs a deliberate action, then he knows that he has done it when it is complete.
  (a) goal(A, G, S) $\Rightarrow$ know($A,\prec$goal(@A@, !G!, @S@)$\succ$,S)
  (b) plan(A, P, S) $\Rightarrow$ know($A,\prec$plan(@A@, !P!, @S@)$\succ$,S)
  (c) occur(I,deliberate(A, E)) $\Rightarrow$
      know($A,\prec$occur(@I@, deliberate(@A@, !E!))$\succ$,end(I)).

KPG.2. Negative introspection: If A does not have a plan or a goal then he knows that he doesn't. If A does not perform a deliberate action, then he knows that he has not performed the action deliberately.
  (a) $\neg$goal(A, G, S) $\Rightarrow$ know($A,\prec\neg$goal(@A@, !G!, @S@)$\succ$,S)
  (b) $\neg$plan(A, P, S) $\Rightarrow$ know($A,\prec\neg$plan(@A@, !P!, @S@)$\succ$,S)
  (c) $\neg$occur(I,deliberate(A, E)) $\Rightarrow$
      know($A,\prec\neg$occur(@I@, deliberate(@A@, !E!))$\succ$,end(I)).

KPG.3. A can deliberately perform only his own acts. (Of course, he can deliberately *trigger* other events, but only by performing an act of his own.)
      occur(I,deliberate(A, E)) $\Rightarrow$ A=actor_of(denotation(E)).

(Keep in mind that "deliberate" takes a string as argument, while "actor_of" takes an actual event as argument.)

KPG.4. The deliberate performance of an action is an occurrence of the action.

$$\text{token\_of}(K,\text{deliberate}(A, E)) \Rightarrow \text{token\_of}(K,\text{denotation}(E)).$$

KPG.5. If A plans to perform P, then he believes that he will deliberately perform P.

$$\text{plan}(A, P, S) \Rightarrow$$
$$\text{believe}(A,\prec\exists_I \text{ precede}(@S@,\text{start}(I)) \wedge$$
$$\text{occur}(I,\text{deliberate}(@A@, !P!)) \wedge$$
$$I \sqsubset \text{real\_chronicle}\succ,$$
$$S).$$

KPG.6. If A plans to perform P, then A believes that P will be a valid plan to accomplish one of his goals.

$$\text{plan}(A, P, S) \Rightarrow$$
$$\text{believe}(A, \prec\exists_{G,S1} \text{ precede}(@S@, S1) \wedge$$
$$\text{goal}(@A@, G, S1) \wedge$$
$$\text{true\_in}(S1,\text{valid}(@A@, \downarrow P\downarrow, G))\succ,$$
$$S).$$

KPG.7. Knowledge of the axioms: If ϕ is an instance of one of the axioms in this chapter, and P spells out ϕ, then "know(A, P, S)" is an axiom.

Axioms KPG.1 and KPG.2 state that an agent knows what are and are not his own goals, plans, and deliberate actions. These are plausible as long as we exclude unconscious goals from consideration. This exclusion is justifiable since robots presumably do not have two levels of goals, and the effect of humans' unconscious goals on their behavior and mental states is hard to characterize in any theory, let alone a formal one. See Section 10.3.3 for an example of a proof that uses KPG.2 on deliberate actions. Axioms KPG.3 and KPG.4, that an agent is the actor of his own deliberate actions and that the deliberate performance of an action is an occurrence of that action, are basic necessary properties of deliberate actions. Axiom KPG.5 states that an agent believes that he will deliberately execute his plans. The converse, that any deliberate action of the agent is part of some plan, likewise seems plausible, and is important for motivation analysis. However, it seems to be tricky to state this rule correctly; it would not be correct to say that if A performs E deliberately, then E is part of some plan P that A is performing deliberately, since A may end up not being able to execute later parts of P. Axiom KPG.6, that an agent only adopts plans that he believes to be valid for some future goal, is obviously an approximation. A more accurate statement would be that the agent believes that the plan has some reasonable chance of forwarding his goals as a whole; however, this would be difficult to represent. Note that we have added the agent A as an argument to the state function "valid." Similarly, we will add the agent A as an argument to "feasible." Axiom KPG.7, that an agent knows the axioms of plans and goals, allows us to infer that the agent can reason about plans and goals; it is analogous to axiom KNOW.4 from Chapter 8.

These axioms can be used to justify inferences like example 2.a in the chapter introduction, in which we infer that Elly believes that the border between two countries will be open from the fact that she is planning to do so. Table 9.3 shows a precise statement of the inference.

9.3.2 Knowledge Needed for Plan Execution

In many cases, an agent is initially ignorant of information that he needs to achieve a given goal, but he knows how to acquire the information. In that case, he may plan to acquire the necessary information and then to use that information in further steps of planning. For example, if Debby wants to read *Moby Dick* but does not know where her copy is on her bookshelf, then she can form the plan "Look through the bookcase; take the book from its place; read it." Here the purpose of the first step of looking though the shelf is to determine the place of the book, a datum needed for the second step of the plan, grasping the book.

A theory of such plans must address the following issues:

- What information is necessary to carry out a primitive action? This is known as the *knowledge-preconditions* problem for actions.[2]

- What information is necessary to carry out a complex plan? This is the knowledge-preconditions problem for plans.

- What actions of the agent provide him with information? This is the information-acquisition problem.

In this section we will discuss the knowledge-preconditions problems for actions and plans. We have considered information acquisition through perception in Section 8.7; we will discuss information acquisition through communication in Section 10.3.

It should be noted, at the outset, that the failure of a knowledge precondition has different consequences than a failure of a physical

---

[2] This term was introduced in [McCarthy and Hayes 1969]

Table 9.3 Inferring Beliefs from Plans

Given:

- In situation s0, Elly plans to cross the border from Bosnia to Herzogovinia.
  plan(elly,≺cross(elly,bosnia,herzogovinia)≻,s0).

- Elly believes that it is only possible to cross from X to Y if the borders are open.

$$\text{believe(elly, } \prec\forall_{S1,A,X,Y} \text{ true\_in}(S1,\text{feasible(cross}(A,X,Y))) \Rightarrow$$
$$\text{true\_in}(S1,\text{open(border}(X,Y)))\succ,\text{s0).}$$

Conclude:

- Elly believes that the border between Bosnia and Herzogovinia will be open at some future time.
  believe(elly,≺∃$_{S1}$ precede(s0,$S1$) ∧
  true_in($S1$, open(border(bosnia,herzogovinia)))≻,s0).

Proof: From axiom KPG.4, Elly believes that she will eventually cross from Bosnia to Herzogovinia deliberately. By axiom PL.1, this can only occur if crossing is feasible; and by axiom KPG.6, Elly knows that it can only occur if it is feasible. By hypothesis, Elly believes that the crossing is feasible only if the border is open. Using axioms KPG.7, KPG.3, and consequential closure on belief (BEL.1), it follows that Elly believes that, at the time when she crosses, the border will be open.

precondition, and the logical treatment must therefore take a different form. If a physical precondition to an event is not satisfied in a situation, then the event cannot occur. If the event is perceived to occur, then we can infer that the physical precondition was satisfied at the start. If the knowledge preconditions of an action are not satisfied, the action may still occur, though it cannot be deliberately performed. For instance, an agent who does not know which U.S. city is largest can nonetheless perform the action of going to the largest city, but he cannot deliberately go to the largest city. Thus, knowledge preconditions, like deliberate actions, are properties of action descriptions rather than the actions themselves.

We will use the predicate "kp_satisfied(A, P, S)," meaning that the knowledge preconditions for action or plan description P (a quoted string) are satisfied for agent A in situation S. An agent can perform an action deliberately only if its knowledge preconditions are satisfied.

KPS.1. occurs(I,deliberate(A, E)) $\Rightarrow$ kp_satisfied(A, E,start(I)).

Two general types of axiomatizations have been proposed for knowledge preconditions for primitive actions. The first is simply to enumerate the knowledge preconditions for each type of action description. We would express the statement "To move to a place described as P, one must know where the place is" in the form

kp_satisfied(A,$\prec$travel_to($\downarrow P \downarrow$)$\succ$,S) $\Leftrightarrow$ know_val(A, P, S).

The statement "To grasp the object denoted by string O, one must know where that object is located" can be expressed in the form

kp_satisfied(A,$\prec$grasp($\downarrow O \downarrow$)$\succ$,S) $\Leftrightarrow$
know_val(A, $\prec$value_in(@S@,place($\downarrow O \downarrow$))$\succ$, S).

A second solution is that an agent knows how to perform a primitive action E if E is "directly executable"; that is, E can be used as a direct call to a robotic control system. For example, if the agent can execute an action routine "tap(N)", to tap the ground N times, then the action "tap(14)" is directly executable, and the agent knows how to do it. An agent A knows how to perform an action description E that is not in the form of a direct robotic call if he knows that E can be carried out by doing $E1$, where $E1$ is directly executable. For example, A knows how to perform the action e1 = tap(cardinality({ S | planet(S) })) if he knows that e1 is carried out through the action "tap(9)," but not if he is unsure whether e1 is the action "tap(9)" or "tap(5)". In general, agent A knows how to perform a primitive action described as $\prec$f(t1 ...tk)$\succ$ if f is a primitive routine for A and A knows the value of t1 ...tk.[3]

KPS.2. kp_satisfied(A,$\prec \downarrow ACT \downarrow (\downarrow T1 \downarrow, \ldots \downarrow Tk \downarrow)\succ$,$S$) $\Leftrightarrow$
primitive_routine(ACT, A) $\wedge$
know_val($A, T1, S$) ... know_val(A, Tk, S).

Thus, we have reduced the problem of knowledge preconditions for action to the problem of knowing the values of terms. This solution

---

[3]This account follows [Morgenstern 1988]. The theory was originally proposed by Moore [1980] in the context of a possible-worlds theory of knowledge. In that context, an executable description of an action was considered to be a rigid designator for the action. The proposal in [McCarthy and Hayes 1969] pointed in a similar direction.

eliminates the need for many specialized knowledge precondition axioms: the knowledge preconditions can be derived directly from the syntactic form of the action description. It also provides an intuitive justification of the knowledge preconditions; they require just that the actor know precisely what action it is that he wants to do. The solution has its costs, however. First, knowing the value of a term is generally a less precise concept than knowing enough to perform an action; to a degree, we have reduced a relatively well-defined problem to a much vaguer one. Second, as we have seen in Section 5.2, the concept of a robotic primitive is not absolute. There are levels of descriptions of actions, and a primitive at one level may involve a number of steps, including the gathering of knowledge, at a lower level. This analysis of knowledge preconditions, therefore, must be considered as relative to a given level of robotic primitives. (The dependence of the representation on the level chosen for robotic primitives is an implicit issue throughout the analysis of planning, but it appears in a particular direct form here.)

Waiting actions require a separate definition. The knowledge precondition for "wait_until(A)" is that the robot knows that A will eventually hold and that he will know when it holds. The knowledge precondition for "wait_while(E)" is that the robot knows that E will eventually occur and that he will know when it ends. The action "wait(T)" is handled by axiom KPS.2; the knowledge precondition for "wait(T)" is that the value of T be known. (We assume that the robot has an internal clock.)

KPS.3. kp_satisfied(A,$\prec$do(A,wait_until($\downarrow Q \downarrow$))$\succ$, S) $\Leftrightarrow$
     know(A, $\prec \exists_I$ start(I)=@S@ $\wedge$
              occurs(I,do(A,wait_until($\downarrow Q \downarrow$))) $\wedge$
              $\forall_{S1 \in I}$know_fluent(A, !Q!, $S1$)$\succ$,
       S).

KPS.4. kp_satisfied(A,$\prec$do(A,wait_while($\downarrow E \downarrow$))$\succ$, S) $\Leftrightarrow$
     know(A, $\prec \exists_I$ start(I)=@S@ $\wedge$
         occurs(I,do(A,wait_while($\downarrow E \downarrow$))) $\wedge$
         $\forall_{S1 \in I}$ know_whether(A,
                   $\prec \exists_{I1}$ end($I1$)=@$S1$@ $\wedge$
                       occurs($I1$, $\downarrow\downarrow E \downarrow\downarrow$)$\succ$, S)$\succ$,
       S)

(Note: In the third line of KPS.4, the doubly imbedded antiquotes of @$S1$@ are scoped to the internal string delimiters. The double antiquotes of $\downarrow\downarrow E \downarrow\downarrow$ are scoped to the external string delimiter.)

We now define the knowledge preconditions for a complex plan, with sequence and conditional operations. (Knowledge preconditions for plans with loops can be defined analogously.) An agent will be able to carry out a physically feasible plan if the knowledge preconditions for each primitive action are satisfied at the time when he has to perform it and he knows the value of each conditional when he has to compute it. Therefore, the knowledge preconditions for the plan at its start are that the agent must know now that he will know the knowledge preconditions for each primitive action by the time he must take it, and that he will know the value of each conditional. For example, the knowledge preconditions for performing the sequence "sequence$(E1, E2)$" are satisfied in S if the knowledge preconditions of $E1$ are satisfied in S, and it is known in S that the knowledge preconditions of $E2$ will be satisfied after $E1$ has been executed.

KPS.5. kp_satisfied$(A, \prec\text{sequence}(\downarrow E1\downarrow, \downarrow E2\downarrow)\succ, S) \Leftrightarrow$
  [kp_satisfied$(A, E1, S) \land$
  know$(A, \prec \forall_{S2} \text{ occurs}([@S@, S2], \downarrow E1\downarrow) \Rightarrow$
            kp_satisfied$(@A@, \downarrow E2\downarrow, S2)\succ, S)$].

The knowledge preconditions for A performing the conditional action "cond$(P, E1, E2)$" are satisfied in situation S if the following conditions are satisfied: (i) A knows whether P is true or false in situation S; (ii) If P is true in S then the knowledge preconditions for $E1$ are satisfied; if P is false, then the knowledge preconditions for $E2$ are satisfied.

KPS.6. kp_satisfied$(A, \prec\text{cond}(\downarrow P\downarrow, \downarrow E1\downarrow, \downarrow E2\downarrow)\succ, S) \Leftrightarrow$
  [know_fluent$(A, P, S) \land$ [true_in$(S, \text{denotation}(P)) \Rightarrow$
  kp_satisfied$(A, E1, S)$] $\land$ [¬true_in$(S, \text{denotation}(P)) \Rightarrow$
  kp_satisfied$(A, E2, S)$]].

To employ these definitions in a nontrivial way, it is necessary that the agent have a theory allowing him to predict what he will know at future times. For example, suppose that, in situation s0, Leo is in room 1, he knows that block B is either in room 2 or in room 3, and he has the goal that block B should be in room 4. Leo has two primitive actions: The action "move(R)" moves himself and anything he is holding to room R. It has no preconditions. The action "pickup(X)" has the effect that Leo is holding X, and the precondition that Leo and X be in the same room. Leo knows all relevant physical and epistemic axioms. He also knows that, for any object, he knows whether the object is in the same room as himself. This last fact can be stated as follows:

know(leo, $\prec \forall_{S1, X}$ know_fluent(leo,
                $\prec$eql(place(leo), place(@X@))$\succ, S1)\succ$, s0).

(Note: in the above formula, the doubly imbedded antiquoted expression @X@ is scoped to the internal string delimiters.)

Leo then knows that he can achieve his goal by executing the following plan:

```
sequence(move(room2),
         cond(eql(place(leo),place(blockb)),
              sequence(pickup(blockb),move(room4)),
              sequence(move(room3),pickup(blockb),
              move(room4)).
```

The physical axioms are sufficient to show that the plan is physically feasible and that if it is carried out, then the goal will be achieved. The conditions that Leo knows the physical axioms and knows that he will know whether the block is in the same room are needed for the knowledge preconditions, to guarantee that Leo will know which branch to take when he comes to the conditional.

An agent A is able to perform a plan P if he knows that P is feasible and that P's knowledge preconditions are satisfied. He is able to achieve goal G if there is a plan P that he is able to perform and that he knows will lead to G. Formally, we define the predicates "can_do(A, P, S)," meaning that A can perform plan P in situation S, and "can_achieve(A, G, S)," meaning that A can achieve goal G in situation S, using the following axioms:

KPS.7. can_do(A, P, S) ⇔
        know(A,≺true_in(@S@,feasible(@A@, ↓P↓)) ∧
        kp_satisfied(@A@, !P!, @S@)≻,S).

KPS.8. can_achieve(A, G, S) ⇔
        can_do(A, P, S) ∧
        know(A,≺true_in(@S@,lead_to(↓P↓, ↓G↓))≻, S).

Note that the condition that A knows of the feasibility and success of the plan is a separate requirement than that the knowledge preconditions are satisfied. Consider, for example, the following example:[4] Nicholas has received two packages. He knows that one is a bomb and the other is innocuous, but he does not know which is which. He also knows that the bomb can be deactivated by putting it in the toilet, but unfortunately he has only one toilet available, and it will not hold both packages. We would like to be able to conclude that Nicholas is not able to deactivate the bomb, and indeed the above definition of

---

[4]This example is a modification of a problem proposed by Bob Moore, cited in [McDermott 1987a].

"can_achieve" will support that conclusion. There does exist a valid plan whose knowledge preconditions are satisfied; namely, either the plan "Put package A in the toilet" or the plan "Put package B in the toilet." However, Nicholas does not know which of these plans is valid. Conversely, there is a plan that Nicholas knows will work — the plan "Put the package with the bomb in the toilet" — however, the knowledge preconditions of this plan are not satisfied.

(It is possible to design a planner that solves this problem without explicitly reasoning about knowledge and knowledge preconditions; see [Pednault 1988]. However, such a planner implicitly uses meta-level (syntactic) categorizations of the plan involved. Certainly, in any theory that treats plans as event types rather than as descriptions of event types, it must be possible to prove the result, "There is a plan with a single action that defuses the bomb.")

9.3.3 Planning and Acting

All the planning we have discussed so far has been suitable for a setting where a top-level goal is presented in a starting situation, and the planner can find a plan, complete or partial, described entirely in terms of constraints on sequences of primitive actions, that is provably valid for the goal. Executing the plan then requires only finding a particular sequence of primitive actions that satisfies the constraints. In reality, it is only in rare, tightly controlled environments that it is possible or practical to plan with this degree of detail and certainty. Rather, a plan is partially developed at the start. Its full expansion into primitive actions is interspersed with its execution. Thus, the planner plans only primitive actions that will be executed soon; later parts of the plan are sketched only dimly. For example, an agent who is planning to go to a destination will not plan out every individual step, but only the basic outlines of his route; the individual steps will be planned only as they have to be taken. This is partly because individual steps must be chosen in response to circumstances that are unknown but very unlikely to affect the larger plan, and partly because even if all future steps could be planned with certainty, to do so is just a waste of computational resources. Interleaving planning with execution also makes it possible for the agent to respond more flexibly to errors — unanticipated obstacles or opportunities — discovered in his world model during execution.

This kind of planning has proven to be hard to implement and even harder to formalize. Here, we will only describe some of the central issues involved.

- *Plan representation*: In the plans we have discussed so far, it is necessary to describe only the primitive actions to be carried out, with constraints on when and whether each should be executed. By contrast, in representing a plan that will be expanded or modified at a later time, it is necessary to record a variety of information to guide the later stages of planning. In particular, it is necessary to represent the purpose of each part of the plan. Typically, these functions are represented in terms of a subgoal or subtask hierarchy. The purpose of a lower-level task is either as a component of a supertask or to achieve a precondition of some later task. (See Figure 9.4.) Other kinds of information to be recorded include constraints of various kinds among parts of the plan, and multiple alternative plans, to be chosen among at a later stage of expansion.

  It is also important, of course, to record which parts of the plan tree have already been accomplished and which are still pending. It may be desirable, for the sake of memory efficiency, to forget (i.e., drop from the plan tree) any portion of it that has already been accomplished.

- *Modification operators*: Additional modification operators are needed to maintain the plan during execution. In particular, a piece of the plan tree may disappear without ever being carried out, either because its purpose has been accomplished without it being necessary to carry it out, or because it has been determined to be impossible or impractical, or because all its supertasks have either been accomplished or disappeared.

- *Actions of general purpose*: An agent may wish to carry out an action whose purpose is not well specified but merely serves to put him in a stronger position. For example, an agent may wish to have more money available than he needs for planned activities, just in case additional expenses arise. An agent may answer the telephone without knowing which, if any, of his goals will be advanced by so doing.

- *Evaluation*: Open-ended planning typically takes place in an uncontrolled and partially known environment in which success cannot be predicted with absolute certainty; it can only be made more or less certain. The evaluation must thus be probabilistic.

- *Plan maintenance*: Finally, there is the central question of search and control, determining what parts of the planning tree to expand or modify and how far to expand them.

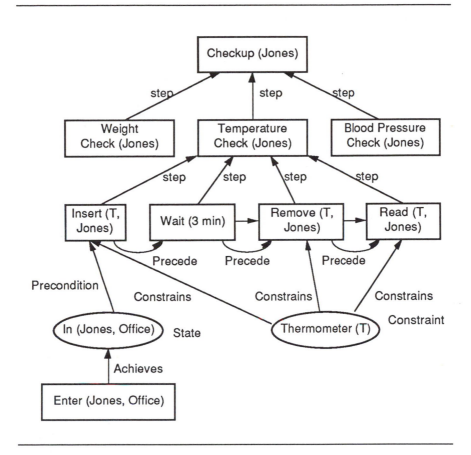

Figure 9.4 Hierarchy of tasks

9.3.4 Reactive Planning

A recent trend in planning research has been to study planning systems that perform relatively little inference or prediction of future states, but instead rely on a library of rules that specify an appropriate action given a goal and a current world state. There is wide variation among such systems in the richness of the world model maintained and of the inferences performed, if any. (Some systems, such as Agre and Chapman's PENGI [1987] have no internal world model whatever; they rely on immediate perceptions.) We will briefly discuss Firby's [1989] RAP system, which is notable among reactive planners for using a relatively high-level planning language and world model.

In Firby's system, a plan consists of a number of RAPs (Reaction Action Packages). A RAP consists of the following parts:

1. A *task* to be achieved by the RAP.

2. A *success* criterion, which may be verified when the RAP has succeeded in carrying out its task.

3. A number of *methods* for carrying out the task. Each method consists of

    (a) A *context*, a world state that must hold for the method to be appropriate.
    (b) A *task network* consisting of a set of subtasks or primitive actions with constraints on their performance.

Table 9.4 shows one simple RAP. (The LISP-like notation is Firby's. Symbols beginning with a question mark are variables. The example is slightly simplified from Firby's; the original had an additional clause whose significance depended on interpreting negation as failure. The logical translation in Table 9.5 is our interpretation, not Firby's.)

The RAP system maintains an agenda of tasks to be performed and a world model. The world model is updated by perceptions, which may be obtained as the direct results of a particular perception task, or may be side effects of the robot's activities. The task agenda is initialized to contain the robot's top-level goals. The robot then repeatedly chooses a task from the agenda to perform, based on scheduling criteria. If the task is primitive, it is executed by a direct command to the effectors. Otherwise, the robot chooses one of its methods whose context is currently satisfied and adds the task network for that method to the agenda. If all parts of a task network have been accomplished, the success criterion of the supertask is checked. The supertask has been successful if the criterion holds; otherwise it has failed. When a task fails, the method of which it was part is held to have failed, so that all other tasks associated with that method are removed from the task agenda.

We can characterize the above RAP in terms of a set of axioms like those of Table 9.5.

The formal interpretation of the central components of a RAP is thus quite straightforward. Such a characterization would be useful in trying to relate a RAP to a physical model of the domain. (The complete RAP language gets a great deal more complicated than this, with many programming bells and whistles. Formalizing these would be a lengthy project in robotic programming language semantics.) Characterizing or justifying the control structure in formal terms, by contrast,

Table 9.4 Sample RAP

```
(DEFINE-RAP
    (INDEX (load-into-truck ?object))
    (SUCCESS (location ?object in-truck))
    (METHOD
        (CONTEXT (and (size-of ?object ?size)
                        (<= ?size arm-capacity)))
        (TASK-NET
            (t1 (pickup ?object)
                ((holding arm ?object) for t2))
            (t2 (putdown ?object in-truck))))
    (METHOD
        (CONTEXT (and (size-of ?object ?size)
                        (> ?size arm-capacity)))
        (TASK-NET
                (t1 (pickup lifting-aid)
                    ((holding arm lifting-aid) for t2))
                (t2 (pickup ?object)
                    ((holding arm ?object) for t3))
                (t3 (putdown ?object in-truck)))))
```

The condition ((holding arm ?object) for t2) attached to t1 in the first method signifies that t1 should accomplish the state "(holding arm object)" and that this condition should be maintained until the beginning of t2. The conditions in the second method are analogous.

---

would be difficult. One can imagine a formal analysis of a RAP system analogous to the analysis of TWEAK in Section 9.2, which would show that a robot with a given set of RAPs could achieve the associated tasks, given certain constraints on the world, but no such analysis has been found, or, so far as I know, sought. Rather, the justification sought for systems like RAP would be empirical — that they do well enough under circumstances that arise in practice.

9.3.5 Characteristic Goals

In understanding the behavior of an agent, it is important to know what its top-level goals are likely to be. Motivation analysis depends

Table 9.5 Axiomatic Partial Characterization of a RAP

RAP.1. $\text{occurs}(I, \text{load\_into\_truck}(X)) \Rightarrow$
$\text{in-truck}(\text{value\_in}(\text{end}(I),\text{place}(X))).$
(Success condition)

RAP.2. $\text{occurs}(I,\text{load\_into\_truck}(X)) \Leftrightarrow$
$[\ \text{occurs}(I,\text{lit1}(X)) \lor \text{occurs}(I,\text{lit2}(X))\ ].$
(The task is accomplished by one of two methods)

RAP.3. $\text{occurs}(I,\text{lit1}(X)) \Rightarrow \text{size\_of}(X) \leq \text{arm\_capacity}.$
(Context for first method)

RAP.4. $\text{occurs}(I,\text{lit1}(X)) \Rightarrow$
$\exists_{I1,I2}\ \text{occurs}(I1,\text{pickup}(X)) \land$
$\text{occurs}(I2,\text{putdown}(X,\text{in\_truck}) \land$
$\quad \text{end}(I1) \leq \text{start}(I2) \land$
$\quad \forall_S\ [\ \text{end}(I1) \leq S \leq \text{start}(I2) \Rightarrow$
$\quad \text{true\_in}(S,\text{holding}(\text{arm},X))\ ].$
(Task net for first method)

RAP.5. $\text{occurs}(I,\text{lit2}(X)) \Rightarrow \text{size\_of}(X) > \text{arm\_capacity}.$
(Context for second method)

RAP.6. $\text{occurs}(I,\text{lit2}(X)) \Rightarrow$
$\exists_{I1,I2,I3}\ \text{occurs}(I1,\text{pickup}(\text{lifting\_aid})) \land$
$\quad \text{occurs}(I2,\text{pickup}(X)) \land$
$\quad \text{occurs}(I3,\text{putdown}(X,\text{in\_truck}) \land$
$\quad \text{end}(I1) \leq \text{start}(I2) \land \text{end}(I2) \leq \text{start}(I3) \land$
$\quad \forall_S\ [\ \text{end}(I1) \leq S \leq \text{start}(I2) \Rightarrow$
$\quad \text{true\_in}(S,\text{holding}(\text{arm},\text{lifting\_aid}))\ ] \land$
$\quad \forall_S\ [\ \text{end}(I2) \leq S \leq \text{start}(I3) \Rightarrow$
$\quad \text{true\_in}(S,\text{holding}(\text{arm},X))\ ].$
(Task net for second method)

entirely on such knowledge; without it, any action could be explained as a top-level goal in its own right. Knowledge of top-level goals is also important in interacting intelligently with other creatures and in predicting one's own future goals, so as to plan for them in advance.

A partial taxonomy of human high-level goals has been proposed by Schank and Abelson [1977]. They propose five general categories of top-level goals in humans:

1. *Satisfaction goals*: There are only a small number of these: hunger, thirst, sleepiness, sexual desire, and so on. A satisfaction goal generally persists until satisfied by an appropriate action (e.g., eating, drinking, sleep, sex), and then reappear after a characteristic time interval. Except for sex, the satisfaction of these goals cannot be indefinitely postponed, and they hold for all humans under all circumstances.

2. *Preservation goals*: The goals of preserving life, health, and property. These are almost always held. Schank and Abelson also distinguish a class of "crisis goals," preservation goals that are under direct threat and therefore must be addressed immediately, such as the preservation goals that are active when one is about to be run over or when one's house is on fire. Crisis goals generally take precedence over any other goal.

3. *Entertainment goals*: These are activities undertaken "for fun." Satisfying them may take from minutes to months to satisfy. They tend to be of lower priority than satisfaction or preservation goals. Examples: read a book, see a movie, visit the Himalayas.

4. *Achievement goals*: Large-scale ambitions whose accomplishment typically requires an extensive structure of actions extending over a long time.[5] Examples: become president, bring up children, write a novel.

5. *Delta goals*: Certain changes of state can be top-level goals in themselves. The most common of these are the gaining of money, property, or knowledge.

Schank and Abelson discuss a number of heuristic rules that characterize these categories of goals along a number of dimensions, such as the relative priority of the goals, the ease with which an agent will substitute one goal for another, and the emotional reaction of an agent to the failure of a goal. For instance, an agent will easily substitute one entertainment goal for another. This is more difficult, though sometimes possible, with achievement goals and delta goals. With satisfaction goals, it is easy to substitute a new argument (eat salmon instead of eat steak), but not to substitute a new type of goal (sleep instead of eat.) Goal substitution among preservation goals takes the form of giving up on less important goals in order to preserve more important goals; for example, spending one's savings to

---

[5]There are occasionally achievement goals that do not require many actions, such as Prince Charles's (presumptive) goal of being king of England, which requires on his part only that he outlive his mother and that he avoid serious offense to his country.

maintain one's health. (These rules can be used to predict behavior only in extreme cases, where one goal is overwhelmingly more important than others. Ordinarily, people continually choose between goals, and it is essentially impossible to know how they will choose without a detailed knowledge of the individual and the circumstances.)

The above taxonomy is not by any means complete. For example, people often have goals for others, such as the betterment of family members, friends, or society (or the injury of enemies). Given the diversity of human desires, it might seem hopeless to arrive at any taxonomy or any necessary conditions for human goals. On the other hand, there are certainly limits on top-level goals that are commonsensically known. A man with a top-level goal of putting a tulip in his glove compartment every day when the Mets score an odd number of runs would be recognizably peculiar.

Also important to an understanding of human behavior is a theory of interactions among goals and actions that will predict, or at least constrain, what actions an agent will perform given a situation and a collection of goals. Making such a choice often involves a complex evaluation, estimating the expected costs and the expected gain of achieving or postponing the various goals. Nonetheless, there is some commonsense consensus on how this calculation should be made. It would be generally agreed, for example, that a man who played chess while his house burned down around him was exercising poor judgment. A similar, deeper example would be to infer that a subsistence farmer in a hard winter will not eat his seed grain until he is in immediate danger.

A related, difficult, issue is the formulation of internal constraints on the set of goals held by an agent at a time, similar to the constraints on an agent's beliefs discussed in Chapter 8. For example, axioms such as the following might seem plausible:

- If G is a goal of A, and A believes that G implies Q, then Q is a goal of A.

- If G is a goal of A, then $\neg G$ is not a goal of A.

- If A believes that G will be a goal of A, then it is a current goal of A that he should be able to achieve G at the future time when he wants it.

- If A has a goal that G should be a goal of A's, then G is a goal of A.

9.4 References

Planners: Most of the AI analysis of plans and goals has, naturally, been in the context of planning programs. The following planning programs were particularly notable: GPS [Newell and Simon 1963] introduced the concepts of means-end analysis and of recursively calling the planner to achieve preconditions. QA3 [Green 1969] constructed plans by applying general theorem-proving techniques to situation-calculus axioms. STRIPS [Fikes and Nilsson 1971] used a GPS strategy applied to a fixed representation for actions. It also used a general-purpose theorem prover to compute dependencies among states in a single situation from state-coherence axioms. (The PLANNER language [Hewitt 1969; Sussman, Winograd and Charniak 1970] appears in retrospect as more an early version of a logic-programming language than a theory of planning.) HACKER [Sussman 1973] learned plans in the blocks world by a process of incremental debugging. BUILD [Fahlman 1974] was a powerful specialized planner for the blocks world. ABSTRIPS [Sacerdoti 1975] extended STRIPS by introducing task reduction and levels of abstraction. NOAH [Sacerdoti 1975] likewise used task reduction, and introduced nonlinear planning. Nonlinear planners with task reduction were further extended in NONLIN [Tate 1977]; in NASL [McDermott 1978b], which also studied the integration of planning and execution; and in DEVISER [Vere 1983], which incorporated a metric language of time and time intervals. MOLGEN [Stefik 1981], which constructed plans for biological experiments, highlighted the use of constraints on variable bindings in planning. TWEAK [Chapman 1987], as described in the text, provides an exceptionally clean theory of nonlinear planning, but does not incorporate task reduction. SIPE [Wilkins 1988] is a state-of-the-art planner that combines task reduction, nonlinear planning, and constraint posting. FORBIN [Miller, Firby, and Dean 1985] incorporates advanced techniques for temporal reasoning in the planner. In particular, FORBIN works in domains where it is possible that multiple events may occur simultaneously. [McDermott 1990] describes a complete linear planner for plans that may include actions with situation-dependent effects.

Theoretical analysis: [Georgeff and Lansky 1987] is a collection of a number of papers dealing with the logic and representation of plans. Particularly relevant to the issues discussed here are [Lifschitz 1987], which gives a formal account of the STRIPS program; [Manna and Waldinger 1987], which studies plan construction using methods from automatic programming, and, in particular, addresses the problem of constructing plans with conditionals; [Drummond 1987], which develops a plan representation capable of expressing conditionals and

loops; and [Cohen and Levesque 1987] which describes how an agent
will maintain and pursue his goals. [McDermott 1985] is a (very difficult) study of the logical structure of a task-reduction planner that
interleaves planning and acting. [Pednault 1988] provides an analysis for TWEAK-like plans that include actions, like toggling a switch,
whose effect depends on the starting state. [Dean and Boddy 1988]
demonstrate that predicting the effect of such a plan is NP-hard, and
gives a polynomial-time partial solution.

Knowledge preconditions: Knowledge preconditions for plans
are studied in [McCarthy and Hayes 1969], [Moore 1980], and [Mor-
genstern 1987].

Reactive planning: The RAP system discussed in the text is taken
from [Firby 1989]. Other important studies include [Agre and Chapman 1987; Brooks 1986; Kaelbling 1987; Hendler 1989; Georgeff 1988;
and Schoppers 1987].

Motivation analysis: The representation of plans and goals for
motivation analysis has been studied in [Charniak 1975; Rieger 1975;
Schank and Abelson 1977; Wilensky 1978; Wilensky 1980; Dyer 1985;
and Kautz and Allen 1986].

9.5   Exercises

(Starred problems are more difficult.)

1. (a) Translate the STRIPS representation of blocks-world events in
        Table 5.11 into the TWEAK representation.
   (b) * Show how TWEAK could construct a plan to get from state
        A to state B in Figure 5-2 using the actions defined in part a.

2. Show that if A can achieve G in S, then A knows that he can
   achieve G in S.

3. * Formalize the following inference:

   Given that Nicholas knows the following:

   (a) Either package A or package B contains a bomb.
   (b) The package containing the bomb weighs 5 pounds while the
       other package weighs 3 pounds.
   (c) If he lifts the package, then he will know its weight.
   (d) If the bomb is put in the toilet, then it will be defused.
   (e) It is possible to put a package in the toilet iff the toilet is empty.
   (f) The toilet is currently empty.

Infer: Nicholas can achieve the goal of defusing the bomb.

4. * Formalize the following inference:

> Joe is at his workshop. He has to build a desk, but his only record of the dimensions is at home. His customers, who are the only people who know the dimensions, are out of town. Infer that Joe will have to go home to get the dimensions.

5. * Consider the following plan:

> Step 1. Take a taxi to the train station no later than 3:30.
> Step 2. Buy a ticket to Miami within 5 minutes of arriving at the station.
> Step 3. When the train to Miami is announced, go immediately to the track where it leaves, and get on the train.

(a) Construct a representation for this kind of plan, and axiomatize the events that constitute carrying out such a plan.

(b) Define the conditions for the physical feasibility of a plan described in the language constructed in part a. The definition should support inferences like "If the train leaves at 3:50 and the taxi takes longer than 30 minutes to get to the station, then the above plan is infeasible."

(c) Define the knowledge preconditions of a plan described in the language of part a.

Chapter 10
Society

The phrase aroused my interest because of its enigmatic quality: "He brought in a second actor." I stopped; I found that the subject of that mysterious action was Aeschylus and that, as we read in the fourth chapter of Aristotle's Poetics, *he "raised the number of actors from one to two" ... With the second actor came the dialogue and the indefinite possibilities of the reaction of some characters on others. A prophetic spectator would have seen that multitudes of future appearances accompanied him: Hamlet and Faust and Segismundo and Macbeth and Peer Gynt and others our eyes cannot yet discern.*

Jorge Luis Borges, "The Modesty of History" in *Other Inquisitions*

This final chapter deals with commonsense knowledge about the interrelations and interactions among agents. In this domain more than any other, commonsense understanding far outstrips any existing formal model in richness and sophistication. Such an understanding is vital for story understanding, in automated teaching and in intelligent interactive systems. In this chapter, we discuss some issues in human and social interactions that have been studied in the AI literature: common knowledge, plan interaction, communication, ethical values, and possession.

The last three of these issues — communication, ethics, and possession — share a number of characteristics. All three issues arise continually in life in a complex society. All are virtually universal among human societies[1] and, apparently, appear in rudimentary form among some nonhuman species. All three are determined, at least to

---

[1] There are some nomadic hunting societies that carry virtually nothing with them on their travels. Property is an irrelevant concept to these. As far as I know, all societies have some language and some concept of the permitted and the prohibited.

some degree, by social convention,[2] but within the society they can often be extremely rigid and inescapable. It is easy to develop a representation for any of these issues that will cover the simplest cases; however, giving a deep theory of any raises profound and unresolved philosophical controversies.

10.1 Common Knowledge

Suppose that Tom and Huck are hiding together, and they witness Joe murder Dr. Robinson. Then Tom, Huck, and Joe each know the proposition "Joe murdered the doctor." Moreover, Tom and Huck each know the proposition "Tom, Huck, and Joe each know that Joe murdered the doctor"; Joe, however, does not know this. Further, Tom and Huck each know the proposition "Tom and Huck each know that Tom and Huck each know that Joe murdered the doctor," and so on *ad infinitum*. In short, Tom and Huck have a complete understanding between them about the fact.

The technical term for this is *common knowledge:* Tom and Huck have common knowledge that Joe murdered Dr. Robinson. To represent this, we introduce the syntactic operator "common_know(SAA, P)," meaning that the set of agents denoted by string SAA have common knowledge of sentence P. (A third temporal argument can be added when necessary.) Thus, "Tom and Huck have common knowledge that Joe murdered Dr. Robinson" is represented

common_know($\prec$
{Tom, Huck}$\succ$, $\prec\exists_I$ occur(I,murder(joe, robinson))$\succ$)

It is possible for every pair of agents in a set to have common knowledge of a fact without there being common knowledge of the fact over the set as a whole. For example, if A and B share a secret ϕ, and each independently tells it to C, then each of the sets { A, B }, { B, C }, and { A, C } has common knowledge of ϕ, but the set { A, B, C } does not. For example, A does not know that B knows that C knows ϕ. (See Exercise 1 for an example where this distinction makes a big difference.)

Unlike simple knowledge, common knowledge is opaque in the agent argument[3]; the members of a set may share knowledge under one description of the set but not another. For example, the secret hand-

---

[2]In defense of the statement that ethical values or property are to some degree a matter of social convention, let me point out that I am including in these categories such rules as "Don't drive through red lights" or "A person is considered to have paid a bill as of the moment the biller receives his check, not when the check clears."

[3]Lesperance [1989] argues that the same should be true of single agents.

shake of the Masons is (I presume) common knowledge among the Masons: All Masons know it, know that all other Masons know it, know that other Masons know that all Masons know it, etc. Nonetheless, it does not follow that if Joseph and Dominic are both Masons, then Joseph knows that Dominic knows the secret handshake; Joseph may not know that Dominic is a Mason. Another example: In Renaissance Venice, the Council of Three were secretly chosen; they met masked and did not know each other's identity (according to Mark Twain). They presumably shared a large body of common knowledge. The same three individuals (being prominent Venetians) undoubtedly knew each other, and may, indeed, have shared common knowledge in mufti. The two bodies of common knowledge, however, were quite separate. In the first case, each of them knew that all the members of the Council of Three knew the facts; in the other case, each of them knew that each member of the set { Leonardo, Giuseppe, Pietro } knew the facts. Thus, in a modal theory, the agent argument is an opaque argument; in a syntactic theory, it is a string that denotes a set of agents; in a possible-worlds theory, it is a fluent ranging over sets of agents, whose value may vary from one possible world to another.

Table 10.1 shows some basic axioms of common knowledge in a syntactic language.

Axioms CK.1 and CK.2 establish the basic properties of common knowledge: If agents AA have common knowledge of ϕ, then they all know ϕ, and they all know that they all know ϕ, and so on. Axiom CK.1a, that common knowledge is veridical, is a direct consequence of CK.1 and KNOW.3, that knowledge is veridical. Axioms CK.3 and CK.4 are the usual consequential-closure principle, analogous to axioms KNOW.1 and KNOW.2 of knowledge. Axiom CK.5 states that, if agents AA have common knowledge of ϕ and agents BB have common knowledge that BB is a subset of AA, then agents BB have common knowledge of ϕ. We can use this rule to justify inferences like the following: If Masons have common knowledge of the Masonic handshake, and Joseph and Dominic have common knowledge that they are Masons, then Joseph and Dominic have common knowledge of the Masonic handshake.

Finding an appropriate set description for a set of agents with common knowledge can raise substantial difficulties. For example, consider three strangers who are standing together and together witness a rabbit eating a carrot. Then it is clear that the three people have common knowledge that the rabbit ate the carrot, but under what description of one another? One solution would be to say that the common knowledge is shared among "the people here now," but that involves positing a common language of indexicals among agents. It

Table 10.1 Axioms of Common Knowledge

CK.1. If P is common knowledge among SAA, then every agent in SAA knows P.

  [common_know$(SAA, P) \wedge A \in$ denotation$(SAA)] \Rightarrow$
  know(A, P).

CK.1a (Veridicality) If P is common knowledge among SAA, then P is true.

  common_know$(SAA, P) \Rightarrow$ true(P).

CK.2. (Positive introspection) If P is common knowledge among SAA, then it is common knowledge among SAA that P is common knowledge among SAA.

  common_know$(SAA, P) \Rightarrow$
  common_know$(SAA, \prec$common_know$(!SAA!, !P!)\succ)$.

CK.3. (Consequential closure) Common knowledge is closed under implication.

  [common_know$(AA, P) \wedge$
  common_know$(AA, \prec \downarrow P \downarrow \Rightarrow \downarrow Q \downarrow \succ)$] $\Rightarrow$
  common_know(AA, Q)

CK.4. (Common knowledge of the axioms) Basic axioms are common knowledge.

  If P spells out an axiom (of logic, knowledge, time, or whatever), then
    $\forall_{SAA}$ common_know(SAA, P)
  is an axiom.

CK.5. (Common knowledge among a subset)

  [common_know$(SAA, P) \wedge$
  common_know$(SBB, \prec \downarrow SBB \downarrow \subseteq \downarrow SAA \downarrow \succ)$] $\Rightarrow$
  common_know(SBB, P).

---

is worthwhile distinguishing situations where this question does not arise, because all the agents involved know each other. We will represent the state in which all the agents in set AA know one another by common names and have common knowledge of this fact using the state type "acquainted(AA)."

To represent common knowledge in a possible-worlds semantics, we use an accessibility relation "ck_acc$(FAA, W1, W2)$," where $W1$ and

$W2$ are possible worlds and FAA is a fluent that ranges over sets of agents in different worlds. FAA thus corresponds to a particular description of some set of agents. The relation ck_acc($FAA, W1, W2$) holds if $W2$ is consistent with everything that is common knowledge in $W1$ to the set of agents described by FAA. The statement that agents AA have common knowledge of ϕ in $W1$ is expressed by asserting that ϕ is true in every accessible world.

10.2 Multiagent Plans

An agent in a society of many agents must consider his neighbors' actions and reactions in forming and evaluating his plans. Interactions among plans can be divided into a number of basic categories:

- *Cooperation*: A set of agents with a common goal cooperate on a common plan. The structure and analysis of such a plan may be considerably more complicated than the analysis of a single-agent plan. In many cases, there will not be any single agent that knows all steps of the plan. Step-by-step validation of the plan, such as we have seen in single-agent plans, therefore becomes largely irrelevant; there is no agent who knows enough to carry out such a validation. Instead, the analysis centers around the ways in which subtasks are divided among the various agents. Another new issue that becomes important in cooperative plans is the communication of relevant information between agents. This type of planning has much in common with the programming of distributed computer systems [Smith and Davis 1980].

- *Influence*: In a plan of influence, the planner tries to get others to perform actions that further his goals. Here, the other agents are analogous to external physical events that the agent is trying to control. The difference is that the agents are governed by psychological and social rules, rather than physical rules. A major aspect of this planning is predicting how another agent will respond to a request, discussed in Section 10.3.2. Section 10.3.3 shows how a simple plan of influence, involving making a request, can be validated.

- *Contingent interaction*: Other agents intend to perform actions, purely for their own purposes, that may aid or hinder the plan of the planner. Again, as in plans of influence, the other agents may be considered as external events that can be affected in a number of ways.

- *Direct conflict*: Another agent specifically wishes to prevent the planner from accomplishing his goal (or vice versa). Here, the planner must assume that the opponent will always perform the action that he (the opponent) considers most obstructive. Such planning often involves an exchange of hostile, destructive, or deceptive actions.

A single plan may involve different kinds of interactions. For example, a group of agents may cooperate on a plan that involves influencing some other agents and conflict with others. There are also many cases that fall on the borderline. For example, the workings of a company are, in some respects, a cooperative activity of the employees; in some respects, an influencing of the workers by the boss; and in some respects, a conflict between the workers and the boss.

Research in representing and reasoning about such plans is currently in a primitive stage, though some intriguing work has been done. Citations are given in the chapter reference list.

10.3 Communication

The most central type of interactions among intelligent agents are communications, also known as *speech acts*. (We use the terms associated with speech — "speech," "speaker," "hearer," and so on — to apply to any mode of communication: speech, writing, telegraphy, etc.) Speech acts may be divided into five categories: *declarative* acts, which convey information, such as stating "Paris is the capital of France"; *interrogative* acts, which ask for information, such as asking "What is the capital of France?"; *imperative* acts, which make a request or issue a command, such as asking "Please go away"; *exclamatory* acts, which express an emotion, such as crying "Alas!"; and *performative* acts, which, by social convention, bring about a condition, such as "I now proclaim you man and wife" or "I hereby cede my rights to Sherwood Forest." These categories are (nearly) mutually exclusive and exhaustive; almost every speech act belongs to exactly one of the categories.

Another well-known categorization associated with speech acts is the division into *locutionary, illocutionary* and *perlocutionary* acts [Austin 1961]. Unlike the previous categorization, these are categories of speech-act *types*, rather than of *tokens*; any given speech-act token may be described in any of these ways. A locutionary speech act describes the act in terms of the physical characteristics of the acts and the symbols used. An illocutionary speech act describes the act in

Table 10.2 Speech Act Categories

Locutionary:	Shouting "I'm mad as hell!" Whispering "Te amo." Writing "John Hancock."
Illocutionary:	Declaring allegiance to the king. Asking for a raise. Proposing a merger between General Soap and Urumchi University Press.
Perlocutionary:	Boring the audience. Converting a student to Marxism. Charming a guest.

terms of its content. A perlocutionary speech act describes the act in terms of the effect on the hearer. Table 10.2 gives some examples of each:

In this section, we will study locutionary and illocutionary descriptions of declarative, interrogative, and imperative speech acts.

10.3.1 Locutionary Descriptions

Locutionary acts are physical actions that produce sequences of signs in speech, writing, sign language, or other physical medium. We introduce the function "speak(P)," mapping a string of phonemes P to the action of speaking P, and the predicate "pronunciation(S, P, L)," meaning that phonemes P are an acceptable pronunciation of string S in language L. Thus, we can express the statements "Humphrey Bogart said 'Here's looking at you'" and "Lincoln spoke the Gettysburg Address" in the forms

$\exists_P$ pronunciation(P, ≺Here's_looking_at_you≻, english) $\land$
occur(i202, do(bogart, speak(P))).
$\exists_P$ pronunciation(P, gettysburg_address, english) $\land$
occur(i624, do(lincoln, speak(P))).

where "gettysburg_address" is a constant denoting the string ≺Fourscore_and_seven_years_ago ...≻.

Speech can accomplish communication only to someone who is present to hear it. Since hearing is a perception, we may apply the theory of perception developed in Section 8.7. For example, we can express a rule such as "If hearer AH is within distance d_hear of speaker AS, then he can hear whether AS is speaking and what he is saying" in the following form:

$$[\ \forall_{S \in I}\ \text{distance(value\_in}(S,\text{place}(AH)),$$
$$\text{value\_in}(S,\text{place}(AS))) \leq \text{d\_hear} \wedge$$
$$\text{bpc}(AH, B, \text{behavior}(I))\ ] \Rightarrow$$
$$[\ \text{occurs}(I,\text{do}(AS,\text{speak}(P))) \Leftrightarrow \exists_{AS1}\ \text{occurs}(B,\text{do}(AS1,\text{speak}(P)))\ ].$$

10.3.2 Illocutionary Speech Acts

An illocutionary description of a speech act characterizes its content. We introduce the event type, "illoc(AS, AH, M, P)", the event of AS communicating P in mode M to AH. (For simplicity, we assume a single speaker and hearer.) In a declarative act, P will be a sentence in a formal language, and M will be the constant "declarative." (Of course, declarative speech acts may be carried out without speaking an entire natural-language sentence. For instance, a question can often be answered in a single word. We assume, however, that the content of any declarative speech act can be expressed as a sentence in a formal language.) In an imperative act, P will be a term in a formal language denoting the action type that the speaker wants the hearer to perform, and M will be "imperative." We will treat interrogatives as special types of imperatives in which the speaker is requesting the hearer to communicate an answer to his question.

For example, the statement "Becky told Amelia that all crows are black" may be represented

occur(i202, illoc(becky, amelia, declarative,
            $\prec \forall_X$ crow$(X) \Rightarrow$ black$(X) \succ$)).

The statement "Becky told Amelia where Joseph was" is interpreted as "Becky told Amelia a true statement of the form 'Joseph is at X' for some constant X," and is thus represented

$\exists_{X,P}\ P = \prec \text{value\_in(start(i202),place(joseph))} = \downarrow X \downarrow \succ \wedge$
        constant$(X) \wedge$ true$(P) \wedge$
        occur(i202, illoc(becky, amelia, declarative, P)).

The statement "Becky asked Amelia to pass the salt" is represented,

occur(i202, illoc(becky, amelia, imperative,
  $\prec$do(amelia,pass(salt42))$\succ$))

The statement, "Amelia asked Becky where Joseph was" is interpreted as "Amelia requested that Becky communicate a true sentence of the form 'Joseph is at X,' where X is a constant," which is represented

occur(i202, illoc(amelia, becky, imperative,
  $\prec$ { I | $\exists_{X,P}$ occur(I, illoc(becky, amelia, declarative, P)) $\wedge$
    P=$\prec$value_in(start(i202), place(joseph))=$\downarrow X \downarrow \succ$ $\wedge$
    true(P) $\wedge$ constant(X) }$\succ$)).

(Note: the down arrows surrounding X in the formula above are scoped to the inner string delimiters.) Table 10.3 shows some basic properties of illocutionary acts.

Axioms IL.1 and IL.3 characterize the relation between locutionary and illocutionary acts. They can serve as the basis for executing an illocutionary act as a locutionary act in a task-reduction planner. The functions "meaning_of(S, K)" and "mode_of(S, K)" in these axioms specify the relation between the string spoken and the content communicated; the content of these functions would be specified by a theory of natural-language semantics. Axioms IL.6 and IL.8 state some necessary conditions that declarative and imperative speech acts be sincere. Additional conditions could be added. For example, we could define a declaration of P to be sincere if the speaker both believes P and believes that the hearer will believe that the speaker is sincere. We could define a request of P to be sincere if the speaker desires P and believes that his requesting P will make the hearer more likely to perform P [Searle 1969].

By combining these axioms with the axioms of belief in Chapter 8, we can justify[4] the plausible inference that if A declares ϕ to B, then B will believe ϕ. Assume that A declares ϕ to B. By IL.2, A and B have common knowledge that A has declared ϕ to B. By axiom CK.1, B knows that A has declared ϕ to B. Using rule BEL.14, we can presume that B will apply IL.4 and infer that A believes ϕ, and that he will further apply rule BEL.13, and infer that ϕ is true.

Stronger initial information will support stronger conclusions. For example, assume (i) that A declares ϕ to B; (ii) that A and B have common knowledge that A is speaking sincerely; and (iii) that A and B have common knowledge that A knows whether ϕ is true. Then it

---

[4]Modulo the limitation that our notation "plausible" doesn't actually refer to any particular theory of plausible reasoning.

Table 10.3 Axioms for Illocutionary Acts

IL.1. token_of(K, illoc(AS, AH, M, P)) $\Rightarrow$
  $\exists_S$ token_of(K,do(AS,speak(S))) $\wedge$
    P=meaning_of(S, K) $\wedge$ M=mode_of(S, K).
  An illocutionary act communicating P in mode M involves
  speaking a string whose meaning is P and mode is M.

IL.2. [occur(I,illoc(AS, AH, M, P)) $\wedge$
  true_in(start(I),acquainted({AS, AH}))] $\Rightarrow$
  common_know($\prec${@AS@, @AH@}$\succ$,
      $\prec$occur(@I@,illoc(@AS@,@AH@,$\downarrow M \downarrow$, !P!))$\succ$,
      end(I)).
  The occurrence of an illocutionary act is a matter of common
  knowledge to speaker and hearer.

IL.3. true_in(start(I), acquainted({AS, AH})) $\Rightarrow$
  [occur(I,illoc(AS, AH, M, P)) $\Leftrightarrow$
  common_know($\prec${@AS@, @AH@}$\succ$,
      $\prec\exists_{S,K}$ token_of(@K@,do(@AS@,speak(S))) $\wedge$
      @I@=time_of(K) $\wedge$!P!=meaning_of(S, K) $\wedge$
      $\downarrow M \downarrow$=mode_of(S, K)$\succ$,
      end(I))].
  A communication of P from AS to AH occurs just if they
  have common knowledge that AS spoke some string S that
  means P.

IL.4. plausible(token_of(K,illoc(AS, AH, M, P)), sincere(K)).
  Illocutionary acts are typically sincere.

IL.5. token_of(K,illoc(AS, AH,declarative,P)) $\Rightarrow$ sentence(P).
  The content of a declarative act is a sentence.

IL.6. [token_of(K,illoc(AS, AH,declarative,P)) $\wedge$ sincere(K)] $\Rightarrow$
  believe(AS, P,start(time_of(K))).
  The speaker believes a sincere declarative speech act.

IL.7. token_of(K,illoc(AS, AH,imperative,P)) $\Rightarrow$
  sort_of(denotation(P))=event $\wedge$
  actor_of(denotation(P))= AH.
  The content of an imperative act is a description of an action
  by the hearer.

IL.8. [token_of(K,illoc(AS, AH,imperative,P)) $\wedge$ sincere(K)] $\Rightarrow$
  goal(AS, P,start(time_of(K)))].
  If an imperative act is sincere, then the speaker wants the
  specified action to be carried out.

---

is possible to infer that A and B have common knowledge of ϕ when the communication is complete (Exercise 3).

In an analogous way, one would like to support the inference that if A requests something from B then, under suitable conditions, B will perform it. Such an inference is necessary to construct plans that involve the cooperation of agents who do not necessarily share the planner's goals. The problem is to spell out the requisite conditions. So far, this has only been done for very idealized microworlds. Section 10.3.3 shows the validation of a simple plan of influence involving a request, using an *ad hoc* assumption that this particular hearer always carry out the requests of the speaker immediately, if possible. (Schank and Abelson [1977] discuss a sequence of request forms, in increasing order of power and decreasing order of ease: asking; invoking a theme relating the two actors (e.g., "We've always been friends"); informing the hearer of the reason for the request; bargaining with the hearer; threatening the hearer; and overpowering the hearer.)

10.3.3 Sample Verification of a Plan of Influence

In this section, we illustrate how a simple plan of influence in a toy world can be verified. This verification combines primitives and rules from Chapters 5, 8, 9, and 10.

Assume that, in the blocks world of Section 5.3, block A is clear and on top of block B and the hand is above them. Fred manipulates the hand. Jack wishes block B to be clear. Show that Jack can satisfy his goal by asking Fred to pick up block A.

We must here assume that branches in time correspond only to Jack's actions, not to Fred's. Therefore, feasibility for blocks-world actions should be defined in domain-specific axioms, not in terms of branching time. For example, the feasibility of a pickup would be defined in the following rule:

true_in(S,feasible(pickup)) $\Leftrightarrow$
true_in(S,clear(hand)) $\wedge \exists_X$ true_in(S,under_hand(X))

An alternative approach would be to distinguish between what Fred could do in given situation (any physically feasible action) and what he would do (what Jack asks). See Chapter 5, exercise 7.

Assumptions:

i. Starting situation.
   true_in(s0, clear(hand)) $\wedge$ true_in(s0, under_hand(blocka)) $\wedge$
   [$\forall_X$ true_in(s0, beneath(blockb, X)) $\Leftrightarrow$ X =blocka].

ii. (Definition) A hand command is "pickup" or "putdown" or "move(L)."
    hand_command(E) $\Leftrightarrow$
    [E = $\prec$pickup$\succ$ $\vee$ E=$\prec$putdown$\succ$ $\vee$ $\exists_L E$=$\prec$move($\downarrow L \downarrow$)$\succ$].

iii. All the hand's activities are deliberate activities of Fred's.
    hand_command(E) $\Rightarrow$
    [token_of(K,denotation(E)) $\Leftrightarrow$ token_of(K,deliberate(fred,E))].

iv. Fred executes a hand command if Jack asks him to and it is physically possible to do so.

    [hand_command(P) $\wedge$ E=denotation(P)] $\Rightarrow$
    [occurs(I, E) $\Leftrightarrow$
    $\exists_{I1}$ meet($I1, I$) $\wedge$ occur($I1$,illoc(jack, fred, imperative, P)) $\wedge$
    can_do(fred,P,start(I))].

v. Fred and Jack are permanently acquainted.
    true_in(S,acquainted(fred, jack)).

vi. The sentence "Please execute a pickup" is under all circumstances a request for a pickup.
    pronounctation(P,$\prec$Please_execute_a_pickup$\succ$, english) $\Rightarrow$
    mode_of(P, K)=imperative $\wedge$ meaning_of(P, K)=pickup.

vii. Jack can always speak any string.
    $\forall_{S,P}$ true_in(S, feasible(do(jack,speak(P)))).

viii. If Jack speaks a string, then it will be common knowledge between him and Fred that he has spoken the string. (Note: This assumption is a quick and dirty device to get around specifying the conditions under which a speech of Jack's is known by Fred, and the frame axioms associated with those conditions.)

    occur(I,do(jack,speak(P))) $\Rightarrow$
    common_know($\prec$\{jack,fred\}$\succ$,
    $\prec$occur(@I@,do(jack,speak(!P!)))$\succ$, end(I)).

ix. If Jack now says "Please execute a pickup," then the only illocutionary act that he will complete at any time during his speech is to request a pickup.
    [pronunciation(P, $\prec$Please_execute_a_pickup$\succ$, english) $\wedge$
    token_of(K,do(jack(speak(P)))) $\wedge$ start(time_of(K)) = s0 $\wedge$
    token_of($K1$,illoc(jack, $A2, M, R$)) $\wedge$
    end(time_of($K1$)) $\in$ time_of(K))] $\Rightarrow$
    $K1 = K$.

x. In s0, Fred has completed any blocks-world action that he started previously.
[E=pickup $\wedge$ E=putdown $\wedge$
E=move(L) $\wedge$ occur(I, E) $\wedge$ start(I) < s0] $\Rightarrow$
end(I) $\le$ s0.

xi. Jack knows about all blocks-world events.
[hand_command(E) $\wedge$ occurs(I,denotation(E))] $\Rightarrow$
know(jack, $\prec$occur(@I@, $\downarrow E \downarrow$)$\succ$, end(I)).

xii. Fred and Jack have common knowledge of all the blocks-world axioms plus asssumptions i through xi, above.

To prove: Jack can accomplish block B being clear.
can_achieve(jack, clear(blockb), s0).

Proof: Let plan0 be the plan,

$\prec$sequence(do(jack, speak($\prec$Please_execute_a_pickup$\succ$)),
wait_while(pickup))$\succ$.

By the definition of "can_achieve" (axioms KPS.8, KPS.7), we can prove the desired result "can_achieve(jack, clear(blockb), s0)" by showing that Jack knows that plan0 is feasible, that it leads to clear(blockb), and that its knowledge preconditions are satisfied. Since Jack knows all the axioms (assumption xii and CK.1) and we assume consequential closure on knowledge (axiom KNOW.1), it suffices to show that it follows from the axioms that plan0 is a valid plan to accomplish clear(blockb) and that all the knowledge preconditions are met.

From PL1.a it is easily shown that a plan consisting of two actions in sequence is feasible just if the first step is feasible in the starting situation, and the second step is feasible at the end of the first step. In our case, the first step is "do(jack(speak($\prec$Please_execute_a_pickup$\succ$)))," which, by assumption vii, is always feasible. Given the frame axioms on the blocks world, the state of the blocks changes only if a pickup, putdown, or move is executed. Assumption iii states that such events are actions of Fred's. Assumption iv states that Fred will perform such an action only if Jack asks him to. Assumption ix states that Jack does not complete any such request between s0 and the completion of speaking "Please execute a pickup." Assumption x states that in s0, Fred is not in the middle of an action. Therefore, it follows that Fred does not perform any hand actions until the completion of Jack's speaking. Therefore, using the frame axioms of the blocks world, the blocks remain as they were at the start throughout Jack's speech.

Assumptions vi, viii, and xii guarantee that the conditions of IL.3 are satisfied, and that Jack's speech is a request to Fred for a pickup.

By assumption iv, Fred will execute the requested pickup if he can do so; that is, (by definition of "can_do"), if he knows that it is feasible and that its knowledge preconditions are satisfied. Since "pickup" is a constant, the knowledge preconditions are always satisfied. By the axioms of the blocks world, the pickup is currently feasible. Moreover, since Fred knew the state of the blocks at the start (assumption xii), and he knows that he has not committed any deliberate acts (KPG.2), applying assumptions iii and xi, KNOW.1, and the blocks-world frame axioms he knows that the blocks are in the starting position and that the pickup is feasible. Since he knows that the pickup is feasible and that its knowledge preconditions are satisfied, he can execute the pickup; hence, by assumption iv, he will. By the blocks-world axioms, this will result in block B being clear.

Thus, the plan plan0 is feasible and results in block B being clear. By axiom KPS.5, the knowledge preconditions of plan0 are that the knowledge preconditions of the speech are satisfied in the initial situation, and that Jack know that the knowledge preconditions of the "wait" are satisfied in the middle situation. But the speech involves only a constant argument, and so has no knowledge preconditions. By axiom KPS.4, the knowledge preconditions of the action "wait while the pickup takes place" are that Jack is sure that the pickup will take place, and that he will know when it has taken place. Jack can determine that the pickup will take place from the argument above, since Jack knows all the premises of that argument. Assumption xi says that Jack will know when the pickup does take place. Thus, the knowledge preconditions are satisfied.

Finally, again, Jack knows all the premises of the above argument (assumption xi) so, by axiom KNOW.1, he knows that plan0 is feasible, that it accomplishes the goal, and that its knowledge precondition are satisfied. Thus, Jack can achieve block B being clear. Q.E.D.

10.4 Ethics

The responsible builder of an autonomous robot will design its planning module so that it perfers doing right to doing wrong. Further, though the prudent robot will not assume that all other agents are as moral as itself, in order to avoid paranoia it must assume that most other agents rarely break important prohibitions.

A crude representation of ethical valuation can be developed along the following lines: We will consider ethical qualities as characteristics of an action type E in a situation S. We introduce the predicates

Table 10.4 Axioms for Ethical Predicates

ETH.1.   If E is obligatory in S, then it is permitted. Equivalently, it is never obligatory both to do E and not to do it.
$\text{obligatory}(E, S) \Rightarrow \text{permitted}(E, S)$.

ETH.2.   It is always possible to avoid all prohibited actions.
$\forall_S \exists_C \forall_{I,E} [I \subset C \wedge \text{start}(I)=S \wedge \text{occurs}(I, E)] \Rightarrow \text{permitted}(E, S)$.

ETH.3   Obligatory actions are better than prohibited ones.
$[\text{obligatory}(EO, S) \wedge \neg\text{permitted}(EP, S)] \Rightarrow \text{goodness}(EO, S) > \text{goodness}(EP, S)$.

ETH.4   Actions can be assumed to be permitted, unless there is reason to believe them prohibited.
$\text{plausible}(\text{true},(\text{permitted}(E, S)))$.

ETH.5   Prohibited actions are generally avoided.

$\text{plausible}(\neg\text{permitted}(E, S),$
$\qquad \forall_I [I \subset \text{real\_chronicle} \wedge \text{start}(I)=S] \Rightarrow$
$\qquad \neg\text{occurs}(I, E))$.

"permitted(E, S)" and "obligatory(E, S)". (Our use of first-order predicates implies that we assume that the ethical qualities of an action are transparent under substitution of equals.) Obligation and permission are dual relations; it is obligatory to do E in S just if it is not permitted not to do E. Formally, we can express this dual relation as follows:

$$\text{obligatory}(E, S) \Leftrightarrow \neg\text{permitted}(\text{nonoccurrence}(E), S).$$

Another representation of ethical values uses a measure space of "goodness" and a function "goodness(E, S)" mapping an event type E and a situation S to a measure of goodness.

Table 10.4 shows some plausible, though perhaps optimistic, axioms on obligation, permission, and goodness.

The main body of a theory of ethical values would be a specification of what acts are permitted, obligatory, prohibited, good, or bad. This would involve both specific rules (e.g., "Killing people is prohibited except under very rare circumstances") and general rules (e.g., "If doing

A will leave everyone happier than doing *B*, then, in general, *A* is a better action than *B*.") Formulating such a collection of rules is far beyond the scope of this book.

10.5 Possession

The following crude theory of possession will handle simple cases. We assume that an object *O* is owned by at most one agent at a time. The owner of *O* can change only by virtue of a transfer by its current owner. Use of *O* by agents other than the current owner are permitted only if the owner permits it. Table 10.5 shows the formal statement of this theory.

This theory is completed by a specification of what actions constitute the use of an object and how the owner of an object permits some particular use of it.

10.6 Appendix A: Conceptual Dependency

Conceptual dependency (CD) is one of the oldest and most influential representations of commonsense knowledge. It focuses on the representation of primitive human actions for the purpose of representing narrative text. Since it deals with issues spanning a number of our chapters, we have postponed discussing it to this final appendix.

CD was developed by Roger Schank and his associates and students over a number of years [Schank 1969, 1975; Schank and Abelson 1977] during which time it underwent continual development. It was not defined within a formal setting. Therefore, our account below, which integrates CD with the theories we have developed in this book, is to some extent a *post hoc* reconstruction. (Our account closely follows the formalization of CD in [Charniak and McDermott 1985].)

CD is primarily concerned with the characterization of primitive human actions. The basic function is the "action(*ACTOR, ACTION, OBJECT, SOURCE, DESTINATION*)," which maps its arguments to an event type. *ACTOR* is the actor of the event. *ACTION* is one of eleven[5] constants denoting different types of primitive actions. The meanings of *OBJECT, SOURCE*, and *DESTINATION* vary with particular action types. The primitive acts and the meanings of these arguments are shown in Table 10.6.

---

[5] The exact number and list varied over time.

Table 10.5 Axioms of Possession

Nonlogical symbols:

owner_of(O): Function. The fluent of the owner of O over time.

transfer(O, A): Function. The action of transferring possession of O to agent A.

use_of(E, A, O): Event type E constitutes a use of object O by agent A.

permits(A, E): State type. Agent A permits event type E.

POS.1. Causal axiom of transference: If the owner of O transfers O to $A2$, then $A2$ becomes the owner.
occurs(I,do(value_in(start(I), owner_of(O)),
$\qquad$ transfer($O, A2$))) $\Rightarrow$
$A2$=value_in(end(I), owner_of(O)).

POS.2. Only the owner can transfer possession.
occurs(I,do($A1$, transfer($O, A2$))) $\Rightarrow$
$A1$=value_in(start(I), owner_of(O)).

POS.3. Frame axiom of transference: Ownership can change only by an act of transference.
[precedes($S1, S2$) $\wedge$
$A1$ = value_in($S1$,owner_of(O)) $\neq$
$\qquad$ value_in($S2$, owner_of(O))] $\Rightarrow$
$\exists_{IT,A2}$ intersect(IT,[$S1, S2$]) $\wedge$
occurs(IT, do($A1$,transfer($O, A2$))).

POS.4. Use by others is permissible only if the owner allows it.
[$A2 \neq$ value_in(S,owner_of(O)) $\wedge$ use_of($E, A2, O$)] $\Rightarrow$
[permitted(E, S) $\Leftrightarrow$
true_in(S,permits(value_in(S,owner_of(O)),E))].

The object of an mbuild or mtrans action is a mental construct. The same problems of referential opacity that we have seen in connection with knowledge and belief therefore arise here as well. We will assume a syntactic theory, in which these objects are strings of characters. CD theory distinguishes between the "mental places" of long-term memory and short-term memory. Thus, the action mtrans may be used either for remembering a fact (transferring information from long-term to short-term memory) or for communication (transferring it from one agent to another).

Table 10.6 Primitive Action Types in CD

ptrans — To move *OBJECT* from *SOURCE* to *DESTINATION*.
propel — To exert a force on *OBJECT* in direction *DESTINATION*.
move — To move body part *OBJECT* to *DESTINATION*.
grasp — To grasp *OBJECT* with body part *DESTINATION*.
ingest — To consume *OBJECT* with body orifice *DESTINATION*.
expel — To emit *OBJECT* from body orifice *SOURCE*.
speak — To make sounds *OBJECT*.
mtrans — To transfer information *OBJECT* from *SOURCE* to *DESTINATION*.
mbuild — To mentally construct (imagine, consider, come to believe) *OBJECT*.
attend — To focus sensory organ *OBJECT* on object *DESTINATION*.
atrans — To transfer possession or control of *OBJECT* from *SOURCE* to *DESTINATION*.

Second, CD defines a number of fluents. These are less central to the theory than the primitive acts, and are often generated *ad hoc*. The following are commonly used:

- place(O) — The place of physical object O.

- mloc(M, P) — Mental location P contains mental object M.

- owner_of(O) — Agent owning object O.

- health-val(A) — Physical state of agent A. Characterized in terms of an integral measure space, running from "dead" through "sick" to "perfect-health".

- happiness(A) — Emotional state of agent A. Characterized in terms of an integral measure space, running from "miserable" to "indifferent" to "content" to "ecstatic".

We define the function "change(F, D)" to be the event of fluent F changing in direction D, where D is either "pos" or "neg". For example, "change(happiness(abel),pos)" is the event of Abel becoming happier.

Finally, CD defines a number of causal connectives. The arguments of these connectives fall into three categories:

- Tokens of physical events or actions.

Table 10.7 Causal Connectives in CD

- result(E, S) — Action E brings about state S.

- enable(S, E) — State S makes action E possible.

- disable(S, E) — State S make action E impossible.

- initiate(S, M) — Action or state S initiates mental state M.

- reason(M, E) — Mental state E is the reason for action E.

- instrumental($E1, E2$) — Action $E1$ is instrumental to action $E2$.

- Tokens of physical states or state changes.

- Tokens of mental actions, mental states, or changes to mental state.

Table 10.7 shows the causal connectives used in CD. We abbreviate the above category as "actions," the second as "states," and the third as "mental states."

Using these primitives, augmented with primitives defined earlier or defined *ad hoc*, we can now represent some simple narratives. Table 10.8 shows the CD representation of the following story:

> Marie saw Jessica pushing a toy wagon. Marie wanted to have the wagon. Marie took the wagon from Jessica. Jessica was upset and started to cry.

10.7 References

Common knowledge: Common knowledge has been studied in a variety of fields, including psychology, economics, game theory, philosophy, and computer science, particularly the theory of distributed systems. [Halpern and Moses 1984] is a particularly important and readable paper. Among other results, it shows that a distributed system cannot attain common knowledge of a fact in a series of communications unless it can attain common knowledge of the fact in a single communication. It also discusses several weakenings of the concept

Table 10.8 CD Representation of a Story

Events and states:

EV1: Jessica pushes a wagon.
   token_of(ev1, action(jessica, propel, wagon1, $\perp$, $\perp$)).

EV2: Marie looks at Jessica push the wagon.
   token_of(ev2, action(marie, attend, eyes(marie), $\perp$, ev1)).

MS3: Marie knows that Jessica pushes the wagon.
   token_of(ms3, mloc(mind_of(marie), ev1)).

MS4: Marie wants to have the wagon.
   token_of(ms4, goal(marie, eql(owner_of(wagon1), marie))).

EV5: Marie takes the wagon from Jessica.
   token_of(ev5, action(marie, atrans, wagon1, jessica, marie)).

ST6: Marie has the wagon.
   token_of(st6, eql(owner_of(wagon1), marie)).

MS7: Jessica is upset.
   token_of(ms7, change(happiness(jessica), neg)).

EV8: Jessica cries.
   token_of(ev1, action(jessica, expel, tears, eyes(jessica), $\perp$)).

Causal connections:

   initiate(ev2, ms3).
   initiate(ms3, ms4).
   reason(ms4, ev5).
   result(ev5, st6).
   initiate(st6, ms7).
   reason(ms7, ev8).

Actual occurrence of these events in this order:

   [time_of(ev1) $\cup$ time_of(ev2) $\cup$ time_of(ms3) $\cup$ time_of(ms4) $\cup$
   time_of(ev5) $\cup$ time_of(st6) $\cup$ time_of(ms7) $\cup$ time_of(ev8)] $\subset$
   real_chronicle.

contains(time_of(ev1), time_of(ev2)).
start(time_of(ev2)) $\leq$ start(time_of(ms3)) $\leq$ start(time_of(ms4)).
end(time_of(ev1)) $\leq$ start(time_of(ev5)).
start(time_of(ms4)) $\leq$ start(time_of(ev5)).
meet(time_of(ev5), time_of(st6)).
start(time_of(st6)) $\leq$ start(time_of(ms7)).
contains(time_of(ms7), time_of(ev8)).

that are more easily attainable. [Vardi 1988] contains a number of other papers on the subject. Common knowledge has not been extensively studied in the context of commonsense reasoning. As far as I know, the observation that the agent argument of common knowledge is opaque is original here.

Multiagent planning: [Bond and Gasser 1988] contains a number of important papers on multiagent planning. See particularly [Smith and Davis 1980; Georgeff 1983, 1984, 1986; Rosenschein 1982 and Stuart 1985] on cooperative planning, and [Morgenstern 1987] on plans of influence. The use of a theory of plan interaction in narrative understanding is studied in [Wilensky 1978, 1980] and [Dyer 1985].

Communication: High-level AI theories of communication have been extensively studied from many points of view and different degrees of formality. The representation discussed here derives largely from [Morgenstern 1988]. Other important works include [Appelt 1982; Perrault and Allen 1980; Cohen and Levesque 1987; Cohen and Pollack 1987], and [Litman 1985]. The classic philosophical studies of speech acts are [Austin 1961] and [Searle 1969]. See also [Wittgenstein 1958] to get an idea of what a complete commonsense theory of communication and language would have to include.

Ethics: [Sanders 1989] discusses a representation for ethical valuations, possession, and emotions. The formal treatment of ethical values is called *deontic* logic. Deontic logic has been applied to legal reasoning by McCarty [1983]. Philosophical studies of deontic logic include [Von Wright 1968; Prior 1967].

Possession: Many representational systems for narratives (e.g., [Schank 1975]) have used a theory of possession essentially equivalent to the simple one here. Theories that deal with certain aspects of property in greater detail have been developed for use in legal reasoning: see, for example, [McCarty and Sridharan 1980, 1981].

Conceptual dependency: Conceptual dependency was first introduced in [Schank 1969]; this version of the theory had the basic form of actions, with actor, object, source, and destination, but had only one action primitive: "trans." The standard version of CD is presented in [Schank 1975] and [Schank and Abelson 1977].

10.8 Exercises

(Starred problems are more difficult.)

1. * The following is known as the "cheating husbands" problem.

There was once a community with a distinctive system of conventions for dealing with marital infidelity.

(a) Every woman knew of every man in the community, except her own husband, whether or not he was faithful to his wife.

(b) A woman who knew that her husband was unfaithful was obliged to shoot him at midnight as soon as possible when she found out. If a woman shot her husband, the fact was immediately common knowledge.

(c) All women had common knowledge of rules a and b. All women were perfect logical reasoners.

At the time in question, there were k adulterous husbands. One day, at a meeting of the entire community, one of the husbands made the following public statement, witnessed in common by the entire community: "It must be admitted that at least one of us husbands has committed adultery."

k nights later, every adulterous husband was shot by his wife.

Provide a formal justification for the actions of the women.

2. Express the axioms of common knowledge CK.1–CK.5, using the accessibility relation ck_acc.

3. Justify the following inference: Assume (i) that A declares ϕ to B; (ii) that A and B have common knowledge that A is speaking sincerely; and (iii) that A and B have common knowledge that A knows whether ϕ is true. Infer that A and B have common knowledge of ϕ when the communication is complete.

4. Express the following statements using the primitives of Section 10.3.

(a) Mr. Martin said to Mrs. Barrows "I'm sitting in the catbird seat."

(b) Mr. Martin told Mr. Barrows that he had taken cocaine.

(c) Mrs. Barrows told Mr. Martin to leave her apartment.

(d) Mrs. Barrows asked Mr. Martin whether he was drunk.

(e) Mr. Fitweiler told Mr. Martin that Mrs. Barrows had told him (Fitweiler) that Martin had taken cocaine.

5. * Validate the following plan of influence [Morgenstern 1988].

John wishes to call Mary, but doesn't know her phone number. However, he does know that Harry knows her number, and that Harry will tell him the number if asked. He therefore constructs the following plan: Ask Harry for Mary's number; wait for Harry to answer the question; dial the number that Harry states.

Bibliography

The chapters where a work is cited are indicated by the numbers in brackets at the end of a listing.

IJCAI is an abbreviation for Proceedings of the International Joint Conference on Artificial Intelligence. AAAI is an abbreviation for Proceedings of the National Conference on Artificial Intelligence, an annual conference of the American Association of Artificial Intelligence.

Addanki, Sanjaya, Roberto Cremonini, and J. Scott Penberthy. [1989]. Reasoning about Assumptions in Graphs of Models. In [Weld and de Kleer 1989] 546–552. [1]

Agre, Philip E., and David Chapman. [1987]. Pengi: An Implementation of a Theory of Activity. *AAAI*. [9]

Allen, James. [1983]. Maintaining Knowledge about Temporal Intervals. *Comm. ACM* 26:832–843. Reprinted in [Weld and de Kleer, 89]. [4]

Allen, James. [1984]. Towards a General Theory of Action and Time. *Artificial Intelligence* 23:123–154. [5,7,9]

Allen, James, and Pat Hayes. [1985]. A Common-Sense Theory of Time. *IJCAI* 528–531. [4]

Ambler, A. P., and R.J. Popplestone. [1975]. Inferring the Position of Bodies from Specified Spatial Relations. *Artificial Intelligence* 6:157–174. [6]

Andrews, P. [1986]. *An Introduction to Mathematical Logic and Type Theory: Truth through Proof*. New York: Academic Press. [2]

Appelt, Douglas. [1982]. Planning Natural-Language Utterances to Satisfy Multiple Goals. SRI Artificial Intelligence Center Technical Note 259. Menlo Park, Calif. [2,10]

Austin, J. L. [1961]. *Philosophical Papers*. Oxford University Press. [1,10]

Ayer, A.J. [1946]. *Language, Truth, and Logic*. 2d ed. London: Gollancz. [1]

Baker, Andrew. [1989]. A Simple Solution to the Yale Shooting Problem. *Proc. First Int'l. Conf. on Principles of Knowledge Representation and Reasoning*, 11–21. San Mateo, Calif.: Morgan Kaufmann Publishers. [5].

Ballantyne, A. M., and W. W. Bledsoe. [1977]. Automatic Proofs of Theorems in Analysis Using Nonstandard Techniques. *J. ACM* 24 (no. 3):353–374. [4]

Ballard, Dana, and Christopher Brown. [1982]. *Computer Vision*. Englewood Cliffs, N.J.: Prentice Hall. [6]

Barwise, Jon. [1975]. *Admissable Sets and Structures in an Approach to Definability Theory*. New York: Springer-Verlag. [2]

Barwise, Jon, and John Etchemendy. [1987]. *The Liar: An Essay into Truth and Circularity*. Oxford University Press. [2]

Barwise, Jon, and John Perry. [1983]. *Situations and Attitudes*. Cambridge, Mass.: MIT Press. [2]

Bobrow, Daniel, ed. [1985]. *Qualitative Reasoning about Physical Systems*. Cambridge, Mass.: MIT Press. [4,7]

Bobrow, Daniel, and Terry Winograd. [1977]. An Overview of KRL, a Knowledge Representation Language. *Cognitive Science* 1 (no. 1):3–46. Reprinted in [Brachman and Levesque 1985]. [1].

Boggess, Lois C. [1979]. Computational Interpretation of English Spatial Prepositions. U. of Illinois Coordinated Science Lab, Tech. Rep. T-75. [6]

Bonissone, P. [1987]. Plausible Reasoning. In S. Shapiro, ed. *Encyclopedia of Artificial Intelligence*. New York: Wiley and Sons. [3]

Borning, A. [1977]. ThingLab — An Object-Oriented System for Building Simulations Using Constraints. *IJCAI* 497–499. [4]

Brachman, Ronald. [1985]. On the Epistemological Status of Semantic Networks. In [Brachman and Levesque 1985]. [1]

Brachman, Ronald, and Hector Levesque, eds. [1985]. *Readings in Knowledge Representation*. San Mateo, Calif.: Morgan Kaufmann Publishers. [1]

Brachman, Ronald, Hector Levesque, and Ray Reiter. [1989]. *Proc. of the First Int'l Conf. on Principles of Knowledge Representation and Reasoning (KR89)*. San Mateo, Calif.: Morgan Kaufmann Publishers. [1]

Brooks, Rodney. [1981]. Symbolic Reasoning among 3-D Models and 2-D Images. *Artificial Intelligence* 17 (nos. 1-3):285–348. [4,6]

Brooks, Rodney. [1982]. Solving the Find-Path Problem by Good Representation of Free Space. *AAAI* 381–386. [6]

Brown, F., ed. [1987]. *The Frame Problem in Artificial Intelligence. Proc. of the 1987 Workshop*. San Mateo, Calif.: Morgan Kaufmann Publishers. [5]

Bundy, Alan. [1978]. Will it Reach the Top? Prediction in the Mechanics World. *Artificial Intelligence* 10:129–146. [7]

Bunt, H. [1985]. The Formal Representation of (Quasi-)Continuous Concepts. In [Hobbs and Moore 1985], 1–36. [7]

Burge, T. [1977]. Belief *De Re*. *J. Philosophy*, June, 338–362. [2]

Bylander, Tom, and B. Chandrasekaran. [1985]. Understanding Behavior through Consolidation. *IJCAI*, 450–454. [7]

Carnap, Rudolf. [1967]. *The Logical Structure of the World: Pseudoproblems in Philosophy*. Translated by Rolf A. George. Berkeley, Calif.: University of California Press. [1]

Chapman, David. [1987]. Planning for Conjunctive Goals. *Artificial Intelligence* 32:333–378. [9].

Charniak, Eugene. [1981]. A Common Representation for Problem-Solving and Language-Comprehension Information. *Artificial Intelligence* 16 (no. 3): 225–255. [9]

Charniak, Eugene. [1983]. The Bayesian Basis of Common Sense Medical Diagnosis. *AAAI* 70–73. [3]

Charniak, Eugene. [1988]. Motivation Analysis, Abductive Unification, and Nonmonotonic Equality. *Artificial Intelligence* 34:275–296. [3]

Charniak, Eugene, and Drew McDermott. *Introduction to Artificial Intelligence*. Reading, Mass.: Addison-Wesley. [1,10]

Charniak, Eugene, Christopher Risebeck, Drew McDermott, and James Meehan. [1988]. *Artificial Intelligence Programming*. 2d ed. Hillsdale, N.J.: Erlbaum Associates. [1]

Cheeseman, Peter. [1985]. In Defense of Probability. *IJCAI* 1002–1009. [3]

Chou, Shang-ching. [1986]. Methods and Examples in Mechanical Theorem Proving. Tech. Rep. No. 53, Institute for Computing Science, University of Texas at Austin. [6]

Church, Alonzo. [1956]. *Introduction to Mathematical Logic*. Princeton University Press. [2]

Cohen, Paul R. [1985]. *Heuristic Reasoning about Uncertainty: An Artificial Intelligence Approach*. San Mateo, Calif.: Morgan Kaufmann Publishers. [3]

Cohen, Philip, and Hector Levesque. [1987]. Persistence, Intention, and Commitment. In [Georgeff and Lansky 1987]. [9]

Cohn, A. G. [1985]. On the Solution of Schubert's Steamroller in Many Sorted Logic. *IJCAI*, 1169–1174. [2]

Collins, John W., and Kenneth Forbus. [1987]. Reasoning about Fluids Via Molecular Collections. *AAAI*, 590–595. Reprinted in [Weld and de Kleer 1989]. [7]

Craig, John J. [1986]. *Introduction to Robotics: Mechanics and Control*. Reading, Mass.: Addison Wesley. [6]

Davidson, Donald. [1967]. The Logical Form of Action Sentences. In *The Logic of Decision and Action*, ed. Nicholas Rescher. Pittsburgh University Press. Reprinted in *Essays on Actions and Events*. Oxford University Press, 1980. [5]

Davidson, Donald. [1974]. Belief and the Basis of Meaning. *Synthese* 27:309–323. Reprinted in *Inquiries into Truth and Interpretation*. Oxford University Press. [8]

Davidson, Donald. [1975]. Thought and Talk. In *Mind and Language*, ed. S. Guttenplan. Oxford University Press. Reprinted in *Inquiries into Truth and Interpretation*. Oxford University Press, 1984. [1,8]

Davis, Ernest. [1984]. A High Level Real-Time Programming Language, NYU Tech. Report No. 145. [5]

Davis, Ernest. [1986]. *Representing and Acquiring Geographic Knowledge*. London: Pitman Publishing. [4,6]

Davis, Ernest. [1987a]. Reasoning, Common Sense. In *The Encyclopedia of Artificial Intelligence*, ed. S. Shapiro. New York: John Wiley. [1]

Davis, Ernest. [1987b]. Constraint Propagation with Interval Labels. *Artificial Intelligence*, 32:281–332. [4]

Davis, Ernest. [1988a]. A Logical Framework for Commonsense Predictions of Solid Object Behavior. *AI in Engineering*, 3 (no. 3):125–140. [7]

Davis, Ernest. [1988b]. Inferring Ignorance from the Locality of Visual Perception. *AAAI*, 786–790. [8]

Davis, Ernest. [1989a]. Order of Magnitude Reasoning in Qualitative Differential Equations. In [Weld and de Kleer 1989]. [4]

Davis, Ernest. [1989b]. Solutions to a Paradox of Perception with Limited Acuity. In [Brachman, Levesque, and Reiter 1989]. [8]

Davis, Martin, and Reuben Hersh. [1972]. Nonstandard Analysis. *Scientific American* (June) 78–84. [4]

Dawes, Robyn M. [1988]. *Rational Choice in an Uncertain World*. Harcourt Brace Jovanovich. [3]

de Kleer, Johan. [1975]. Qualitative and Quantitative Knowledge in Classical Mechanics. Tech. Report 352, MIT AI Lab. [6,7]

de Kleer, Johan. [1986]. An Assumption-Based Truth Maintenance System. *Artificial Intelligence*, 28:127–162. Reprinted in [Ginsberg 1987], 280–297. [1]

de Kleer, Johan, and Daniel Bobrow. [1984]. Qualitative Reasoning with Higher-Order Derivatives. *AAAI*, 86–91. Reprinted in [Weld and de Kleer 1989]. [4]

de Kleer, Johan, and John Seely Brown. [1985]. A Qualitative Physics Based on Confluences. In [Bobrow 1985]. [4,7]

de Kleer, Johan, and John Seely Brown. [1986]. Theories of Causal Ordering. *Artificial Intelligence*, 29:33–62. Reprinted in [Weld and de Kleer 1989]. [7]

Dean, Thomas. [1984]. Planning and Temporal Reasoning Under Uncertainty. *IEEE Conf. on Knowledge Representation*. [4]

Dean, Thomas. [1985]. Temporal Reasoning Involving Counterfactuals and Disjunctions. *ICJAI*, 1060–1062. [5]

Dean, Thomas, and Mark Boddy. [1988]. Reasoning about Partially Ordered Events. *Artificial Intelligence*, 36:375–387. Reprinted in [Weld and de Kleer 1989]. [5]

Dean, Thomas, and Keiji Kanazawa. [1988]. Probabilistic Temporal Reasoning. *AAAI*, 524–529. [5]

Dean, Thomas, James Firby, and David Miller. [1989]. Hierarchical Planning Involving Deadlines, Travel Times, and Resources. *Computational Intelligence*, 3. [9]

DeMillo, R. A., R. J. Lipton, and A. J. Perlis. [1979]. Social Processes and Proofs of Theorems and Programs. Comm. ACM, 22:271–280. [1].

Dennett, Daniel. [1978]. *Brainstorms*. Cambridge, Mass.: MIT Press. [8]

Dennett, Daniel. [1981]. Beyond Belief. In *Thought and Object*, ed. Andrew Woodfield. Oxford University Press. [2,8]

Downs, Roger M., and David Stea. [1973a]. *Cognitive Maps and Spatial Behavior: Process and Products*. Chicago, Ill.: Aldine Publishing Co. [6]

Downs, Roger M., and David Stea. [1973b]. *Image and Environment*. Chicago, Ill.: Aldine Publishing Co. [6]

Doyle, Jon. [1979]. A Truth-Maintenance System. Tech. Memo 521, MIT AI Lab. [4]

Doyle, Richard. [1989]. Reasoning about Hidden Mechanisms. *IJCAI*, 1343–1349. [7]

Drummond, Mark. [1987]. A Representation of Action and Belief for Automatic Planning Systems. In [Georgeff and Lansky 1987]. [9]

Dyer, Michael. [1983]. *In-Depth Understanding: A Computer Model of Integrated Processing for Narrative Comprehension*. Cambridge, Mass.: MIT Press. [9,10]

Etherington, David, and Ray Reiter. [1983]. On Inheritance Hierarchies with Exceptions. *AAAI*, 104–108. Reprinted in [Ginsberg 1987]. [3]

Fagin, Ronald, and Joseph Halpern. [1985]. Belief, Awareness and Limited Reasoning. *IJCAI*, 491–501. [8]

Fahlman, Scott. [1974]. A Planning System for Robot Construction Tasks. *Artificial Intelligence*, 4:1–49. [7,9]

Faltings, Boi. [1987a]. Qualitative Place Vocabularies for Mechanisms in Configuration Space. Tech. Rep. UIUCDCS-R-87-1360, University of Illinois at Urbana. [6,7]

Faltings, Boi. [1987b]. Qualitative Kinematics in Mechanisms. *ICJAI*, 436–442. Reprinted in [Weld and de Kleer 1989]. [6,7]

Faltings, Boi, Emmanuel Baechler, and Jeff Primus. [1989]. Reasoning about Kinematic Topology. *IJCAI*, 1331–1336. [7]

Feys, R. [1937]. Les Logiques Nouvelles des Modalites. In *Revue Neoscholastique de Philosophie*. Vol. 40, 517–553, 1937, and vol. 41, 217–252, 1938. [2]

Fikes, Richard E., and Nils J. Nilsson. [1971]. STRIPS: A new approach to the application of theorem proving to problem solving. *Artificial Intelligence* 2:189–208. [5,9]

Fine, Terrence L. [1973]. *Theories of Probability: An Examination of Foundations*. New York: Academic Press. [3]

Firby, James. [1989]. Adaptive Execution in Complex Dynamic Worlds. Research Report No. 672, Yale University. [9] .

Fleck, Margaret. [1987]. Representing Space for Practical Reasoning. *IJCAI*, 728–730. [6]

Fodor, Jerry. [1975]. *The Language of Thought*. Harvard University Press. [1]

Forbus, Kenneth. [1979]. A Study of Qualitative and Geometric Reasoning in Reasoning about Motion. Tech. Report No. 615, MIT AI Lab. [6,7]

Forbus, Kenneth. [1985]. Qualitative Process Theory. In [Bobrow 1985]. [7]

Forbus, Kenneth. [1986]. Interpreting Measurements of Physical Systems. *AAAI*, 113–117. [7]

Forbus, Kenneth. [1989]. The Qualitative Process Engine. In [Weld and de Kleer 1989]. [7]

Forbus, Kenneth, Paul Nielsen, and Boi Faltings. [1987]. Qualitative Kinematics: A Framework. *IJCAI*, 430–435. [7]

Funt, Brian. [1989]. Problem Solving with Diagrammatic Representations. *Artificial Intelligence* 13:201–230. Reprinted in [Brachman and Levesque 1985]. [7]

Gaifman, Haim. [1983]. Towards a Unified Concept of Probability. *Proc. Int'l. Conf. for Logic, Philosophy, and Methodology of Science*. Amsterdam: North-Holland Publishing.

Gaifman, Haim. [1986]. A Theory of Higher Order Probabilities. In [Halpern and Moses 1986] 275–292.

Gallin, D. [1975]. *Intensional and Higher Order Modal Logics*. New York: American Elsevier. [2]

Geertz, Clifford. [1983]. Common Sense as a Cultural System. In *Local Knowledge: Further Essays in Interpretive Anthropology*. New York: Basic Books. [1]

Gelernter, H. [1963]. Realization of a Geometry-Theorem Proving Machine. In *Computers and Thought*. eds. E. Feigenbaum and J. Feldman. New York: McGraw Hill.

Gelsey, Andrew. [1987]. Automated Reasoning about Machine Geometry and Kinematics, *Third IEEE Conf. on Artificial Intelligence Applications*, 182–187. Reprinted in [Weld and de Kleer 1989]. [6,7]

Genesereth, Michael, and Nils Nilsson. [1987]. *Logical Foundations of Artificial Intelligence*. San Mateo, Calif.: Morgan Kaufmann Publishers. [1,2,3].

Gentner, Dedre, and Albert Stevens, eds. [1983]. *Mental Models*. Hillsdale, N.J.: Erlbaum Associates.

Georgeff, Michael. [1988]. An Embedded Reasoning and Planning System. Australian Artificial Intelligence Center. [9]

Georgeff, Michael, and Amy Lansky, eds. [1987]. *Reasoning about Actions and Plans: Proc. 1986 Workshop, Timberline, Oregon*. San Mateo, Calif.: Morgan Kaufmann Publishers. [9]

Gettier, E. [1967]. Is Justified True Belief Knowledge? In *Knowledge and Belief*, ed. A. P. Griffiths. 144–146. Oxford University Press. [8]

Ginsberg, Matthew L. [1986]. Counterfactuals. *Artificial Intelligence*, 30:35–79. [2]

Ginsberg, Matthew L., ed. [1987]. *Readings in Nonmonotonic Reasoning*. San Mateo, Calif.: Morgan Kaufmann Publishers. [3]

Goodman, N. [1961]. About. In *Mind*. 1–24. [2]

Green, Cordell. [1969]. Application of Theorem Proving to Problem Solving. *IJCAI*, 219–240. [5,9].

Grice, H. P. [1957]. Meaning. *Philosophical Review* 66:377–388. [3,10]

Grosof, Benjamin. [1988]. Non-monotonicity in Probabilistic Reasoning. In [Lemmer and Kanal 1988]. [3]

Gupta, A. [1982]. Truth and Paradox. *J. Philosophical Logic* 11, no. 1. [2]

Haas, Andrew. [1983]. The Syntactic Theory of Belief and Knowledge. Bolt, Baranek, and Newman, Report No. 5368. [8]

Haas, Andrew. [1986]. A Syntactic Theory of Belief and Action. *Artificial Intelligence* 28 (no. 3):245–292. [8]

Halmos, Paul. [1960]. *Naive Set Theory*. New York: Van Nostrand Reinhold. [2]

Halpern, Joseph, ed. [1986]. *Theoretical Aspects of Reasoning About Knowledge*. San Mateo, Calif.: Morgan Kaufmann. [8]

Halpern, Joseph, and Yoram Moses. [1985]. A Guide to the Modal Logics of Knowledge and Belief. *IJCAI*, 480–490. [8]

Hanks, Steven, and Drew McDermott. [1987]. Nonmonotonic Logic and Temporal Projection. *Artificial Intelligence* 33:379–412. [5]

Harel, D. [1979]. First-Order Dynamic Logic. In *Lecture Notes in Computer Science*, eds. Goos and Hartmanis. Vol. 68. New York: Springer-Verlag. [5]

Hayes, Patrick. [1977]. In Defense of Logic. *IJCAI*, 559–565. [1]

Hayes, Patrick. [1978]. The Naive Physics Manifesto. In *Expert Systems in the Micro-electronic Age*. ed. D. Michie. Edinburgh, Scotland: Edinburgh University Press. Revised and reprinted in [Hobbs and Moore 1985]. [1,4,5,6,7]

Hayes, Patrick. [1979a]. Naive Physics 1: Ontology for Liquids. Originally written 1979. Reprinted in [Hobbs and Moore 1985]. [6,7]

Hayes Patrick. [1979b]. The Logic of Frames. In *Frame Conceptions and Text Understanding.* ed. D. Mentzing. Berlin: Walter de Gruyter and Co. Reprinted in [Brachman and Levesque 1985]. [3]

James Hendler. [1989]. Abstraction and Reaction. *Workshop on Knowledge, Perception, and Planning, IJCAI.*

Hewitt, Carl. [1969]. PLANNER: A language for proving theorems in robots. *IJCAI*, 295–301. [9].

Hintikka, Jaako. [1962]. *Knowledge and Belief.* Ithaca, N.Y.: Cornell University Press. [2,8]

Jaako Hintikka. [1969]. Semantics for Propositional Attitudes. In *Reference and Modality*, ed. L. Linsky. 145–167. Oxford University Press. [8]

Hinton, Geoff. [1979]. Some demonstrations of the effects of structural descriptions in mental imagery. *Cognitive Science* 3. [6]

Hobbs, Jerry. [1985a]. Introduction. In [Hobbs and Moore 1985]. [1]

Hobbs, Jerry. [1985b]. Granularity. *IJCAI*, 432–435. Reprinted in [Weld and de Kleer 1989]. [1]

Hobbs, Jerry. [1985c]. Ontological Promiscuity. *Proc. 23rd Annual Meeting of the Association for Computational Linguistics* (July). Chicago, Illinois. [2]

Hobbs, Jerry. [1987]. World Knowledge and Word Meaning. *Proc. TINLAP-3.* Las Cruces, N.M. [1]

Hobbs, Jerry, and Robert Moore, eds. [1985]. *Formal Theories of the Commonsense World.* Norwood, N.J.: ABLEX Publishing. [1]

Hoffman, Christoph. [1989]. *Geometric and Solid Modeling: An Introduction.* San Mateo, Calif.: Morgan Kaufmann Publishers. [6]

Hofstadter, Douglas. [1979]. *Godel, Escher, Bach: An Eternal Golden Braid.* New York: Basic Books. [2]

Hofstadter, Douglas. [1985]. *Metamagical Themas.* New York: Basic Books. [2]

Hughes, G. E., and M. J. Cresswell. [1968]. *An Introduction to Modal Logic.* London: Methuen and Co. [2,8]

Hummel, Robert, and Michael Landy. [1986]. Evidence as opinions of experts. *Proc. Workshop on Uncertainty in AI*, 135–143. Philadelphia, Pa.

Iwasaki, Yumi, and Herbert Simon. [1986]. Causality in Device Behavior. *Artificial Intelligence* 29:3–32. Reprinted in [Weld and de Kleer 1989]. [7]

Edwin T. Jaynes. [1979]. Where Do We Stand on Maximum Entropy? In *The Maximum Entropy Principle*, eds. Raphael D. Levine and Myron Tribus. Cambridge Mass.: MIT Press. [3]

Johnson-Laird, P. N., and P. C. Wason. [1970]. A Theoretical Analysis of Insight into a Reasoning Task. *Cognitive Psychology* 1:134–148.

Joskowicz, Leo. [1987]. Shape and Function in Mechanical Devices. *AAAI*, 611–618. Reprinted in [Weld and de Kleer 1989]. [6,7]

Joskowicz, Leo, and Sanjaya Addanki. [1988]. From Kinematics to Shape: An Approach to Innovative Design. *IJCAI*, 347–352. [7]

Kaelbling, Leslie P. [1986]. An Architecture for Intelligent Reactive Systems. In [Georgeff and Lansky 1987].

Kahn, K., and G. A. Gorry. [1977]. Mechanizing Temporal Knowledge. *Artificial Intelligence*, 87–108.

Kahneman, Daniel, and Amos Tversky. [1982]. On the Study of Statistical Intuition. *Cognition*, 11:123–141. [3]

Kanal, Laveen N., and John F. Lemmer. [1986]. *Uncertainty in Artificial Intelligence*. Amsterdam and New York: Elsevier Science Publishers. [3]

Kaplan, David. [1968]. Quantifying In. *Synthese* 19:178–214. [2]

Kaplan, David, and Richard Montague. [1960]. A Paradox Regained. *Notre Dame Journal of Formal Logic* 1 (no. 3):79–90. Also in [Montague 1974]. [2,8]

Kautz, Henry. [1986]. The Logic of Persistence. *AAAI*, 401–405. [5]

Kautz, Henry, and James Allen. [1986]. Generalized Plan Recognition. *AAAI*, 32–37. [9]

Kilmister, C. W., and J. E. Reeve. [1966]. *Rational Mechanics*. New York: American Elsevier. [7]

Kolmogorov, A. N. [1950]. *Foundations of the Theory of Probability*. Translated by Nathan Morrison. New York: Chelsea Publishing.

Kolodner, Janet. [1984]. *Conceptual Memory: A Computational Model*. Hillsdale, N.J.: Erlbaum. [3]

Konolige, Kurt. [1982]. A First Order Formalization of Knowledge and Action for a Multi-agent Planning System. In *Machine Intelligence* 10, J. E. Hays and D. Michie. [8]

Konolige, Kurt. [1985]. Belief and Incompleteness. In [Hobbs and Moore 1985]. [2,8]

Kosslyn, Stephen. [1980]. *Image and Mind.*   Harvard University Press. [6]

Kowalski, Robert. [1979]. *Logic for Problem Solving.* New York: Elsevier Publishing. [1]

Kripke, Saul. [1963a]. Semantical Considerations on Modal Logic. *Acta Philosophica Fennica, Modal and Many-Valued Logics* 83–94; Reprinted in *Reference and Modality*, ed. L. Linsky. London: Oxford University Press, pp. 63–72. [2]

Kripke, Saul. [1963b]. Semantical Analysis of Modal Logic. *Zeitschrift fur Mathematische Logik und Grundlagen der Mathematik*, Vol. 9, pp. 67–96. [2]

Kripke, Saul. [1972]. Naming and Necessity. In *Semantics of Natural Language.*   eds. D. Davidson and G. Harmon. Dordrecht, Holland: D. Reidel Publishing Co. pp. 253–355; Published as a book by Harvard University Press, 1980. [1, 2]

Saul Kripke. [1975]. Outline of a Theory of Truth. *Journal of Philosophy* 72:690–716. [2]

Kube, Paul. [1985]. Cognitive Propositional Attitudes. Chapter 5 in Commonsense Summer: Final Report, ed. J. Hobbs. Report No. CSLI-85-35, Center for the Study of Language and Information, Stanford University. [8]

Kuipers, Benjamin. [1975]. A Frame for Frames. In *Representation and Understanding.* eds. D. Borbow and A. Collins. New York: Academic Press. [3]

Kuipers, Benjamin. [1977]. Representing Knowledge of Large Scale Space. Tech. Rep. 418, MIT AI Lab. [6]

Kuipers, Benjamin. [1978]. Modelling Spatial Knowledge. *Cognitive Science* 2 (no. 2):129–154. [6]

Kuipers, Benjamin. [1985]. Commonsense Reasoning about Causality: Deriving Behavior from Structure. In [Bobrow 1985, pp. 169–204]. [7]

Kuipers, Benjamin. [1986]. Qualitative Simulation. *Artificial Intelligence* 29:289–338. Reprinted in [Weld and de Kleer 1989] [4,7].

Kuipers, Benjamin, and Charles Chiu. [1987]. Taming Intractible Branching in Qualitative Simulation. *AAAI*, 1079–1085. Reprinted in [Weld and de Kleer 1989]. [4]

Kuipers, Benjamin, and Tod Levitt. [1988]. Navigation and Mapping in Large-Scale Space. *AI Magazine* 9 (no. 2):25–46. [6]

Ladkin, Peter. [1987]. Models of Axioms for Time Intervals. *AAAI*, 234–239. [4].

Lavin, Mark. [1979]. Analysis of Scenes from a Moving Viewpoint. In *Artificial Intelligence: An MIT Perspective*, eds. Patrick Winston and Richard Henry Brown. Vol. 2, MIT Press, pp. 185–208. [6]

Lehnert, Wendy. [1981]. Affect and Memory Representations. *Proc. Third Conf. Cognitive Science Society*, 78–83. Berekley, Calif. [8]

Lemmer, John F., and Laveen N. Kanal. [1988]. *Uncertainty in Artificial Intelligence 2*. Amsterdam and New York: Elsevier Science Publishers. [3]

Lenat, Doug, and R. F. Guha. [1988]. The World According to CYC. MCC Tech. Rep. No. ACA-AI-300-88. [1]

Lenat, Doug, Mayank Prakash, and Mary Shepherd. [1986]. CYC: Using Common Sense Knowledge to Overcome Brittleness and Knowledge Acquisition Bottlenecks. *AI Magazine* 6 (no. 4):65–85. [1]

Levesque, Hector. [1984]. A Logic of Explicit and Implicit Belief. *AAAI*, 198–202. [9]

Lewis, C. I., and C. H. Langford. [1932]. *Symbolic Logic*. New York: Dover. [2]

Lewis, D. [1973]. *Counterfactuals*. Harvard University Press. [2]

Lifschitz, Vladimir. [1985]. Closed-World Databases and Circumscription. *Artificial Intelligence* 27:229–235. Reprinted in [Ginsberg 1987]. [3]

Lifschitz, Vladimir. [1987a]. Formal Theories of Action. In [Brown 1987]. [5]

Lifschitz, Vladimir. [1987b]. On the Declarative Semantics of Logic Programs with Negation. In [Ginsberg 1987]. [3]

Lifschitz, Vladimir. [1987c]. On the Semantics of STRIPS. In [Georgeff and Lansky 1987]. [5,9]

Lifschitz, Vladimir, and John McCarthy, eds. [1989]. *Formalizing Common Sense: Papers by John McCarthy*. Norwood, N.J.: Ablex Publishing. [1].

Malik, J., and T.O. Binford. [1983]. Reasoning in Time and Space. *IJCAI*, 343–345. [4]

Manna, Zohar, and Richard Waldinger. [1987]. A Theory of Plans. In [Georgeff and Lansky 1987]. [9]

Marcus, Ruth. [1986]. Rationality and Believing the Impossible. *J. of Philosophy* 80:321–330. [8]

Mason, M. T. [1986]. Mechanics and Planning of Manipulator Pushing Operations. *Int'l J. Robotics Research* 5. [7]

Mates, Benson. [1972]. *Elementary Logic*. Oxford University Press. [2]

Mavrovouniotis, M. L. and G. Stephanopoulos [1988]. Formal Order-of-Magnitude Reasoning in Process Engineering. *Computer Chemical Engineering* 12:867–880. Reprinted in [Weld and de Kleer 1989].

McCarthy, John. [1959]. Programs with Common Sense. In *Proc. Symposium on Mechanisation of Thought Processes* 1. London. [1]

McCarthy, John. [1963]. Situations, Actions, and Causal Laws. Stanford AI Project Memo No. 2, July. [1,5]

McCarthy, John. [1968]. Programs with Common Sense. In *Semantic Information Processing*, ed. M. Minsky. pp. 403–418. Cambridge, Mass.: MIT Press. Combined from [McCarthy 1959] and [McCarthy 1968]. [1]

John McCarthy. [1980]. Circumscription — A Form of Nonmonotonic Logic. *Artificial Intelligence* 13:27–39. Reprinted in [Ginsberg 1987]. [3]

John McCarthy. [1986]. Applications of Circumscription to Formalizing Common-Sense Knowledge. *Artificial Intelligence* 28:86–116. Reprinted in [Ginsberg 1987]. [3]

McCarthy, John, and Patrick Hayes. [1969]. Some Philosophical Problems from the Standpoint of Artificial Intelligence. In *Machine Intelligence 4*, eds. B. Meltzer and D. Michie. Edinburgh: Edinburgh University Press. pp. 463–502. Reprinted in [Ginsberg 1987]. [1,5,9]

McCarthy, John, M. Sato, T. Hayashi, S. Igarashi. [1978]. On the Model Theory of Knowledge. Computer Science Tech. Rep., STAN-CS-78-657, Stanford University, April. [8]

McCloskey, Michael. [1983]. Naive Theories of Motion. In [Gentner and Stevens 1983, pp. 299–324]. [7]

McDermott, Drew. [1974]. Assimilation of New Information by a Natural Language Understanding System. MIT AI Tech. Rep. [6]

McDermott, Drew. [1976]. Artificial Intelligence meets Natural Stupidity. *SIGART Newsletter*, No. 57. Reprinted in *Mind Design: Philosophy, Psychology, Artificial Intelligence*. ed. J. Haugeland. MIT Press. 1981. [1]

McDermott, Drew. [1978a]. Tarskian Semantics, or No Notation Without Denotation! *Cognitive Science* 2 (no. 3):277–282. [1]

McDermott, Drew. [1978b]. Planning and Acting. *Cognitive Science* 2:71–109. [9]

McDermott, Drew. [1982a] A Temporal Logic for Reasoning about Processes and Plans. *Cognitive Science* 6:101–155. [5,7]

McDermott, Drew. [1982b]. Nonmonotonic Logic II: Nonmonotonic Modal Theories. *J. Association for Computing Machinery* 29 (no. 1):33–57. [2,3]

McDermott, Drew. [1985]. Reasoning about Plans. In [Hobbs and Moore 1985, pp. 427–448]. [9]

McDermott, Drew. [1987a]. A Critique of Pure Reason. *Computational Intelligence* 3:151–160. [1]

McDermott, Drew. [1987b]. Spatial Reasoning. In *The Encyclopedia of Artificial Intelligence*, ed. S. Shapiro. New York: John Wiley. [7]

McDermott, Drew. [1989]. Regression Planning. Research Report No. 752, Yale Computer Science Dept. [9]

McDermott, Drew, and Ernest Davis. [1984]. Planning Routes through Uncertain Territory. *Artificial Intelligence* 22:107–156. [4,6]

McDermott, Drew, and Jon Doyle. [1980]. Non-Monotonic Logic I. *Artificial Intelligence* 13:41–72. [3]

Meehan, James. [1976]. *The metanovel: Writing Stories by Computer.* Research Report No. 74, Yale Computer Science Dept. [4]

Miller, David, James Firby, and Thomas Dean. [1985]. Deadlines, Travel Time, and Robot Problem Solving. *IJCAI*, 1052–1054.

Minsky, Marvin. [1975]. A Framework for Representing Knowledge. In *The Psychology of Computer Vision*, ed. P. Winston. New York: McGraw-Hill. Reprinted in part in [Brachman and Levesque 1985]. [1,3]

von Mises, Richard. [1964]. *Mathematical Theory of Probability and Statistics.* New York: Academic Press. [3]

Montague, Richard. [1974]. *Formal Philosophy.* ed. Richard Thomason. New Haven, Conn.: Yale University Press. [1]

Moore, Robert. [1980]. Reasoning about Knowledge and Action. Tech. Note 191, SRI International, Menlo Park, Calif. [2,8]

Moore, Robert. [1982]. The Role of Logic in Knowledge Representations and Commonsense Reasoning. *AAAI*, 428–433. Reprinted in [Brachman and Levesque 1985]. [1]

Moore, Robert. [1985a]. A Formal Theory of Knowledge and Action. In [Hobbs and Moore 1985, pp. 319–358]. [8]

Moore, Robert. [1985b]. Semantical Considerations on Nonmonotonic Logic. *Artificial Intelligence* 25:75–94. [3,8]

Moore, Robert, and Gary Hendrix. [1980]. Computational Models of Belief and the Semantics of Belief Sentences. Tech. Note 187, SRI International, Menlo Park, Calif. [8]

Moravec, Hans. [1988]. Sensor Fusion in Certainty Grids for Mobile Robots. *AI Magazine* 9 (no. 2):61–74. [6]

Morgenstern, Leora. [1987]. Knowledge Preconditions for Actions and Plans. *IJCAI*, 867–874. [9]

Morgenstern, Leora. [1988]. Foundations of a Logic of Knowledge, Action, and Communication. Ph.D. Thesis, New York University. [2,8,9,10]

Morgenstern, Leora. [1990]. Knowledge and the Frame Problem. In *The Frame Problem in Artificial Intelligence.* eds. K. Ford and P. Hayes. Greenwich: JAI Press. [8]

Morgenstern, Leora, and Lynn Stein. [1988]. Why Things Go Wrong: A Formal Theory of Causal Reasoning. *AAAI*, 518–523. [5]

Morris, Paul H. [1988]. The Anomalous Extension Problem in Default Reasoning. *Artificial Intelligence* 35:383–399. [5]

Nagel, Ernest, and James Newman. [1958]. *Godel's Proof.* New York: New York University Press. [2]

Newell, Alan. [1981]. The Knowledge Level. *AI Magazine* 2 (no. 2):1–20. [1]

Newell, Alan, and Herbert Simon. [1963]. GPS, A Program that Simulates Human Thought. In *Computers and Thought*, eds. E. Feigenaum and J. Feldman. New York: McGraw-Hill, pp. 279–298. [5,9]

Nielsen, Paul. [1988]. A Qualitative Approach to Mechanical Constraint. *AAAI*, 270–274.

Nilsson, Nils. [1980]. *Principles of Artificial Intelligence.* San Mateo, Calif.: Morgan Kaufmann Publishers.

Nilsson, Nils. [1986]. Probabilistic Logic. *Artificial Intelligence* 28:71–87. [3]

Novak, Gordon. [1977]. Representation of Knowledge in a Program for Solving Physics Problems. *IJCAI*, Cambridge, Mass. San Mateo, Calif.: Morgan Kaufmann. pp. 286–291. [6,7]

Pearl, Judea. [1988a]. *Probabilistic Reasoning in Intelligent Systems: Networks of Plausible Inference.* San Mateo, Calif.: Morgan Kaufmann Publishers. [3]

Pearl, Judea. [1988b]. Embracing Causality in Causal Reasoning. *Artificial Intelligence* 35:259–271. [7]

Pednault, Edwin P. D. [1988]. Extending Conventional Planning Techniques to Handle Actions with Context-Dependent Effects. *AAAI*, 55–59. [9]

Perlis, Donald. [1985]. Language with Self-Reference I: Foundations. *Artificial Intelligence* 25:301–322. [2]

Perrault, C. Raymond, and James Allen. [1980]. A Plan-Based Analysis of Indirect Speech Acts. *American J. of Computational Linguistics* 6 (no. 3–4):167–182. [10]

Peshkin, M. A., and A. C. Sanderson. [1987]. Planning Robotic Manipulation Strategies for Sliding Objects. *Proc. Int'l. Conf. on Robotics and Automation.* [7]

Piaget, Jean. [1952]. *The Origin of Intelligence in Children.* New York: International Universities Press. [1]

Piaget, Jean, and Barbel Inhelder. [1967]. *The Child's Conception of Space.* New York: Basic Books. [6]

Polanyi, Michael. [1958]. *Personal Knowledge: Towards a Post-Critical Philosophy.* University of Chicago Press. [8]

Pratt, V. [1976]. Semantical Considerations on Floyd-Hoare Logic. *Proc. Seventeenth FOCS,* IEEE, 109–121. [5]

Prior, A. N. [1967]. *Past, Present, and Future.* Oxford: Clarendon Press. [5]

Putnam, Hilare. [1962]. It Ain't Necessarily So. *Journal of Philosphy* 59 (no. 22):658–71. [1]

Putnam, Hilare. [1975]. The Meaning of 'Meaning'. In *Mind, Language, and Reality,* Cambridge University Press. [1]

Pylyshyn, Zenon. [1984]. *Computation and Cognition: Toward a Foundation for Cognitive Science.* Cambridge, Mass.: MIT Press. [6]

Pylyshyn, Zenon. [1987]. *The Frame Problem and Other Problems of Holism in Artificial Intelligence.* Norwood, N.J.: Ablex Publishing. [1,5]

Quine, W. V. O. [1953]. Two Dogmas of Empiricism. In *From a Logical Point of View.* Harvard University Press. [1]

Quine, W. V. O. [1969]. Propositional Objects. In *Ontological Relativity,* 137–160. New York: Columbia University Press. [2]

Raiman, Olivier. [1986]. Order of Magnitude Reasoning. *AAAI,* 100–104. Reprinted in [Weld and de Kleer 1989]. [4]

Randell, D. A., and A. G. Cohn. [1989]. Modelling Topological and Metrical Properties in Physical Processes. In [Brachman, Levesque, and Reiter 1989]. [6]

Reichgelt, Hans. [In preparation.] *Knowledge Representation: An AI Perspective.* Norwood, N.J.: Ablex Publishing. [1]

Reiter, Ray. [1978]. On Closed World Data Bases. In *Logic and Data Bases*, eds. H. Gallaire and J. Minker. New York: Plenum Press. Reprinted in [Ginsberg 1987] [3].

Reiter, Ray. [1980a]. A Logic for Default Reasoning. *Artificial Intelligence* 13:81–132. Reprinted in [Ginsberg 1987]. [3]

Reiter, Ray. [1980b]. Equality and Domain Closure in First-Order Databases. *J. Association for Computing Machinery* 27:235–249. [3]

Requicha, Aristides A. G. [1980]. Representations for Rigid Solids: Theory, Methods, and Systems. *ACM Computing Surveys* 12 (no. 4):437–464. [6]

Requicha, Aristides A. G. [1983]. Towards a Theory of Geometric Tolerancing. *The Int'l J. Robotics Research* 2 (no. 4):45–60. [6]

Rescher, N., and A. Urquhart. [1971]. *Temporal Logic*. New York: Springer-Verlag. [5]

Retz-Schmidt, Gudula. [1988]. Various Views on Spatial Prepositions. *AI Magazine* 9 (no. 2):95–108 [6]

Rieger, Chuck. [1975]. The commonsense algorithm as a basis for computer models of human memory, inference, belief, and contextual language comprehension. *Theoretical Issues in Natural Language Processing I*. [9]

Rieger, Chuck, and M. Grinberg. [1977]. The Declarative Representation and Procedural Simulation of Causality in Physical Mechanisms. *IJCAI*, 250–256. [7]

Riesbeck, Christopher K. [1980]. 'You Can't Miss It!': Judging the Clarity of Directions. *Cognitive Science* 4 (no. 3):285–303. [6]

Abraham Robinson. [1966]. *Nonstandard Analysis*. Amsterdam: North-Holland Publishing. [4]

Roseman, Ira. [1982]. *Cognitive Aspects of Discrete Emotions*. Ph.D. Thesis, Psychology Dept., Yale University. [8]

Rosenschein, Stanley, and Leslie Kaelbling. [1986]. The Synthesis of Digital Machines with Provable Epistemic Properties. In [Halpern 1986]. [8]

Rowat, Peter F. [1981]. Representing Spatial Experience and Solving Spatial Problems in a Simulated Robot Environment. Tech. Rep. 79-14, University of British Columbia Computer Science Dept. [6]

Russell, Bertrand. [1903]. *Principles of Mathematics*. London: Kimble and Bradford. [1]

Russell, Bertrand. [1940]. *Inquiry into Meaning and Truth*. London: George Allen and Unwin. [1]

Russell, Bertrand. [1948]. *Human Knowledge: Its Scope and Limits*. New York: Simon and Schuster. [1,8]

Ryle, Gilbert. [1949]. *The Concept of Mind*. New York: Barnes and Noble.

Sacerdoti, Earl. [1975]. *A Structure for Plans and Behavior*. New York: American Elsevier. [9]

Sacks, Elisha. [1987]. Hierarchical Reasoning about Inequalities. *AAAI*, 649–654. Reprinted in [Weld and de Kleer 1989]. [4].

Sacks, Elisha. [1988]. Qualitative Analysis by Piecewise Linear Approximation. *Artificial Intelligence in Engineering* 3:151–155. [4].

Sanders, Kate. [1989]. A Logic For Emotion. *Proc. Conf. for Cognitive Science*. Ann Arbor, Mich. pp. 357–363. [8].

Schank, Roger. [1975]. *Conceptual Information Processing*. Amsterdam: North-Holland Publishing. [8]

Schank, Roger. [1982]. *Dynamic Memory: A Theory of Reminding and Learning in Computers and People*. Cambridge, Mass.: Cambridge University Press. [3]

Schank, Roger, and Robert Abelson. [1977]. *Scripts, Plans, Goals, and Understanding*. Hillsdale, N.J.: Lawrence Erlbaum Associates. [1,9]

Schmolze, James G. [1986]. Physics for Robots. *AAAI*, 44–50. [7]

Schubert, L. [1978]. Extending the expressive power of semantic networks. *Artificial Intelligence* 11:45–83. [1]

Schwartz, Jacob, Micha Sharir, and John Hopcroft. [1987]. *Planning, Geometry, and Complexity of Robot Motion*. Norwood, N.J.: Ablex Publishing. [6]

Shafer, G. [1976]. *A Mathematical Theory of Evidence*. Princeton, N.J.: Princeton University Press. [3]

Shannon, C. E., and W. Weaver. [1949]. *The Mathematical Theory of Communication*. Urbana, Ill.: University of Illinois Press. [3]

Shoham, Yoav. [1985a]. Naive Kinematics: One Aspect of Shape. *IJCAI* , 436–442. [6,7]

Shoham, Yoav. [1985b]. Ten requirements for a theory of change. *New Generation Computing* 3. [5]

Shoham, Yoav. [1987]. A Semantical Approach to Non-monotonic Logics. *IJCAI*, 389–393. Reprinted in [Ginsberg 1987]. [3]

Shoham, Yoav. [1988]. *Reasoning about Change: Time and Causation from the Standpoint of Artificial Intelligence*. Cambridge, Mass.: MIT Press. [2, 3, 5, 7]

Shoham, Yoav, and Drew McDermott. [1988]. Problems in Formal Temporal Reasoning. *Artificial Intelligence* 36:49–62. [5]

Shore, John E., and Rodney W. Johnson. [1980]. Axiomatic Derivation of the Principle of Maximum Entropy and the Principle of Minimum Cross-Entropy. *IEEE Transactions on Information Theory* IT-26 (no. 1):26–37. [3]

Simmons, Reid. [1986]. 'Commonsense' Arithmetic Reasoning. *AAAI*, 118–124. Reprinted in [Weld and de Kleer 1989]. [4]

Skinner, B. F. [1971]. *Beyond Freedom and Dignity*. Knopf. [8]

Smullyan, Raymond. [1978]. *What is the name of this book?* Englewood Cliffs, N.J.: Prentice Hall. [2]

Sobocinski, B. [1953]. Note on a Modal System of Feys-Von Wright. *J. Computing Systems* 1:171–178. [2]

Stefik, Mark. [1981]. Planning and Metaplanning (MOLGEN: Part 2). *Artificial Intelligence* 16:141–169. [9]

Struss, Peter. [1989]. Problems of Interval-Based Reasoning. In [Weld and de Kleer 1989]. [4]

Sussman, Gerald J. [1975]. *A Computational Model of Skill Acquisition*. New York: American Elsevier. [9].

Sussman, Gerald J., and Guy L. Steele. [1980]. CONSTRAINTS — A Language for Expressing Almost Hierarchical Descriptions. *Artificial Intelligence* 14:1–40. [4]

Sussman, Gerald, Terry Winograd, and Eugene Charniak. [1970]. The Micro-planner Reference Manual. AI Memo 203, AI Lab, M.I.T. [9]

Sutherland, I. E. [1963]. SKETCHPAD, A Man-Machine Communication System. MIT Lincoln Labs Tech. Report No. 296. [4]

Tarski, Alfred. [1956]. The Concept of Truth in Formalized Languages. In *Logic, Science, and Metamathematics.* Oxford University Press.

Tate, Austin. [1977]. Generating Project Networks. *IJCAI,* 888–893 [9]

Thomason, Richmond. [1980]. A Note on the Syntactical Treatments of Modality. *Synthese* 44:391–395. [8].

Thomason, Richmond. [1987]. The Context Sensitivity of Belief and Desire. In [Georgeff and Lansky 1987, pp. 341–360]. [8]

Thorpe, Charles E. [1984]. Plan Relaxation: Path Planning for a Mobile Robot. *AAAI,* 318–321. [6]

Turner, Raymond. [1984]. *Logics for Artificial Intelligence.* New York: John Wiley and Sons. [2,3].

Tversky, Barbara. [1981]. Distortion in Memory for Maps. *Cognitive Psychology* 13 (no. 3):407–433. [6]

van Benthem, J. F. A. K. [1983]. *The Logic of Time.* Dordrecht: Reidel. [4,5]

Vardi, Moshe [1988]. *Proc. Second Conference on Theoretical Aspects of Reasoning About Knowledge.* San Mateo, Calif.: Morgan Kaufmann Publishers. [8]

Vere, Steven. [1983]. Planning in Time: Windows and Durations for Activities and Goals. *IEEE PAMI-5/3,* 246–267. [5]

Vilain, Marc. [1982]. A System for Reasoning about Time. *AAAI.* [5]

Vilain, Marc, and Henry Kautz. [1986]. Constraint Propagation Algorithms for Temporal Reasoning. *AAAI,* 377–382. Revised (with Peter van Beek) and reprinted in [Weld and de Kleer 1989] [4]

von Wright, George H. [1968]. *An Essay in Deontic Logic and the General Theory of Action.* Amsterdam: North-Holland Publishing. [10]

Wallace, Richard S. [1984]. Three Findpath Problems. *AAAI,* 326–329. [6]

Walther, C. [1987]. *A Many Sorted Calculus Based on Resolution and Paramodulation.* London: Pitman Press. [2]

Waltz, David. [1975]. Understanding line drawings of scenes with shadows. In *The Psychology of Computer Vision*, ed. P. Winston. New York: McGraw-Hill. [4]

Waltz, David. [1980]. Towards a Detailed Model of Processing for Language Describing the Physical World. *IJCAI 7*, 1–6. [6]

Wang, Y. [1986]. On Impact Dynamics of Robotic Operations. Tech. Rep. CMU-RI-TR-86-14, Robotics Institute, Carnegie Mellon University. [7]

Weld, Daniel. [1986]. The Use of Aggregation in Causal Simulation. *Artificial Intelligence* 30:1–17. Reprinted in [Weld and de Kleer 1989]. [4]

Weld, Daniel. [1988a]. Comparative Analysis. *Artificial Intelligence* 36:333–374. Reprinted in [Weld and de Kleer 1989]. [4]

Weld, Daniel. [1988b]. Exaggeration. *AAAI*, 291–295. Reprinted in [Weld and de Kleer 1989]. [4]

Weld, Daniel, and Johan de Kleer. [1989]. *Qualitative Reasoning about Physical Systems*. San Mateo, Calif.: Morgan Kaufmann Publishers. [4,7]

Whorf, Benjamin. [1956]. *Language, Thought, and Reality: Selected Writings of Benjamin Lee Whorf*, ed. J. B. Carroll. New York: John Wiley. [1]

Wilensky, Robert. [1983]. *Planning and Understanding*. Reading, Mass.: Addison-Wesley. [9,10]

Wilkins, David E. [1988]. *Practical Planning: Extending the Classical AI Planning Paradigm*. San Mateo, Calif.: Morgan Kaufmann Publishers. [9]

Wilks, Yorick. [1976]. Philosophy of Language. In *Computational Semantics*, eds. E. Charniak and Y. Wilks. Amsterdam, New York, Oxford: North-Holland Publishing. [1]

Williams, Brian. [1985]. Qualitative Analysis of MOS Circuits. In [Bobrow 1985, pp. 281–346]. [7].

Wilson, N. L. [1959]. Substances without Substrata. *Review of Metaphysics* 12:521–539. [8]

Wing, Jeannette, and Farhad Arbab. [1985]. Geometric Reasoning: A New Paradigm for Processing Geometric Information. Carnegie-Mellon Tech. Rep. CMU-CS-85-144. [6]

Winograd, Terry, ed. [1980]. Special Volume on Non-Monotonic Logic. *Artificial Intelligence* 13 (nos. 1 and 2). [3]

Wittgenstein, Ludwig. [1958]. *Philosophical Investigations*. Oxford University Press. [1]

Woods, William A. [1975]. What's in a Link: Foundations for Semantic Networks. In *Representation and Understanding: Studies in Cognitive Science*, eds. D. G. Bobrow and A. M. Collins. New York: Academic Press. Reprinted in [Brachman and Levesque 1985]. [1]

Wos, Larry, Ross Overbeek, Ewing Lusk, and Jim Boyle. [1984]. *Automated Reasoning: Introduction and Applications*. Englewood Cliffs, N.J.: Prentice Hall. [1]

Zadeh, Lotfi. [1963]. Fuzzy algorithms. *Information and Control* 12:94–102. [3]

Zadeh, Lotfi. [1987]. Commonsense and Fuzzy Logic. In *The Knowledge Frontier: Essays in the Representation of Knowledge*, eds. N. Cercone and G. McCalla. New York: Springer-Verlag, pp. 103–136.

Zadrozny, Wlodek. [1989]. Cardinalities and Well-Orderings in a Common-Sense Set Theory. In [Brachman, Levesque, and Reiter 1989]. [2]

Glossary

These ambiguities, redundancies, and deficiencies recall those attributed by Dr. Franz Kuhn to a certain Chinese encyclopaedia entitled Celestial Emporium of Benevolent Knowledge. *On those remote pages it is written that animals are divided into (a) those that belong to the Emperor, (b) embalmed ones, (c) those that are trained, (d) suckling pigs, (e) mermaids, (f) fabulous ones, (g) stray dogs, (h) those that are included in this classification, (i) those that tremble as if they were mad, (j) innumerable ones, (k) those drawn with a very fine camel's hair brush, (l) others, (m) those that have just broken a flower vase, (n) those that resemble flies from a distance.*

Jorge Luis Borges, "The Analytical Language of John Wilkins," *Other Inquisitions*

This glossary lists most of the formal notations used in this book. Omissions fall primarily into the following four categories:

- Symbols that are highly specific to a problem or to a narrow microworld, such as "john," "table," and "heat_flow."

- Standard mathematical notation that is infrequently used, such as "$\sin(X)$".

- Grouping symbols: parentheses, brackets, and commas.

- Notations that are dependent on a particular structuring of symbols, rather than on the use of a particular symbol, such as $\alpha^{\mathcal{I}}$, meaning the interpretation of α under interpretation $\mathcal{I}$.

An entry in this glossary consists of the following four parts, separated by periods.

1. The symbol and its use. A prefix symbol is followed immediately by its arguments. For a symbol that is not a prefix, we first list the symbol, then illustrate its placement relative to its arguments.

As in the text, object-level variables are represented by italicized capital symbols; metalevel variables are represented by Greek letters.

2. The category of the symbol. This is one of the following:

   - First-order logical symbol
   - Constant symbol
   - Function symbol
   - Predicate symbol
   - Special symbol; a symbol that appears inside a first-order formula, but is not interpreted in a standard way; syntactic sugar
   - Modal operator
   - Metalevel symbol
   - Symbol associated with plausible reasoning.

3. Explanation of the symbol, including the sorts or categories of its arguments.

4. Reference to the page where the symbol is defined.

Some symbols are given more than one definition. Some of these are symbols that have different categories in different theories, such as "know," which can be either a modal operator or a predicate with a string argument. Others are symbols that have been overloaded, such as square brackets, which can be used for grouping, to indicate a closed interval, or to indicate the sign of a quantity.

$\neg\phi$.
Logical. Negation of sentence ϕ. [p. 31]

$\vee$. $\phi \vee \psi$.
Logical. Boolean operator: Formula ϕ or formula ψ. [p. 31]

$\wedge$. $\phi \wedge \psi$.
Logical. Boolean operator: Formula ϕ and formula ψ. [p. 31]

$\Rightarrow$. $\phi \Rightarrow \psi$.
Logical. Boolean operator: Formula ϕ implies formula ψ. [p. 31]

$\Leftrightarrow$. $\phi \Leftrightarrow \psi$.
Logical. Boolean operator: Formula ϕ if and only if formula ψ. [p. 31]

$\dot{\vee}$. $\phi \dot{\vee} \psi$.
Logical. Boolean operator: Either formula ϕ or formula ψ but not both. [p. 31]

$\forall \mu \alpha(\mu)$.
Logical. Universal quantifier: Formula α holds for all values of variable μ. [p. 36]

$\exists \mu \alpha(\mu)$.	Logical. Existential quantifier: Formula α holds for some value of μ. [p. 36]
$\exists^1 \mu \alpha(\mu)$.	Logical. Unique existential quantifier: Formula α holds for a single value of μ. [p. 47]
0.	Constant. Zero. [p. 155]
∞.	Constant. Infinite quantity. [p. 151]
$\perp$.	Constant. Null value. [p. 44]
$\emptyset$.	Constant. The empty set. [p. 49]
[ ]. $[L, U]$.	Function. Closed interval from quantity L to quantity U. [p. 151]
[ ]. $[X]$.	Function. Sign of quantity X, or interval containing X in some fixed partition. [p. 161, 168]
+. $X + Y$.	Function. Sum of quantities X and Y. [p. 155]
{ }. $\{X1, X2, \ldots Xk\}$.	Function. The set containing $X1, X2, \ldots Xk$. [p. 48]
$-X$.	Function. Negative of differential quantity X. [p. 155]
$-$. $X - Y$.	Function. Difference of quantities X and Y. [p. 155]
$-$. $S - T$.	Function. Difference of sets S and T. [p. 50]
$\cup$. $S \cup T$.	Function. Union of sets S and T. [p. 50]
$\cap$. $S \cap T$.	Function. Intersection of sets S and T. [p. 50]
$<>$. $< X1, X2 \ldots >$.	Function, Tuple of entities $X1, X2 \ldots Xk$. [p. 50]
$\cdot$. $X \cdot Y$.	Function. Product of quantity X with quantity Y. [p. 157]
ΔX.	Function (relative to two implicit situations). Change in parameter X from one situation to the other. The value of ΔX is in the differential space of the range of X. [p. 161]
$\|\|$. $\|S\|$.	Function. The cardinality of set S. [p. 158]

∂X.

Function. Sign of the derivative of parameter X. ∂X is a fluent whose range is the differential space of the range of X. [p. 166]

$\sim A$.

Function. Negation of state A. $\sim A$ is a state. [p. 224, 402]

$()$. (X, Y).

Function. Open interval from quantity X to quantity Y. [p. 152]

$=$. $X = Y$.

Predicate. Entity X is equal to entity Y. [p. 43]

$<$. $X < Y$.

Predicate. Quantity X is less than quantity Y. [p. 147]

$\in$. $X \in S$.

Predicate. Entity X is an element of set S. [p. 48]

$\subseteq$. $S \subseteq T$.

Predicate. Set S is a subset of set T. [p. 50]

$\ll$. $X \ll Y$.

Predicate. Quantity X is negligible as compared to quantity Y. [p. 180]

$\neq$. $X \neq Y$.

Predicate. Entities X and Y are not equal. [p. 43]

$\sim$. $X \sim Y$.

Predicate. Sign X is compatible with sign Y. [p. 161]

$\propto_{Q+}$. $F \propto_{Q+} G$.

Predicate (sort of; see text). Parameter F is qualitatively proportional to parameter G. [p. 322]

$\propto_{Q-}$. $F \propto_{Q-} G$.

Predicate (sort of; see text). Parameter F is inversely qualitatively proportional to parameter G. [p. 322]

$\{ \mid \}$. $\{ \mu \mid \alpha(\mu) \}$.

Special. The set of all μ such that α holds. [p. 48]

$\prec\succ$. $\prec ABCDE \succ$.

Special. String of characters ABCDE. [p. 78]

$@$. $\prec @X@ \succ$.

Special. Splice the name of X into a character string. [p. 370]

!. ≺!X!≻.	Special. Splice X with an extra level of quotation into a character string. [p. 370]
↓. ≺↓X↓≻.	Special. Splice string X into a character string. [p. 370]
$\iota(\mu)\alpha(\mu)$.	Special. μ is a variable, and α is an open formula. The unique μ such that $\alpha(\mu)$ holds. [p. 48]
⊨. ⊨ ϕ.	Metalevel. Sentence ϕ is universally valid. [p. 29]
⊨. $\mathcal{I}$ ⊨ ϕ.	Metalevel. Sentence ϕ is true in interpretation $\mathcal{I}$. [p. 29]
⊨. Γ ⊨ ϕ.	Metalevel. Sentence ϕ is a semantic consequence of set of sentences Γ. [p. 29]
⊢. Γ ⊢ ϕ.	Metalevel. Formula ϕ can be proven from set of formulas Γ. [p. 29]
ab(X).	Predicate. Entity X is abnormal (used in nonmonotonic inference). [p. 113]
abut(**RR, PP, FF**).	Predicate. Regions **RR** and **PP** abut in boundary **FF**. [p. 258]
acquainted(AA).	Function. State of all the agents in set AA having common knowledge of their respective names. [p. 438]
action($ACTOR, ACTION, OBJECT, SOURCE, DESTINATION$).	Function. In conceptual dependency, the event type of agent $ACTOR$ performing action type $ACTION$ on object $OBJECT$ taking it from location $SOURCE$ to location $DESTINATION$. [p. 450]
active(S, P).	Predicate. Process P is active during situation S. [p. 323]
actor_of(E).	Function. The agent who is the actor of event type E. [p. 410]
after(θ, ϕ).	Modal. The state that follows if event ϕ occurs in a situation where state θ holds. [p. 231]
always.	Constant. The set of all situations. [p. 224]

angle(**X,Y,Z**). Function. The angle formed by the rays $\mathbf{Y} - \mathbf{X}$ and $\mathbf{Y} - \mathbf{Z}$. [p. 251]

angle($\hat{E}, \mathcal{C}$). Function. The angle between direction $\hat{E}$ and the x axis of coordinate system $\mathcal{C}$ (in two dimensions). [p. 298]

angle($\mathcal{F}, \mathcal{C}$). Function. The angle between the x axes of coordinate systems $\mathcal{F}$ and $\mathcal{C}$ (in two dimensions). [p. 298]

apply($O, A1 \ldots Ak$). Function. Combines a string O, which spells out an operator, with strings $A1 \ldots Ak$, which spell out arguments, and returns the string that spells out the application of O to $A1 \ldots Ak$. [p. 78]

assumptions($\mathcal{S}$). Metalevel. In natural deduction, the assumptions of proof step $\mathcal{S}$. [p. 87]

atrans. Constant. In CD, the action type of transferring possession. [p. 452]

attend. Constant. In CD, the action type of focusing a sensory organ. [p. 452]

before(I, J). Predicate. Interval I ends strictly before interval J begins. [p. 148]

believe(A, ϕ, S). Modal. Agent A believes sentence ϕ in situation S. (S may be omitted if time is not an issue.) [p. 356, 381]

believe(A, P, S). Predicate. Agent A believes the sentence spelled out by string P in situation S. (S may be omitted if time is not an issue.) [p. 356, 367]

believing(A, ϕ). Modal. The state of agent A believing sentence ϕ. [p. 381]

believing(A, P). Function. The state type of A believing the sentence spelled out by P. [p. 381]

bel_acc($A, W1, W2$). Predicate. Possible world $W2$ is accessible from world $W1$ relative to the beliefs of A. [p. 72, 365]

border(**RR, PP**,S). Predicate. In TOUR, path **PP** is on the border of region **RR**. S is a Boolean, indicating

	whether the forward direction of **PP** goes clockwise or counterclockwise around **RR**. [p. 281]
boundary(**AA**).	Function. The boundary of region **AA**. [p. 258]
bounded(**RR**).	Predicate. Region **RR** is bounded. [p. 255]
bpc($A, B1, B2$).	Predicate. Behavior $B2$ is compatible with the perceptions of agent A in behavior $B1$. [p. 388]
bulk(**RR**, $\tilde{D}$).	Predicate. Region **RR** is bulk with radius $\tilde{D}$ (see text for formal definition). [p. 343]
can_achieve(A, G, S).	Predicate. Agent A can achieve goal G in situation S. [p. 422]
can_do(A, P, S).	Predicate. Agent A can perform plan P in situation S. [p. 422]
card(S).	Function. Cardinality of set S. [p. 158]
change(F, D).	Function. Event type of quantity-valued fluent F changing in direction D. [p. 452]
circle(**O**, $\tilde{D}$).	Function. The circle with center **O** and radius $\tilde{D}$. [p. 251]
CIRC(T, μ).	Plausible. The circumscription of theory T in predicate μ. [p. 111]
ck_acc($FAA, W1, W2$).	Predicate. Possible world $W2$ is accessible from world $W1$ relative to the common knowledge of FAA. FAA is a fluent ranging over sets of agents. [p. 439]
clock_time.	Constant. The fluent that gives the clock time in a given situation. [p. 190]
close(X, Y).	Predicate. The difference between quantities Y and X is negligible as compared to their magnitude. [p. 180]
colinear(**X, Y, Z**).	Points **X, Y, Z** are colinear. [p. 251]
common_know(SAA, P, S).	
	Predicate. The agents in the set denoted by string SAA have common knowledge of the sentence spelled out by string P in situation S. [p. 438]

complement(**RR**). Function. The complement of region **RR**. [p. 255]

concs($\mathcal{S}, \mathcal{D}, \mathcal{E}$). Plausible. In default logic, the conclusions from the set of sentences $\mathcal{S}$ using default rules $\mathcal{D}$ in extension $\mathcal{E}$. [p. 116]

concurrent($E1 \ldots Ek$). Function. The event type of event types $E1 \ldots Ek$ occurring concurrently. [p. 228]

cond($A, E1, E2$). Function. The event type "If state type A holds, then event type $E1$, else event type $E2$." [p. 225]

cond(θ, ϕ_1, ϕ_2). Modal. If state θ, then event ϕ_1, else event ϕ_2. [p. 231]

congruent(**AA,BB**). Predicate. Regions **AA** and **BB** are congruent without reflection. [p. 255]

conj(Q). Function. Conjugate of quaternion Q. [p. 302]

connected_component(**CC, XX**).
  Predicate. Region **CC** is a connected component of region **XX**. [p. 255]

connected(**XX**). Predicate. Region **XX** is connected. [p. 255]

contains(I, J). Predicate. Interval I contains interval J. [p. 149]

content($\mathcal{S}$). Metalevel. In natural deduction, the content of proof step $\mathcal{S}$. [p. 86]

coor1(**P**, $\mathcal{C}$). Function. Maps a k-dimensional point **P** and a coordinate system $\mathcal{C}$ onto a $k + 1$-by-1 column array consisting of the coordinates of **P** in $\mathcal{C}$ followed by 1. [p. 297]

coordinates(**P**, $\mathcal{C}$). Function. The coordinates (a k-tuple) of k-dimensional point **P** in coordinate system $\mathcal{C}$. [p. 247, 295]

cylinder($\tilde{L}, \tilde{R}, \mathcal{F}$). Function. The right circular cylinder of height $\tilde{L}$ and radius $\tilde{R}$ with the bottom face in the x-y plane of coordinate system $\mathcal{F}$ centered at the origin. [p. 274]

d_belief(A, ϕ). Modal. The degree (a real number) to which agent A believes sentence ϕ. [p. 370]

dbl_quote(S).	Function. String S with an extra level of quotation (a string). [p. 81]
dboundary(**RR**).	Function. Boundary of two-dimensional region **RR** directed counterclockwise around **RR**. [p. 276]
dboundary(**RR**).	Function. Boundary of three-dimensional region **RR** directed outward from **RR**. [p. 343]
declarative.	Constant. Declarative mode of illocutionary acts.
dedge(**X,Y**).	Function. Directed edge from **X** to **Y**. [p. 276]
deliberate(A, E).	Function. Event type of the deliberate performance by A of the action denoted by string E. [p. 414]
delta(X).	Function (relative to two implicit situations). Change in parameter X from one situation to the other. The value of delta(X) is in the differential space of the range of X. [p. 160]
denotation(S).	Function. The entity denoted by string S. [p. 81]
deriv(P).	Function. The derivative of parameter P with respect to time. deriv(P) is a parameter whose range is in the differential space of the range of P. [p. 165]
diameter(**RR**).	Function. The diameter (a length) of region **RR**. [p. 249]
direction(**X,Y**).	Function. The direction of the ray from **X** to **Y**. [p. 251]
dir_cosines($\hat{D}, C$).	Function. Maps k-dimensional direction $\hat{D}$ and coordinate system C to the k-tuple of directional cosines. [p. 295]
disable(S, E).	Predicate. In CD, state S makes event E impossible. [p. 453]
distinct($X_1 \ldots X_k$).	Predicate. Entities $X_1 \ldots X_k$ are all unequal. [p. 43]
dist(**X,Y**).	Function. The distance (a length) between points **X** and **Y**. [p. 249]

do(A, E).   Function. The event type of agent A performing action type E. [p. 410]

during(I, J).   Predicate. Interval I starts after and ends before interval J. [p. 148]

empty(**RR**).   Function. State of region **RR** being empty. [p. 343]

enable(S, E).   Predicate. In CD, state S makes event E possible. [p. 453]

end(I).   Function. Maps an interval I to its least upper bound. [p. 151]

eql(F, G).   Function. The state type of fluent F being equal to fluent G. [p. 189]

equal(I, J).   Predicate. Intervals I and J are equal. [p. 148]

event_part($K1, K2$).   Predicate. Event token $K1$ is part of event token $K2$. [p. 192]

expel.   Constant. In CD, the action type of emitting something from the body of the agent. [p. 452]

FALSE.   Metalevel. Falsehood. [p. 32]

feasible(P).   Function. State of plan P being feasible. [p. 398]

filled_liquid(**RR**).   Function. State of region **RR** being filled with liquid. [p. 343]

finishes(I, J).   Predicate. Interval I starts after interval J, but they end together. [p. 148]

fixed(O).   Predicate. Object O is immovable. [p. 334]

flow_through(**F**).   Function. Fluent of the flow of liquid through directed face **F**. [p. 343]

future(ϕ).   Modal. State ϕ will hold at all future times. future(ϕ) is a state. [p. 231]

goal(A, G, S).   Predicate. In situation S, agent A has the goal denoted by string G. [p. 414]

goes_through(**FF, PP**).   Function. Event type of region-valued fluent **FF** going through region **PP**. [p. 262]

goodness(E, S).   Function. The ethical value (a quantity) of event type E in situation S. [p. 449]

grasp.   Constant. In CD, the action type of the agent grasping an object. [p. 452]

H(S).   Plausible. Entropy. S is a probability distribution defined on a frame of discernment. [p. 131]

happiness(A).   Function. In CD, the fluent of agent A's happiness over time. [p. 452]

health_val(A).   Function. In CD, the fluent of agent A's health over time. [p. 452]

horizontal(**PP**).   Predicate. Planar surface **PP** is horizontal. [p. 255]

illoc(AS, AH, M, P).   Function. The event type of agent AS performing an illocutionary act with agent AH being the hearer, M being the mode, and string P being the content. [p. 442]

imperative.   Constant. The imperative mode of an illocutionary act. [p. 442]

ind.   Constant. The interval of all quantities. [p. 161]

infinite_on_left(I).   Predicate. Interval I is unbounded below. [p. 151]

infinite_on_right(I).   Predicate. Interval I is unbounded above. [p. 151]

influence(P, Q).   Function. The influence of process P on parameter Q. influence(P, Q) is a fluent ranging over the differential space of Q. [p. 323]

ingest.   Constant. In CD, the action type of consuming an object. [p. 452]

initiate(S, M).   Predicate. In CD, action of state S initiates mental state M. [p. 453]

inside(**II**, **RR**).   Predicate. Region **II** is an inside of region **RR**. [p. 251]

instrumental($E1, E2$).   Predicate. In CD, action $E1$ is instrumental to action $E2$. [p. 453]

intersect(I, J).   Predicate. Intervals I and J have more than a single point in common. [p. 207]

interval(I).   Predicate. I is an interval. [p. 150]

is_constant(S).   Predicate. String S is a constant. [p. 80]

is_inside(**II, BB**).   Predicate. Region **II** is inside the box **BB**.

is_meaningful(S).   Predicate. String S is meaningful (a term or a formula). [p. 80]

is_sentence(S).   Predicate. String S is a sentence. [p. 80]

is_symbol(S).   Predicate. String S spells out a single symbol. [p. 80]

is_term(S).   Predicate. String S is a term. [p. 80]

join(I, J).   Function. If I and J are intervals that meet, join(I, J) is the interval that starts with the beginning of I and ends with the end of J. [p. 149]

know(A, ϕ, S).   Modal. Agent A knows sentence ϕ in situation S. (S may be omitted if time is not an issue.) [p. 373]

know(A, P, S).   Predicate. Agent A knows the sentence spelled out by string P in situation S. (S may be omitted if time is not an issue.) [p. 373]

know_acc($A, W1, W2$).   Predicate. Possible world $W2$ is accessible from world $W1$ relative to the knowledge of agent A. [p. 377]

know_fluent(A, F, S).   Modal. In situation S, agent A knows the current value of fluent F. [p. 382]

knowing(A, ϕ).   Modal. The state of agent A knowing sentence ϕ. [p. 381]

knowing(A, P).   Function. The state type of agent A knowing the sentence spelled out by P. [p. 381]

know_val(A, τ, S).   Modal. Agent A knows the value of term τ in situation S. [p. 378] know_val(A, T, S).   Predicate. Agent A knows the value of the term spelled out by string T in situation S. [p. 378]

know_whether(A, ϕ, S). Modal. Agent A knows in situation S whether sentence ϕ is true. [p. 378]

know_whether(A, P, S). Predicate. Agent A knows in situation S whether the sentence spelled out by string P is true. [p. 378]

kp_satisfied(A, E, S).   Predicate. The knowledge preconditions of the action spelled out by string E are satisfied for agent A in situation S. [p. 419]

L(ϕ).   Modal. ϕ is necessarily true. Used in this book as a generic modal operator. [p. 60]

label(S).   Metalevel. In natural deduction, the label of proof step S. [p. 86]

leads_to(P, G).   Function. A state in which the execution of plan P will lead to the accomplishment of goal G. [p. 398]

liquid_at_rest(**RR**).   Function. The state type of all the liquid in region **RR** being at rest. [p. 343]

liquid_in(**RR**).   Function. The fluent of the quantity of liquid in region **RR**. [p. 342]

lower_bound(X, I).   Predicate. X is a lower bound for interval I. [p. 151]

M(ϕ).   Modal. ϕ is possibly true. Used here as a generic modal operator. [p. 60]

mbuild.   Constant. In CD, the action type of making a mental construction. [p. 452]

meaning_of(S, K).   Function. The meaning of string of phonemes S in speech-act token K. meaning_of(S, K) is a string of symbols in a formal language. [p. 443]

measure($\tilde{M}, \mathcal{C}$).   Function. The measure (a real number) of length $\tilde{M}$ in coordinate system $\mathcal{C}$. [p. 295]

meets(I, J).   Predicate. Interval I ends as interval J begins. [p. 148] mloc(M, P).   Function. In CD, the fluent of mental location P containing mental object M. [p. 452]

mode_of(S, K).   Function. The mode of string of phonemes S in speech-act token K. For example, mode_of(S, K) may be "declarative" or "imperative." [p. 443]

monotonic(QD, QI, QF, SG).

     Predicate. Parameter QD depends on parameter QI in the direction indicated by sign SG for fixed values of parameter QF. [p. 163]

motionless(O).   Function. The state of object O being motionless. [p. 345]

move.   Constant. In CD, the action type of moving a body part. [p. 452]

mtrans.   Constant. In CD, the action type of communicating information from one mental location to another. [p. 452]

name_of(X).   Function. A constant string denoting entity X. [p. 81]

neg.   Constant. The interval of negative quantities. [p. 161]

null.   Constant. The event type of a no-op. [p. 226]

obligatory(E, S).   Predicate. Event type E is obligatory in situation S. [p. 449]

occurs(I, E).   Predicate. Event type occurs during interval I. [p. 192]

occurs(I, ϕ).   Modal. Event ϕ occurs during interval I. [p. 231]

occurs_exclusively(K).   Predicate. Event token K constitutes all that occurs during its time period. [p. 230]

occurs_in(I, E).   Predicate. Event type E occurs some time during interval I. [p. 412]

Odds(E).   Plausible. The odds on event E. [p. 129]

Odds($E \mid F$).   Plausible. The odds on event E given event F. [p. 129]

on_path(**PP**, $X_1, \dots X_k$). Predicate. In TOUR, places $X_1 \dots X_k$ appear in that order on path **PP**. [p. 281]

opening(**OO, XX, II**). Predicate. Region **OO** is an opening of barrier region **XX** into interior region **II**. [p. 261]

ordered(X, Y). Predicate. Quantities X and Y are ordered with respect to one another. [p. 150]

origin($\mathcal{C}$). Function. The origin (a point) of coordinate system $\mathcal{C}$. [p. 251]

OU($E|F$). Plausible. The update in the odds of event E given event F. [p. 130]

overlaps(I, J). Predicate. Interval I overlaps interval J from the left. [p. 148]

overlap_of(I, J). Function. The common subinterval of overlapping intervals I and J. [p. 149]

overlap_reg(**XX, ,YY**). Predicate. Regions **XX** and **YY** overlap. [p. 251]

owner_of(O). Function. The fluent of object O's owner (an agent) over time. [p. 451]

P(E). Plausible. The *a priori* probability of event E. [p. 120]

P($E \mid F$). Plausible. The conditional probability of event E given event F. [p. 120]

past(ϕ). Modal. State ϕ held at all future times. past(ϕ) is a state. [p. 231]

pc($A, L1, L2$). Predicate. Layout $L2$ is compatible with layout $L1$ relative to the perceptions of A. [p. 387]

permits(A, E). Function. State type of agent A permitting event type E. [p. 451]

permitted(E, S). Predicate. Event type E is permitted in situation S. [p. 449]

place(O). Function. The fluent of the region occupied by object O over time. [p. 328]

planar(**RR**). Predicate. Region **RR** lies in a plane. [p. 255] plan(*A*, *P*, *S*).   Predicate. In situation *S*, agent *A* intends to carry out the plan described in string *P*. [p. 414]

plausible(Γ, φ).   Plausible. Generic plausible inference. Sentence φ is a plausible inference given Γ, in the absence of evidence against φ. [p. 101]

pos.   Constant. The interval of positive quantities. [p. 161]

position(*O*).   Function. The fluent of solid object *O*'s position over time. In each situation, position(*O*) is a rigid mapping. [p. 328]

possible_occur(*S*, *E*).   Predicate. It is possible for event type *E* to occur starting in situation *S*. [p. 213]

precedes(*S*1, *S*2).   Predicate. Situation *S*1 precedes situation *S*2. [p. 190]

present_in(*O*, *S*).   Predicate. Entity *O* exists in situation *S*. [p. 191]

prevent(*E*).   Function. The event type of preventing event type *E*. [p. 215]

prim_change(*I*, *F*).   Predicate. Primitive fluent *F* changes during interval *I*. [p. 204]

prim_fluent(*F*).   Predicate. *F* is a primitive fluent. [p. 204]

prim_state(*F*).   Predicate. *F* is a primitive state. [p. 204]

primitive(*E*).   Predicate. Event type *E* is primitive. [p. 230]

primitive_component(*KP*, *KC*).
      Predicate. Event token *KP* is a primitive component of compound event token *KC*. [p. 230]

primitive_routine(*ACT*, *A*).
      Predicate. *ACT*, a function from arguments to an action type, is a primitive robotic routine for agent *A*. [p. 419]

process(*P*, *A*).   Predicate. *P* is a process of type *A*. [p. 323]

prohibited(*E*, *S*).   Predicate. Event type *E* is prohibited in situation *S*. [p. 449] pronunciation(P, S, L). Predicate. String of phonemes P is an acceptible pronunciation of string of characters S in language L. [p. 441]

propel. Constant. In CD, the action type of exerting a force on an object. [p. 452]

ptrans. Constant. In CD, the action type of moving an object. [p. 452]

quat(**P**, $\mathcal{F}$). Function. The quaternion corresponding to point **P** in coordinate system $\mathcal{F}$. [p. 302]

real_chronicle. Constant. In a branching theory of time, the chronicle that actually occurs. [p. 213]

reason(M, E). Predicate. In CD, mental state M is a reason for action E. [p. 453]

rectangle($\mathcal{C}, IX, IY$). Function. The rectangle of points with coordinates in $IX \times IY$ in coordinate system $\mathcal{C}$. [p. 251]

regular(**RR**). Predicate. Region **RR** is regular. [p. 258]

result(S, E). Function. In the situation calculus, the result of performing action type E in situation S. [p. 217]

result(E, S). Predicate. In CD, event E results in state S. [p. 453]

scale$_U(X)$. Function. The measure of quantity X relative to unit quantity U. [p. 156]

sequence($E_1 \ldots E_k$). Function. Event type of the occurrence of event types $E_1 \ldots E_k$ in sequence. [p. 225]

sequence($\phi_1 \ldots \phi_k$). Modal. Event of the occurrence of events $\phi_1 \ldots \phi_k$ in sequence. [p. 231]

set(S). Predicate. S is a set. [p. 49]

shape(O). Function. The shape (a region) of object O. [p. 328]

sign(X). Function. The sign (an interval) of differential quantity X. [p. 161] simply_connected(**RR**). Predicate. Region **RR** is simply connected. [p. 256]

sincere(K).   Predicate. Speech-act token K is sincere. [p. 443]

solid(O).   Predicate. O is a solid object. [p. 342]

solid_coating(**RR**, $\tilde{D}$). Function. The state of region **RR** being the "coating" within distance $\tilde{D}$ of solid objects. [p. 343]

some_future(ϕ).   Modal. State ϕ will be true at some point in the future. some_future(ϕ) is a state. [p. 231]

some_past(ϕ).   Modal. State ϕ will be true at some point in the past. some_past(ϕ) is a state. [p. 231]

sort_of(O).   Function. The sort of entity O. [p. 45]

speak(P).   Function. The event type of speaking the phoneme string P. [p. 441]

speak.   Constant. In CD, the action type of making a sound. [p. 452]

star(**X**, $< \mathbf{PP}_1, S_1 >, \ldots, < \mathbf{PP}_k, S_k >$). Predicate. In TOUR, places $\mathbf{PP}_1 \ldots \mathbf{PP}_k$ meet at place **X**. Moreover. the directed paths $\mathbf{PP}_i$ with sense S_i occur counterclockwise around **X**. [p. 281]

start(I).   Function. The greatest lower bound (a quantity) of interval I. [p. 151]

starts(I, J).   Predicate. Interval I starts with interval J, but finishes first. [p. 148]

subst($SNEW, SVAR, SOLD$). Function. The result (a string) of substituting $SNEW$ for every occurrence of variable symbol $SVAR$ in string $SOLD$. [p. 80]

success(P, G).   Function. The fluent giving the degree to which plan P will succeed in achieving goal G in each starting situation. [p. 409]

sum_over(S, F).   Function (second order). The sum of F over set S. F is a function from S to some differential quantity space. [p. 158] surf_norm(**PP, X**).   Function. The surface normal (a vector) pointing out of region **PP** at surface point **XX**. [p. 263]

Th(S).   Metalevel. The set of first-order consequences of theory S. [p. 116]

time_of(K).   Function. The time interval in which event (or state) token K occurs. [p. 191]

token_of(K, E).   Predicate. Event (or state) token K is a token of event (state) type E. [p. 191]

tolerance(**CC**, $< \mathbf{EE}_1, \tilde{D}_1 >, \ldots < \mathbf{EE}_k, \tilde{D}_k >$).
     Predicate. Directed edges $\mathbf{EE}_1 \ldots \mathbf{EE}_k$ approximate directed curve **CC** within tolerances $\tilde{D}_1 \ldots \tilde{D}_k$. [p. 275]

transfer(O, A).   Function. Action type of transferring possession of object O to agent A. [p. 451]

true_in(S, A).   Predicate. State A is true in S. S is a situation, a possible world, or a layout. [p. 56, 73, 188, 365, 389]

true_in(S, ϕ).   Modal. State A is true in situation S. [p. 231]

TRUE.   Metalevel. Truth. [p. 32]

true(P).   Predicate. String P spells out a true sentence. [p. 81]

tuple($X_1 \ldots X_k$).   Function. The tuple of $X_1 \ldots X_k$ in order. [p. 50]

twilight_zone.   Constant. Imaginary situation that results from an impossible event "occurring." [p. 400]

two_d(**FF**).   Predicate. Region **FF** is two dimensional. [p. 258]

unit_length(C).   Function. The unit of length in coordinate system C. [p. 251]

upper_bound(X, I).   Predicate. Quantity X is an upper bound of interval I. [p. 151]

use_of(E, A, O).   Event type E constitutes a use of object O by agent A. [p. 451] valid(P, G).   Function. State type of plan P being a valid way to accomplish goal G in a situation. [p. 398]

value_in(S, F).   Function. Value of fluent F in S. S is a situation, a possible world, or a layout. [p. 58, 73, 160, 188, 365, 387]

value_in(S, τ).   Modal. Value of term τ in situation S. [p. 231]

volume(**RR**).   Function. The volume of region **RR**. [p. 263]

w0.   Constant. The real world. [p. 74]

wait(T).   Function. The action of waiting for time duration T. [p. 410]

wait_until(Q).   Function. The action of waiting until state Q becomes true. [p. 410]

wait_while(E).   Function. The action of waiting until event E is complete. [p. 410]

while(A, E).   Function. Event type E occurs repeatedly as long as A holds at the beginning of each iteration. while(A, E) is an event type. [p. 225]

while(θ, ϕ).   Modal. Event ϕ occurs repeatedly as long as θ holds at the beginning of each iteration. [p. 231]

x_axis($\mathcal{C}$).   Function. The positive x direction in coordinate system $\mathcal{C}$. [p. 251]

z_coor(**P**, $\mathcal{C}$).   Function. The z coordinate (a real number) of point **P** in coordinate system $\mathcal{C}$. [p. 256]

z_y_z_euler($\mathcal{F}, \mathcal{C}$).   Function. The Z-Y-Z Euler angles (a triple of real numbers) of the orientation of coordinate frame $\mathcal{F}$ relative to coordinate frame $\mathcal{C}$. [p. 274]

Index of Names

General Index